The Seven Chakras

A Guide to the Root, Sacral, Solar Plexus, Heart, Throat, Third Eye, and Crown Chakra

Your Free Gift
(only available for a limited time)

Thanks for getting this book! If you want to learn more about various spirituality topics, then join Mari Silva's community and get a free guided meditation MP3 for awakening your third eye. This guided meditation mp3 is designed to open and strengthen ones third eye so you can experience a higher state of consciousness. Simply visit the link below the image to get started.

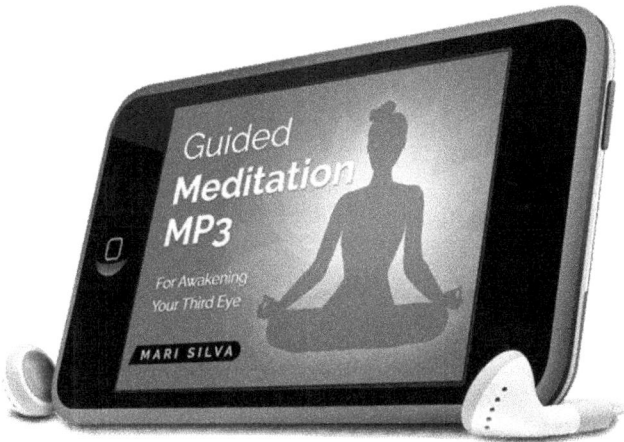

https://spiritualityspot.com/meditation

Table of Contents

Part 1: Root Chakra

The Ultimate Guide to Opening, Balancing, and Healing Muladhara

MARI SILVA

Root Chakra

THE ULTIMATE GUIDE TO OPENING,
BALANCING, AND HEALING MULADHARA

Introduction

When your work on aligning and balancing your chakras, it's essential to start with the first chakra – Muladhara, or the root chakra. This chakra is tasked with keeping you grounded in the physical world. When it is out of balance, you can experience physical pain in the lower half of your body and find it challenging to stay focused and stable. You can also feel exhausted, depressed, and stressed—like you're being forced to rush through tasks without giving them the attention they deserve.

In this guide, we'll look at everything you need to know about your root chakra and cover tips on clearing, opening, and balancing it. With the knowledge that you pick up from this guide, you'll have a good idea of what to do should your Muladhara ever get blocked or imbalanced.

In the first chapter, we'll look at the basics; understanding what chakras are, focusing on the root chakra in particular, and why it must be aligned.

In the second chapter, we'll look at the tell-tale signs and symptoms of a blocked root chakra so that you can remedy the situation when needed. Following that, the third chapter will look at what meditation techniques you can use when working on opening your Muladhara, and the fourth chapter will specifically look at mantras and affirmations you can use throughout this process.

Chapter five will look at how you can use mudras and pranayama to enhance your meditation and make it easier to balance your root chakra. Chapter six will look at how yoga can help you balance your Muladhara and offer you several asanas (yoga poses) you can implement.

In chapter seven, we'll look at how you can use crystals and stones in conjunction with your chakra meditation and yogic exercises. We'll explore various options available and how they should be used. The following chapter will cover aromatherapy and essential oils and their use in balancing your Muladhara and will suggest specific essential oils you can use.

Chapter nine looks at how you should tailor your diet and nutrition for a healthy root chakra. In chapter ten, you'll be provided with a weekly sample routine you can follow for healing your Muladhara. This schedule will incorporate everything you will have learned in the previous chapters to understand how they all come together to unblock your chakra.

Finally, you'll find a bonus chapter that will explain how you can move beyond your root chakra to the other chakras in your body. This chapter will prepare you for unblocking the rest of your chakras to help you balance yourself physically and spiritually.

Unlike other guides on Muladhara, this guide is perfect for both beginners and experienced yogic practitioners. It doesn't matter if this is the first time you've heard the term "chakra" or if you've been working to balance them for years; everyone will be able to benefit from this very detailed guide.

All that's left for you to do is to turn the page and use this easy-to-follow guide to get started with balancing your chakras, so you can finally live the life you were meant to!

Chapter 1: What Is Muladhara?

Before you can start with unblocking and balancing your root chakra, it's a good idea to fully understand what chakras are and why it's so necessary to balance them.

What Are Chakras?

Chakras are a concept that stems from Tantra and early Hinduism. The word "chakra" literally means "disk" or "wheel" in Sanskrit and refers to different energy centers found in the human body. There is some debate about how many chakras there are in a person's body, with some traditions saying there are as many as 88,000.

Chakras are energy centers in the body.
https://pixabay.com/es/vectors/chakra-meditaci%c3%b3n-aura-energ%c3%ada-5628622/

However, most belief systems concur that seven main chakras run up your body along your spine. They start with the root chakra, which we'll discuss in detail in this chapter and book, and extend to the crown chakra, located at the crown of your head.

The concept of chakras originates from the idea that each person has two bodies in two parallel dimensions. The first one is the tangible body, which is located in the physical world. The second is the energy body, or subtle body, connected by energy pathways (or channels) known as *nadi*. These energy channels are connected and directed by nodes of psychic energy – or more commonly known as the chakras.

The physical body can affect the energy body (and vice versa), and this interaction is what allows you to balance your chakras.

Each of the seven major chakras has different physical and psychological effects on your body, meaning that any unbalanced chakra has a particular effect on your body. Learning what to look out for is the first step toward achieving a balanced body in both realms.

To start the balancing process, you should ideally start from the base one and carry on unblocking each chakra in order until you get to your crown chakra. So, to get you started, let's begin with understanding the root chakra.

What Is the Root Chakra?

As we've already told you, the Muladhara is found at the base of your spine. The word "Muladhara" —the Sanskrit term— means "root," hence its English name.

This chakra acts as the root of your body and is linked to the element of earth, which represents a person's ability to feel rooted and stable in life. It is connected to your familial relationships and sense of security. A healthy root chakra enables you to feel confident, safe, and secure as you go through the journey of life.

This chakra also supports your bone structure, acting as a connective chakra to the physical world around you. When the root chakra is blocked or unbalanced, all the other chakras in your body may go out of alignment.

The Root Chakra symbol.
https://pixabay.com/es/illustrations/chakra-mandala-chakra-ra%c3%adz-1340058/

In Hindu scripture and yogic texts, Muladhara is said to be the chakra from which the three main nadis (Ida, Pingala, Sushama) emerge. It is considered to be the home of the god Ganpati - which is to say Ganpati governs it, and his influence on your life is considered to be spiritually emanating from the Muladhara. Along with being the god who brought good luck and removed obstacles, Ganpati is also the son of Shiva, who is described as the omniscient yogi who first taught yoga to Hindu sages.

The root chakra is where everything in your body begins. It is the home of your emotions. However, an unbalanced root chakra will lead to swings in your emotional state, including feelings of anger, insecurity, and restlessness. It can also cause your fear, panic, and anxiety levels to spike as a result of what your body sees as a threat to your safety and security.

An unbalanced root chakra is common for people who have had negative personal struggles, such as troubles with their financial situation, interpersonal relationships, and worries about ensuring their survival needs are met.

Another way the root chakra influences you is through its role in maintaining the constant flow of one's creativity. It acts as the root of creative intention in your body and, when in balance, ensures that a person feels confident to develop their ideas and inspiration. The "root" of your creativity is clear, allowing you to be able to bring your ideas to reality.

It allows you to stand up for yourself and your ideas and ensures you don't let the fear of failure hold you back. However, when unbalanced, it can make it challenging to bring your creative ideas to fruition, and there's a greater fear of defeat that can often stop you from trying in the first place.

Root Chakra and Sexuality

As mentioned above, your root chakra is located at the base of your spine – specifically, on your pelvic floor. This location also means that it significantly impacts your sexuality and sex life.

As we've discussed, one of the major effects of an out-of-balance root chakra is fear. When you're afraid, you're unable to open yourself up to intimacy, making it challenging to trust and connect with sexual partners. A blocked root chakra makes your sex life unsatisfying because you're unable to appreciate sex with a person you trust completely.

The root chakra also has physiological effects on your body. This is especially true for women who have experienced trauma in childhood. The root chakra responds by shutting down in women who are afraid of sex, whether it is because of previous traumas or worry about a painful first experience. A dormant root chakra also means the muscles in your pelvic floor tighten and can lead to a reduction in vaginal lubrication.

For women who have a sexual experience when their root chakra is closed, the tense pelvic floor muscles can cause pain and, in the case of first times, bleeding. This pain sets a precedent, causing you to expect it to reoccur the next time you have sex. This fear leads to an out-of-balance root chakra, which means both physiological and psychological reactions.

This combination of fear and physiological effects (tightened pelvic muscles) leads to long-term sexual dysfunction, which cannot be resolved until the root chakra is opened and balanced. For men, the fear and lack of trust in their partner leads to an unsatisfying sex life that, once again, requires their root chakra to be aligned and opened to remedy.

Understanding the Root Chakra in Depth

A red, four-petalled lotus with a yellow square in the center represents the Muladhara. Each petal has one of four Sanskrit letters (va, scha, sha, and sa) written in gold. Depending on the yogic tradition, these letters either symbolize the four vrittis (thoughts that surface in the mind) – natural pleasure, greatest joy, blissfulness in concentration, and delight in controlling passion – or represent dharma, artha, kama, and moksha.

At the center of the lotus, the syllable lam is placed within the yellow box. This is the bija mantra, or Vedic seed mantra, associated with the root chakra and will be discussed in further detail in other chapters in this book.

In some depictions of the root chakra symbol, eight spears point out from the sides and corners of the square towards the petals.

The root chakra is associated with the Hindu deity Ganpati, as discussed above, and the god Indra, who is the king of heaven and the god of the sky, weather, lightning, rains, and thunder.

As it is linked to the earth element, the root chakra is also associated with the color red (or pink), which symbolizes the earth. Additionally, it is linked to the sense of smell, and its musical note is C.

In your root chakras, you carry not only your own experiences but also ancestral memories, both good and bad. Thus, generational traumas can even affect people who have never experienced a similar level of hardship during their own lifetime, but balancing this chakra helps heal these deep-rooted traumas.

When energy flows unimpeded through your root chakra, the kundalini energy is awakened. The kundalini energy is the divine feminine energy associated with the goddess and lies dormant in the Muladhara until the chakra is opened. Energy flow through this chakra also gives the other six chakras a strong base they can lean on, which is why it's essential to start opening up your root chakra before any other.

Unbalanced Root Chakras

With an unbalanced root chakra, several physical and emotional problems can be prevalent in your lower body, including:

- Weight gain or weight loss
- Problems with the colon and bladder
- Constipation
- Pain in the pelvis
- Problems with your lower leg or feet
- Pain in the lower back
- Prostate problems in men
- Sleeping problems
- Weakened immunity, making it easier for you to fall ill

Psychological and emotional symptoms of an imbalanced root chakra include:

- Depression
- Anxiety disorders
- Eating disorders
- Lack of confidence and self-esteem
- Sudden inability to focus
- Fear and loss of your sense of security
- Erratic behavior
- Negativity and cynicism
- Feeling extremely overwhelmed, like you're constantly living in survival mode
- Lack of energy and a constant feeling of lethargy

You may also develop self-control issues, which is one of the reasons an unbalanced root chakra can lead to eating disorders - controlling your food intake can lead to a temporary feeling of regaining control but can actually lead to severe medical problems.

Furthermore, an imbalance may also lead to spiritual issues, such as an existential crisis or crisis of faith, loss of will, and a feeling of doubt about your place in the universe around you. It can lead to you losing interest in being part of the world.

A balanced root chakra, on the other hand, is linked to:

- A healthy survival instinct
- A sense of belonging among the people around you
- The ability to connect with loved ones and feel grounded in your life
- Stability and security

A healthy root chakra is essential for giving you the will to live and care for yourself and restore focus to your life. With a stable root chakra, you'll be able to thrive and truly meet your potential.

Balancing your root chakra is key to regaining this sense of stability in your life. This book will explore ways to do so in detail in the following chapters, but some methods you can try include:

- Yoga
- Meditation
- Aromatherapy
- Crystal healing

You can also use movement, sound, and touch to balance your root chakra.

Movement is exactly what it sounds like - getting out of your home and moving around. As the root chakra is linked to the earth, it's recommended you engage with nature. Even something as simple as walking through a garden or hiking can help.

Another way to unblock your root chakra is by connecting to the ground with your feet. To do so, stand with a tennis ball on the ground in front of you. Then, shift one foot onto the ball, putting your weight on the other foot. Move the foot on the ball in a circular motion, allowing your ankle to move. When you feel grounded, change sides.

If spending time in nature isn't possible, other forms of movement, such as dance and pilates, can help as well.

You can also use sound to heal your chakras, including using singing bowls, sound baths, and gong sounds. As we'll cover later in the book, you can also use mantras. The root chakra's vibration frequency is 432 Hz; using sound at this vibration can help especially well.

Finally, you can also use touch to balance your chakra. This involves touching your body and being touched; one option is to try self-massage.

Alternatively, you can ask a loved one for a massage or visit a professional. Being connected with another person by touch is a matter of trust, especially when being massaged. This helps you connect with other people better, allowing you to balance your root chakra.

You can also try other touch-based activities, including hugging (self-hugging is also an option), cuddling, and sex with a trusted partner. You should try touching your body through self-massages and self-hugs because this type of touch reinforces your love for yourself.

Besides self-touch, you should also set aside time to spend alone. You can work on your self-confidence and discover your true self. Use this time to manifest what you want from your life or spend it doing things that you enjoy but are otherwise unable to do due to a lack of time, such as reading a book, enjoying music, or going for a run. Essentially, you should do what helps whatever helps you to connect better with your inner, true, authentic self.

Why You Should Align Your Root Chakra

A balanced root chakra helps you feel more connected to the people around you and more secure in yourself and your place in the world.

However, there's more to it than just that.

An aligned, balanced root chakra ensures you feel a zest for life. It makes you enthusiastic about experiencing the world around you and rescues you from boredom and feelings of stagnation. It's also essential for you to feel energetic and able to complete your daily routine.

The root chakra also provides energy to the rest of the chakras in your body, so getting it balanced is critical for getting any of your chakras onto the same path.

Now that you understand your root chakra, it's time to look at it in further detail. The next chapter will explore the effects of a blocked root chakra and look at what can cause it.

It will also look at other issues with the root chakra, including the effects of a weak or overactive Muladhara. It will give you some symptoms to keep an eye out for and includes a questionnaire you can use to determine whether your root chakra is in balance.

Once you've worked out the state of your root chakra, you can then look at ways to address any imbalance that may exist. Other chapters will explore, in detail, some popular ways to treat imbalanced chakras and open closed Muladharas, including how to meditate, to open it, what mantras and affirmations you can use, and what mudras and pranayamas are recommended for your root chakra.

We also look at some yoga poses and sequences that can balance your Muladhara and list some crystals and stones you can incorporate into your meditation and yoga practice. Furthermore, you'll be able to learn how to use aromatherapy and essential oils to encourage the balancing process, and you'll be informed about which essential oils are best for this chakra.

One important thing this book will explore is how to tailor your diet to ensure your root chakra is balanced. Your diet and nutrition can have a significant impact on the state of your chakras, and this book will provide you will all the information you need to continue having a healthy diet while also taking care of your Muladhara.

By the time you're done with this book, you'll truly be a root chakra expert. You'll know how to balance your root chakra and be ready to move on to understanding the other chakras in your body.

So, what are you waiting for? Now that you know your root chakra, all that's left for you to do is turn the page and continue reading!

Chapter 2: When Your Root Chakra Is Blocked

The root chakra represents anything that keeps us grounded. Once we begin to feel discombobulated, overly anxious, nervous, or a bit airy and flighty, it means that our root chakra is blocked, and something needs to be done immediately to rectify that. What you need to feel grounded tends to vary from one individual to the next, and sometimes it can be a matter of meeting the basic needs required for survival: nourishment, a roof over one's head, good friends, etc. For others, it can be an intense emotional need that is not met and feels amorphous and intangible to explain to others.

A blocked chakra can be why you're feeling stressed.

Feelings of emotional safety can be just as important as physical safety for some, whereas, for others who are more practical-minded, it may not be the most essential thing. In all cases, once you feel as though the metaphorical rug has been swept out from underneath you, you lose your balance, and all that helps to make you feel grounded. This vivid sensation means that your root chakra has not only been thrown out of whack but that it is blocked, which will create other problems that will reverberate throughout you emotionally and physically. This chapter is dedicated to exploring these feelings further and will help reveal how to go about doing the hard work of undoing some of the damage.

Causes and Symptoms

A few ideas have been mentioned in the intro to help outline why a chakra might become blocked. However, it might be helpful to further illuminate exactly why and how the Muladhara chakra may be blocked, so you can feel more empowered in knowing what to do about it. By the same token, it will also be helpful to delineate the lines between a blocked chakra or one that is simply overactive since there tend to be some subtle but noticeable differences between the two.

By now, you understand that a root chakra that is in good shape and balanced induces feelings of peace, safety, and emotional stability. It can be a very Zen state of affairs, and you won't be feeling on edge, sad, or experiencing extreme emotional states. Conversely, an overactive Muladhara chakra will go into overdrive when you're feeling as though the basic needs you require to survive and feel comfortable aren't being met. Everything from overwhelming feelings of insecurity, hunger, and simply physical pain will throw you off, leaving you anxiety-ridden and frightened. For some people, it may even contribute to physical ailments such as back pain, prostate issues, and so on.

A blocked chakra can also have a debilitating effect but may attack less aggressively when compared to an overactive one. Suppose you find yourself feeling unmoored, your ability to concentrate shot to hell, or completely disconnected from loved ones and the experiences around you. In that case, you definitely have a blocked chakra that needs to be resolved.

A real-world illustration of these differences may help you better understand how to tackle each scenario and recognize the symptoms that come along with it. For example, an individual - let's call him Matt - has long had a toxic relationship with his brothers and sisters. They're a large family, so the dynamics between different siblings vary in addition to their relationships with their parents. There tends to be a great deal of strife between Matt and his siblings - sure, some are kind and supportive, but others are manipulative and competitive. As they get older, each one marries and has a home of their own, but internal squabbling arises when a fight over unclaimed inheritance comes up. The money is one issue and can be stressful, especially since Matt's finances are in a bit of a tough spot due to the pandemic.

However, what makes everything far worse is the amount of bad energy and toxic manipulation that comes about, with his siblings backstabbing one another and creating strife to secure their share of the money. Matt finds himself distracted and unable to focus on work. He has trouble sleeping and feels a bit lost as though he's regressed - like a confused child left alone in the woods. It takes a while for him to get out of this funk and even longer for people to learn enough empathy to get off his case. Matt realizes that if he doesn't catch himself, his spaciness may further hinder his ability to work and provide for his family.

Furthermore, the insults begin to dig deeper and prevent him from feeling safe in his own skin. This is when he starts to feel anxious, scared, and confused. The stress is so prevalent that he begins to develop various health issues, and his body isn't able to function in quite the same way. In fact, it starts to feel as though his body is also rebelling against him when he finds himself at the doctor looking for treatment for his back pain and emerging migraines.

In the scenario briefly outlined above, it is clear that Matt's first reaction is one that is informed by a blocked root chakra - an inability to concentrate and daydreaming more than usual gets to him. It affects his ability to feel grounded and secure, which are classic symptoms of a blocked chakra.

However, as the family drama heats up, he begins to feel less and less safe, more frightened, and deeply upset. His system goes into overdrive and begins experiencing the symptoms of an overactive root chakra that are hard to quiet down. Hopefully, this example helps illustrate to you the different ways someone can experience a root chakra that is not properly balanced and understand how one scenario can move into another quite seamlessly, even in the same individual.

Of course, the things it takes to make someone feel safe and secure will vary, and not everyone will react in the same way in a given situation. At the same time, you can clearly identify the ways different physical and emotional symptoms can manifest once the root chakra becomes off-kilter. By understanding the causes of your inability to feel grounded, you will be able to find a solution for the root chakra and how to become more balanced over time.

To further illustrate how the root chakra can affect you, it may be helpful to quickly list some of the common symptoms and their impact on your life. The root chakra is, after all, the center that holds together every thought and feeling you have about yourself, and it informs your self-esteem above all else. Any problems you may feel stem from this, which is why remaining mindful of your body is exceedingly helpful:

In addition to prostate problems, an unbalanced root chakra can affect your colon health and your bladder. Drinking herbal tea and meditating are highly recommended in that case.

- Inflammation throughout the body is another big problem. You may find that your gut feels a bit swollen, and you can't enjoy food normally. Or the nerves in your wrists are inflamed, and you can't type normally. This is a classic sign of an unbalanced chakra that needs a combination of medical attention and a mindful reset through healthy practices such as yoga.

- Cramping and pain in the left arm or foot are other common ailments people tend to suffer from when the root chakra is experiencing turbulence. Of course, a medical professional should attend to anything to do with the left arm right away. Furthermore, it's a clear sign from the universe that you need to slow things down a bit and become more mindful of how your body reacts to certain situations.

- Feeling on edge or anxious is another common symptom, but if you leave it untreated, you can develop a full-on anxiety disorder. These can be accompanied by panic attacks, bouts of depression, etc. The root chakra is strongly connected to anything affecting your mental health, so leaving it dormant for a long time is bound to make things harder to remedy later. Of course, treatment with a mental health professional is key, but taking on other measures to help care for your mental health, such as meditation, yoga, and other self-care practices, will help heal your root chakra over time.

When in Doubt

So, you've read everything here, and maybe it seems clear. Or maybe not so much. Maybe you doubt yourself and are unclear about the extent to which the root chakra may be off. Is it another chakra, or are you just having a bad day? Part of the work you're doing for yourself here is giving yourself a chance to listen to your body and figure things out, slowly and deliberately. In light of this, taking a short quiz might be a helpful step to take. Don't worry; this isn't a cheesy, woman's magazine-style quiz that you take while waiting for your dentist appointment. Treat the quiz as a vital tool in this workbook to help you make sense of things and take stock of where you are at the moment.

1. Out of these colors, which one do you find the most upsetting at the moment?

   - Red
   - Orange
   - Blue
   - Black

2. How would you describe your personality in general?

   - Loving
   - Happy
   - Grounded

- Wise

3. Which of these words best describe your current emotional state?

    - Nervous
    - Sad
    - Happy
    - Angry

4. How do you feel about your finances?

    - Fine
    - Could stand to make more money
    - Feel unsafe
    - Content with what you currently possess

5. How are you currently dealing with any negative feelings you may have?

    - Going shopping
    - Reading
    - Listening to music
    - Keeping to yourself and ignoring texts or phone calls for awhile

6. Describe your approach to food:

    - I eat even though I'm not hungry
    - I can't eat at all and avoid food unless necessary
    - I take the time to cook and meal prep healthfully
    - I help prepare food for my partner/children/etc., but I don't have the energy to do anything for myself.

7. Which statement describes how you feel about the future?

    - I feel anxious
    - I can't think that far ahead; my mind feels blank
    - I'm optimistic

- I find myself thinking about other people's future (kids, partners, etc.), but not my own

8. How would you describe your energy levels?

   - Adequate

   - Sluggish

   - Avoiding major events or work functions

   - Finding it hard to do even the most straightforward of tasks (changing into fresh clothes, cooking, cleaning, etc.).

9. When you meet a new person, do you

   - Feel as though you can openly share your likes and dislikes

   - Feel utterly confident in your personality

   - Get influenced easily by the opinions of others

   - Prefer to listen and keep quiet rather than become engaged in different layers of conversation

10. Which of these statements best describe how you feel about your career?

    - Unhappy and unclear as to what my professional aspirations are

    - The job is fine, but maybe I don't make enough money

    - I don't work hard enough, so I lost out on that promotion

    - I want to switch careers but feel overwhelmed

11. Describe your relationship with others

    - People don't respect your boundaries

    - You feel like a doormat, but you're not sure why

    - You are able to express your needs to others healthfully and don't get pushback from the people in your life

    - You feel like everyone is manipulative and out to get you

12. Which statement best describes your relationship with the earth?

- I feel connected to nature and worry about climate change
- I enjoy nature but can't bring myself to go out these days
- I can't find peace in nature; it makes me nervous
- I feel disconnected and don't harbor any negative or positive associations with the earth

13. Which statement best describes your relationship with groups?

- I feel comfortable in groups and enjoy meeting new people
- I used to feel comfortable in groups but now try to avoid them
- Groups give me anxiety
- I feel insecure in groups and do not trust new people easily

14. If you struggle with excessively negative emotions, how often do you find yourself feeling overwhelmed?

- All the time
- Only in the face of certain triggering situations
- Rarely
- Even if I'm feeling overwhelmed, I try to incorporate calming methods to help mitigate some of the pain

15. Do you suffer from recurring health problems? Write down what you can in the space below.

Key

So, this is a fairly straightforward quiz, and you can probably glean from the information listed above the various issues you could be suffering from. It should also help you realize the severity of the situation and whether or not you need immediate intervention. The first question about color may seem a bit confusing, but it helps set the stage: if the red color upsets you the most, it is a clear indication that your root chakra is off. Orange is another strong indicator you may not be feeling well, but the effects on you may be gentler. Many of these feelings are on a scale, but if you find yourself answering more than usual in the more extreme negative sense, you should try to figure out an action plan to help you mitigate the worst of your symptoms. To help you do so, try to keep a journal of different events or anecdotes that have led you to feel uncomfortable or ill. Once you see everything written down clearly in front of you, you'll be able to tackle the problems one by one. It's hard work, but it's feasible, and it's important to remember that you shouldn't do everything on your own. Looking to a primary physician and a mental health professional is definitely one way to begin the healing and start to align your chakras to achieve a more balanced sense of being.

Altering Your Mindset

The root chakra is critical to helping us formulate a strong connection to the ground beneath us. Without it, we will not be able to harness our full energy both mentally and physically. A blocked chakra - or an overactive one - causes us to lose clarity and confidence in our choices and actions. As such, it has a tremendous impact on our health and wellbeing, and its influence cannot be overstated. Once we become disassociated with the landscape surrounding the people populating our lives, we end up missing out on the emotional and spiritual sustenance we need to survive. This could mean any spiritual needs that help keep you afloat – or even practical everyday needs that impact your capacity to go about daily life normally.

For this reason, altering one's mindset is absolutely crucial in trying to get the chakras balanced. There is something to be said for the fact that everyone on this planet, without exception, is going through some kind of major realignment to respond to the stresses of contemporary life. Naturally, living through a global pandemic, the subsequent economic fallout, unanswered calls for social justice, and political unrest will bring forth a myriad of issues. People are just becoming reacquainted with the earth and the energies that feed into it, so it makes sense that many are trying to realign their chakras. Most struggles you are currently experiencing in an inability to meet your needs and help others achieve that same goal boils down to blocked chakras that need reactivation.

Sadly, feeling constantly victimized or experiencing an inability to trust others is so prevalent these days that it has become a permanent feature of our political discourse. If only more people would try to unblock their chakras! All jokes aside, much of the trouble you experience as an individual can end up affecting others in your orbit. No matter how we try to self-isolate or treat ourselves as islands unto ourselves, other people are bound to be affected by our behavior or inability to be mindful. Altering your mindset and becoming more grounded and aware of your actions will help spread positivity in other areas of your life, minimizing pain –something the world needs a bit more of now. Trusting that you deserve to have your basic necessities covered is not a selfish act - in fact, it can encourage other people to do the same or ask others they care about to prioritize healthy habits, which is definitely a good thing.

Chapter 3: How to Meditate on Your Root

Now that you have learned about the symptoms of a blocked root chakra and its causes, we will discuss the main method to balance your Muladhara. Meditation is one of the surest ways to open up your root chakra. Even if you have never practiced meditation before, you are probably familiar with its many benefits. It helps you to be mindful, focused, and self-aware while boosting your mood and reducing stress and anxiety. Meditation can be a tremendous help in managing symptoms of depression, keeping you calm and relaxed, improving your memory, increasing your self-esteem, making you a kinder person, and opening and balancing the root chakra since it focuses on healing the body and mind. Meditation also has many physical benefits like lowering your blood pressure, improving your immunity, helping you handle pain, reducing PMS symptoms, improving digestion, and boosting your metabolism so you can lose or manage your weight. It isn't an exaggeration to say that the benefits of meditation are endless.

Meditation helps balance your root chakra.
https://unsplash.com/photos/rOn57CBgvMo

What Is Meditation?

Meditation is an ancient tradition that originated in the Indus Valley (in modern-day India). It is about practicing certain body movements that help you to relax and focus on the present moment. As more and more people started to take notice of meditation, news of its benefits traveled the world, and now it has become one of the most popular stress-relieving and fitness practices.

Meditation is a very simple activity since it mainly focuses on your breathing, and it doesn't require much effort. We know that many movies have shown meditation being practiced in temples or mountains far away from the rest of the world. However, you can easily meditate in your bedroom because all you need is a quiet spot with no distractions.

Consistency is key to reaping the many benefits of meditation, and – for this reason – it should be incorporated into your daily routine. Many people lead very busy lifestyles and have hectic schedules, but all you need is a few minutes each day. Some people prefer early morning meditation because there are no distractions like phone calls, kids, or outside noise. So, try to wake up 10 or 20 minutes early every day. You can just be by yourself, at peace, focusing on your breathing. There are others who prefer to meditate before bedtime, which can also improve your sleeping pattern. You can meditate at work in your office or outdoors during your lunch break. You can also meditate while you are exercising, doing your chores, walking on a bus, or if you are stuck in traffic. There is always time in your day for meditation; you just need to be serious about it and commit to it. Make it a priority and treat it the same way you would a doctor's appointment. All you need is a few minutes each day. You can also use a meditation app to remind you and even guide you through your meditation session. Once you incorporate meditation into your daily schedule, it will become a habit that you won't be able to break, especially when you start to feel its benefits on your physical and mental health.

Benefits of Meditation on the Root Chakra

"Breathing in, I calm body and mind. Breathing out, I smile. Dwelling in the present moment, I know this is the only moment." - Thich Nhat Hanh

Specific meditation practices target the root chakra as a conduit for healing energy. Root chakra meditation can help you sleep better at night since it calms your mind and releases negative emotions like grief, fear, anxiety, or anger, making you more optimistic and upbeat. Additionally, it improves your relationships and makes you more empathetic towards other people's needs; it also provides you with self-acceptance, enables you to enjoy life, and makes you more aware.

Guided Meditation Exercises to Open Muladhara

This part of the chapter will discuss various meditation exercises to unblock, heal, and balance your root chakra. It is vital that you follow the instruction to the letter to get the best out of each exercise. When performing any meditative exercise, make sure you choose a quiet place to practice with no distractions and *turn your phone off.* You should also ensure the environment is comfortable so you can calm your brain and relax your body.

Always sit in a comfortable position, preferably on the ground, since your root chakra is located at the base of your spine, so you will be able to feel grounded. Make sure that you sit up straight. If you want to stimulate the Muladhara, you can listen to healing music. Since you will be sitting still, your mind may wander. However, it is best to neither ignore nor dwell on these thoughts; simply acknowledge them and then focus back on your breathing.

Now we are going to give you grounding meditation techniques that will enable you to connect with the Earth and activate your root chakra.

Grounding Meditation Exercise #1

1. Find a quiet place.
2. Sit in a comfortable position cross-legged, preferably on a yoga mat (if you are unable to sit on the floor, you can sit on a cushion or a chair).
3. Sit up straight.
4. Place both your hands on your knees with your palms facing upwards.
5. You can use the Gyan Mudra gesture by making the index finger and the thumb touch so they form a circle, or you can opt for the Dhyana Mudra by placing both hands on your lap with the palms upturned and both thumbs touching each other's tips.
6. Ensure your whole body is relaxed, even your facial muscles.
7. Close your eyes.
8. Breathe in deeply through your nose.
9. Feel the air filling your belly and reaching your Muladhara.
10. Now, visualize there is red light at your root chakra (the base of the spine).
11. When inhaling, visualize the red ball growing.
12. Let it unblock your energy.
13. Every time you inhale, imagine the light growing.
14. Imagine the light reaching your feet to keep you grounded.

15. Now you are connected to the Earth.

16. Feel its energy moving through you.

17. Visualize the red light moving to your hip bones and legs.

18. Visualize the red ball of light-emitting energy to heal your body.

19. You are feeling your muscles relaxing.

20. Your blood is flowing through your body with no restrictions.

21. You are surrounded by the red light's healing energy as it contains you with its warmth.

22. Breathe deeply from your belly four times.

23. The fifth time, breathe in deeply and chant "LAM".

24. Breathe out while extending the "M".

25. Practice the breathing and chatting exercise for a couple of minutes.

26. Gradually, start breathing normally.

After you finish meditating, don't get up right away. Remain still and be aware of how you are feeling in your root chakra and legs. Start moving different parts of your body like your arms, shoulders, fingers, and toes while focusing on the sensation in every part of your body. Now slowly open your eyes and get up.

Grounding Meditation Exercise #2

1. Find a quiet spot.

2. Sit in a comfortable position.

3. Focus on your root chakra.

4. Close your eyes.

5. Visualize your favorite tree (if you don't have a favorite tree, then visualize any tree).

6. Imagine the trunk of the tree growing from your root chakra.

7. Inhale and exhale slowly and deeply.

8. Now, feel grounded and connected to the Earth.

9. Each time you breathe out and imagine yourself letting go of the things that you don't need or don't benefit you.

10. Imagine these things moving down to the trunk of the tree and being released into the Earth beneath you.

11. Each time you breathe in, imagine your body being nourished.

12. Repeat the inhalation and exhalation while visualizing the aforementioned thought experiment 5 to 10 times.

13. Feel the Earth beneath you, supporting and embracing you.

Grounding Meditation Exercise #3

1. Find a quiet place.

2. Sit in a comfortable position.

3. Sit up straight.

4. Relax your shoulders and muscles from your forehead to your toes.

5. Feel your heart being opened.

6. Breathe in and out deeply.

7. Feel the air fill your belly.

8. Focus only on your breathing.

9. Slow down your thoughts.

10. Now bring your focus to your root chakra.

11. Visualize a ball of red light at your Muladhara.

12. This red light makes you feel safe.

13. It grounds you to the Earth beneath you.

14. The Earth is supporting you.

15. You are surrounded by the whole universe.

16. Feel strength and peace flowing through you.

17. Feel connected to every part of your being.

18. Visualize energy emitting from the red light.

19. Consume this energy and let it keep you grounded.

Calming Meditation

This meditation should be practiced outdoors, and it is different from the ones we have mentioned so far because you will be walking instead of sitting still.

1. Find a quiet spot outdoors.
2. Stand firmly on the ground.
3. Feel the Earth beneath your feet.
4. Put your hands on your chest.
5. Breathe deeply 3 times.
6. Slowly remove your hand from your chest.
7. Start walking slowly.
8. Focus on the present moment and on every step you are taking.
9. Feel the Earth beneath as you take every step.
10. Breathe deeply with every step.
11. Feel the energy of the Earth flowing into you. Repeat these steps until you feel your energy changing.

Meditation to Heal the Muladhara

This meditation should also be practiced outdoors, like in your yard or at a park.

1. Find a quiet spot outdoors.
2. Take off your shoes.
3. Stand barefoot on the ground.
4. Feel the connection between you and the Earth through your bare feet.
5. Ensure you are standing up straight.
6. Close your eyes.
7. Relax your shoulders.
8. Place both your arms by your side.
9. Gently bend your knees.

10. Focus on your feet's soles.

11. Feel the energy between your feet and the Earth.

12. Feel your feet planted firmly on the ground.

13. Imagine an upward force keeping you in place.

14. Let your awareness move through your body.

15. Feel every part of your body as it is being supported by your base.

16. As your awareness reaches the top part of your spinal cord. Visualize your head's crown separated from your body and being lifted to the sky

17. Remain in this state for a few minutes.

Meditation Exercise While Walking #1

As mentioned, you can incorporate meditation into your daily routine. You can practice this meditation exercise while taking a hike, walking to work, or running errands.

1. Walk normally at your regular pace.

2. You can put your hands on your belly, at your sides, or behind your back (go with whatever makes you comfortable).

3. Count every step you are taking from 1 to 10, then start from 1 again (this step is optional).

4. Focus on how your feet move as you take every step.

5. Feel how your legs and every part of your body move.

6. Since you are walking outside, you may encounter distractions, or your mind may wander. This may happen a few times, but you shouldn't let it frustrate you, simply bring your attention back to your walking.

7. Be aware of the environment around you, and feel everything.

8. Remember that you are outdoors, so make sure you remain safe.

9. Focus your attention on all the sounds around you.

10. Don't try to identify the sounds or even be amused or disturbed by them.

11. Just notice the sounds without getting too invested in any of them.

12. Now focus on what you are smelling.

13. Just like sounds, don't try to identify the smell or feel anything towards it.

14. Now bring your awareness to your vision.

15. Notice the objects and colors around you.

16. Don't let them distract you, just be aware of them (if something distracts you, simply go back to your sense of awareness).

17. Don't drift off; just walk naturally while being mindful.

18. Keep walking while being mindful of your environment and everything around you.

19. You aren't doing anything or changing anything; you are only walking while you are being mindful.

20. Remain in this state for a few minutes.

21. By the end of the meditation, bring your focus back on the practice.● Feel your feet on the ground and how your body moves with every step.

22. After you finish meditating, stand still for a few minutes, and try to keep this awareness sensation with you for the rest of the day.

Meditation Exercise While Walking #2

1. Walk normally for about 10 to 15 steps (preferably in slow steps).

2. Place your hands behind your back or by your side (do whatever makes you comfortable).

3. Now stop and start breathing normally for a couple of minutes (Or for as long as you feel like it).

4. Keep walking for a few steps.

5. Stop and breathe again.

6. Repeat these steps for as long as you like.

7. With each step, feel every movement of your feet, like when you lift your foot or when it touches the floor.

8. Focus on your breathing and your feet's movement on the ground.

9. When your mind wanders, shift the focus back to your breathing and walking.

Meditation Exercise While Commuting #1

We spend a long time on buses, trains, or in our cars. Sometimes we can feel stressed, especially when we are stuck in traffic. To relax and enjoy your commute, practice mindful meditation. It is important to note that you should ensure your safety while performing. This exercise should be practiced while driving.

1. Set your phone to silent.

2. Turn off your radio.

3. Shut your windows to avoid distractions.

4. Start by breathing deeply.

5. Be aware of the silence and your surroundings.

6. Focus on your surrounding while driving and keep your eyes on the road.

7. Never take your eyes off the road (this is vital for your safety).

8. Use your peripheral vision to be aware of your surroundings.

9. Be aware of the scenery, sounds, and sights while you are on the road.

10. Pay attention to your driving and what each part of your body is doing.

11. Feel your feet on the pedals.

12. Feel your hands on the steering wheel.

13. Feel the sensation as you are in the driver's seat.

14. Now notice how you are feeling in every part of your body (Do you have a headache? Are your shoulders tense?)

15. Now feel all the pain, tension, and stress leave your body.

16. While driving, you may get stuck in traffic, or someone may cut you off (if this happens, you need to be able to identify all your feelings at this very moment. Do you get angry, anxious, or frustrated?)

17. Try to understand why you feel these negative emotions.

18. Once you understand why you are reacting this way, it may very well lead to a change in your perspective, and you'll start feeling different and opt for a more positive attitude.

19. When you stop the car at a stop sign or traffic light, breathe deeply to calm yourself.

20. Whenever your mind wanders, bring it back to the present moment.

Meditation Exercise While Commuting #2

This meditation exercise is practiced on public transportation.

1. You can be seated or standing up.

2. You can keep your eyes opened or closed (if you close your eyes, ensure your surroundings are safe).

3. Focus on your breathing.

4. Be aware of the sounds around you, how your body is feeling, and the movements of the vehicle.

5. Now, pay attention to the people around you.

6. Just like you, they may also be experiencing something internal.

7. This will help you connect to them and feel less isolated.

Meditation Tips and Tricks that Every Beginner Should Know

1. You can record yourself reading the guided meditation mentioned here and listen to it when you are alone.

2. If you are a beginner, we recommend you practice for a couple of minutes every day for a week and pick it up from there.

3. Make meditation an early morning ritual.

4. Don't be frustrated or angry with the thoughts that creep in when you are meditating. Whatever you feel or think of while meditating is part of you, so treat it with love and kindness.

5. Notice how you feel during every meditation session.

6. Don't fight your thoughts and simply bring your mind back when it wanders.

7. Practice gratitude after every meditation and end it with a smile.

8. Use technology to help you, like mediation apps.

9. You may struggle with meditation at times. Don't be frustrated; it happens. Be kind and patient with yourself.

10. Try doing some stretches before meditation.

11. You can listen to music while meditating.

12. To keep track of your progress and experience, keep a journal to write down your feelings and thoughts before and after every session.

13. After you finish every session, take a few minutes to sit still and feel all the new sensations in your body. You can also do a few stretches or write in your diary to conclude the mediation session.

Chapter 4: Muladhara Mantras and Affirmations

In this chapter, we are going to discuss mantras and affirmations and their role in opening your root chakra. Many people think that affirmations and mantras are the same things, but they are both different. So, let's take a look at mantras and affirmations and the difference between them.

What Are Mantras?

Mantra isn't an English word; in fact, it is derived from two Sanskrit (an ancient Hindu language) words, "*manas*" and "*tra*," which mean mind and vehicle, respectively. Mantras are sounds, words, or phrases that you repeat to yourself so you can stay focused. They are regarded as tools for our minds that are powerful enough to calm our thoughts, so we are able to meditate or practice yoga. Whether you are anxious, depressed, or overwhelmed with thoughts, chanting mantras can be a great tool for meditation, especially for beginners. Mantras also help shift our awareness to ourselves so we can focus inward.

Repeating mantras has a huge impact on the way we think and feel, and they can influence the way we live our lives. The practice of repeating mantras can also reduce stress and anxiety, make you more self-aware and self-compassionate, calmer, improve your concentration, provide you with a better outlook on life, and improve your mood.

What Are Affirmations?

Affirmations are statements that may be short and simple – but hold a lot of power. They are sentences that focus on the goals you want to achieve, and repeating them motivates you to take action. The more you say these affirmations, the more you start believing them. They become engraved in your subconscious and are so powerful you find yourself changing your behavior and taking action to realize these goals. Affirmations can alter the way you think and replace negative thoughts with positive ones.

Many of us don't know that we have more negative than positive thoughts throughout the day, which can damage our mental health. Affirmations help you become aware of the negativity in your mind, so you start actively thinking positively, gradually pushing out the negative thoughts in your head.

They have many benefits, like changing your thought patterns, behavior, and how you see the world around you. They also motivate you and help you stay focused on your goals. Additionally, affirmations increase your energy and positivity and motivate you to change yourself and the way you live your life. You will also find yourself happier as your negative thoughts are replaced with positive ones and more appreciative of the simpler things in life. Your health will also thrive because leading a positive and happy life is good for your heart's health and can reduce the risk of strokes and heart attacks.

Affirmations vs. Mantras

As previously mentioned, many people confuse affirmations and mantras. Affirmations are positive short sentences that help change your thought patterns. They are usually statements that you say to yourself and about yourself, like stating something nice about yourself or something you hope to be or achieve. On the other hand, mantras are sounds or words that have a specific vibration that allows you to create a relationship and harmony with the universe.

You can say your affirmations anywhere, anytime, and either say them once or repeat them 100 times. Mantras should be uttered on specific occasions, like while you are meditating or practicing yoga. You can say your mantras once, they don't have to be repeated, and you should be only focused on them.

Both affirmations and mantras can heal a blocked root chakra releasing healing energy that can balance your root chakra, and mantras can increase your energy and make you feel secure.

Affirmations

In this part, we are going to provide you with affirmations that will help open your root chakra but first, we need to provide tips on how to use affirmations.

1. Don't state your affirmations in the past tense or the future; you want things to happen now, so always use the present tense.

2. Make affirmations part of your daily routine and set time to repeat them every day. You can repeat them any time during the day, and anywhere you like.

3. Use positive words and thoughts. Believe that what you want is being realized, which will influence your thoughts and make you believe that no matter what happens, you will succeed.

4. Don't use affirmations on things that you aren't sure of, as self-doubt will prevent you from achieving your goal.

5. It is best to repeat the affirmation out loud while looking in the mirror.

6. You can also write them down or say them in your head.

Affirmations to Open Your Root Chakra

- I am ready to achieve my goals.
- I am healthy and full of life.
- I feel the earth under my feet.

- I am connected to every part of my body.
- I am one with the Earth.
- I treat my body with love and respect.
- I am open to new opportunities.
- The world is my home.
- I know I am enough.
- I deserve to be loved and cared for.
- I am self-disciplined.
- My body is my home.
- I love my body.
- I am grounded.
- I am wise, and I trust myself.
- I am independent.
- I am safe.
- I deserve to be here.
- I have everything I need.
- I deserve respect.
- I am grateful for the strength in my body, mind, and soul.
- Mother Earth nourishes my body and soul.
- The universe will guide me, and I trust it.
- Mother Earth fulfills my needs.
- I am financially secure.
- The Earth protects me.
- I am responsible for my own happiness.
- My body is flourishing.
- I vibrate positive energy.
- I exhale and let go of fear and anxiety.

- I am free of fear and doubts.
- My life is built on love, peace, and trust.
- My body is healthy.
- I feel protected and safe.
- I am not attached to anything that doesn't serve me.
- My root chakra is open.
- Life is good.
- I belong here.
- I attract positive energy.
- My body makes and keeps me safe.
- In stillness, I find comfort.
- I deserve to feel secure.
- I am always grounded, even when my world is falling apart.
- I am firmly rooted to the Earth beneath me.
- I nurture my body.
- I believe there is good in the world.
- My needs are always met.
- The people in my life support me.
- My life keeps getting better.
- I am where I am supposed to be.
- I keep building myself up; nothing will ever break me.
- I don't live in fear.
- I am always at peace.
- I am awake.
- I am calm.
- I am happy.
- I am nourished.

- I am brave.
- I am wealthy.
- I am steady.
- I am strong.
- I am successful.
- I am grateful.
- I am content.
- I am in control.
- I am stable.
- I breathe in trust and breathe out doubt and fear.
- My energy rises with the sun every day.
- My body supports my well-being.
- My body is a safe place where my spirit flourishes.
- I admire my peacefulness and calmness in the chaos.
- I have all the tools to make me a successful person.
- I am capable of taking care of myself.
- I am always my truest self.
- I live in the moment.
- I feel empowered.
- I breathe in peace.
- I trust in the Universe's plan for me.
- The Universe loves and supports me, and I appreciate everything it is doing for me.
- I find pleasure in living in the present.
- I make the right choices.
- I have everything I need to thrive.
- Amazing things happen in my life every day.
- I trust timing; everything will come at the right time.

- My body takes care of me.
- My body is a temple.
- I am healthy.
- I am well.
- Radiant energy flows through me.
- I am proud of the person I have become.
- I can build my own world.
- I feel safe where I am.
- I create beauty around me.
- My mind is stable.
- I respect my body, and I treat it right.
- I wake up energized every day.
- I am perfect the way I am.
- I am grateful for nature's guidance.
- I believe in myself.
- I am abundant.
- I am a tree that is planted on the earth.
- I am whole.
- I will fulfill my purpose in life.
- My body is healthy.
- I am very confident in my own abilities.
- I love my life.
- I can handle whatever life throws at me.
- Everything is perfectly fine in my life.
- I believe in the goodness of others.
- I take care of my body, and my body takes care of me.
- I have faith in myself.

- I have it in me to make my life great.

- My ancestors' strength is empowering me.

Although these affirmations will help open your root chakra, you probably want to create your own to help you through personal situations. We will provide you with tips to come up with your own.

How to Create Your Own Affirmations

1. You first need to recognize your negative thoughts, feelings, traits, or anything that is holding you back and is affecting your self-confidence. You may have thoughts like *"I am not smart"* or *"I don't have it in me to be successful"*.

2. Write down the negative thought or trait, which will be therapeutic in itself, whilst remaining objective about what you've written.

3. You can then throw the piece of paper away to help get rid of these thoughts and prepare yourself to replace them with positive ones.

4. Now you will come up with your own affirmations by creating statements that contradict your negative thoughts. For instance, if one of your negative thoughts is that you can't lose weight, create an affirmation that says, *"I can lose weight, and I have the right tools to reach the body I want."*

5. When you read your affirmation, it will feel strange at first which is pretty normal. You have been consumed with negative thoughts for so long that it will feel strange when you start adopting a different thought pattern.

6. Keep repeating your affirmations, and you will plant the seed of positivity in your subconscious and will eventually see them growing and your life flourishing.

7. When creating your affirmation, don't use the negative like "don't, can't, or not." For instance, instead of saying "I am not afraid," say *"I am fearless."*

8. If you can't connect with your affirmation or find it hard to believe in it, you can opt for a less firm tone like *"I am ready to believe that I can lose weight"* or "I am open to the idea of working hard to get the promotion."

9. You can later change your words to a firmer and self-assured tone, as mentioned previously.

10. Try to begin your affirmations with the words "I am".

11. Remember to be very specific with your goals and affirmations.

12. Keep repeating them throughout the day, and you will notice a huge difference in your life.

Mantras

LAM Mantra

The "LAM" mantra is associated with the root chakra. The vibration released when repeating this mantra helps heal and unblock your Muladhara. Chanting the LAM mantra helps ground and connect you to the earth by creating a vibrational frequency that can cleanse your root chakra.

LAM is a Bija mantra, and Bija is a Sanskrit word that means *seed*. The Bija refers to one syllable mantras. You won't find English meaning or translation for any of the Bija mantras. All Bija mantras can be chanted loudly or silently and release powerful vibrations. LAM is pronounced as *lahm* or *luhm*. In other words, make an "ah" or "uh" sound when pronouncing the "a" in LAM.

Chant the LAM mantra whenever you need to boost your energy. It will also make you feel secure and that you belong where you are. Additionally, it can increase your self-esteem, improve your finances, and provide you with prosperity. You can chant this mantra during guided meditation.

Vam Mantra

The Vam mantra is also a Bija mantra, and it is pronounced like "vum," just like how you pronounce "thumb." This mantra helps increase your creativity and sexual pleasure. You can chant it while meditating.

Ram Mantra

The Ram mantra is pronounced like the English word "rum." Chanting this mantra will reduce your anxiety and increase your self-confidence. You can chant it alongside longer mantras.

Yam Mantra

Yam is pronounced as "yum." Chanting this mantra promotes love and acceptance.

Ham Mantra

Ham is pronounced like "hum" in "humming. This mantra helps improve your communication skills.

Aum Mantra

The Aum mantra is pronounced like the "U" in "Uber." This mantra helps make your purpose clear and purifies your faith.

Om Mantra

The Om mantra makes you mindful and physically and emotionally aware. When chanting Om, you may find yourself releasing various syllables and vibrations.

- *Anagata* is a stage that you experience when chanting Om. You will find yourself immersed in total silence.

- A is pronounced as "aahhh," releasing this sound from the back of your throat. It helps connect you to your original self.

- M is pronounced as "mmmm." You release this sound with your mouth closed, and you will feel the vibration in your mind and all through your body. It will make you one with the universe.

- U is pronounced as "oooh." It is associated with the energy released from the universe and the mind. You say it from the back of your tongue to your lips. The vibrations released from this sound provide clarity and keep you balanced

Aham Prema

Aham Prema is different from the other mantras we have mentioned as it is more than one syllable. It is pronounced as "*ah-hem-pree-mah.*" The Aham Prema means "I am Divine Love." It is easily pronounced and uttered, and it should be chanted 108 times. Every one of us has divine love deep inside. Chanting this mantra will help you to connect with this love. The Aham Prema mantra will put your soul, mind, and body in a calming and relaxing state. Begin your day by chanting this mantra. If, throughout the day, you find yourself stressed, chanting this mantra will help reduce your stress and put you in a state of tranquility.

Om Mani Padme Hum

The Om Mani Padme Hum is pronounced as "*ohm-mah-nee-pahd-may-huum.*" It is a very popular mantra, mainly because it is easy to utter, and it has proven to be very effective. It means "Praise to the Jewel in the Lotus." According to the Dali Lama, this mantra has a vast and great meaning. All Buddha's teachings are found in this mantra. It is a very powerful mantra that makes us feel compassionate, relaxed, fulfilled, and less obsessed with our physical being. It releases energy that makes us loving and kind towards others and ourselves.

Aum Gum Shreem Maha Lakshmiyei Namaha

The Aum Gum Shreem Maha Lakshmiyei Namaha is pronounced as "*ohm-guum-shreem-mah-ha-lok-shmee-yay-na-mah-ha.*" It means "My salutations or adoration to the great Lakshmi." Chanting this mantra allows you to ask the goddess Lakshmi for help to increase your wealth and provide you with prosperity. You should chant this mantra on a regular basis to bring abundance and prosperity into your life.

Tips for Chanting Mantras

- The most popular and powerful mantra is "Om." You can chant this mantra throughout the day anywhere – while doing your chores, cooking, showering, or meditating.

- You can chant your mantras out loud or quietly as if you are sending its vibrations to your heart. When you chant quietly, you will be focused only on your mantra.

- You should always chant your mantra even if you don't feel like it. Chant through all your negative emotions.

- Study various mantras through books or recordings, or you can consult a yogi to help you out.

- Learn how to pronounce each mantra correctly, and learn about their translation as well (the ones that have translations anyway), as this will help you connect with the mantra while chanting it.

Make mantras and affirmations part of your daily routine until they eventually become a habit, and watch your life transform and feel your root chakra open up.

Chapter 5: Mudras and Pranayama for Your Root

This chapter discusses two other useful additions to help enhance your meditation routine and help balance the Root chakra, namely mudras and pranayamas. Both of these techniques are used in meditation, yoga, and mindfulness exercises designed to balance, heal, and unblock the chakras. The exercises you'll find below are beginner-friendly, although it may take some time to master them if this should be your first encounter. However, when you get them right, you will rejuvenate your root chakra, and with it, your entire body.

What Mudras Are and How to Use Them

Mudras are symbolic hand gestures predominantly stemming from Hindu and Buddhist meditative practices. They are also used in ceremonies and dances and are represented in art, such as sculptures and paintings. Their origins indicate that they were most likely developed for spiritual purposes to help practitioners manifest their inner intentions. Whenever you want to manifest energy, desires, or anything else in your life, you just have to call upon the specific mudra that allows you to do so.

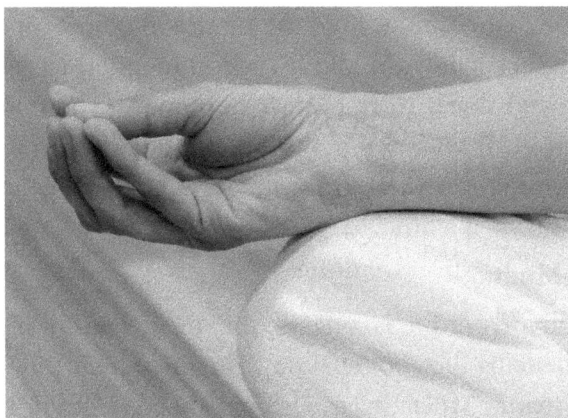

Mudras are symbolic hand gestures.

What makes mudras so efficient is that anyone can learn and use them. Unlike yoga and other complex meditative and breathing techniques that need professional guidance, forming mudras is as easy as pressing two fingers together. A mudra is performed using both hands. It can involve touching the fingers of one hand to another, touching the fingers of the same hand, wrist movements, bending the elbows and shoulders, or slowly moving the entire body. The purpose of these movements is to aid the flow of natural energy through your body.

Most mudras are performed when you are in a padmasana posture. However, you can use another position more comfortable for you, like either sitting or standing, so long as your feet are grounded and accessing natural energy. This helps you focus on your mindfulness practice and heal from the inside out. Because, apart from channeling natural energy and growing your spirituality, mudras have many other therapeutic effects.

Essentially, mudras can help you achieve anything you want, including balancing, healing, or unblocking your root chakra. Forming a mudra designed for these purposes allows you to connect with nature and ultimately activate this energy center.

Mudras for Root Chakra

When doing a mudra for the root chakra, it's crucial not to force the flow of vital energy by pressing your fingertips together too forcefully.

For however long you want to hold the mudra, the fingertips should only be pressed together lightly. While it's recommended to start with a 10-minute session and slowly work toward 20 minutes, you don't have to do this in one session. If you aren't comfortable holding a mudra this long, you can try forming it several times throughout the day and keeping it only for 3-4 minutes at a time.

Muladhara Mudra

The Muladhara mudra is one of the most commonly used hand gestures for balancing the root chakra. It's named after this center - using the Sanskrit word Mulaadhaar, which means "foundations." This indicates that it helps the root chakra ground and stabilize you during mindfulness and spiritual practices. It keeps you connected to nature and its energy - just like it does with trees and other plants - nourishing them through their development and maintaining them in good health throughout their lives. This brings countless physical benefits and mental ones, nourishing your thought processes.

Here is how to do Muladhara mudra:

1. Sit comfortably in a place where you won't be disturbed and try to relax.

2. Bring your palms together with your thumb pointing towards your chest and the other fingers pointing upwards.

3. Fold your little fingers and ring fingers towards your palm, interlacing them.

4. The middle fingers should be left extended, touching at the fingertips.

5. Lock the index fingers and thumbs together, allowing them to form a circle around each other.

6. Alternatively, you can position your hands by bending them towards the root chakra, with the extended middle fingers pointing in that direction.

Gyana Mudra

The name of this mudra means knowledge, which is why it is often used in conjunction with meditation or yoga to gather wisdom. By grounding you to the earth, Gyana mudra helps seal this knowledge into your mind through energy coming from nature. It also helps channel the energy towards your body by opening the root chakra, allowing the vital force to flow through uninterrupted.

Here is how to do the Gyana mudra:

1. Start by getting into a comfortable position, such as padmasana, or by sitting in a chair with your feet touching the ground. Keep your back straight, and your shoulders relaxed.

2. Place your hands on your knees, with your palms facing upward. Stretch your fingers a little, then relax them.

3. Move your index finger towards your thumb and let them touch at the tips, forming a ring. The other fingers should remain straight.

4. Close your eyes and start focusing on your breathing technique.

Keep in mind that you should always bend your index finger towards the thumb and not the other way around. The thumb should never be bent as it represents the source of universal wisdom. The index finger symbolizes your individual consciousness; therefore, bringing it to the thumb allows you to tap into that universal source.

Prithvi Mudra

Prithvi mudra is another hand gesture that involves touching your thumb, only in this case with your ring fingers. Prithivi is the Sanskrit word for "earth. "Through this hand position, you are essentially helping your body to become grounded. It's often used in meditation, yoga, and similar chakra healing exercises. It eradicates physical and mental symptoms of a hurt root chakra, including lack of energy, weakness, loss of appetite, weight loss, and much more.

Here is how to do Prithivi Mudra in a few simple steps:

1. Assume a comfortable position by sitting straight with your feet planted firmly on the ground. Alternatively, you may also begin in the padmasana posture.

2. Make sure your back is straight but relaxed, and bring your hand onto your knees, palms facing upwards.

3. Start forming the mudra by bending your ring fingers towards the thumbs and letting them touch at the tips. Make sure to do this with both hands at the same time.

4. With the tip of the ring finger, apply slight pressure to the thumb while keeping your other fingers straight. They shouldn't be strained, but they shouldn't be bent either.

5. Beginners should maintain the position of their fingers for at least five minutes. Once your fingers get used to the position, you can start to expand the time to ten minutes or more.

Bhumisparsha Mudra

The name of this hand gesture literally means "touching the earth," which references Buddha himself as its first practitioner. According to the saying, the great Buddha used this technique to ground himself to the earth and harness its energy for spiritual enlightenment. And just as it kept the other forces from taking the enlightenment from Buddha, Bhumisparsha mudra will also keep the negative energy out of your root chakra. It empowers you with focus and wisdom, allowing you to overcome any challenges you may face throughout your life.

In this mudra, the left hand (placed on your lap) represents creative knowledge. The right hand (pointing toward the ground) illustrates practical skills. This indicates that through the grounding effect, you'll also become more productive. Apart from this, the regular practice of Bhumisparsha mudra has numerous mental, emotional, and physical benefits. Here are some of them:

1. Improved focus and long-lasting mental clarity, particularly when combined with other relaxing exercises.

2. When you are "touching the earth," you also become more resilient and learn to control your emotions even through tough times.

3. It either drives away negative energy coming from harmful emotions or transforms them into something productive.

4. Reduced stress and anxiety levels are also quite common results of this practice. This may also help alleviate physical symptoms related to these states of mind.

Here is how to perform Bhumisparsha mudra:

1. You can start from a comfortable position of your choice. Padmasana posture is a common choice - but if you are more comfortable with simply sitting straight in a chair or standing, feel free to do so.

2. Close your eyes while trying to relax your body and mind. Inhaling and exhaling a couple of times deeply should help you with this, aiding in bringing certain thoughts into focus.

3. When your mind has achieved the state of awareness you want to be in, you can start forming the mudra.

4. Place your left hand in your lap, with your palm facing upward. Then put your right hand on your knee, with your thumb pointing toward the ground.

5. Keep the hand in this position for at least ten minutes or for as long as you are comfortable.

6. Visualize how energy travels from the ground towards your hand and then to your root chakra. Focus on the sensation it brings and place any other feelings or thoughts in the background.

7. When everything else has faded, and you can feel only the natural energy traveling through your body, you may go on with your meditation or yoga session.

If you have trouble concentrating on the sensations with your eyes closed, you can choose to keep them open. Try finding one point in the room to focus on, and keep your eyes fixed on it through the entire exercise.

This mudra is recommended as a daily exercise, both in the morning and before going to sleep. Ten minutes is usually enough for grounding you, especially if you combine it with meditation and pranayama techniques. However, if you are dealing with too many negative emotions at the same time, you may feel it's not long enough to calm you down, in which case, try doing it for 20 minutes.

What Is Pranayama?

Pranayamas are breathing techniques based on ancient yogic practices, meditation, and various other purposes. Its name comes from the combination of the Sanskrit words *prana* (also known as the universal life force) and *ayama,* which means control. Most experts recommend you do them as soon as you wake up before you have breakfast. This provides your mind and body with revitalizing energy, so you'll be ready for the day's challenges. If you do them later in the day, wait at least two hours after your last full meal to avoid discomfort.

By controlling the duration, frequency, and timing of your breathing, you'll be on your way to achieving your ultimate goal - to balance the mind and body. Most of the techniques involve deep breathing, which funnels more oxygen into your body, effectively cleaning it from negative energy and all its physical and mental symptoms. The benefits of pranayama are also noted in a balanced chakra system. Each of the seven main chakras can be balanced, healed, or unblocked by several pranayama techniques.

Pranayama Techniques for Root Chakra

There is a wide range of pranayama and other breathing practices you can use to perfect meditative and yogic techniques to increase the positive effect of mindfulness exercises on your root chakra.

Nadi Shodhana

Also called alternate nostril breathing, Nadi shodhana is one of the best techniques for grounding and balancing the root chakra. Its name comes from the Sanskrit words *nadi* (means "channel") and *shodhana*(means "cleaning"). This indicates that it has a deeply purifying effect on the nadis in your body and mind, effectively calming you down and balancing your energy.

Nadi shodhana is recommended for beginners or anyone struggling to relax before meditation or any other root chakra balancing exercise. Alternating the exhale and inhale allows the air to move freely through your body - including your brain, where it balances out the left and right hemispheres. This action grants both emotional security and mental clarity, which helps balance the root chakra.

Here is how to do Nadi shodhana in a few simple steps:

1. Start by sitting in a comfortable position with your back straight. Relax your shoulders by bringing them forward, then close your eyes. Remember to keep your mind and heart open to the experience.

2. Put your right forefinger and middle finger between your eyebrows and press gently down. Your ring finger should be on your left nostril and your thumb on the right one.

3. Use your thumb to close the right nostril and inhale from your left nostril. Hold your breath for a few seconds, then close the left nostril with your ring finger while simultaneously opening the right one.

4. Exhale through the right nostril, taking a few seconds of pause before inhaling through the same nostril.

5. Now, close the right nostril again. Open the left one and exhale through it. Repeat the entire cycle for 5-10 minutes, breathing naturally, without exertion.

Sitali Pranayama

Sitali pranayama is a breathing exercise with a calming effect. Its name comes from the Sanskrit words *sitali* (means "cooling"), *prana* ("vital energy" or "life force"), and *ayama* (means "exertion"). This points to the soothing effect of the practice, which is designed to still your body and mind for root chakra meditation. It's used after certain practices to keep a clear state of mind while you contemplate your values and anything else related to the root chakra. The cooling aspect also has a healing effect on the root chakra, helping to erase negative energy from this center. Sitali pranayama may reduce fever and excessive hunger and alleviate symptoms of several pulmonary and endocrine conditions.

This extremely easy breathing technique only requires a few steps to complete:

1. Find a quiet place where you won't be disturbed and won't disturb others. Sit in a comfortable position, with your spine

straight and your shoulders relaxed.

2. You may choose to close your eyes or leave them open.

3. Now, roll your tongue in your mouth while inhaling deeply. The air should travel only through the tongue as if it was a straw.

4. If you find the previous technique too challenging to execute, you may also opt for a modified version, in which the air is drawn in through the closed teeth.

5. Exhale through your tongue or teeth and feel the vibrations the air makes as it passes through them.

6. Repeat this for at least five minutes and as many times as you find useful to keep yourself calm.

7. With a last deep exhale, slowly start resuming your regular day-to-day activities.

Ujjayi Pranayama

Ujjayi Pranayama, or "victorious breath," is another technique for preparing your body and mind for relaxation and mindfulness exercises. Its name comes from the Sanskrit word *ujji,* which means "victorious." The exercise forces the air through constricted airways, which raises one's body temperature, making you more comfortable and ready to relax before your session. The passing air's vibration has a grounding effect and helps unblock your root chakra.

Here is how to practice Ujjayi Pranayama:

1. In a quiet place, assume a standing or sitting position. If you opt for the latter, sit on a chair with your back straight and your feet planted on the ground.

2. While you are starting to relax, focus on the stillness coming from within. Make sure your breath stays even while you inhale and exhale slowly and deeply.

3. Feel the effects of your inhale in your lungs and abdominal area, including energy pooling and focus. Exhale, feeling the air leaving these areas of your body.

4. Continue this technique for a couple of minutes until you are truly relaxed.

5. When you are ready, switch to the second part of the exercise - the visualization. Start this by envisioning roots traveling down from your feet to the ground.

6. Inhale deeply, imagining that you are absorbing nature's energy from the ground, and ascend towards your root chakra. Focus on sensing how the energy gets absorbed in this center and distributed through your body.

7. Retain your breath for a couple of seconds before exhaling, when you can take another short pause. Now, you should feel the air traveling downwards from the root chakra to your feet and back to the ground.

8. Feel the heaviness of the grounding effect in your limbs as you repeat the exercise a few times in a row.

Optionally, you can take in more natural energy and distribute it from your root to other chakras - unblocking the flow of energy in them. This boosts the overall well-being by being overly stimulating. You can repeat this a few times in a row as well.

Chapter 6: Muladhara Yoga Poses and Sequences

The benefits of yoga have been much ballyhooed in the West for the past few decades. Of course, it is an ancient practice that has deep roots in the East and has been cultivated by "yogis," or people who specialized in Eastern spiritual medicine for centuries. Long before an understanding of yoga became widespread in the United States and elsewhere, people in India have looked to this unique and spiritual form of exercise to help cure a whole plethora of ailments that can plague the body and mind. Of course, balancing the root chakra is precisely one of these issues that yoga helps to assuage, provided that the right poses are used and practice is consistent. This chapter will help elucidate the ways in which you could turn to yoga to help balance your root chakra and engender a feeling of well-being and calm. There are many poses you can learn, which will be outlined below.

Disclaimer

Before beginning to officially explain the different poses and sequences you can use for your practice, it's worth noting that you need to start out gently. If you're new to yoga or have some trouble with flexibility or mobility - which is bound to happen if your root chakra has been off balance for a long while or suffer from other physical ailments -

be extra careful. You may purchase bolsters to help you meet the required movement halfway without sacrificing its core benefit. Furthermore, there are different adaptations you can try for each pose or sequence to make things further adaptable for your condition. The key here is to have yoga work for you, not the other way around.

Yoga Poses and Sequences

Garland Pose

This pose, called Malasana in Sanskrit, is known for its strengthening capacity for the pelvic floor, which is especially helpful for women. In addition, it provides an excellent stretch for the ankles, groin, and back, which in turn facilitates healthy digestion. To do this pose, you start by squatting and keeping your feet as close together as possible. If you can't keep your feet right on the floor, use a blanket to help soften your stance.

The garland pose.
https://pixahive.com/photo/malasana-garland-pose/

Next, as you squat, be sure to keep your thighs wide apart so that your body, in effect, takes the shape of a slightly flattened flower. The space between your thighs should be wider than your torso. As you squat, exhale, and lean your upper body slightly forward, it will fit comfortably between your thighs.

Once you've mastered that first part comfortably, you will need to bring your palms together, resting your elbows on the insides of your knees. This simple movement will help lengthen your torso and add a more gratifying stretch.

You can choose to end here or further deepen the stretch by pressing your inner thighs against the sides of your torso. Then, stretch your arms forward, swing them to your sides, and press your shins into the armpits. You can then press the fingertips of your hands into the floor or grab your ankles for balance. This is a more complicated move, so you may need to train yourself for a while before being able to do this, which is completely fine. In all cases, you can either stop here or at the step just before this and hold the pose for approximately thirty seconds before standing up again, slowly, and gently rolling your arms, legs, and torso as you do so.

Easy Pose

Easy pose, referred to as *Sukhasana* in Sanskrit, is essentially how it sounds: a simple move that any beginner can master, regardless of their health issues, and it has many benefits. Any classic picture or drawing of a "yogi" will invariably be shown seated in this exact yoga posture. While it is essentially a seated cross-legged pose, there is more to it than meets the eye. In all cases, it is meant to induce a feeling of comfort and calm, and you can remain in an easy pose for however long it takes for you to feel more centered and grounded.

This pose should come rather naturally to you since we've been practicing it in one shape or another since childhood, without even realizing it. You can use a yoga mat, or if that's not gentle enough, pull out a blanket to help ease you onto the ground. Then, extend your legs in front of you, and sit up straight. A good posture here is absolutely critical, and you won't benefit from this pose if you're hunched over. Next, cross your legs in front of you at the shins.

Your knees will be set wide apart, and you can place each foot right beneath your opposite knee, making sure to fold your legs towards you. If this move is too intense, you can keep the bottoms of your feet facing each other. Then, place your hands on your knees with your palms down. Now, you can relax. Make sure that your head, neck, and the length of your spine are straightened while keeping your neck relaxed; you don't want any tension in this part of your body. If you like, you can either look straight ahead or close your eyes, taking a few deep, slow breaths. You can remain in an easy pose for as long as required, and it is an especially good way to meditate for a few minutes. Whenever you're ready to move on in your sequence, or need to get back to your daily routine, simply release and uncross your legs, getting up slowly.

Standing Forward Fold

Uttanasana, also referred to as the standing forward fold, is another pose that can incorporate different modifications to suit your physical needs. It's not terribly complicated, but it does provide a deeper stretch. At the same time, it engages more muscles and joints, so you don't want to overdo it if you're not feeling flexible or agile.

The standing forward fold is a great pose that helps to stretch the body while allowing you to feel more energetic. It provides an intense stretch, working the hamstrings and the back. However, if it hurts, then you're probably doing it wrong. A good standing forward fold pose should feel relaxing, so don't push too hard. In fact, the more you relax throughout this pose, the deeper the stretch will be - if you do the opposite of that, then you might feel a bit sore or tense.

To start, stand tall with your hands on your hips, your feet close together - essentially a mountain pose or *tadasana*. Then, breathe out slowly, bending forward at the hips. Bend your elbows and hold onto each one with the opposite hand, slowly bringing your head down as you bend over. You might not be able to keep your heels fully pressed to the floor, and that is fine. It takes time to be able to deepen the stretch in such a manner - just start slow and gradually build your way to greater flexibility over time.

As you bend over and hang your head low, be sure to keep your knees a bit loose and not locked together; if you're able to keep your knees straight, then great. To deepen the stretch, try to bring your arms down, keeping your fingertips at the same level as your toes, and press your palms onto the yoga mat. If you can't do that quite yet, you can just keep your elbows crossed near your head, holding onto the opposite side of each with your hands.

Once you've reached a comfortable stance, inhale and then exhale, lightly lengthening your torso as you do so. Each exhalation will allow you to fold deeper into the pose, especially as you let your head hang loosely against your body. Hold this pose for however long you feel is helpful to you, but in general, it's recommended to keep steady for roughly a minute.

When you're ready to get up, place your hands back on your hips, then draw your tailbone slowly up while keeping your back flat and inhaling. Slowly stand up straight.

Child's Pose

Similar in some ways to the easy pose, the child pose - or *balsana* - is a pretty good movement to practice, especially if you're a beginner. It is an excellent pose to help you feel relaxed and focused while experiencing a deep stretch that engages your muscles directly.

To start, sit down on your mat, bringing your legs underneath you. However, make sure that your knees are kept far apart - your knees shouldn't be locked when trying to relax into this position. Then, bring your arms straight ahead of you and slowly put your belly between your thighs, pressing your forehead to the floor. Keep your shoulders, face, and eyes relaxed. If this is a hard move for you to do, you can place a block or bolster in front of you and rest your head. Or use your palms to form two fists stacked one upon another, bringing your forehead to rest on them. To benefit from this pose, inhale and exhale slowly for at least five breaths, keeping your forehead centered comfortably ahead of you. You need to get as relaxed as possible in this pose to benefit from the deep stretch while also feeling mentally grounded.

Creating a Sequence

You can create a calming, gentle sequence using all the moves above or incorporating one or two in a streamlined Sun Salutation sequence that will generally take you five to ten minutes at a time. Also, be sure to listen to your body: one day, you may be able to do the standing forward fold easily without a problem; other days, you may find yourself only able to do the garland pose and hold that for a few minutes at a time. It's hard to know how your body will feel on any given day, and there are some moves that will come more naturally to you at one point and others that will feel hard. It's important to go with the flow and figure out how to induce a feeling of calm and comfort, as opposed to pursuing lots of strenuous activity that will only have the opposite effect.

Therefore, listening to your body and what it needs on a given day is important before assessing the best sequence to do to heal your root chakra. If you don't have the time to do a full session of restorative yoga, incorporating one or all of the poses listed above, then you should feel free to adapt certain movements in a manner that befits your current schedule and capacity. For example, you can simply sit in a child pose for a few minutes as you meditate or complete a pranayama session.

To have a clearer idea of the different kinds of variations you can take on, go to the last chapter, and choose the yoga positions that best suit you. As long as you're aware of what it takes to complete any one of the poses listed in this book, you should be well on your way to creating a routine that works well for you. In general, it will help if you pay attention to poses that focus on the lower back since that is where your root chakra is based. Any movement that engages this part of your body will help you accomplish precisely what you need in order to feel more grounded.

Stability, Balance, and the Muladhara

Consistently incorporating yoga sequences into your daily self-care routine will increase your body's ability to feel balanced and enhance your stability both mentally and physically. A few minutes of yoga on any given day will make you feel better, but the key to feeling more rooted, and healing the root chakra in general, lies in sticking to your practice.

Of course, yoga shouldn't be used as a stand-alone practice if it does not completely fit within your daily routine. It should be used alongside other healthy, mindful interventions to help keep your chakras aligned. For example, you may try the standing forward fold pose while practicing visualization techniques. Since the color red is often associated with the root chakra, try visualizing that and maintain the pose for as long as you can - perhaps two minutes. Visualization is an excellent way to help you lock into more complex feelings, allowing you to face them head-on while becoming more grounded and soothing a blocked or overheated root chakra. When combined with yoga, visualization exercises are great mechanisms to allow you to feel more connected to yourself. They provide an important way for you to slow down and think about what you need emotionally and spiritually at any given moment.

Think of yoga as a tool - one of many in your toolbox that helps you feel better whenever you need to. There are some clear-cut techniques you can use to balance your root chakra instead of suffering through the endless streams of stress and their negative impact. Maybe you can combine yoga with an in-depth meditation session, one that could use sound vibrations to help induce a feeling of calm. Or simply play a recorded meditation video or audiotape, and remain in a child's pose for a few minutes, inhaling and exhaling slowly until you feel calm and comfortable.

However you decide to approach things, remember that yoga is one strong way in which you can develop a deep relationship with the Muladhara chakra so that you can feel more at home in your body. As described elsewhere in this book, an overactive root chakra, or one that is blocked, will leave you feeling rather disassociated from your body. This, in turn, affects your capacity to feel grounded, calm, and focused, causing all sorts of disruptions in your work, relationship with yourself, and others. Consistent use of yoga sequences - or even a few simple poses - used alone or in conjunction with another mindful practice will allow you to heal over time.

Not to put too fine a point on it, but consistency is really key to healing the root chakra. While you don't have to employ hyper-involved, complex yoga sequences or meditative practices to achieve a sense of calm, a balanced approach is key. Again, listening to your body and your needs at any given point is important when figuring out the ways in which yoga can help calm the root chakra. How you choose to treat your body has a tremendous impact on your overall well-being. While there are a lot of factors we cannot control (which directly affect our health), being able to incorporate simple, low-cost solutions will help you feel empowered in the face of the biggest obstacles that affect you.

Everyone needs to feel safe and present, and when we are constantly interrupted by our phones or work that never seems to end, sometimes putting down a yoga mat is the only sense of peace you can achieve. Many of the poses listed here and elsewhere in the book are meant to guide you, but nothing is prescriptive. At the end of the day, only each person will know exactly what they need to feel balanced and to help calm the root chakra. So, you should feel free to experiment and try new ideas whenever you can. Yoga, meditation, or visualization techniques are all processes and not finite solutions in and of themselves. Therefore, you would need to keep trying and experimenting in order to see which combination of movement or techniques best work for you. Finding peace or a sense of fulfillment isn't easy - if it were, then there would be no reason to do all this work. It's something that we all strive to achieve, and yoga is one way to help you accomplish just that.

Chapter 7: Using Crystals and Stones

Crystals and stones can add another layer to your root chakra balancing meditation or yoga practice. Moreover, you can use them in your daily life and tap into their energy anytime you need a little extra help dealing with difficulties. In this chapter, you'll find out how and which crystals can help balance the root chakra. You'll also learn how to take care of your crystals, so they will always be full of positive energy.

How Crystals Can Help Balance the Root Chakra

The basic purpose of chakra healing with crystals is to keep your chakras open and free to conduct your essential energy. Each chakra serves a specific purpose in your body, and the root chakra, as you know by now, is responsible for keeping you connected to the earth. Anxiety, despondency, and all the other symptoms of a blocked root chakra that you've studied can be avoided with the correct crystals and gemstones. Stones and crystals vibrate at the same frequency as human energy due to their molecular composition. They work by enhancing your body's inherent healing abilities.

As part of nature, crystals and stones contain pure, positive energy. Holding them will allow you to channel their power to reconnect with nature and balance or clear away any blockage in your root chakra. Not only that, but they can also absorb the harmful energy from your body.

The Difference Between Stones and Crystals

While their functions may sound very similar, crystals and stones provide two very different types of healing. During the crystallization process, crystals such as diamonds, amethysts, or quartz, are formed in angular shapes with jagged edges. They are often translucent, with a high level of shine and a natural resilience thanks to their solid state.

Amethyst crystal.
https://unsplash.com/photos/jLWLxX6i3R8

Stones, on the other hand, are often composed of different minerals, except for semi-precious gemstones, which are typically cut from one single block of minerals. Stones like agate are much smoother and rounder than crystals. They also have a denser structure and wider color variations.

Due to their differences in composition and density, crystals and stones often give off different vibrations. Consequently, they will often align with different types of energies. Nevertheless, it's still possible for a person to be drawn to both groups if they contain the power the person lacks in their energetic system.

Using Crystal and Stones for the Root Chakra

Balancing root chakra with crystals and gems should be based on stabilizing your physical and emotional state. Once your energetic homeostasis has been reestablished, you can move on to elevate the functions in your energy centers, starting from your root chakra.

Crystals and stones in earthy colors work best to empower your root chakra and kickstart your healing process. Look for red and brown variations as these have the deepest connection with the earth. Blacks have a grounding effect as they are reminiscent of the color of wet soil. The shape and form you'll use may depend on the purpose of the crystal, but it's a good idea to opt for the most natural formations. That being said, the choice also depends on which rocks you are drawn to.

Here are some of the most powerful stones and crystals that work with the root chakra.

Garnet

Garnet, particularly red garnet, is an incredibly rare and powerful stone, shining in different shades of red that speak to your root chakra. It raises the energy in this center, contributing to the balance of your overall well-being. Garnet is recommended for channeling strength and courage through specific exercises or daily life. You can place garnet in the corner of the room you spend the most time in for the latter. Or you can keep it close to your body in the form of a talisman to have constant access to its power.

Hematite

With its naturally rugged edges and natural brightness, Hematite is an excellent tool for replacing negative with positive energy. It borrows the energy from your root chakra, cleanses it, and returns it to the chakra, effectively restoring its balance. Keep it in your hand if you have trouble concentrating during mindfulness exercises. Empowering yourself with Hematite during a session will help you to stay grounded and keep only relevant thoughts in focus. You can also take advantage of its power by keeping it on your desk at your workplace to improve your productivity.

Black Obsidian

Black Obsidian is as rich in raw natural power as is the soil that nurtures our plants. Its mirror-like surface reflects the state of your root chakra but can also protect it if needed. Carrying this stone with you will repel any falsity or negativity threatening your energy, allowing you to rely on the wisdom that comes from the root chakra. Just knowing that you can always trust your gut empowers this base energy center, which, in turn, grows your intuition even more. Wear Black Obsidian in jewelry, preferably as a ring, so you can always check the reflection of your energy.

Red Jasper

Another stone in earthy red colors, Red Jasper, has a nourishing effect on your root chakra. It can be a source of endurance, inspiration, and resilience to overcome adversities and heal yourself emotionally, mentally, and physically. Wear Red Jasper as a pendant to keep it as close to your body as possible to increase your confidence. If you are going through tough times, place a Red Jasper crystal ball in your room and allow it to restore your vitality and reconnect you to your inner power.

Bloodstone

Bloodstone can turn you into a true warrior with its blood-red freckles painted over a green background. It unblocks the root chakra, allowing vital energy to flow towards the upper chakras, raising its level throughout the body. Bloodstone balances out your emotions, making you feel more secure in yourself and invincible even when it comes to the toughest emotional challenges. Hold this stone in your hands during meditation to ease anxiety, or wear it as a talisman to shield yourself from negative emotions.

Carnelian

Carnelian is known for its energizing effects - something your blocked or unbalanced root chakra would really need. It can replace sluggishness with vibrancy and boost your mood and productivity so you can return to the top of your game. Keep it on your desk at your workplace to ensure you'll have the strength to complete all your assignments and perhaps challenge yourself by taking on some new ones. You can also use Carnelian to inspire you if you have trouble clarifying your intent in spiritual or meditative practices for balancing or healing the root chakra.

Black Tourmaline

This mysteriously dark stone has a protective effect on your energy, aimed at the point where it enters your body, the root chakra. Here, Black Tourmaline repels all the negativity directed at you, so no one will be able to lower your vibes. Helping you where you need the most, Black Tourmaline restores your sense of safety and heals you from traumatic experiences. Wear it as jewelry to achieve this effect. If negativity has already entered your body, you can transform it into positivity by using this stone during meditation, yoga, or other chakra healing exercise.

Tiger's Eye

If you are looking for the ultimate protection for your root chakra, Tigers Eye can definitely deliver this and much more. This stone incorporates all the earthy colors -a true indication of its power. By looking at it, you are reminded of the natural strength that lies within you, strengthening your root chakra and making you believe that you can overcome everything. Wear Tigers Eye as a bracelet to show that you can always keep your head high. Placing the stone in the corner of your space will ensure you are protected from toxic energy as long as you are in that room.

Smoky Quartz

The shimmery Smoky Quartz clears a blocked chakra from all the negativity and reestablishes its connection with the upper centers. Its power lies in being both the messenger of nature and the universe, granting a level of wisdom that is unparalleled. It can clarify your path and purpose in life and show you the energies you need to let go of in order to move on. For all these reasons, Smoky Quartz is particularly recommended for meditation and other mindfulness exercises. If you want your root chakra to stay connected to both sources of wisdom, place this stone near the entrance of your home.

Smokey quartz.
https://pixabay.com/es/photos/cristales-cuarzo-ahumado-macro-3129390/

Black Onyx

Similar to the other black stones, the Black Onyx can also be used to guard your root chakra. This stone maintains the energetic balance of the root center and deters negativity from entering your body. Black Onyx also has the ability to restore mental clarity and physical strength, further improving the grounding effects of the root chakra. Use this stone during meditation to channel your thoughts from your subconscious to your conscious mind. Pairing it with another black crystal will be even more beneficial in bringing forth any negativity.

Moss Agate

Moss Agate is believed to cleanse your root chakra with the power of a spring shower, thanks to its unusual combination of light and dark colors. By removing your stress, you'll be able to be more productive and obtain abundance in your emotional and spiritual lives. Moss Agate's coolness also acts as a grounding stone, reminding you not to be overcome by powerful emotions. Wear it as a talisman or piece of jewelry to remind yourself to be more patient. Use it during a mindfulness exercise or other spiritual practice to connect with your inner self or spiritual guide.

Cleansing and Caring for Your Crystals and Stones

Regardless of how many crystals or stones you have or how often you use them, they'll only help you if you also take care of them. Since many of them can absorb negative energy, it's crucial to cleanse them after each use. Since crystals and stones are constantly busy protecting you, they don't even get the chance to purify themself as those you use only occasionally may do.

Besides cleansing, you'll also need to learn how to store and recharge your rocks with natural energy. While they can connect to the positive vibrations of nature on their own, they'll also need to be in touch with your vital energy. So, make sure you charge them regularly through different sources to keep them at full capacity.

Purifying your crystals and stones is necessary even before their first use because they can pick up negativity anytime. How often you need to perform a cleansing and recharging ritual after the first use depends on how often you are using your gems. If you are going through tough times and rely on your crystals to soak up all the negative emotions, you'll need to clean them more often.

Depending on your preferences and their functions, cleansing and recharging your stones and crystals can be done in several ways. Here are some of the most common ways to keep your rocks full of positive energy.

Using Moonlight

Both the full and new moon are full of radiant energy you can use for cleansing and recharging. The new moon will provide them with elevating energy, which can come in handy if you are looking to use your crystals for personal growth in the future. The full moon gives you the ability to release pent-up emotions and end relationships that aren't working out.

Put the crystals on a windowsill at night, ensuring they will be exposed to moonlight. For the best results, leave them to soak up the moon's energy throughout the entire night. The best part about this method is that it can be applied to any crystal and stone.

Using an Eclipse

Just as the power of moonlight can purify your stones, so can its absence. In fact, both lunar and solar eclipses are known for releasing an enormous amount of power - and in a way, they herald a new beginning.

You can use this fresh and supercharged energy in your crystals to motivate you to move forward with your life, even if you have to make radical decisions.

Similar to the previous method, you'll need to place your crystal outside to be exposed to the lunar or solar eclipse and its energy. It's important to note that if you are doing this during a solar eclipse, you should only use it on gems that won't get damaged by the sunlight when it emerges.

Soaking in Saltwater

Saltwater has played a part in chakra healing as long as they've existed to humankind- and it also works for rejuvenating crystal energy. Soaking your stones in saltwater strips them of toxic energy and provides them with a gentle flow of fresh energy. Although the most natural form of salt water is the sea and the ocean, you can also use manually salted water if this is the only form available.

Place your crystals in a large bowl, pour salt water over them, and leave them to soak up the power for 12-24 hours. After that, take your gems out of the water, dry them, and they'll be ready to use. Unfortunately, not all crystals fare well in water, so make sure you don't use this method on them.

Smudging

Smudging is a very simple yet efficient method for purifying your crystals. It's an ancient technique applicable to any stone. Smudging involves burning healing plants or herbs and using their smoke to cleanse the object of your choosing. Lavender, cedar, and sweetgrass are just some of the popular choices of materials to use for smudging. Sage is also often used as it has a soothing effect - which, when infused into the crystals, provides an extra healing element for your chakras.

Gather your herbs in a bundle and light them on one end. As they start to smoke, start waving them over your crystal. You can do this either inside beside an open window or outside in the open air, so the negative energy can leave the space as fast as possible. Continue smudging for at least 30 seconds.

Basking in Sunlight

Just as the sun has the power to revive nature in springtime, it can also give new life to your stones and crystals. Just feeling the warmth emanating from a freshly recharged stone can work wonders on your chakras.

When you know that the weather will be sunny the entire day, place the gems outside in the morning and collect them when night falls. Be careful whilst doing this with darker stones, as they might fade and lose some of their vibrating capacity. These should be left out for no more than three hours at a time.

Using Sound Frequencies

Essentially, sound is made up of vibrations, which crystals and stones absorb, changing their own vibration. It's a convenient, safe, and effective method for purifying your gems. Chanting, bells, and other methods are often used for raising vibrations in crystals. For the best result, it's a good idea to do this a couple of times a day, a few minutes at a time.

Larger Stones

Some larger stones can transfer some of their vibrations to smaller ones, providing you with another simple way to cleanse and recharge your healing crystals. All you need to do is to leave the small gems on top of the larger ones for a couple of hours. If their shape doesn't allow this, you can simply put them in a bag together and wait until the transfer is over.

Stone Burial

Crystals used for balancing or healing the root chakra will particularly benefit from being buried. This allows them to soak out natural energy from the soil and ground you when it's needed. The soil will also absorb any bad energy contained in your crystals.

Find a place you'll bury your stones, make a hole of a few inches, place your stone in it and cover it with soil. Leave it for 24-72 hours, depending on the future purpose and previous use of the item.

Chapter 8: Root Chakra Aromatherapy

To understand root chakra aromatherapy, it is necessary to grasp the fundamental concept of vibrational energy. Our bodies are composed of many atoms that vibrate at various distinct wavelengths. When we are physically or mentally stressed, our body's vibrations get out of sync very quickly. Vibrational therapy can help the body reclaim its fundamental natural rhythm. Many therapies will help you balance your inner chakras, such as yoga, traditional Chinese medicines, aromatherapy, etc. In this chapter, you'll learn about root chakra aromatherapy.

Essential oils are used for root chakra aromatherapy.
https://pixabay.com/es/photos/aceites-esenciales-aromaterapia-spa-1433692/

In root chakra aromatherapy, essential oils are used to alter our deep vibrations and spiritual health. We rely on the oils' energetic or vibrational attributes instead of their physicochemical capabilities. All kinds of essential oils have the power to affect our physiological, psychological, spiritual, and intellectual health. When our Muladhara (Root Chakra) is disturbed or blocked due to unbalanced vibrations in the body. Then, it is preferable to balance these vibrations with the help of essential oils before it converts into physical sickness.

How Aromatherapy Helps Balance Muladhara

Aromatherapy is a procedure in which essential oils heal a person's mental and physical health. It includes using various essential oils such as cedarwood, sandalwood, white fir, lavender, etc. Essential oils are extracted from roots, bark, peels, flower petals, herbs, and trees.

One of the most commonly reported benefits of this type of therapy is relieving strain, nervousness, and distress, which are commonly present in our everyday lives. Another important benefit that you'll notice from using these essential oils is a greater feeling of calmness and serenity. They also help with improving your sleep quality and are very beneficial for people who have been suffering from chronic or persistent pain. The numerous benefits of these magical essential oils don't end here; they are also beneficial for long-term health issues linked to memory loss.

Why Is Aromatherapy Appropriate for Root Chakra?

Humans have been using plants for their amazing medicinal qualities since ancient times. Soothing energy from the oils is experienced when you inhale the aroma, use them directly on your body, or massage your face with them. There are many methods for using essential oils in your daily life. Each plant has its unique therapeutic characteristics that connect to your body's natural energy points.

Each chakra has an essential oil that works best to heal it. The qualities of aromatherapy given below to indicate its appropriateness for root chakra:

Helps You Calm Down

When you are dealing with overwhelming thoughts, massaging essential oils into your body can help you calm down. You can also breathe in their lovely aromas, and because the aroma causes your eyes to expand and your body to create enzymes that make the tissue in your vascular system rest. It also causes your bloodstream pressure to drop, which leads to a steadier heartbeat.

Helps Improve Sleep

According to research, two out of every five people do not get enough sleep. On the other hand, aromatherapy may considerably assist in soothing the body and brain. It prepares your body for rest and helps you relax if you use essential oils every night.

Helps with Stress

Coping with your stress is essential in making it to the end of the day when everything is getting out of hand. Essential oils can help you in reducing your stress. Oils from wood, such as frankincense and sandalwood, may be ideal if your distress is making your life difficult.

Instead of grabbing coffee or sugary items to boost your energy in the morning, it is more appropriate to use aromatherapy by infusing essential oils into your daily life.

Essential Oils for Balancing Your Root Chakras

Aromatherapy offers potent therapeutic effects that help people feel comfortable and secure. You can use essential oils in aromatherapy, such as sandalwood, cedarwood, patchouli oil, and many more. Some of them are discussed below:

Cedarwood Essential Oil

Cedarwood essential oil is obtained from the cedar tree's branches, leaflets, trunk, and seeds. It possesses various qualities that make it an amazing choice for helping with the opening and balancing of Muladhara. One of the biggest benefits is that it helps reduce inflammatory issues in bones, which can cause severe pain and agony. Another notable medical benefit of cedarwood essential oil is its ability to relieve spasms. This oil can treat almost all forms of spasms. It can also be used as a health tonic because it enhances metabolism. It corrects the functioning of the kidney and liver, which in turn enhances general well-being.

Another therapeutic aspect of cedarwood oil is that it acts as a *diuretic*, so it increases urination, assisting in the release of extra water and toxins (such as uric acid) from the body. Cedarwood oil not only corrects menstruation but also regulates the menstruation cycle. So, it's ideal for those who have blocked or irregular menstruation. Menstruation's discomfort and side effects, such as sickness, exhaustion, and mood changes, can also be balanced by using cedarwood oil daily.

Moreover, cedarwood oil can be used to relieve discomfort. It helps to eliminate coughing and removes phlegm from the nasal passages and lungs. It also helps with migraines, red and swollen eyes, and other cold symptoms. Cedarwood oil is a powerful sedative with a relaxing and soothing impact on the psyche. It relieves tension and anxiety while reducing skin irritation. This function also aids in promoting good, restful, and undisturbed sleep.

Frankincense Essential Oil

Essential oils, such as frankincense oil, have been used in aromatherapy for hundreds of years for their medicinal and healing characteristics. Frankincense oil has been known to regulate breathing and heart rate when there is a turmoil of emotions and/or stress. It possesses anti-anxiety and anti-depression properties, yet it has no harmful side effects or causes undesirable sleepiness, unlike pharmaceutical drugs. As a matter of fact, this oil has immune-enhancing properties that may aid in the destruction of harmful germs. It can keep germs from growing on your skin, mouth, or in your house.

Moreover, this oil can strengthen skin and increase a person's skin tone, elasticity, and defense systems against infections or blemishes. It may be used to tone and lift skin, cure wounds, and minimize the appearance of scars and acne. According to research, frankincense oil can help increase memory and cognitive abilities. Using frankincense during pregnancy improves the memory of a mother and child. In addition to this, Frankincense oil lowers the symptoms related to menstruation and menopause by regulating hormone levels. In premenopausal women, frankincense oil can help regulate estrogen production.

The many benefits of Frankincense oil don't end here because it also aids in bowel motions in the digestive tract. It may also assist in easing stomach discomfort and cramping and drain out retained water from the belly that causes bloating. Lastly, it can help with worry and stress, holding you awake at night. It has a soothing and anchoring smell that might assist you in falling asleep easily.

Sandalwood Essential Oil

The next oil on our list is Sandalwood essential oil, famous in aromatherapeutic practices because of its great medical properties. It helps balance the root chakra because Sandalwood essential oil is a natural cure for improving mental sharpness and brain function. It helps you to stay cool under pressure and think more clearly. Moreover, Sandalwood essential oil is a gentle antibacterial that can help prevent the skin from any bacterial illness. It has several active components that effectively alleviate inflammation.

In addition to this, Sandalwood essential oil is famous for its relaxing effects. Smelling the essential oil can assist in producing a sense of relaxation and calm, which can help reduce anxiety and depression-related issues. Another sought-after benefit of Sandalwood is that it also helps relieve anxiety, which is one of the classic signs of a blocked root chakra—this moderate nervous system soothing aids in alleviating insomnia and encourages better sleep.

Patchouli Essential Oil

Patchouli oil has a long and complicated history, much like its aroma. Patchouli oil is extracted from the meticulously wilted leaflets of the patchouli plant. It is a green shrub that grows to approximately three feet tall and is related to the mint plant.

Interestingly, Patchouli has a unique and powerful scent. Like many of the other essential oils for the root chakra on our list, it has an earthy and woody fragrance. It does, however, have a musky, sweet, and somewhat spicy aroma. Patchouli essential oil helps to repair and regulate the root chakra by instilling emotions of security and tranquility. This oil can also help us feel less insecure, alone, and anxious. Our root chakra is frequently blocked due to a lack of fundamental necessities, namely protection and stability. As a result, patchouli is one of the most effective essential oils for unblocking, balancing, and aligning.

Vetiver Essential Oil

It is also known as the "oil of calmness." It is one of the most widely suggested essential oils for regulating the root chakra. It has a natural scent that is sometimes compared to chopped grass on a hot summer day. It has an earthy, smoky, and woody fragrance. Vetiver oil is extracted from matured and submerged in roots from the vetiver plants. It is now commonly grown in many tropical places.

It is well-known for its grounding properties and capacity to aid the body, brain, and soul-center and for regulation of chakras. Similarly, vetiver also promotes quiet and tranquility. This assists in the reduction of stress, anxiety, and uneasiness. One of the most prevalent signs of a blocked root chakra is emotional instability. Vetiver helps develop a feeling of connection and significance in one's life. It can also aid with muscular pains and burns on a physical level.

Basil Essential Oil

This oil is extracted from basil leaves. Basil Essential oil has a pleasant, fragrant, refreshingly flowery, and cleanly grassy aroma described as breezy, bright, and refreshing. Basil, which is said to have a calming influence on the psyche, has been used for various purposes and is available in a variety of teas, dried powders, and oils. Its anti-inflammatory, oxidative, antibacterial, antiviral, and antidepressant properties make it a popular ingredient in Asian traditional medicine.

It is used in aromatherapy to relieve or eliminate headaches, exhaustion, melancholy, and the discomforts of asthma and inspire psychological perseverance. It helps people with impaired attention, allergies, clogged sinuses, or viruses. Furthermore, the perfume made from Basil repels insects. It kills germs that generate smells in rooms, efficiently deodorizing stale indoor air, such as automobiles and even dirty furniture. Its digestive characteristics provide relief from uneasiness, spasms, nausea, diarrhea, and all indicators of metabolic abnormalities.

Basil essential oil is said to rejuvenate, stimulate, and encourage the restoration of scarred or lackluster skin when used topically. It's commonly used to help the skin's suppleness and resilience. It is also helpful in regulating oil production, calming acne outbreaks, relieving dryness, and soothing symptoms of skin infections and other disorders.

Sweet Basil oil is recognized for adding a pleasant and refreshing aroma to any ordinary shampoo, boosting circulation, controlling scalp oil production, and promoting healthy hair development to halt or stop hair loss. It efficiently eliminates any buildup of dead skin, grime, oil, environmental pollutants, and germs from the scalp by moisturizing and cleaning it. Sweet Basil Oil aids in the appearance and feel of silky, glossy strands by demonstrating these cleaning and clarifying capabilities.

White Fir Essential Oil

It has a clear, crisp scent similar to a forest. It can be used directly or aromatically to promote relaxation, stabilization, and even revitalizing benefits for the person with an unbalanced root chakra. It is a unique essential oil that can soothe skin, reduce tension, and improve the surrounding environment.

It can open your root chakra by reducing your anxiety, unsettlement, and laziness. Some of the most prominent benefits of this essential oil are that it has a serene and soothing aroma that can be of great benefit after an intensive activity. Massage white fir oil onto the skin after strong regular activity to get these advantages. Moreover, when tired or lazy, you can simply use the "white fir" essential oil for an energizing effect. When you're also feeling unsettled, you can use white fir to evoke feelings of stability.

How to Use Essential Oils for Root Chakra

Aromatherapists usually recommend dispersing essential oils into the atmosphere or water. They also recommend directly applying them to various body areas that are close to the chakra you are seeking to regulate. On the other hand, the root chakra is one of the simplest chakras to open and balance because it does not require the use of water or air dispersion. To activate this chakra and feel more rooted and connected to the soil, apply suggested root chakra essential oils *straight to the bottoms of your feet.*

Some Precautions to Consider

Before you start using the essential oils, you have to keep a few things in mind. This is because essential oils are quite potent and immensely helpful in opening chakras. However, you must be cautious while using them. Following are some of the precautions that you should take:

1. Essential oils should not be used on newborns or children under the age of three or pregnant and breastfeeding women. Anyone with cerebral or neurological issues or major health difficulties should not use them without consulting their doctor or aromatherapist.

2. No one should take essential oil injections. They are quite harmful. Avoid applying essential oils directly to eyelids or eye regions unless prescribed medical guidance is given. Essential oils should not be splashed or rubbed directly to the nose or ears. To massage the prohibited regions, you may still use a blend of essential oil diluted to 10% in vegetable oil.

3. To ensure there is no allergic skin response, do a test on the inside crease of the elbow and wait 24 hours. Never use an essential oil unless you have first learned how to use it properly. Always seek the advice of a health expert if you have any doubts.

After using an essential oil, wash your hands properly. Make sure that you are taking them in exact proportion (as was recommended) and according to the instructions for each one of them. Essential oils should be kept out of the reach of children and animals.

Chapter 9: Muladhara Diet and Nutrition

Crystals, meditations, yoga, affirmations, pranayamas, and mantras aren't the only things that can open your root chakra. Eating the right food can open and balance your Muladhara, as well. Food and chakras are connected because chakras are the energy centers in our bodies, and food provides one's physical body with energy. So, when we eat the right food, our chakras remain open, which eases the energy flow in our bodies. Additionally, food has a very specific vibration that our chakras feed on, ultimately activating them.

A healthy diet is essential to balance your root chakra.
https://unsplash.com/photos/qKbHvzXb85A

Food plays a huge role in balancing the root chakra more than any of the other six chakras. This is because it is the base chakra, and it is connected to the Earth, where food comes from. Anything that comes from the Earth contains its energy which will stabilize and balance your root chakra.

We all know the many benefits of eating healthy meals every day, but now you can add balancing your root chakra to these benefits. You should mainly focus on meat, legumes, nuts, grains, and root vegetables. These foods will increase the energy flow in the Muladhara.

Best Foods for the Root Chakra

When it comes to choosing the best food for healing and opening your root chakra, think red. Red is the color associated with the Muladhara, so it makes sense that all food with the same color balances the base chakra.

Disclaimer: Before we go any further, it is important to note that we aren't nutritionists. You should always check with your health specialist before making any drastic changes to your diet, especially if you have any underlying conditions.

Red Foods

As mentioned, all-natural red foods are perfect for your root chakra. In fact, incorporating red ingredients into your meals is the fastest and easiest way to help restore the Muladhara. The root chakra is responsible for your adrenals, your bone, and skin health which all require vitamin C. You'll find this vitamin in various red fruits and vegetables like apples, strawberries, tomatoes, cherries, grapes, beets, red plums, guava, red currants, red cabbage, raspberries, rhubarb, watermelon, chard, cranberries, and pomegranates.

Red Meats

Red vegetables and fruits aren't the only food that energizes the root chakra, but red meat can do the same job as well, especially since red meat contains iron and protein, which can provide the body with more energy to keep us grounded. Veal, venison, beef, lamb, and goat are some excellent choices.

Eggs

Since we are still on the subject of proteins, we can't forget about eggs. They contain protein and vitamins that are very beneficial to the root chakra. So, make sure to add chicken eggs and quail eggs to your diet.

Proteins

Chicken, fish, and pork also play a huge role in activating and energizing the root chakra.

Food Containing High Protein

If you are a vegan, don't worry, we haven't forgotten about you. You can open your root chakra without consuming red meats or eggs since there are many other vegan foods that can do the same job as soy products, tofu, cashew, beans, cacao nibs, edamame, spinach, chickpeas, green peas, black eye peas, broccoli, lentil, quinoa, peanut butter, tahini, walnuts, almonds, peanuts, chia seeds, hemp seeds, hemp milk, tempeh, black beans, amaranth, pumpkin seeds, spirulina, and sunflower seeds.

Hot Peppers

Do you like spicy food? Then you will surely love this ingredient. Hot peppers are known for being fiery, which usually gives a physical reaction that makes us more aware of our bodies. This fiery feeling also boosts our energy. Next time you are cooking and want to add a little kick to your dish, you should try red jalapenos, poblanos, chipotles, sweet red cherry peppers, hatch peppers, anchors, or serranos.

Root Vegetables

Can you think of a food that will provide you with Earth energy more than root vegetables? Root vegetables grow underground, which makes them the best ingredients to keep us grounded and connected to the Earth. Mother Earth is always looking out for us and providing us with healing powers. So, when you experience a deeply blocked chakra, dig through the earth to find remedies in vegetables like garlic, ginger, yam, onions, potatoes, radish, carrots, turnips, parsnips, rutabaga, turmeric, celery, shallots, and dandelion root tea.

Grains

No one can deny the health benefits of grains, and balancing the root chakra is one of them. Buckwheat, whole oats, and bulgur are carbohydrates that provide the body with fibers and the energy it needs to activate the root chakra. Make sure that you only buy whole grains and check the ingredients first.

Spices

Add horseradish, cayenne, chives, and paprika to your dishes whenever you feel any symptoms of a blocked root chakra.

Adding these foods to your diet will do wonders to your root chakra. It is essential to note that you should add naturally red food to your diet, not artificially colored food or red dye. In addition to artificial colors being harmful to health, you won't reap any benefits since the food isn't really red. In other words, you can't trick your chakra.

Recipes for the Muladhara

Now that you have learned about all the food that can balance your root chakra, we have now arrived at the most interesting part of this chapter. We are going to provide you with some easy, healthy, and delicious recipes that will benefit the Muladhara.

Stuffed Potatoes

This recipe will help you if you feel unsettled and will stabilize your root chakra.

Ingredients:

- 4 potatoes (sweet or russet)
- 2 cloves of garlic
- 1 ½ red onions
- 1 cup of mushrooms
- 1 cup of kale
- Grapeseed oil (or any oil you prefer)
- 1 cup of kidney beans

Seasoning

- Salt
- Pepper
- Parsley

Instructions:

1. Heat the oven to 350 F.
2. Wash the potatoes.
3. Poke some holes in the potatoes.
4. Cover them with the oil.
5. Pour a small amount of salt on the potatoes.
6. Put the potatoes in the oven for an hour.
7. Now, sauté the garlic gloves and ½ of the red onion.
8. Once they are translucent, add the kidney beans.
9. Sautee this mix for 3 minutes.
10. Now add the chopped red onion, the kale, and the mushrooms.
11. Add the salt, pepper, and parsley.
12. After the potatoes are done, cut them down from the middle.
13. Next, add the sauteed mix to the middle of the potatoes.
14. Bake in the oven for about 10 minutes.

Sweet Potato and Parsnip Soup

Ingredients:

- 2 large sweet potatoes
- 2 large parsnips
- 2 tablespoons of red curry paste
- 1 cup of vegetable stock
- 1 cup of unsweetened almond milk
- 1 ½ tablespoon of minced fresh ginger
- 1 diced onion

- 1 teaspoon of grated garlic
- 1 tablespoon of coconut oil
- 1 chopped jalapeno
- 1 handful of chopped roasted nuts
- 1 bunch of chopped fresh coriander

Instructions:

1. Peel and dice the sweet potatoes and parsnips.
2. Get a large saucepan.
3. Add the coconut oil.
4. Heat it over medium-high.
5. Add the ginger, garlic, onion, and jalapeno to the saucepan.
6. Sautee them for 5 minutes or until the onion becomes clear.
7. Add the curry paste and mix it with the ingredients for 1 minute.
8. Now add the sweet potatoes (you can add carrots along with the potatoes as well).
9. Add salt and pepper.
10. Stir them together for a while.
11. Pour the almond oil.
12. Add the vegetable stock.
13. Boil the mixture.
14. Next, set the heat to low.
15. Leave the mixture to simmer for 20 or 25 minutes.
16. Check the vegetables with a fork to make sure that they are tender.
17. Now, get a blender.
18. Add soup in batches and puree.
19. After it is pureed, taste it to see if it needs seasoning.
20. Add chopped roasted nuts and coriander (optional).
21. Add salt and black pepper (optional).
22. Remove the soup from the heat.

23. Leave it for a few minutes to cool down.

24. Put the vegetables in broth and maple syrup in a blender.

25. Puree until they have a smooth and creamy texture.

26. Serve and enjoy.

Root Vegetable Soup

Ingredients:

- 4 peeled medium carrots
- 2 cups of unsweetened coconut milk
- 2 tablespoons of coconut milk yogurt (unsweetened)
- 1 ½ knob of peeled fresh ginger
- 1 teaspoon of cinnamon
- 1 diced yellow onion
- 1 sweet potato, medium (you can also use yam)
- 1 teaspoon of curry powder
- 1 tablespoon of coconut oil, unrefined
- 1 teaspoon of sea salt
- 1 cup of vegetable broth, low sodium
- ½ teaspoon of ground black pepper
- ½ teaspoon of ground nutmeg
- A small amount of sprigs paisley

Instructions:

1. Add the coconut oil to a large pot.

2. Warm the oil over medium heat.

3. Add the sweet potato, carrots, ginger, garlic, and onion.

4. Sauté them for 10 minutes.

5. Next, add the cinnamon, coconut milk, nutmeg, curry, salt, pepper, and vegetable broth.

6. Bring the pot to a boil.

7. Now reduce the heat a little so the mixture can simmer.

8. Cover the pot and leave the vegetables to cook for 15 to 20 minutes

9. Now remove the pot and put the mixture in a blender

10. Puree the soup for a couple of minutes or until it looks smooth

11. Put the soup in bowls

12. Garnish each bowl with a sprig of fresh parsley and a dollop of coconut yogurt

Red Curry Coconut Squash Soup

Ingredients:

- 4 minced garlic cloves (you can use less if you want)
- 2 pounds of butternut
- 1 medium chopped yellow onion
- 2 teaspoons of ground coriander
- 2 tablespoons of coconut oil (you can also use olive oil)
- 2-3 tablespoons of vegan red curry paste (preferable Thai)
- 1 quart of vegetable broth
- 1 teaspoon of cumin
- ½ cup of unsweetened coconut flakes (to be used for garnish)
- ¼ cup of chopped fresh cilantro (to be used for garnish)
- ¼ teaspoon of sea salt
- 1 tablespoon of lime juice, fresh
- ¼ teaspoon of red pepper flakes, crushed

Instructions:

1. Put the oil in a pot on medium heat.

2. Now add the red pepper flakes, cumin, salt, garlic, coriander, onion, and curry paste.

3. Stir the ingredients to mix them together.

4. Leave it to cook for 5 minutes.

5. Now add the butternut squash.

6. Cook for 1 minute.

7. Add the broth and bring to a boil.

8. Now reduce the heat and let it simmer for 15 to 20 minutes.

9. During this time, get a medium skillet.

10. Put the coconut flakes in the skillet and let them toast over medium-low heat, and stir.

11. Keep stirring until the edges turn golden brown.

12. Next, remove it from the heat.

13. Check the squash; if they are soft, remove them from the heat.

14. Leave it for a few minutes to cool down.

15. Now put the soup in a blender and blend it until it becomes smooth.

16. Put the smooth soup in a large pot.

17. Add the lime juice to the soup and stir.

18. Garnish the soup with fresh cilantro and toasted coconut flakes.

Beet Smoothie

Ingredients:

- 1 cup of strawberries
- 1 cup of beats (cut into cubes)
- ½ cup of vegan milk
- ½ cup of vegan yogurt

Instructions:

1. Put all the ingredients in a blender.

2. Blend them for 1 or 2 minutes or until it forms a "smoothie" texture.

3. Pour it into a glass and enjoy.

Tofu Quinoa Bowl

Ingredients:

- 2 cups of tofu, cubed
- 3 peeled and chopped garlic cloves
- 2 cups of broccoli, chopped
- 2 teaspoons of ginger
- 2 teaspoons of Bragg's Liquid Amino
- 2 teaspoons of turmeric
- 2 teaspoons of soy sauce
- 1 ½ cups of water
- ½ of a large, chopped onion
- 1 cup of quinoa
- 1 tablespoon of honey
- 1 tablespoon of cranberries
- 1 chopped sprig of parsley
- 1 cup of cauliflower
- 1 tablespoon of olive oil
- 1 tablespoon of chopped walnuts
- 1 teaspoon of fennel seeds
- ½ cup of lime juice
- 1 tablespoon of chopped almonds
- Salt and pepper

Instructions:

1. Add water to a saucepan and bring it to a boil.
2. Now add the soy sauce, ginger, quinoa, lime juice, and turmeric.
3. When the ingredients boil, reduce the heat to medium-low.
4. Leave it until the quinoa becomes fluffy.

5. Remove the pan from the heat.

6. Add the olive oil to a sauté pan on medium-high heat.

7. Next, add the garlic.

8. Leave it to sauté for one minute while stirring.

9. Now add the Bragg's Liquid Amino, tofu, fennel seeds, and onions.

10. When the tofu becomes brown, remove the sauté pan from the heat.

11. Now add the ginger, honey, broccoli, walnuts, soy sauce, almonds, cauliflower, turmeric, and dried cranberries.

12. Leave the ingredients to sauté until the cauliflower and broccoli are cooked.

13. Next, remove the pan from the heat.

14. Add the ingredients in the sauté pan to the saucepan.

15. Fold it into the quinoa **gently.**

16. Add salt and pepper to your liking.

17. Garnish the dish with parsley

Root Vegetable Chips

Ingredients:

- 1 sweet potato
- Sea salt
- 2 large beets
- 3 tablespoons of coconut oil
- 2 parsnips

Instructions:

1. Preheat the oven to 150 C.

2. Peel the vegetables.

3. Slice them.

4. Add the oil and salt.

5. Mix them together.

6. Leave them to bake for 25 to 40 minutes.

7. When the chips dry out, it means they are done.

8. Leave them to cool down so they can become crunchy.

Chocolate Beetroot Brownies (Gluten-Free)

Ingredients:

- 4 tablespoons of de-oiled cocoa
- 1 grated beetroot
- 1 organic egg
- 2 teaspoons of baking soda
- 2 tablespoons of maple syrup
- 1 teaspoon of vanilla
- 175 almonds (you can also use peanuts or cashew)
- A pinch of sea salt
- 5 tablespoons of coconut sugar

Instructions:

1. Preheat the oven to 180 C.

2. Mix the eggs and vanilla together using a whisk.

3. Now, add all the ingredients to a large bowl

4. Mix until the dough becomes very sticky.

5. Get a 9x9-inch baking pan.

6. Line it with parchment paper.

7. Next, spread the dough evenly in the tin.

8. Leave it to bake for 35 minutes.

9. Dust the brownies with more cocoa.

Roasted Root Vegetables with Crispy Tofu

Vegetable Ingredients:

- 6 tablespoons of olive oil
- 2 teaspoons of lemon zest, grated
- 2 teaspoons of dried thyme with 1 teaspoon of tea
- 3 tablespoons of chopped fresh parsley
- 4 peeled and sliced carrots
- 3 peeled and cubed potatoes
- 2 cubed and peeled sweet potatoes
- 3 tablespoons of balsamic vinegar

Tofu Ingredients:

- 2 eggs
- 1 teaspoon of garlic powder
- 454 g of firm tofu (1 block)
- 4 tablespoons of fresh parsley
- 1 teaspoon of soy sauce (reduced sodium)
- ½ cup of flour
- 1 tablespoon of maple syrup

We recommend that you prepare the tofu first.

Tofu Preparation:

1. Cut the block of tofu into small cubes.
2. Add the soy sauce, maple syrup, and garlic into a large bowl.
3. Next, add the tofu cubes and stir until the tofu is covered with the sauce.
4. Cover the bowl and leave it to marinate for 15 minutes (it may take longer).
5. Preheat the oven to 400 F.

6. Get 2 deep plates

7. Put the flour in one and the eggs in the other

8. Beat the eggs

9. Flour the tofu cubes.

10. Next, soak them in the whisked eggs, then flour them again.

11. Prepare a baking sheet lined with parchment paper and add the tofu cubes to the sheet.

12. Leave them to bake for 20 minutes, flipping them halfway through.

Instructions:

1. Preheat the oven to 400 F.

2. Add 6 teaspoons of olive oil and 2 teaspoons of thyme into a large bowl.

3. Mix them together.

4. Next, add the potatoes, sweet potatoes, and carrots and toss to coat.

5. Now place the vegetables on a sheet lined with parchment paper in a single layer. Season with salt and pepper to your liking.

6. Leave the vegetables to bake for 40 minutes.

7. Add the tofu after 20 minutes (they should be golden and crisp when they are done), and make sure to stir frequently.

8. When the vegetables are golden-brown, it means they are done.

9. Add the balsamic vinegar to a small bowl.

10. Next, add the rest of the thyme and olive oil to make a vinaigrette.

11. Before you serve the dish, pour the vinaigrette on the roasted vegetables.

12. Now sprinkle lemon zest and parsley.

Make sure that you follow all the instructions exactly as mentioned, but you can experiment with different ingredients if you like. However, make sure that you opt for ingredients from the ones we have mentioned at the beginning of the chapter to activate your root chakra. Remember to use red food when cooking and enjoy healthy and delicious meals that will heal your root chakra.

Chapter 10: Muladhara 7-Day Routine

The balance of Muladhara is essential for intellectual, physiological, and spiritual well-being. When your root chakra is operating poorly, you might feel unsupportable, untrustworthy, unwilling to be realistic, and unproductive. Without the sustaining energy of a healthy root chakra, you may lose your feeling of belonging and enthusiasm just by being a member of the universe.

According to tradition, there are numerous techniques to stimulate, regulate, and reactivate the root chakra. Some are movement, sound, meditation, affirmations, breathwork, and touch. Here is a seven-day routine to help you balance your Muladhara:

Day-1 Activity

It is your first day trying to balance your inner chakra; it's the Root Chakra. Let's just keep it simple so you don't get tired on the first day.

Start your day with light movement while walking outside your home. You can go for a morning walk in that park or any open landscape. While walking, listen to birds chirping and smell the musky and grassy fragrance of flowers and plants. You'll feel energetic.

Before going to work or school, take a bath by using a fragrant essential oil; it will calm your nerves and help you balance your root chakra.

During the day, if you are busy and cannot take time out for meditation, then you can perform the simple root chakra. Visualize the color red and take long and steady breaths. You can perform this at any time of the day or anywhere.

Your last activity for the day has to be Mantra Affirmations. These are the positive statements you will say aloud to yourself. This will help you open your root chakra, positively affecting your mental health. This affirmation could be anything such as "It's okay, everything will be fine."

Day-2 Activity

Start your day by performing yoga. Stick to Sukhasana poses. They are the easiest. This is an excellent method to begin your day since it will help you create a purpose and stay centered.

Find a suitable sitting pose with your legs folded in front of you to achieve this posture. Raise your hands to your sides and softly place your hands on your lap or the top of your thighs. Release any tightness in your neck by extending it across the curvature of your vertebrae and dropping your shoulders downward. Close your eyes and inhale deeply into your core to help you concentrate on your purpose.

If you still have negative thoughts, you could also go running in the evening. It will not keep you fit and physically healthy, but it will help you maintain your mental health. Running means you are doing a movement, and thus this movement will help you open your clogged Root Chakra.

You can end your day by using essential oils for the root chakra. Massage it directly to the bottom of your feet. You also can use a diffuser to diffuse its fragrance in your room. By inhaling their scent, you can feel relaxed.

Day-3 Activity

On day three, you can perform the following two yoga poses:

A child's pose is a relaxing pose in which your body completely relaxes in on itself. You may practice submission and acceptance in this posture since the earth holds you underneath you. This is a stabilizing position that you may use at any point in your practice, especially when you need to realign with your breath. Take a sitting posture at the rear of the floor. Bring your chest to the floor and succumb to your body's weight. You can spread out with your elbows on either side of the body or extend. Take deep breaths and feel your spine move along with your breath.

The second pose is a Garland pose. This crouch position allows you to directly connect with the earth while also soothing your spirit and soul. It strengthens your lower spine and feet while also allowing your pelvis to expand up from sideways. Fold both of your legs until your knees are facing up into the sky, one at a time. The rear of your thighs ought to be nearer to your knees. Bend over and lift your body to a 45 ° angle, making sure your toes are facing outwards. If your heels begin to rise, a bundled sheet can be positioned under them for more stability.

Next, you can go out to the park or any other place where you can smell nature's earthy fragrances and listen to nature's sounds. This smell and sound will remove your worries and stress for the whole day. If you are going to a park, walk barefoot on the grass. It will soothe your body ache, and it will also open your root chakra.

Day-4 Activity

On day four, perform pranayama. It is responsible for guiding the flow of energy throughout physical existence. This is beneficial for root chakra restoration and vibrational frequency purification. Here are two effective practice exercises:

Alternate Nose is a term used to describe a person who breathes via a separate nasal cavity that equalizes the brain, physique, and spirit. Proceed by resting in a cross-legged position. Breathe deeply and fully while placing one palm on your knee. Close your nostril with your other hand and take deep breaths through the other. Now alternate between both nostrils and fully breathe. Exhale entirely via the left nostril after inhaling through your nose. This cycle should be repeated 15 times.

Cooling Breathing is a great way to keep your body cool during the summer heat and hot flushes. Start by deep breathing while closing your eyes. Make an "O" shape with your mouth when you're ready. Bend your tongue horizontally and push it out of your mouth considerably. Inhale slowly and deeply through your mouth as if you were sipping through a tube. Repeat the movement for another five minutes, focusing on the soothing feeling.

After performing pranayama, you may do some light movements. It will be enough for the day. For instance, if you enjoy gardening, spend some time in the garden. While gardening, you'll indirectly perform Mudras, which means touching the earth or soil. It will ease your unbalanced root chakra.

Day-5 Activity

Start Day 5 with some movement first. Today's movement will be dance. It will be a fun exercise for you. You can play any sound you like or any song that makes you move. You may dance with someone, or you can even dance alone. It will ease the stress in your body.

Your next activity will be meditation exercises. Meditation transmits calming energy throughout the entire body. It aids enlightenment by establishing a connection with one's inner consciousness and God, linking to a higher spirituality of global energy, whether mother earth, divinity, or enlightened awareness. Meditation also brings tranquility and serenity. It is good for all chakras – not only the root chakra. Here are two effective meditation methods:

Begin by reclining your back in a relaxed posture for Body Scan Meditation. Relax your body by taking a few breaths deep into your belly. Start by focusing your attention on your toes and noting any sensations there. Relax through the discomfort rather than resist it. Squeeze into any stress or discomfort in your body and envision it fading. Work your way up through your parts of the body until you've completed a full scan of your entire body.

You could also practice Targeted Meditation. You can start it by focusing on anything specific, including your breath. Simply sit in a relaxed posture, relax your muscles, and breathe deeply into your belly button. Shift your focus to the target you've chosen. Pay attention to the exterior and internal feelings you feel when you inhale and exhale if you've decided to concentrate on your Breathing.

Lastly, you take a bath and add some essential oils to it. You have to spend at least 4o minutes in the bath so that the mixed essential oils will work properly.

Day-6 Activity

On day six, you may start your day with positive affirmations. Such as:

- It will be a wonderful day.
- If anything goes wrong, I will try to make it right.
- If anything is bothering me, I will let it go.

You can say as many positive affirmations as you need to hear. Hearing positive statements will have a positive effect not only on your mental health – but also on your chakras as well.

Next, perform the following yoga poses:

Today, you'll perform a Standing Forward Bend pose. It helps you relax your thoughts and establishes a sense of tranquility and focus on your practice. This position physically stretches the quadriceps and releases stress throughout the back.

Begin in a Mountain Pose by bringing your feet close together. Extend your knees gently and hinge from your pelvis to fold your legs. Put your hands on the floor next to you. You can also grasp onto either elbow if you want to relax even more into this posture. Push out your backbone with each inhalation and bend a little more with each breath.

Day-7 Activity

It is the last day of balancing your root chakra. You will do some movement today as well. But today, you will do a different kind of movement, i.e., hiking.

It is primarily a leisure activity that involves walking in nature. Hiking is a natural activity that enhances physical health, is inexpensive, convenient, and helps you balance your root chakra. Hiking in the woods offers several advantages, including beautiful vistas, fresh air, and the sounds and fragrances of nature. All of these advantages will help you in maintaining your root Chakra.

1. Begin slowly. Beginners should go on a short neighborhood trek. Work your way up to trails that have hills or varied terrain.

2. Make use of poles. Pressing into the ground and driving yourself forward forces your upper body muscle fibers to work harder, which results in a more intense aerobic exercise.

3. Make your way to the hills. Even a little incline will raise your heart rate and cause you to burn more calories. It's believed that a five to ten percent elevation results in a 30 to 40 percent increase in calorie expenditure.

4. Increase the volume. Muscles may be worked while increasing balance and stability on uneven terrain.

5. Put a weight on yourself. Extra weight should be added to your daypack.

6. Get into a rhythm. On days when you can't go to the trails, power-walk on steep terrain while carrying a weighted backpack to maintain your hiking abilities and fitness level.

When you reach your destination, massage the bottom of your feet with soothing essential oil or do some yoga and meditation there. However, there are many other things that you could do to balance Muladhara. You may use crystals in your daily life, wear the red color, or you can also use mudra in your daily life.

Mudra is often referred to as a type of yoga called touch yoga. It indicates touching the earth while doing yoga. It helps to balance potent connections with the root chakra or Muladhara. This type of yogic practice has origins in the Buddhist tradition. It is something you may perform when you're feeling lost or detached.

How to do it: place one palm over your chest, then place the other palm on the ground. Then, take ten or more slow deep breaths.

Another effective strategy to balance root chakra is to use the color red. Because the color red is associated with the root chakra, it is believed that merely wearing it can help to energize the root chakra. You may notice how your energy transforms when you put on a red dress, red shawl, or red lipstick. As red color adjusts your frequency and modifies your energy, engaging with color is the simple and easiest approach to energize or balance your root chakras.

You can also use crystals. They assist any chakra, but they usually originate from the earth, so they have earthy characteristics of the root chakra. It can not only balance root chakra, but it can also strengthen root chakra. Crystals may be used in a variety of ways, including decorating your house with them, donning them as jewelry, and you can also meditate with them. Many crystals, like Red Jasper, Bloodstone, and Hematite, are specifically connected to the root chakra. We hope that you use all these additional things to balance the root chakra.

Some Things to Consider

You may have wondered what it feels like to really release the Muladhara. Well, people will feel secure, relaxed, and assured when the root chakra awakens and energies flow freely. Experiencing rooted, linked, and protected emotions are all signs of the chakra opening. You may also experience warmth, healthy changes in your meals and sleeping habits.

Perhaps you feel curious to know more about what is referred to as the "root chakra sensation." The root chakra is opening and flowing if you feel sensation in your root chakra's parts. The soles of the hands, the bottoms of the feet, and the pelvic girdle are common body parts to feel these feelings during root chakra balancing.

You need to be more aware of the overactive Muladhara. The indications of a clogged Muladhara energy are remarkably similar to those of a hyperactive root chakra. A hyperactive root chakra might have a negative impact on one's health. Panic, worry, and terror are all mental symptoms of a root chakra dysfunction. Low levels of self-esteem, severe anxiety, and eating problems are also frequent in such people.

Sometimes people report feeling pain or feeling that their root chakra is hurting. The presence of discomfort in the pelvic area is normally a symptom of the unbalanced root chakra. You have to understand how to open and balance your root chakra – you must understand that your basic need to survive involves being healthy.

Bonus: From the Root Up

Representing the foundation of your well-being, the root chakra plays a strong significant role in your life. But learning how to unblock and balance it means much more than having a strong chakra. It means having the vital life force travel up to your other chakras uninterrupted and with more power than it ever did before. Raising your energy to the upper chakras is just as essential as taking care of your roots. At the same time, nurturing those chakras may help keep negative energy from permeating your root chakra. In this chapter, you'll get an insight into the upper chakras, see how their blockages affect your health, and what you can do to unblock them.

Sacral Chakra

Located just below your belly button, the sacral chakra is linked to sensuality, pleasure, creativity, desire, and self-worth. It's represented by the color orange and is linked to the element of water. Physically, the sacral chakra plays a role in keeping your lower abdominal area healthy. When this chakra is blocked, you may experience tiredness, lower back pain, urinary tract infections, impotency, and other issues with your genital area.

Emotionally, this center determines how you express your feelings in your relationships as well as how much creativity you bring into them. If you lack desire in your relationships or are unable to express it, this may be a sign of this chakra being blocked. You may also find it hard to find joy in other areas of your life as if nothing could inspire you to unleash your creativity.

Here are some great ways to unblock your sacral chakra:

- **Yoga:** Hip opening poses, like the frog pose, the pigeon, or the cobra pose, can work wonders on your sacral region. They will release physical tension and improve blood and energy circulation in this area. For the best results, try going as deep with them as you can and holding them for the maximum allocated time.

- **Meditation:** Try meditation or other mindfulness techniques designed to raise your emotional intelligence and unlock the issue that keeps you stuck in one place with your emotions.

- **Diet:** Eat orange foods like carrots, sweet potatoes, oranges, mango, pumpkin, and papaya to heal your sacral chakra.

- **Crystals:** Garnet, carnelian, orange calcite, bloodstone, and other orange stones vibrate at the same level your sacral chakra needs to reestablish its energetic balance. Keep them near you during meditation. Or, better yet, place them on your lower abdomen to channel their energy to you.

Solar Plexus Chakra

The solar plexus chakra is an energy center affecting the upper abdominal area, or, to put it simply, your gut. When it's functioning properly, you'll have more confidence in your intuition as well as more self-esteem. The energy of this center also affects your digestion and your core muscles. If blocked, you may experience bloating, increased or decreased appetite, ulcers, stomach pain, acid reflux, and other digestive issues, as well as muscle cramping.

On the mental and emotional front, a blockage in this chakra comes out in the following ways - a loss of self-esteem, powerlessness, worthlessness, and eating disorders. Feeling unsatisfied with your life may also signify a disbalance in this region.

You can unblock your solar plexus chakra through the following methods:

- **Yoga:** Some of the most effective poses for this chakra are the warrior pose, the bow pose, and the boat pose. All of these engage your core muscles which stimulate energy flow in this area. They are also great for strengthening your balance which helps regain your confidence.

- **Meditation:** Use mediative strategies that draw in positive energy, giving you back the confidence, courage, and self-discipline you need. Combine them with pranayama or other deep breathing techniques for an even more powerful effect.

- **Diet:** Yellow foods work best for healing this chakra, so try eating bananas, bell peppers, and pineapples. Improve your gut health with yellow digestion stimulating foods like ginger.

- **Crystals:** Yellow quartz, citrine, yellow tiger's eye, and yellow calcite are closely associated with solar chakras energy. Place them on your upper abdomen while lying down, or wear them on a necklace, ensuring they reach your stomach.

Heart Chakra

As its name suggests, this chakra is located in the center of your chest, near your heart. Closely associated with the color green, it promotes love, kindness, and compassion primarily directed toward yourself – and then at others. Consequently, when this chakra is blocked, you'll likely have trouble expressing your feelings, and you may lack empathy for other people's emotions.

Feeling lost is also common, particularly if the blockage is caused by a relationship ending or the death of a loved one. Circulatory issues, high or low blood pressure, and an irregular heart rate can also be symptomatic of an unbalanced heart chakra.

Here are some effective ways to unblock your heart chakra:

- **Yoga:** Heart opening poses, such as the camel or the eagle pose, are particularly recommended for heart chakra-related issues. You may also want to try other sequences that engage your chest, shoulders, and back, renewing black flow in these regions.

- **Meditation:** Try meditation techniques that bring out unconditional love, compassion, generosity, and the ability to find goodness in yourself and others.

- **Diet:** Eating your greens will be extremely beneficial for your heart chakra. You have kale, spinach, romaine lettuce, cucumber, and many more green veggies to choose from. Kiwis are also associated with this energy center.

- **Crystals:** Look for shiny green stones, like jade, emerald, green calcite, peridot, or watermelon tourmaline, to gain natural healing energy. Wear them over your heart, and they'll be guaranteed to heal, unblock, or cleanse your heart chakra.

Throat Chakra

As its name suggests, this is located in the throat area and is associated with the color blue. It's responsible for your ability to communicate. Everything you feel in your body and mind is linked together in this chakra. Physically, it affects the base of your skull, your ears, cheeks, lips, tongue, jaw, the lower part of your neck, upper part of the back, and shoulders. Blockages in this chakra are probably the most noticeable as they often cause the loss of your voice, thyroid issues, or mouth, teeth, and gum infections.

Not only that, but you may experience a loss of ability to communicate verbally, speak without thinking, and use negative words. The tendency to dominate conversations or have the last word, anxiety to speak in front of others, and unwillingness to listen to others are also common signs of a blocked throat chakra.

Use these methods to unblock your throat chakra:

- **Yoga:** Some of the recommended poses for this chakra are the plow, fish, and queen pose, as well as others designed to release the tension from your neck, shoulders, and upper back and keep the energy flowing to these areas.

- **Meditation:** Focus on meditative exercises that will help you communicate your needs to others. This may not be through words, but other creative means of becoming more mindful can teach you.

- **Diet:** Blueberries, blackberries, and blue-green algae work best for realigning the throat chakra. Other non-blue foods like kelp, wheatgrass, ginseng, and teas have a soothing effect on your throat and may help restore energy flow to this center.

- **Crystal:** You can harness energy to nurture your throat chakra from blue stones like aquamarine, celestite, lapis lazuli, and turquoise. Hold them at the base of your throat or on your shoulder while meditating. Or wear a small stone on a tight necklace to keep it close to the throat.

Third Eye Chakra

The third eye chakra is located between your physical eyes and represents a clear link to your intuition. Associated with the color indigo, it prompts the development of your imagination and higher wisdom. Its function affects your brain and your eyes, through which its blockage often manifests as problems with your vision, frequent headaches, memory loss, and mental fog. On the emotional front, the signs of a blockage may include issues comprehending reality, being narrow-minded, trouble trusting one's intuition, and unwillingness to tap into the deeper wisdom that lies within.

Here are a few ways to unblock your third eye chakra:

- **Yoga:** There is no specific yoga poses for unblocking, realigning, or healing this chakra. Instead, focus on movements or sequences that feel good for the body. This may vary from time to time, so make sure to listen to the cues from your body and mind, so you can cater to your intuitive needs.

- **Mediation:** You'll need mediation and other mindfulness techniques designed to realign you with your intuition. Combining these with affirmations may even be more helpful for you to open your mind and start believing in yourself.

- **Diet:** Purple food is best associated with the third eye chakra, so look to incorporate as much you can into your diet. Eat purple lettuce and carrots, eggplants, plums, and grapes to nourish this center.

- **Crystals:** This chakra requires energy from stones that are dark purple or almost on the blue side of purple, like sugilite, amethyst, and sapphire. You can incorporate these stones into head accessories, wear them as earrings or hold them close to you while meditating on your third eye chakra.

Crown Chakra

Closely associated with intelligence, deep awareness, enlightenment, and the color violet, the crown chakra is definitely one that demands a lot of attention. And even more so because it's connected to all the other energy centers. Due to this, it's also often symbolized by the color white, which is the universal color of a higher power. This means that even though it's on the top of your head, the crown chakra doesn't always affect only what lies beneath it physically, but it also affects all the other organs in your body.

While the physical symptoms linked specifically to this center may be fewer than with the other chakra, signs like sensitivity to light and sounds and neurological issues may indicate problems in this department. Spiritual and mental symptoms, on the other hand, are numerous. From the lack of spiritual growth to stubbornness and skepticism to focusing on the material things in life - all these signs may be due to a misaligned crown chakra.

Here are some helpful ways to unblock your crown chakra:

- **Yoga:** The headstand, the lotus, and the butterfly poses are all great for restoring blood circulation in your head and the energy flow to your crown chakra. Make sure to start your session with deep breathing, so you can focus.

- **Mediation:** Grounding exercises will help steer your mind away from inconsequential things and towards what's important. Combine them with mudras linked to the crown chakra to get even better results.

- **Diet:** Interestingly enough, the crown chakra diet relies on the lack of food rather than specific foods to eat. Fasting just enough not to let your body run out of fuel can work wonders in clearing your head. Start by fasting for 12 hours during the night, and slowly increase your period of not eating.

- **Crystals:** Light purple and clear and white stones like diamonds, selenite, moonstone, and quartz vibrate at the same frequency as your crown chakra, which means they can provide you with a higher power. Rest them on your head while meditating or wear them throughout the day similarly to the ways described for the previous chakra.

Final Thoughts

Not all the symptoms described for the individual chakras stand for a blockage on that specific chakra. They may be the manifestation of a blocked root chakra that doesn't let the energy flow towards another chakra, affecting its functions. Before you start working on any of the chakras, make sure the issue truly lies within them.

Additionally, as you know, the vibration of your energy always depends on your current feelings. This means that what looks and feels wrong today may not feel the same tomorrow.

Established patterns of blockage can be resolved using a method from those described above for each chakra. If a symptom appears continuously, this may be an indication of serious trauma and blockage to the chakra. This usually requires you to combine several healing methods for an extended period.

Conclusion

As the chakra associated with groundedness and stability, Muladhara is responsible for catering to your basic needs. Apart from encouraging you to find adequate food and shelter to protect yourself from the elements, it also prompts you to explore your spiritual, physical, and emotional needs. Unfortunately, it can't do any of this correctly when it's blocked or overwhelmed by negative energy stemming due to a hostile environment or unpleasant experiences. Mulling on past experiences is when you start experiencing symptoms like insecurity, anxiety, lack of focus, sleeplessness, and many other emotions associated with a blocked root chakra.

Since the basic function of Muladhara is to keep you grounded, it's a good idea to start with exercises designed to do just that. Using the quiz you'll find in this book, you can check the state of your root chakra. If you perceive any of the symptoms described beforehand, you can proceed to learn techniques that can rectify the problem. If you aren't familiar with mindfulness techniques, you can start with simple pranayama exercises. These deep breathing techniques will help you ease into meditation or yoga sessions designed to open or heal a blocked root chakra.

Little by little, you can start enriching your practice with positive affirmations and mantras that will further help you express your intent.

You'll learn to channel your energy in a positive direction and keep the negativity away from your base chakra. Using healing crystals and stones adds another layer to your Muladhara nourishing practices. Earthy color and natural elements, such as stones made from one mineral, will provide you with the purest form of energy to use to nourish your chakra system. If you learn how to recharge your crystals naturally, you will have an endless supply of raw power, motivating you to work through any obstacle in life.

And, of course, you mustn't forget about diet and nutrition. Eating natural foods can help you feel more connected to the earth, effectively unblocking or balancing your root chakra. Focus on the color of the food you eat - just as you do with the crystals you choose to have around you. Always look to please Muladhara with lots of red foods, preferably in raw form, as it contains more of the precious nutrients you need. You may also pamper yourself with aromatherapy during your baths and showers or use essential oils to open your root chakra through mindfulness exercises.

While you can't add all these elements into your schedule at once, incorporating them into your daily routines bit by bit will work wonders on your root chakra. Feel free to mix and match yoga poses to assemble fun sequences. Add different mantras, affirmations, mudras, pranayama, and meditation exercises to create a unique session for each day, so you won't get bored with any of them. It's all about focusing on your basic needs and doing what feels right for you. Because ultimately, this is what your energetic essence is based on. Not only will keeping it healthy balance the Muladhara, but it may also open the possibility of raising the upper chakras. Remember, all your chakras are connected in a complex energy system and are in constant communication with each other. Nurturing one means nourishing all of them.

Part 2: Sacral Chakra

The Ultimate Guide to Opening, Balancing, and Healing Svadhisthana

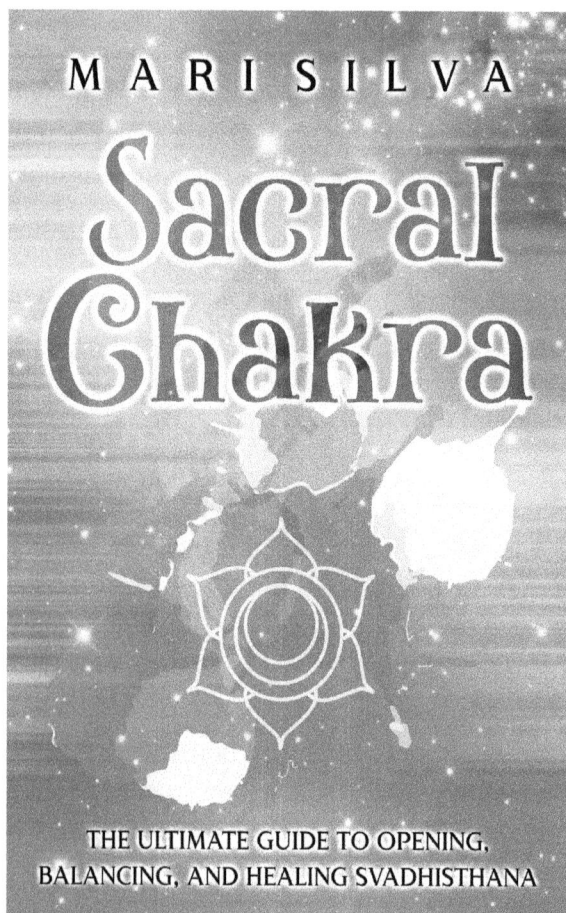

MARI SILVA

Sacral Chakra

THE ULTIMATE GUIDE TO OPENING, BALANCING, AND HEALING SVADHISTHANA

Introduction

"You can relieve pain and suffering by learning to take better care of your chakras." ~ Catherine Carrigan

There is a lot of mystery and confusion surrounding the chakras because they are esoteric and not easily understood by most people. However, if you take the time to learn about them and how to activate them, you will unlock a whole new level of health and wellbeing!

The sacral chakra, located in the lower abdomen, is the second chakra of your energy body. It governs creativity, sexuality, and passion and is often associated with emotional and physical blockages. This guide aims to help you learn about the sacral chakra, how to tell if it is blocked, and what you can do to open and balance it.

Whether you're starting your journey toward health and happiness or have been walking the path for some time, this guide will be an invaluable resource as you continue along your journey. The first chapter of this guide provides background information on the sacral chakra, including its history, mythology, and associated colors, elements, and symbols. The second chapter will explore how the sacral chakra can become blocked or imbalanced.

The third chapter discusses meditation and visualization to help you activate your sacral chakra, followed by mantras and affirmations in the fourth chapter. The fifth chapter explores the power of mudras and pranayama, while the sixth chapter provides yoga poses and sequences specifically designed to help heal and activate the sacral chakra.

In the seventh chapter, we explain the use of crystals and stones to help heal and balance the sacral chakra. The eighth chapter discusses Svadhisthana-specific aromatherapy, and in the ninth chapter, we will explore diet and nutrition for the sacral chakra. Finally, the tenth chapter provides a 7-day sacral chakra routine to help you get started on the path to activating and balancing your sacral chakra.

A bonus chapter at the end of the guide explores how to balance your energy, the sacral chakra to the upper chakras. By cultivating awareness and understanding of your sacral chakra, you'll find that you can unlock a whole new level of health, happiness, and wellbeing in your life.

Whether you are new to the world of chakras or have been working with them for some time, this guide will provide everything you need to know about the sacral chakra and explain how to activate, balance, and heal it for optimal health and wellness. So, why wait? Let's get started on your journey toward activating and balancing the sacral chakra today.

Chapter 1: What Is Svadhisthana?

Chakras are energy centers that receive, process, and transmit information throughout your body. When they are balanced and aligned, these energy centers work together to keep you in a state of wellness and wellbeing. When there's an imbalance, it can manifest in very real physical and mental health issues.

If you're only just starting to learn about the chakras and how to balance them, a great place to begin is with Svadhisthana. Svadhisthana is the second chakra and one of seven chakras in the body. The word Svadhisthana means "dwelling place of the self." So, your Svadhisthana is where you reside in your body. It's also known as the sacral chakra because it's located just below your navel in the pelvis.

This chapter gives you a general overview of chakras, explains the energy body, and discusses the roles chakras play in the energy flow through the body. The chapter focuses on the second chakra and explains what it represents, its associated colors and elements, and how to keep it in balance. By the end of this chapter, you should understand what Svadhisthana is and be well on your way to keeping it balanced.

Chakras in Our Body

There are seven spinning energy nodes within the subtle body known as chakras. They are the seat of our emotions and desires and contribute to our physical health. In yoga practice, we often focus on aligning the chakra system to promote balance and wellbeing through asanas (poses), pranayama (breath work), and meditation.

These are your seven major chakras, each associated with a different aspect of your personality, emotions, or physical functions. For example, the root chakra is located at the base of the spine and is associated with your feelings of safety and security. From bottom to top, the seven major chakras are:

- Muladhara (root)

- Svadhisthana (sacral)

- Manipura (solar plexus)

- Anahata (heart)

- Vishuddha (throat)

- Ajna (third eye)

- Sahasrara (crown)

We improve our mental and physical wellbeing by aligning the energy flowing through our chakras and keeping them balanced. Various meditation techniques and other mind-body practices are helpful because they help clear out any blockages in the chakras and strengthen their ability to absorb and transmit energy. Ultimately, by learning to listen to the messages from our chakras, we can better understand ourselves and pave the way for greater happiness and health in our lives.

The Energy Body

The energy that flows through our bodies, or our life force, is called prana. It's a unique and fascinating force in our physical world. At its simplest level, prana refers to the subtle energy that permeates everything around us. We can think of this energy as an invisible "life force" that infuses all living things. However, the energy body also has other important qualities beyond its physical presence.

In some ancient traditions, it is believed that prana plays an essential role in maintaining physical and mental health because the energy body is intimately connected to emotions and intuition. It helps regulate stress levels and facilitate communication between different parts of the psyche.

Therefore, while we usually focus on its tangible effects, like giving life to plants or driving vital processes within our bodies, we should also recognize prana's important role in fostering our mental health and overall wellbeing. For this reason, many yoga and meditation practices focus on cultivating awareness of the energy body and learning how to control the flow of prana within us.

By nurturing the energy body through meditation, mindfulness practices, and other holistic activities, we unlock our full potential for happiness and purpose. After all, as modern science consistently tells us, a healthy mind makes a healthy body.

The Role of Chakras

We all have seven major energy centers in our energy body called chakras, which are funnel-shaped spinning vortices of energy and light that correspond to major nerve bundles and glands in the physical body. They read and interpret the energy coming into us, internally and externally, and keep us healthy as long as they stay open, balanced, and flowing freely.

The word "chakra" comes from the Sanskrit chakra, meaning "wheel" or "disc." Each chakra is associated with a particular body area and a particular emotion or aspect of our personality. When unbalanced or stressed, our chakras become closed off or blocked, leading to emotional or physical illness.

The role of the chakras is to help us interpret and regulate the energy we receive from ourselves, others, and our environment. We cultivate greater self-awareness and improve our overall wellbeing by learning to work with our chakras. Through practices like yoga, pranayama, or meditation, we also help activate and unblock our chakras to continue to perform their vital function of helping us thrive.

Svadhisthana - The Sacral Chakra

In Sanskrit, "Svadhisthana" means "one's place" or "one's abode." It's all about enjoying life and going with the flow. It's where we truly feel at home in our bodies and at peace with ourselves. This chakra is about feeling grounded in who you are as a sexual being, enjoying pleasure, connecting with others, feeling creative, and experiencing joy.

The Svadhisthana chakra is one of the most important energetic centers in the body. This chakra, located in the sacral area, governs creativity and sexuality and influences self-expression, confidence, and emotional balance. It is important to stay mindful of how we express ourselves physically and emotionally to maintain our Svadhisthana chakra.

By being aware of the internal processes and patterns that drive our behaviors, we can more effectively manage our emotions and work through any challenges. Whether we embrace a more spiritual path or explore more worldly experiences, staying attuned to our Svadhisthana chakra will help us lead vibrant lives full of creativity and joy.

Origins and Early Scriptures

Svadhisthana has an ancient and rich history in Vedic texts like the Upanishads. Early scriptures reveal that this energetic portal has always been seen as a source of vital energy and insight, allowing us to fully experience our physical bodies and our inner selves.

The word "Svadhisthana" first appeared in the Taittiriya Upanishad, one of the earliest of the Vedic scriptures. In this text, it is described as a symbolic representation of the "semen that is contained in the testes" and is closely linked with the second chakra in its location and function.

Over time, the Svadhisthana has expanded to include all the creative and emotional realms, including the expression of sexuality. Most spiritual traditions recognize Svadhisthana as an important chakra for self-expression, creativity, and emotional balance.

Location and Corresponding Body Parts

The Svadhisthana is located in the sacrum, a small triangular-shaped bone at the base of the spine. The sacrum is where the spinal cord meets the pelvis, and it's also the point of origin of many of the body's nerves and organs. The sacral plexus, a network of nerves that innervates the lower abdomen and pelvis, is also located in this area.

The subtle body is also linked to Svadhisthana, and this chakra corresponds with many internal organs in the lower abdomen, including the bladder, kidneys, and reproductive organs. This chakra also governs the lymphatic system, a network of tissues and organs that fight infection and remove waste from the body.

As one of the most important energetic centers in the body, Svadhisthana plays a crucial role in our physical, mental, and emotional health. By learning to work with this chakra and strengthening it through various practices, we cultivate a greater sense of balance and wellbeing in all aspects of our lives.

Symbol, Color, and Associated Element

Sacral chakra symbol.
https://pixabay.com/images/id-2533094/

In many spiritual traditions, there is a belief that there is more to reality than what meets the eye. The physical world is seen as merely one small part of a much larger picture, and our human bodies are viewed as vehicles for the soul. This concept is represented in the Svadhisthana symbol, depicting a swirling *vesica piscis*.

This symbol is often used to represent the energetic portal between the physical and spiritual realms. It reminds us that we are all connected to something greater than ourselves, and there is more to life than that which we can see and touch. Meditating on this symbol helps us open our minds and hearts to the infinite possibilities beyond the physical world.

Svadhisthana is commonly associated with the color orange, representing vitality and creativity. Orange represents many facets of our being - from physical vitality and strength to creativity and passion. Whether we are engaging in artistic expression, exploring new ideas, or simply engaging in movement and activity, the power of Svadhisthana helps us bring our ideas to life and manifest them into reality.

The element associated with Svadhisthana is water, as it should be. Water is essential for all life on earth, providing nutrients, cooling us down in summer heat, and making plant growth possible. In addition, water is crucial in many natural processes by interacting and combining with other elements.

For example, evaporation forms rain clouds or reduces a body of water to a mere trickle. Similarly, ice and snow have a powerful impact on our environment during the colder months. All these aspects make water an essential component of life on earth - and one that perfectly embodies the energy of Svadhisthana.

Traits and Functioning

Svadhisthana is often seen as a gateway to the subconscious mind and our more primal impulses. It governs many aspects of our lives that we may not even be aware of, such as sexual desires, creativity, and emotions. Therefore, it's essential to keep this chakra in balance. When Svadhisthana is out of balance, we could find ourselves consumed by our primal impulses and unable to control our emotions or behavior.

However, when this chakra is in balance, we harness the powerful energies associated with it to bring our latent talents and desires to fruition. Whether through artistic expression, physical activity, or sexual intimacy, Svadhisthana is responsible for helping us unleash our creative potential and enjoy the fullness of life in all its aspects.

This chakra is not only about physical pleasures. Svadhisthana is also responsible for our ability to connect with others emotionally and helps us forge stronger and more meaningful connections bringing us a greater sense of fulfillment in our relationships. Therefore, keeping this chakra strong and healthy is important if we want to enjoy all the aspects of life that Svadhisthana governs.

Benefits of Aligning Svadhisthana Chakra

Svadhisthana chakra is essential to maintain optimal physical, mental, and emotional health. This subtle energy center, located in the sacral or pelvic region of the body, is responsible for regulating feelings of vitality, pleasure, power, and desire. When this chakra is balanced, we feel confident and energized. However, when it is out of alignment or blocked, we may experience feelings of stagnation or depletion.

Fortunately, there are many simple ways to cultivate balance in the Svadhisthana chakra and unlock its many benefits. Some strategies include practicing meditation techniques that focus on the root energy of this center, engaging in activities that stimulate the senses and promote creativity, eating a healthy diet that includes plenty of fresh fruit and veggies, and incorporating grounding exercises into your daily routine. Whether you're looking to promote peak performance at work or simply enhance your overall sense of wellbeing, aligning the Svadhisthana chakra can help you get there.

Emotional Wellbeing

One of the main benefits of aligning your Svadhisthana chakra is improved emotional wellbeing. This subtle energy center is often called the "emotional body," as it governs our ability to process and express our emotions healthily. When this chakra is unbalanced, we may experience frustration, anger, or confusion. So, by learning to cultivate balance in this area, we can achieve greater harmony in our relationships and daily life.

Most of us could stand to improve our emotional wellbeing. We all go through tough times, and sometimes it feels like our emotions are out of control. If you're looking for a way to regain control, aligning your Svadhisthana chakra is good. The more aligned this chakra is, the better equipped you'll be to manage your emotions healthily and constructively – whether you're dealing with work-related stress, conflict in your personal life, or any challenges that come your way.

Creativity and Expression

Regardless of whether you're an artist, musician, or writer, aligning your Svadhisthana chakra can help you tap into your creative potential. This chakra is considered the seat of creativity, and focusing on it accesses the wisdom that lies within yourself and opens you up to new possibilities in your work and life.

Many of us struggle with creative blocks at some point or another. If you're feeling stuck, aligning your Svadhisthana chakra can help to jumpstart your creative process. Whether you're a writer, artist, or anything in between, this chakra holds many answers and insights you seek.

Aligning your Svadhisthana chakra opens you up to new levels of creativity and expression you never knew were possible. With this chakra in balance, you'll access your full creative potential and overcome the obstacles that once seemed impossible.

Improved Relationships

Whether you're looking to improve your love life or build stronger bonds with family and friends, aligning your Svadhisthana chakra can help. This energy center governs our ability to give and receive love, and when it is out of balance, we feel disconnected or alone.

If you're struggling in your relationships, aligning your Svadhisthana chakra is the key to turning things around. When this chakra is balanced, we give and receive love more easily, leading to more fulfilling and satisfying relationships.

If you're looking for a way to improve your love life or build stronger bonds with those around you, aligning your Svadhisthana chakra is a good place to start. By working on this energy center, you open yourself up to more love and connection in all aspects of your life.

Improved Physical Health

In addition to promoting emotional and creative wellbeing, aligning your Svadhisthana chakra also leads to improved physical health. This energy center governs our ability to enjoy pleasure and vitality, and when it is out of balance, we feel exhausted or disconnected from our bodies.

If you want to enhance your physical health, aligning the Svadhisthana chakra should be one of your priorities. When this chakra is balanced, we connect with our bodies on a deeper level and tap into vitality and pleasure. With this chakra in balance, you can achieve greater health and wellbeing and positively impact every area of your life.

Greater Sensory Awareness

Our senses of smell, taste, sight, touch, and hearing are all governed by our Svadhisthana chakra. When this chakra is out of balance, we find ourselves disconnected from our senses or unable to enjoy the full range of sensations life offers. This energy center is essential to connect with your five senses, and when it is balanced, you open yourself up to a greater range of sensory experiences.

Whether you're looking to improve your ability to taste, smell, see, touch, or hear, aligning the Svadhisthana chakra can help. With this chakra in balance, you connect with your senses on a deeper level, and tap into a wealth of sensory experiences you might not even realize were possible.

Enhanced Intuition

The Svadhisthana chakra is also associated with our intuition, and when it is in balance, we can tap into our innate sense of knowing and understanding. Connecting with this energy center, you unlock your inner wisdom and intuition so that you always know what's best for your work and life.

With this chakra in balance, you can access your intuition with greater ease and clarity and use it to guide your work and life in the direction you want to go. If you're looking for a way to enhance your intuition and tap into your inner wisdom, aligning your Svadhisthana chakra is the perfect place to start.

Overall Wellbeing

When our Svadhisthana chakra is out of balance, it has a ripple effect on every area of our lives. If you're struggling in any area of your life, then chances are your Svadhisthana chakra is out of balance. However, focusing on this energy center restores your overall sense of wellbeing and observe greater contentment in every aspect of your life.

The Svadhisthana chakra plays an important role in our emotional, creative, and physical wellbeing, so we may experience challenges in all areas when it is out of balance. By focusing on it and bringing it into balance, you restore your overall wellbeing and find greater peace and contentment in your life.

The chakras are focal points of energy located in the energy body. The energy body is an ethereal counterpart to the physical body, which can only be seen with the third eye. Each chakra acts as a center that receives and processes life energy, or prana. They are responsible for receiving and exchanging prana, directing it throughout the body, and distributing it to the different organs.

There are seven major chakras in total—the root, sacral, solar plexus, heart, throat, crown, and third eye—and each is associated with a different color and symbol. Energy flows through the chakras from one end to the other, from the root chakra up through the crown. The Svadhisthana Chakra is located about two inches below the navel in the lower abdomen.

Remember that this is a journey, not a destination. When you're ready to start working on your Svadhisthana chakra, there is no right way to go about it, and there is no perfect balance that you're aiming for. The goal is simply to become more aware of your energy center and start working on it so that you can experience the benefits of a balanced Svadhisthana chakra.

Do your best to stay positive and patient as you work through this process, and remember the benefits are well worth the effort. With a little time and patience, you can achieve a greater sense of wellbeing, vitality, and pleasure by aligning your Svadhisthana chakra.

Chapter 2: Is Your Sacral Chakra Blocked?

Are you experiencing physical, emotional, or spiritual blocks in your life? If so, your sacral chakra could be clogged and in need of healing. Located in the lower abdomen, roughly two inches below the navel and slightly behind the belly button, the sacral chakra is one of the seven energy centers in our bodies known as chakras.

This powerful energetic vortex plays a key role in our relationships, creativity, and senses of personal power, sexuality, pleasure, and comfort. When our sacral chakras are blocked or out of balance, we feel anxious, disconnected from others, and stuck in unhealthy patterns. This chapter will help you identify symptoms of a blocked, weak, overactive, or out-of-balance sacral chakra.

At the end of this chapter, there is a quiz to help you determine whether or not your sacral chakra needs healing.

Blocked Sacral Chakra

The sacral chakra, the Svadhisthana, is an important energy center in the body. Located in the lower abdomen and associated with water, this chakra plays a key role in your overall health and wellbeing. However, when the sacral chakra becomes blocked or imbalanced, it leads to negative symptoms, health issues, anxiety, and depression. It also affects your ability to connect and communicate with others and leads to problems with digestion and sexual functions.

Thankfully, there are various techniques you can use to clear and balance the sacral chakra. Common methods include meditation, visualization exercises, dietary changes, and massage therapy. By focusing on balancing this important energy center, you reclaim your health and wellbeing from the inside out.

Symptoms of a Blocked Sacral Chakra

The sacral chakra governs our creativity, sexuality, pleasure, and sensuality. A blocked sacral chakra manifests as creative stagnant, sexual dysfunction, and low self-esteem. Other symptoms include abdominal pain, constipation, bladder infections, and kidney problems. When the sacral chakra is balanced, we feel creative, confident, and sexually fulfilled. We can express our emotions freely and enjoy healthy relationships.

If you're experiencing any of the above negative symptoms, you can do a few things to help unblock your sacral chakra. Crystals like carnelian and citrine are helpful for a blocked sacral chakra. You can also try yoga poses like warrior II or bridge pose to help promote creativity and confidence.

Causes of a Blocked Sacral Chakra

While many factors contribute to a blocked sacral chakra, some of the most common causes include stress, trauma, and excessive worry or anxiety. Other possible triggers include relationship conflicts and issues surrounding sexuality or intimacy. Some people also suggest childhood trauma or sexual abuse can lead to a blocked sacral chakra.

It is crucial to address these underlying causes to help unblock and heal your sacral chakra by relaxing more often, releasing negative emotions like anger and resentment, seeking better support from friends and family members, and making healthy lifestyle choices like eating well-balanced meals and getting enough exercise. With time and patience, your sacral chakra will be restored to its natural state of balance and harmony.

Real-Life Story: Tracy's Sacral Chakra Healing

A woman named Tracy recently sought help for a blocked sacral chakra. She struggled with symptoms like low self-esteem, sexual dysfunction, and digestive issues for several years. After consulting with a health practitioner, Tracy learned that her problems were likely due to an imbalanced sacral chakra.

Tracy decided to try several different techniques to unblock her sacral chakra. She practiced meditation and visualization exercises, journaled regularly about her feelings, and took up a more active exercise routine. After about a month of dedicated practice, Tracy noticed her sacral chakra had started clearing, and she was feeling more confident, creative, and fulfilled.

If you're struggling with a blocked sacral chakra, know that you are not alone. By taking time to address the underlying causes of this imbalance, you can begin to clear and heal your sacral chakra naturally.

Weak Sacral Chakra

While a blocked sacral chakra can cause many negative symptoms and affect your health, wellbeing, and relationships, a weak sacral chakra can also be problematic. A weak sacral chakra makes you feel disconnected from your emotions, leading to numbness or loneliness. You may also find it difficult to express your emotions openly or be creative in your pursuits.

Additionally, a weak sacral chakra puts you at risk of health issues like digestive disorders, menstrual problems, infertility, and low libido. It can also make you more susceptible to addictions, as you may turn to substances or activities to fill the emptiness you're feeling inside.

Symptoms of a Weak Sacral Chakra

If your sacral chakra is weak, it can cause several symptoms, including anxiety, mood swings, difficulty focusing on tasks at hand, difficulty managing stress, and apathy. Furthermore, a weak sacral chakra also leads to physical problems such as digestive issues, POTS (postural orthostatic tachycardia syndrome), low energy levels, and frequent infections.

Suppose you struggle with these symptoms or others related to your sacral chakra. In that case, it is important to seek the guidance of a trained healthcare professional to help you address underlying causes and work toward restoring balance to your chakra system. With proper care and attention, you can reclaim your strength and creativity and find joy in living life to its fullest potential.

Causes of a Weak Sacral Chakra

As with a blocked or overactive sacral chakra, several possible causes of a weak sacral chakra. These include childhood trauma or abuse, a negative attitude toward sexuality or intimacy, and excessive stress and anxiety. Some medications or medical treatments and an unhealthy diet can also contribute to a weak sacral chakra.

It is crucial to identify the underlying causes and address them with the help of a trained professional to restore balance to your sacral chakra. In some cases, this requires seeking therapy or counseling to work through past traumas. In other cases, making simple lifestyle changes, like eating a more balanced diet or getting regular exercise, is enough to help support your sacral chakra and promote healing.

Real-Life Story: Maria's Sacral Chakra Healing

Maria had been struggling with weak sacral chakra symptoms for several years. She had always felt emotionally distant from others and had difficulty connecting with her creativity. Over time, these feelings impacted her health as well. Maria realized she was always experiencing digestive issues and was chronically tired.

After doing some research and discussing her symptoms with her doctor, Maria decided to focus on healing her sacral chakra. She began an active exercise routine and ate a nutrient-rich diet filled with whole grains, fruit and vegetables, and healthy fats. Within a few months, Maria noticed her digestion had improved, her energy levels were higher, and she was feeling much happier and more in touch with her emotions.

Overactive Sacral Chakra

The overactive sacral chakra is characterized by insecurity, a lack of self-confidence, and an inability to let go of certain feelings or opinions. When the sacral chakra is overactive, we feel overly emotional or sexual and prone to addiction or self-destructive behaviors.

If you suspect that your sacral chakra is out of balance, you can do a few things to restore harmony. First, spend time near bodies of water like lakes or oceans. You can also meditate on the color orange or wear orange clothing. Finally, eat foods associated with water, like cucumbers or oranges.

You help bring your sacral chakra back into balance and restore harmony to your life by taking these steps.

Symptoms of an Overactive Sacral Chakra

When one of the chakras becomes overactive, it leads to various symptoms. For example, an overactive root chakra can cause anxiety or insecurity, while an underactive solar plexus chakra causes digestive issues. Other symptoms of an overactive chakra include insomnia, headaches, and racing thoughts.

If you are experiencing any of these symptoms, it is important to seek a qualified spiritual healer to help balance your chakras. With the help of a trained professional, you can restore peace and harmony to your mind and body.

Causes of an Overactive Sacral Chakra

When this energy center becomes overactive, physical and emotional symptoms manifest, including increased stress levels, insomnia, low libido, depression, chronic pain, and fluid retention. If you experience any of these symptoms and suspect that your sacral chakra is out of balance, engage in activities that help activate and open the body's natural healing energies.

A few simple strategies include taking a yoga class or massage treatment. These strategies are focused on stimulating the pelvic area, practicing deep breathing exercises, or guided meditations to ground yourself in your body's present moment and spend time engaging in creative pursuits like painting or journaling.

By reconnecting with your body through these practices, you can help restore harmony to your sacral chakra and reclaim your sense of joy and vitality.

Real-Life Story: Sarah's Sacral Chakra Healing

Sarah struggled with an overactive sacral chakra for several years. She had always been an emotional person. Sometimes she would get so overwhelmed by her feelings causing her to act impulsively or lash out at those around her.

In addition to her emotional struggles, Sarah dealt with chronic pain and digestive issues. She had seen several doctors, but none of them could find the root cause of her problems.

Frustrated and feeling hopeless, Sarah decided to seek a spiritual healer specializing in chakra healing. After several months of regular energy work and a detoxifying diet, Sarah finally regained her sense of balance.

Her emotional outbursts subsided, her chronic pain improved, her energy levels were higher, and she felt much more positive and in tune with her body. Today, Sarah regularly sees her healer and follows a healthy lifestyle that keeps her sacral chakra in balance.

Out of Balance Chakra

The sacral chakra is responsible for our creativity, sexuality, and sense of pleasure. When this energy center is out of balance, it leads to physical, mental, and emotional symptoms. You feel tired, anxious, or depressed and have trouble concentrating or sleeping. Your body feels out of alignment, and you experience pain or discomfort.

There are several ways to balance your chakras - meditate, practice yoga or Tai Chi, or receive energy work from a certified practitioner. You can also use crystals and essential oils to help balance your chakras. By taking some time to focus on balancing your chakras, you can restore harmony and wellbeing to your mind, body, and spirit.

Symptoms of an Out of Balance Sacral Chakra

When the sacral chakra is out of balance, it leads to many physical, emotional, and psychological symptoms. Some of the most common signs of an out-of-balance sacral chakra include chronic pain, low libido, digestive issues, and depression. When the sacral chakra is out of balance, we feel disconnected from our feelings and desires or find it difficult to express ourselves emotionally. We also feel creatively blocked or find it hard to enjoy our hobbies and interests.

If you are experiencing any of these symptoms and suspect that your sacral chakra is out of balance, many strategies can help to restore harmony. Some simple methods include spending time in nature, practicing meditation or mindfulness, and engaging in creative pursuits.

Causes of an Out of Balance Sacral Chakra

There are many potential causes of an imbalanced sacral chakra. One common cause is a lack of physical affection in childhood. If you were not given enough hugs or affection as a child, it could have led to feelings of deep insecurity and a belief that you are not worthy of love. This can block your ability to experience pleasure and creativity as an adult.

Another common cause of sacral chakra imbalance is sexual, emotional, or physical trauma. If you have experienced any trauma, it is essential to seek professional help to heal the wounds. Once the traumas are healed, your sacral chakra will likely become balanced.

Finally, if you are constantly suppressing your creativity or sexuality, it can also lead to an imbalanced sacral chakra. If you have been repressing your true desires for a long time, it is important to start exploring these feelings to help align your chakra.

Real-Life Story: Jennie's Sacral Chakra Healing

Jennie is a 38-year-old mother of two who has always been a creative person. She loves to sing, write, and dance and has always been passionate about expressing herself creatively. Unfortunately, Jennie's career had always taken priority, and she rarely had time for her hobbies.

For years, Jennie was frustrated about this imbalance in her life. She felt stuck and unhappy but didn't know how to make time for her creative pursuits. Eventually, Jennie began seeing a therapist to help her deal with her discontent.

After several months, Jennie's therapist helped her realize that she was repressing her creativity to cope with low self-worth. As a child, Jennie was told by her parents and teachers that she was not good enough, and this belief led her to suppress her creativity.

Once Jennie started exploring her creativity again, she felt more balanced and fulfilled. She made time for her hobbies and even pursued a career in the arts. Thanks to her newly balanced sacral chakra, Jennie is happy and thriving.

Checking Your Sacral Chakra Balance – The Quiz

Keeping your chakras balanced is essential to maintaining harmony in your mind, body, and spirit. Take this quick quiz if you suspect your sacral chakra is out of balance. There are four possible answers to each question, so be sure to choose the one that best describes you.

1. **When you were growing up, how often did you receive physical affection from your parents or caregivers?**
   a) Often
   b) Sometimes
   c) Rarely
   d) Never

2. **How do you express your emotions?**
   a) I am very open and honest about my feelings.
   b) I tend to keep my emotions to myself.
   c) I have a hard time expressing my emotions.
   d) I tend to get emotional very easily, even when it may not be appropriate.

3. **How do you feel about your creative abilities?**
   a) I am very confident in my creative abilities and often use them in my work or hobbies.

b) I am somewhat confident in my creative abilities and enjoy expressing them in my free time.

c) I am not confident in my creative abilities, but I try to use them in my free time.

d) I am not very confident in my creative abilities and rarely express that part of myself.

4. **When was the last time you tried something new?**

a) Within the past month.

b) Within the past year.

c) More than a year ago.

d) I can't remember.

5. **How do you feel about your sexuality?**

a) I am very comfortable with my sexuality.

b) I am somewhat comfortable with my sexuality.

c) I am uncomfortable with my sexuality.

d) I am very uncomfortable with my sexuality.

6. **Do you have any fears or hang-ups regarding intimacy?**

a) No, I am very open to intimacy.

b) Some, but I am working on overcoming them.

c) Yes, I have a lot of fears and hang-ups when it comes to intimacy.

d) I don't think about intimacy.

7. **How would you describe your energy level?**

a) High

b) Moderate

c) Low

d) I don't notice my energy level.

8. **Do you enjoy being around people or being alone?**

a) I enjoy being around people and often feel antsy when I'm alone for too long.

b) I enjoy being around people but don't mind spending time alone if necessary.

c) I don't enjoy being around people, but I don't mind it if necessary.

d) I prefer to spend my time alone and often feel drained after being around people for too long.

9. **Are you able to let go of things easily?**

a) Yes, very easily.

b) Sometimes, it can be hard, depending on what's going on in my life.

c) No, I have a hard time letting go of things.

d) It depends on what the thing is that I need to let go of.

10. **Do you live impulsively or plan everything out ahead of time?**

a) I don't live impulsively and rarely make decisions on a whim.

b) I try to plan things out as best I can but sometimes go with my gut instinct.

c) I always try to plan things out ahead of time as much as possible.

d) I don't plan things out ahead of time or make decisions on a whim.

Key to the Sacral Chakra Quiz

If you mostly answered the questions above with As, your sacral chakra is most likely open and balanced. It means you have a good sense of creativity, sexuality, and self-worth. You likely enjoy trying new things and feel good about who you are. You are also comfortable in your skin and enjoy being around people.

If you answered mostly Bs to the questions above, your sacral chakra is probably open and balanced but could use some work. It means you likely have a good sense of creativity, sexuality, and self-worth, but there are some areas where you could improve.

If you answered mostly Cs to the questions above, your sacral chakra is probably blocked. It means you may have difficulty expressing yourself creatively, feel uncomfortable around others, experience low energy levels, lack motivation, and have difficulties with intimacy.

If you answered mostly Ds to the questions above, your sacral chakra is probably overactive. It means you likely have excessive or over-the-top sexual desires, an overabundance of creative ideas, and a high energy level. You also find it difficult to focus on one thing and can be easily distracted.

If you are experiencing any symptoms of a blocked, out-of-balance, or overactive sacral chakra, it would be helpful to seek the help of a therapist or other professional to guide you on your journey toward healing and balance. Whether through meditation, therapy, or other techniques, there are several ways to work on healing and opening up your sacral chakra to regain balance in your life.

Chapter 3: Sacral Meditation and Visualization

"Meditation is not evasion; it is a serene encounter with reality." - Thich Nhat Hanh

Meditation is a process of calming your mind, becoming aware of your thoughts and emotions, and developing inner peace. Meditation has been proven to have many health benefits, including reduced stress and anxiety, increased focus, better sleep, and improved immune function. Meditation can be done anywhere, at any time, and it's an activity anyone can enjoy.

There are many different ways to meditate. You can practice mindfulness meditation by focusing on your breath, using a mantra, or performing seated or walking meditation. Additionally, you can use many different objects as tools for meditation - from music to candlelight to art. These are all things that help us open the lower chakras and integrate the energies of Svadhisthana into our daily lives.

This chapter on sacral meditation and visualization delves into more detail about the different methods used to open this chakra and gives some helpful tips to get started. So, let's dive in.

Meditation and Visualization

Meditation and visualization are two of the most common practices used to open the sacral chakra. Meditation is a practice that has been around for thousands of years. It is an exercise that allows you to focus your mind on one thing or thought while clearing your mind of all other thoughts. Meditation is often done with the aid of mantras, which are sacred sounds spoken or chanted during meditation. Mantras are used to clear the mind, open the chakras, and bring about spiritual growth.

Visualization is when you visualize yourself doing something in your mind's eye. You see yourself doing it as if it was real, even though it is only happening inside your head. Visualization helps you become more in tune with your emotions and feelings so that they don't control you. Instead, they serve as a guide for your life decisions and actions.

It is important to work both meditation and visualization into your daily practice to open the sacral chakra. Together, the two help clear any blockages that might prevent you from fully accessing your creative potential.

Overall Benefits of Meditation and Visualization

Before discussing specific methods for opening the sacral chakra, it's essential to discuss the many health benefits that meditation and visualization offer. Both practices have been proven to improve health in many ways, including:

Relaxation

The first and most obvious benefit of meditation is relaxation. Meditation is an effective way to reduce stress and anxiety. When you focus your mind on one thing, it allows your body to relax and release any tension it is holding onto. Meditation leads to improved sleep, increased energy, and a general feeling of wellbeing.

Improved Focus

A common complaint in today's society is that there are simply too many distractions. We are constantly bombarded with information from the media, and it is difficult to focus on one thing for a long period. Meditation has been proven to help improve focus and concentration, making it easier to get tasks done without being side-tracked.

Better Sleep

Are you struggling with sleeplessness? Studies have shown that meditation helps improve the quality of your sleep, meaning you'll feel more rested and refreshed when you wake up in the morning. It also helps reduce anxiety and stress, two of the most common causes of insomnia. The calming influence of meditation can help you doze off faster and stay asleep longer.

Increased Immunity

When we are stressed or anxious, our bodies go into a state of fight or flight. This is a primal survival mechanism that was once essential for our ancestors to survive in the wild. Unfortunately, this mechanism has not evolved to adapt to the stresses of modern life.

As a result, when we are in this state of chronic stress, our bodies go into overdrive and produce damaging stress hormones that wear down the immune system. This leads to several health problems, including colds, flu, and other illnesses.

Meditation has been proven to help the body recover from this state of chronic stress, giving the immune system a much-needed break. As a result, people who meditate regularly are less likely to get sick.

Unblocking, Healing, and Balancing the Sacral Chakra

While meditation and visualization offer many health benefits, they can also be used to open blocked chakras. When this happens, we tap into the immense healing potential of our subtle energy body. This leads to dramatic improvements in mental, emotional, and physical health.

The sacral chakra is closely connected to our emotions, so many of the benefits we receive when this chakra opens are related to emotional healing. For example, we are better equipped to deal with difficult emotions like sadness, anger, and fear. We may also discover that we are more open to new experiences and more creative than before.

If you are looking for a way to open your sacral chakra, you can try a few different methods. The following section explores some of the most effective ways to meditate and visualize to achieve this desired result.

Guided Meditation Exercises for Opening the Sacral Chakra

Guided meditation is a powerful tool to find inner peace and clear the mind of distractions. One of the best ways to open and balance your sacral chakra is to engage in guided meditation exercises specifically designed to target this energy center. These exercises typically involve deep breathing and visualization, helping you focus on your breath and all the sensations associated with it.

You can use specific visualizations, like imagining a glowing orange sphere deep within your abdomen – or simply focus on any sensations that arise, from vibrations to tingling or warmth. With regular practice, these guided meditation exercises help you open and strengthen your sacral chakra, allowing you to feel more grounded, centered, and in touch with your intuition.

Visualizing the Mind as a Lake

Imagine your mind as a lake or pond. Visualize the waters as calm and clear, with gently rippling waves. Allow yourself to sink below the surface and feel the peacefulness of the water enveloping you. Imagine the water infusing your body with vitality and renewed energy as you breathe in. Let go of anything that no longer serves you as you exhale, watching as it dissipates into the water. Continue this visualization for several minutes until you feel a sense of peace and balance within yourself.

Visualizing the Sacral Chakra as a Lotus Flower

Visualize the sacral chakra as a lotus flower, vibrant and alive. The lotus flower grows in muddy water, but it emerges clean and pure. This symbolizes that even when our lives are filled with challenges, we can rise above them and blossom into our true potential. Just as the lotus flower turns to face the sun, so, too, should we turn toward the light of our divine nature. By visualizing the sacral chakra as a lotus flower, we bring balance and harmony into our lives.

Slowly move your focus back into the present moment when you feel ready. Slowly open your eyes and return to normal awareness. You may wish to spend a few moments journaling about your experience or practicing creative visualization exercises to further integrate the energy of the sacral chakra into your life.

The Sacral Chakra Unblocking Exercise

This exercise may be right for you if you want a more hands-on approach to opening your sacral chakra. This practice involves gently massaging and applying pressure to the body area associated with this energetic center to help clear blockages and open your energy flow.

Start by finding a comfortable seat. You can sit on the floor with your legs crossed or on a chair, but place your feet flat on the ground if you choose a chair. Take a few deep breaths and allow your body to relax. Begin by massaging your lower abdomen in a clockwise direction with both hands. Spend a few minutes massaging in this way, applying gentle pressure and taking care to focus on any areas that feel tense or blocked.

Next, visualize the energies of your sacral chakra opening and flowing freely. Imagine you are breathing energy in through this center, infusing your body with vitality and healing. Imagine you are breathing in the energy of growth and expansion with each inhale. When you exhale, imagine you are releasing the tension or negativity from the sacral chakra, watching it float away on the exhalation. Continue this visualization for a few minutes until you feel your sacral chakra opening and the energies flowing freely.

When you have finished, take a few deep breaths, and allow your body to relax. If you aren't sure of the best way to do this, spend a few minutes writing about your experience or performing creative visualization. With time and patience, you can learn to open and balance your sacral chakra and experience a greater sense of wellbeing, creativity, and connection in your life.

The Emotional Healing Meditation

If you struggle to understand, connect with, and heal the emotional energy held within your sacral chakra, this guided meditation will be helpful for you. This practice helps you identify and release any negative emotions holding you back from achieving balance in this area of your life.

Start by finding a comfortable seat. You can sit on the floor with your legs crossed, or you can choose to be seated on a chair, again with your feet flat on the ground. Close your eyes and allow your body to relax. Begin by taking a few deep breaths, imagining you are breathing in the light of love and healing. As you exhale, imagine you are releasing the tension or negativity from your body.

When you are ready, visualize the energy of your sacral chakra. Imagine it as a ball of light glowing in the center of your lower abdomen. See the light of this chakra as being a beautiful, radiant orange.

Now, focus on any emotions you harbor in the sacral chakra - emotions like guilt, shame, sadness, or anger. Simply allow yourself to become aware of these emotions without attaching judgment to them. Breathe into these emotions, and imagine that the light of love and healing surrounds you.

Allow yourself to feel these emotions fully, and then imagine releasing them. Visualize the emotions floating away on your exhale, replaced by the light of love and healing. Continue to breathe deeply and focus on releasing the emotions you hold in the sacral chakra.

When you have finished, take a few deep breaths, and allow your body to relax. Spend a few minutes writing about your experience or performing creative visualization. With time and patience, you'll learn to release the negative emotions holding you back from achieving balance in your sacral chakra and experience greater health, happiness, and fulfillment in your life.

Mindful Meditation Practices for Commuters and Outdoor Walks

Walking is a great way to reduce stress and get some exercise, but it's easy to zone out and not be present in the moment - this is where mindful meditation comes in. Mindful meditation is about being present in the moment and paying attention to your thoughts, feelings, and sensations without judgment. It helps you focus on the here and now, which can be very helpful when you're walking outdoors.

There are many ways to practice mindful meditation, but one simple way is to focus on your breath. Also, as you walk, pay attention to the sensation of your feet hitting the ground and be aware of the feeling of your breath going in and out. If your mind wanders, that's okay. Gently bring your attention back to your breath. With more mindful meditation practice, you'll find more peace and calm in your everyday life.

Tips for Building a Meditation Practice

- **Time and Place:** It's crucial to have a regular time and place for your meditation practice. It helps you develop a habit and makes it easier to stay consistent. Make sure you pick somewhere quiet where you won't be disturbed when deciding on your time and place.

- **Breathing:** One of the most important aspects of meditation is your breath. Make sure you breathe deeply and slowly. If your mind begins to wander, simply bring your attention back to your breath. The goal is not to clear your mind but rather to focus on the present moment.

- **Posture:** It's important to maintain a good posture when meditating. This helps keep your body relaxed and allows you to focus your mind. You can sit on a chair, on the floor with your legs crossed, or even lie down if you prefer. The important thing is that you are comfortable and relaxed.

- **Start Small:** Don't try to meditate for hours on your first try. Start small, with a few minutes of meditation each day. Gradually work your way up to longer periods as you build your practice. Don't get discouraged if you don't see results right away. Keep at it, and it will become easier.

- **Record Yourself:** If you find it hard to focus or get distracted easily, record yourself reading your guided meditation. Then, listen to the recording later and use it to help you focus and stay on track. It is also helpful to have the recorded voice of someone else leading you through the meditation.

- **Use a Timer:** Using a timer is useful if you're new to meditation. You don't have to worry about how long you've been meditating. Simply set a timer for the desired amount of time and focus on your breath until it goes off. Try to avoid one that has a loud tick. Over time, wean yourself off of the timer and focus on your internal clock instead.

- **Setting Goals:** When you're meditating, it's essential to stay focused on your goals. If you have a specific aim, like reducing stress or improving your concentration, keep that goal in mind as you meditate. This helps keep you motivated and focused. While it's important to start small, you also need to be consistent to reap the benefits of meditation. It's favorable to meditate every day, even if it's just for a few minutes.

- **Find a Community:** If you're struggling to stick to your meditation practice, look for a community of like-minded people. Many groups and classes are available to help you learn more about meditation and be successful in your practice. Joining an online community or finding a regularly practicing buddy is another promising option.

Along with these tips and suggestions, it's imperative not to forget to be patient with yourself. The more you practice, the better you will become. Meditation is a journey, not a destination.

Meditation is a powerful tool to help you tap into your inner resources and achieve your goals. It helps you increase your focus and concentration, reduce stress, and achieve success when used correctly. However, meditation and visualization are not one-size-fits-all. What works for someone else may not work for you, so it's essential to experiment and determine what works best for you.

There's no right or wrong way to meditate or visualize. The most important thing is to find what works for you and stick to it. With practice and consistency, you'll be amazed at how much meditation and visualization can help you achieve your goals.

Chapter 4: Svadhisthana Mantras and Affirmations

Do you want to manifest positive changes in your life? Then consider using mantras and affirmations. These powerful tools can help you create the reality you desire by focusing your mind and opening your heart.

Mantras and affirmations are two powerful tools to help you manifest what you want in life. These powerful tools can be very effective and bring about the changes you want to see in your life if used correctly.

Mantras are a series of words or sounds repeated over and over again with meaning. These words are often from an ancient language and have been used for centuries by people who believe in them. They are usually said out loud but can also be said silently.

Affirmations are positive statements you make about a situation, an outcome, or yourself. An affirmation is usually written down to be repeatedly read until it becomes ingrained into your subconscious mind.

This chapter will explore the power of mantras and affirmations and their role in manifesting. It will also discuss choosing effective affirmations and using them in your everyday life.

Mantras and Affirmations

Mantras have been used for centuries by people who believe in them because they have been proven to work repeatedly. The effect of Mantras on your mind is similar to hypnosis or meditation. When you repeat a mantra, the meaning behind the words becomes embedded in your subconscious mind and eventually affects how you think and feel about different aspects of your life.

Affirmations work similarly to mantras. When you repeat an affirmation to yourself, it also becomes embedded in your subconscious mind and changes how you think and feel. It is especially effective if you pair your affirmations with visualizations or even a quiet meditation time.

Mantras and affirmations are used to manifest what you want in life. You can use them to change your mindset, attract abundance, improve your relationships, heal your body, etc. The sky is the limit.

Benefits of Mantras and Affirmations

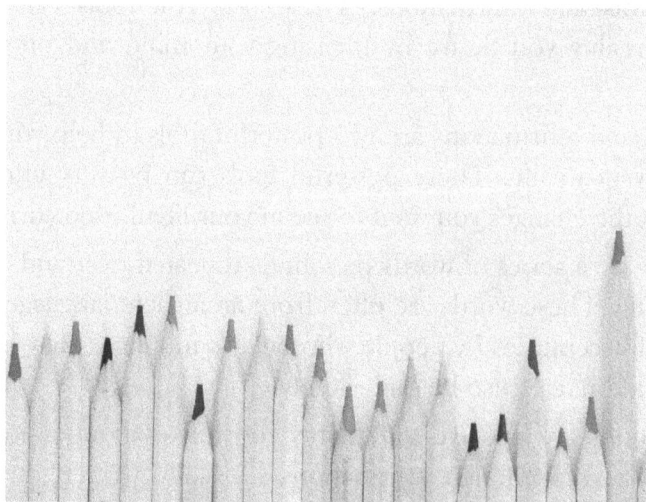

Svadhishana mantras increase creativity
https://www.pexels.com/photo/close-up-photography-of-colored-pencils-743986/

Many different benefits are associated with practicing Svadhisthana mantras and affirmations. These techniques help balance and energize the second chakra responsible for creativity, sexuality, and emotions. By tapping into this energy center, you unlock your full potential in these areas of your life.

Svadhisthana mantras and affirmations can boost your mood and help you manage stress more effectively. They also provide a calming influence over emotional imbalances like anxiety or depression. Altogether, these techniques offer a powerful tool to empower yourself and live an energetically balanced life.

Here are some of the most notable benefits you can expect from using Svadhisthana mantras and affirmations:

- Increased creativity.

- More energy and motivation.

- Greater clarity of thought.

- A calmer mind and reduced stress levels.

- Improved focus and concentration.

- An overall feeling of wellbeing.

When you use mantras and affirmations to balance your chakras, expect to see an improvement in all areas of your life. Clearing and energizing your body unlocks the full potential of all your energy centers.

Part 1: Affirmations for the Sacral Chakra

When working with affirmations, choosing ones that resonate with you personally is crucial. The more connected you feel to your affirmations and how they make you feel, the more powerful they will be while helping to manifest what you want to create in your life.

Here are some examples of affirmations you can use to work with the sacral chakra:

- I am open to new opportunities and experiences.

- I welcome abundance and prosperity into my life.

- I release all fear and doubt.

- My creativity is limitless, and I express it in all that I do.

- I am confident and comfortable in my skin.

- I love and approve of myself just the way I am.

- I am worthy of love, respect, and happiness.

- My relationships are healthy, supportive, and fulfilling.

These are a few examples to get you started. Feel free to tweak them or create your own from scratch. Remember, it is vital to choose affirmations that resonate with you on a personal level.

This next section looks at how you can create your affirmations for the sacral chakra.

How to Write Your Affirmations for the Sacral Chakra

To write your affirmations for the sacral chakra, it is important to consider the qualities this energy center governs. These include creativity, passion, joy, and intuition, among others. With this in mind, craft a short statement or phrase that captures each idea and speaks about how you want to feel.

It is also important to have an intention behind them when crafting affirmations. For example, you may start with a simple declaration like "I am creative" or "I am filled with passion." Use these as the foundation for more specific assertions such as "My creative energy flows freely at all times" or "I am passionate about embracing my unique voice and style." Consider why you want to work on strengthening your sacral chakra, what specific benefits you hope to achieve, and how you ultimately want to feel when utilizing these techniques.

Think about the different areas of your life where you would like more creativity and passion; this will help you get started with your sacral chakra affirmations. For example, do you need help finding new inspiration in your writing or art projects? Are there areas of your personal life where you would like more joy and spontaneity? Do you want to connect more deeply with your intuition and trust the guidance that is coming to you? You can create affirmations that will support you while achieving your specific goals by having a clear intention in mind.

Tips for Coming Up with Original Affirmations

There are many ways to create affirmations to promote authenticity and open communication. Moreover, it is helpful to focus on the qualities or traits you admire most in yourself and others. For instance, if you value confidence and creativity, you may come up with an affirmation like, "I am a naturally confident person who can overcome challenges with ease." It is important to reflect on these qualities while creating your affirmations to come from a genuine place of self-acceptance.

Another key component of engaging affirmations is specificity. While it may feel like enough to simply state something like "I am a kind and compassionate person," digging deeper into this idea can help you craft more meaningful sayings that resonate more deeply within yourself. Consider focusing on actions that demonstrate kindness, like showing compassion for other people, offering advice without judgment, or helping friends and family members in need. These more concrete statements serve as reminders that you are living following your values and beliefs.

Finally, phrase your affirmations so that they feel natural for you. While certain forms of structured meditation focus specifically on repeating particular phrases throughout the day, taking a more organic approach to affirmations can also be beneficial. Keep your affirmations in mind throughout the day and let them come to you organically, rather than forcing yourself to adhere to a rigid plan.

Part 2: Mantras for the Sacral Chakra

In addition to crafting affirmations for the sacral chakra, it is also helpful to utilize mantras regularly. These Sanskrit words can be repeated aloud or internally and often focus on a single syllable intended to resonate with the energy of this particular chakra. The mantras listed below can be used to support the sacral chakra when you work on opening yourself up to new inspiration, embracing your innate creativity, and developing a more passionate approach to life.

1. Vam Mantra for Svadhisthana Chakra

The first mantra for the sacral chakra is "*vam.*" This word is pronounced like "*vahm,*" and it means "I," making it the perfect mantra for promoting a sense of self-acceptance and inner strength. This mantra can be repeated whenever you feel disconnected from yourself, and it is especially powerful when chanted with a focus on the abdomen and the lower back area.

The vam mantra is specifically designed to activate and balance the sacral chakra. The word "*vam*" also means "water" in Sanskrit and represents this chakra's fluid, creative energy. By repeating this mantra regularly, we help open the flow of creative energy in our lives. We find our sexual relationships blossom, and our creative endeavors flow more easily as we do so. Chant the vam mantra for yourself today and see what changes you notice in your life.

2. Mantra for the Sacral Chakra: "Om Mani Padme Hum"

The second sacral chakra mantra is "om mani padme hum." This phrase is pronounced like "*oh-muh-nee-pahd-may-hoom,*" meaning "jewel in the lotus." This mantra is associated with Buddhist tradition and is often used as a meditation tool. By focusing on the energy of this mantra, we activate our sacral chakra and help develop a deeper connection with our innate creativity.

This mantra is also said to represent the path of spiritual development. We remind ourselves that we are on a journey toward enlightenment by repeating this mantra. The lotus flower in this mantra symbolizes our potential for growth and transformation, while the jewel represents the wisdom we can gain through this process.

3. Mantra for Svadhisthana Chakra: "Muladhara"

The third sacral chakra mantra is "Muladhara." This word is pronounced like "*moo-lah-dah-rah,*" meaning "root support." This mantra is intended to help us ground and balance our energy, making it the perfect mantra for those who feel as though their sacral chakra is out of balance.

This mantra can be repeated anytime you feel ungrounded, scattered, or lacking in energy. By repeating this mantra with intention, you help realign your energy and bring yourself back into balance. The word "*Muladhara*" is also thought to represent the four corners of the Earth, reminding us that the ground supports us beneath our feet.

4. Namo Mantra

The fourth sacral chakra mantra is "*namo.*" This word is pronounced like "nah-moh," which means "bow to the divine in me." This mantra is intended to help us connect with our inner wisdom and can be repeated anytime you are looking for guidance or support in your life.

This mantra reminds us that we all have access to divine guidance, and we can connect with this guidance by turning inward. The word "namo" also represents humility, reminding us that we are all part of the same divine energy. As you repeat this mantra, you will find it helps open your mind and heart, allowing you to embrace the universe's wisdom.

5. So Hum Mantra

The fifth sacral chakra mantra is "*so hum.*" These words are pronounced like "soh-hoom," meaning "I am." This mantra reminds us that we are all connected to the divine and are made of the same energy as the universe. It can be repeated anytime you are looking for a way to connect with your inner wisdom or wish to tap into the divine energy surrounding us.

This mantra is also said to be the universe's sound and is often used as a meditation tool. We help quiet our minds and connect with the peace and stillness that lies within by repeating this mantra. We can also use this mantra to connect with the energy of all life, reminding us that we are a part of something much bigger than ourselves.

6. Maha Mrityunjaya Mantra

The sixth sacral chakra mantra is the "maha mrityunjaya mantra." This is pronounced like "*muh-huh-muh-ree-toon-jah-yuh,*" meaning "great death conqueror." This mantra can be used to help us overcome fear and anxiety and is often recommended for those dealing with difficult life transitions. It is said to contain the power of transformation and helps us let go of old patterns and ways of being that no longer serve us.

This mantra is also said to represent the cycle of life and death, reminding us that change is an inevitable part of existence. As we repeat this mantra with intention, we release the fear and anxiety holding us back. The word "mahamrityunjaya" also represents the three aspects of the divine, reminding us that a higher power always supports us. You find strength and balance reentering your life as you repeat this mantra.

7. Om Namah Shivaya Mantra

The seventh sacral chakra mantra is the "om namah shivaya" mantra. Pronounced as "*ohm nah-muh-shee-vuh-yuh*" it means "I bow to Shiva." This mantra reminds us that we are all connected to the divine and are made of the same energy as the universe. It can be repeated anytime you are looking for a way to connect with your inner wisdom or wish to tap into the divine energy surrounding us.

Tips for Using These Mantras

Now that you know some of the most popular sacral chakra mantras, here are a few tips to help you use them correctly:

1. Find a quiet space where you can relax and focus on your mantra. Ideally, this space should be as still and as quiet as possible.

2. Take a few deep breaths before you begin to help calm your mind and relax your body.

3. Clear your mind of all other thoughts, and focus only on your mantra.

4. Repeat your mantra slowly and clearly, with intention.

5. Allow your mantra to sink in, and notice how it makes you feel.

6. Be patient with yourself, and don't worry if your mind wanders during meditation. Simply bring your attention back to your mantra as soon as you notice it has drifted.

7. If possible, practice this technique every day, and add more mantras as you feel ready.

8. You should begin to notice the benefits of using these mantras after only a few weeks of practice. They can help you release stress, connect with the divine, and find more peace in your daily

life. With time and practice, you may discover that these mantras become an important part of who you are.

The sacral chakra is located near the sacrum at the base of your spine and is associated with creativity, energy, passion, pleasure, and sexuality. Using the right sacral chakra affirmations and mantras, you help balance this energy center and bring more harmony into your life. Repeat these mantras and affirmations daily, and see how they make you feel, and you'll be surprised at the positive changes you encounter.

Whether you are looking for a way to relax and connect with your inner wisdom or bring more healing energy into your life, these mantras are a great place to start. Remember to be patient with yourself, and practice regularly for the best results. With time and commitment, you should notice a difference in your life.

Chapter 5: The Power of Mudras and Pranayama

In many spiritual traditions, mudras and pranayama are powerful tools for opening and balancing the body's chakras. Mudras involve specific hand postures and gestures that harness the energy of the mind, body, and spirit to help align these energy centers. Pranayama is deep breathing that helps activate and circulate the flow of vital life force (chi) throughout the body.

When practiced together regularly, mudras and pranayama enhance our sense of wellbeing by helping us to achieve balance and harmony at a physical and energetic level. So, if you are looking to tap into your inner power by energizing your chakras, then mudras and pranayama are certainly worth exploring.

This chapter explains these two useful additions to help enhance your meditation routine and balance the sacral chakra. First are the mudras that help to balance the energy of this chakra. The second is pranayama which is a powerful tool to enhance energy flow. It also provides instructions on performing pranayama breath work for chakra balancing to get the most from your meditation experience.

Mudras

There are seven main chakras, or energy centers, in the body. Each chakra is associated with a different color, element, and set of emotions. Balancing the chakras helps promote physical, mental, and emotional wellbeing. One way to balance the chakras is through the mudras, or hand gestures.

Mudras can be used during meditation or when you feel out of balance. Each mudra is associated with a different chakra. For example, the Apana Mudra is associated with the Root Chakra - it helps to ground and center you, promoting stability and security. The Anahata Mudra is associated with the Heart Chakra - it helps open and balance the heart chakra, promoting love, compassion, and understanding.

For the sacral chakra, the Svadhisthana Mudra is recommended. This mudra helps increase our capacity for pleasure and creativity. Several other mudras are used to balance the sacral chakra. Incorporating these mudras into your meditation routine will help you achieve greater balance and harmony physically, emotionally, and mentally.

Experiment with different mudras to determine which ones work best. There is no right or wrong way. Just let your intuition guide you and trust that you'll find the perfect mudra for balancing your chakras.

The Power of Mudras

Mudras are essential tools used to balance and heal the sacral chakra, or the energy center associated with emotions. These ancient gestures have been used in yoga and meditation practices for thousands of years, as they help to facilitate a connection to the divine energy surrounding us. We direct this powerful energy to flow through our bodies and restore balance to our sacral chakra by placing certain fingers together or moving them in specific ways.

Regardless of whether you use mudras before meditation or want to incorporate them into your daily life, their ability to tap into the sacral chakra makes them an incredibly powerful tool for achieving happiness, health, and peace of mind. If you're looking for a way to harness the power of your chakras, then mudras are certainly worth exploring.

Mudras for Unblocking Sacral Chakra

You can try several mudras to unblock the sacral chakra and improve your energy flow. Some of the most common include yoni mudra, varun mudra, and ksepana mudra. These mudras can help you balance your sacral chakra and improve energy flow in your lower abdomen.

Whichever mudra you choose depends on what you want to achieve. If you seek a simple and easy way to unblock the sacral chakra, yoni mudra is a good place to start. For a mudra to increase energy flow in the body, try Varun mudra or *ksepana mudra*. No matter which mudra you choose, focus on your breath and visualize the area of your body you want to open. You should notice a difference in your energy levels and overall sense of well-being with regular practice.

Mudras for Healing Sacral Chakra

Many mudras can be used to heal the sacral chakra. Some of the most common include Prithvi mudra, Apana mudra, and yoni mudra. These mudras can help unblock the sacral chakra and improve energy flow in the body.

Prithvi mudra is used to increase the earth element in the body. This mudra can help balance the energy in the lower abdomen, improving physical and emotional health. Apana mudra is a mudra used to increase the earth's energy and water in the sacral chakra. This mudra helps with health issues associated with imbalances in the sacral chakra, like urinary problems or reproductive issues.

The Different Mudras

When we activate and open our sacral chakra through mudras, we find more joy in life by simply being present in the moment and enjoying all it has to offer. There are many different mudras for the sacral chakra, and each is associated with a different element of emotion. Some of the most common mudras for balancing the sacral chakra include:

For every mudra we exemplify, we'll also explain the meaning behind the name and the chosen hand gesture, and their connection to the sacral chakra.

1. Shakti Mudra - The Gesture of Energy

"Shakti" is a Sanskrit word that translates to "power." So, the Shakti Mudra is a mudra of power and strength. It helps activate the kundalini energy, or the life force residing at the base of the spine. This mudra is often used to increase creativity, improve self-esteem, and balance the sacral chakra. When we activate this mudra, we tap into our natural power and draw upon it to achieve our goals.

To perform the Shakti Mudra, begin by sitting in a comfortable position with your spine straight. Place your hands on your knees with your palms facing upward, wrapping your thumbs with your index and middle fingers. Extend your little and ring fingers and touch their tips together. The shakti mudra is now completed, and you can hold it for as long as you like.

Breathe in and out slowly and deeply as you focus on the sacral chakra. Visualize a ball of orange light spinning in your lower abdomen. Imagine the ball of light growing larger and brighter as you exhale. Continue to breathe deeply and focus on the sacral chakra until you feel your emotions balancing.

2. Yoni Mudra - The Gesture of the Universal Womb

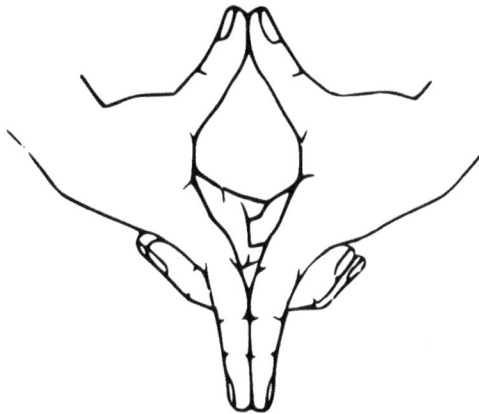

Yoni mudra.
https://pixabay.com/images/id-6170665/

The yoni mudra is an ancient yogic practice believed to stimulate the sacral chakra, located in the lower pelvic region. This practice involves forming a circle with the thumb and pointer finger and tracing a continuous line from your navel all the way up to your solar plexus. Yoni mudra helps clear any blockages or imbalances in your sacral chakra by connecting the energy from the root of your body to its potential at your heart.

Performing the yoni mudra: Sit with your spine straight and your hands resting in your lap with your palms upward. Touch the tip of your thumbs and forefingers together to form a diamond. Interlace your remaining fingers with the forefingers facing down towards the ground. Envision a red ball of energy spinning in the pelvis, tap into it with your mind's eye, and continue to breathe as you deeply focus on your sacral chakra.

The yoni mudra is one of the most common mudras for the sacral chakra, so it's a good place to start if you're new to mudras. Whether you want to improve creativity and intuition, initiate new romantic relationships, or unblock emotional trauma, this simple yet powerful mudra can help you achieve those goals. It opens a way for you to tap into your inner wisdom and the powerful energy of your sacral chakra.

3. Varun Mudra - The Gesture of Water

Varun mudra.
https://pixabay.com/images/id-7202715/

Varun mudra is a gesture representing the water element. This mudra is commonly used to balance the sacral chakra and increase energy flow in the body. Its name comes from Varuna, a Hindu deity associated with water and the ocean. The act of the Varun mudra evokes the creative and nurturing power of water, making it a perfect mudra for anyone seeking healing or creativity.

To perform the Varun mudra, simply sit in a comfortable position with your back straight. Hold your hands out in front of you with your palms facing up. Touch the tips of your pinky fingers and thumbs together, and extend your other fingers. Focus your attention on the area between your navel and pubic bone to balance the sacral chakra with the Varun mudra. Visualize a ball of blue light spinning in this space. Imagine the ball of light growing larger and brighter as you breathe in and out. Continue to focus on your breath and the water energy in your body until you feel your sacral chakra opening.

If you need a quick and easy way to balance your sacral chakra, Varun mudra is a great place to start. This mudra is simple and can be done anywhere, making it a great option for busy schedules. Remember to take deep, slow breaths as you practice getting the most benefit from Varun mudra.

3. Ksepana Mudra - The Gesture of Sealing

Ksepana mudra.
Schlum, CC BY-SA 4.0 <https://creativecommons.org/licenses/by-sa/4.0>, via Wikimedia Commons: https://commons.wikimedia.org/wiki/File:Mudra-Naruto-Chevre.svg

Ksepana mudra is a gesture that seals in the energy of the sacral chakra. This mudra is commonly used to clear energy blockages in the body and increase energy flow in the lower abdomen. It can also balance the energy in other chakras, such as the crown chakra or heart chakra.

To perform the ksepana mudra, sit with your spine straight and hands on your knees. Link the fingers of both hands. Release the pointer fingers, pointing them straight, and fold the thumbs over the opposite pointer finger. Now, press your fists into your lower abdomen just above the pubic bone.

Imagine a ball of white light spinning in your lower abdomen as you breathe in and out. Focus on your breath and the energy of the sacral chakra until you feel your lower abdomen opening. Ksepana mudra is a great way to increase energy flow in the body and clear any blockages preventing the free flow of energy.

Pranayama

Breathing is an essential function of life, but it's also a powerful tool that can be used to promote physical and mental wellbeing. Pranayama is a yoga technique involving controlled breathing to calm the mind and body. The practice is helpful to focus the mind during meditation, and it's also an effective way to release tension and promote relaxation.

When the nervous system is balanced, it's easier to achieve a state of calmness and focus. Controlled breathing helps regulate the nervous system, which is one of the benefits of pranayama.

Additionally, controlled breathing helps improve circulation and promotes detoxification. Therefore, pranayama is an important part of yoga practice and is highly beneficial for those seeking to improve their overall health and wellbeing.

There are many benefits to this practice, but one of the most important is that it helps open and balance the sacral chakra. In particular, pranayama will help release any trapped emotions or stagnant energy. As a result, this practice is highly beneficial for anyone seeking to open creativity or experience more emotional freedom.

Pranayama helps control and direct the flow of energy in the body. We can move stagnant energy and open the flow of vital life force energy in the body by focusing on the breath and deepening the inhalations and exhalations. In addition to promoting creativity, pranayama also boosts immunity, increases energy levels, and helps quiet the mind.

The Different Types of Pranayama

Pranayama practice is an essential part of any yoga experience, targeting the different energy centers (or chakras) in your body and helping you achieve better physical, mental, and spiritual wellbeing. Some yogis use various pranayama techniques, such as alternate nostril breathing (Nadi shodhana), mula bandha, and belly rolls to activate the sacral chakra. These can be practiced individually or combined for a powerful effect on your energy body. Regardless of your technique, incorporating pranayama into your practice helps you unlock and balance your sacral chakra for optimal health and vitality.

Here are a few simple pranayama techniques to open and balance your sacral chakra:

1. Ujjayi Breath - Victorious Breath

Ujjayi is a breath control technique that helps calm the mind and promotes relaxation.

Performing Ujjayi Breath

Take a deep inhalation through your nose. Exhale through the mouth while making a "ha" sound. Constrict the muscles at the back of your throat to create a slight snoring sound as you exhale. Repeat this breath for 3-5 minutes.

2. Nadi Shodhana - Alternate Nostril Breathing

Nadi shodhana is a pranayama technique that helps cleanse and purify the energy channels (or nadis) in the body. Before meditation, this practice is often used to clear the mind and prepare for focused introspection.

Performing nadi shodhana

Sit comfortably with your hands in a mudra (hand position that helps direct energy flow). Using your right thumb, close your right nostril and take a deep inhalation through your left nostril. Close your left nostril with your ring finger and release your right thumb. Exhale through your right nostril, and inhale again through the same side. Finally, close your right nostril and release your left nostril, exhaling through the left side. Repeat this breath for 3-5 minutes, then switch sides and repeat the process.

3. Mula Bandha - Root Lock

Mula bandha is a yogic technique that helps lock the energy in the lower body and direct it upward towards the higher chakras.

Performing Mula Bandha

Simply contract the perineum (between your anus and genitals) as you inhale and exhale. This helps direct your body's prana (vital energy) toward the sacral and solar plexus chakras.

4. Belly Rolls

Belly rolls are a simple but effective pranayama technique for stimulating the sacral chakra.

Performing Belly Rolls

Simply inhale deeply and expand your belly. Exhale and roll your pelvis forward, tucking your tailbone and rounding your back. Repeat this breath for 3-5 minutes to open the hips and sacral chakra.

While these pranayama techniques are some of the most basic in yoga, they have also shown to be very effective in promoting sacral chakra balance. In addition to practicing pranayama, use mudras (hand gestures) to open and balance your sacral chakra. Mudras are an important part of yoga, as they help direct the flow of energy in the body and balance different energy centers.

This chapter covered a few of the most effective pranayama and mudra techniques for opening and balancing your sacral chakra. Check out the rest of this book to learn more about other practices for the sacral chakras.

Chapter 6: Sacral Yoga Poses and Sequences

Do you want to balance your sacral chakra and achieve greater overall health and wellbeing? Yoga may be the perfect solution. With its focus on breathing, meditation, and asanas (or poses), yoga can help you open and heal your sacral chakra while improving strength, flexibility, and mental clarity.

Yoga is a practice that engages the sacral chakra and helps harmonize physical and emotional needs and improve wellbeing in many aspects of life. Furthermore, regular yoga practice has been proven to boost the immune system, reduce stress and anxiety levels, improve sleep quality, etc.

So, yoga is the perfect solution if you're looking for a way to balance your sacral chakra and find greater health and wellbeing overall. With so many different practice styles available today, there's truly something out there for every yogi at every level.

This chapter will discuss the benefits of yoga for the sacral chakra and offer some specific poses and sequences to help you open and heal this chakra. We'll also provide tips on how to get started with yoga and find the right style for you. So, whether you're new to yoga or a longtime practitioner, there's sure to be something here to help you on your path to greater health and wellbeing.

Yoga's Benefits in Balancing Svadhisthana

Yoga can be a great tool for balancing the sacral chakra. Certain yoga poses help increase circulation and opens the hips, which help release blockages causing an imbalance in the sacral chakra. In addition, breathing exercises and meditation help focus and calm the mind, promoting feelings of safety and security. Help keep your sacral chakra balanced by incorporating yoga into your daily life.

Here are a few of the many benefits yoga offers by balancing the sacral chakra:

- **Improved Circulation:** The poses and sequences used in yoga help increase circulation, allowing for a more balanced energy flow throughout the body.

- **Increased Flexibility:** Yoga poses help to stretch and open the muscles and joints, increasing flexibility. This is especially helpful in releasing tension in the hips and lower back, closely related to the sacral chakra.

- **Reduced Stress and Anxiety:** Through breathing exercises, meditation, and focused attention, yoga can help focus the mind and promote calm and relaxation. In turn, this reduces stress and anxiety levels, promoting a sense of wellbeing.

- **Improved Sleep Quality:** The relaxation techniques learned in yoga also help improve sleep quality by promoting a sense of calm and peace before bed.

- **Balanced Hormones:** The endocrine system, which controls the body's hormones, is closely connected to the sacral chakra. You can maintain a healthy hormone balance by keeping this chakra in shape.

- **Elevated Mood:** Regular yoga practice improves mood and overall mental wellbeing. It is likely due to the increased focus on breathing and meditation and the release of endorphins during physical activity.

As you can see, there are many benefits to incorporating yoga into your life to balance the sacral chakra. If you're looking for specific poses and sequences to help open and heal your sacral chakra, the next section will provide some suggestions.

Asanas for Opening and Balancing the Sacral Chakra

The sacral chakra governs our ability to connect with others and experience pleasure. Asanas, or yoga poses, help balance this chakra by opening the hips, legs, abdomen, and lower back and stimulating the energy flow in those areas. Some of the most effective asanas to open and balance the sacral chakra are the Goddess pose (Utkata Konasana), Reverse Warrior Pose (Viparita Virabhadrasana), Cross-Legged Twist Pose (Parivrtta Sukhasana), Uttanasana (standing forward fold), Marjaryasana (cat and cow pose), and Balasana (child's pose).

You can increase your vitality, joy, creativity, intuition, and emotional health by focusing on these postures during your practice each day. So, if you're looking to balance your sacral chakra and improve your overall wellbeing, start incorporating the following asanas into your regular practice today.

Utkata Konasana (Goddess Pose)

The Goddess pose is a standing posture that opens the hips, thighs, and chest while strengthening the legs and lower back. This pose also helps stimulate the energy flow in the sacral area, making it an excellent asana to open and balance the sacral chakra. Keep your back straight while pushing the hips forward and down when performing this pose.

Instructions:
1. Begin by standing with your feet about a foot apart and turn your toes outward.
2. Bend your knees and lower your hips down toward the ground. Your thighs are parallel to the ground, and your arms are stretched in front of you.

3. Hold this position for several deep breaths, feeling the stretch in your hips and lower back.

4. Straighten your legs and return to standing to release the pose.

Depending on your flexibility, this pose can be performed with or without props. If you have any knee pain, place a yoga block or a blanket under your heels to protect them from the ground. You can also perform this pose with your back against a wall for extra support if needed.

Viparita Virabhadrasana (Reverse Warrior Pose)

The reverse warrior pose is a great way to stretch the muscles in your hips, abdomen, and lower back while opening the chest. This asana helps balance the sacral chakra with regular practice by stimulating the energy flow in your hips and lower back. It is a great pose for beginners, as the reverse warrior can be performed in many ways to increase its effectiveness.

Instructions:

1. Begin by standing with your feet together and turning your right foot outward.

2. Bend your left knee slightly and keep your right leg straight, with the right heel in line with the left heel.

3. Point your right arm straight up toward the ceiling and slowly lean back, stretching your body's right side.

4. Hold this pose for several breaths, feeling the stretch in your hips and abdomen.

5. To release the pose, straighten your right leg, and return to standing.

The key to correctly performing this pose is to keep your back straight and your front knee bent at a 90-degree angle. The reverse warrior pose can also be performed with a chair if you need extra support. Remember to keep your shoulders square and aligned over your hips, making sure not to hunch your shoulders forward as you lean back.

Parivrtta Sukhasana
(Cross-Legged Twist Pose)

The cross-legged twist pose is a gentle and relaxing posture that helps stretch the hips, lower back, and abdomen. As a staple for any yoga practice, this pose can be performed in various ways, depending on your flexibility. The cross-legged twist helps open and balance the sacral chakra, increasing creativity and emotional health when performed correctly.

Instructions:

1. Begin by sitting in a cross-legged position on the ground.

2. Place your right hand on the ground behind you and twist your torso to the left, looking over your left shoulder.

3. Hold this pose for several breaths, feeling the stretch in your hips and lower back.

4. Untwist your torso and return to sitting cross-legged to release the pose.

The cross-legged twist pose is great for beginners but can also be performed with props if you need extra support. If your hips are tight, place a yoga block under your right buttock to help tilt your pelvis. You can also place a blanket under your knees for extra comfort.

Uttanasana (Standing Forward Fold)

The standing forward fold is a simple but effective posture that helps stretch the hamstrings, lower back, and hips. The forward fold is often used as a resting pose at the end of yoga practice, but it also has many therapeutic benefits to help balance your sacral chakra. It is said that the standing forward fold helps increase creativity and emotional stability.

Instructions:

1. Begin by standing with your feet together and slowly bending forward, keeping your back straight as you lower down.

2. Allow your head and neck to hang freely, pushing your hips toward the ground as much as possible.

3. Hold this pose for several breaths, feeling the stretch in your hamstrings and lower back.

4. Slowly roll your spine back up to standing and return to the starting position to release the pose.

The standing forward fold can also be performed with a yoga block under your hands for extra support if needed. Remember to keep your shoulders relaxed as you lower down, focusing on keeping your back straight and aligned with your legs throughout the pose.

Ardha Matsyendrasana (Half Fish Pose)

Half fish pose.
lululemon athletica, CC BY 2.0 <https://creativecommons.org/licenses/by/2.0/>, via Wikimedia Commons https://commons.wikimedia.org/wiki/File:Ardha_Matyendrasana_-_Half_Lord_of_the_Fishes_Pose_-_Bound_Arm_Variation.jpg

The half-fish pose is a deep twist that helps stretch the shoulders, chest, and neck. This pose can also be therapeutic for the lower back, hips, and sacral chakra. This pose helps increase emotional stability and creativity by opening the second chakra. With regular practice, you'll experience the many benefits of this powerful asana.

Instructions:

1. Begin by sitting on the floor with your legs extended in front of you.

2. Bend your right knee and place your foot on the floor next to your left thigh.

3. Place your left hand on the floor behind you and twist your torso to the right, looking over your right shoulder.

4. Hold this pose for several breaths, feeling the stretch in your shoulders, chest, and neck.

5. Untwist your torso and return to a sitting position with your legs extended in front of you to release the pose.

You can also perform this pose using a yoga strap around your back if needed. Place a blanket under your knee for extra support if you have tight hips. Remember to keep your sitting bones grounded and spine long as you twist into the pose.

Marjaryasana (Cat and Cow Pose)

The cat and cow pose is a combination backbend that helps stretch the spine, neck, and shoulders. While this posture is used to warm up the body for more intense yoga practice, it also has many therapeutic benefits making it a great pose for beginners. The cat and cow pose helps increase emotional stability and creativity by opening the second chakra.

Instructions:

1. Begin on your hands and knees, your wrists directly beneath your shoulders and knees aligned with your hips.

2. Inhale as you drop your belly down and arch your back toward the ceiling, looking up at the sky.

3. Exhale and bend your spine back toward the ground, lowering your head and tucking your chin into your chest.

4. Continue moving between these two poses for several breaths, feeling the stretch in your spine and neck with each inhale and exhale.

5. Lift your head back up to neutral and return to the starting position to release the pose.

Remember to keep your breath smooth and even as you move between the cat and cow poses. If you have any lower back pain, take it slow at first. Focus on moving slowly and mindfully as you breathe into the stretch.

Balasana (Child's Pose)

The child's pose is a resting pose that helps stretch the hips, thighs, and ankles. It is called the child's pose because it resembles a young child's position when sitting back on their heels. The main goal of this pose is to relax the mind and body, releasing any tension or stress you are feeling.

Instructions:
1. Begin on your hands and knees, your wrists directly beneath your shoulders and your knees aligned with your hips.
2. Exhale, sit back on your heels, and lower your forehead to the floor.
3. Extend your arms out before you, letting your palms rest on the floor.
4. Stay in this position for several breaths, breathing deeply and focusing on releasing tension or stress.
5. Inhale and return to the starting position on your hands and knees to release the pose.

It may be difficult to sit back on your heels if you are new to yoga or have tight hips. Use a blanket or yoga block to prop up your heels if this is the case. Be sure to keep your sitting bones grounded and your spine long as you rest in this pose.

Sequencing and Alternative Poses

Once you have learned the basic yoga poses, you can start putting them together into sequences. These sequences can be as simple or as complex as you like, depending on your goals or experience level. You can also use different poses to target specific body areas, like stretching the upper back and shoulders or toning the legs and glutes.

There are many different sequences you can try, but here are a few popular options to get you started:

Sequence 1:

1. Marjaryasana (Cat and Cow Pose) – 5-10 breaths

2. Balasana (Child's Pose) – 5-10 breaths

3. Uttanasana (Standing Forward Fold) – 5-10 breaths

Sequence 2:

1. Uttanasana (Standing Forward Fold) – 5-10 breaths

2. Ardha Matsyendrasana (Half Fish Pose) – 5-10 breaths on each side

3. Paschimottanasana (Seated Forward Fold) – 5-10 breaths

Adding Variety

If you have been practicing yoga for some time, you'll find your body becomes accustomed to doing the same poses in the same order every day. Therefore, it's important to mix things up and add variety to your practice. Here are a few ways that you can do this:

1. **Vary the Order of Your Poses** – Do the cat and cow pose first instead of last, or alternate between the standing and seated forward folds.

2. **Add New Poses** – If you're feeling adventurous, add new poses to your sequences. There are hundreds of yoga poses to choose from, so you're sure to find some that suit your level and goals.

3. **Hold Poses for Different Lengths of Time** – Instead of holding the standing forward fold for a full 5-10 breaths, hold it for just 2 or 3. This will keep your practice interesting and challenging.

4. **Use Props** – Props, like yoga blocks or straps, help deepen your stretch or get into poses that would otherwise be difficult.

5. **Practice with a Friend** – Practicing with a friend makes your practice more enjoyable and motivating. It's also a great way to learn new poses and get feedback on your form.

Practicing yoga is a great way to improve your flexibility, strength, and overall wellbeing. By adding variety to your practice, you keep your body and mind challenged and maintain your motivation and progress.

Alternate Poses

While the basic yoga poses and sequences are a great starting point, there are many other options for creating your practice. If you're looking for something different, these simple alternatives are some of the most common poses:

1. Instead of a seated forward fold, try a reclined twist – This pose is a great way to release tension in the lower back and spine.

2. Instead of the child's pose, try a supported backbend – This pose is a gentle way to open the chest and heart.

3. Instead of the cat and cow pose, try a spinal roll – This is an easy way to loosen up the spine and release built-up tension in the back, neck, and shoulders.

4. Instead of a standard side plank, try a dolphin plank – This pose is a great way to build strength in the core and upper body.

5. Instead of a pose for the shoulders, try a forward fold instead – This is an easy way to release tension in the neck and upper back.

Yoga beyond the Asanas

When many people think of yoga, they often picture standing poses, twists, and extensions - activities that seem to require quite a bit of effort and muscle engagement. However, the truth is that yoga is about far more than mere physical postures. At its heart, yoga is a practice of connecting one's mind and body, developing greater awareness and focus, and ultimately achieving balance and harmony in all aspects of life. This holistic approach has particular resonance in healing the sacral chakra, which runs along the center axis of the lower belly and is associated with pleasure and desire.

Incorporating other practices such as pranayama (breathing exercises), meditation, or mudras into your yoga routine, you help open your body on a deeper level by facilitating flow through this key energy center. Whether you work these elements into your regular asana practice or simply use them as standalone methods for balancing your energy centers, they will help ground you physically while relieving stress and tension. Keeping your sacral chakra open will also allow you to reconnect with your genuine desire for life in all its beauty.

Hopefully, the information presented in this chapter has helped introduce you to the various aspects of yoga and its many benefits, but there is always more to learn. If you're interested in deepening your practice and learning more about yoga's potential for healing and growth, consider enrolling in a yoga teacher training program or seeking other resources to help you on your journey.

Chapter 7: Using Crystals and Stones

Crystals are a powerful tool used for healing and balancing your chakras. Each crystal has different properties and is used in different ways to help you heal, balance, and strengthen your chakras.

Crystals are formed by natural processes over thousands of years, and each crystal is unique and comes with its own specific energy. They can help with many aspects of your health, including emotional balance and spiritual enlightenment.

Since ancient times, people have used crystals in many cultures to help heal physical ailments, mental and emotional issues, during meditation, seeking spirituality, and much more.

This chapter focuses on using crystals and stones to balance your sacral chakra. It discusses the properties of different stones and crystals, what makes them good for this chakra, and how to use, cleanse, and care for them.

The Role of Crystals in Balancing the Sacral Chakra

Sacral chakra healing uses crystals in many different ways. The role of crystals in this healing process is to help clear any blockages and re-energize the chakra, helping to restore balance and optimal function.

Balancing the sacral chakra with crystals is done using various methods. Some popular methods include using crystals in meditation, carrying them with you, or placing them on your body. When a crystal is placed directly on the body over the sacral chakra, it allows the crystal's energy to flow into the chakra and clear any blockages or imbalances.

Here are a few ways crystals help balance the sacral chakra:

Restore Equilibrium to the Chakra

Crystals help restore the energetic equilibrium of the sacral chakra by clearing blockages and restoring balance. For example, carnelian is a powerful sacral chakra stone that helps increase motivation and creativity. Citrine is another sacral chakra crystal that promotes positive change by dissolving old patterns and beliefs. We can release old hurts and blockages and make way for new levels of creativity, pleasure, and vitality by working with sacral chakra crystals.

Promote Fertility and Abundance

For centuries, people have used crystals for their purported magical properties. Today, many people still believe that crystals promote creativity, fertility, and abundance. While there is no scientific evidence to support these claims, some people find that working with crystals helps them connect with their creative side. Others use crystals as a way to focus their intention on manifesting abundant blessings in their life. Still, others carry crystals to increase their chances of conceiving a child.

Whether or not crystals have magical powers, working with them can be a fun and empowering way to connect with your intentions and infuse your life with positive energy. They are a unique tool for healing and self-discovery and, when used correctly, help lift your vibration, increase creativity, and attract abundance.

Releases Stress and Traumas

Stress and trauma are among the most common causes of imbalanced sacral chakras. These negative energies have a draining effect on our energy, making us feel anxious, overwhelmed, and disconnected from our true selves. We can work with the healing power of crystals to restore balance to our sacral chakra and release these toxic energies from our bodies.

Certain crystals, like jade or aquamarine, have increased mindfulness and reduced stress by relaxing the mind and body. Like amethyst or orange calcite, other crystals help release past traumas and negative beliefs that fuel anxiety and upset. Therefore, working with crystals is a powerful tool for healing the sacral chakra for anyone looking for an effective way to get back in touch with their truest feelings and emotions.

The Difference between Stones and Crystals

Stones and crystals are often used interchangeably, but there is a difference between the two. Stones are natural rocks that have been cut or polished. They are found in a variety of colors, shapes, and sizes. Stones are typically used for their physical appearance and are mainly used in jewelry or decor. On the other hand, crystals are naturally occurring or man-made substances with a crystalline structure. They have many different purposes and are often used as tools for healing or meditation.

When it comes to balancing the sacral chakra, there is no difference between using stones and crystals. Both are used to clear blockages and restore energetic balance, which comes down to personal preference. Some people prefer the look of stones, while others find crystals more powerful. Ultimately, it is up to you to decide which stone or crystal is best suited to your needs.

What Makes a Stone or Crystal Good for the Sacral Chakra?

The sacral chakra is a key energy center located in the lower abdomen just below the navel. This energetic center influences many aspects of our lives, from creativity and sexuality to relationships and happiness. It is important to work with crystals and stones that resonate with the sacral chakra to support the health of this vital energy center.

Generally, orange or yellow crystals and stones are thought to be particularly beneficial for this chakra. These include carnelian, citrine, and tiger's eye. Additionally, any stone or crystal with an earthy or organic feel promotes balance in the sacral chakra. It is also essential to note that certain crystals must be avoided when working with the sacral chakra, like quartz and amethyst.

Understanding what makes a particular stone or crystal effective for our energy centers can make more informed choices when selecting healing stones and crystals. Therefore, choosing a stone or crystal that resonates with our sacral chakra helps us unlock its power and cultivate greater health and happiness in all areas of life.

Color and Appearance

The sacral chakra is associated with the color orange, and many stones and crystals exhibit this hue. However, other colors are also effective for balancing the sacral chakra. For example, red stones are often used to stimulate energy and passion, while yellow stones promote creativity and joy. Typically, any stone or crystal that is brightly colored and visually appealing is likely to help balance the sacral chakra.

It is imperative to go with your intuition and choose a piece you are drawn to when choosing a stone or crystal. Its connection to emotions makes the sacral chakra an important energy center to keep in balance. Working with stones and crystals of various colors helps restore harmony to this vital area of your being.

Properties and Formation

Many people practice crystal healing using stones and crystals with particular properties that align and revitalize this energy center. Different stones and crystals have unique physical characteristics, like materials and structures that form crystals or a sharp, pointed shape.

These properties play an important role in forming a stone or crystal for the sacral chakra. For example, quartz is one of the most common materials used in crystal healing for its strong vibrations and beneficial effects on energy flow. Additionally, some stones like red jasper radiate heat naturally when held against the skin at this chakra, resulting in feelings of warmth and excitement.

Consider properties like those mentioned when selecting a stone or crystal for your sacral chakra, and optimize its strength and alignment with your body's energies.

Stones and Crystals Good for the Sacral Chakra

Many stones and crystals are used to support the health of the sacral chakra, but some are more commonly used than others. Below is a list of some stones and crystals widely regarded as beneficial for the sacral chakra.

Carnelian

Properties: Carnelian is an agate stone known for its vibrant orange color, often associated with the sacral chakra. In addition to its bright hue, the carnelian also has several other properties that make it an effective crystal to balance the sacral chakra. For example, carnelian is known to boost creativity, passion, and drive. This stone also helps balance the sacral chakra by enhancing energy flow and reducing blockages.

Uses: Carnelian is often worn as jewelry or placed in the home or workplace to support the health of the sacral chakra. A carnelian is placed on or near this energy center during meditation or yoga practice for maximum effect. Carnelian can also be used in crystal healing grids or placed in the home or office areas that need an extra boost of sacral chakra energy.

Snowflake Obsidian

Properties: Snowflake obsidian is a volcanic glass with a black base and white spots or streaks that resemble snowflakes. This stone has several beneficial properties for the sacral chakra, including grounding the energy, reducing stress, and promoting calm. Snowflake obsidian also helps release emotions like anger and resentment that block energy flow in the sacral chakra.

Uses: Snowflake obsidian can be worn as jewelry or held during meditation, yoga, or other practices to promote the flow of energy in the sacral chakra. For best results, snowflake obsidian is placed on or near the sacral chakra during these activities. This stone is also used in crystal grids or kept in the home or office areas where stress or tension is common.

Citrine

Properties: Citrine is one of the most important stones for the sacral chakra due to its bright orange hue and association with creativity and abundance. This stone is known for its ability to align the sacral chakra with the lower chakras, allowing energy to flow smoothly and reducing blockages resulting in stagnation. Citrine also enhances creativity, confidence, and joy.

Uses: Citrine can be worn as jewelry, held during meditation or yoga, or placed in the home or office to support sacral chakra health. This stone can also be added to crystal healing grids or placed in areas where anxiety, stress, or tension are common to promote calm.

Amber

Properties: Amber is a fossilized tree resin used for centuries to support the health of the sacral chakra. This stone helps balance the sacral chakra due to its ability to cleanse and purify energy. Amber is also associated with creativity, fertility, and abundance.

Uses: Amber can be worn as jewelry or placed in the home or office to help cleanse the sacral chakra. Place amber on or near the sacral chakra during meditation or yoga for best results. Amber can also be used in crystal healing grids or placed in the home or office areas that need an extra boost of sacral chakra energy.

Other Stones and Crystals

Many other stones and crystals are helpful for the health of the sacral chakra. Some suggested stones include amethyst, moonstone, tiger's eye, and garnet. Consider consulting with a qualified crystal therapist or energy healer to learn more about these or other crystals and stones that support the sacral chakra.

How to Choose, Cleanse, and Care for Your Stones or Crystals

When cleaning and taking care of your stones and crystals for the sacral chakra, there are a few important things that you should keep in mind. The first step is to choose the right stones or crystals, emphasizing those that resonate most strongly with the energy of this chakra. Some good options include orange calcite, carnelian, and tiger's eye.

As you care for your crystals and stones, pay attention to their color and clarity. Ideally, they should be bright and smooth-looking, with no visible cracks or mineral lines. Once you have chosen your stones or crystals, you must cleanse them by placing them in a bowl of cold water overnight or in direct sunlight for a few hours. This will clear out any lingering negative energies from previous owners or environments.

Once you are ready to use your stones or crystals for the sacral chakra, you must engage all your senses as you meditate or focus your energy on this goal. Use as many images, sounds, smells, etc., to feel fully connected and balanced with these healing gems.

1. Choosing Your Stones or Crystals

Choose stones that resonate with the energy of this particular chakra. Another important consideration is color. Since this chakra is associated with the color orange, it is best to opt for stones in shades of orange or red. Additionally, pay attention to other properties of particular crystals or stones, like how they feel in your hands or which attributes they are believed to improve. Choosing appropriate stones can be a powerful way to enhance your spiritual energy and balance your sacral chakra when done properly.

2. Cleaning Your Stones or Crystals

One way to keep your sacral chakra in balance is to regularly cleanse your stones and crystals. It removes any built-up negativity and allows the positive energy of the stone to flow more freely. There are a few different ways to cleanse your stones.

One method is to place them in sunlight for a few hours. Alternatively, cleanse them with water (either by placing them under running water or soaking them in a bowl of water overnight) or using sound (ringing a bell near them or singing).

If you're unsure which method to use, simply hold the stone in your hand and ask how it would like to be cleansed. Whichever method you choose, your stones must be regularly cleaned to keep your sacral chakra in balance.

3. Caring for Your Stones or Crystals

Once you've chosen and cleansed your stones or crystals, you must take good care of them to maintain their positive energy. Avoid exposing them to harsh chemicals or extreme temperatures, which damage their surface. It is also important to cleanse them regularly, as discussed above.

In addition to these care tips, it's advisable to engage in other practices associated with the sacral chakra. For instance, spending more time in nature, cooking delicious foods, or practicing yoga or dance increases your creative and sensual activities. Taking care of your stones and crystals and engaging in activities that nurture your sacral chakra keep this energy center balanced and healthy.

As you can see, using crystals and stones is a powerful way to enhance your spiritual energy and balance your sacral chakra. Many different stones and crystals are used for this purpose, so take some time to experiment and determine which ones work best.

Look for stones and crystals that resonate with the energy of the sacral chakra and which are colored orange or red. Additionally, be sure to cleanse them regularly using one of the above methods. Remember to care for your stones frequently and engage in activities that nurture your sacral chakra. Using these tips as you use your crystals and stones will improve your spiritual energy and bring balance to your sacral chakra.

Chapter 8: Svadhisthana Aromatherapy

Aromatherapy helps open the sacral chakra.
https://pixabay.com/images/id-3321811/

Ayurveda and essential oils go hand in hand. Essential oils have been used in Indian medicine for thousands of years, with great results. Ayurveda is a holistic system that uses all the tools at our disposal to achieve balance; diet, exercise, meditation, yoga, and herbs. Essential oils are among the most potent of these tools.

According to Ayurveda, the use of aromatic oils helps open the sacral chakra and bring out the positive emotions associated with it. Aromatherapy helps balance the energy centers of your body and brings about harmony within you. This chapter explores some of the best essential oils for Svadhisthana, their properties, and how to use them.

The Role of Essential Oils in Achieving Balance for the Sacral Chakra

Essential oils provide a highly concentrated dose of plant medicine directly into your bloodstream for immediate absorption into your cells. This allows your body to access and utilize the healing benefits of these oils quicker than if you were to take them in internally.

In addition, these oils can be diffused, inhaled, or applied topically for targeted effects on specific areas of the body, making them an ideal choice for treating imbalances in the sacral chakra. Moreover, there are plenty of choices for aromatherapy to balance Svadhisthana, and each oil has unique properties that make it ideal for opening up Svadhisthana.

Essential oils are a helpful tool to achieve sacral chakra balance. For example, ylang-ylang oil is known for promoting happiness and contentment. On the other hand, Jasmine oil helps alleviate sexual tension and insomnia. Diffusing these oils or applying them topically to the lower abdomen encourages the flow of creative energy and aligns our whole selves.

The Role of Smell in Aromatherapy

One of the most important senses in aromatherapy, obviously, is smell. The ability to smell is crucial to promoting balance and wellness in the sacral chakra because that sense is closely linked to our subconscious mind and where the sacral chakra is located.

We unlock and balance this powerful energy center within us by using specific scents and aromas daily. For example, essential oils like ylang-ylang and orange are believed to support the second chakra by bringing more joy, sensuality, and creativity into our lives.

So, if you're looking to enhance this aspect of your being, don't underestimate the power of smell. You can live a more vibrant and balanced life with the right scents and essential oils through your sacral chakra.

The Benefits of Essential Oils for the Sacral Chakra

Many people rely on essential oils to maintain a healthy balance and connection in this energy center. Essential oils are natural plant extracts prized for their fragrance and healing properties. Using specific oils like jasmine or ylang-ylang on or near the sacral chakra promotes joy and optimism, improves your ability to express yourself creatively, and activates your libido.

Whether used in meditation practices or blended into a relaxing bath time ritual, these essential oils help bring your sacral chakra back into alignment. So, if you're looking for a natural way to boost your overall wellbeing and stimulate greater creativity and vitality in your life, look no further than the powerful benefits of essential oils for the sacral chakra.

1. Relieve Anxiety and Stress

Whenever you're feeling anxious or stressed, using aromatherapy is a helpful way to find relief. The scents of certain essential oils calm and soothe the mind, easing anxiety symptoms and promoting a sense of peace. The sacral chakra is closely connected to our emotional state, and the healing properties of essential oils bring this energy center back into balance.

2. Boost Your Libido

Healthy sex life is an important part of a balanced sacral chakra. So, if you want to add a little extra spice to your love life, use certain essential oils to enhance your libido. These specific oils increase passion and arousal, promoting a more energized sacral chakra.

3. Enhance Creativity and Imagination

The sacral chakra is known as the "powerhouse of creativity." Using specific essential oils will stimulate your imagination and tap into your creative potential. These oils are also used to assist the manifestation of dreams and goals, increasing clarity of thought and helping you achieve greater success in all areas of your life.

As you can see, the benefits of essential oils for the sacral chakra are plentiful. Whether to relieve stress and anxiety, boost your libido, or enhance your creativity, these powerful plant extracts are a fabulous tool to achieve greater balance in your life.

How to Use Essential Oils for Svadhisthana

Essential oils are used in several ways for opening and balancing the sacral chakra. Some of the most popular methods include:

Inhalation

Inhalation of essential oils is a great way to harness the therapeutic benefits of these powerful plant compounds. Breathing in the aromatic vapors, we directly stimulate the medulla oblongata, the part of the brain responsible for regulating powerful subconscious processes like heart rate and respiration.

Essential oils contain constituents that target specific health concerns, like inflammation and chronic pain. Therefore, inhalation is particularly helpful for Svadhisthana, the sacral chakra. The sacral chakra is linked to physical and emotional wellbeing and governs sexual desire and creativity.

Using inhalation techniques to dedicate time each day exclusively to Svadhisthana helps us tap into this energy center and experience greater joy and pleasure. Whether we use an essential oil diffuser or simply take a few deep breaths before bedtime, inhalation provides a simple and effective way to promote balance within our vital energy centers.

Topical Application

The topical application involves adding your oil to a carrier oil or lotion before massaging it onto your skin. This allows your body to absorb the oil's beneficial properties more slowly over time. It's important to be aware of any potential skin sensitivities when using essential oils topically. So, it's always a good idea to do a small skin test before using an oil for the first time.

The Svadhisthana chakra is only one area of the body that benefits from natural remedies using the topical application of these oils. Essential oils are an excellent way to bring this chakra back into alignment, promoting physical and mental wellbeing. Some of the most useful essential oils for Svadhisthana include ylang-ylang, patchouli, sandalwood, geranium, clary sage, lavender, rosemary, and cedarwood.

These powerful plant extracts have properties well known to restore balance to this important energy center in the body. For example, ylang-ylang has been known to improve self-esteem and reduce stress levels by affecting dopamine levels in the brain. Patchouli oil is traditionally used as an aphrodisiac due to its ability to boost libido and enhance sexual energy. Sandalwood oil has long been revered for its calming and relaxing properties, which ease anxiety and promote peace and wellbeing.

Diffusion

Diffusion is a great way to enjoy the benefits of essential oils without directly applying them to your skin. This method involves using an oil vaporizer or diffuser to disperse the fragrant oils into the air around you. It is particularly helpful for promoting mental wellbeing, as diffusing essential oils creates a calming and relaxing environment.

At its most basic level, diffusing essential oils stabilizes this chakra by promoting a sense of relaxation and calmness. Additionally, many essential oils hold healing properties that can aid in addressing specific issues related to Svadhisthana, like balancing sex hormones or stimulating sexual desire. Overall, using diffusers with essential oils is one way to bring balance and harmony back into your life.

Aromatherapy Massage

An aromatherapy massage is a powerful tool to promote healing and balance in the body. One of its key benefits is that it works directly on the sacral chakra. Aromatherapy massage unblocks and stimulates the sacral chakra, restoring its natural flow of energy and allowing our bodies to release any toxins or toxic emotions trapped within it.

Whether your goal is physical healing, emotional wellbeing, or both, an aromatherapy massage can be a powerful aid to balance and revitalize your sacral chakra. It's important to choose an essential oil that will support your specific needs. Some of the most popular oils used in aromatherapy massage for Svadhisthana include ylang-ylang, sandalwood, patchouli, rosemary, and geranium. These oils are proven to help release stress, increase libido, and improve self-esteem.

Essential Oils for Svadhisthana

Many different essential oils help to balance the sacral chakra. Here are some of the most popular and effective options:

Ylang-Ylang

Properties: Ylang-Ylang is a sweet-smelling flower that has long been revered for its healing properties. This oil is said to help promote happiness and peace while also promoting a sense of self-love and acceptance. This powerful oil is rich in nutrients like fatty acids and antioxidants, making it a highly effective treatment for conditions like stress, anxiety, and depression. In addition, its aromatic properties make it a great tool for relaxation and meditation.

Uses: Ylang-Ylang oil is most often used in aromatherapy massage or diffusers. It can also be added to bathwater, diluted with a carrier oil, or even applied topically to the skin. It is crucial to use small amounts and observe caution when applying it to the skin when using ylang-ylang essential oil. Highly concentrated essential oils can irritate if used in large amounts or applied directly to the skin.

Sweet Orange

Properties: Sweet orange essential oil is a powerful tool for balancing the sacral chakra, which governs feelings of pleasure, creativity, sexuality, and emotional wellbeing. Due to its bright, uplifting aroma and numerous therapeutic properties, sweet orange oil is used to reduce energy blockages in this important energy center and restore balance to the body and mind. Its key properties include antiseptic, aphrodisiac, tonic, antidepressant, anti-inflammatory, and sedative effects.

Uses: This versatile oil used in aromatherapy treatments or blended with other oils for various topical applications promotes deep relaxation and stress relief. Whether applied topically or diffused into the air for aromatherapy purposes, sweet orange essential oil is an excellent choice for those wanting to tap into the healing power of nature.

Tangerine

Properties: Like sweet orange, tangerine essential oil is also useful to balance the sacral chakra. This oil promotes creativity, pleasure, and sexual vitality. Tangerine essential oil is also a great choice for improving their mood or reducing stress and anxiety. This oil has a refreshing, uplifting aroma that helps clear the mind and promote feelings of well-being. In addition to its emotional benefits, a tangerine essential oil also has antiseptic, anti-inflammatory, and detoxifying effects.

Uses: Tangerine essential oil improves emotional and physical health and is used in many ways, like in a diffuser or diluted with a carrier oil and applied topically. It can also be added to baths or used in massage. It is important to start with a small amount and gradually increase as needed when using tangerine oil for the sacral chakra. Moreover, consult with a healthcare provider before using any essential oils if pregnant or breastfeeding.

Patchouli

Properties: Patchouli is a powerful herb and has been used in traditional Chinese medicine for thousands of years. This oil is often used for healing purposes, as it reduces inflammation and improves circulation. Patchouli essential oil is also reputed to promote peace, calm, and wellbeing. Due to its aphrodisiac properties, it is an excellent option to enhance libido and boost sexual health.

Patchouli oil awakens and balances this chakra, including grounding, rejuvenating, and calming effects with its many healing properties. Additionally, patchouli is commonly used in aromatherapy to enhance passion and sensuality, making it a popular choice for those wishing to open up and connect with this aspect of themselves.

Uses: Patchouli essential oil is one of the most versatile oils available, with many ways to use this oil successfully. When used in aromatherapy treatments or diffusion, patchouli oil can be added to a diffuser or blended with other oils for a relaxing and grounding experience. Patchouli oil must be diluted with a carrier oil and applied to the skin for topical applications. This oil can also be added to baths or used in massage.

Whether used in a diffuser or applied directly to the skin, patchouli essential oil is a powerful tool for promoting overall health and wellbeing. Whether you want to increase your libido or merely feel more grounded and connected to your true self, patchouli oil will help you unlock your sacral chakra and unleash your full potential.

Vetiver

Properties: With its rich hormone-like compounds, vetiver is well-known for calming and soothing this part of the body, helping to create calmness and balance. In addition, vetiver has also been used to support healthy digestion and even treat skin ailments like eczema and fungal infections. Overall, whether you are looking for relief from anxiety or simply want to boost your overall mood, vetiver essential oil is a valuable tool for promoting the health of your sacral chakra.

Uses: Vetiver essential oil used in various ways promotes optimal health and balance. This oil is often paired with other oils, like ylang-ylang or lavender, to enhance its relaxing effects. Vetiver can also be diffused in your home to create a calming and soothing atmosphere. As with all essential oils, it is important to dilute the oil with a carrier oil before applying directly to the skin. Vetiver oil can also be added to baths or used in massage.

Essential oils are an effective tool for enhancing energy levels and targeting the sacral chakra. In particular, oils like orange, jasmine, and ylang-ylang are famous for strengthening this energy center, associated with joy, pleasure, sensuality, creativity, and spirituality. These oils can be used in various ways to get the most out of their healing properties. Whether diffused into the air or applied directly to the skin, they revitalize your sacral chakra, and you'll rediscover a sense of balance and wellbeing.

So, if you're searching for a natural way to boost your energy levels and enhance your spiritual connection to the world around you, look no further than essential oils. With only a small amount of time and effort on your part, they could change your life forever.

Disclaimer: Always read the label of the essential oil and use caution when using them around pets, people with allergies, pregnant women, or children. The safety and efficacy of essential oils are not guaranteed by any means, so consult with a qualified healthcare professional before making any changes to your routine. As always, this is not intended as medical advice. We recommend that you speak with your doctor before making any changes to your diet or lifestyle.

Chapter 9: Diet and Nutrition

The sacral chakra is a key energy center in the body, responsible for regulating our bodily functions and emotions. It's crucial to make healthy dietary choices and focus on nutrition that benefits the sacral chakra to keep this important chakra in balance. Together, diet and nutrition play an essential role in keeping the sacral chakras balanced and in good health.

Diet and nutrition are powerful tools for improving the health of the chakra system and maintaining overall balance in human bodies and minds. While many different foods help balance the sacral chakra, this chapter focuses on some of the best foods for this chakra. We also touch on a few simple recipes to help you unblock and balance the sacral chakra.

The Relation between Food and the Sacral Chakra

Food plays an important role in our overall health and wellbeing. From providing us with much-needed nutrients to helping us feel energized, healthy food is essential for keeping us functioning at our best. But the connection between our food and our bodies goes even deeper than this. The foods we eat also have a significant impact on the sacral chakra.

Foods high in fiber, like fresh fruit and vegetables, can help to open this chakra and promote vitality and wellbeing. On the other hand, fried or overly processed foods limit the chakra's flow and make us feel sluggish or uninspired. So, whether it's to boost your creativity or find more joy in your everyday life, try to ensure that you feed your body well to feed your sacral chakra healthily.

The Importance of a Healthy Diet

A healthy diet is crucial to keep the sacral chakra in balance. Foods rich in color and flavor, like fruit and vegetables, are particularly beneficial. Orange and red foods are especially helpful in promoting a healthy sacral chakra, so incorporate carrots, sweet potatoes, and tomatoes into your diet.

In addition to eating plenty of fresh produce, it's also important to stay hydrated. The water element is closely associated with the sacral chakra, so drink plenty of water throughout the day to keep your energy flowing. Following these simple tips will keep your sacral chakra healthy and balanced.

Food and Dieting

There is more to consider than the food you put into your body for those interested in dieting and losing weight. The body's energy plays a role in how successful you'll achieve your goals. It's essential to also focus on balancing your sacral chakra when trying to lose weight.

One way to do this is by eating foods associated with the water element, such as blueberries, salmon, and cucumbers. Additionally, using crystals like carnelian or moonstone helps balance this chakra. So, taking a holistic approach to dieting increases your chances of success.

Benefits of Fasting

Fasting for the sacral chakra offers many benefits. Perhaps the most obvious is that it helps resolve blocks and imbalances in this energy center. Going without food or other material comforts, we gain insight into our underlying cravings and yearnings, allowing us to make better choices in our day-to-day lives. Furthermore, we foster greater awareness and spiritual growth by experiencing a state of deprivation and focusing more intently on the moment.

It is possible to enjoy a more balanced and meaningful existence when we break free of unhealthy habits and gain control over our impulses. However, it is important to practice safe fasting techniques and seek advice from a healthcare professional before trying this method. With the right preparation and support, fasting is a powerful tool for promoting a healthy sacral chakra.

Detoxing and Cleansing

When purifying and energizing the sacral chakra, there are many different approaches. One popular method is detoxing and cleansing with food. Foods like fruit and vegetables are naturally high in antioxidants and other nutrients that help to balance this energy center. Like regular exercise and meditation, other lifestyle choices promote the free flow of energy within the body.

Additionally, spending time in nature, disconnecting from technology, and focusing on your passions are great ways to clear out excess energies. Detoxing and cleansing benefits are many, including improved energy levels, emotional stability, and overall wellbeing. With some simple tweaks to your daily routine, you can revitalize the sacral chakra and improve overall wellbeing.

Foods to Avoid for a Healthy Sacral Chakra

Certain foods and other substances can aggravate or otherwise disrupt the sacral chakra if you consume them too often. Caffeine and alcohol are two of the biggest culprits, as they can lead to dehydration and imbalance in this energy center. Processed foods and artificial additives are highly problematic as they prevent the free flow of energy within the body.

It's crucial to be aware of how various foods and substances affect your body to make informed choices about what to eat and avoid. The better you understand the role of diet in sacral chakra health, the easier it is to maintain a balanced and healthy energy center. You can promote a healthy sacral chakra and enjoy greater overall wellbeing by being mindful of your foods and other choices.

Color Theory and Orange Foods

In color theory, orange is often associated with the sacral chakra. This energy center is located in the lower abdomen, and it plays a key role in physical and emotional health. Therefore, orange foods support the optimal functioning of this chakra, promoting good digestion and boosting moods. Some healthy orange foods include carrots, sweet potatoes, pumpkin, peaches, mangoes, cantaloupe, oranges, and butternut squash.

With their high carotenoids and vitamin C levels, these foods provide the necessary nutrients to nourish the sacral chakra and promote a sense of joy and wellbeing. The potential benefits include increased energy levels, better moods, and improved digestion. In addition to including more orange foods in your diet, another viable option is using aromatherapy or meditation to balance this energy center further.

Including these foods in your diet will help unblock and balance the sacral chakra, promoting overall wellbeing. If you don't include many orange foods in your diet already, it would be a good idea to start adding a few more into your meals and snacks. With a little effort, you can easily incorporate these foods into your diet and enjoy the many benefits they offer.

Foods that Unblock or Balance the Sacral Chakra

Foods traditionally used to unblock or balance the sacral chakra include yellow fruits and veggies like papaya, mangoes, ginger root, and lemons. These foods are effective due to their bright color and natural sweetness. Similarly, they stimulate the reproductive hormone production and energize the body to focus on the navel during meditation.

1. Carrots

One way to help heal the sacral chakra is by eating carrots. Carrots are physically grounding and contain beta-carotene, which helps balance hormones and boosts fertility. Additionally, the sweetness of carrots restores our natural sense of pleasure and vitality. A simple way to incorporate more carrots into your diet is by adding them to salads, soups, and stir-fries.

2. Peaches

Peaches are a wonderful food for nurturing the sacral chakra. Unlike many other fruits, high in sugar and acid, peaches are relatively low in both properties. Plus, they contain many essential nutrients like vitamin C and antioxidants, supporting overall health and balancing the body's energy systems.

But beyond their physical benefits, peaches also have a soothing and sensual energy that is perfect for awakening the sacral chakra. Their perfume-like smell has long been cherished by perfumers, while their soft texture and delicate flavor can instantly transport you to sunny summer days spent relaxing with friends on a patio or lounging under a tree at the beach.

3. Sweet Potatoes

It is essential to incorporate foods that help energize, support, and maintain the sacral chakra, like the sweet potato. With its vibrant color and deliciously sweet flavor, this root vegetable nourishes the body and mind. Sweet potatoes are rich in many nutrients beneficial to the sacral chakra, including vitamins A and C, magnesium, copper, and other key minerals.

Eating sweet potatoes stimulates our creativity by encouraging us to experiment with new flavors and explore new possibilities. Whether enjoyed as part of a satisfying breakfast or simply baked as an after-dinner treat, regular consumption of sweet potatoes is an easy way to nurture our sacral chakras and promote happiness, health, and vitality.

4. Papaya

Few foods are more effective than papaya for balancing the sacral chakra. This sweet, juicy fruit contains a wide range of vital nutrients and bioactive compounds that support the healthy functioning of this energy center. From potent antioxidants to energizing enzymes like bromelain, the nutrients in papaya help unblock the flow of life force through this essential chakra. Its soft texture and sweet flavor make eating papaya a pleasure and a practice that supports overall health and wellbeing.

This juicy, yellow fruit is rich in antioxidants and vitamin C, which help improve our reproductive system's health. Papaya has been traditionally used in Ayurvedic medicine to remedy menstrual imbalances and fertility issues. It has a sweet, light taste making it perfect for smoothies or salads. With its natural sweetness and smooth texture, papaya is a great way to help balance the sacral chakra and support overall health.

5. Mangoes

The color orange is often used to represent the sacral chakra, and mangoes are the perfect fruit to help balance this energy center. Mangoes are not only a delicious and exotic treat, but they also contain vitamins A and C, which promote creativity. In addition, mangoes are often used in Traditional Chinese Medicine to improve circulation and increase libido.

With their sweet flavor and creamy texture, mangoes make a delicious addition to smoothies, yogurt, or oatmeal. Or, for a quick and easy snack, you can simply enjoy them on your own or with a dollop of whipped cream. Consider adding mangoes to your diet if you're looking for a way to add extra zest to your life. They will help balance your sacral chakra, but they'll also leave you feeling satisfied and energized.

Whatever way you choose to eat mangoes, this tropical treat helps balance the sacral chakra and promotes overall health and wellbeing. This delicious fruit is a great way to enjoy the benefits of the sacral chakra while also indulging your senses.

Recipes for Healthy and Fun Meals that Balance the Sacral Chakra

One of the best things to balance the sacral chakra is incorporating foods that align with this energy center. One way is by adding orange ingredients, such as sweet potatoes, papaya, and mangoes, to your regular diet. Not only are these foods delicious and satisfying, but they also help energize the sacral chakra and stimulate your creativity.

Orange-Papaya Smoothie

Ingredients:

- 1 cup papaya, cubed
- 1 orange, peeled and juiced
- 1 cup plain yogurt
- 2 tablespoons honey

Directions:

1. Combine all ingredients in a blender and blend until smooth.
2. Pour into glasses and serve immediately.

Sweet Potato Fries

Ingredients:

- 1 large sweet potato, cut into fries
- 1 tablespoon olive oil
- 1/2 teaspoon garlic powder
- 1/2 teaspoon paprika

Directions:

1. Preheat the oven to 400°F.
2. Toss sweet potato fries in a large bowl with olive oil, garlic powder, and paprika.
3. Spread onto a baking sheet and bake for 15-20 minutes, or until fries are crispy and tender.

Mango Salad

Ingredients:

- 1 head butter lettuce, rinsed and dried
- 1 mango, peeled and cubed
- 1 bell pepper, chopped
- 1 avocado, pitted and cubed

- Juice of 1 lime
- 1 tablespoon olive oil

Directions:

1. Toss together lettuce, mango, bell pepper, avocado, and lime juice in a large bowl.
2. Drizzle with olive oil and serve immediately.

Orange Vegetable Stir-fry

Ingredients:

- 1 tablespoon olive oil
- 1 orange, peeled and diced
- 1 head of broccoli, chopped into florets
- 1 red pepper, diced
- 1/2 teaspoon ginger
- 1 tablespoon soy sauce

Directions:

1. Heat olive oil over medium-high heat in a large wok or frying pan.
2. Add orange and stir-fry for 2 minutes.
3. Add broccoli, red pepper, and ginger.
4. Stir-fry for 3-5 minutes, or until vegetables are tender.
5. Add soy sauce and continue to stir-fry for 1 minute.
6. Serve immediately.

Peach and Basil Salad

Ingredients:

- 1 head lettuce, rinsed and dried
- 2 peaches, pitted and cubed
- 1/4 cup slivered almonds
- 1/4 cup chopped fresh basil

- 2 tablespoons olive oil

- 2 tablespoons honey

Directions:

1. Toss together lettuce, peaches, almonds, basil, olive oil, and honey in a large bowl.

2. Serve immediately.

Carrot Cake Muffins

Ingredients:

- 1 cup whole wheat flour

- 1 teaspoon baking powder

- 1/4 teaspoon salt

- 3/4 cup milk

- 1/4 cup vegetable oil

- 1 egg, beaten

- 2 large carrots, shredded

Directions:

1. Preheat the oven to 350 degrees.

2. In a large bowl, mix flour, baking powder, and salt.

3. Add the milk, vegetable oil, and egg and stir until well combined.

4. Fold in the carrots.

5. Pour batter into a greased muffin tin and bake for 15-20 minutes, or until a toothpick inserted into the center of a muffin comes out clean.

Sweet Potato Brownies

Ingredients:

- 1 cup sweet potato puree

- (About 2 large sweet potatoes)

- 3/4 cup sugar

- 1/4 cup vegetable oil
- 3 tablespoons cocoa powder
- 1 teaspoon vanilla extract

Directions:

1. Preheat the oven to 375°F.
2. Mix sweet potato puree, sugar, vegetable oil, cocoa powder, and vanilla extract in a large bowl.
3. Pour batter into a greased 8x8 inch baking dish and bake for 20-25 minutes, or until brownies are set and a toothpick inserted into the center comes out clean.

These recipes are just a few of the many ways you can incorporate orange ingredients into your diet to help balance the sacral chakra. Adding these foods to your routine unblocks creativity and encourages positive emotions.

As you can see, many different ways are readily available to incorporate orange ingredients into your diet to support the health and function of your sacral chakra. Whether you choose to eat these foods alone or incorporate them into your favorite recipes, you benefit from their properties to unblock and balance this important energy center. So, why not give them a try today and determine how you feel? Whether you want to improve your creativity, boost your mood, or simply enjoy a healthy and delicious meal, these foods will help.

Disclaimer: The information provided in this chapter is for educational purposes only and is not intended to replace or substitute for professional medical advice. If you have any concerns or questions about your diet and healthcare, please speak to your doctor or registered nutritionist for advice.

Chapter 10: Svadhisthana 7-Day Routine

We must make opening and healing our sacral chakra a priority in our lives. It means dedicating some time each week to activities that support Svadhisthana, like yoga and meditation. At the same time, we need to avoid behaviors that hurt this important energy center - overworking or over-indulging.

Set aside at least an hour each day for activities that strengthen your sacral chakra with these goals in mind. For instance, practice yoga or relaxation exercises like deep breathing and progressive muscle relaxation. Additionally, incorporate rest periods into your routine as stress and fatigue slow down the Svadhisthana healing process.

Following this simple daily routine will ensure that the energy of your sacral chakra remains strong and balanced throughout the week.

As we approach the end of this book, it's time to put all of the information you have learned about Svadhisthana into practice. We have created a weekly routine to open and heal the sacral chakra in this final chapter. We'll start each day with a yoga sequence to help energize and activate the chakra. Move on to some mantras, affirmations, and mudras to help focus and direct your Svadhisthana energy. We finish with a meditation exercise to help you relax and let go of the tension or stress you are holding onto.

Defining Your Sacral Chakra Weekly Routine

Setting up a consistent routine is a key part of achieving optimal wellness and balance. One area in particular that greatly benefits from a thoughtful routine is your sacral chakra. So, to get your sacral chakra in top shape, it's essential to establish a few key habits for your week. These may include journaling your feelings in different areas of your life or simply spending time meditating to connect with this powerful energy center within you.

Additionally, incorporating movement like yoga or dance into your schedule is a great way to engage with the energy of the sacral chakra and release any trapped or stagnant feelings within you. With dedication and persistence, establishing a little bit of self-care each day, you experience all the joys life has to offer.

Monday - Yoga Poses, Orange Clothes, Creating Something New

Yoga Poses: Camel pose, cat, and cow pose

Orange Clothes: Wear something orange to help you feel more connected to your sacral chakra.

Creating Something New: Attempt a new creative project or simply start a journal in which you document your thoughts and feelings.

On Mondays, start your day by doing some energizing yoga poses. Include twists to help detoxify the body and hip openers to release stagnant energy. As you move through your practice, focus on your breath, and think about the qualities of the sacral chakra, which are creativity, pleasure, and flow.

After your yoga practice, take a moment to reflect on your feelings. If you're feeling creative, it's a great time to start a new project. If you feel happy, do something that brings you joy. If you're feeling that life is flowing well, go with the flow and see where the day takes you.

Tuesday - Meditation, Mudras, Affirmations

Meditation: Practice guided meditation to help you connect with your sacral chakra and release the tension or stress you are holding onto.

Mudras: Try mudras like the Apana Mudra and Lakshmi Mudra to help balance and energize your sacral chakra.

Affirmations: Use positive affirmations to help you strengthen your connection with Svadhisthana and evoke creativity, pleasure, and flow.

On Tuesdays, begin your day with a meditation exercise. Sit in a comfortable position and focus on your breath as you connect with your sacral chakra. As you meditate, think about the qualities of this powerful energy center within you and repeat affirmations that evoke the same qualities.

After your meditation, move on to mudras and focus on feeling balanced, energized, and open. You can also incorporate some of the affirmations you repeated during your meditation into this part of your routine.

Wednesday - Journaling, Orange Foods, Art

Journaling: Write about how you're feeling in different areas of your life or simply spend time meditating to connect with your sacral chakra.

Orange Foods: Eating orange foods helps you feel more connected to your sacral chakra and promotes creativity and pleasure.

Art: Create something beautiful or simply admire the beauty around you.

On Wednesdays, start your day by journaling about your feelings. Journaling is a great way to connect with your sacral chakra and release the pent-up emotions lurking beneath the surface.

Also, eat lots of orange foods throughout the day, including fruit, vegetables, and even spices like turmeric and saffron. Not only will this help you feel more connected to your sacral chakra, but it also promotes creativity and pleasure.

End your day by doing something creative or simply admiring the beauty around you. This can be as simple as taking a walk in nature or visiting an art gallery. Whatever you do, make it a moment of pure joy and beauty.

Thursday - Pranayama, Mantra, Poetry

Pranayama: Practice pranayama exercises like Ujjayi and Nadi Shodhana to help balance and energize your sacral chakra.

Mantra: Chant the Svadhisthana mantra to help you connect with this powerful energy center.

Poetry: Write a poem or read poetry that speaks to your soul.

On Thursdays, begin your day with pranayama exercises. It will help you feel more connected to your sacral chakra and release the stagnant energy blocking the flow of this power source.

After your pranayama, focus your attention on connecting with Svadhisthana by chanting the Svadhisthana mantra or simply repeating it in your mind.

End the day by writing a poem or reading poetry that speaks to your soul. It can be something wholly personal or a poem written by someone else. Either way, it's blissful to connect with this beautiful art form and to let it soothe your soul.

Friday - Yoga, Visualizations, Gratitude

Yoga: Practice yoga poses that help open and balance your sacral chakra.

Visualizations: Focus on visualizing and imagining yourself living a life of pleasure, creativity, and joy.

Gratitude: Take some time to reflect on all the things you're grateful for in your life.

On Fridays, start your day with a yoga practice that helps you open and balance your sacral chakra. It can be a mix of different poses you feel drawn to or a specific sequence you've wanted to try.

After your yoga practice, spend some time visualizing and imagining yourself living a life of pleasure, creativity, and joy. It can be anything from traveling to different places, pursuing a creative passion, or simply enjoying your everyday life.

End the day by reflecting on all the things you're grateful for in your life. This can be anything from your health to your family and friends and material possessions. Whatever you're grateful for, make sure to take a moment and appreciate it fully.

Saturday - Mudras, Crystals, Orange Clothing

Mudras: Use mudras like the Shakti Mudra and Apana Mudra to help connect with your sacral chakra.

Crystals: Work with crystals like carnelian and orange calcite to help balance and energize your sacral chakra.

Orange Clothing: Wear orange clothing, jewelry, and accessories to help promote a sense of pleasure and joy in your life.

On Saturdays, start your day using simple mudras to help connect with your sacral chakra. This can be anything from the Shakti Mudra to the Apana Mudra.

After your mudra practice, work with crystals like carnelian and orange calcite that help to balance and energize your sacral chakra. Either hold these crystals in your hand or place them near you as you go about your day.

End the day by wearing orange clothing, jewelry, and accessories to promote a sense of pleasure and joy in your life. It can be anything from wearing an orange scarf or ring to simply surrounding yourself with predominantly orange objects.

Sunday - Self-Reflection, Art, Journaling

Self-Reflection: Take some time each week to reflect on how you can live a more pleasurable life.

Art: Create a piece of art that expresses your creativity.

Journaling: Write about your experiences with pleasure, creativity, and joy in your journal.

On Sundays, start your day by reflecting on how you can live a more pleasurable life. It can be anything from making small changes in your daily routine to pursuing a long-term goal you're passionate about.

After your period of self-reflection, create a piece of art that expresses your creativity. This can be anything from painting or drawing to writing poems or songs. There are no limits to what you can create, so let your imagination run wild.

End the day by writing about your experiences in your journal with pleasure, creativity, and joy. It can be anything from recounting a memory that made you happy to brainstorming ways to bring more pleasure into your life. Whatever you decide to write about, reflect on your experiences with pleasure, creativity, and joy.

As you can see, various ways will work with your sacral chakra. Mix and match these activities to create a routine that works best. If you need help creating a routine, the next section gives some tips and ideas to get started.

Creating Your Own Chakra Routine

Having a grounded and balanced energy is essential for your health and wellbeing, which is where chakras come in. You can create a balanced state of being, physically and emotionally, by learning to identify and energize your chakras. There are many different ways to work with your chakras, including visualization exercises and guided meditations.

One simple strategy is to create your chakra routine. A chakra routine involves activities like yoga, journaling, or aromatherapy that target specific areas of the body and mind. Whether you decide to use only one or several techniques, the key is to remain consistent so that you'll see the results. With practice and patience, you'll be on your way to creating the ultimate chakra routine that will bring harmony and balance into every aspect of your life.

Selecting Your Poses

Selecting yoga poses that will work with your chakras can be daunting at first. However, there are many different ways you can go about it. One option is to create your chakra routine by selecting specific poses corresponding to each of the seven main chakras. For example, you might choose a pose like the Camel Pose or Anahata Chakra Pose to open your heart chakra.

Alternatively, if you are working with your root chakra, you might choose poses like the Garuda Pose or Muladhara Chakra Pose. Ultimately, the best way to select your poses is to experiment and determine what feels right. There is no one-size-fits-all approach when working with your chakras, so trust your intuition and let your body guide you.

A few essential things to keep in mind when selecting your poses:

1. Make sure you warm up before you start. Warming up helps prepare your body for physical activity and prevents injuries.

2. Start with basic poses and gradually work your way to more advanced ones. It's important to listen to your body and not overextend yourself.

3. Focus on what each pose does for you and your body rather than trying to achieve a certain shape or form.

4. Pay attention to your breath. Your breathing is a key component of all yoga poses, so ensure that you can breathe deeply and fully in each pose.

Choosing Your Meditation Technique

Another important aspect of creating your chakra routine is to choose a meditation technique that will help you connect with your chakras on a deeper level. There is no wrong or right way to meditate, so experiment with different techniques and discover what works best for your body and mind. A few options particularly effective for chakra meditation include:

1. **Guided Visualization:** This involves focusing on a particular image or mental representation of each chakra.

2. **Chakra Affirmation:** Repeating a certain phrase or mantra corresponding to each chakra helps you strengthen the energy of that area.

3. **Chakra Mantra:** Similar to affirmation, use a mantra or phrase corresponding to each chakra. The key is to focus on the words and their meaning and not merely repeat them mindlessly.

4. **Chakra Sound Meditation:** This involves making a sound corresponding to each chakra. For example, you might make a "ha" sound for the root chakra and a "so" sound for the crown chakra.

5. **Chakra Symbols:** Focus on drawing the chakra symbols in the air with your hands or a w, and or even print out copies of the symbols and meditate on them.

Incorporating Chakra-Healing Activities

In addition to yoga and meditation, many other activities benefit your chakras. For example, you could incorporate aromatherapy, crystals, or even color therapy into your routine. Here are a few ideas to get you started:

- **Aromatherapy:** Different essential oils are used corresponding with each chakra. For example, use lavender oil for the crown chakra or rose oil for the heart chakra.

- **Crystals:** Different crystals have specific properties, and you can use them to help balance each chakra. For example, amethyst is often used for the crown chakra, while garnet is often used for the root chakra.

- **Color Therapy:** Different colors are used to help balance each chakra. For example, wearing orange clothing or surrounding yourself with orange objects to help balance the sacral chakra.

Reflecting on Your Weekly Routine

At the end of each day, take a few minutes to reflect on your chakra routine and the effect it is having on your life. This is a very powerful way to help you stay on track and reap the full benefits of your routine. Some questions to ask yourself could include:

1. How did I feel after completing my routine?
2. Did I notice any changes in my energy levels or mood?
3. What do I want to create or bring into the world?
4. Am I fueling my creative passions?

5. Did I enjoy the activities I chose?
6. How can I make my routine even better?
7. What are the biggest challenges I faced this week?
8. How can I overcome them?
9. What were my successes this week?
10. What can I do to replicate them?

Additional Tips

- **Keep a Journal:** Journaling is a great way to track your progress and reflect on your experiences.

- **Find a Friend:** It is often helpful to be with someone else who is also interested in chakra healing. This way, you support and motivate each other.

- **Join a Group:** Many groups online and in-person focus on chakra healing. Joining one is a great way to find inspiration and connect with like-minded people.

- **Don't Get Discouraged:** Remember, balancing your chakras is a process, and it can take time to see results. Trust that the work you are doing positively impacts your life, even if the effects might not be immediately obvious.

- **Set Realistic Goals:** It's important to set realistic and achievable goals and that it does not become something you feel you "should" do. Realistic goals help you stay motivated and avoid feeling overwhelmed.

Chakra healing is a powerful tool to improve your physical, mental, and emotional wellbeing. You can balance your chakras and experience a wide range of benefits by incorporating a weekly routine of yoga, meditation, and other practices. Remember, this is not a quick fix, and it will take time, dedication, and patience to see results. But, with the right mindset and motivation, your chakra healing journey will create lasting positive change in your life.

Bonus: From Svadhisthana to the Upper Chakras

"When you touch the celestial in your heart, you will realize that the beauty of your soul is so pure, so vast, and so devastating that you have no option but to merge with it. You have no option but to feel the rhythm of the universe in the rhythm of your heart." - Amit Ray

Balancing the sacral chakra can be a challenge, but it is essential for moving up to the higher chakras. When the sacral chakra is balanced, a person's creativity and sexual energy are in harmony. Once you have achieved harmony in this area of your life, you can focus on the higher levels of consciousness.

The higher chakras include the Solar Plexus, the Heart chakra, the Throat Chakra, the Third Eye chakra, and the Crown chakra. Each chakra has a unique role in our lives, and balancing them is an important part of achieving spiritual enlightenment. This chapter provides an overview of the higher chakras and offers tips on balancing them.

The Possibilities of Balancing the Sacral Chakra

Once the sacral chakra is balanced, several possibilities could open up for you. For example, you may find it easier to express yourself creatively. Also, you may find that you have more energy and enthusiasm for life, or your relationships improve as you become more open to intimacy and closer emotional connections.

Everyone experiences the benefits of a balanced sacral chakra differently, but these are a few common possibilities. So, if your goal is to make some positive changes in your life, balancing your sacral chakra is a great place to start. However, the possibilities are endless, and the only limit is your imagination.

A balanced sacral chakra means you are ready to move to the higher chakras. It's important to learn more about each chakra and how to balance them if you are interested in exploring your spiritual self.

Moving Up to the Higher Chakras

Moving up to the higher chakras after working with and balancing the sacral chakra can seem a bit daunting. However, with focus and intention, it is possible. Start with exercises that cultivate greater awareness of your thoughts and emotions - activities like meditation and journaling are great ways to open yourself up to this important work.

Spending time in nature or doing activities like yoga or stretching are excellent ways to keep your energy freely flowing as you move up through the chakras. Ultimately, it is important to approach this process with an open mind and curiosity. If you go into it with skepticism and resistance, your progress will not be as smooth or effective as you hoped.

Suppose you approach it with openness and willingness to learn. In that case, you will discover more about yourself and unlock even greater levels of growth, healing, and transformation as you continue on this journey of discovery.

The Role, Symbol, Use, and Blockage
Symptoms of Higher Chakras

Solar Plexus Chakra – Manipura

Role: The Solar Plexus chakra is about self-confidence and personal power. It is the seat of your will and character and relates to your metabolism. The Solar Plexus chakra is about taking control of your life, setting boundaries, and achieving your goals.

Symbol: The symbol for the Solar Plexus chakra is a triangle inside a lotus. The lotus signifies that this chakra can blossom and grow like a flower. The triangle symbolizes its need for balance and harmony to reach its potential fully.

Use: The Solar Plexus chakra is responsible for your power, confidence, and will. When this chakra is open, you'll feel in control of your life and achieve your goals. You'll be able to set boundaries and feel like the master of your destiny.

Blockage Symptoms: When this chakra is blocked, you will feel powerless and not in control of your life. You have trouble setting boundaries or saying "no" to others and also suffer from digestive problems or feel like your metabolism is out of balance.

How to Unblock: Exercises that build confidence and self-esteem will open the Solar Plexus chakra. Stand in front of a mirror and list all the things you love about yourself. Practice yoga or stretching exercises and spend time in nature or with people who make you feel good about yourself to help your body feel strong and healthy.

Heart Chakra – Anahata

Role: The Heart chakra is all about love and compassion, as this is where we feel our emotions. The Heart chakra is also related to your perception of the world around you and how you see yourself. This chakra is about balance within yourself and in your relationships with others.

Symbol: The symbol for the Heart chakra is a lotus with twelve petals. The twelve petals represent the twelve letters of the Sanskrit alphabet, which are the foundation of creation. The Heart chakra color is green, representing balance and harmony between people.

Use: The Heart chakra is linked to our emotions and how we express our feelings to others. When this chakra is open, you'll feel a deep sense of love for those around you. You'll also have compassion for yourself and others and always see the beauty in the world.

Blockage Symptoms: When this chakra is blocked, you'll have trouble expressing your emotions, be afraid of showing your true feelings to those closest to you, or feel emotionally cut off from others. You could also experience physical pain in the heart or chest area.

How to Unblock: One way to open the Heart chakra is to spend time in nature. Surround yourself with beauty and allow yourself to feel the peace and calm that comes with it. You can also work on forgiveness for yourself and others. Talk to a therapist or friend about your feelings and learn to let go of the past.

Throat Chakra – Vishuddha

Role: The Throat chakra is about communication and self-expression. It is related to your ability to speak your truth and be heard by others. The Throat chakra is also about creativity and self-expression through art or writing.

Symbol: The symbol for the Throat chakra is a circle with a downward-pointing triangle inside it. The triangle represents the water element, the source of all life. The color of the Throat chakra is blue, representing communication and expression.

Use: The Throat chakra is responsible for your ability to communicate effectively. When this chakra is open, you'll feel confident speaking in front of others and sharing your thoughts and ideas. Also, you'll comfortably express yourself creatively through painting, writing, or music.

Blockage Symptoms: When this chakra is blocked, you have trouble expressing yourself to others or communicating your desires and wishes. You keep your thoughts and feelings bottled up or rush to speak without thinking things through first. You also have trouble with your vocal cords or thyroid gland.

How to Unblock: One way to open the Throat chakra is by expressing yourself creatively. Find a form of self-expression that speaks to you and develop it as much as possible. You can also try singing or chanting to help clear out blockages in your Throat chakra. Finally, work on your communication skills and learn to listen more than you speak.

Third Eye Chakra – Ajna

Role: The Third Eye chakra is about your intuition and ability to see things. It is associated with your understanding of the world around you and making wise decisions based on that understanding. The Third Eye chakra also rules your imagination and creativity.

Symbol: The symbol for the Third Eye chakra is a lotus with two petals. These two petals represent the dual nature of creation and destruction, like night and day of birth and death. The color of the Third Eye chakra is indigo, a deep purple representing intuition. The Om mantra is also associated with the Third Eye chakra since this mantra promotes intuitive thinking.

Use: The Third Eye chakra is your gateway to intuition, imagination, and wisdom. When this chakra is open, you see clearly and make wise decisions based on that clear perception. You'll also access your creative side and use your imagination freely.

Blockage Symptoms: When this chakra is blocked, you have trouble making decisions based on your intuition. You also cannot use your imagination or see things and experience physical symptoms such as headaches, eye problems, or seizures.

How to Unblock: One way to open the Third Eye chakra is meditation. Sit in a comfortable position and focus on your breath. Visualize a bright light shining through your Third Eye chakra as you inhale and exhale. Practice yoga poses that open up the Third Eye chakra, like the Camel pose or the Child's pose. Finally, use aromatherapy with essential oils like lavender or frankincense to open this chakra.

Crown Chakra – Sahasrara

Role: The Crown chakra is about spiritual connection and enlightenment. It is said to be the gateway to cosmic consciousness. The

Crown chakra will help you see beyond the physical world and connect with the divine.

Symbol: The symbol for the Crown chakra is a lotus flower with 1,000 petals. This symbol represents the many aspects of the universe that are all connected. The color of the Crown chakra is violet, representing spirituality and connection to the divine.

Use: The Crown chakra is your gateway to enlightenment and connection with the universe. When this chakra is open, you'll sense that you feel a oneness with all that exists. Moreover, you'll access your higher consciousness and connect with the divine.

Blockage Symptoms: When this chakra is blocked, you feel disconnected from the world and yourself and experience physical symptoms like headaches, migraines, or depression. You also find it difficult to connect with your higher self or the divine.

How to Unblock: One way to open the Crown chakra is meditation. Sit in a comfortable position and focus on your breath. Visualize a bright light shining down from above as you inhale and exhale. Practice yoga poses that open the Crown chakra, like the Corpse pose or the Camel pose. Finally, use aromatherapy with essential oils like sandalwood or lotus to open this chakra.

Now that you know a little bit more about the role of each chakra, let's look at ways to open and balance them.

Ways to Open and Balance Chakras

There are many ways to open and balance your chakras, ranging from specific exercises and meditation techniques to dietary and lifestyle changes. The most important thing is to be consistent in your practice, as this is the key to reaping the full benefits of chakras.

1. Practice Meditation Regularly

One of the simplest and most effective ways to open and balance your chakras is through regular meditation. Focusing on one or more specific chakra during meditation sessions helps these energy centers to align with each other. This allows for a greater energy flow throughout your body, increasing vitality, wellbeing, and peace.

In addition, research has shown that regular meditation also has positive effects on overall health and disease prevention, making it a great choice for anyone looking for an effective way to open and balance their chakras. Start with just a few minutes each day, and gradually increase the duration as you become more comfortable if you're new to meditation.

It's crucial to focus on your breath. Simply sit comfortably, close your eyes, and breathe deeply. Imagine your breath flowing in and out of you with each inhalation and exhalation.

2. Use Crystals

Crystals have long been used in various spiritual practices to focus energy and promote healing. Each crystal contains its vibrational energy and is directed toward specific chakra points to encourage energetic flow and promote balance. Popular crystals for working with the chakras include amethyst, rose quartz, and obsidian.

Simply hold a crystal in your hand as you focus on opening the corresponding chakra. You can also place a crystal directly on the corresponding chakra point for more powerful effects. With regular practice, you can learn to harness the power of crystals to keep your mind, body, and spirit aligned and achieve spiritual growth and happiness.

3. Incorporate Healthy Foods into Your Diet

Certain foods impact your chakras, and incorporating more of these items into your diet help open and balance these energy centers. For example, green vegetables cleanse and open up the Heart chakra, while eating yellow and orange fruit and vegetables stimulates the Solar Plexus chakra.

These foods are not only packed with nutrients essential for good health, but they also contain compounds that promote balance in the chakra system. In addition to eating a healthy diet, you can also use supplements and essential oils to encourage balance in your chakras.

While adding more chakra-friendly foods to your diet is a good idea, it's also important to pay attention to the quality of the food. Processed foods and those high in sugar and fat must be avoided, as they contribute to blockages in the chakras and reduce the flow of energy throughout the body.

4. Get Plenty of Exercise

One of the most important things you can do to keep your chakras balanced is to get plenty of physical exercise. Exercise moves energy through the body and gives you a sense of well-being. It also helps to ground you and keep you centered. It is easier to be emotionally and spiritually healthy when you are physically healthy.

There is no shortage of exercise options available, so find something you enjoy and feels good and right for you. Walking, running, biking, swimming, yoga, and dancing are great ways to move your energy. However, it's imperative that you do not over-exercise, as this can lead to an imbalance. Find a healthy balance that works for you and stick with it.

5. Connect with Nature

Another great way to open and balance your chakras is by connecting with nature. Spend time outside in the sun, go for a walk in the park, or sit under a tree. Breathe in the fresh air and feel the warm sun on your skin. Let nature ground you and provide a sense of peace and balance. It's also important to clear your mind, so leave your stressful thoughts or worries behind.

You can also open and balance your chakras through meditation when you are out in nature. Focus on your breath and allow your mind to be quiet. Listen to the sounds around you and focus on the sensations of your body. Connecting with your breath helps you connect with the present moment and gather a sense of calm. By taking some time for yourself to focus on your breathing, you open and balance your chakras.

6. Get a Chakra Reading

You can always get a chakra reading if you are looking for more specific ways to open and balance your chakras. A chakra reading provides insight into which of your chakras are out of balance and what you can do to correct the problem. It can also give you a better understanding of each chakra's role in your overall wellbeing.

Chakra readings are usually done with the assistance of a trained intuitive or chakra healer. This person connects with the energy around you and feels where there are blockages or imbalances in your chakras. Once they have identified the problem areas, they will help you find ways to open and balance these chakras.

As you extend your search to open and balance your chakras, it might be helpful to consult with a professional. Chakra readings are done in person or remotely and often incorporate crystals, aromatherapy, and Reiki. However, it is essential to consult a qualified practitioner you feel comfortable with if you're interested in exploring this option.

After your sacral chakra is balanced, you can move up to the other higher chakras, such as the Solar Plexus, Heart, Throat, Third Eye, and Crown. Visualization, journaling, and getting a massage are the best-recommended ways to open and balance these chakras.

Most importantly, when opening and balancing your chakras, you must be patient and consistent with your practice. It takes time and effort to clear blockages and bring harmony back into your life. But, by committing yourself and your wellbeing, the positive changes in your life will be well worth the effort.

Conclusion

Known as the Svadhisthana, the sacral chakra is located at the base of the spine, just above the tailbone. The color associated with this chakra is orange, and its element is water. It is associated with sexuality, creativity, pleasure, and emotions. We can enjoy life through our senses and experience pleasure in all aspects of life when this chakra is balanced. The sacral chakra also affects our physical health by increasing digestion and assimilation of nutrients from the food we eat.

It's important to eat foods high in protein such as beans, nuts, seeds, and whole grains like quinoa or brown rice for this chakra to be well-balanced. Vegetables like carrots or sweet potatoes are also good choices for this chakra because they provide our bodies with vital energy. Another important thing to remember when eating healthy is always avoid processed foods that contain artificial flavors or colors because these harm our emotions if consumed frequently enough over time.

The first chapter in this guide focused on the history and background of the sacral chakra. In the second chapter, we explored what it means to have a blocked sacral chakra and how to identify if this applies in your case. Chapter three discussed different meditation and visualization techniques to help clear energy blockages and restore balance to the sacral chakra.

In chapter four, we looked at ways to use mantras and affirmations to influence energy flow in this area. The fifth chapter explored how mudras and pranayama are used to improve the health of the sacral chakra. In chapter six, we provided yoga pose suggestions and sequences to help open and balance the sacral chakra.

The seventh chapter focused on using crystals and stones to support the health of the sacral chakra. Chapter eight looked at how essential oils used in an aromatherapy diffuser help balance and heal the sacral chakra. Chapter nine explored how diet and nutrition play a crucial role in keeping the sacral chakra healthy and balanced. Finally, in chapter ten, we created a 7-day sacral chakra routine to help you strengthen and maintain your sacral chakra.

This guide covered many tips and techniques to keep your sacral chakra healthy and well-maintained. Whether you need to heal a specific issue or merely want to learn more about this energy center, these suggestions will assist you on your journey. Your sacral chakra will stay healthy and balanced with regular practice and attention provided by this guide.

Part 3: Solar Plexus Chakra

The Ultimate Guide to Opening, Balancing, and Healing Manipura

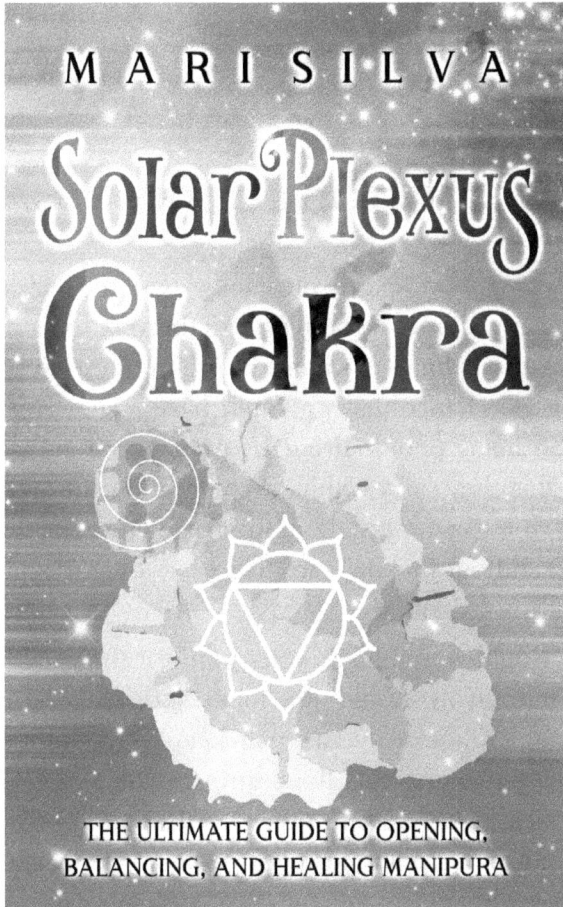

MARI SILVA

Solar Plexus Chakra

THE ULTIMATE GUIDE TO OPENING, BALANCING, AND HEALING MANIPURA

Introduction

Chakras are part of an excellent energy system that allows us to experience life as we should by tapping into the very force that keeps our hearts beating and our lungs breathing. Without these wonderful energy centers, there is no chance that we could have a shot at a full, healthy, and long life. So many people live each day without being aware of the energy centers that they carry within them and how they affect their lives in real-time. If they knew just how important the chakras were, they would never go without making sure that everything was in balance and alignment, not for a second.

Just as you would never leave your home without taking a bath or brushing your teeth, you should also make sure that you practice good spiritual hygiene. How exactly can you keep your spirit hygienic? By making sure that the energy that flows through you and in you continues to have no obstacles in its way. In other words, you must make sure that your energy centers remain open, active, and in balance at all times. Clearly, you are already taking the first step necessary to help you achieve this, and that is by choosing to educate yourself on this subject.

The fact that you are presently reading this means that you already have some knowledge of the chakra system. The solar plexus chakra is a very important one that is relevant to whether you stand in your own power and continue to achieve all that you must achieve in your present incarnation. Most people are interested in how to open their third eye chakra or activate their crown chakra, but they don't realize that the solar plexus is vital. You're reading this book, though, which means you are definitely smarter than most people.

Simply put: you'll find this book is a very pleasant read that is easy to understand and assimilate. You're not going to be left scratching your head wondering just what you've just read, unlike other books on the subject. By the time you come to the final pages of this book, you'll become an expert on making sure your solar plexus chakra works exactly as it should. Packed full of very useful information, you'll find all you learn here to be practical. When you apply what you learn from the pages of this book, you are sure to get results. If you are ready to stand in your own power, let's proceed.

Chapter 1: What Is Manipura?

What Are Chakras?

Chakra is a Sanskrit word that means "disk" or "wheel." A chakra is basically a spinning disk or wheel of energy that allows prana (or chi or life-force if you prefer) to flow through your energetic and physical body. You have seven of these chakras, starting from the bottom of your spine and going to the top of your head. While they're lined up along your spine, they also protrude out in front of and behind you. You can't see these wheels of energy with your regular vision, but they're there, and you can also feel them out energetically and intuitively. The energy that they all run on is known as prana, and this is basically what keeps us alive and thriving.

Within a Chakra

The chakra contains all your thoughts and feelings. It's a container that holds everything you've ever experienced, all you can remember, and all you've ever done in your lives – present, concurrent, past, and potentially future. The thing about the chakras is that they're not only excellent at storing energy, but they can also process prana, converting it into forms of energy that you need. They can even release this energy so that you can continue to live the life you want to. We will show you how to manifest whatever you desire in life if you're not satisfied with what you've lived so far.

You may have heard of the term "chakra healing." This is the process of deliberately connecting with the energy you've stored in each chakra, so you can understand exactly how your choices in the past continue to affect your current and future circumstances. You can get in touch with the prana you carry to help you figure out where you're at in life and what has to change if you want to experience something different. Prana helps you figure out what you want to do at all times, and it also has a very clear effect on your health, your progress in your professional life, how well your love life is going, and so on. Your subtle energy body is why your physical body and life are the way they are. Suppose you want to see better experiences in your physical life. In that case, it's a smart call to work on your energy body first, which means working with your chakras to heal and balance them.

Why Chakras Matter

The chakras in your body are connected to the body's nervous system, and you have seven of these energy centers, each with their nerve bundles, connected to relevant organs in your body and your mind and soul. Suppose you understand that, fundamentally, everything is energy. In that case, you will also understand why it is vital that your energy centers - the chakras - remain open, working in balance (not overactive or underactive) and allowing energy to flow freely. Imagine you have a sieve, but the holes are clogged with old food or something. When you have too much blockage, you won't be able to use the sieve as the water or fluid will always remain in it instead of passing through as it should. This stagnant water will remain there, becoming the perfect breeding ground for mold and all sorts of dangerous microbes. It's basically the same with the chakras, except it's a lot easier to unclog your sieve. Unclogging your energy centers is another ball game entirely.

If you didn't already know this, your mental, spiritual, and physical selves are all connected. This implies that whenever there's some sort of blockage in one of your chakras, you'll feel it in all aspects of your life. For instance, let's say a man just lost his daughter, and he's grieving terribly. Unable to move past it, he could get something like bronchitis, which would affect his respiration, which means he would experience pain and discomfort. On the surface, you might think there's no connection between the illness and the heart chakra, but that's not the truth of the matter. Grief keeps the energy from flowing freely in the heart's energy center. This lack of flow is very likely to manifest as a physical problem as well. If he could realize that there's a connection between his illness and his grief, then it would be easier for him to let go to become whole again.

What Is the Energy Body?

You have more than one body, believe it or not. We will focus on the energy body here, as the other bodies are beyond the scope of this book. So, what exactly is your energy or subtle body? Your energy body is your invisible body which acts as a template or framework for your physical one. It is visible to those with active third eye chakras, who have the gift of seeing energies. This body shows up as a field of energy that extends beyond your physical body for up to 5 inches or even more, the more powerful it is. It's connected to your physical body. This implies that if you've got bad habits like smoking or drinking too much, it's likely to affect your energy body. In the same way, if you take care of your physical body, your energy body will thank you for it. However, you can feed your energy body, too - all it needs is pure prana, and to get access to the life force, the onus is on you to make sure your energy centers are all open and able to receive all the energy needed to run this body which actually runs your life.

Your energy body is also sometimes referred to as the "etheric double" or "etheric body," or "plasma body," because it is entirely composed of ether. It has arms, legs, and a head, like your physical body. Ether is also known as plasma, and it is basically matter's fourth state. Indians refer to this body as the *pranamaya kosha*, which translates to "prana's container" or "prana's vehicle." They call it this because your physical body can access prana and use it as needed thanks to the energy body, which gives off a unique aura - the same one that some psychics can perceive. This aura is sometimes called the etheric aura.

When you have a well-developed energy body, meaning you not only access and use prana at will but have developed all of its senses, you'll be able to achieve such feats as psychokinesis and all other psychic abilities that many think are impossible but are in fact very real.

The energy body is as real as your physical one. You can perceive it by using Kirlian photography, developed in 1939 by Doctor Semyon Davidovich Kirlian and his wife and partner. The camera works to form an electric field that vibrates at a high frequency.

Your energy body has several channels through which energy can flow. They're known as *nadis* or, if you prefer, meridians. The energy flows through this channel, ultimately being collected by the energy centers or chakras, which act as power plants to distribute said energy to all aspects of you that need it the most. When you're dealing with a very troubling disease, it's often because one or some of your chakras are not functioning as they should. The energy meridians are responsible for channeling the energy you receive from life into the relevant organs in your body.

Another important role your energy body plays is to connect your emotional (or astral body) and your physical body. Remember, you have more than just one body. Without your energy body, you would not be able to tell what is going on with you emotionally. You would also find it difficult to embark on astral trips out of your physical body. Your energy body also makes it easy for you to download all the activities taking place during an astral projection or a dream into your physical body's memory. It is also thanks to the energy body that you were able to detect energies and receive downloads from spirits on very important things that you must know.

What Is the Manipura?

Your Manipura is also known as your solar plexus chakra. In the popular 7 chakra system, this one is your third energy center. Your solar plexus is deeply connected with your digestion, specifically your digestive fire. I'm specifying digestive fire because not only does that fire help you move food along, but it also helps you process the thoughts, feelings, and the sensory impressions you get from your surroundings and people around you.

In this author's humble opinion, not enough people pay enough attention to this particular energy center. If you want to feel like your entire mental and physical health are in balance, then you must make sure that you are paying attention to what your Manipura chakra is up to. This particular energy center is responsible for keeping your entire being in balance. This energy center allows you to decide that you'll achieve a particular thing and gives you the drive that you require to make it through every obstacle in the process. It is literally the fire lit under you to drive you to accomplish great things.

The word *Manipura* comes from mani, meaning "gem," and *pura*, meaning city. So quite literally, this energy center is known as the city of gems. You pronounce the word *mahn-ee- poo-rah*. Remember that inner fire we keep talking about? In Ayurveda, it is known as Agni. Your Manipura chakra is the seat of Agni. Below are the relevant correspondences for this chakra:

Location: Just above your belly button

Seed Sound: RAM

Element: Fire

Color: Yellow

Sense: Sight

Mudra: Matangi Mudra

Symbol: Lotus with ten petals

Affected Organs: Central nervous system, skin, digestive organs, liver, and pancreas

Gemstones: Sunstone, yellow tourmaline, tiger's eye, yellow topaz, yellow jasper, citrine.

The Vedas on the Manipura

The Vedas teach that the period of life in which the Manipura reigns supreme is from age 15 to 21 years old. At this time, you'll start to reveal who you are as a formal person, in terms of your goals and dreams, what you intend to accomplish, how disciplined you are, and much more.

This chakra also becomes particularly active when you're aged 10, 17, 24, 31, 38, and 45. *How do you know this?* Because it's the chakra responsible for making you feel like you "ought to do something" with your life; still, not everyone has a clue what that "something" is! So, the usual story is people begin to try all sorts of things and, as a result, they run into a whole lot of suffering.

The Seat of Your Personal Power and Your Authentic Self

Your solar plexus chakra is where your personal power lies. In other words, if you ever feel like you're low on confidence and self-esteem, there's a huge chance you need to work on your Manipura. This is where your true self resides, which also implies that if you ever feel like you need to be anyone other than who you really are, your Manipura chakra must be out of balance and likely suffering from blocks.

This energy center controls the level of freedom you feel. If you feel like you're bound by societal constraints or someone else's expectations, or even your unreasonably high expectations, the chances are that this chakra isn't working the way it should. It's the reason you know who you are. Knowing who you are means you fully understand what you won't stand for and what you will and won't accept. Some people in life float around being shoved around by other people's desires, and they wind up doing and saying things that are completely out of character for them. Suppose they took a moment to work on their Manipura each day. In that case, they would slowly but surely begin to get a sense of who they really are. They wouldn't allow themselves to be taken for a ride anymore when they could be the one behind the driving wheel instead. When it comes to willpower and drive, you should look to this chakra. Have you found it difficult to get started with something? Or have you noticed that you start with good intentions, but you never get to the finish line because you get distracted along the way? Well, guess what? Your Manipura could use some tender loving care. As the very seat of your soul, it deserves to be looked after with love.

Analyzing the Manipura Symbol

Manipura symbol.
Atarax42, CC0, via Wikimedia Commons: https://commons.wikimedia.org/wiki/File:Chakra3.svg

The symbol for this chakra has ten petals in a lotus flower. Each of these petals has its own letters in Sanskrit:

- Pha

- Pa

- Na

- Dha

- Da

- Tha

- Ta

- Nna

- Ddha

- Dda

What exactly do these petals represent? Sadness, silliness, fear, shame, self-deceit, spiritual ignorance, betrayal, thirst, disgust, and jealousy. These are all known as the ten mental modifications or *vrittis*.

You see the Manipura's seed in the middle of the symbol, right in the middle of a yellow circle. You'll also see an upside-down red triangle. This is meant to represent the Agni, and it is the fire this chakra is known for. With this fire, all the karma you've got from your past and present lives are purified, and the purification process leads to higher consciousness as you continue your spiritual evolution.

The Function of the Manipura

This energy center helps you establish your autonomy as a unique person. It helps you exercise your will and personal power to accomplish whatever you want to. It's also responsible for your body's metabolism, so if nothing you're doing is working to help you burn food and fat faster, you should consider addressing these issues energetically by working with the solar plexus. This center is connected to your mid-back, stomach, gallbladder, liver, adrenal glands, intestines, kidneys, and more.

If you have a functioning Manipura, you should notice that you have no spontaneous problems without feeling like your whole world is being upended just because something new and unexpected is happening to you. You'll also find that in all you do, you act effectively, doing things in the fastest and most efficient way, not wasting a bit of energy or time. You know how to be confident in who you are and all you do, and you don't let the naysayers get to you.

This chakra is also responsible for your ego's development, and as it awakens in your teenage years, it is what drives you to seek power and a sense of identity. It causes you to want respect from others, be acknowledged for who you are and what you do, and lord that over others. When this chakra is too active, you may become the sort of person who wants to control everyone around them. You act and think selfishly, no one's got higher shoulders than you, and you don't care what effect your choices have on others.

Chapter 2: Is Your Solar Plexus Blocked?

How Chakras Generally Get Blocked

Remember the point about the physical body affecting energy and vice versa? In the same way, your emotions and mind can also affect Manipura. *Why is this relevant?* Because there are certain things you may be doing, thinking, or feeling that lead to blockage, overactivity, or weakness in your solar plexus chakra. So, let's talk about what could block it, for starters.

Your chakras don't exist in a vacuum. They share a strong connection with every aspect of who you are, spiritually, physically, emotionally, and mentally. Each energy center is a container for the various parts of who you are, including your psyche.

Think of your energy system of chakras as being a river that flows in a straight line. There are seven different divisions of this river, and when one of these is blocked off, that will inevitably affect the other divisions. The blockages are caused by our refusal to release the things that no longer serve us, our choice to allow fear to dominate us, or by not processing emotions as they should be processed.

If you make a habit of suppressing things instead of feeling them, they will continue to demand your attention by popping up randomly. That's why you may experience sudden outbursts of anger or a sudden desire to cry even if it appears there's no reason to do that at the moment. If you refuse to honor your feelings, it will cause a blockage that will eventually demand your attention by affecting every other aspect of your life, including your finances, health, friendships, and other relationships. Of course, one can only block out life force for so long before that constant disconnection leads to one's inevitable, ugly end. You don't need to let things get to that point before doing something about your blocks.

Louise Hay of Hay House is an author who talks about this with grace and clarity, penning such lovely books as <u>You Can Heal Your Life</u>. She noted that the thoughts and emotions we have are the true sources of all disease and that your body acts as a mirror for what's going on with you emotionally and spiritually. In the same way, your chakras reflect your beliefs and emotions, especially regarding what each center is concerned with. You can trace all the pain and disease you're dealing with by looking at the chakras, seeing which ones your uncomfortable experiences are connected to, and then making a conscious effort to heal them.

What Blocks the Manipura

Your Manipura is the reason you're able to set boundaries. You can't set boundaries if you aren't confident in yourself. You can't be confident in yourself if you don't know who you are. Also, if you have no idea who you are, you won't even know what you want, let alone have the drive and motivation to go after it. All of these things are connected to the Manipura, and they all share one connection; feeling like you're unworthy. This is what blocks your solar plexus chakra.

Be, Come

Just one of the ways you could choose to help yourself with this feeling of low or no self-worth is by deciding right now that you are more than enough. Notice, I'm not asking you to *do* anything in particular. I'm asking that you simply *be* enough. Notice that the word become has *be* before *coming*. As the saying goes, *"First be it, then it will come."* In other words, rather than try to do the things that people with high self-worth do (which is going to feel very uncomfortable and will be obvious to one and all that you're faking it), simply *decide* that you are the sort of person who is worthy and more than enough.

It's basically like method acting. Since you are actually embodying the idea that you are worthy, you have no choice but to do the things that people *who think they are worthy* do. You'll find yourself naturally thinking, speaking, and acting like that. You won't have to even think about the process! Of course, not everyone will find the process of method acting or just assuming they're someone else easy, so take a deep breath if this method is not for you. There are lots more you can do, and you'll learn as you read along.

Signs You've Got a Blocked, Overactive, or Weak Manipura

When this third energy center is out of balance, you will experience some issues with your digestion. For instance, you could suffer from ulcers or even diabetes. You may notice that your food never gets digested promptly, and it's almost like you have a persistent lump just sitting in your stomach like a bezoar.

Other issues include struggling with portion control because you can't help but eat too much, irritable bowel syndrome (IBS), constant acid reflux, gastroesophageal reflux disease (GERD), and other eating disorders. Also, your skin, liver, belly, gallbladder, and spleen can be terribly affected by some disease or dysfunction because the solar plexus is in charge of those, too.

Remember how the Manipura is supposed to help you with boundaries? Your skin is a boundary of some sort, separating you from the world, acting as a gatekeeper to let in what's good for you and keep out the bad stuff. So, when your skin has trouble, this could be a sign that you need to look at the other ways in which you're allowing your boundaries to be violated.

Now let's talk about emotions. When you've got an underactive - or even a fully blocked - solar plexus, you may notice this in terms of feeling too full of yourself, having a big ego, or severely lacking confidence. When you're far too connected to what you look like and constantly bothered about how others perceive you, this could be a sign that things aren't quite as they should be with your solar plexus, and you need to do some work in it.

Other emotional issues that indicate a weak solar plexus chakra are low self-esteem and depression. If you notice that every little thing seems to make you feel bad, or on the flip side, you don't seem to care about anything, this could point to weakness. You could also be struggling with failing to do things when you should, knowing you're procrastinating but not taking control of your life. You may feel that people are taking you for granted or ripping you off by taking more than they give when you're always the one giving all of yourself to them.

The trouble with this energy center can also present itself in the form of being absolutely shut down to any ideas and opinions other than your own or being unable to think outside the box. You may become quite a pessimist, only seeing the bad in everything and everyone and finding it incredibly difficult to trust. You no longer want to share your thoughts or who you are with anyone else. In fact, your lack of trust could be so bad as to extend to your lack of trust in your own instincts and intuition, which could be very bad for you.

You may also display extreme or sudden aggression – aggression that doesn't match whatever you used as an excuse to get triggered in the first place. When you notice these things, you are experiencing an imbalance (overactivity or weakness) or a complete block of your solar plexus energy center, and you must fix this right away. Typically, this is a sign that your Manipura is overactive. You are hungry for power, absolutely controlling and bossy to others, too wrapped up in yourself to care about the people around you. You have excessive hard-headedness and terrible heartburn. You may also find that new projects may cause you to become very excited, but you don't finish them with the same energy, if at all.

Think of things as being on a spectrum. Your Manipura is about your inner fire, which is used not just for digestion but for going after what you want, standing up for yourself, and having the will to live, among other things.

Let's dig even further into this.

When your chakra is blocked, it could be either partially or totally inactive. When it's underactive, it means it's functioning but not at an optimal level. When it's overactive, it means it's "doing too much." So, when your Manipura chakra is blocked, you have self-confidence issues, you don't remember things easily, you get the sense that all is lost, and you're helpless, you can't see the big picture, you're plagued by insecurity, constantly dwell on your past, can't figure out the next step for yourself in life, and your dream far too much but won't do anything to make those dreams real. Those are all the mental issues. Physically, expect bloating, an uncomfortably full feeling in your belly, and nausea.

When the chakra is overactive, you'll struggle by being stubborn, judgmental, constantly aggressive, demanding, and bossy, and you'll struggle with addictions. You'll also notice illnesses that affect the health of your kidneys and even diabetes or other diseases connected to diabetes.

Under-activity is present when you have self-doubt, helplessness, powerlessness, indecision, insecurity, terrible focus, no planning, no confidence, no willpower, no emotional regulation, no control in any aspect of life, and a terrible self-image and no purpose. This is evidenced by being underweight or overweight, having a terrible appetite, slow digestion, allergies, IBS, celiac disease, and trouble with your adrenal glands.

Signs of Balance in the Manipura

On the flip side, how do you know your solar plexus chakra is open and balanced? You'll notice that you're very passionate about life once more. You're true to who you really are, and you're extremely confident in your person. You have no trouble setting clear and firm boundaries for others, and you recognize if they're not okay with you setting boundaries, then they were just not your *tribe* to begin with! You can act in a way that is true to you and in line with the objectives you've set for yourself instead of doing other people's bidding at your own expense. This doesn't mean you never consider others, but you're aware that you should also consider yourself – *even as you think of them.*

When your Manipura is healthy, you will be driven and motivated. You're in touch with your inner guide, following that still small voice and trusting it to help you see through all forms of self-delusion and other external illusions. You've got no problems trusting your gut because you know it could never steer you wrong. To be clear, it's not that you "have faith" or hope it won't steer you down the wrong path. Instead, you know for sure. Knowledge is a step beyond faith. Also, since you have this implicit trust in yourself, it's easy for you to go after your desires because you know that they aren't misplaced. You can remain grounded at all times, even when a situation is heated or there's a lot of chaos going on around you.

Quiz: How Balanced Is Your Manipura?

1. Do you struggle with digestive issues like excess gas, IBS, GERD, or anything else?
2. Do you have trouble with your weight?
3. Are you plagued by any addiction?
4. Do you have trouble keeping your temper in check?
5. Do you find it hard to connect with your gut feelings?
6. Do you constantly find you're ready to go on the offensive when you perceive a threat?
7. Do you deal with things like inexplicable tension in your muscles or fibromyalgia?
8. Are you struggling with your eating in any way?
9. Do you get the feeling that everyone is better than you?
10. Do you feel clear about who you are and what you want out of life?
11. Do you get the sense that you're always helping and are never/seldom helped?
12. Do you feel like people don't appreciate you?
13. Are you struggling to trust that things will be okay?

14. Do you find it hard to trust that others won't let you down?

15. Are you generally a very stubborn person?

Number of Yes answers:_____

SCORING YOURSELF:

If You Have 8 Yes Answers or More: You have a **blocked** solar plexus chakra, or it's extremely **weak** from overuse. This means you need to balance this chakra if you hope to find your confidence and reconnect with your true self once more.

If You Have 6 to 7 Yes Answers: Your Manipura is **overactive** and on the verge of becoming weak or blocked. You're dangerously close to losing the gifts this chakra offers you. You've got to become mindful of your chakra and act on that to bring it back into balance.

If You Have 4 to 5 Yes Answers: Your Manipura is **fairly overactive.** It appears that this chakra is the most dominant one in your life, and because you're mainly from that center, it keeps you from being able to develop emotionally.

If You Have 2 to 3 Yes Answers: Your Manipura is **fairly open** to the flow of prana, but you've still got to make sure you keep it in check so that your self-esteem doesn't take a hit.

If You Have 0 to 1 Yes Answers: Your Manipura is **balanced.** You're also open to the energy from your sacral and root chakras, which is a good thing.

Benefits of Healing Your Manipura

1. You'll have more empathy and compassion for others, so you'll be a good friend to many.

2. Your positive energy will greatly boost the chances of attracting opportunities into your life.

3. You'll find love and companionship with ease and healthy relationships with all of your family members, both past and present.

4. You'll feel grounded in yourself, bringing stability to your life when you're feeling off-balance or scattered because of all the

activities you like to do spontaneously (like playing music).

5. Your feelings will be stronger than ever before – making it easier for you to move on from the pain in your past, which leads to much better future outcomes for you personally and professionally over time.

6. You'll fill your body with a burst of energy and enthusiasm.

7. You'll feel stronger since a balanced Manipura means more oxygen in your bloodstream, giving you stamina.

8. Your luck will be better than ever. You won't need to worry about bad luck at all because everything that happens to you is just going to be a positive chance for growth (especially if it's something that's going to help make you a better person).

9. You'll have more confidence, which will help you become more positive about yourself.

10. Your voice will sound better, your body will feel lighter, and it will feel good to be in the sun - not to mention that you won't feel sick from being out in the hot weather.

11. You'll have better focus and concentration at work, which makes the difference when you want to focus on something productive or creative, like writing a book or painting a beautiful piece of art.

12. It will be easier to get along with your friends as you'll have more energy to play with them, and you will also find it easy to make new friends.

13. You'll have a great time at work – not just because you're in a better mood, but because of the deeper connections that you make with everyone else who is around you.

14. You'll discover yourself to be more driven and motivated than ever before – which is great when balancing all the different activities in your life.

15. Your energetic body will be balanced, so you won't need to worry about any of your physical ailments getting worse over time.

16. You'll feel better about yourself as a person. You'll feel more connected to your community, which also helps you feel better

about being a world citizen.

17. You'll become more compassionate and loving toward yourself in turn, which will allow you to be more comfortable with your own spirit and the world around you.

It goes without saying that this list only scratches the surface of the benefits that come from healing your solar plexus chakra. It's very important to focus on healing this chakra when you want to experience major positive changes in your life (like with any other chakra).

Chapter 3: Building a Strong Chakra Foundation

While you can focus on opening and balancing your Manipura instead of other energy centers, it is essential and even beneficial for you to make sure that the centers that are lower than the solar plexus are also working as they should. This is because you draw energy into your body through the root chakra, and from there, that energy or life force works its way upwards. Your solar plexus chakra is amazing, but it needs help from all the other chakras, and it can only perform its functions wonderfully well when the others are working as they should. For this reason, we're going to discuss the root chakra and the sacral chakra in this chapter and talk about how you can make sure everything's up to snuff with those two.

While the information you're about to learn concerning the root and sacral chakras is very useful, it's good to do more research on these two outside of just reading this chapter. I'd recommend looking into other books that speak about each of them specifically, to make sure you really do have a solid foundation for you to allow the energy flow and proper functioning of your Manipura.

The Root Chakra

The Sanskrit word for the root chakra is *Muladhara,* which means "root support." You can find this chakra at the bottom of your spine, where it sits in the perineum, the area between your anus and genitals. It's connected to the element of earth, and its color is red, which means you can activate this chakra by putting on things with the color red and even pink. Red is a color that demands attention. It screams power, strength, vitality, confidence, and an undeniable sense of being grounded. It also happens to be the color with the slowest wavelength out of all the other colors we can perceive with our eyes.

This chakra is depicted visually as a lotus that has four petals, each of which represents:

- Your mind
- Your intellect
- Your consciousness
- Your ego

This energy center is a fascinating one, too, because it happens to be connected to the serpent energy known as kundalini, which rests at the base of your spine along with the chakra itself. The serpent is wrapped around itself three and a half times, and you can wake it up if you know what to do - but please don't attempt to do this before you're ready. Kundalini is a topic far beyond the scope of this book, but some interesting things happen when it awakens, so it's worth taking a look at.

What Does the Root Chakra Do?

Thanks to this chakra, you feel a sense of security in your life. It's what connects you to your ancestors and what ties you down to the material universe to know your own identity and feel safe in your being here, now. This energy center is basically akin to your reptilian brain and what it is to you as an entire being. It is the home of all your instincts, which drives you to fight, flee, freeze, or fawn, all of which are the possible solutions to situations that you find threatening. Your Muladhara is the very foundation upon which the remaining six chakras are built. This is why as empowering as it would be to open your Manipura (or as fun as it would be to activate your third eye), you'll be risking a lot of trouble if you don't work your way from the bottom to the top. This root chakra begins to form when you hit the age of seven.

You can think of this energy center as the roots of a tree, connecting you to the earth so that you don't lose your place or sense of being in life. It is the reason you can remain secure even in the face of what you might call challenging situations. It is the very framework upon which the entirety of you is built.

Symptoms of a Blocked Muladhara

So, how can you tell that this chakra is blocked? You'll notice that you tend to feel constantly tired and bored with life. Nothing enthralls you anymore, and nothing can hold your attention for too long without you feeling simply tired. Your mind lacks focus as you feel scattered in all your thoughts.

Your Muladhara's imbalance could cause you to feel like you're constantly floating somewhere that isn't the present. You feel like there's too much going on, causing you to disengage in mind and body. You may even get to the point where your nerves get better, and you break down. Paranoia is no stranger to you either because you have to question everything since you feel so unsure and unsafe, not being rooted as you should. This could cause you to experience horrible self-talk and even treat others poorly, even though you're only projecting what you feel onto innocent people.

You might experience issues with your feet, legs, lower back, spine, bladder, and colon when your root chakra isn't functioning properly. If you've been struggling with chronic back pain, it might be good to look into what's going on energetically with your root energy center.

Other ways you can be affected by your Muladhara include being overwhelmed by anxiety and stress. You may not feel confident in who you are, and so you continue second-guessing yourself to the point where you never make any progress no matter what you want to accomplish. You may also struggle with financial trouble, a poverty mindset, and disbelief in abundance. Since you don't believe that good can come your way monetarily speaking, you're probably not going to do what you must to make sure you can do more than just keep the lights on. As far as you're concerned, to strive for more than that would only lead to disappointment and heartache – this couldn't be further from the truth.

Healing Your Muladhara

There are many ways to heal your root chakra and bring it back into balance. It's all up to you to figure out what works best, but keep an open mind as you may be surprised at what brings you the most results.

Meditation and Visualization: You'll find there's no faster way to begin working on your energy centers than by practicing meditation and supercharging that with visualization if you want to. Meditation is a practice that forces you to be in the here and now. In other words, it grounds you in the present moment. When you have an unbalanced root chakra, you'll notice that you're always in the future or in the past. Everything happening around you goes unnoticed, and that's a sad thing because it is in the present that you find the many presents that life has to offer you. There's a reason it's called the present – and a blocked Muladhara means you're missing out on all of that because you're stuck regretting the past or fearing and worrying about the future. This is no way to live at all.

So, when you meditate, your mind is forced to be still and stop wandering all over the place. You're forced to slow down and just be. You connect with your essence– neither your mind nor your body because those are only tools. You connect with who you really are, and who you are is spirit, ever-present, always here and now, even long after your mind and body have passed away. This is a great way to bring yourself back to feeling grounded and secure because the home we all seek is truly within us, and it could never be home if it weren't safe, and we didn't feel supported. Meditating will help you see that you are home – you've always been home. There's no reason to be afraid because nothing at home could ever hurt you.

So, here's a quick practice you can use to begin bringing your Muladhara back into alignment:

1. Put on loose and comfortable clothing.

2. Find somewhere you will not be disturbed or distracted for at least fifteen minutes.

3. Sit in a comfortable position you can hold for the next fifteen minutes, or if you prefer, you can relax in a recliner or lie down if you're absolutely certain you're not going to fall asleep.

4. Shut your eyes, and bring your attention to your breath.

5. Part your lips slightly.

6. Don't try to change how you're breathing; just notice it.

7. Now, take a long, deep breath through your nose, hold it for a beat, and then release it through your slightly parted lips.

8. Do this repeatedly, and pay attention to how the breath connects with your nostrils and lips, feeling it as it fills your chest and belly and leaves you.

9. There will be times when your attention will have wandered off as you do this. There's nothing wrong with this; it happens to the best of us. Just notice when you've drifted, feel thankful and glad you noticed, and lovingly bring your attention back to the breath. You mustn't beat yourself up for getting distracted, as this will take away from the meditation. Just come back to the breath as many times as necessary.

10. When you feel calm and relaxed, it's time to visualize. Imagine there's a cord made up of brilliant red light that shoots out like a beam from your Muladhara, extending down past the earth and into its very core.

11. Feel the energy from the earth connecting with the energy in your root chakra.

12. Visualize the energy from the earth, terminating in your root chakra as a red ball of light. What does it look like to you? Is it moving? Fast or slow? Do you notice any splotches of darkness in there?

13. As you breathe in, imagine that the inhale pulls in more of the energy from the earth, infusing your Muladhara richly.

14. Imagine that you're expelling all the darkness in the Muladhara with each exhale. See it leaving your root chakra and going into the earth's core to be discarded.

15. You notice your Muladhara spinning faster, looking more radiant and beautiful as you breathe in.

16. As you breathe out, feel the warmth that settles in it, and let that radiate all through your body. Feel what it's like to be at home, at peace, at one with one and all.

17. Imagine that the beam of light connecting you to the earth slowly dissipates into nothing when you're ready. Notice all that's there now is your root chakra, looking balanced, beautiful, and brilliant.

18. You can return your attention to just your breath when you're ready.

19. When you feel ready, come out of the meditation, intending to feel at ease.

Root Chakra Foods: Another thing you can do is eat the right foods for the Muladhara. You shouldn't indulge in unnatural foods just because they're red. You want to eat only natural and healthy meals. The best things to help you bring back balance to this chakra include foods like sesame seeds, pumpkin seeds, red apples, strawberries, beets, pomegranates, red carrots, yams, potatoes, kidney beans, cherries, tomatoes, and other naturally red foods. You must eat them *mindfully*. Just chewing and swallowing isn't enough. As you chew, imagine that they are brilliant, red energy that goes down and makes its way straight to your root chakra, balancing it out for you. Chew slowly and with love and gratitude in your heart, trusting that they will do their bit to help you feel better.

Walk Barefoot: You can do this one with ease. When you walk around barefoot on the natural earth, you feel a sense of oneness with the ground, and you feel as though nothing could possibly shake you or rip you off your foundation. This does wonders for your root chakra. You're not supposed to walk like you're trying to get somewhere. You're walking slowly, just for its sake, for the pure pleasure of feeling your feet connect with the ground as they're supposed to. This is known as grounding, and it's a great way to return to the present and feel at peace whenever you feel flustered and frustrated with your life. You can also practice mindful breathing as you walk to really supercharge the experience. You only need a few minutes each day to benefit from this, and not only will your nervous system thank you, but you'll also get the curious feeling that Mother Nature has missed you and loves having you around. In my book, that's a good feeling!

Affirmations: You can also work with affirmations, which are basically statements you can make each day. The key to these affirmations is to say them with feeling, as though they were true, here and now. So, try the following on for size:

- I am safe
- I am secure
- I am here
- I am now
- I am grounded; my foundation is strong
- I am at peace
- I am content with all things
- I am nourished by the earth
- I am supported fully and unconditionally
- I belong
- I am at home in my body
- I am at home in this life
- I am home

The Sacral Chakra

The sacral chakra is also known as the *svadhisthana* in Sanskrit, which means "the home of the self." This is where your creativity lies and springs from. This is where your sexuality comes from and your deepest, truest desires. You can find this chakra resting just below your belly button, in the area where you have your reproductive organs, kidneys, and bladder. Naturally, being the second chakra, it is just above the root chakra. It's connected to the element of water, representing the idea of the importance of being in the *flow state* if you want to thrive in life. Water is all about releasing, allowing things to be as they are, and changing you mightily, just as water flowing in a river will change all the stones along its path and make them smooth and beautiful.

Water is also the perfect representation of our emotions which flow back and forth just like the element itself. So, if you want an accurate picture of the state of your sacral chakra, you should consider your dominant emotions and how you deal with them. Also, think about how you connect with others on an emotional level.

This chakra is orange in color, and its symbol is the crescent moon, which further connects this chakra to water, seeing as the moon has a profound influence on the waters of the Earth. It's also a strong reminder of the connection between this chakra and women's menstrual cycle. This energy center is also known as the seat of your sexual organs, and it's where your yin energy is stored – yin energy being the divine feminine in one and all, whether you're a man or a woman or identify as something else.

What Does the Sacral Chakra Do?

The sacral chakra is the reason you can express yourself, and it's also the seat of your sexuality. If you've ever had a desire in your life, sexual or otherwise, it was inspired by this energy center. If it's something that will please you, allow yourself to loosen up and play, or if it's something you feel passionate about, you have the svadhisthana to thank for making it possible for you to feel these things and enjoy them.

There are two dominant aspects to this chakra – sex and fun. The first is self-explanatory. The second refers to such things as new hobbies, new ways to play, new things to create and explore, etc. It's all about the things you do to enjoy yourself, not what you *must do*, which many people slog through with no pleasure. However, if you work consciously with this chakra, you'll be able to find the fun in everything, no matter how tedious it might be to you.

Symptoms of a Blocked Svadhisthana

When this chakra isn't balanced, you don't feel quite right. First, you may notice a permanent sense of detachment from everything. Also, you fail to react, not to positive or negative news. You're basically the "meh" emoji when your chakra is blocked. You might also notice that you're no longer as creative as you used to be, which can be quite an issue if you happen to work in a field that demands your steady creativity.

Emotionally, you feel that you're completely isolated from everyone else. When fun things come your way, you're afraid to let loose and enjoy yourself – whether that's from a fear of looking silly, not being in control, or something else. You're bogged down all the time by fatigue, you feel anxious, and you also suffer greatly from being lonely because no one likes that sort of energy. Also, you'll have to struggle to connect with your partner in the bedroom because your libido's gone away on leave and with no notice about when it will be back.

When you find it difficult to want to move your body, have fun, connect with others, and express yourself creatively, it could well be that your sacral chakra is crying out for some help, and you should do something about it. It doesn't just affect you mentally and emotionally but physically as well. In fact, you may have to deal with chronic back pain, hip problems, trouble with your joints, arthritis, chronically low energy, premenstrual syndrome (PMS), anemia, trouble with your kidneys and spleen, cysts on your ovaries(if you're a woman), trouble with your genitals, and the list goes on.

At other times, it could be that your sacral chakra is overactive. You'll know this is the case when you tend to indulge in extreme sexual fantasies, or you indulge in regular sexual fantasies all the time. You could also notice that you have addictions, especially to mind-altering substances and food. If you notice you've got nothing but sex on the brain and always have to have your favorite consciousness-altering vice, then this could be your sacral chakra asking for balance. It would be a good thing to work on this energy center so you can return to normal before things take a turn for the worse in your life.

Healing Your Svadhisthana

There are several methods you could use to help you restore regular working conditions to this energy center. Try them all on for size, and make sure you make this a daily practice so that you never have to worry about whether you're doing okay in your svadhisthana or not. Let's begin.

Meditation and Visualization: We've already gone over how powerful meditation is, so let's jump right into what you need to visualize to balance the sacral chakra. Work your way through steps one through nine in the previous meditation for the root chakra, and then proceed with the following when you hit that calm, relaxed point:

1. Imagine that, where your sacral chakra should be, you have a brilliant ball of orange light that pulses with power.

2. Sit with this ball and notice how you feel as you observe it.

3. Look at the ball. Do you see any blockages in the form of darkness? Or is it moving far too slowly? What do you notice?

4. As you breathe in, imagine you're breathing in a pure orange light that goes into you through the sacral chakra itself, energizing it.

5. As you breathe out, imagine that the darkness leaves through the sacral chakra, causing it to glow brighter and move even faster.

6. Continue breathing and visualizing in this way until you notice there is no longer any darkness in the chakra and that it's moving nicely.

Sacral Chakra Foods: You can also opt for meditative eating here. You'll be eating naturally orange foods, like oranges, carrots, mangos, pawpaw or papaya, butternut squash, sweet potato, melons, pumpkin, etc. Eggs are also excellent, as are seeds and nuts. Remember, take your time as you chew and swallow. Imagine that you're literally chewing on brilliant orange energy that goes down to the sacral chakra to clear out and balance it so you can feel better at last.

Creative Practices: Sometimes, all you need to do is have some fun. So do something creative. That doesn't mean you need to be the next Ernest Hemingway or write a movie or something as dramatic as that.

You could do the simple stuff like choose to take a different route to work, brush your teeth with your other hand, and roll around in a circle on your bed before you get out of it... anything counts! Think about kids and the way that they are, for instance. There's absolutely no logical reason why little Tammy needs to try to loop her arm under her thigh to get her lollipop into her mouth, but she's doing it anyway. . . because it's fun! What could you do differently? Also, if you have some creative skills that you may have abandoned because "life happened," it's a good idea to get back to them. However, I should caution you against being hard on yourself because you're not as good at it as you used to be. The idea is to have fun. That's it. You could also choose to learn a new skill. You just might surprise yourself.

Affirmations: Try on the following affirmations for size:

- I am creative
- I am free
- I am boundless
- I feel passion with no remorse
- I am safe expressing myself
- I am safe to be me
- There's nothing safer than being who I am in each moment
- I am emotionally balanced
- I am in touch with my feelings
- I love to feel
- I feel free and honor my emotions.

Chapter 4: Manipura Mantras and Mudras

Mantras or Affirmations?

Cultivating positive thoughts daily can be an effective way to control anxiety, improve mood, and enhance self-esteem. Affirmations are a great way to help you accomplish all this and whatever else you set your mind to. But what are affirmations, really?

Affirmations are profound yet simple words or phrases that encourage you to think positively about yourself, your goals, and your dreams. They can be anything from "I am successful!" to "I am a great person." The idea behind them is simple but powerful. You can reprogram your mind to believe in them by repeating them daily. In other words, affirmations help you start speaking your truth and ultimately achieve what you desire.

Mantras are words or phrases repeated silently and mentally to bring about the desired outcome. They are similar to affirmations, yet they have a more religious, spiritual, and mystical feel to them. They can be used for various purposes – such as stress relief, cleansing the mind of negative thoughts, meditation, and more. The best part about mantras is that they can be very powerful in their own right. For example, "Om

Namah Shivaya" is an example of a mantra that you can use to focus the mind on positive aspects of life. It will help you come to know who you really are better the more you chant it.

Both affirmations and mantras are deeply personal and inspirational acts that can change your life for the better. They both help you replace fearful thoughts and negative self-talk with positive beliefs and affirmations. They create a sense of optimism, hope, and excitement, and they are both helpful in improving self-esteem and in the pursuit of goals and dreams.

So, which one should you choose? The truth is that both are effective tools that positively impact one's life. While mantras have a spiritual element to them, affirmations focus more on the physical world around us. Ultimately though, it doesn't matter much which one you choose because you can get great value from either of them by repeating them regularly.

Mantras on the Brain

How do Sanskrit mantras affect the human brain? How Sanskrit mantras affect the human brain is a complicated and surprising phenomenon. Even though Sanskrit, the language from which these mantras are written, isn't widely known outside of India, the brain seems to recognize it and reacts to it.

The structure of Sanskrit allows the human brain to remember and recite these ancient phrases and mantras. The sounds of particular words or syllables frequently repeat with each new phrase; this gives a rhythm and a cadence to each mantra. In addition, each sentence written in Sanskrit has meaning for the reader. Combined, these two elements become something powerful – much more powerful than English or any other modern language commonly used today.

Sanskrit mantras literally and figuratively help the human brain to focus on whatever the goal of the mantra is. The complex nature of the language allows a person to concentrate on many different sounds that are all combined into one sentence. By increasing concentration and focus, our brains can enter into an alpha state that induces deep relaxation and stress relief. At the same time, a Sanskrit mantra can be so easy to remember and repeat aloud that after only one or two times of chanting a particular mantra, your brain will begin to memorize it. Through repetition, your brain will tone down its alertness level while simultaneously increasing its ability to relax deeply.

What's even more amazing is that through the use of Sanskrit, a person can actually chant mantras while meditating. This means that you can improve your memory and concentration skills simultaneously as you enhance your ability to meditate deeply by simply repeating a mantra out loud in Sanskrit.

Ultimately, whether or not you believe in how well-structured Sanskrit helps the brain activity, it's important to note that the science behind mantras affecting the brain is still being studied. Regardless of whether there are benefits to chanting Sanskrit, it's fairly safe to say that these ancient phrases have their own power no matter what language they are written in.

Why Use Mantras and Affirmations?

Using mantras and affirmations can do wonders for your life. Using them opens up space in your mind to think about what really matters to you. Repeating these personal changes to yourself helps you reprogram your thoughts and enhance your self-perception.

Affirmations are a great way to start this process because they simply begin with something that is already true – like "I am a great person" or "I can achieve anything I set my mind to." You can begin with the stuff that's already true and then work your way into the things you would like to be true by using that energy. By repeating these phrases daily, you can change how you think about yourself concerning your goals and dreams.

Mantras are well worth your time, too. They create a direct link between you and the power of the Universe. They allow you to feel at one with nature, your goals, and your dreams. They help you make yourself more in tune with life on Earth by directly connecting you to the source of all creation. At the same time, they help calm your mind and profoundly reduce stress. These are powerful tools to achieve peace of mind, inner harmony, and happiness for both body and soul.

Besides self-esteem, other benefits include physical health and spiritual benefits. By using mantras, you can improve your immune system, reduce the symptoms of stress, and improve your ability to focus. Mantra meditation also helps you increase your energy levels while improving blood circulation and increasing blood flow to certain parts of the body.

The best part about mantras is that they help you gain more control over your life by helping you achieve balance in thought and action. Regularly performing a mantra meditation can effectively help you achieve peace of mind and improve physical health, mental health, and spiritual well-being. You'll be able to achieve a better sense of purpose and direction in your life and peace and joy.

Affirmations for Your Solar Plexus

The lovely thing about affirmations is that you can *come up with your own*. In fact, I support you doing this strongly because when you do so in your own words, you'll feel the truth of them even more, allowing them to take hold of your life. You have to simply make sure that you're stating them *in the present tense* as if they're already true because that's how it works. If you phrase them in the future, that will make whatever you're affirming remain in the future, forever out of your grasp – and we don't want that, obviously. Also, you should only ever state them using positive words – meaning, nix the word "not" from your affirmations. For instance, you shouldn't affirm, "I am not fighting with anyone today," because your subconscious mind will only remember, "Fight with everyone today. Got it?" Instead, you should say, "I get along with everyone well today."

So, when it comes to creating affirmations for your solar plexus, the odds are you'll know better than anyone else what to say. For instance, let's assume Sandra has issues with her Manipura. Those issues show up for her because she tends to blow up easily at people. Really, the reason she acts in that way is because that's how she feels on the inside, and other people are getting the spillover of her inner anger, so to speak. So, she could create mantras like the following:

- I am at peace with myself.

- I am at peace with everyone around me.

- My soul is at rest.

- I see the beauty in everyone.

- I see the beauty in myself.

- I allow myself to be at ease; I flow with one and all.

Do you see how this works? If you just work with many generic affirmations, you may not really target whatever needs to change. So, in light of the many symptoms that accompany solar chakra issues, what could you craft for yourself right now as an affirmation? Take out a sheet of paper and write them down, then stick them somewhere you'll see them every day so you can say them out loud and with feeling. The feeling is the secret. It's not about the words but what the words imply. It's why "hi" is a super short word, but it can communicate all kinds of things depending on who says it, when, and how they say it. So, focus on feeling as if what you're saying is already true.

But I'm Lying!

No, affirmations aren't lies. They're a process to help you manifest whatever you seek. Your brain doesn't know the difference between what you're feeling and what you're actually experiencing. With the mechanism of words, you're generating a feeling within yourself and training yourself how to reach for and maintain this state of mind. Eventually, you will no longer need affirmations because they're true. You're not lying at all. You're simply taking advantage of the wonderful power of the subconscious mind to manipulate your energy body back into wholeness, so don't ever feel like a fraud or like you're fooling yourself. Instead, feel those words as being true and your present reality, and watch your reality morph to conform to the feeling you've been embodying by working with the affirmations you've got.

Back to Mantras

What mantra should you use when working with your solar plexus chakra? I suggest using the seed sound of this energy center, which is

RAM. This sound is known as the bija. It's supposed to vibrate along with the same energy that powers the solar plexus chakra, so using this sound will help you bring things back into alignment. As you chant this mantra, if you're sensitive to subtle energies, you will feel it working on your energy pathways, clearing them out. Please note that the correct way to pronounce this mantra isn't "ram," as in the animal or the verb, but R-Ah-M, that's the Ah sound you get from the first syllable of the word avocado.

The RAM mantra is from the Vedic scriptures between 1500 BCE and 500 BCE. It's one of the bija mantras mentioned in the scriptures, and you can work with it while envisioning something shaped like a lotus in your mind's eye. Give this lotus a bright, yellow aura, and see it turn like a wheel behind your belly button.

Another mantra you can use is the vowel sound OO as in "zoo." Chant this in time with your breath to help your solar plexus chakra get to work on healing itself.

Mudras

Mudras are widely used in India today as part of Yoga practices designed for both mental and physical health. They are hand movements that have a deep, spiritual significance. Traditionally, mudras have been seen to help open up the third eye and achieve higher levels of awareness. The hands and fingers are very important in Hinduism because they represent the element of sattva – the state of purity and compassion.

Mudras were devised in India thousands of years ago. Through the practice of these ancient arts, the yogis learned how to transform their lives in many different ways. Each mudra was developed to help the yogi achieve greater mastery over his mind and body.

In Sanskrit, *Mudra* is a compound word that means "seal" or "sign." According to ancient beliefs, when a person uses a specific mudra, they are sealing or imprinting certain energies within his body. This process creates an inner cycle of energy that keeps certain vibrations alive within his own physical body and throughout all of creation.

From an energetic perspective, mudras allow practitioners to tap into ancient wisdom found in Indian culture. Mudras help you improve your ability to meditate more deeply by connecting with your own inner self and spiritual energy. They also help you to become more aware and in tune with your surroundings and environment.

Mudras are a different but related set of hand positions that are used in yoga. Like yoga postures, mudras are typically physical poses that can be practiced for as little as a few minutes or several hours. The practice of mudras includes physical movements and breathing patterns, and mental concentration. There are many different types of mudras anyone can practice.

The practice of mudras involves taking the fingers and hands into certain positions to improve health and well-being, bring about feelings of relaxation, achieve inner peace, and then some. You can use the following mudras to help your Manipura come back into alignment and balance (note that you can use them when you're sitting in meditation).

Rudra Mudra:

Rudra mudra.
Schlum, CC BY-SA 4.0 https://creativecommons.org/licenses/by-sa/4.0 , via Wikimedia Commons: https://commons.wikimedia.org/wiki/File:Mudra-Naruto-Coq.svg

Your ring and index fingers and your thumbs should be connected at the tips (ring to ring, index to index, thumb to thumb). Next, extend the remaining two fingers so that they're relaxed. This mudra will require both hands. You can hold it for just 5 minutes at a time, three times a day or more. This is a good one to boost your concentration and heal your Manipura.

Agni Mudra:

Agni mudra.
*Chatsam, CC BY-SA 3.0 https://creativecommons.org/licenses/by-sa/3.0 , via Wikimedia
Commons: https://commons.wikimedia.org/wiki/File:Mudra_Coq.svg*

This is also known as the "fire hand" gesture. You want to bend your ring finger to allow your thumb to rest on top of it. Your thumb should hold that finger in place while the rest of your fingers remain pointing straight out. Please make sure you're not using too much pressure to keep the ring finger in position. You should ideally do this while sitting down, two or three times a day, for five minutes at a time. You can do it for longer if you like, but no longer than 15 minutes.

Guru Mudra:

Guru mudra.
*Schlum, CC BY-SA 4.0 https://creativecommons.org/licenses/by-sa/4.0 , via Wikimedia Commons:
https://commons.wikimedia.org/wiki/File:Mudra-Naruto-Cheval.svg*

Interlock all your fingers except your two forefingers. While your hands are clasped together, extend your forefingers out, and put their tips together. This one is great not just for waking up your solar plexus chakra but also for developing great ideas and psychic powers, detoxing your body, dealing with overeating, helping you feel lighter, and so much more. It will also bring you abundance in your life, so that's an added plus!

Pushan Mudra: This is known as the "giver of good health." It's also called the "gesture of digestion," and it's no surprise then that it helps your solar plexus chakra a lot when you do this. Its literal English meaning is "one who nourishes," and it's great for waking up the Manipura and balancing it. You can also use it to help you to let go and receive. Here's how to do it: For your right hand, bring the tips of your thumb, middle, and index fingers together. Let the other two fingers extend outwards, and keep your palm facing the sky. For your left hand, bring the tips of your thumb, ring, and middle fingers together. Let the other fingers extend outwards, and your palm should face the sky too. You can do this for 5 minutes at a time each day while you're sitting in meditation for explosive results.

Chapter 5: Meditation and Visualization

We've already touched briefly on the topic of meditation and visualization, but we're going to really get into it here.

What Is Meditation?

Meditation is the process of grounding yourself in the moment.
https://pixabay.com/images/id-3053488

Meditation is the process of focusing on the here and now, grounding yourself in the moment so that you don't allow your mind to run away with you as it typically does. It's about channeling all your focus onto one particular thing, which could be anything from the way a candle flame looks, your hands, a leaf, your breath, or even a sensation or an emotion. It's about picking one thing and sticking to it so that the chatter in your mind is silenced, allowing you to connect with the divine energy of life. This is a very good thing for your chakras, as you can imagine.

Meditation is a state of mind, body, and soul that concentrates on one's breathing to achieve a deep sense of tranquility and inner peace. It's a form of self-help that's easy to learn and practice and an invaluable stress-reliever that improves moods and sleep quality.

Meditation doesn't have to be complicated – all you need is your body, your breath, and a little time every day. Meditation is also known to improve the attention span of children with ADHD and reduce heart disease risk factors such as high blood pressure levels.

Meditation is good for your solar plexus chakra because it helps you focus on what is happening within your body, mind, and life rather than what happens around you from moment to moment and how to deal with such circumstances when they arise. Inwardly focusing leaves less time for worrying about the external environment, so meditation helps balance both sides of the spectrum, balancing out the solar plexus chakra.

If you have some type of impulsive behavior, then meditation can help you resolve it by getting you to look inwardly and get a better sense of what's going on inside yourself. This makes you better able to respond appropriately rather than reacting automatically to the environment around you.

What Is Visualization?

What is visualization, and how does it work with meditation? The mind is a powerful force and can affect all of your life. How you think impacts how you feel and what you do in life. When meditation is combined with visualization, it can help to create a richer experience for the mind.

Visualization, simply put, is projecting images in your head as if they are happening right now. You can use it with meditation to create scenes around the body that connect its parts to locations on Earth or other planets within our solar system during meditative practice. It's an important tool used to energize various places in the body, like an acupuncture point or chakra, for more balance and insight into self-healing abilities.

Visualization can also be used in the form of guided imagery. Guided imagery is a form of storytelling that helps you to see things that are not real or objects that are not there. These images have a powerful effect on the mind and emotions because they trigger the mind's own inner resources for healing and balance.

There are many ways one can use visualization in meditation, but one of the most important is during an empowerment practice. Empowerment brings energy into a person so they can embark on new challenges and opportunities in life. If your goal is to do something important, like start a business or study for school, visualize yourself doing it and all that comes with it. Right now, what you're seeking to empower is your solar plexus chakra, so let's focus on that. You're about to receive a set of guided visualization meditations you can use to work on your solar plexus chakra, and I recommend that you record them in your own voice so you don't have to keep coming back to the book to figure out what you should visualize next because that can take you right out of it. Also, make sure you won't be bothered for the duration of these exercises and that you're wearing comfy clothes.

Guided Visualization for Balancing the Manipura

Now, get comfortable wherever you've chosen to sit. Make sure you're feeling good; this position is one you can remain in for the duration of this visualization. If you find that you need to make adjustments during this meditation, that's fine. Do so mindfully and with love. There's no room for judgment here. When you're settled, you may resume the meditation.

Whenever you've noticed your mind has traveled off to some other land, bring it back with love and kindness. Don't be upset with yourself. This is a practice. You can keep your eyes shut through this meditation, or leave them half-open, your gaze unfocused and soft.

Now, notice your breath. Pay attention to the way your chest rises and falls. Notice how there's a natural rhythm to your breath, and just sit with that. If you notice your attention is drifting off, you can bring your mind back to your breath or let it come back to your solar plexus and sit there.

If you have thoughts as you sit, it's okay. You can allow them in and allow them to leave when they want to by simply bringing your mind back to the meditation. Now, it's time to yawn. Do this three times. It doesn't matter whether you feel like yawning or not. Just take three nice, deep yawns. Take your time with this. There's no rush involved.

Once you've finished yawning, come back to your breath and pay attention to what's happening. Now, breathe deeply, allowing your belly to fill with air first and then letting your lungs fill up next. Slowly, allow the air to escape, and then do this again. In and out. Take another breath, and allow your attention to be drawn toward the base of your spine.

At the base of your spine, imagine that you have a red ball of light. Pay attention to this light as it grows and glows from within you to the outside. Notice how the lights glow around your entire body. Now move your attention from the root chakra to the sacral chakra. Notice the orange ball of light and allow it to grow and encompass your entire body. Now move your attention to your solar plexus. Notice that you have a fairly small ball of light that glows yellow. As you breathe in, notice how this light grows. As you exhale, notice how you're starting to glow with a yellow light. Allow this yellow light to encompass your entire stomach and your chest. Feel it as it grows to cover your entire upper and lower bodies. Know that this is the light that drives you.

This light is the embodiment of your dreams and aspirations. It is the fire that drives you to fulfill your destiny in life. Feel how warm and powerful it is as it moves through your whole body, beginning with your abdomen. Notice how it washes over your throat, head, and lower body. Feel this yellow energy infusing you with passion, enthusiasm, and fun. Feel your inner self awakened to the challenge of life, ready to take things head-on with a smile on your face. As you breathe out, feel the relief of knowing that you have overcome every obstacle that could possibly come your way already. Now you may begin to chant RAM... RAM... RAM...

It is now time to bring your breath back to its normal state. Notice that the yellow light still surrounds you. Pay attention to the way the light pulses powerfully from your solar plexus. With each pulse on your inhale, notice how infused you are with so much passion and joy for life. Now repeat the following affirmations, either out loud or in your mind, if you prefer:

I can feel my personal power, and it is great. I am strongly driven to bring all my dreams to pass. I am on the path to fulfilling my destiny. Everything I touch turns to gold. I am successful in all that I do. I know what it is I want to accomplish, and I remain focused. Ideas come to me easily and quickly. I implement these great ideas with great success. I always see the results of my labor. My word is my bond, and I always do what I say I will. I am always willing to do the most in order to achieve my big dreams. I firmly believe in what I want to accomplish. I firmly believe in myself and my abilities. I confidently go after my dreams because they are a done deal.

Now continue to bask in this pure yellow light and silence as you allow it to energize you, body, mind, and spirit. Inhale this yellow light and allow it to charge your being. Let it fill you up from head to toe and feel the thrill of it moving around you.

Now we are close to the end of this visualization, and you need to come out as slowly as you can. First, return your attention to your breath. Pay attention to its rhythm as your chest rises and falls with each inhale and exhale. Gently wiggle both your toes and fingers to shift your awareness fully into your body. You can move your arms and legs around to really feel grounded in the present if you like. Now, slowly and gently, open your eyes while you continue to keep your attention on what's happening within you energetically. Take one more deep breath in and out and feel gratitude for the shifts you have just accomplished.

Guided Visualization for Unblocking Your Solar Plexus Chakra

This visualization will help you open your solar plexus chakra to feel more confident and empowered in all aspects of your life. It will help you make strong connections between your mind and body, positively affecting all areas of your life.

You'll begin by taking a few deep breaths and moving your hands and legs around if you would like until you find a comfortable position to remain in for this exercise. Take a moment to center yourself and then shut your eyes and get comfortable in your seat. Inhale deeply through your nose, allowing the energy of each breath to fill every part of your body. Fully exhale until you have expelled all the air out of your lungs. Gently wiggle both your hands for one final time just to ensure that you are still grounded in the present moment and that you have full access to all parts of your body. Inhale and exhale deeply as you fully settle down in your body three more times.

For the next step in this visualization, you'll imagine that you have an orb of yellow light just one foot in front of you. This orb is your own personal source of power, and you must work with it carefully and respectfully. The orb represents your belief system, and it is how you tell yourself how things are going to be from one day to the next. It is what keeps your mind focused on positive ideas to continue to live a happy and fulfilling life. Focus on its size, shape, and overall appearance before moving on to the next part of the visualization.

Now, imagine that you are holding one hand upward. As your hand reaches out to contact the orb, you'll feel it pushing back on your palm. This push represents all of the negative things that you believe about yourself. If you believe that you cannot change, then that is exactly what will stay fixed in place for an indefinite amount of time. The goal of this visualization is not to change every thought that you have ever had. Instead, make some changes to get back on track with making your life better in as many ways as possible and allow the solar plexus chakra to work as it should once more.

Now, imagine that you have a much larger orb of energy surrounding your body, centered in your solar plexus itself. This orb is filled with glowing, radiant yellow light, representing your confidence and personal power. Every time you get a negative thought trying to latch on to your energy, this orb will push it back out of the way until there is no more room for negativity within your mind. This visualization represents how important it is always to think positive thoughts and repel any negativity before it has a chance to take over completely.

Feel the energy in the room starting to change as the negativity that was once part of your life floats away into nothingness. Feel your own personal power growing as you replace thoughts of hopelessness and fear with good things. See the color of the orb near you brighten and intensify as your personal power becomes more accessible than ever before. Allow your personal orb to completely engulf the one in front of you as your solar plexus glows even brighter than the sun. Feel that raw power.

Feel the energy of this chakra move around your body like a wave that forms from your solar plexus outward toward your extremities and then back again. Allow yourself to get used to how it feels inside of you and notice how much lighter you feel without all of that negativity weighing down on you. When the bright energy is moving, imagine that it has become part of the rhythm in which your heart beats. Make a note of how much stronger it seems now that all of those negative beliefs are gone for good.

Once the orb is glowing brightly and your glowing energy is moving around your body, you can decide to open your eyes. When you open them, notice how much lighter and more confident you feel than before. Hold on to that feeling as a constant reminder to focus on positive thoughts.

Useful Tips and Tricks for Working with Guided Meditations

Using imagery has been proven to increase the likelihood of success for guided meditation sessions. If you are having a hard time getting your mind to focus on something, try thinking about it in an image rather than a word. Although sometimes words can be easier, try thinking about them as if you are seeing them through the filter of an image of your choosing. Remember that image is by no means necessary, and you can always just say the word that is meant to represent that concept instead. When you visualize yourself doing something or seeing something, it's actually much easier for your mind to concentrate on getting the task done than attempting to listen to someone over sounds that you don't understand.

Many people prefer to listen to a guided meditation on a continuous loop. This can be achieved easily if you use headphones while doing your practice. If you want to do this, it's useful to set up two separate tracks in an audio editing program like Audacity. You can make each track one hour long. Use the first track as your background music, then add the sound of a repetitive mantra throughout the meditation. This will make it much easier for you to focus on what is being said during your session instead of just becoming distracted by the background music or noise around you. The repetition could also help trigger more positive thoughts than would otherwise be available were you to simply read them off a book or something. Also, you can play this audio file just as you're dropping off to sleep to get maximum effects.

Some people find it easier just to listen for five minutes every day rather than attempt longer meditations at first. I would advise that you make this a daily practice. You'll achieve a lot more practicing for five minutes once or twice a day than by attempting to cram in five days' worth of meditation in one day. It's a practice, not a test you have to cram for and ace only to forget everything you've learned after you have finished. So, it is in your best interest to decide – right here and now – that you'll never skip a single day of meditation and visualization to help your solar plexus chakra function the way it's supposed to. If you can keep this up for at least 30 days, you won't even need to remind yourself to do it. You may notice that you're doing it while waiting in line at the grocery store or stuck in traffic, or anywhere you can find a few minutes at a time to help your solar plexus chakra stay balanced. You may not even need a recording to do this.

You'll love incorporating a little something known as "breath-work" into your meditation and visualization techniques. The results are going to be *astronomical*. What exactly is breath-work, and why does it matter? Keep reading to find out more.

Chapter 6: Solar Plexus Pranayama and Yoga

What Is Pranayama?

Pranayama is the fourth limb of yoga, and it means "control of air" or "extension of breath." It translates as "breath control." It's a powerful form of meditation that can help calm the mind, heal the body, and achieve many other benefits. The goal of pranayama is to link breath with emotional centers in the body. When these two are connected, they can combat physical effects such as depression and stress.

Pranayama is based on the principle that, like electricity, prana (the Sanskrit word for "energy") flows through the body. The flow of prana can be blocked through poor posture, anxiety, or tiredness. While it's hard to change your circumstances, a little bit of effort can transform your life.

This yogic technique mobilizes and regulates the prana, or life force. Pranayama is traditionally practiced in balancing the mind and body. The breathing techniques used in this practice can help calm an overactive mind and body, clear your headspace, reduce anxiety levels, lower blood pressure, and relieve stress levels and tension in the muscles. There are many different types of pranayama techniques that anyone can practice regardless of age or gender.

Why Pranayama Matters

Pranayama is the most important component of yoga and is actually considered to be an essential technique. There's a reason you do yoga poses backward, upside down, and in strange positions. It's because they all activate different energy centers in the body. Also, immersing yourself in zero gravity (like lying down) can calm your mind, help you sleep, and heal your body. In conjunction with yoga poses and meditation, Yogic breathing techniques allow us to access the power of our brain waves and subconscious mind to facilitate the changes we seek to enjoy. This ability helps us stay grounded and connected with our surroundings. It's also why we sleep when we're tired or stressed out.

Pranayama is an important part of yoga because it is one of the techniques used to control your breathing. Yoga is all about finding peace within, and pranayama is one of the four main components (along with asana, pratyahara, and Dharana) that help you find inner peace.

Pranayama is one of the most effective ways to use the breath to achieve greater physical and mental health. It is a powerful tool that can help you relax and turn off your mind's constant chatter. Pranayama effectively reduces stress levels and protects against stress-related disorders and illnesses because it impacts both the mind and body on a deep level by altering brainwave patterns through slowed breathing.

When you are stressed or anxious, you breathe in an irregular and shallow way. You also have a greater likelihood of contracting infectious illnesses if you have a weakened immune system. Therefore, pranayama is important for overall fitness and health.

Bhramari Pranayama for Your Manipura

One of the best forms of breath-work you can do for your Manipura is known as the *Bhramari Pranayama*, which means "bumblebee breath." This is an excellent form of breathwork that will help you to heal your mind, and, more than that, it has an actual effect on your nervous system as well by calming it down. You're going to make a sound reminiscent of the bumblebee, a soft humming sound that causes vibrations to move all through your body. These vibrations help your nervous system switch over to the parasympathetic system, which your body uses to rest and digest. It also affects your vagus nerve.

Why does the vagus nerve matter? Because it's responsible for kickstarting the processes that make resting *and* digestion possible. In other words, it's directly connected to the inner fire of the solar plexus chakra. This nerve shoots out of your brain stem, down your neck, and into your belly. It also makes up the pathway for hormones to move through your brain-gut axis. As you know, the brain-gut axis is why you can feel mentally at peace with yourself. In fact, your gut determines your mood, and that's why you have to be particular about the sort of food you eat. Your gut is responsible for creating about 95 percent of your body's serotonin, which is a neurotransmitter that helps you with neural functions and mood stabilization.

To meditate with this form of pranayama, you can work either with higher tones or lower tones. Since you're working on the solar plexus chakra, it's good to work with both tones, as your solar plexus chakra is close to the heart chakra, which is the energy center that sits smack dab in the middle of all the others. Another smart thing to do is to try to hum in the key of E. Why E? Because this is the tone that corresponds specifically to the solar plexus chakra, and so you'll be focusing all of the energy being generated from the breath-work to that particular energy center. If you want to work on other energy centers with this form of pranayama, you can too. It's a matter of adjusting the tone and focusing on the energy center in question, but this book is all about the solar plexus, so we'll turn our attention there instead.

How to Do the Bumblebee Breath

1. Find somewhere quiet where you'll neither be distracted nor disturbed for the next fifteen minutes. Make sure you're wearing comfortable clothing that's loose so you can breathe easily.

2. Sit in a comfortable position. You can place both hands on your lap or use your index fingers to plug your ears while pointing your elbows to your sides.

3. Take three full inhales and exhales through your nostrils as you settle down and get comfortable.

4. Bring your attention to your solar plexus chakra. If you want to, you may visualize it.

5. Breathe in deeply and, as you breathe out, press down on the cartilage of your ears to block them and create a humming sound, just like a bee.

6. If you're visualizing the solar plexus chakra, imagine that bright yellow energy goes into it as you breathe in and as you breathe out, imagine the solar plexus getting brighter and more beautiful.

7. Breathe in and out just like this for 6 to 7 repetitions (1 repetition has both an inhale and exhale).

8. You may take a break, then continue breathing in this way for the next five minutes or until you feel like you've done enough work for the session.

What Is Yoga?

Yoga is an ancient practice that's been around for more than 5,000 years, originating in India. It's based on the idea of connecting to your inner self. Those who practice it believe that yoga unites all aspects of your mind and body through breathing and poses, or *"asanas."* Practicing yoga makes you feel calmer and more relaxed. Yoga does not just exercise but a way to live a happy life.

Yoga is more than just a physical exercise; it's a discipline that can help you find balance in your life with meditation and breathwork. Yoga has been proven to reduce stress, anxiety, and depression. It can also be an effective way to maintain flexibility and engage muscle groups for strength-training purposes. There are many different kinds of yoga to suit everyone's needs, from beginners to advanced practitioners.

How Yoga Helps Your Solar Plexus Chakra

The solar plexus chakra governs your relationship to the material world and your passions. The feeling of well-being you'll experience through practicing yoga can help you discover your true passions. Your solar plexus chakra is the chakra that controls your ability to feel, think and act from a place of intuition and inspiration instead of fear, confusion, and hesitation by feeding your body with what it needs to feel healthy, happy, and fit.

Yoga is also a practice that allows us to know just what we truly need in life. In yoga, our needs are not dependent on others but on ourselves. Only you can satisfy your needs in a way that will truly make you happy. Yoga can give you the necessary skills to fulfill your own needs.

The physical benefits of yoga may also help your solar plexus chakra. This chakra governs how your body and mind respond to stress and anxiety or its lack. The different poses of yoga help to alleviate stress and anxiety, not only on a mental level but also on a physical level, by making you more flexible and stronger both mentally and physically so that you can handle stressful situations more easily with less pain and discomfort. Many people find that as it improves their health and fitness level, it also helps them to have a more positive outlook on life. According to yogic philosophy, once we learn how to handle stress and anxiety in our daily lives, we become more balanced and less prone to illness.

Yoga is also an ancient healing practice that dates back thousands of years before Western medicine was developed. Yoga practice is now the fastest growing form of alternative medicine in the U.S., surpassing traditional medicines like herbal remedies and doctor's office visits by a wide margin. Yoga has been so beneficial because it can help you control your thoughts and emotions by learning how to adapt your behaviors, resulting in better health and more peace of mind.

Yoga Poses to Balance and Heal the Manipura

Dhanurasana – The Bow Pose

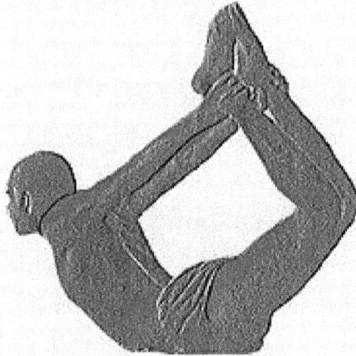

The bow pose.
Adishankaracharya108, CC BY-SA 4.0 https://creativecommons.org/licenses/by-sa/4.0 , via Wikimedia Commons: https://commons.wikimedia.org/wiki/File:Dhanur%C4%81sana_%E2%97%A6_Bow_I_yoga_%C4%81sana.jpg

This pose is part of the 12 fundamental poses in Hatha Yoga. Here's how to do it:

1. Lie on your stomach either on a carpeted floor or on your yoga mat. Make sure that you place both hands by your sides, palms up to the sky, and your chin touching the ground.

2. Breathe out and, as you do, bend both knees so that you draw your heels up to your rear end as close as you can get them. Please make sure that both knees are at least hip-width apart from each other.

3. Now, raise both hands and grab onto your ankles. Please, make sure you're holding your ankles, not the tops of both feet. It's just your fingers that should be wrapped around them. Keep your thumbs free and flex your toes to point outward.

4. Breathe in and raise your heels so they move away from your rear end while you continue to hold on to your ankles. At the same

time, you should raise your thighs, head, and chest, moving away from the ground. Please make sure that, as you do this, you turn your shoulders as needed. It should feel comfortable. Only your core will be on the floor when you do this right.

5. Push down to the ground to make the most of this stretch. You'll really feel it in the back muscles. Keep your gaze straight out before you and remain in this pose for at least 15 seconds while you breathe mindfully and remain balanced.

6. Breathe out as you come out of the pose by bringing your feet, thighs, torso, and head back down to the floor, naturally letting go of your ankles. Rest for some seconds, then start the process over again if you feel so inclined.

Parivrtta Trikonasana – The Revolved Triangle Pose

Revolved triangle pose.
Kennguru, CC BY 3.0 https://creativecommons.org/licenses/by/3.0 , via Wikimedia Commons: https://commons.wikimedia.org/wiki/File:Parivrtta-Trikonasana_Yoga-Asana_Nina-Mel.jpg

This pose will require some great balance. Don't beat yourself up if you don't get it right away. It will pay off in heaps of gold the more you practice. Here's how to do it:

1. Start off in a standing position, with your feet pointing out in front of you. Keep them at least three feet apart (adjust as needed).

2. Make sure that your hips are squared to face the front of the mat you're using.

3. Your right foot should be out before you, while your left foot is behind you and turned out by 45 degrees.

4. Breathe in deeply, and place your hands on your hips.

5. Bend forward at the hips as you go hinge over the front right foot. At some point, your spine will start to round, which means you need to pull back a bit. You don't want it round.

6. Breathe out and take a moment to figure out what you want to do with your left hand; it can go outside the right foot, inside it, or just beneath your right shoulder.

7. Take a deep breath in and let your right hand go to your sacrum to check that it's nice and even.

8. Breathe out with your hand where it is as you twist your upper body so that your chest is out and open to your right-hand side. If you notice you're losing the even level of your sacrum, you can fix this by either shifting your left hip backward or pulling your right hip forward.

9. Take a deep breath as you raise your right hand to the sky, so your chest is really open now. The right shoulder should be in alignment with the left one.

10. Breathe out and look up to the sky at your extended fingertips.

11. Remain in this position for a few deep breaths or for as long as a minute.

12. Gently untwist your torso while breathing out to come out of the pose.

You can then do the same thing on the other side. Please make sure that you plant your heel firmly in the ground to don't lose your balance or hurt yourself as you do this pose.

Utkatasana – The Chair Pose

Chair pose.

This pose is also called the standing squat, power pose, or thunderbolt pose. Here's how to do it:

1. Start off by standing straight and tall. Your big toes should be in contact with each other. Root yourself firmly into the ground. Both hands should be by your sides.

2. Bend both knees. You want to keep going until your thighs are just about parallel to the ground. Both feet should be together, although it's okay if there's a slight separation between them. If that's the case, you need to make sure that an equal distance separates your knees.

3. To be sure that you're as low as you should be, you can check by brushing the tips of your fingers against the mat.

4. Now, remaining in that position, raise your arms to the sky.

5. Hold the pose for 5 breaths or 10 if you're feeling beastly.

6. Take a deep breath in, straighten both legs, and rise through your arms to come out of the pose.

A Quick Note

Please be aware of the fact that yoga it's not just about holding the poses. It's about keeping your attention centered on the solar plexus chakra as you move through each pose and hold it because that's what you're attempting to bring healing and balance to.

You need to think about all the information in this book when you're working with any element. In other words, rather than just practice pranayama on its own, you can incorporate it with your yoga poses, work with the breath, and the different mudras outlined. You can also work in your mudras with poses that allow you to. If you want more out of yoga, you should take a quick peek at the final chapter, where you will find a lot of moves and a whole sequence you can work with.

Chapter 7: Using Crystals and Stones

Crystals.
https://unsplash.com/photos/cVt0u781VGo

Before jumping into this, please note that crystals and gemstones aren't a substitute for proper healthcare with your medical health professional. Please don't attempt to self-diagnose or treat your symptoms using only stones. Your doctor knows best what will work for you.

The solar plexus chakra is all about being grounded. It's about self-confidence, courage, and taking the initiative. It is associated with our ability to have insight into ourselves, take responsibility for our actions, and know that we are not victims of circumstance. If you've ever felt like something is not right or that a situation will never get better, your solar plexus chakra may need some attention.

If your solar plexus chakra has gone out of balance, it can manifest as a lack of direction, feeling gutless or depressed all the time. When this happens, it's important to act on that instinct and find ways to balance out this energy center so that you can feel more grounded. Crystals and gemstones are a great way to help heal the solar plexus. But the question is, what makes these two things different from each other?

Difference between Crystals and Gemstones

Let's talk about gemstones first. Gemstones are also called gems, for short. These minerals are rather rare indeed, and often they've been polished to look good being worn as jewelry. They often have a mineral base, as is the case with rubies and diamonds, but gemstones can have organic bases as well, as is the case with amber.

Gems are considered precious or semiprecious, and it all comes down to their translucency and other things like color. Gemstones are sorted into various classes depending on how rare they are, their chemical makeup, and how they're cut. They're raw, natural, dug right from the earth, and then run through a set of processes to make them look really good.

Now let's move on to crystals. The thing about them is that while some gemstones can be crystals, no crystal is classed as a gemstone. Why is that? Well, gemstones can be crystalline in their structure, but crystals cannot take on the composition of gemstones. One of the things that makes them both seem so alike (and what confuses pretty much everyone) is that the colors of each of these stones could both be impure and pure.

It's the light that passes through them both that gives them their unique colors, which present in different ways based on the way the atoms are arranged in the stone, and that's why you get so many different colors of the same stone or crystal. For instance, you can get quartz as clear or rose-colored versions. You can also get sapphire in pink and blue. Another thing that makes the colors of these stones and crystals pure or impure is the process that jewelers use to get rid of impurities. This process works with heat, and depending on how it is applied, it can affect how expensive the crystal or stone is. Either way, it shouldn't matter because both gemstones and crystals have magickal properties that can be very useful for your chakras.

Why Crystals and Stones?

Why should you use crystals and gemstones to heal your solar plexus chakra? Crystals are one of nature's sources of raw healing power, just like plants, because they absorb sunlight rays that turn into heat and light upon coming into contact with them. The solar plexus chakra is often referred to as the power chakra, and it controls how you take action and manifest your thoughts into things that happen in your life. Many emotional issues can build up in this chakra, so it's important to keep yours strong and balanced. Crystals are a great way to heal emotional issues because they work with the body's energy systems.

Crystal and gemstone healing is an alternative medicine that incorporates the idea that these stones have healing and spiritual power properties. Some believe that crystals improve your life by strengthening chakras, the energy centers in your body. Chakras are the conduits for energy flows between your physical body, mind, and spirit. With them, you can strengthen your intentions and goals and change the energy flow within you.

Stones for Your Manipura

Lemon Quartz: The lemon quartz crystal is perfect for any solar plexus chakra work, especially if you're looking to work through issues with self-worth, control, and discipline. It's a potent stone that encourages change and will help you to manifest your desires with passion and strength. If you're feeling lethargic or dull-witted, restore your zest for life by wearing a lemon quartz necklace or carrying one in your pocket. It will lift your mood and bring out the fight in you. Paired with rhodonite and black tourmaline, lemon quartz will raise your energy levels while keeping you grounded.

Citrine: Citrine is my favorite stone to use in layouts. It's a yellow type of quartz that is nice and translucent, so it fits well with various layouts, including circular. But it also has this beautiful golden yellow color that makes you feel warm and happy. In general, citrine is a very "sunny" kind of stone with yellow or golden hues. You can also use it for wealth or abundance layouts because it's also a very "money" kind of stone. So, this is an excellent choice, no matter if you want to use it for prosperity or healing. So how do you use this stone? Citrine is a very soothing stone. You can use it to calm and relax your mind in general or prepare yourself for meditation. You can also use it for meditation. You can put a citrine in the center of your layout and then surround it with various stones that represent your chakras or meditate around it on any given day.

Yellow Jasper: Yellow jasper assists in clearing excess energy from the solar plexus chakra and helps to restore balance to this area. It will also help you maintain a healthy sense of self-worth. Sunlight yellow jasper promotes the health of your nervous system, balances your solar plexus chakra, and calms anxiety. It is also said to help you share your feelings with others constructively. The colors of sunlight yellow jasper are browns, yellows, and oranges. Its frequency is high spiritual light energy that triggers the first or root chakra located at the base of the spine. The meaning of yellow jasper is strength.

Golden Heliodor: Heliodors have a very bright and rich golden color. Their beauty makes them worthwhile to work with, even if they're not fully translucent. Heliodors help alleviate chronic conditions of the liver, gallbladder, pancreas, kidneys, and other areas of the body. They bring positive energy and vitality into your life by cleansing wounds and activating your immune system. Golden heliodor is like supercharged beryl, affecting all the chakras equally throughout your whole body. It encourages you to focus on the future and to bring out your true self. It's a gentle stone, which makes it particularly powerful for children. The heliodor is a stone of creativity that can be used to heal any chakra, and it is particularly awesome for the solar plexus.

Tiger's Eye: Tiger's eyes will protect your energy field and keep your aura strong and clear. It's said to help you gain self-confidence, making it easier for you to work on issues related to self-esteem, and helps you to become more aware of how you talk to yourself. Tiger's eye is also helpful in finding or attaining the things you want through the use of visualization. This can help you manifest your desires and know the steps needed to get from A to B.

Amber: Amber is a great stone for the solar plexus because it has both physical and emotional effects. Did you know that amber is fossilized tree resin? Amber helps to heal and balance the body on an emotional level, which can make it helpful to fight depression or anxiety. It also makes for a great solar plexus chakra healing talisman because of its grounding effects. Amber is a protective stone that will help you to shield your energy field from unwanted negative energies.

Sunstone: Sunstone is a grounding stone that helps the solar plexus chakra balance the heart chakra. It's also one of my favorite stones to create energy, both positive energy and energy for manifestation. It's also a great stone to help you reach your goals and dreams. If you're in a slump or feeling blocked, wear sunstone to help bring out your inner happy self again. It will give you a boost of sunshine and happiness to help you reconnect with your joy of living.

Sunstone is a stone that stimulates metabolism, and it's also a great stone if you have an underactive thyroid. It energizes the thyroid and helps it to function better. Sunstone is also one of my favorite stones to help with emotional issues. This can be related to depression, insomnia, or self-esteem issues in particular.

Yellow Tourmaline: Yellow tourmaline is a wonderful stone for the solar plexus chakra. It's a stone that allows you to be your own best friend and support yourself as you achieve your dreams. Yellow tourmaline is a very spiritual stone, so it will help you feel grounded even if you're working on things with a spiritual or metaphysical slant. It will help you feel stable and confident in your own abilities, which will help your energy shine more brightly.

Pyrite: Pyrite is a stone that's said to help the solar plexus chakra balance emotions. It supports healing and can aid in digestion, so it can help with chronic digestion or problems with the intestines. It aids by balancing the nervous system and alleviating pain. It will also cause you to be more aware of your own emotional state.

Mookaite: Mookaite will help you to feel more relaxed, happy, and upbeat. It's a great stone for the solar plexus chakra because it will make you more aware of your feelings. Mookaite can make it easier for you to speak out even if you're afraid of embarrassing yourself in front of others.

When You Buy Your Stones

When you buy a new gemstone, you trust that it was properly cut and graded. It's up to the merchant to know if the gem has been cut correctly and if it's genuine. They need to be able to tell the quality of cuts without actually having their own cutter on staff.

While you can't always know what the gem has gone through in its life, it's important to make sure the gem is cleaned often and kept in a safe environment. When you're buying from an online retailer, it's important to know how they keep their stones since they don't have any cleaning staff on call. Digital photos of the stone are good because they help show its clarity, transparency, and color. You can usually see the inclusions, major scratches, and other defects that may not be visible to the naked eye. A professional gemologist will often have a loupe (a magnifying glass) to help see these fine details. You can also request a physical inspection of the stone you're buying before you make a purchase just to be sure.

When you get your new stone home, it's important to keep it away from any moisture, heat, or direct sunlight because these things can cause your precious stone to fade or change color. Keep it in a soft pouch or an airtight bag while traveling. Keep it in a velvet-lined box or pouch with a desiccant pack to soak up any moisture when you're at home. It's also important to clean your gemstone regularly.

When you clean your stone, it's important to be careful with your tools so you don't scratch the surface. Never use household cleaners or window cleaners. If your stone is too dirty or has had surface dirt on it for too long, it may not be worth cleaning – this can also cause damage to gemstones as well. Also, make sure that the gemstone doesn't get scratched in everyday life.

How to Cleanse Your Crystals and Gemstones

Crystals and gemstones are beautiful, precious objects imbued with healing properties. They can also hold a lot of negativity from a person's energy or environmental factors like pollution. It's important to cleanse them periodically so they're free from negative energy, which can be achieved through some easy techniques.

1. Gather together crystals or gemstones that you want to cleanse and use a piece of white paper or parchment to place them on.

2. Focus on your crystals or gems while saying: "I cleanse and charge this crystal" or "I charge this stone with love and cleansing. Thank you." The charged crystal or gemstone will absorb the energy of your words and receive the cleansing process.

3. Hold a large quartz crystal in your hand, and then with your other hand, grasp the left side of it at its base and imagine you're pulling off the skin of negative energy with your right hand and throwing it away. This is done to remove negative vibrations and thoughts that might have attached to the stone or stored in it due to environmental factors like pollution or radiation.

4. Hold the crystal or gemstone in your hand and focus on a pink light coming from your heart chakra and streaming through your hand into the stone to infuse it with love and warmth. Imagine purifying white light entering your body and surrounding you completely. When you feel complete, imagine the energy being absorbed into the crystal or gemstone, so it's renewed with positive, loving energy.

5. After cleansing, you can cleanse your crystals and gemstones using this method as often as you like.

6. Keep them on your altar to charge them for the week, or make sure you keep them close to you by placing them in a pouch in your wallet so it absorbs the energy of your intention.

You can also cleanse them by burying them in the earth for 24 hours, washing them with saltwater or water from the sea, placing them under the sun or under the moon, or burying them with potted plants. You can also light some sage and pass the stones and crystals through the smoke. After you're finished cleansing them, you can now work on your solar plexus chakra with them. Here are several ways you can work with them:

1. Sit with them in your hands as you meditate.

2. Place them on your lap (if you're sitting) or around your head (if you're lying down) while you perform your meditation and mudras.

3. Place them around you as you practice your pranayama.

4. Place them around you while you do your yoga poses.

5. You can also just meditate on them by looking at them and focusing on everything you see and sense from them.

6. You can wear them as jewelry or carry them with you everywhere you go.

Chapter 8: Manipura Aromatherapy

Before we begin this chapter, please note that aromatherapy isn't meant to be used to cure disease and pain but should be used as a supplement to whatever treatment you are recommended to take by your professional medical practitioner. Please do not resort to using or ingesting essential oils to heal or fix anything you think may be wrong due to what you learned from this chapter.

The Ins and Outs of Oils and Smells

Aromatherapy is a form of alternative medicine in which fragrant plants, their essential oils, and related compounds are used for healing. It is based on the premise that the sense of smell gives access to the part of the brain where memories are stored and to primitive centers of emotion and instinct.

Aromatherapy involves the use of essential oils as a form of medicine. Essential oils are complex mixtures of chemical compounds derived from various plant parts. The oils used in aromatherapy were first extracted from the plant through steam distillation or cold pressing methods. Today, essential oils can be refined using various techniques, including distillation, expression, or expression with subsequent crystallization (decoction).

Essential oils are very volatile. This means that they tend to evaporate easily and disperse into the air. They are soluble in alcohol and vegetable oils – but not so much in water. However, this can be resolved by mixing essential oils with a "carrier oil" or a "base oil" to make an aromatherapy massage oil or a diluted aromatherapy skin spray. The base provides a medium for transporting the active ingredients in the essential oils. It also provides a feel and odor of the oil to not smell like alcohol. The base oils used for this purpose are generally chosen for their similarity to the essential oils, but they can be substituted for each other to produce different effects.

The therapeutic effects of aromatherapy are produced by inhaling a volatile substance that is absorbed through the olfactory epithelium in the olfactory mucosa in the upper respiratory tract. As a result, the essential oils can pass through the mucosa and reach the local blood circulation. Because of their high vapor pressure, they are transported by the blood to various organs such as the brain, heart, and lungs.

The essential oils contained in aromatherapy skin sprays or massage oils are absorbed through the skin and mucous membranes. The diffusion of essential oils into the bloodstream is promoted by diffusion through a layer of skin oil under the epidermis. The essential oils are introduced into different regions of the body that are not sensitive to their volatile natural state. The skin or mucous membranes combine with the essential oil to produce a complex mixture, including carriers for other plant parts. Once released into the body, essential oils interact with receptors in organelles of respiratory, cardiac, skeletal muscles, brain cells, and receptor molecules. The blood then transports this complex mixture of plant parts, carriers, and other substances to various parts of the body.

Aromatherapy is based on the premise that our brains associate scents with emotions, physical reactions, memories, places, or people. Based on this principle, essential oils used in aromatherapy have been reported to positively affect behavior and emotions through the sense of smell.

The main goal of aromatherapy is to improve relaxation, reduce stress, and alter moods. The positive effects of aromatherapy on physiological functions such as heart rate, blood pressure, breathing rate, and respiration are also claimed. Aromatherapy can be used in many different ways, and we're going to talk about how it can help you heal and balance your solar plexus chakra for the better. What oils work well for this chakra and why?

Aromatherapy and Your Solar Plexus Chakra

There are several ways you can work with essential oils to help you balance the energy of your Manipura. If you have an overactive Manipura, then you would be better off working with oils that are cooling with feminine, yin elements. If you notice that your solar plexus chakra is a little too active, you can work with a warming, yang oil instead. Let's look at the different oils that can help you restore regular activity to this energy center without further ado.

Ginger: It helps with digestion and stimulates the function of your stomach and liver. Not only that, but it can soothe a headache and fight nausea. It is also known to relax your throat muscles. Some other benefits of the ginger essential oil include treating acid reflux, reducing inflammation, and helping to beat insomnia in bed. How does it help your solar plexus chakra and its energies? The ginger essential oil can help to relieve symptoms of depression, anxiety, and stress by increasing serotonin levels in the brain. Also, ginger essential oil stimulates circulation and enhances the heart's health. It is not only a powerful food with powerful antioxidants, but it can also help you detox your body and help you if you have already been exposed to toxins in your environment. You can also use ginger essential oil to relieve migraines, facial tightness, and neck tension. You may be wondering how ginger essential oil can help your solar plexus chakra. When you use it to reduce anxiety, it naturally helps your positivity levels.

Lemon: You can use lemon in your cooking or juice it. You can also add lemon essential oil to a bath to allow it to relax your body and mind. The lemon essential oil has powerful antioxidants and nutrients that boost your immune system, protect your heart and your brain, and let you live a healthier life. This citrus fruit is pure happiness in a bottle. Lemon essential oil's supply of vitamin C also supports the healthy development of your skin, hair, and nails. How does it help the Manipura chakra? Lemon essential oil is a mood-booster and can lift your spirits by improving your mental clarity. Also, it can help you to overcome fatigue and stress, which is why it helps you with the solar plexus chakra energies.

Black Pepper: You can use black pepper essential oil to protect you from free radicals. It helps your body absorb the nutrients you need to feel rejuvenated once again. It also helps with respiratory problems, but it is most commonly used as a digestive aid. Black pepper essential oil can help to promote the healthy digestion of your food and make sure that your immune system is strong and protected. How does it help the solar plexus chakra? Black pepper essential oil will help you to make the right decisions quickly and confidently. It can also promote a sense of happiness because it can help to relieve stress and boost your mood. Black pepper essential oil is also known to promote mental clarity and focus, which makes it one of the best oils for solar plexus chakra energies.

Cedarwood: You can use cedarwood essential oil in a diffuser to help relieve sore muscles and ease your mind. It will make you feel better because it has relaxing properties, but the aroma of cedarwood essential oil can clear your home of any odors and leave it smelling fresher than ever before. Cedarwood helps your body to fight off infections, but it is also known to be an antidepressant. How does it help the solar plexus chakra? Cedarwood essential oil has been known to be a good antidepressant. It can improve your mental health and let you feel relaxed and refreshed after a long stressful day. It is also known to treat respiratory infections, headaches, and any other pains that you may be experiencing in your body. How does cedarwood work to unblock your solar plexus chakra? It can help remove stagnant energy and promote trust emotions in your relationships.

Rosemary: Rosemary essential oil is known to be a natural antidepressant and is often used in aromatherapy to make you feel stronger, more confident, and focused. It also helps your body to produce more of the hormone serotonin. Rosemary's scent of pleasant freshness can help with depression because it promotes feelings of joy and trust in your life. Rosemary essential oil can help to unblock your solar plexus chakra and relieve symptoms of depression and stress. It can help you to feel good about yourself and make you feel more confident.

Chamomile: Chamomile essential oil can be used to soothe a headache, help you fall asleep, and make you feel relaxed after a long stressful day. It is also known to relieve anxiety and stress. Chamomile essential oil can also help promote clear skin, as it has anti-inflammatory properties and will build up your skin's natural defenses. Chamomile helps the body expel toxins, eases the symptoms of PMS, and promotes mental health. It will help you feel calmer and happier, which can help you with the Manipura chakra energies.

Cypress: Cypress essential oil has strong antiseptic properties that make it a powerful cleanser. It helps relieve a sore throat and earaches, but it is also known to be an antidepressant. Cypress essential oil soothes your mind by improving your mental clarity. It will also improve your mood and keep you calm throughout the day. How does it help with the solar plexus chakra? Cypress essential oil promotes feelings of happiness, confidence, and relaxation.

Geranium: Geranium essential oil helps you to relax and de-stress. It will make you feel more focused, and it can calm you down if you are experiencing anxiety. The geranium essential oil also helps your skin heal wounds by promoting cell regeneration. It will also improve your skin's texture and tone. Geranium essential oil is good for your digestion, helping you digest your food properly and promote your body the healthy growth of your body. The geranium essential oil will help you to feel positive and confident in yourself. It will also encourage feelings of happiness and joy for everyone around you, improving both your own and your loved ones' mental health.

Sandalwood: Sandalwood helps reduce depression, stress, and anxiety symptoms. It is known as one of the most calming oils because it relieves tension built up in your muscles. Sandalwood essential oil has a sweet scent and can help to improve your mood. It is also known to treat respiratory infections, asthma, and bronchitis. Sandalwood essential oil will help you to feel centered in your body, which will help you with

Manipura chakra energies.

Ylang-Ylang: Ylang-ylang essential oil has a powerful scent that can be both calming and uplifting at the same time. It is commonly used in aromatherapy to treat stress, anxiety, and depression. Ylang-ylang can also help treat respiratory infections, colds, and fevers. Ylang-ylang oil will help you to feel relaxed so that you can release tension throughout your body. You'll feel more confident in yourself and your relationships with others.

How to Meditate with Essential Oils

Essential oils are energized with the same kind of life energy that flows through your body. When you inhale essential oils during meditation, they will help you to explore your Manipura chakra.

1. Sit comfortably on a pillow or directly on the floor. You should be in a position that allows you to remain relaxed while you meditate. For example, if sitting on the floor makes your back hurt, sit on a pillow so that your posture is still straight but comfortable.

2. Close your eyes and clear your mind of all thoughts. If you find it difficult to do this, simply focus on the sound of your breath.

3. Take deep breaths, filling your lungs with oxygen. As you inhale, imagine you are receiving life energy from the earth through the top of your head. Imagine it flowing down to the soles of your feet. As you exhale, allow this life energy to flow back into the ground beneath you through the bottom of your feet.

4. While you inhale, think of the colors associated with both the sun and moon. As you exhale, think of the color yellow. Imagine that the color is filling your body and reaching your Manipura chakra, helping to unblock any blockages that you might have.

5. Feel your body relax as you breathe in this color and let it fill your body. Continue to breathe deeply until you feel relaxed and energized simultaneously.

6. Now, visualize a bright yellow light burning at the solar plexus. This bright light is your life energy, which will help you to

unblock misaligned energy in your Manipura chakra. Imagine all the cells in your body becoming illuminated, like when you use a flashlight shining through a dark room.

7. Visualize yellow sunlight filling every cell and flowing into your Manipura chakra until it feels full and glowing.

8. Be sure to breathe in and out through your nose to not interrupt the color's flow. Now bring your attention to the essential oil you're using. You should have this already applied to your jawline or collar. Only a drop or two will do. Envision that the smell of this oil is part of the yellow light.

9. Feel the light flowing into you through your nose, filling your body and reaching your Manipura chakra. Imagine the energy from the oil's scent going into your body through your chest and spreading into every cell in your body. Feel healthy and energized as they fill you with health and vitality.

10. Take a moment to enjoy this feeling of strength, warmth, and expansion.

11. Now, imagine that there is a gap between your hands. Visualize this gap as a slightly open door. A large yellow flower in the doorway that you can see but cannot touch.

12. Think of this flower as a symbol of your creative abilities. It represents your potential and can help you to achieve all of your dreams and goals once you have mastered the skills it requires.

13. Now, focus on how the essential oil's energy flows into the gap between your hands as you exhale. Feel that you are filling your body with this energy and also filling the large yellow flower with energy.

14. Visualize the flower as it starts to close, like a small door. You can see energy radiating from the flower, and it looks like a sunflower.

15. Now, visualize your Manipura chakra as a large yellow sunflower that opens up when you inhale. Feel the life force inside you expanding and growing stronger every time you breathe in.

16. Once you have visualized this for long enough to feel complete, say "Thank you" to the flower and slowly come out of your

meditation.

Ways to Incorporate Essential Oils into Other Yoga Practices

As well as being used in your meditation sessions, essential oils can be used in a wide range of yoga practices. You can use them to unblock your Manipura chakra during asanas or pranayama.

Pranayama: Adding a few drops of essential oils to your own yoga pranayamas can help you to unblock your Manipura chakra. By using your breath in this way, you'll breathe in the oil's life energy. The oil and your breath qualities will combine to create pleasant energy that will uplift and revitalize you.

Asanas: You can use essential oils in your asanas in various ways. By adding a drop to your yoga mat, you can enjoy the scent while you do your asanas. You can also add one or two drops to an unscented moisturizer and apply it before doing any practice.

If you continue to explore new ways to unblock your Manipura chakra, the energy flow through your body will increase, and you'll feel happier and more vital all day long.

Chapter 9: Diet and Nutrition

Before we begin with this chapter, please note that I'm not a nutritionist, so you should always check in with your medical health professional before you make any changes to your diet, as suggested in this chapter, especially when you have underlying conditions that could become worse.

The solar plexus chakra is related to the lower stomach. When you think about this, it makes sense that the foods that serve this region should then be mainly made up of natural products with a high amount of healthy fats and protein sources. It also means that some foods can negatively affect your emotions and experiences if they are unbalanced or unhealthy.

This chakra is responsible for your personal power, vitality, and ability to meet challenges of all kinds. It is connected to rebirth, transformation, and the process of adaptation. This chakra can control the organs of elimination and their functions as well.

If this chakra is balanced as the center of your metabolism, it can help your awareness of balance in all areas of your life (mental, physical, and spiritual). When unbalanced, you may have problems with your relationships related to food habits and physical health.

How Yellow Foods can Unblock Your Solar Plexus Chakra

Yellow foods are related to the sun. They have a warming effect on your body, as they are stimulants that help you feel more awake and more alert. They have a healing effect on the nervous system. Foods with yellow in them often help alleviate mental fatigue and boost concentration. This means they are good for meditators and those who feel listless or uninspired.

When the solar plexus chakra is unblocked, you'll experience increased strength, vitality, and self-esteem. You'll feel more optimistic and cheerful. You'll also tend to be more self-confident, outgoing, and spontaneous. In addition, you will find that you have a better memory and ability to learn new things. Yellow foods can unblock the solar plexus chakra by helping to increase your metabolism and give those important mental faculties all the energy they need to burn brightly regardless of age or lifestyle factors. They are full of vitamins A and C as well as beta carotene.

The reason yellow foods work so wonderfully well at restoring balance and proper function to your solar plexus chakra is because it shares the same color as that energy center. This is no coincidence, you see. It works out this way because there was a correspondence between the color of the foods and the color of your chakra. Color is an expression of energy, and so the fact that they share the same colors tells you that these things are energetically matched and will be of great benefit to each other. You can wear a yellow shirt and trust that it will help you with your solar plexus chakra, or you can stay in a room that is painted yellow and soak in the vibrations of the color, allowing it to work on every block that you're experiencing, if you do this consciously, of course. It is also the same reason that most of the gemstones and crystals that we've mentioned happened to be yellow, or at least close to it. Everything in life has been intelligently designed in this way by source energy.

One thing you have to understand about food is that it is energy. I'm not just talking about this in the literal sense of the word, where you know that if you eat food, you'll feel stronger and have the energy to do stuff. I am talking about the fact that food is light and life. It is a sad state of affairs that these days most people will eat even when they're not hungry and eat more than they need to at every sitting. The end result is obesity and all other related diseases. This is not how we were designed to live as human beings. You know how the saying goes. Eat to live, don't live to eat.

Eating Mindfully

It is a very good idea to decide here and now that you will eat mindfully no matter what. It shouldn't just be about empowering your solar plexus chakra, although that is a very good thing to do as well. When you eat the right foods, you won't even have issues with this chakra - or at least whatever problems you have will not be caused by the foods you're consuming. So, now, make a commitment to yourself to do better with your diet and nutrition.

Every food has its natural color for a reason. What is the energy of that color? When you consume the food, it will naturally affect the chakras that are connected to the color of the food being eaten. However, when you choose to eat these foods mindfully, you can supercharge the energy you receive from them and get even more radical benefits.

When you eat mindfully, you focus on how the food feels and tastes in your mouth. You're not in a hurry to chew and swallow, and you're not distracted by the television or a book or something. You're very aware that the food that you are taking in is light and energy and that it has the power to change your being radically on a physical, spiritual, and mental level. So, if you want to eat mindfully, you should go slow and pay attention to the colors and textures of the food. You can also visualize while eating. Imagine, if you'll, that the food you are chewing is a yellow light that goes right down through your esophagus into your solar plexus chakra. See and feel the food supercharging that chakra and clearing all blockages with which you may struggle. When you eat in this manner, you'll discover that your food does far more than simply keep your body going.

Foods for the Manipura

Consider adding the following foods to your diet:

- Corn
- Lemon
- Natural grass-fed butter
- Bananas
- Papayas
- Pineapples
- Kombucha
- Yams
- Grapefruit
- Butternut squash
- Cumin
- Turmeric
- Chamomile
- Oats
- Mangos
- Quinoa
- Squash

Recipes for Your Manipura

Pineapple Muffins

This is a weird but absolutely divine treat that you can have either for breakfast or as a pick-me-up in the middle of the day. They pack a lot of lovely flavors and will help you start off on the right foot if you have them first thing in the morning.

You'll Need:

- ¾ cup milk
- ¼ cup melted butter

- ½ cup sugar
- 1 cup wheat flour
- 1 cup all-purpose flour
- ½ teaspoon salt
- 1 teaspoon baking powder
- 1 can of crushed pineapple (about 400 mL)
- 1 beaten egg

Instructions:

1. To prepare, preheat your oven to 375 degrees Fahrenheit.
2. Grab a large bowl and mix the salt, baking powder, flour, and sugar.
3. Drain your pineapple. Hold on to a quarter of the juice because you'll need it later.
4. Add your pineapples, milk, egg, a quarter of pineapple juice, and melted butter. Mix them until they're nicely combined.
5. Grab a muffin pan and line that up with your muffin liners.
6. Pour the mix into the tins.
7. Slide the pan into the oven and let it sit there for 30 minutes, or until you slide in a toothpick and it comes out clean.
8. Allow it to cool for a bit, and then enjoy.

Apple, Fennel, and Chickpea Salad

This is another lovely delight that you are sure to enjoy. You can prep this really quickly, and it will last you anywhere from a day to two, as long as you store it in your fridge.

You'll Need:

- Fresh basil (optional)
- ¾ cup chickpeas (should be rinsed thoroughly and then drained)
- 2 red apples (peel them, then chop them
- 2 cups of fennel (thin slices)
- ½ cup celery (thin slices)

- 1 teaspoon Dijon mustard
- 1 pinch of salt
- 1 tablespoon maple syrup
- ¼ cup plain yogurt (thick, plain)
- 2 teaspoons lemon juice

Instructions:

1. Grab a bowl and then whisk all the ingredients for your dressing together: the salt, lemon juice, maple syrup, yogurt, and mustard. You want the mix to be nice and smooth when you've finished.
2. Grab another large bowl and throw in your apple, chickpeas, celery, and fennel. Mix them properly.
3. When it's time to serve, you can simply dress the salad and mix the ingredients properly together.
4. Garnish with fresh basil if you like, and enjoy.

Chickpea Curry

This is a lovely one for the solar plexus, and it's quite the comfort meal. You can have this along with some rice or couscous if you like. Quinoa is also an option.

You'll Need:

- Rice, quinoa, or couscous (cooked)
- 1 teaspoon sriracha (if preferred)
- 1 tablespoon coconut oil
- 1 tablespoon garlic (chopped finely)
- 1 tablespoon ginger (fresh, minced)
- 1 onion (medium, sliced thin)
- 2 teaspoons tomato paste
- 2 teaspoons maple syrup
- ½ cup tomatoes (diced)
- 2 teaspoons curry powder
- 1 cup coconut milk

- ¼ teaspoon red pepper (crushed)
- ¼ cup cilantro (fresh, chopped)
- 1 can chickpeas (about 500mL, drained)
- 2 teaspoons soy sauce (low sodium)
- Salt (to taste)
- Pepper (to taste)

Instructions:

1. Grab a large saucepan and put it on the stove on medium heat.
2. Melt your coconut oil in the pan.
3. Add in your onions and cook them until they're nice and brown. This shouldn't take longer than 5 minutes, 7 minutes max.
4. Add the tomato paste, maple syrup, soy sauce, broth, red pepper, and curry. Mix that all up nicely.
5. Now throw in your chickpeas and cover the saucepan. Allow things to come together to a boil, and then lower the heat.
6. Let it simmer on low heat for the next ten minutes. You want it to cook until everything is tender. Please leave your saucepan partially open.
7. Now, add in your cilantro and milk, and let the mix simmer for five more minutes.
8. Take the saucepan off the heat, then add in your pepper, salt, and sriracha.
9. Serve this with your rice or whatever else you want.

Banana Almond Cookies

The awesome thing about this recipe is that you don't need traditional flour to make it happen. Also, they're incredibly healthy and delicious to boot! You can simply work with almonds by grinding them to the point where they resemble flour itself. You need to throw a cup or two of almonds into the blender and then blend it until you've got a very fine flour. If you don't care for blending your own nuts, you can simply buy almond flour from the store.

You'll Need:

- ½ teaspoon sea salt
- ½ teaspoon cinnamon
- 1 teaspoon baking powder
- 1 teaspoon vanilla extract
- ¼ cup brown sugar
- ¼ cup almond butter
- 1 cup almond flour
- 1 egg
- 1 banana (ripe, mashed)

Instructions:

1. Preheat your oven to 375 degrees Fahrenheit.
2. Grab a bowl, and then throw in all your dry ingredients. Mix thoroughly.
3. Grab another bowl and throw in the wet stuff. Mix properly.
4. Working with the good process, mix the dry mix and wet mix until it's all nice and smooth. Mix them together by beating.
5. Now, grab this dough and place it onto your baking sheet. Ideally, you want to use 2 tablespoons of dough for each cookie so that the results are nice and even.
6. Pop them into the oven and let them sit for 15 minutes. If you like them crisp, then let them sit in there for longer but be careful not to burn them.
7. Wait for them to cool, and then enjoy.
8. To store the leftovers, please place them in a Ziploc bag or a Tupperware container to retain their delicious texture.

Solar Smoothie

This smoothie is not only ridiculously delicious, but it's going to do wonders for your Manipura as you drink it consciously.

You'll Need:

- 2 kiwis (fresh, chopped)
- ½ cup kale
- ½ an avocado (chopped)
- ¼ of a lime (fresh, squeezed)
- 1 cup spinach (fresh)
- 1 teaspoon spirulina
- ¾ cup coconut water/almond milk/cold water
- Ice (just a handful will do)

Instructions:

Throw all of this into your blender and blend until you have a smooth mix. Drink and enjoy right away. This is a good one to have with your cookies.

Tips for Mindful Eating

First of all, always begin your meals with a healthy dose of raw foods. Start with fresh fruit and vegetables. You can also add some sprouted grains and whole grains like quinoa or brown rice to your diet. They are very healthy, but they are also more filling and satisfying.

Food is not a mere necessity. It is a way to communicate with our environment, other people, and even the earth itself. When you go for a meal, consider what you're about to eat and why eating is important to you. In the end, recognize that our food comes from Mother Earth, so it's important that we show gratitude by eating consciously.

Enjoy every sensory experience. By being aware of each movement involved in eating, you are participating in the meal rather than just ingesting it. When you do this, life can become pleasurable and satisfying. For example, you can use chopsticks instead of a fork. When eating with chopsticks, your hands must be clean so take a moment before the meal to wash them thoroughly. After that, hold the chopsticks firmly in one hand while picking up the food with another hand. Now bring the food to your mouth. You can make the meal flow by watching what the food does as it travels from hand to mouth. With practice, you will discover how to enjoy every sensory experience in eating and be fully present with each moment.

Use your hands. Food is sometimes about tactile pleasure (such as raw food) or taste. Whatever your favorite way of eating, you can use that sense to connect more deeply with food. Certain cultures still eat with their hands to this day, and honestly, food just hits different when you eat with nothing but clean hands. The taste of the food doesn't have to compete with the taste of metal or plastic or wood, and you're more conscious of the process of eating this way. Try it with loved ones and notice how much more connected you are to each other when you eat with just your washed hands.

When eating, relax your shoulders and neck and breathe fully to help you enjoy the sensations of contact with food. Pay attention to the taste of the food on your tongue and explore what it can do to you on a deeper level.

Eat slow. When we eat quickly, we fill our stomachs too quickly, creating an unbalanced gut which can lead to digestive disorders such as indigestion and heart disease. Eating slow also gives the body more time to digest the food and regulate cellular processes. Slow eating will especially benefit people with chronic stress since they tend to eat too fast.

Eat *happy foods*. There are a lot of studies around the benefits of bright light in our diet, but there is some evidence that eating *happy foods* that make us feel joyful may have health benefits as well. One study found that eating cookies made people feel good. The mood boost of eating the food may contribute to emotional health and help you to cope with stress. These foods are generally very nutritious, so they offer a bonus in that way. A diet rich in these "happy foods" can help us cope with stress and contribute to our physical health. Just make sure your happy foods aren't *junk food*.

Love your leftovers. Plan your meals so that leftovers can be eaten for several days in a row. This way, you'll get to eat the same food without getting bored and without having waste. Legumes and rice are great for savory leftovers, and fruits are delicious cold. Make sure to pick foods that reheat or warm well to enjoy them every day.

Chapter 10: Solar Plexus Seven-Day Routine

At last, we have come to the final chapter of this book. Doubtless, you have just received a lot of information, and you may be wondering what to do with it all. Where do you even begin? You have absolutely no reason to fuss because you are about to get a seven-day routine that will help you figure out what to do to help your solar plexus chakra find balance. It is recommended that you be consistent in your practice for this to work.

Some people, for instance, will not do anything for several days in a row, only to try to pile in five days' worth of practice into a few hours in one day. This is absolutely not the way to go because you will not get consistent results this way – if you do get any results. Now, sometimes life will get in the way. You may need to attend a special event, or you may have to deal with an emergency at work or with your kids. In this case, it is completely okay if you have to skip one day, but the important thing is you don't set yourself back by thinking you must start again from day one.

There are two simple rules that you can follow to make sure you stay consistent to get the results you want for your solar plexus. Rule number one is that you must not skip more than one day in a row. Rule number two is that you must not start over from day one when you skip a day. It is far more beneficial for you to carry on as if you hadn't missed a beat because you will feel more motivated to continue than if you feel like you have to keep starting from the beginning and you've not made any progress since.

Another important thing for you to keep in mind: you will unblock or balance your solar plexus chakra at your own rate. In other words, you must never try to compare yourself with someone else. Attempting to make comparisons is a recipe for disaster. Besides, you will not get a medal for being the fastest one to open or unlock your solar plexus chakra. This is not a race, and you should not treat it like one!

I hammer on about this point of not turning this into some sort of weird competition because if you do, you'll put unnecessary pressure on yourself to perform. The trouble with doing this is when it comes to spiritual and energetic matters, things will happen in their own time, and they absolutely *cannot be rushed.* If you hurry through this process, you run the very real risk of overcorrecting, for starters. Or, on the flip side, you might find that you were not experiencing any results at all, which may dissuade you from bothering to pursue this path of finding spiritual balance. You must be patient with yourself; try not to keep track of someone else's progress or to keep up with them. This is a journey you must make on your own.

Also, remember that some days you may experience a shift within yourself energetically, while other days, you may not notice anything at all. There is nothing unusual about this. Do not fall into the trap of assuming that nothing is happening because you've not noticed anything yet. As a matter of fact, it is not uncommon to come out of a meditation process only to go and scream your head off at something that you thought you would be able to handle. Please always be gentle and loving toward yourself because the important thing is that you showed up to make it happen.

As much as possible, you should stick with the routine we've outlined here. However, if you notice that you were intuitively led to do something else, please do not ignore your gut because there is a reason you are getting that nudging. Your soul knows even better than a book what it is you need at any given point in time, and so if you feel led to do something other than what you should be doing for that day or that session, go ahead and do so.

You must embark on this routine with no expectations in mind about what should or should not happen. Having expectations is a recipe for disappointment, and you do not want that at all because it will impede your progress. The correct attitude to adopt instead is one of open-mindedness where you are fine whether or not something happens. When you simply keep your mind open and free of expectations, you allow your subconscious and your soul free reign to do what needs to be done to correct the imbalances and blockages you're dealing with in your solar plexus chakra. You also keep yourself from falling into the trap of trying to form-fit your experience into some preconceived notion you have.

Here's a final note on visualization. If you find that you have trouble imagining or envisioning something in your mind's eye, then this is where you want to pay attention. Instead of picturing an actual image for right now, what you can do is simply sense the energy that is being discussed. For instance, if you cannot envision a yellow ball or a yellow flower that's opening and closing, you can simply imagine the energy connected to your solar plexus chakra and feel it growing larger or smaller, stronger, or stronger weaker. In the long run, however, it is much more beneficial for you to learn to train your imaginal faculties to reproduce pictures with accuracy in your mind.

A simple exercise to train your imaginal sight is to pick a simple object around you. Now study just one small section of that object and look at it closely as you can, noticing every blemish in every detail. After doing this, close your eyes and try to replicate the section you have studied in your mind. Open your eyes once more and study another small section of that object. Then close your eyes and recreate that new section. The better you get at this, the more of the object's surface area you can cover. You can begin doing this for entire rooms full of things with time. If you intend to supercharge your meditation and visualization exercises, this is a practice worth doing to have true, concrete, and rapid results with your chakras.

Day 1

1. When you wake up in the morning, chant RAM out loud for five minutes before doing anything else.

2. Take five more minutes to practice the bumblebee breath.

3. Later in the day, take ten minutes to contemplate the following affirmations: "I am at peace with myself. My soul is at rest." Say these words out loud, and then give yourself 30 seconds in between each repetition to really mull over what those words mean to you.

4. Do the rudra mudra while meditating with some essential oil for the solar plexus chakra on your collar or your jaw, just beneath both ears. Hold this mudra for five minutes while you visualize energy moving from both hands and from the oil straight to your solar plexus chakra.

5. Do the bow pose for five minutes while practicing the bumblebee breath. Take breaks as needed during this time.

Reflection: *What does peace mean to me?*

Day 2

1. When you wake up this morning, chant the OO vowel sound first. Do this out loud and for five minutes.

2. As soon as you step out of bed, go right into the chair pose. Do that for five minutes, taking breaks between five or ten breaths in the pose.

3. Later in the day, sit with your hands in the Agni mudra as you contemplate the following affirmations and what they mean to you: "I see the beauty in myself. I see the beauty in everyone."

4. Perform the guided visualization meditation for balancing your Manipura (from chapter five). It will help if you record the meditation in your voice first, then play it back.

5. Sit with a crystal if you've got one for your solar plexus chakra, and practice the bumblebee breath as you breathe its energy into your solar plexus chakra and breathe out all blocks and negative thoughts.

Reflection: *What makes me feel powerful?*

Day 3

1. Start your day off by saying and contemplating the following affirmation: "I allow myself to be at ease. I flow with one and all." Do this for ten minutes, and think about what that really means to you.

2. As soon as you step out of bed, take five minutes to flow from the chair pose to the revolved triangle pose. Remember to follow the instructions as outlined in chapter six, and please take breaks in between.

3. Apply your preferred essential oil to your preferred spots, and then sit in meditation for ten minutes while your hands are doing the guru mudra. Do the bumblebee breathe throughout and envision yellow energy from your hands and the oil feeding your solar plexus chakra.

4. Prepare a solar plexus meal (you can just munch on one food item if that's all you've got or if it's easier) and eat it mindfully. Imagine its yellow light going down into your solar plexus to sort it out.

5. As you fall asleep tonight, chant RAM repeatedly until the Sandman comes.

Reflection: *How can I play more every day?*

Day 4

1. Begin your day by chanting RAM for five minutes, then switch to OO for five minutes.

2. For the next ten minutes, alternate between the boat pose, chair pose, and revolving triangle pose. Please take breaks as needed and don't push harder than necessary. Harder doesn't mean better.

3. Prepare a meal for your solar plexus chakra. Do so mindfully, and then eat it mindfully. Thank it for nourishing and replenishing this energy center.

4. Do the guided visualization for unblocking your solar plexus chakra (from chapter five) with crystals in your hand and your

essential oil. Use the bumblebee breath.

5. Chant the following mantra for ten minutes while doing the pushan mudra: "Play is my energy; play is who I am."

Reflection: *What is my life's purpose? What matters the most to me in life?*

Day 5

1. Begin your day by chanting OO for ten minutes while your hands are in the guru mudra.

2. Contemplate and repeat the following affirmation today for just ten minutes: "Fun and fulfillment are my birthright." You can augment this with essential oil of your choosing.

3. Meditate on a crystal today and visualize it infusing you with its energy for five minutes.

4. For at least five minutes, do something creative. You could sketch something, write something, imagine things around you have a different color than they actually do... it doesn't matter. Just create.

5. End your day chanting RAM for fifteen minutes, then go right to bed.

Reflection: *Who am I? What is my true nature?*

Day 6

1. Begin your day by chanting RAM for fifteen minutes. Keep your hands in the Agni mudra.

2. Prepare a meal for your Manipura. Place your hands over it before you eat and mindfully chant RAM. As you do this, envision yellow energy coming out of your mouth and palms and infusing the food with powerful yellow light. Chant just five times, and then eat mindfully.

3. Do the bow, chair, and revolving triangle pose for just ten minutes, alternating from one to the next. Please make sure you take breaks in between. Holding a pose for longer than needed doesn't mean faster or better results.

4. Do something creative for ten minutes. Please don't judge whatever you're doing. Remember, you are fun. So have fun with this.

5. End your day by chanting OO in your mind as you drift off to sleep.

Reflection: *Where does my true power lie?*

Day 7

1. Chant RAM in your mind for 7 minutes while doing the rudra mudra, then chant OO in your mind for another 7 minutes, switching to the guru mudra.

2. Practice the bumble bee breath while you envision yourself as being nothing but a beautiful ball of yellow energy for ten minutes.

3. Do something creative for 15 minutes. If you notice that you've spent more than 15 minutes and you still want to keep going, do that. Stop as soon as you sense you should, instead of trying to force it.

4. Prepare a meal, bless it with both hands by infusing it with energy as you chant OO, and then eat it mindfully. Remember to thank it for nourishing you when you're done.

5. End your day once more, imagining yourself to be a ball of bright yellow light for fifteen minutes this time while you do the bumblebee breath and the Agni mudra. You may supercharge this with your crystals and oils.

Reflection: *How do I express my divine creativity more and more each day?*

If you really want to have explosive results, you can repeat this routine for the next 21 to 30 days and see where you wind up. If you stick with this, you'll find that you're a completely different person by the time you've finished! I haven't yet met one person who did not experience dramatic changes for the better when doing this routine. The key here is *consistency*. Know that there will be some days when you really don't feel like doing any of this stuff. However, it is worth it just to do it anyway. You have absolutely nothing to lose and everything to gain!

Bonus: From Manipura to the Upper Chakras

So, you've learned that it is important for you to establish a clear and strong foundation by first working with your root chakra, moving up to your sacral chakra, and then moving to your solar plexus chakra. No doubt you are already aware that other energy centers need to be addressed as well. Just because this book only addresses the solar plexus chakra does not mean that is where you should end your journey toward developing your energy self. So, I figured that I would give you a bonus section in this book that would allow you to continue your work with your energy centers so that you don't feel like you may just stagnate upon clearing the solar plexus. Without further ado, let's take a quick look at the heart chakra, throat chakra, third eye chakra, and crown chakra.

The Heart Chakra

The heart chakra is the center or root of loving-kindness and compassion in most people's systems. The heart regulates feelings, emotions, love, and relationships. It tells us what we value most in life and how to treat ourselves when we don't feel like our needs are being met. This chakra is considered to be the center of our conscious mind. Its color is green.

Our hearts are where we store our memories and our relationships. Our hearts also hold a lot of pain and sadness from events that may have happened in our lives, but this pain can be transmuted into a positive vibration and heart-based energy. The key to opening the heart chakra is forgiveness. Forgiveness is an ability that most people cannot tap into because it requires an act of forgiveness within ourselves first.

The ability to forgive others is a powerful tool for spiritual growth, but the ability to forgive ourselves gives us a true sense of freedom and self-love, which is the bonding glue that can connect all people.

A good way to express love and compassion in our daily lives is to show kindness and gratitude toward others less fortunate than ourselves. Think of someone in your life who has helped you retain some sort of grounding or stability that you have needed during a difficult time in your life.

Symptoms of a Blocked Heart Chakra

- A sense of loss or emptiness in the heart

- Difficulty with accepting oneself as a person

- Feeling like something is holding you back from being who you want to be

- Difficulty being loving and compassionate toward other people

- Lack of self-love and self-care, low level of positive emotion in life.

How to Balance Your Heart Chakra

- Engage in acts of kindness toward yourself and others

- Show self-care by reading, meditating, working in your garden, and doing things that you enjoy doing

- Be aware of your own needs, desires, and wants. Express yourself when you need to.

- Laugh a little more and set aside time for humor each day

- Practice forgiveness toward yourself and others

The Throat Chakra

The throat chakra is the center of self-expression, communication, and creativity. This chakra's color is blue, and it regulates what we can create and release into the world, whether it is poetry or a painting. The throat chakra also regulates our ability to express love through words. Our vibrational frequency around speaking our truth and communicating with others comes from this center of the body. The throat chakra is also the creative writing, singing, and music center. Recording that creative self-expression on film or in journaling can help us clarify our path and bring more self-love into our lives. If you feel stymied or unsure what direction to go in life and your creativity is blocked, try doing a little more intuitive writing.

The key to opening the throat chakra is self-expression. We express ourselves through speaking our truths, communicating with others, singing, or creative writing. It is important to express yourself in some way so you can free the creative energy that exists within all of us. This will help us feel better about ourselves and open our hearts further.

Symptoms of a Blocked Throat Chakra

- Low confidence in yourself
- Lack of self-expression
- A feeling of being imprisoned or blocked in some way
- Difficulty embracing your true identity
- Have a sense of not being seen for who you really are by others.
- Feeling like you are playing a role or need to conform to the expectations of others.
- Feel like your life is not going anywhere, or you don't know what direction to go in life.
- Lack of passion and inspiration in life.

How to Balance Your Throat Chakra

- Visualize the color blue emanating from your throat chakra

- Write down what you are feeling, speak what is coming to you, and sing or dance.

- Find time for solitude where you can be by yourself and be quiet

- Do things that make you feel creative. Get your hands dirty in the garden, spend time with nature, or go on a creative walk

- Spend more time speaking only the truth and meaning what you say. Be careful to avoid gossiping and spreading rumors.

- Find someplace to express yourself creatively, whether it's in a journal, a blog, or artwork.

The Third Eye Chakra

This is also known as the third eye chakra, and its color is indigo. The third eye chakra is located at the center of the forehead and regulates our intuition, imagination, inspiration, and insight. Third eye energy connects us to our divine nature and heaven. When this area is blocked, it can lack intuition or imagination because we do not get those messages from our higher self. When we are not able to access our intuition, it leads to a lack of direction in life.

The key to opening the third eye chakra is meditation. This center of our body regulates our imagination, psychic ability, and creativity. Intuition is a powerful tool that we can tap into each day to help us understand what we need in our lives. Our intuition provides us with messages from the universe, and it helps us decide what direction to take in life. It also helps us interpret dreams, visions, and hunches that can lead us down a new path or show us something important about ourselves.

Many people have been taught to ignore their intuition and have become skeptical in nature because they grew up in a culture that taught them not to believe in psychic ability. But it doesn't mean that we cannot harness the power of our intuition. As a result, we can become confused and not know what is right for us anymore. We may believe that being psychic is something only other people do or that we are crazy for thinking like this. Instead, we can practice daily meditation to help us connect with our own intuition. When we are in tune with our intuition and receive messages from the universe, it is more likely that we will receive guidance from the universe instead of being led down a detour.

Symptoms of a Blocked Third Eye Chakra

- A lack of connection with your intuition
- A lack of imagination
- Lack of creativity and imagination
- A lack of being able to trust in what you feel and your gut instincts.
- Difficulty becoming inspired by ideas and thoughts.
- Feeling like life is a little boring or mundane.
- Feeling that there is no point to anything you do because nothing makes a difference.
- Lack of feeling connected with the world.
- Feeling like you lack purpose in life or don't know why you are here. You may feel disconnected from the world around you.
- Feeling like you are missing out on certain opportunities or insights in life.

How to Balance Your Third Eye Chakra

- Start meditating daily
- Visualize the color indigo or turquoise emanating from your third eye chakra.
- Spend time in nature. The power of the universe flows through all living things in the natural world.
- Do something creative like painting, drawing, singing, or dancing.

- Write a journal entry of your dreams and visions; do intuitive writing.

- Pay attention to your dreams because they are messages from your higher self to help you on your journey in life.

- Do something creative like writing, painting, singing, or dancing.

The Crown Chakra

The crown chakra is located at the top of the head and regulates our connection to the higher realms and the divine. When this center is blocked, it can feel disconnected from the spirit or not have a connection with God. Those who do not have a connection with their spirit may feel that something is missing from their lives. People who are blocked at this center will feel disconnected from themselves, others, and their true divine nature.

The key to opening the crown chakra is about feeling connected to the world and with yourself. People have not been taught to embrace their true divine nature in the past. This can confuse us about who we are and why we are here. To learn more about our divine nature and connect with it, we can begin a transformation journey of self-discovery that opens up our hearts and our minds forever.

To help open your crown chakra, you can visualize the color purple or pink emanating from it. Remember, the color violet is one of the strongest colors for opening your crown chakra.

Symptoms of a Blocked Crown Chakra

- Feeling disconnected from yourself or your spirit

- Feeling like you don't exist in this world.

- Feeling like you are not connected to anyone or anything

- Feeling lost, like you don't know what to do or who you are. You may feel hopeless and worthless.

- A lack of being able to connect with others on a deeper level.

- Difficulty finding your purpose in life.

How to Balance Your Crown Chakra

- Start embracing your true divine nature as a spiritual being having an earthly experience. This can help you learn more about yourself and why you are here.

- Start doing something creative like painting, singing, dancing, or writing. This will help you to open up your spirit and feel more connected with it.

- Spend time in nature. The power of the universe flows through all living things in the natural world.

Conclusion

You've finally come to the end of this book, and I'm fairly certain that you've learned a whole lot and are about to change in so many ways you could never have imagined possible. This is good. Embrace it! It's one thing to know all you know now, but it's another thing entirely to put it into practice. That's where the real magic lives, you know.

The fact that you took the time to read through this book and intend to do something about your current state says a lot about you. You're the sort of person who knows when it's time to do something different and, clearly, when you make up your mind, you'll make it happen. I'm so happy and proud that you've come this far, and I can't wait for you to see the way you become radically different.

Choosing to work on your solar plexus chakra will inevitably affect the other chakras, which means you'll experience some other interesting and pleasant side effects that we didn't cover in this book. It's different for everyone, but it's always worth it. Please practice the seven-day routine, and after you've done that once or twice, you can switch things up. The point is, you should never stop taking care of your energy body, not if you want to enjoy your life more than you ever thought possible. I get the sense you already know that, and that's what you're already planning. You now have all you need. Now go make the change, and you'll love who you become. That's a guarantee.

Part 4: Heart Chakra

The Ultimate Guide to Opening, Balancing, and Healing Anahata

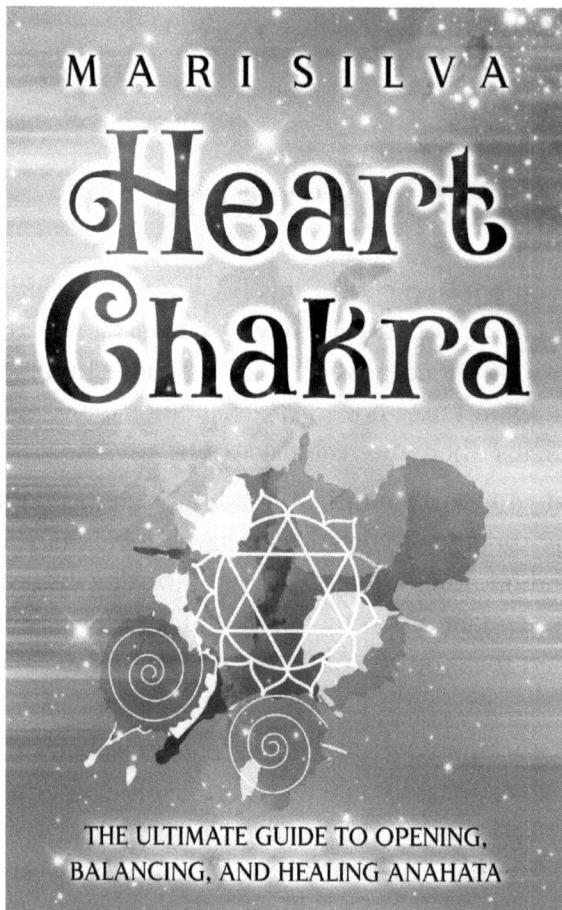

MARI SILVA

Heart Chakra

THE ULTIMATE GUIDE TO OPENING,
BALANCING, AND HEALING ANAHATA

Introduction

You've probably heard about the chakra system if you're into spirituality and meditation or have considered trying out energy healing sessions. You may have also learned that they play a significant role in revitalizing the body and promoting energy flow. All healers stress the importance of maintaining balanced and unblocked chakras because of how they affect our physical and emotional health.

The word "chakra" refers to the energy centers found throughout the body. Each chakra is associated with either a major organ or a set of nerves in the body. To maintain optimal function, these chakras have to be balanced. Many mental, emotional, and physical ailments that correspond to that specific body part occur when they get obstructed or blocked.

Although there are believed to be over 114 chakras in the body, seven main ones run along the spine. They begin at its root, extending up to the crown of the head. The heart (or Anahata chakra) is his book's main focus; it is located at the center of the chest, near the heart.

In this book, you'll learn more about the chakras and the origins of the Anahata. The first chapter covers in-depth its characteristics, symbolism, and function. Then, you'll find out what to expect if the heart chakra gets blocked and how you can determine if you need to balance yours.

We explore various methods to open your heart chakra and balance it. You'll find out all about mantras and mudras and how you can use them in your spiritual practices. The following chapter will teach you how to build a strong visualization and meditation practice for opening the Anahata. Chapter 6 covers using yoga and pranayama to balance the heart chakra. Then, you'll learn about the difference between stones and crystals and the qualities that make a stone or crystal good for Anahata, such as its color, properties, or formation. The final two chapters recommend food choices, recipes, and additions to one's diet that could help to balance the Anahata. Also, a weekly routine is provided to practice keeping opening and healing the Heart chakra. You'll also find The book also includes a bonus chapter that gives you insight regarding your possibilities now that the heart chakra is balanced and how you can move up to higher chakras.

Although highly educational and full of indispensable information, this book is also a very interesting read. It is suitable for both beginners and more experienced individuals who wish to brush up on their knowledge surrounding the Anahata. The book is very easy to understand and follow. It also includes hands-on methods and step-by-step instructions to guide you through new practices. It is the perfect read for anyone who wishes to learn more about the heart chakra and obtain extensive knowledge of balancing and unblocking it. Read on if you wish to maintain your physical, mental, emotional, and spiritual health.

Chapter 1: What Is Anahata?

Chakras.
mpan, CC0, via Wikimedia Commons:
https://commons.wikimedia.org/wiki/File:Chakras_map.svg

Before we talk about the heart chakra (Anahata), we should first understand a little more about what chakras are, their purpose, and what they do. If you are familiar with yoga or meditation, you'll have heard of them. *"Chakara"* is derived from the Sanskrit word *"Cakra,"* which means wheel or circle. According to yogis, the chakra is the center of the spiritual energy in your body.

Everyone has seven chakras located along their spine.

The Root Chakra (Muladhara Chakra)

The Sacral Chakra (Svadhishthana Chakra)

The Solar Plexus Chakra (Manipura Chakra)

The Heart Chakra (Anahata Chakra)

The Throat Chakra (Vishuddha Chakra)

The Third Eye Chakra (Ajna Chakra)

The Crown Chakra (Sahastrara Chakra)

Chakras originated between 1500 and 500 BC in India and were named by the Buddhists and Hindus. Each of the seven chakras corresponds to vital organs and nerves in the human body. Each chakra impacts an aspect of our lives, be it our emotions, mental health, physical health, or spiritual well-being, and each one is responsible for the energy flow in our bodies. This they do by giving, receiving, and storing energy.

Although chakras are invisible since they exist in the astral body, each emits a certain color. It is also believed that chakras are very small and have shapes, but no one knows exactly what that shape is. Everyone has a different idea. Some people believe that they look like ice cream cones, while others believe they are similar to spinning discs or a lotus flower. You can believe whatever you want since chakras can't be seen unless you are a psychic.

Chakras should always be open and balanced. If they are blocked or become unbalanced, this can affect you negatively and upset your emotional well-being. For instance, if your heart chakra is blocked, you'll be consumed with negative emotions like fear, anger, jealousy, or hatred. For this reason, you should maintain your chakras' balance and ensure they are always open through yoga, meditation, journaling, and exercising. When your chakras are open, you'll become more aware of their presence and how they impact every aspect of your life, including your career and personal relationships.

The Energy Body

A schematic drawing of the body showing the energy centers and channels gives you an idea of where the chakras are. They are responsible for the movement of prana (life-giving force) through the body. There are hundreds of these channels in our bodies. These channels house our chakras. Although there are hundreds of them, the seven chakras mentioned above are the biggest and most well-known ones. These energy bodies move in a circular motion which is why they are called chakras.

Chakras work as channels to distribute energy to every system in our bodies. Lifeforce energies flow unhindered when they are open and balanced. Energy should never be motionless or stagnant; it should always be moving. It is the same as water; if it is stagnant, it becomes useless and even harmful. When our energy channels (chakras) are blocked, our lifeforce energy becomes stagnant, and we begin to feel it in our body, mind, heart, and soul.

The Anahata

Anahata is a Sanskrit word; you won't find a word in the English language that can capture its exact meaning. However, it can be roughly translated to unstruck, unhurt, or unbeaten. Like all the other Chakras, Anahata originated in India and was first mentioned in the Hindu Vedas scriptures (Indian sacred books and the first literary records we have on the Indo-Aryan civilization). According to the Veda texts, Anahata is symbolized by the image of Anahata Nada (unstruck sound). The Anahata Nada is pure and created from within. It's a sound of the universe that only the heart can only create. If you open your heart and focus on the silence within, you may be able to connect to the Anahata Nad vibration, which will connect you to everything around you.

Anahata is associated with two of the most popular Hindu deities, Shakti and Shina. It is also the fourth of the seven main chakras, and being in the center of our chests places it in the perfect location to act as a bridge between the lower and upper chakras. This gives the Anahata a special role, making it stand out from other chakras. The lower chakras are responsible for our mental, emotional, and physical well-being. In contrast, the upper ones are responsible for our spiritual side, focusing on divine guidance, divine insight, and our soul's purpose. The heart chakra stands in the center between the physical world and the cosmos, or body and spirit, to integrate these energies.

Why is the Anahata the bridge between the lower and upper chakras? Because the Anahata chakra is located at the heart – which is where *every aspect of ourselves exists*. The heart connects us to ourselves, the world around us, and the spiritual world. We close our eyes to pray and reach the divine through our hearts, we connect to our spiritual side through our hearts, and we love, hate, and feel all different emotions through the heart. It is the center of our being, giving the Anahata its special role.

Air is this chakra's element, and it brings connection, love, and compassion to everything around us. Air is quite similar to love as you'll find it and feel it everywhere you go. Like the air, our minds can move freely and wander wherever they want. The Air element is associated with our thoughts, movements, feelings, and emotions.

The Anahata, just like the heart, is responsible for our emotions, soul, and our relationships with the divine, other people, and ourselves. As a result of its unique role, the heart chakra has two colors and is a fascinating symbol.

Interesting Fact: *The Earth has a heart chakra too! The Anahata of our planet is believed to be located in England in two towns: Shaftesbury and Glastonbury. Just a few miles from these towns, standing tall is one of the most mysterious and enchanting monuments, Stonehenge. Many tales took place in the Earth's Anahata, like the legend of Arthur.*

The Anahata Symbol

Anahata Symbol.
Morgan Phoenix, CC BY-SA 3.0 https://creativecommons.org/licenses/by-sa/3.0 via Wikimedia Commons: https://commons.wikimedia.org/wiki/File:Anahata_Mandala.svg

The heart chakra symbol represents its special role in connecting the upper and lower chakras. As you can see from the illustration above, the heart chakra symbol is a green lotus consisting of 12 petals. Each petal represents one of the heart's 12 divine qualities.

- Kindness
- Empathy
- Love
- Compassion
- Harmony
- Forgiveness
- Peace
- Understanding
- Clarity
- Bliss
- Purity
- Unity

At the center of the lotus, you'll find a shatkona, a six-pointed star. As you can see, this star consists of two opposite triangles integrating, which represents the unity of the upper and lower chakras created by the Anahata. The star also symbolizes male and female unity.

The Anahata symbol is green because it is one of the two colors of the heart chakra; the other color is pink. Green symbolizes love, transformation, life, the Earth, growth, and harmony. Green is nature, and you can find it everywhere you look. It nurtures our souls and soothes our minds. Many positive feelings are associated with green, like empathy, openness, compassion, and development. Interestingly, green is the fourth color in the rainbow, and Anahata is the fourth chakra. We feel hopeful, optimistic, and harmonious when we see this color. Green is also connected to good health.

The Traits and Functions of the Heart Chakra

The Anahata represents positive and beautiful feelings like joy and compassion. In the heart chakra, our deepest feelings lie our truths that can never be described or put into words. The heart chakra represents love and not just any type, but unconditional love. Through love, the Anahata heals us and makes us whole. It helps us see that love is a healing force and that it is always the answer. When you see and feel love in everything around you, you start to see the world differently and become kinder and more compassionate, not just towards the people in your life but also yourself. The fourth chakra also allows us to develop deep and meaningful relationships with other people that focus on respect and empathy.

This chakra makes us at one with the world because it facilitates our bond with people and animals. It helps us see how we are all connected, leading us to show love to everyone we meet. It helps you develop romantic relationships and create long-lasting friendships. You'll be able to love yourself and everyone in your life unconditionally and unselfishly. And in so doing, you'll treat everyone around you with understanding and respect. You'll be thoughtful towards other people's feelings and respectful of their boundaries and thoughts. The heart chakra gives you wisdom and makes you more emotionally mature, so you start treating others with the love and compassion they deserve.

The heart chakra raises your empathy level, which leads you to be more sympathetic and empathetic towards other people's pain and sufferings. You'll become a warm person that people feel safe around. There is no denying that there are many negative emotions around us, and there will always be people who will hurt you, lie to you, and take advantage of you. Don't give in to these negative feelings and let them consume you. They will generate negative energies that move through your body, replacing the positive emotions inside you and destroying your heart, mind, body, and spirit.

That said, love heals, and the heart chakra will help you forgive and forget. It will give you the power to put the past behind you and move on from the pain others have caused you. You'll become a bigger person who understands that we are all humans and make mistakes. You won't hold grudges or hold on to the pain; you'll feel your feelings and then let go. You'll know better things are coming your way, so why live in the past? Forgiveness is a choice, and you can either live with the bitterness and pain of the past or choose love and open your heart to it, which this chakra helps you do. You'll no longer be a slave to the past and live with painful memories and heartaches. You won't let the ghost of the past hover over your present life, ruining all your happy and special moments.

Do you remember how you reacted to the world around you when you were a child? We allowed ourselves to feel and express all our emotions, whether hope, love, compassion, or even fear. We were never ashamed of our feelings. However, as we grow up, we become more reserved and vulnerable with our emotions. The heart chakra will help you feel, accept, and express your different emotions with no shame, just like children. It will also help you let go of all your childhood issues to move on from them and become a better adult for them.

The Anahata is responsible for our emotional responses and everything we feel deep inside, like our ideas, thoughts, and inspiration. It also enables you to heal, be grateful, and show generosity to the people in your life. You become someone who can create healthy relationships.

The Anahata functions as a bridge between the lower and the upper chakras. When the heart chakra is balanced, it will provide you with harmony and enhance your experience with the divine because deep inside our hearts lie unconditional self-acceptance.

Our life force energy is usually stagnant, but by practicing meditation, pranayama, or any techniques to unblock our chakras, it begins flowing through the Anahata. We experience various emotions like joy, self-love, and motivation, and we begin to understand our purpose in life. Additionally, it helps us let go of our egos because it humbles us and shows us that we are all connected.

The heart chakra isn't only responsible for our emotions and soul; it also has a huge impact on our physical health. It maintains the health of our immune system, blood plasma, respiratory system, thymus gland, and circulatory system. Additionally, it is connected to our vital organs and body parts, like the heart, upper back, lungs, thorax, shoulders, rib cage, and the skin and hands, due to the heart's connection to our sense of touch.

The Benefits of Aligning the Heart Chakra

All chakras should be open, aligned, and balanced. When the Anahata is aligned, you'll find yourself experiencing positive emotions like love and self-acceptance. You'll feel good and will be eager to experience everything life has to offer. Whatever challenges life throws your way, you'll be able to handle them with a positive and "can-do" attitude. You won't let depression take over; you'll feel at peace even when nothing is going your way. You'll also easily be able to resolve all your relationship problems. Wherever you look, you'll see love and beauty. You'll become one with the world around you and connect with yourself and the people you love.

A balanced heart chakra provides you with self-acceptance and self-love. You'll fully accept and love all your flaws, whether in your looks or body, and you'll also be able to acknowledge your weaknesses. No one is perfect, and you won't have to try to be; you'll just be yourself. An open Anahata will get you there. You'll let go of hatred and will only choose love. You'll no longer be stubborn or let your ego get in the way; you'll happily admit when you are wrong and apologize when you make a mistake. You will find yourself a more generous and charitable person – always willing to lend a hand. You won't judge others and be more understanding of their shortcomings.

You'll become calmer and find joy and peace inside of you. Your communication skills will improve drastically; you'll become a better listener and someone straightforward and able to get their point across clearly. You'll experience a sense of purity and become more intuitive. Your spiritual energy will also increase. Your physical health will improve, your heart will become stronger, your thyroid gland's health will improve, and you'll notice an increase in your upper body strength.

You won't seek revenge or even wish them ill if someone hurts you. This will set you free as you'll no longer be driven by anger, negativity, or hatred. An open heart chakra will give you the courage to be open and vulnerable with those closest to you. You'll no longer be afraid of intimacy and letting someone in. You'll trust others and be your true self around them. You won't isolate yourself from people but will be happy to be around the ones you love.

Sounds like a lot of change, right? All in all, you'll become a better person who is sympathetic to other people's feelings and needs. You'll be confident and strong enough to be your most authentic self and live your own truth. When your heart is open and filled with positivity, you'll be emotionally, mentally, spiritually, and physically healthier. You'll be a happier person, and every aspect of your life will improve.

The Beatles said it best: *All we need is love.* Open your heart chakra and let love, joy, and compassion surround you. You may be now thinking, "I don't feel joy" or "I am unable to trust or be intimate with the people I love." You may not know it, but your chakra may be blocked. Don't fret. For every problem, there is a solution. Learn how to unblock your heart chakra in the next chapter.

Chapter 2: When Your Heart Chakra Is Blocked

Spiritual well-being recognizes our need to find a deeper purpose and meaning in life. Our spiritual health connects us to those around us and guides us to something, or an entity, much larger than life. It allows us to make decisions and go on about our daily life with a clearer mind. When we are spiritually healthy, our actions and behaviors become aligned with our morals, values, and beliefs.

Everyone can reap the benefits of maintaining good spiritual health. In doing so, they will build compassionate relationships and will be able to keep inner peace. When you are in a good spiritual state, you can acknowledge your own perception of life and cultivate your meaning of it. You are also tolerant and accepting of other people's beliefs. Those who don't sit well in their spirituality are rather closed-minded and highly intolerant of opposing mindsets. Those who struggle spiritually also find it difficult to stay in tune with their beliefs and values, making it impossible to develop a true sense of self.

People who can maintain good spiritual health are hopeful and always see the glass as half full. They can forgive, commit, and accept themselves cultivating a clear sense of value and self-worth. In retrospect, people who need to reinvigorate their spirituality are likely to feel void, anxious, self-critical, apathetic, and struggle to lose a sense of purpose and meaning.

The Heart Chakra and Spiritual Wellness

Negative emotions constantly plague our lives. Aside from political, economic, and global crises, which undoubtedly leave us spiritually damaged, our relationships and daily activities can compromise our spiritual wellness. Holding grudges, being emotionally repressed, anxiety, romantic frustration, avoidance, and lamenting past events are among the symptoms everyone experiences. These symptoms, essentially, are all associated with the heart chakra.

If you've been experiencing any negative emotions like these, it's safe to say that your Heart Chakra is blocked. An obstructed heart chakra, which hinders the flow of energy throughout the entire body, is enough to create a plethora of emotional ailments and impediments to ourselves and those around us.

It's not healthy to be in constant pain, disappointment, and loneliness. They are signs of spiritual blockages, and these feelings also affect one's physical and mental health, which shows how important it is to keep the chakras balanced.

Each Chakra is responsible for certain aspects of our wellness and is responsible for the function of the part of the body they're located in. Each Chakra is linked to sensations and emotions in the body's vast energetic system. This is why the balancing of each Chakra plays an equal role in ensuring our overall well-being.

Unluckily, the body's energetic flow can be easily hindered as our chakras are quick to become blocked. If we allow ourselves to be influenced by negative emotions and experiences, this obstruction will likely occur. When energy doesn't flow effectively, our body's vitality is affected. Thus, a blocked heart chakra can leave us with cardiovascular and circulatory issues and problems like bronchitis and lung problems.

The Anahata, or heart chakra, is linked to social and romantic connections and love. The fourth Chakra serves as a link between the mundane and the higher aspirations. The heart chakra is the most prone to obstruction. When blocked, our contentment, fulfillment, relationship, and happiness are significantly weakened.

This chapter will explore the causes behind a blocked heart chakra. Then, we will list off the common symptoms of a blocked Anahata chakra and an overactive one. Finally, you'll come across a short quiz that will help you identify the current status of your Heart Chakra and how healthy it is.

Causes of a Blocked Heart Chakra

There are several reasons why the heart chakra may be blocked, making it impossible to give a sole reason behind this experience. The cause behind a blocked heart chakra varies greatly from one person to the other and can be identified by poor energy levels and a general feeling of being out of balance. If you suspect that you're struggling with an obstructed Anahata chakra, you'll need to reflect deeply on what may be contributing to your ailment.

Generally speaking, a blocked heart chakra results from prominent negative and hateful emotions in one's life. Physical and mental illnesses, emotional turmoil and upset, stress, and conflict can cause the chakra system to fall out of balance. All seven chakras exist within a single network and are interconnected. So, when one Chakra becomes obstructed, all the others are subject to imbalances and blockages. This disruption in the body's vitality and energy causes the affected person's body, mind, and spirit to suffer.

The primary emotion behind a blocked heart chakra is pain. This intense emotion usually results from an incredibly traumatic or negative experience. The burden that goes with this feeling places a heavy burden on the mind and body, causing stoppages in the energy flow throughout the body and putting a halt to the flow of love and compassion.

Love is the most powerful emotion we know, as it contributes the most energy when it comes to our spiritual network. This means that without love, our well-being will be highly unbalanced. Even though the chakras are not visible to the naked eye, we can easily identify an energetic blockage through its manifestation in many emotional and physical ailments.

However, before we delve deep into the symptoms of an unbalanced heart chakra, we must first learn about the different states of the Chakra.

Underactive vs. Overactive Chakras

Each of your chakras can exist in three main states: overactive, balanced, or underactive (blocked). When one of your chakras is overactive, it's giving out way too much energy, resulting in an imbalance to that Chakra. When it's balanced, it operates efficiently and harmoniously. It is giving out just the right amount of vibrational energy. When a chakra is underactive or blocked, it's subject to some type of obstruction. An underactive chakra is deficient and gives out low vibrational energy, which also causes an imbalance in that Chakra.

As we mentioned, negative behaviors and emotions, like a lack of exercise, unhealthy diets, stress, physical and emotional conditions, conflicts, and emotional distress, can imbalance the Chakra. These causes can promote an over-abundant or deficient distribution of vibrational energy from the affected Chakra.

This is an overview of the symptoms that the three states of the heart chakra accompany:

Symptoms of an Overactive Heart Chakra: jealousy, over-generosity, self-sacrificial tendencies, codependency.

Symptoms of a Balanced Heart Chakra: loving and compassionate interactions, tolerance, openness, connection, peace of mind, and warmness.

Symptoms of an Underactive Heart Chakra: bitterness, intolerance, commitment issues, trust issues, lack of compassion, and lack of empathy.

As you can see, the qualities associated with the heart chakra are amplified and exaggerated when it's overactive, just right when it's balanced, and deficient when it's blocked. These are the three states of giving and receiving love and connecting with the world and people around us.

Signs Your Heart Chakra Is Overactive

You Struggle with Setting Boundaries

You need to set boundaries intentionally in all your relationships and interactions, whether with yourself or others. Boundaries are essential for self-protection and preservation, healing, and self-love. They help you know and assert your self-worth. If you have an overactive chakra, you may find it hard to set and maintain healthy boundaries. When your Chakra is imbalanced, you tend to overlook your own needs and emotions. This can make it very difficult to pinpoint the boundaries you need to set and when to set them. Even when you can identify them, setting them and upholding them can be quite taxing. This is especially the case when others are challenging your boundaries.

You Always Come Second

Helping others and caring about them is not a bad thing. However, it should never be at the expense of your energy and well-being. Your Heart Chakra is likely overactive if your needs and desires always come second to others. You always feel the need to help others and take care of them until you are left feeling neglected, tired, and depleted.

You Find It Hard to Receive Love

The heart chakra is all about giving and receiving love and compassion. Finding it hard to receive love from others is a sign of both blocked and overactive Anahata chakra. This is because overactivity prompts you to direct all your energy and attention to giving others rather than being open to receiving nurturing and loving gestures from those around you. This may not seem like a problem. However, it will likely leave you feeling drained and resentful of others because they don't reciprocate your care.

You Are a People Pleaser

Being a people pleaser means that you feel a constant need to please others and seek validation from them to feel emotionally fulfilled. Instead of being self-sufficient and accepting, you replenish your confidence or worth through constant positive feedback from others. This is a sign that your heart chakra is overactive and may cause you to do everything to please others regardless of your own needs.

You Are Rather Needy

This can be a touchy subject to acknowledge. However, if people repeatedly point out that you are needy or desperate, or if you've come to discover that you give off these qualities in your relationships, it is a sign your Heart Chakra is overactive. This point is highly connected to those mentioned above and is associated with people-pleasing tendencies. Besides seeking other people's validation, you may be desperate for their care, affection, or nurturing energy.

You Tolerate Abuse

Tolerating physical, verbal, or emotional abuse is a sign of an overactive heart chakra. You tend to stay in toxic relationships because you always manage to come up with excuses for their behavior or are too scared to lose them. Once again, you are trying to provide them with loving and nurturing energy while neglecting your needs.

You Are Codependent

When you're codependent in a relationship, you lose all your sense of self, identity, and worth. You struggle to make your own decisions and cannot pinpoint your wants and needs. Codependent individuals also usually have very low self-esteem. This is a symptom of an overactive Anahata chakra.

Signs Your Heart Chakra Is Blocked

You're Stuck in a Past Relationship

We're not talking about fresh breakups and wounds here. If you can't get over an old relationship or breakup, you are likely experiencing a blockage in your Heart Chakra. You may be dwelling on your mistakes or reevaluating the separation, telling yourself what could've gone differently so this connection could've been preserved.

You're Holding Grudges

Grudges are a very normal part of being hurt. However, at some point, the feeling is supposed to become less intense so you can move on. However, if you find it hard to forgive and let go of grudges, then this is a sign that your heart chakra is underactive. The more you hold onto

---

your grudges, the more you reinforce your pain and ward off joy and happiness from your life.

You Have Trust Issues

This is not easy to do. However, if you don't want to impact all your relationships negatively, you must not let the trust issues from unpleasant past experiences dictate your interactions and impressions of others. Having a blocked heart chakra may be why you find it hard to trust others and confide in them. It can cause you to believe that others are devising schemes against you to betray you again.

You're Excessively Shy

Shyness is not a negative personality trait. When it's excessive, it can influence your relationships and self-esteem. It may cause you to self-sabotage fruitful friendships and relationships.

You Feel Lonely

Loneliness is a normal feeling everyone is bound to experience from time to time. However, excessive amounts of loneliness could signify that your Heart Chakra is underactive. As counterintuitive as it sounds, you may resort to self-isolation to protect yourself from emotional turmoil, even if it makes more sense to connect with others. Chances are past negative experiences with relationships are the reasons behind your loneliness.

You Have Commitment Issues

Commitment issues spring up for many reasons. Whether you are afraid of feeling confined, worry about choosing the wrong person, or doubt your significant other, you may feel unable to commit to a relationship. If you want to build healthy relationships with those around you, you need to start working on healing and balancing your Heart Chakra.

You're Very Defensive

Being constantly on defense and on edge can make it hard for you to feel at ease and comfortable around others. Past emotional pain or trauma is the main reason behind overly defensive behavior and tendencies. This is a sign that you need to unblock your Heart Chakra.

Quiz: How Healthy Is Your Heart Chakra

The signs that we mentioned above can help you identify the state of your Chakra. However, if you're still in doubt, take this short quiz to help you determine whether your heart chakra is overactive, balanced, or blocked.

I find it easy to forgive others.

I rarely get mad at people anyways. I always find excuses for their actions.

I take my time to process my emotions, but I forgive them eventually.

I tend to hold grudges, and it can be very hard for me to forgive those who hurt me.

I know the limits to all my relationships, and I'm not afraid to uphold them.

I usually find it hard to distinguish whether people are overstepping my boundaries. When I know they are, I'm hesitant to call them out.

I know my boundaries. If someone oversteps their limits in our relationship, I make sure to communicate with them.

My boundaries are very rigid. I barely let anyone in.

I always prioritize other people's wants and needs.

Their happiness and contentment are my priority, even when it's at the expense of my well-being.

I like to care for others and help them when they need me. However, I'm not scared to say no when my needs and wants are in jeopardy.

I usually find it hard to empathize with others, so I don't truly know when they need my help.

I seek nurturing relationships.

I seek relationships in which people make me feel validated, nurtured, and loved. I sometimes worry that I may come off as needy or desperate.

I seek relationships where I give and receive equal amounts of care, affection, and nurturing.

I find it difficult to accept attention and love from others.

Maintaining limits and personal space, beliefs, and thoughts are important to me in any relationship.

I am easily influenced and swayed by others' decisions, thoughts, and beliefs. When in a relationship, I depend on my significant others to make important decisions.

Maintaining my identity and sense of self is important to me. While it would be nice to have things in common, my significant other and I don't need to share the same interests, thoughts, beliefs, etc.

I'm rather closed off and hyper-independent.

I accept that everyone has their own take on life.

I usually agree with other people's arguments and opinions in conversations, even when they don't align with my own. I'm afraid they'd judge me or like me less if I express myself.

I am tolerant and accepting of different worldviews, but I'm not scared to speak my truth.

I get very defensive when it comes to my opinions and beliefs. I don't accept other people's opinions easily.

I stand up to myself in the face of any form of abuse.

I find it hard to abandon the person because there is always a reason behind their behavior.

I know when to leave toxic relationships.

I never trust anyone enough to let them hurt me.

I am open to receiving love, care, and affection from others.

I don't usually know how to respond to these gestures because I'm used to being the one who gives in any relationship.

My efforts must be reciprocated in all relationships.

It's not easy for me to accept positive gestures from others.

I am quick to jump into relationships.

I trust people very easily, and I usually find myself speeding into friendships and romantic relationships.

I usually take things slow until the person proves that I can trust them.

I'm afraid they will let me down or betray me, so I never commit to relationships.

I love being around others and ensuring they're fulfilled.

Helping others and giving with no restraints makes me feel good, so I like being around people.

I like hanging out with others and being a source of trust and help, but I can tell when my social battery runs out.

I feel on edge around other people, so I tend to self-isolate.

Results

Mostly As: You likely struggle with an overactive heart chakra.

Mostly Bs: Your Heart Chakra is balanced.

Mostly Cs: Your Heart Chakra is probably blocked and underactive.

Today's world is incredibly demanding and fast-paced. We're all consumed by technology and are preoccupied with corporate life, education, and daily routine. Under all that pressure, most of us forget about something fundamental -: spiritual health. Everyone knows the importance of having good physical, mental, and emotional health. However, unfortunately, the need for good spiritual well-being isn't discussed enough. Many people don't realize that maintaining spiritual balance is vital to living vigorously.

Achieving spiritual health can be done by balancing the chakras, especially the Anahata. Everyone's goal should be to align all chakras and keep them open. We should all aim to promote a healthy and easy flow of energy between all the chakras because all six others are affected when one is weakened. They should all work together harmoniously to ensure our mental, physical, emotional, and spiritual well-being.

Chapter 3: Start with a Strong Chakra Foundation

In the previous chapter, you read about Anahata's role in your well-being and how much you rely on this chakra to develop positive emotions. Now, it's time for you to see how much it affects your other energy centers - and, more importantly, how their functions affect your heart chakra. A blockage in its center may not be the sole cause of a closed Anahata, and even though the heart chakra can be opened without opening the other chakras, it is highly beneficial for the lower chakras also to be open. In this chapter, you'll see how the balance of your other chakras allows the energy to flow up freely into Anahata. Moreover, working on the self by balancing all of the other chakras first will help heal and strengthen an already-open heart chakra.

Your surroundings affect your focus.

Importance of Strong Chakra Foundations

As you may remember, your chakra system is a complex network of interwoven lines, and your energy is concentrated in the seven main points. Not only does each line affect all the others, but so do the centers themselves. For instance, without positive emotions, your actions towards your environment can become unkind, which may cause you to feel unhappy with your surroundings. This can cause depression, and lack of sleep, which, in turn, lead to physical conditions. Physical problems will cause you discomfort, so your motivation and productivity levels decrease. This further lowers the positive energy level in your body. Soon you'll get to the point that all you feel is hatred, fear, and jealousy towards those who find inspiration to move forward with their life. A prime example of this would be the development of eating disorders - which affect the solar plexus and the heart chakra. An eating disorder is often rooted in emotional instability, a characteristic regulated by the sacral chakra. If negativity keeps piling up and this center is becoming affected, it's only a matter of time before your root chakra becomes affected as well. The example refers to the downward flow of negative energy, but there can also be reversed pathways. In these, the issue starts with your root center and slowly travels towards Anahata.

The Role of Polarity in Balancing the Chakras

Even though the seven chakras correlate to different body parts and carry diverse forms of energy, these differences naturally balance each other out. This is called polarity and represents the basis of all spiritual and physical dimensions. Anything that happens in one place gets reflected in another, which is true for the body's dimensions and energy centers. This means that apart from each center being in harmony, the lower chakras should be in balance with the upper ones. The largest polarity is between your root and heart chakras, located at the opposite end of your energetic system. Still, its existence can vastly distinguish between being aligned with yourself or not. Therefore, establishing polarity is the main goal when trying to heal the heart chakra. However, sometimes it's also necessary to align your other centers and unlock them. A similar balance exists between the third and fifth and the second and sixth chakras.

To understand what this polarity looks like in practice, you must observe the two centers contributing to the balance. For example, a clear pattern is revealed by examining the sixth and second chakras and the pathway between them. The second from the lower center, the sacral chakra, reflects your creativity and feelings. It rules over all the emotions we experience during our relationships and their physical counterparts - the hips, the kidneys, the bladder, the lower gastrointestinal tract, and reproductive organs. If this chakra is affected, the desire to experience positive emotions lowers, and your creativity level decreases. All this imbalance in your sacral chakra is mirrored in an imbalance in your Third-eye chakra. The energy centering here determines your mood and affinity for spiritual growth. It also aligns with your neurons traveling in your spine, affecting your sleep patterns and cognitive functions.

Apart from all the methods recommended for nourishing your sacral chakra, you also must pay attention to your Third eye. When your Third eye chakra is affected, you are in no mood to seek new relationships and positive emotions. Even if all your other chakras (including Anahata) are open and properly balanced, you won't be able to form a trust-filled relationship if your sixth chakra is blocked. In the rest of the chapter, you'll find the signs of blockage for each chakra, followed by a few tips and tricks on unblocking them. This will give a much broader understanding of how they affect your body and each other.

Keeping in mind the importance of the polarity between the chakras, it becomes much easier to find a solution to your blocked or unbalanced heart chakra. Remember to start with your physical symptoms to see if they point to another energy center. After doing the same with your emotions and pinpointing a few problematic areas, you can proceed with clearing them out. Nourishment and activities designed to unblock any of the lower channels can restore the balance in Anahata. If the block persists, you can look at the polarity between the root and heart chakras. You may find that doing something that benefits the former positively impacts the latter.

The Pathway to Anahata

The energetic pathway to Anatha starts from the root (Muladhara) chakra, envelopes the sacral (Svadhishthana) and solar plexus

(Manipura) chakras, finally culminating at your heart center (Anatha). If any of the lower chakras are blocked or unbalanced, the energy flow is interrupted, and everything affected by your heart chakra suffers. Here are the signs of blockage for each chakra, from the root to the heart centers, and how to remedy them.

The Root Chakra

Also called Muladhara, the root chakra is an energetic center at the base of the spine. It's represented by the color red and the earth element. Its name means foundation, and its role is linked to safety, groundedness, and foundation. Besides providing the foundation for your entire life, Muladhara can grant an overall sense of security. A blocked root chakra may rob you of stability in various areas of your life, including the emotional one, usually because of an overwhelming sense of being in danger caused by emotional or physical neglect and abuse, childhood traumas, or current financial instability.

Signs of a blocked root chakra may include:

- Overthinking, overanalyzing every situation in your life
- Fear or panic from future events or the recurrence of past negative experiences
- Depression or anxiety due to being unmotivated to set and complete goals and insecurity
- Lack of sleep and inability to process your experiences, emotions, and throughout through your dreams
- Being emotionally disconnected from everything and everyone around you
- Failure to trust that things will work out, especially if you are forced into a new experience
- Feeling anger and frustration at your inability to cope with issues the same, you see others can do
- Lack of confidence to seek out new experiences that could help you grow spiritually and emotionally

- Being slothful and not even trying to make an effort to move forward with your life and achieve your dreams

Ways to open Muladhara may include:

- Either by using the color red in your decorations at your home and workplace or by wearing red clothes as often, you can

- Eating red foods - with the focus being on fruits and vegetables, including berries, beets, and red cabbage

- Mediating specifically on the root chakra while chanting the sound "LAM."

- Performing other grounding exercises - meditations, deep breathing, journaling, etc.

- Doing yoga poses that promote stability, such as the children's pose, the standing forward fold, or the squat.

- Walking barefoot in your home can also help you feel closer to nature and grounded in your present situation.

Take a proactive approach in facing your past traumas - whether through family, friends, professional therapy, or any other type of support system.

The Sacral Chakra

The sacral chakra, or Svadhisthana, is an energetic center associated with the color orange and the water element. Located slightly below your navel, it represents your ability to relate to emotions. Whether directed towards yourself or to or from others, intimacy, passion, trust, creativity, fluidity, sexuality, and the need for procreation are just some of the sensations linked to this chakra. Svadhisthana is often blocked by emotions lingering from past traumatic events in your relationships, such as guilt, shame, or anger. Being in conflict with your feelings or disconnected from your passionate and creative sides may also impede its balance. Since many of your emotions and actions towards others are governed by Svadhisthana, your ability to form new relationships (caused by a blocked heart chakra) may also affect the functioning of this center.

Here are some signs of a blocked sacral chakra:

- A long-lasting creative block that prevents you from being more flexible in different areas of your life
- Guilt and shame caused by past traumatic experiences - widespread in sexual trauma and toxic relationships
- Toxicity in your current relationships due to your unwillingness to break the perpetual cycle of seeking out these types of arrangements
- Feeling that you are undeserving of the love, trust, and compassion from others, much less from yourself
- Believing that others do not care about your happiness and health - translates to you not managing as well
- Being unmotivated to set goals and work towards them
- Lack of sexual desire or intimacy in general
- Either the lack of emotions or feelings directed toward inappropriate things
- Seeking out addictive devices and other tools of self-destruction
- Being insecure about everything and everyone in your life
- The constant need to control everything around in your environment
- Physical symptoms related to your bladder and kidneys

Ways to open up your sacral chakra may involve:

- Either by using the color orange in your decorations at your home and workplace or by wearing orange clothes as often, you can
- Eating orange foods - with the focus being on fruits and vegetables, including mangoes, carrots, and pumpkins
- Mediating specifically on the sacral chakra while chanting the sound "VAM."
- Doing hip-opening yoga poses that promote a healthy sacral area

- Walking barefoot in your home can also help you feel closer to nature and grounded in your present situation

- Taking conscious steps to build healthy relationships - both on the emotional front and the sexual one

- Reciting affirmation that you are deserving of love from yourself and others

- Use your creativity to make your day to day experiences easier so you can have a fuller and more balanced life

The Solar Plexus Chakra

Also known as Manipura, the solar plexus chakra is an energetic center found in the middle of your abdomen. Linked to the color yellow and the fire element, this chakra gives home to your self-esteem, often determining how much control you have over your life. It represents an endless source of inner power, vitality, and independence if unblocked. It can be sabotaged by low self-esteem coming from past traumatic experiences such as abuse, neglect, bullying, or being victimized. Eating the wrong foods and generally believing you aren't strong enough to face life's challenges may also cause issues with this center. In addition, the solar plexus chakra also affects the functionality of your gastrointestinal tract, either slowing it down or speeding it up drastically, even at a minor blockage in your energy. This is caused by the lack or abundance of your inner fire called "tapas."

Some signs of a blocked solar plexus chakra may include:

- Feeling anxious about even the minor changes in your life and highly fearful about the larger ones

- Being powerless to confront past traumas or to shed the influence they have on your present and future life

- Having a victim mentality, even in situations where you aren't one

- Willingly relinquishing the power over your life to others, saying you don't have control over anything anyway

- Inability or unwillingness to accept you are capable of achieving so much more in life
- Displaying egoistic tendencies or unnecessary aggressivity in your relationships with others
- Frequent bouts of pain or discomfort in your stomach and upper abdominal area
- Problems with your liver, pancreas, and spleen

Here are some ways to resolve these issues and open your solar plexus chakra:

- Either by using the color yellow in your decorations at your home and workplace or by wearing yellow clothes as often as you can
- Eating yellow foods - with the focus being on fruits and vegetables, including citrus, cauliflower, and yellow peppers
- Mediating specifically on the solar plexus chakra while chanting the sound "RAM."
- Doing hip-opening yoga poses that promote healing in the solar plexus area
- Performing other yoga exercises that stimulate the healthy production of tapas, including the boat pose, the cobra, the bow poses, or the sun salutations.
- Reciting affirmations about having enough power to overcome life's challenges
- Journaling about what makes you special - a unique individuality, the ability to see good people, etc.
- Practicing mindfulness exercises and breathing techniques such as the Bhastrika Pranayama (or bellows breath) or the Kapalabhati Pranayama (the breath of fire).

The Heart Chakra

Since the heart chakra will be discussed more thoroughly through this book, only a rundown on how its blockage manifests concerning the chakras and how to resolve this will be presented here. Located in the middle of the body, Anahata represents the central point in your energetic system. Anahata is often depicted as representing your ability to develop feelings such as compassion and love. However, its malfunction can be felt by lacking much more than simply these emotions. Its association with the heart, the color green, and air points to affinity towards nature and its polarity with the root chakra. Whether it's blocked by the lack of love, day-to-day stress, or deep-seated trauma, Anahata will affect the lower chakras as well.

Similarly, holding on to negatives caused by a blockage in the lower centers will affect the heart chakra. Only by keeping open all the chakras will you be able to access the unlimited source of positive emotions offered by Anahata.

Signs of a blocked Anahata manifesting in the lower centers may include:

- The lack of commitment stemming from intimacy issues often bleeds into the lack of goals in personal life.

- The increasing tendency to hold grudges and your lack of compassion makes you hard to deal with professionally.

- The unwillingness to let go past hurts causes anxiety, sleeplessness, or depressive thoughts, often progressing to physical symptoms.

- Due to being closed off, you cannot maintain relationships, depriving yourself of a cluster of new spiritual experiences.

- Despite being lonely, your ability to love decreases daily, leading to all your energetic centers getting blocked, right up to the Crown chakra.

Ways to open the Anatha through the other centers may include:

- Meditating on the chakra, you found issues during your self-inspection.

- Chanting the appropriate sounds while meditating.

- Eating food that promotes the healing of all the lower chakras.

- Wearing colors that represent these centers.

- Reciting affirmations of love for yourself - your body, mind, and spirit.

- Doing different yoga poses associated with the four lower chakras on alternate days of the week.

- Spending time in a natural environment is also beneficial for your entire energetic system.

- Reciting affirmations that open up the individual lower chakras often positively affects the balance of the center above them.

Final Thoughts

Opening your lower chakras establishes a clear pathway for your energy to follow towards the heart chakra. By doing this, you may uncover some hidden issues that need to be resolved before you can put all your negative emotions and memories aside.

Balancing your entire chakra system will relieve you from many burdens and improve your physical and mental well-being. Because just as an emotional burden can manifest in physical symptoms, physical issues will generate negative feelings, including frustration, anger, and self-doubt - should they last for an extended period. So, if you want to ensure your heart chakra receives all the energy it needs, you'll need to start from your lower chakras.

For the best results, we recommend you do all the exercises during the morning hours as soon as you wake up and before you have breakfast. This way, your chakras will be prepared for the day's challenges, and they will be less likely to be blocked by negative energy. If you need to clear them in the evening, you may do the exercises before bed, at least two hours after your last meal.

This chapter can be a great stepping stone for anyone interested in evaluating all their chakras and learning how to recognize their blockage. After all, just as this book is designed to help you heal your heart chakra, so are many others dedicated to the lower centers. They contain more extensive information about specific yoga practices, affirmations, and mindfulness techniques. You'll also get a few tips on opening them, but feel free to do your own research regarding this topic.

Additional ways to open the chakras may include using crystals, mudras, or tones. At the end of the day, everyone's energetic makeup is different. This means that the symptoms and solutions of each chakra blockage may also vary from one person to another. A solution that works for someone else may not bring you the desired results. Having an open mind and being willing to find alternative solutions is crucial for rebalancing your chakras. It can enhance your creativity - which, in turn, will have an immense effect on your emotional center, so you'll want to check them out.

Chapter 4: Anahata Mantras and Mudras

When we stumble across images of world-renowned yoga practitioners like B.K.S, Iyengar, and Tao Porchon-Lynch don't necessarily see the yoga postures we've learned through learning about pranayama or asana. This is because the purpose behind pranayama and other healing-oriented practices is to build a strong connection between one's body and mind. Yoga therapists largely adopt these types of yoga activities as they don't only help in promoting mindfulness, peace of mind, and relaxation. Still, they also aid in numerous aspects of physical health, such as supporting the functions of various vital organs. They can help you improve your mental, emotional, physical, and spiritual well-being.

Mudras is a practice to move your hands to help you focus
https://unsplash.com/photos/ktPKyUs3Qjs

You can do numerous things to boost the vitality and condition of your heart chakra, including meditation, which we will cover in more depth in the following chapter. When we meditate, we can make the most out of the activity by incorporating the use of mantras and mudras. Mantras are phrases or certain words that you can recite to yourself or out loud. The key to mantras is to align your repetition or recitation with the rhythm of your breath. On the other hand, Mudras is a practice that prompts you to move your hands in a way that can help you focus your brain.

How They Work

There are specific mantras and mudras that you can use to help activate each of your chakras. When you do them, they tap into the part of your body that you are targeting. For instance, reciting the mantras and making the mudras that correspond with the heart chakra can help promote healing. Yoga therapists utilize mantras and mudras in their practices because they focus on the areas of the body that have the most nerve endings. While the mudras focus on the hands and fingers, the mantras involve your mouth and lips. Their high sensitivity makes them more efficient in healing and curative support.

For this reason, both mudras and mantras can help you strengthen the correspondence between your physical actions and how your mind works, increasing focus, intention, skill, and more. Individuals who can't do meditative poses due to physical or location-related limitations can benefit significantly from learning mudras and mantras to open their chakras. These practices can serve as great access points to the world of meditation.

Mudras

The hands, especially the fingertips, hold the greatest number of nerve endings in the body. This is why employing them throughout your meditative routine has proven to be the most beneficial physical yoga practice for enhancing the function of the brain. Since this is practical and body-based, it can be easily approached in asana. Mudra makes a great starting point for beginners.

Mantras

Most yoga practitioners chant mantras silently to themselves or aloud. This creates an atmosphere that starts the healing process and reinvigorates the link between the brain and the body parts that you use to make the chant: your lips, tongue, and mouth. Mantras are still as effective if you choose to hum or recite them silently because they allow you to keep your focus throughout the meditation.

Although it was initially an Ayurdevic practice, the rest of the world has started to take an interest in the benefits of mantras. Even those not into yoga and similar meditative practices are now aware of the power of words and how they can influence one's vibrational energies. Using phrases and words is now a prevalent practice among self-help circles and individuals who wish to improve their lives. It is a way to announce an intention to yourself and the universe, influence yourself to adopt a new mindset, or bring positivity into your life. You probably think that mantras are the same as affirmations. To be clear, we will be exploring the difference between both in this chapter.

This chapter illustrates the benefits of mantras and provides one that you can recite and its meaning, pronunciation, and uses. You'll also find some helpful affirmations to help you open your heart chakra. In the second part of the chapter, you'll learn all about mudras and how and when you can use them. Here, you'll find some examples and detailed instructions on mudras that can make you unblock, heal, and balance your heart chakra.

Affirmations vs. Mantras

There come times when we all feel overwhelmed, stressed, and demotivated. Fortunately, mantras and affirmations are both easy yet highly effective practices that help us to control and influence our thoughts and feelings. You can either add both into your daily routine or experiment with a method you feel most comfortable using. However, it's important to highlight that each of these practices focuses on some regions of self-improvement, which is why they're best used together.

What Are Affirmations?

Affirmations are short, positive, and specific statements that you tell yourself. It is an announcement that you direct to yourself, shedding light on your positive qualities or confirming the person you wish to be. They essentially work through the Law of Attraction. Your affirmations can be about anything you desire. For instance, if a person wishes to work on boosting their self-esteem, they can repeat affirmations that stress their self-worth, acceptance, love, and compassion. A good example of an affirmation for building confidence would be: *"I am at peace with everything I am."* In your case, your primary goal is unblocking your heart chakra, so that's where you'll direct your focus.

There are several ways to use your affirmations, such as writing them down or repeating them multiple times during the day. However, when reciting your affirmations, we suggest that you stand in front of a mirror. It may feel odd at first, but looking yourself in the eye as you recite these affirmations will illustrate their power. You can incorporate them into your morning or bedtime routine, so they're easy to follow. Think of them as a self-care routine that needs you to stay consistent so it can work.

What Are Mantras?

Mantras are chants you repeatedly say to yourself during yoga, meditation, or any other spiritual practice. Mantra is a Sanskrit word that translates to "free the mind." These chants can be words or phrases repeated several times in a 10-minute session. You can make up a list of affirmations that would take you three minutes to recite. However, you need to fully indulge in the words of the mantra during the meditation. It won't be enough to say it once or repeat it for just a few minutes.

When verbalizing a mantra, you need to be fully involved and focused. Ultimately, you have to disconnect entirely from everything around you and direct your full attention to the words you utter. While this can be very challenging to do at first, it's something that you'll eventually achieve over time. Because they require so much consciousness and attentiveness, they're best included in the form of meditation.

Designate a quiet and tranquil space to conduct the practice regularly. If you live with a roommate or family members, ask them not to disturb you for the period of your session. Sit in a comfortable position on the floor and bring awareness to your breathing. Start chanting your mantras so they match the rhythm of your breaths. The harmony you create by repeating the mantra generates a vibration that moves throughout your body and frees your mind. Noticing the vibrations of the mantra and how it makes you feel can help you reduce anxiety and stress and promote a sense of inner peace. Besides the harmony of the mantra, the words themselves, which are in Sanskrit, hold immense power. They help the reciter understand who they are and offer insight into their capabilities and abilities.

There are many things that we don't know and can't control in the world, which can cause a great deal of stress and anxiety, which mantras can help us overcome. They allow us to make peace because we can't control everything around us. Not only that, but reciting mantras allows us to understand the world around us and helps us make sense of all its dynamics. Reciting these chants gives you a lot of power. Instead of dwelling on other people's actions and circumstances beyond your control, they encourage you to hold yourself accountable and influence the only thing you can control yourself. Like affirmations, there are mantras designed for each purpose. Each chakra also has its own mantra that helps it maintain its balance.

Heart Chakra Affirmations

Here are some affirmations that you can use to open and balance your heart chakra:

"I am worthy of affection and pure love."

"I am fully open to receiving and accepting love."

"I let go of past hurt and resentment."

"I live harmoniously and peacefully with all other beings."

"I attract loving and supportive partners."

"I build healthy and affectionate romantic relationships."

"I forgive myself for all past mistakes, and I view them as a way to learn and move forward."

"My heart is full of compassion for myself and those around me."

Creating Your Own Affirmations

Writing your own affirmations is not difficult. While the ones above can be of great help, learning to write your own affirmations lets you tailor them to your own needs and experience. It's also worth mentioning that if you wish to tackle other aspects of your life and open your heart chakra, you can do that. Only you can determine the number of affirmations and themes that work best for you.

When writing your affirmations, select a quiet place where you can focus. Choose a negative thought or aspect of your life you wish to challenge and counter it with a positive opposite phrase. For instance, if you've always believed that you're incapable or always make numerous mistakes, you can write affirmations similar to "I'm capable and experienced, or "My mistakes help me grow and learn."

Your affirmations should be short so you don't have trouble remembering them. Don't worry about creating statements that are too short. Even ones that are just four words long can be impactful. It all depends on your word choice and how you say and feel it. Here are some tips that can help you build powerful affirmations:

Make them personal and begin with "my" or "I." Your affirmations are about yourself, so they should reflect just that. *"I attract love"* is much more powerful than *"love finds me."*

Keep them in the present tense. The key behind affirmations is to act as though you are experiencing your desires now. For example, *"I am influential"* is better than *"I will be influential."* Avoid limiting your affirmations, such as *"I will be in a relationship in four months."*

Avoid expressing that you want or need your affirmation to happen. You don't want to declare that you lack it. Instead, you want to announce that you already have what you desire and are thankful for it.

Don't use negative statements. For example, if you don't want to fail, don't say so. A better-worded affirmation would be *"I am successful."* Avoid using words like "don't," "stop," "can't," etc.

Include emotions whenever you can. Example: *"I am **excited** about ranking up at work."*

Believe. If you want your affirmations to work, you must believe in them. This is why you shouldn't create statements out of your scope. For example, if loving yourself sounds unbelievable at the moment, you can start with a statement like *"I accept myself despite my flaws."* When you feel ready or less resistant to the idea of self-love, switch it to a more powerful affirmation like *"I love myself unconditionally."*

Heart Chakra Mantra

There are seven bija (seed) mantras associated with each chakra. Reciting them during your meditative practice allows you to vibrate with the same energy of the chakra you're targeting. YAM is the bija mantra that corresponds to the Anahata chakra.

While bija mantras consist of just one syllable, mantras can generally consist of words and phrases. However, these longer chants are mainly recited for their vibrational significance rather than the meaning of their words. When incorporated into yoga practice, bija mantras can help calm the mind and body, keep them balanced and in alignment, and cleanse them.

When you recite the YAM chant, your focus is directed toward the energy of the heart chakra. The Anahata is where the physical body encounters the spiritual essence, impacting your physical, emotional, and spiritual health.

Pronunciation

The VA, LA, YA, and RA are the semi-vowels, or "antahstha," of the Sanskrit alphabet. The bija mantras are primarily made using these semi-vowels. To generate these sounds, you mainly utilize five tongue positions, each of which stimulates the five elements that aid you in balancing the chakras. According to Ayurvedic belief, the body has 72,000 subtle energy channels or "nadis." There are also 84 reflex points (hard palate: 64, soft palate: 20) found in the mouth, which you can stimulate by chanting the bija mantras. Each point corresponds to several nadis. The chanting prompts energy to flow throughout the body by activating passive parts of the brain. Each element is linked to a unique symbol. When you visualize it during your chanting, it can strengthen your connection with its element.

When chanting the YAM, visualize the heart chakra. A green lotus flower represents it with twelve petals and a shatkona (six-pointed star) inside. The YAM chant sounds like YANG. Press your tongue to the front of the soft palate on the roof of your mouth. You can look up the chant and listen to it if you're still confused.

What Is a Mudra?

A mudra is a sacred, typically physical, gesture. This symbolic practice is significant in various faiths and spiritual activities, including Buddhism, Jainism, and Hinduism. However, the most popular mudras are incorporated into meditative and yoga practices. Those are our main focus in this chapter.

Yogists use mudras to aid the flow of prana, or "life force energy," throughout the body. Mudra is a Sanskrit word that translates into "gesture" or "seal." There are around 400 mudras in total when you account for the numerous traditions and religions. Besides their spiritual use, mudras are often used in Indian dance and choreography.

Each mudra serves a unique purpose and affects the mind and body differently. There are three main types of mudras that you can use: hasta, which refers to hand mudras (these are the most common), *kaya,* which are body mudras, and citta, referring to consciousness mudras.

Mudras are used in meditation and pranayama because of how they influence the prana, serving as a great source of support in the practice.

These two mudras can help you balance and heal your heart chakra:

Hridaya Mudra

Place one index finger at the root of the same hand's thumb. Touch the tips of the middle and ring fingers with the tip of that thumb. Keep your pinky finger pointed upward. Keep your palms facing upward and bring your hands to your knees.

This mudra can help you release emotions that have been weighing you down. It can help you let go of stress and emotions

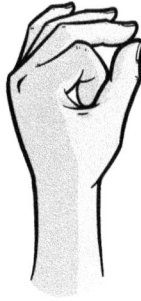

Padma/ Lotus Mudra

Press the bottom of both hands together. Allow the sides of both your pinkies and thumbs to touch. Your index, middle, and ring fingers should be kept far apart. Your hand should look somewhat like a lotus. Bring your hand to the center of your heart before drawing your forearms together. Lift them over your heart, opening your heart.

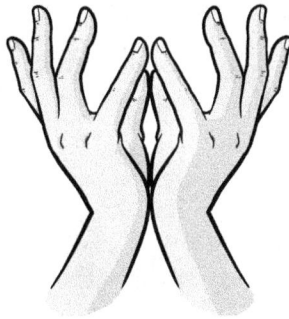

This mudra can help keep you grounded. It is an uplifting gesture that symbolizes purity. Practicing the lotus mudra can help you release negative emotions like loneliness, sadness, and insufficiency.

Mantras, affirmations, and mudras can be great tools for opening and balancing your chakras. They can also help you eliminate negative emotions and enhance certain aspects of your life. Those three simple yet highly effective practices can benefit your daily and spiritual endeavors.

Chapter 5: Meditation and Visualization

Meditating
https://pixabay.com/images/id-198958

Meditation is a brilliant tool for opening up your heart chakra. It's a practice where you allow your mind to relax and your emotions to surface and develop. Yet, many people are reluctant to try it out, not knowing how to add it to their daily schedule, despite it being one of the most accessible mindfulness exercises you can choose. Meditating just a few minutes a day can open, rebalance, or clear out your heart chakra, even if you are unfamiliar with meditation techniques. In this chapter, you'll learn several mediation and visualization techniques, each having a slightly different approach to dealing with Anahata's issues.

Heart Chakra-Unblocking Guided Meditation

"Life can be found only in the present moment. The past is gone, the future is not yet here, and if we do not go back to ourselves in the present moment, we cannot be in touch with life." – Thich Nhat Hanh

This is a relatively simple yet effective guided meditation for opening up your heart chakra. As simple as it is, it still requires preparation time, but only to make it easier for you to clear away anything obstructing this energy center. The preparation consists of reading the script you'll find below a couple of times until you are sure you can read aloud without stumbling, as you'll need to record yourself. There should be a 5-10 second long pause between the paragraphs. If you feel nervous about doing it yourself, you can ask someone else to read it for you while you record it.

When your recording is complete and you feel ready, start your session the following way:

- Sit straight-backed on the floor with your legs crossed or on a chair. You could also do this while lying down if you are awake enough.

- Close your eyes, take a few relaxing breaths, and listen to the recorded directions.

- Inhale deeply, and as you exhale, visualize your heart chakra as a green tree in your chest. Focus on the emerald green light it emits, which radiates towards different parts of your body.

- Then shifting your focus to an individual branch of the luscious tree, visualize yourself climbing it. As you move past the smaller branches laden with thick green leaves, you'll feel their coolness. The sun can't break through them, so you'll always remain safely tucked away in the shade.

- When you reach the top branch and look down, all you see are more lusciously green trees glowing with the same emerald green light.

- Focus on how being there, at the top of the tree, makes you feel. Feel its grounding effect, power, and protecting nature as it's guarding you with its leaves.

- Now imagine this tree being inside of an orb representing your heart chakra. The orb is spinning, and as it does, it imbues your body with the power of the green tree.

- Take a few deep breaths and let yourself become more and more aware of the strength now emanating from the chakra.

- When you are ready, slowly climb down from the tree feeling its protection all the way down.

- Once you reach the ground, look back at the tree and take pride that its power is inside you.

- Then open your eyes and stand up with your green heart chakra now freely transmitting energy into every direction within your body.

A Mindfulness Exercise for Healing and Self-Compassion

Another great way to open or heal your heart chakra is to find compassion for yourself. This will teach you to be kind towards others and allow you to overcome traumatic experiences that damage your heart center. Regularly practicing this exercise will clear away negativity from Anahata and reconnect you with creativity. It also promotes self-expression and spiritual growth.

Here is how to heal your heart chakra through self-compassion:

- Find a quiet space where you'll be able to focus without interruptions and assume a comfortable position.

- Take a deep breath and try to visualize a situation that's causing you anxiety or any negative emotions.

- Now close your eyes, and take a closer look at the situation. Your initial reaction would be to avoid the discomfort it causes, but you are helping yourself overcome it by embracing it.

- Take the time to fully acknowledge what's causing your stress and why. Feel free to say it out loud to enhance the message.

- You must also recognize that experiences like this make you grow and that you aren't alone. And as you would condone anyone who would be struggling the same way you do, you should do it to yourself.

- Affirm to yourself that you are worthy of being loved and that the love has to start from your own self.

- Put your hand over Anahata, and try to release the negativity with a couple of deep breaths.

- Feel the burden lifted from your shoulders and your hand on your chest as a grounding effect. Allow the energy that comes from your hand to heal your heart chakra.

- So, you'll feel the energy all over your body, promoting you to be kind to yourself in the future.

You now have a chance to ask for and cultivate it for yourself, whatever you lacked beforehand - whether it was an inability to forgive past transgression, weakness, lack of compassion or kindness, or anything else.

Anahata Balancing Meditation

Sometimes the emotions are only causing a slight disbalance in the flow of energy through your heart center. In this case, the issue is easier to fix. This simple Anahata rebalancing meditation will restore your energy flow and remove negativity from this center. Here is how to do it in a few simple steps:

- Find a space where you won't be distracted during your session so you can focus on your emotions. You'll need at least 20-30 minutes.

- Sit comfortably either on the ground or in a chair. Keep your back in an upright position with your shoulders tilted slightly forward.

- Take a deep breath and close your eyes. For a few more seconds, continue to focus on your breathing to keep you from being distracted by your racing thoughts.

- When your mind is relaxed enough, switch your focus to the sensations you can feel in your body. Continue to breathe deeply in and out and feel how the air travels to your body.

- When it reaches your heart chakra, the air may cause slight discomfort. If you feel this, try to bring your feelings to the fore at that particular moment.

- Then, start sending positive feelings toward the negative ones in your heart chakra to balance it out.

- Continue the exercise until you feel the discomfort disappearing behind the growing positive emotions.

- When you are ready, open your eyes, and finish your session with an exhale.

Reconnecting with Your Heart Chakra

In this busy world, it's easy to lose track of the state of your chakras. However, without keeping in touch with them, you won't be able to examine them for blockages. Like self-compassion meditation, this one is also based on recognizing what lies within you - only with a slightly different purpose. This exercise will help you reconnect with your heart chakra:

- Start by getting comfortable either by lying flat on your back or sitting with your back straight. Feel free to try out several positions until you find the one that'll make you the most comfortable.

- Start focusing on your breath when you feel that your body and mind have settled down.

- Pause for a few seconds, then open up your collarbones. Put one hand on your heart and the other one on your stomach.

- Notice the space around your heart and what lies within it. You may see that it's growing and shrinking with each breath. This is because the lungs force your belly to expand when breathing in.

- Now take another pause, then move on to the next part - visualizing the green light of your heart chakra. You are breathing in its power, which travels through your body and ultimately ends up in your heart center.

- Feel the warmth of the power you are receiving. This will allow your heart to be open for love. You may feel vulnerable. You must fight this because only by moving on can you find motivation in life.

- Now take yet another pause, after which you can call on your guide. This can be someone you loved in the past and with whom you share fond memories.

- Focus on your loved one's face - bringing it closer and closer, and allowing the green light to envelop them.

- The hardest part comes - you must visualize someone you haven't had the best relationships with. Let them bask in the light as well.

- Finally, you should picture yourself right where you are - only with an open heart chakra. Bring yourself just as close as you did with the other pictures.

- Proceed to cover your own image with compassion, love, and openness now that you are aware of your feelings.

- Once that's done, you'll be able to send these feelings toward others or keep them close to yourself.

After resting for three minutes, open your eyes, get up, and go about your day.

Opening Your Heart with Visualization Meditation

Raising your self-awareness is one of the best ways to open up your heart chakra. Unlike your thoughts, your emotions are far more permanent, which means that bringing them forth is one of the best things you can do for yourself. It doesn't even take much to look around you and understand how you relate to your own feelings and the feelings of others. Often referred to as emotional intelligence, finding kindness, compassion and love are easier than you think - but you must be willing to seek it out.

Here is how to open up your heart in meditation with visualization:

- Start by finding a quiet space where you feel safe and most likely to bring forth love and desire.

- Sit in a comfortable position and close your eyes while trying to relax. The aim is to relinquish control over your feelings.

- Your back should be erect, while your shoulders should be relaxed.

- Take a deep breath and let yourself experience the emotions that come through, no matter how uncomfortable they make you feel.

- Exhale and inhale again, repeating this a couple of times, and allowing some negativity to leave your body and mind with each breath.

- If you feel the tension in any part of the body (except your Anahata), try to let it go.

- Now start focusing on your heart. Feel if there is anything that's making you feel uncomfortable in that area.

- If there is any negativity, try to visualize your breath traveling towards it, relaxing your heart just as it did with your mind.

- Examine the sensations more closely to see how heavy they are and whether they are blocking the energy path or keeping it out of balance.

- Regardless of the weight of your feelings, allow them to come forth fully by sending loving thoughts towards your heart center.

- Now imagine that each of these thoughts nurtures different, positive emotions that will wipe away the negative ones.

- Visualize your thoughts physically traveling to your heart and their breath and removing the uncomfortable feelings one by one.

- Keep repeating it until you feel your heart opening for the new, nurturing feelings. You can even ask your Anahata whether it's ready to move on or not.

- The answer will come instinctively from your emotions. Don't think about it, but let it be the first emotion that surfaces.

- Continue to breathe in and out deeply to let your heart grasp the new emotions it's experiencing.

- When you feel your heart is open enough, bring your hand in front of it in a prayer position and bow your head.

Make sure to express gratitude for all the love and kindness you'll now get to feel before you continue your daily activities.

Easy Meditation Techniques for Busy Days

Contrary to popular belief, not all mediation exercises should be guided and practiced in a quiet room. In fact, at the beginning of your journey, you may find it easier to incorporate a few techniques into your life to make it easier to follow meditation scripts. Trying to quiet your mind while commuting could be good practice, and it won't take you more than a few minutes. Similarly, if you have 5-10 minutes to spare during your lunch hour, you can walk to the nearest park and immerse yourself in nature. This will enhance your visualization skill, and they will be more effective when you get to use them.

Tips and Tricks for Anahata Meditation and Visualization

You probably noticed a few recurring themes in all the mediation and visualization techniques presented above. The first one is that they all require you to find a quiet place where you can work in peace. Whether the duration of a session is five or 45 minutes, you should aim to relax your mind as much as possible. However, this can be quite challenging if people are moving around, distracting noises in the background - not to mention a phone constantly popping up with notifications beside you. You'll need to eliminate them for the best results before approaching your session.

The second thing you may have noticed is that the instructions always point out that your back should be straight. Whether you are standing, sitting, or laying down during your session, slouching can cause your spine and ribs to press on your organs. This makes your activity uncomfortable, and you won't be able to do it properly. Ideally, it's best to do meditations on the ground, but if you prefer to use a yoga mat or sit on a chair (or have to due to medical reasons), feel free to do so.

Wear appropriate clothes for mediation. Once again, what you wear depends on your preferences, but it needs to be clothing that is not restrictive. Yoga attire is also perfectly acceptable. Ideally, the best time to do these exercises is in the morning, when your mind is relaxed right after waking up. You'll also find the effect of the air you breathe more refreshing. There is no better way to rejuvenate your heart center and awaken it than to send positive energy towards it in the morning. If mornings are not going to work for you, there is no harm in doing it during the day. You can use other thought-channeling stimuli for exercises that do not require you to listen to guided meditation. Some people prefer to combine meditation with mantras - something you'll read more about in another chapter of this book. Listening to healing music is another popular choice, as the vibrational frequencies will allow you to feel the sensations spreading through your body. That is, if you don't find this too distracting. If you are used to your thoughts racing all the time, you may find it hard to keep them from distracting you without being in complete silence. While you should acknowledge their existence, you still must learn how to dismiss them.

You may feel that your tight schedule limits your ability to meditate or visualize your chakras. Fortunately, you don't necessarily have to do this as frequently as most guides recommend. Simply recording yourself reading a few guided sessions and listening to them whenever you have time for them will be enough. Whether you do it at night, in the morning, standing in line at the grocery store, or while being stuck in traffic - there are no rules on when to practice compassion and generosity.

If you are keen on trying out some of the mediation or visualization practices described in this chapter, you may also want to look into the next chapter to see which breathing techniques you can use during your sessions. Many are perfect for heart chakra-promoting meditation styles and are incredibly easy to incorporate into any routine.

Chapter 6: Pranayama and Yoga for Your Heart

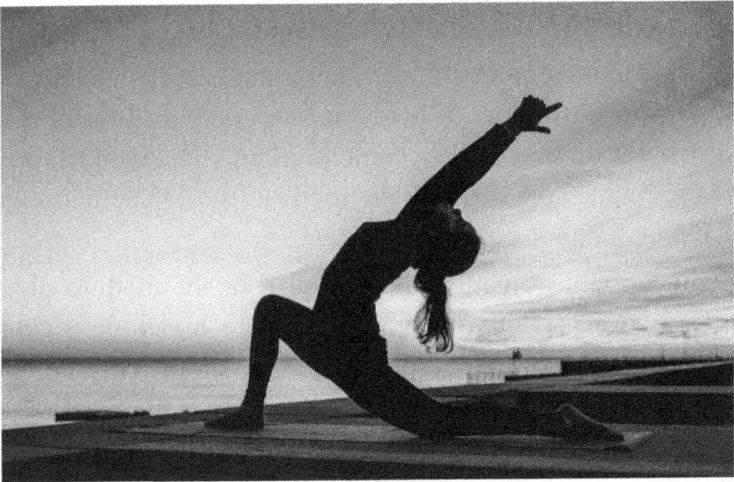

Yoga pose.
https://unsplash.com/photos/F2qh3yjz6Jk

Breathing is an essential part of our lives. It's something we do automatically, whether we're conscious or asleep. In its living state, the human body has to breathe to function and is, in fact, a vital part of our life. The practice of yoga uses this fundamental human function to help us gain control over our mental and physical health. The word

Pranayama comes from the Sanskrit words, Prana, which translates to breath sustaining the body, and Ayama, which means drawing out or extending. Thus, Pranayama means control of breath or extension of breath. Yoga combines Asana and Pranayama techniques to help us attain a deeper sense of peace and calm.

Every cell of our body needs oxygen to function properly, so it's no surprise that practicing controlled breathing techniques can help improve mental and even physical health and have a good overall effect on our well-being. Pranayama techniques aren't easy to grasp at first; however, once you've integrated these methods into your yoga routines, you'll see an almost instant change in your health. This chapter includes a detailed guideline on using pranayama techniques to gain control of your body and incorporate them into your yoga routines to gain control of your heart chakra.

The Science behind Controlled Breathing

Conscious breathing helps us connect with the subtle energy present within ourselves and navigate the different levels of consciousness. Controlled breathing combined with mindfulness helps us connect with different parts of our brains. When you focus on your breathing and let go of every other thought, you become present; your mind lets go of the past and the future and is simply focused on the inhale and exhale of your breath.

While unconscious breathing is controlled by the medulla oblongata, the most primitive part of your brain, conscious breathing is connected with the cerebral cortex, responsible for more evolved thought processes. Controlled breathing thus helps activate the cerebral cortex, which has a relaxing effect on our emotions. In simple words, by controlling your breathing, you're able to control which parts of your mind dominate over others, which will result in the elevation of your thoughts from primitive to evolved.

By practicing different breathing patterns, you can control your emotional state. For instance, slowing your breath makes you relax. When your controlled breathing activates the cerebral cortex, it sends inhibitory impulse signals to the respiratory center of your brain. These signals will overflow into the hypothalamus, which is associated with your emotions, and relax this area.

Pranayama for Balancing Heart Chakra

The heart chakra or Anahata holds more importance than any other of the seven chakras of your body. The central chakra is associated with love, joy, and compassion; Anahata connects the upper and lower chakras, connecting with the spiritual chakras. Your heart chakra must be balanced to achieve a carefree, empathetic attitude. If you feel that your heart chakra may be blocked by negative energy, there are many pranayama techniques you can try to get Qi flowing through your Anahata in no time.

Agni Saar

Pranayama
https://pixabay.com/it/photos/il-kundalini-yoga-yoga-pranayama-4941150

Agni Sara is one of the most effective ways to unblock your heart chakra through pranayama. It is defined as purifying your abdomen by heat generated during breathing. Simple to practice, Agni Saar can be performed by following these steps:

Inhale deeply before contracting your lower abdomen and pelvic floor. Your lower belly should be pulled in and up.

When the whole abdominal wall is completely contracted, suck the diaphragm under your ribs.

Now, release the diaphragm and start inhaling slowly. Release your abdominal muscles as you continue inhaling.

Release your lower belly, inhale, and finally let go of your pelvic muscles.

After you've repeated this three to four times, you'll notice a warm sensation traveling from your abdominal muscles up to your heart.

Anulom Vilom

This technique is perfect for balancing your heart chakra and helps deal with any respiratory or breathing problems you might have. Also known as the alternate nostril breathing technique, Anulom Vilom pranayama helps your lungs function properly for smooth breathing while keeping stress at bay. To practice Anulom Vilom, follow these steps:

- Get into a comfortable position, preferably sukhasana or padmasana.
- Ensure that your spine is straight and your shoulders are pushed backward.
- Use your thumb to block your right nostril and inhale deeply through the left one.
- Now, block your left nostril and exhale slowly through the right nostril.
- Make sure your mind is focused on your breath and not plagued by any other thoughts.

Repeat this process sixty times or for five minutes.

Bhramari

Bhramari pranayama is one of the most commonly used breathing techniques to activate the heart chakra. Also called the bumblebee breathing technique, it can help us connect with our internal sounds and improve our overall brain activity. A bee's humming sound is produced when practicing this technique, which has a soothing effect on our mental and physical health. It is a simple enough technique, which includes the following steps.

- Get into a comfortable meditative position and use your index fingers to plug your ears.

- Keep your spine straight, with your head facing forward.

- Close your eyes, but don't strain them. Keep your mouth closed, but your upper and lower teeth should be apart.

- Inhale deeply for a few seconds.

- As you exhale, create a humming sound in sync with your breath. Make sure you exhale slowly.

- When you're done exhaling, stop producing the humming sound and inhale deeply.

- Keep your ears plugged while doing this, and hum with the next exhale.

- Repeat this process for about five minutes.

Vyana Vayu

Vyana Vayu is one of the five dynamic currents that flow through our chakras. It helps activate the energy of expansion which moves in all directions to connect your physical and spiritual components. This technique mainly targets your heart chakra and helps activate it. Follow these steps to practice it:

- Sit in a comfortable position with your spine straight and your head facing forward.

- Form Anjali mudra (prayer position) with your hands, and bring it close to your heart.

- Think of something or someone you love; this will help open up your heart chakra energy.

- Inhale deeply through your nose while opening your arms as if hugging someone.

- While doing so, imagine a color of your choice flowing out of your heart, through your hands, and out of your fingertips, filling your surroundings with love.

- Exhale slowly and bring your hands back into the prayer position close to your heart.

Continue this process for ten to fifteen rounds until you feel the love engulfing your mind and body.

Benefits of Yoga in Balancing Anahata

When the heart chakra is activated, you'll feel at peace and regard everything with love and compassion. Anahata yoga combines pranayama and asana techniques to stimulate and activate the heart chakra through breathing techniques, controlled postures, and mindful meditation. Many benefits come with Anahata yoga, some of which include:

- It forms a bridge between lower and upper chakras and connects your mental, physical, and spiritual well-being.

- Activating and balancing the heart chakra doesn't just ensure improved health for your heart but also for your lungs, chest, and arms.

- An imbalance in your heart chakra can result in mental health issues, including depression, anxiety, stress, panic disorders, etc. Practicing Anahata yoga will help deal with these issues.

- Anahata poses help release negative energy from your physical body and your mental consciousness.

Recommended Poses for Balancing Heart Chakra

Ustrasana (Camel Pose)

The word ustrasana is a combination of two Sanskrit terms, Ustra, meaning camel, and Asana, meaning pose. So, the word literally translates to camel pose. It is a very common yoga technique used to open your heart chakra, and although it is not very difficult, it is still considered an intermediate-level pose. Certain technicalities in this pose have to be executed perfectly for effective practice. Before getting started, it's recommended that you perform some back-bending warm-up exercises and then follow through with these steps.

Camel Pose
lululemon athletica, CC BY 2.0 <https://creativecommons.org/licenses/by/2.0>, via Wikimedia Commons https://commons.wikimedia.org/wiki/File:Ustrasana_-_Camel_Pose.jpg

- Start with your knees on the ground, wide apart, with your thighs directly perpendicular to the floor.

- Slightly push your buttocks outwards while bringing your elbows together.

- Now, pull up your pubic bone and push your buttocks forward. At this point, you'll start feeling a slight strain in your thighs.

- Next, lift your chest, and rotate your hands outward to grab your heels from behind.

- Open up your chest further by squeezing your shoulder blades as close as possible.

- Hold this pose for five to ten seconds.

- To end the pose, lift both your arms and bring them forward. Sit in a Vajrasana position to relax.

Bhujangasana (Cobra Pose)

Bhujangasana is a Sanskrit word that roughly translates to Cobra (Bhujanga) Pose (Asana). This yoga technique has many positive results, particularly in activating the heart chakra. Not only does this method help reduce stress and fatigue, but it also strengthens your muscles, tones the abdomen, improves the flexibility of your upper and lower back, and helps treat some medical issues related to breathing. Follow these steps to practice the Cobra pose for activating your Anahata.

Cobra Pose
https://pixabay.com/it/illustrations/yoga-posa-del-cobra-posa-di-backbend-5494709

- Lie down flat on your stomach, with your soles facing upwards and toes touching the ground.

- Make sure you keep your legs close together, with your feet touching slightly.

- Place your hand on the ground right under your shoulders, and keep your elbows parallel to your torso.

- Inhale slowly, raising your neck, head, and chest upwards but keep your navel on the ground.

- Now, pull your torso off the ground as well with the help of your hands. However, make sure you're putting equal weight on both hands.

- Slowly curve your spine, and breathe deeply. Be conscious of your breaths and each movement you make.

- If possible, straighten your arms by stretching your back and tilting your head even upwards.

- Maintain this pose for five to 10 seconds.

- Now, exhale slowly and gently, bring your upper body back towards the ground and rest for a few seconds.

Repeat this process four to five times.

Camatkarasana (Wild Thing)

Camatkarasana is a challenging but fun yoga pose that targets your heart chakra. This technique requires strength and flexibility in your shoulders, hip joints, and especially your core. Therefore, warm-up exercises are recommended before you start this exercise. Follow these steps for the Camatkarasana pose.

Wild thing pose.

Mr. Yoga, CC BY-SA 4.0 <https://creativecommons.org/licenses/by-sa/4.0>, via Wikimedia Commons https://commons.wikimedia.org/wiki/File:Mr-yoga-wild-thing.jpg

- Get into a comfortable position and center your body and mind on your breathing.

- Do some warm-up exercises for your shoulders, chest, spine, and neck.

- Now, it's time to activate your chaturanga muscles by doing the downward-facing dog pose and tabletop postures. This will later help with shoulder joint stability during the pose.

- Next, stretch out your front body with postures of a low center of gravity. These can include spring, locust, cobra, half bow, and bow.

- Perform some sun salutations to help strengthen your spine, back body, hips, and shoulders.

- Now, perform some side planks to prepare your body further for Camatkarasana. Ensure that you shift your heels back before shifting from plan to side plank.

- Continue with exercises to further strain your quadriceps, psoas, and obliques through a combination of scorpion tail poses and a downward-facing dog pose.

- Now, inhale deeply and lift up your hips while in the combination of downward-facing dog and side plank pose.

- Exhale slowly while bringing your left foot back on the floor, and keep your knees partially bent.

- Curl your upper back and create a sweeping action with your shoulders into the back of your ribcage.

- Hold this pose for about ten to fifteen breaths, and then return to the downward-facing dog pose. Repeat for the other side.

Matsyasana (Fish Pose)

Matsyasana, or fish pose, is one of the best yoga poses to practice if you're a beginner and want to target the activation of your Anahata. This technique effectively stretches out various body parts, especially those often neglected in yoga asanas.

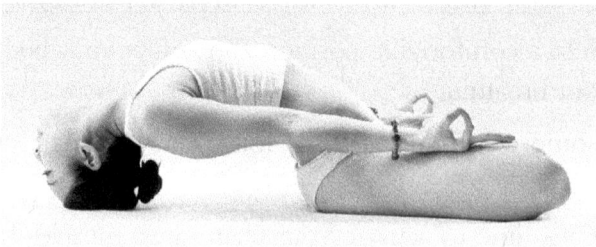

Fish Pose
Mr. Yoga, CC BY-SA 4.0 <https://creativecommons.org/licenses/by-sa/4.0>, *via Wikimedia Commons* https://commons.wikimedia.org/wiki/File:Mr-yoga-fish-pose.jpg

The fish pose helps stimulate two very important regions in your body that are very hard to reach. As well as stimulating the heart chakra, the fish pose also stimulates your Qi to flow through the throat chakra and the crown chakra. Start this method by lying down on your back and following these steps:

- Place your forearms on the mat, and keep your upper arms perpendicular to the ground.

- Puff out your chest by curving your shoulders outward and tucking your shoulder blades behind your back. This will create a back bend effect with your body.

- Tuck your hands under your buttocks or place them on the mat.

- Lower your head towards the ground backward until it reaches your throat.

- Inhale deeply and exhale after a few seconds. Hold this pose for five to ten seconds.

Marjariasana (Cat Pose)

Marjariasana, or the cat stretch technique, incorporates feline grace and stretching into yoga practice. Like the other techniques for heart chakra activation, Marjariasana helps bring flexibility to the spinal cord while strengthening your muscles. It also stimulates the Qi flow through your body and improves blood circulation. To perform the cat pose yoga, follow these steps:

- Kneel on the ground while placing your palms flat on the ground. Form a table with your body where your back will be the tabletop, whereas your legs and hands will act as the legs of the table.

- Your arms should be perpendicular to the ground, with your hands placed on the ground directly beneath your shoulders. Your knees should be wide apart, and you need to look straight ahead.

- Inhale slowly, raise your chin slightly, tilt your head backward, raise your tailbone and move your navel downward. Compress your buttocks, and hold this position for a few seconds.

- Now, exhale slowly and relax your posture. Arch your back like a cat, and bring your chin near your chest. This movement will act as a countermotion. Hold this pose for a few seconds before returning to the first position.

Repeat this process five to six times.

Setu Bandha Sarvangasana (Bridge Pose)

The bridge pose is one of the most commonly back-bending yoga poses practiced by beginners to open up the heart chakra. Setu Bandha Savanga translates to "bridge, all, and limb," in Sanskrit. So, the Setu Bandha Sarvangasana technique uses all your limbs to make a bridge. Follow these steps to perform Setu Bandha Sarvangasana yoga.

- Lie straight on your back with your knees bent apart at hip distance and your legs and feet parallel.

- Now, bring your feet closer to your buttocks and raise your hips such that your lower half is suspended.

- Clasp your hands together underneath your arched back, broaden your chest and balance your body on top of your shoulders.

- Now, exhale slowly, unclasp your hands, and lower your body to the ground. Allow your body to rest for a few seconds before repeating the process.

The heart chakra is one of the essential chakras that, if blocked, can cause you quite a lot of trouble. Many pranayama methods can be used to activate the Anahata. However, yoga is not just about doing poses or performing different breathing techniques. Many levels have to be channeled to activate the heart chakra. So, asana or pranayama techniques alone cannot be enough for this. Instead, you should try to integrate these processes to form a suitable yoga routine that includes meditation, asana, consciousness, mantras, mudras, and other solutions required for opening your Anahata. The last chapter of this book will provide you with a proper routine that integrates all of these solutions for the effective activation of your Anahata.

Chapter 7: Using Crystals and Stones

Crystals and Stones.
Maatpublishing, CC BY-SA 4.0 https://creativecommons.org/licenses/by-sa/4.0 *via Wikimedia Commons:* https://commons.wikimedia.org/wiki/File:Crystals_002.jpg

As discussed in previous chapters, your Anahata, or heart chakra, is where your feelings are centered. Located at the center of your chest, just above your heart, it represents a person's ability to love and to be loved.

And to re-cap, when it's balanced, your heart chakra is linked to empathy, self-care, and the ability to connect to other people. However, it can cause you severe emotional strain when out of balance. It can make you feel alienated from the world around you and make it more common for you to hold grudges.

Additionally, you'll find you have lower self-esteem and may find you have lower energy levels. It can cause you to feel depressed or anxious in severe cases, resulting in physical symptoms like panic attacks, breathing issues, heart palpitations, and more.

Given these issues, it's essential to look for ways to balance your heart chakra. Some options discussed already include:

- Mantras and mudras
- Meditation and visualization
- Pranayama and yoga

However, these are not the only options available to you. Another way you can consider balancing your heart chakra is through the use of crystals and stones.

Understanding Crystal Healing

If you've never experienced crystal healing before, it's natural that you may be a little skeptical about using stones and crystals to balance your heart chakra. Before we can look at the crystal options available to you, we should first look at crystal healing in a bit more detail.

While crystal healing seems like just another New Age fad, crystal healing is hundreds and even thousands of years old. They are used for healing and protection and enhance your meditation by providing you with a focus object that you can use to become aware of your higher self.

The idea behind crystal healing is simple – depending on your concerns, you use specific crystals to help balance and realign your body's systems. The idea is to use the unique frequency and energy field each crystal has and balance your body's energy field in a way that helps deal with your concerns.

It should be noted that each crystal has a different effect, and you need to know what you're using – you cannot simply choose the closest stone or crystal to you and use it to unbalance your heart chakra or improve your ability to meditate. You'll need to choose one that is meant to address your specific concerns.

Stones vs. Crystals

As you may have noticed, we've used the terms stones and crystals interchangeably when it comes to crystal healing. This may lead you to wonder whether there's any difference between the two and if one is better than the other.

The short answer is no. In crystal healing, gemstones and crystals are as good as each other – the only difference is that you choose a stone or crystal that addresses your specific concerns.

However, while there isn't a difference between the two in terms of crystal healing, there is a difference in their mineral makeup.

When we talk about stones in the context of healing, we generally mean gemstones, not any old stone you can find on the road. These gemstones have either a mineral or organic base; they are semi-precious and are categorized based on their mineral makeup. Some examples include jade and amazonite.

Crystals are chosen based on their atomic makeup, which gives them their unique structure. They are categorized based on their structure and shape, and some examples include rose quartz, amethyst, and tiger's eye.

Deciding whether a crystal or gemstone is better for you comes down to several considerations, including what benefit you're hoping for. However, one of the most common deciding factors is cost – while individual prices may differ, crystals are generally less expensive than gemstones, making them accessible to more people.

Choosing a Stone or Crystal for the Heart Chakra

Some factors help determine what stones are good for balancing your heart chakra. This chakra is represented by the color green and the air element, both of which play a significant role in choosing the right crystals and stones.

Given its connection to the color green, green stones are good for this chakra. Along with green, pink is also good for the Anahata Chakra, which is why rose quartz is a popular stone to balance it. These types of stones (green and pink) resonate with the ideas of love, compassion, and truth, linked to your heart chakra.

Additionally, your chakra is one of the higher ones and requires a stronger vibration stone/crystal to balance it out, affecting which options are right for you. Finally, stones and crystals for this chakra are chosen based on how much loving energy they have and their ability to help boost your self-worth, happiness, inner strength, and harmony.

Let's look at some stones and crystals that are especially good for the heart chakra.

Rose Quartz

As mentioned above, this is perhaps the most common crystal used for balancing your heart chakra. It is often known as the stone of unconditional love and is full to the brim with loving, compassionate, and soothing energy. Additionally, it's easy to find, which helps boost its popularity.

It's a great option when you're insignificant emotional distress; for example, you might be going through a contentious divorce, a break-up, or any other loss in your life that is causing you a lot of emotional grief. When used correctly, it can:

- Help boost your sense of self-love
- Help you heal from past trauma and pain by allowing you to accept and understand the situations that caused them
- Support you as you move past those negative emotions
- Open your heart to all types of new love, including romantic, familial, and friendly love – and, of course, self-love

Here's how you can use this crystal:

- Wear it in jewelry so you can benefit from its energy all-day
- Place it under your pillow or near your bed to take in the soothing vibrations at night, which will help you sleep peacefully.
- Place it on your heart chakra during healing sessions, and hold it in your hands during meditation.
- Place it on the windowsill of a room to attract peace and healing to the space – ideally, choose a room in which you spend a significant amount of time. If you're looking to bring it to a

workplace, you can keep it on your desk instead or wear it with you in jewelry.

Emerald

Emerald is a common gemstone, and it might even be something you already have in the form of jewelry. Known as the "stone of successful love," it promotes friendship, unconditional love, and unity and helps keep both romantic and platonic partnerships in balance.

When working with emerald for your heart chakra, this stone has healing properties for your physical and emotional hearts. It helps eliminate negativity, enhances psychic ability, and opens clairvoyant channels, making it a good option to use during meditation. It also boosts your clarity of thought, enhances memory, and affects disorders of the spine, lungs, heart, and more.

You can use this stone as a meditation tool to help promote healing of the body, mind, and soul. While you can also wear it as part of jewelry, it's essential to remember that the stone can be scratched easily and should be taken off before you engage in strenuous activities that might damage the stone, such as swimming, playing sports, etc.

This stone:

- Helps protect you from emotional harm
- Boosts self-confidence and self-esteem
- Helps you understand your inner wisdom and insight by bringing things you know unconsciously to the surface
- Helps you understand the messages of the universe

Malachite

This green stone helps balance and clear your heart chakra, relieving any stress you may be carrying and helping you heal yourself and your relationship with others through apologies and learning to let go. The stone is said to attract love and is associated with the Roman goddess Venus. It's also said to be able to attract loving relationships.

You can use this stone by:

- Wearing it in jewelry. At one point in the past, it was worn as a protective amulet, and this is still the best way to carry it with you to experience its effects all day.

- As a décor element that you can repurpose for healing ceremonies. For example, bowls made of malachite are common decor options but can also be used for crystal healing.

Rhodonite

This pink stone is perfect for people looking to move through tough times in their past. Rhodonite is all about helping you develop a healthy sense of healing and boundaries for yourself. It offers you a way to heal from past hurts so that your heart chakra can be unblocked and you can move on, putting out positive vibrations into the world once more.

It helps break down any emotional walls you may have built up, allowing you to continue your journey through life without fear. It can also help combat low energy and fatigue and connect to your heart and circulatory systems. It also boosts your self-worth, self-confidence, and self-love.

Here's how you can use this stone:

- Placing it in your home or office so that it can shine its healing light throughout the property

- Wearing it as jewelry – rhodonite is a gorgeous shade of pink and, combined with the soothing nature of the stone, makes it the perfect option as an accessory.

- If you choose to wear rhodonite as jewelry, consider wearing it as close to your pulse point as possible – this way, the stone's soothing energy radiates directly to your heart chakra.

Rhodochrosite

This is the older sibling of Rhodonite; Rhodochrosite helps with healing, self-esteem, and self-love. The stone is also known as "the stone of the compassionate heart" or the "inner child stone."

This stone acts as a release crystal, helping you cry and confront the pain in your past, allowing you to move on. As suggested by its name, it helps heal trauma from your childhood or past lives and other old emotional wounds.

You can use it by wearing it as jewelry or leaving it in a room you spend a lot of time in, allowing its vibrations to fill the room.

Jade

Another popular stone, jade, helps heal romantic wounds and attracts more loving energy to your life. It's considered the ultimate lucky gemstone and can also attract prosperity and abundance toward you.

The effects of jade as a purifying and protective stone have been known for thousands of years, and it was used by the Mayans, Aztecs, Chinese, and other ancient cultures for its healing properties. In China, it's given so much value that it is placed above gold.

Here's how you can use this stone to balance your chakra:

- Display jade sculptures in your home, allowing the stone's energy to floor the space
- Place stones directly on your heart chakra during a healing session
- Wear jewelry made of this stone if you're looking to attract a romantic partner into your life

Bloodstone

This gorgeous and unique-looking stone is primarily green, shot with red spots and patches through it. It brings overall emotional healing and is particularly effective for healing and balancing the heart chakra.

The emotional healing it promotes helps you work through the trauma that is causing your charka to be blocked so that you can heal healthily. Additionally, it can help with offering calm, relaxing nights of sleep, and the energy it emits can also help soothe the unpleasant side effects of detoxing and/or stopping smoking.

Here are some ways you can use bloodstone to heal your heart charka:

- Place the bloodstone near your bed or under your pillow before you sleep. Then, keep a crystal healing journal in which you write down whatever comes to your mind first thing in the morning. You can use this to understand communications from your subconscious mind better.

- When laying down, put the bloodstone right on your chest, and allow it to work on your heart chakra.

Cleaning Crystals and Stone

While all of the crystals and stones mentioned above effectively treat an imbalance of the heart chakra, some things make their abilities more (or less) effective. One of these factors is how clean a stone is.

Knowing how to clean your crystals and stones is an essential part of crystal healing, as it allows you to restore and "recharge" them. The relaxing act of taking care of your stones can also boost your sense of self-worth and purpose.

Here's how to clean your crystals and stones:

- Washing your stones under running water for about a minute each. Make sure the stone is completely submerged. This is recommended for hard stones, including quartz.

- Submerge and soak your crystal/stone in saltwater for a few hours but no more than two days. Follow this method for hard crystals and stones, like amethyst and quartz.

- Fill a bowl with dry brown rice and bury the stone/crystals inside it. Leave for up to 24 hours before removing. Throw the rice away immediately, as it takes in the negative energy from the stone you were cleaning.

- Leave your stone outside right before nightfall, allow it to sit there, and bring it back into the home before 11 am the next day. Exposure to both sun - and moonlight can help cleanse it of negative energies. When storing your stones outside, place them directly in contact with the earth. When you bring them back in, rinse gently to remove any debris. This is a method that will work for most tumbled stones.

- Smudge your stone with sage. You'll need to light a bundle of sage to do this, moving the stone through the smoke. Continue for 30-60 seconds, depending on how long it has been since the last cleansing of the stone.

- Use sound healing to cleanse a large area of crystals/stones if you cannot clean them one at a time. You can use everything from a tuning fork to a bell or even chanting to achieve sound healing - the sound should simply be large enough to encompass the target area.

Once cleaned, you'll have to reprogram your crystal/stone. To do so, either place the stone on your heart chakra or hold it while you meditate, speaking to the stone while you do so and asking for help with your current need.

Finally, if your crystal feels heavier than normal, you may have to spend time activating it. You'll essentially need to lend some of your own energy to the crystal to rejuvenate it. You can do so by speaking to the crystal, sending life force energy to it via breathwork, or singing to it.

Alternatively, you can take your stone outside into a natural area. There, let it suck up the natural energy of its surroundings to become activated. Finally, you can also consider setting up an activation grid - this involves surrounding the stone you're looking to activate with more energetic alternatives. You can use any stones of your choice for this task - you just have to make sure they surround the main crystal completely, allowing it to take in the grid's vibrations and energy.

Keep in mind, of course, that using crystals and stones as part of balancing your heart chakra is not for everyone. Some people aren't comfortable using these materials, while others simply find that other ways of balancing chakras work better for them.

Ultimately, it's simply a question of what is more effective for you. There's also a chance that none of the methods described above sound just right. In that case, continue to the next chapter, which explores another option for balancing your heart chakra - aromatherapy.

This book will also go into other questions you may have, including what foods are the best to have for the Anahata Chakra. We'll also provide you with a weekly routine for opening and healing this essential chakra - all you need to do is continue reading!

Chapter 8: Heart Chakra Aromatherapy

Incense & Essential Oils
https://unsplash.com/photos/AuhPy2NofM0

Essential oils are widely used in chakra balancing aromatherapy. They act as a mediator between a person's inner energy and the natural world, allowing them to direct positive energy towards themselves. Through this, essential oils can heal the body and mind, promote personal growth, and do much more. This chapter provides a comprehensive insight into the benefits of aromatherapy for your heart chakra. It also contains a list of essential oils recommended for balancing Anahata.

How Essential Oils Help Balance Anahata

To comprehend how essential oils affect your heart chakra, you first must learn a little more about them. These oils are active biochemical compounds extracted from plants and carry their natural vibrational energy. This energy is reinforced when individual components within each extract interact with each other. They can also interact with your body - which is why they are used in aromatherapy. Because as they interact with your energy, they can affect your health and emotional state and promote spiritual well-being. Aromatherapy for Anahata relies on the therapeutic properties of essential oils - even though they are used in smaller quantities. Sometimes, all it takes is a tiny drop on your skin or a few breaths of air infused with essential oil- and your mind becomes clear, and your heart opens.

Each plant has its own distinct vibrational profile, which means the oils extracted from them will affect Anahata differently. Some will help correct a slight imbalance, while others can grant a complete rejuvenation and healing experience. By using essential oils to reshape the old energy patterns, you are empowering yourself to become an open and courageous person who can overcome any challenge. After all, your heart chakra determines some of the critical experiences of your life.

Essential oils are all about replacing negative emotions, thought patterns, and energies with positive ones. The most significant impact on mental, emotional, or physical health can only be achieved by combining essential oils with other heart chakra balancing techniques. For example, using them can help you relax your body and mind before mediation to explore the energy in your heart chakra. Incorporating essential oils into mindfulness practices can also help expand the state, and you'll get more time to learn about yourself. You can reveal the hidden positivity and bring it forward to balance Anahata, creating a foundation for new experiences and personal growth.

Matching the essential oils to the current condition of the heart chakra is the first step in finding the right product. This may be determined by the mental, physical, or emotional symptoms a malfunctioning chakra displays. Excessive and low Anahata functions require different energies, so you must treat them all with different oils. If you aren't sure which essential oil to use, consult a chakra healer and ask them to determine the exact nature of your Anahata imbalance. Make sure to mention whether you have a specific reason, such as opening your heart to others, personal growth, etc.

Essential Oils for Anahata Aromatherapy

Rosemary

Rosemary is used as a therapeutic oil due to its empowering effect on one's spirituality. Inhaling its aroma boosts self-confidence, allowing you to walk a chosen path. It nurtures your heart chakra by lowering the levels of stress-inducing hormones. This alleviates the physical symptoms of repressed emotions such as weight gain, high blood pressure, and other circulatory issues. Use rosemary oil in your diffuser to calm your senses and release negativity from your body during a mindfulness exercise. Or, inhale a homemade aromatherapy spray to combat the effects of acute stress. You can create this by combining six tablespoons of water with 10 drops of rosemary essential oil and two tablespoons of alcohol. Pour it into a spray bottle and spray it into the air around you or the surfaces you are in contact with for longer periods.

Cardamom

Cardamom promotes the release of stress-reducing hormones, giving you the ultimate happiness. Inhaling it can boost your mood and productivity, helping you to see you can achieve your dreams and goals. Since it's a spicy scent, the refreshing scent of citrus oils can further enhance its uplifting effects on Anahata. Mix equal amounts of cardamom drops and lemon oil drops, and place the mixture in your diffuser to have a stimulating meditation or yoga session. Place it into a nebulizer and inhale it deeply as the scent is released. Wear it in aromatherapy jewelry for constant access to openness. The options are nearly limitless, as even children can use this oil.

Bergamot

Bergamot is one of the best oils to encourage the release of deeply hidden emotions you might be harboring from past trauma. Whether it's anger, guilt, shame, or sadness, bergamot encourages you to accept and express it. So, any time you feel disheartened due to past negative experiences, all you need to do is tap into the energy of bergamot oil to uplift your mood. Those allergic to this oil can opt for having it as a flavor in their teas anytime they feel overwhelmed by the memories from past events. Use it in your diffuser to have a clear mind and find all those pent-up emotions during a mindfulness exercise.

Lemon Balm

Also known as Melissa, this essential oil restores mental and emotional clarity, filling you with positive energy. Its invigorating citrusy scent wakes up your senses, allowing you to see the beauty in being independent. If your Anahata is suffering due to you being complacent to other people's emotions but not your own, the unique power of lemon balm will help you see the error of your ways, balancing your heart chakra. Lemon balm relieves the physical symptoms of a blocked heart center, including hypertension, impaired blood circulation, and an overstimulated nervous system. Combine lemon balm with a neutral and nourishing carrier oil and apply topically to get the most of its healing properties.

Neroli

Another incredibly versatile essential oil brings a wide array of benefits to your heart chakra. For one, its soothing effects promote forgiveness, trust, and emotional development, putting you at ease in stressful situations. On the other hand, it also can have a soothing effect. By helping you release pent-up negative emotions directed toward yourself, neroli relieves the symptoms of depression. Neroli oil also acts as a booster for your self-confidence by preventing infection on the skin, improving digestion, and contributing to weight loss. You can wear a few drops of it as a natural deodorant to balance your heart chakra.

Rose

As one of the universal symbols of love, the rose is one of the most commonly used essential oils for nurturing the heart chakra. Not many people can smell the scent of a rose and not be reminded of nature and our connection to it. The natural beauty of the rose can be an excellent tool for self-reflection. It encourages devotion, compassion, and kindness, starting with one's inner self. By motivating you to get in touch with your true feelings, rose promotes opening Anahata for the connection with others.

Rose is also one of the most versatile essential oils for balancing your heart chakra. Diffusing it promotes beauty from within, as its natural anti-aging properties smooth out fine lines, bringing peace to your heart every time you look in the mirror. Pamper yourself by adding a few drops of rose oil mixed with a carrier oil into bath bombs, so you can enjoy its scent while it fizzes out in the water. For everyday use, mix it with water, drizzle some of the mixtures onto the shower floor and let it permeate the air while enjoying your shower. Use it in your diffuser while meditating on matters of the heart or practicing self-healing yoga.

Lavender

Lavender has a calming scent that soothes your nerves and relaxes your mind, letting it deal with hurtful emotions. It promotes self-healing - which is why it's considered one of the best essential oils for balancing Anahata. By taking care of your mental and spiritual well-being, lavender can aid in finding the harmony and support you need for healthy heart chakra functions. Not only that, but this oil is also perfect for nourishing some of the other energy centers associated with Anahata, further promoting its balance.

Some of the most popular uses of lavender oil include adding two to three drops into your bath-water or using it in a diffuser. Put 5-10 drops into your nebulizer and let it permeate the air while meditating or practicing yoga for your heart. Or, even better, get an aromatherapy necklace that diffuses it to your body throughout the day. If you don't want to invest in a necklace, you can also mix the lavender oil with a carrier oil and put one to two drops of the mixture behind your ear. It will give you continuous access to this beautiful scent, giving you the mental clarity to deal with your emotions in challenging situations. Those without not too sensitive skin can even use it without a carrier oil.

Sweet Orange

Sweet orange is another oil that encourages a cheery disposition by helping you deal with anxiety and frustration. Inhaling its sweet citrusy scent encourages you to adapt to any situation, no matter how challenging it may seem. Mix it into your bath bomb or put a few drops into your bath water to disperse your negative emotions and balance your Anahata after a difficult day. It will give you the emotional clarity for dealing with all the irritating situations you have encountered during the day.

Ylang Ylang

Similar to cedarwood, Ylang Ylang also has a rather powerful aroma you can use to bring forth hidden feelings and desires. Reconciling your emotional and physical aspects of yourself allows you to experience greater joy in life. It promotes a sensuality many people possess but are afraid to display. Due to its strength, Ylang Ylang should always be diluted. You can wear one to two drops of this oil topically or use it in an oil diffuser.

Cedarwood

Cedarwood is one of the best aromatherapy oils if your negative energy stems from insecurity and lack of intuitive feelings. This earthy scent will help you feel grounded, bringing your inner convictions forward and securing them in your conscious. Use it occasionally in a diffuser to fortify your intent and will during meditation and yoga practices.

Roman Chamomile

Roman chamomile has a uniquely harmonizing effect on your heart chakra. It promotes hope, peace, and openness and nurtures positive energy within you, helping you dispel fear. It also encourages the development of a deeper appreciation for yourself. This self-development teaches you how to accept others as well. Even though we all have limitations, we can make up for them by being enthusiastic and motivated to reach our goals. It has a centering effect that encourages action but also helps set boundaries. Use roman chamomile topically around your wrist and neck, or spray it diluted onto your pillow for a restful sleep.

Pine

Pine is a refreshing scent that reminds you of the evergreen forests, exactly the color that feeds Anahata. It can assist you in balancing your heart chakra by helping you deal with old traumas, accept painful emotions, and move on with your life. The ability to experience these negative feelings is something many people struggle with, yet bringing them forward in real-time is the best way to release negative energy. Use essential pine oil in a diffuser, preferably during the evening hours.

Tips for Diffusing Essential Oils

You have probably noticed that most oils should be used in a diffuser. While many commercial nebulizing diffusers are on the market, creating a natural mist can have an even more powerful effect. It's also inexpensive and sustainable, making it a favorite for many. You only need to pour distilled water and aloe vera gel into a spray bottle, add up to 20 drops of essential oil, and you'll have a mixture you can spray anywhere you like. You can spritz it around your space before starting your yoga practice or sprinkle it on your mat or clothes.

Disclaimers and Final Thoughts

Essential oils can open your heart and allow you to nourish positive emotions like love, kindness, compassion, and courage. They'll also assist you in developing healthy practices, including mindfulness and reaching out to others. Whenever you find yourself depressed, anxious, or fearful, you can use aromatherapy to balance your heart chakra. Combined with regular mindfulness exercises, essential oils will help you calm your body and mind so that you can reflect on your situation. You'll realize that it's much better to concentrate on unconditional positive feelings than fixating on negative ones.

Choosing the essential oils you'll use in aromatherapy often comes down to your intuition. Anahata will tell you what it needs - you just need to listen and preferably opt for pure essential oils. Because of their many benefits for your physical and mental health, essential oils can be a valuable instrument in opening, healing, or balancing Anahata. From uplifting your mood to relieving symptoms of stress to giving you the clarity, you need to see the value of positive emotions; their effects are invaluable. However, each essential oil has its own intended purpose and, like most things, must be used with caution.

While pure organic oils contain fewer potentially harmful elements, they are still a very concentrated form of natural chemicals. Make sure to read the labels to understand exactly how much and which method to use. For example, labels will often warn against using the product in a certain way, whether topically or through inhalations. They will also tell you whether they are suitable for children and, if so, in what quantities.

Despite all the advantages, not all oils are harmless, especially not in larger quantities. Some essential oils are suitable for children above a certain age but not for babies and pregnant women as they can cause developmental disabilities. One of the Anahata-balancing essential oils discussed in this chapter and which you need to avoid during pregnancy is rosemary. Even if this does not apply to you, it's still a good idea to be mindful about using essential oils around children and pregnant women.

Allergies are another reason to be careful about using natural oils. Due to the industrial environment and the lack of natural elements people often live in, more and more people are developing allergies to plants and plant products. If you have asthma, your ability to use essential oils may be limited. Always ask for your doctor's advice on which oils you can use. If you are going to use oil on your skin or in your bath, you should always do a patch test beforehand. It's recommended to do this even if you haven't been diagnosed with allergies. Proceed with the application only if there is no reaction to the test. Dilute the product according to the instructions or use an online tool for calculating dilution rates.

Some essential oils are suitable for people of all ages but can be extremely toxic for animals. Make sure you do thorough research on how oils may affect your live-in pets, especially if you'll use them in a diffuser. Avoid contact with animals when applying essential oils topically.

Keep in mind that different issues may warrant the use of different essential oils. The oil used to balance the heart chakra at one particular time may not be right again the next time a different issue causes an imbalance. For example, a lemon essential oil can help clear your mind when you are depressed but won't be of much help when you are feeling stressed out.

Chapter 9: Anahata Diet and Nutrition

From the previous chapters of this book, you've learned about how taking care of your body and mind with dedicated exercise can contribute to the health of Anahata. There is another essential part of your life that you need to pay attention to - and this is how to nourish your heart through a balanced diet and nutrition plan. This chapter is dedicated to all the wonderful foods ideal for introducing into your diet to nurture this chakra. By incorporating them into your everyday diet, you'll soon feel a range of benefits - and balancing your heart chakra is only one of them. You'll also feed the other chakras and improve your fitness levels and overall physical health.

The Importance of a Healthy Anahata Diet

As one would expect, eating unhealthy foods does not do you much good and equally affects your Anahata badly. For one, you are not feeding your body with the nutrients it needs, and sooner or later, this causes a physical reaction, which leads to a blocked heart center. Consuming meals with a low nutritional value can lead to addictive behavior, which results in mental health issues, such as anxiety, depression, and much more. The addiction may also be caused by an unhealthy relationship with food, indicative of prior issues with your heart chakra. It's not uncommon for people to use food (or the lack of it) as an emotional crutch in hard times. However, by doing so, you are only giving yourself a false sense of security and not truly addressing the issue. Even though you may feel like you are feeding your soul with the foods you crave, you aren't. You make things worse, causing negative energies to completely unbalance or block Anahata.

Like all things in life, foods vibrate at a certain frequency. By eating them, you transfer their vibrations onto your body, causing your vibrational energy to drop or rise, depending on the type of food you choose. Raw, natural foods are the healthiest as they can balance, open, or heal your chakras. Not only that, but each energy center in your body is susceptible to different vibrations found in certain foods. While a well-balanced diet is beneficial to your entire chakra system, eating the specific items linked to the chakra you want to nourish will provide even better results.

Which diet is best for each chakra is determined by several factors:

- The functions of the chakra
- The color associated with the chakra
- Personal preferences
- The nutritional profile of the food
- Underlying conditions

As you'll see in the continuation of this chapter, all these elements play a crucial role in making your heart chakra thrive. Except for any underlying conditions, all these can be addressed simply by implementing a few simple changes into your diet.

The Color Theory

The color of the food is one of the primary determining factors for a chakra healing diet. Each chakra resonates with a different color - which is where their associations come from. Anahata is linked to the color green because it resonates with the elemental vibration of nature. So, if you have issues with this center, it makes sense to use green foods to heal, clear, or unblock it. So many elements in nature represent the color green. From the luscious forests to the phytoplankton in the ocean, its purifying effects are everywhere. Putting it into your body promotes the connection with nature, opening up your heart to new, positive energies, emotions, and experiences.

Another reason green food is recommended for an Anahata-based diet is due to its nutritional profile. Different nutrients nourish each chakra, and for Anataha, these are phytochemicals. These are natural compounds produced at various stages in plant growth. Amongst them are vitamins, minerals, and antioxidants your body needs to function at its best. Food abundant in phytochemicals includes green veggies and fruit, grains, nuts, and legumes in various colors.

Here is the list of greens containing the most phytochemicals:

Cruciferous Vegetables: Broccoli, cabbage, Brussel sprouts, and bok choy.

Leafy Vegetables: Spinach, chard, watercress, collard greens, and kale.

Other types of veggies: peas, cucumber, and zucchini.

Bitter Edible Plants: Mustard greens, dandelion, and arugula.

Microgreens: Sprouts with more nutrients than their parent plant.

Green Fruits: Avocado, green grape, lime, kiwi, guava, and green apple.

There are also superfoods, which contain even more phytonutrients in smaller packaging and can boost your nutritional intake. Some of the food from this category include:

Spirulina: A green algae that nourish your heart chakra directly, and it also has blue in it, which boosts your creativity, leading to a higher sense of self-satisfaction, which again feeds Anahata.

Moringa: Also known as drumstick tree, this plant contains nutrients that can help combat depression and other harmful emotions caused by negative energy. Its vitamin content promotes better cognitive functions and a fulfilled life.

Wheatgrass: Contains a form of life chlorophyll that aids nutrition and promotes overall health and well-being. Chlorophyll also contains enough magnesium to provide enough energy to get through stressful days.

Seaweed: Packed with phytonutrients and minerals and low in calories, thus, without a doubt, one of the best options for balancing your heart chakra.

Matcha: Typically used as a powder, it contains caffeine which acts as a natural energy booster and has a calming effect at the same time. Instead of making you distressed as regular coffee does, matcha energizes you by giving you the clarity to focus on important tasks.

Green Tea: Full of phytochemicals that actively work to alleviate symptoms of cardiovascular diseases and improve cognitive functions, green tea is one of the best teas to clear your mind.

Barley: Promotes healthier nutrition by reducing cravings and diminishing attachment to food. It also plays a role in reducing the risk of heart diseases.

The final category of greens that must be mentioned here is the green herbs:

Mint: This sturdy plant will provide you with the same resilience that lies within its nutrient-rich cells. They contain fiber and essential oils in high concentrations, which will heal your heart chakra.

Sage: A plant with a calming effect perfect for meditation, visualization, or spiritual cleansing.

Parsley: Rich in antioxidants and vitamins, parsley contributes to your overall health.

Celery Leaves: Contain several vitamins and minerals, boosting your immunity and thyroid functions.

Needless to say, the best way to consume all these foods is in their raw forms. So, keep them as raw as you can, and cook them only if absolutely necessary. There are many ways to incorporate fresh goods into your diet. From smoothie bowls to salads, there are countless combinations to create. Dehydrated food is still considered raw if it isn't processed using a high temperature.

Eating for Better Heart Chakra Functions

There is another compelling reason why eating organic greens nourishes your heart chakra. Your body instinctively feels the connection to nature through these foods and all the benefits they can provide. Just think about how you feel when walking in the park and observing the nature around you. If you listen closely to your body, you'll notice a sense of calm and openness when surrounded by the color green. As you look at the plants and trees, the association with abundance and growth becomes clearer. This inspires you to become ready for new emotions and experiences, nourishing Anahata. So, what better way to embrace this uplifting energy than through green food? Start by incorporating them into your diet, especially if you aren't used to their taste. Experience different flavor combinations until you find the ones you like. Because there will be some that you won't like, for sure, and that's entirely normal. But the ones you do like will gradually start to fill you with new positive emotions, empowering you more and more.

Organic greens are rich in compounds that promote physical health, particularly that of the circulatory system. They contain folates and Vitamin K, essential for protecting your heart. Add in the high 0levels of magnesium, calcium, potassium, iron, and fiber leafy greens contain, and you get an incredibly healthy mixture. Green food is loaded with antioxidants and vitamins and is also linked to the increased production of oxytocin, the hormone of love.

You can also explore other parts of the color spectrum, particularly the regions linked to the lower chakras. If you remember, nourishing these plays a crucial role in providing Anahata with a continuous energy flow. So, feel free to combine your greens with produce that benefits your root, sacral, and solar plexus chakras. Another reason for doing this is that not all the best Anataha nourishing food is green. You probably heard about how cacao makes people feel better, and it's not remotely green. Unlike cocoa, cacao isn't processed at high temperatures. Yet, it can open up your heart in more ways than one.

However, be careful when choosing this product. After initially being extracted from cacao beans by cold pressing, cacao goes through various steps of refinement. Look for raw cacao products to get the most out of this delicious food. Organic cacao contributes to the release of dopamine and serotonin - the hormones responsible for uplifting you in stressful situations. It also contains magnesium, which provides you with energy and improves your cognitive functions - leading to increased productivity and a sense of fulfillment. Magnesium is also a mood booster, chasing away your worries similarly to serotonin and dopamine. The antioxidants in cacao can clear up your skin and protect it from the effects of aging and UV damage. They are also shown to increase immunity and reduce the risk of plaque formation in the arteries.

After lifting your mood and making you feel good about yourself, it's easy to see how cacao can help you reconnect with those around you. After all, who can resist the temptation of cacao offering? So, feel free to share your experience with others and encourage them to switch refined cocoa products to organic cacao. You may all soon find it easier to open up about your emotions, deal with day-to-day stress, and heal from past negative experiences together, effectively growing your emotional intelligence and Anahata.

Fun, Healthy, and Simple Anahata Recipes

Incorporating heart chakra-nourishing food into your diet is easier than you think. Here are some simple recipes for you to try out for breakfast, lunch, and dinner.

Green Superfood Smoothie

There is no better way to prepare your heart chakra for the day ahead than to have a delicious green smoothie for breakfast. This recipe uses kale, green apples, kiwi, mint, wheatgrass, and almond milk. The green veggies, fruit, and superfood are distinctive Anahata balancers, while the herbs add a little zest to the mixture. Wash the kale, the wheatgrass, and apples and cut them into smaller chunks. The size you need depends on whether you use a blender or a food processor to make your smoothie. Toss all the ingredients into the machine and process them until you get a smooth consistency. When finished, pour your smoothie into your favorite cup, and take your breakfast on the go.

Green Goddess Smoothie Bowl

This smoothie bowl is the perfect option if you are looking for a quick and easy yet healthy breakfast with a little more punch. It's also quite refreshing on warm summer mornings. For this, you'll need avocadoes, frozen mangos, frozen bananas, kale, kiwi, coconut milk, and shredded coconut. Wash the kale, and cut the frozen fruit and avocados into chunks. Add them into your blender or food processor and pour coconut milk over them. Blend until the mixture reaches a smooth consistency. It should be thick enough to be eaten with a spoon. Pour it into a bowl and sprinkle the top with the shredded coconut. Add a few thin kiwi slices on the top, and your smoothie bowl is ready to serve.

Heart Healthy Spinach Avocado Salad

Spinach and avocados are the two most recommended foods for opening or balancing Anahata. The spinach raises oxytocin levels, expanding your capacity to feel love and compassion, while the healthy fats in the avocados will keep your heart in check physically. And you need besides these two ingredients are just some red onions, limes, sea salt, and olive oil. Wash the spinach, and cut off the stems if you use mature leaves (you can skip this step with baby spinach). Cut the red onions and the avocados into bite-sized chinks. Sprinkle the spinach with lime juice and olive oil, then season with salt to your liking. Mix it until the spinach is coated. Add in the avocadoes and the onions and mix again until well combined.

Happy Heart Salad

This recipe is ideal for a light summer salad because it contains baby spinach, baby kale, pomegranate seeds, sunflower seeds, and shredded parsnip. Wash and dry the leafy greens, then place them into a bowl. Shred the parsnip and sprinkle it over the veggies, along with the sunflower seeds. Add pomegranate seeds, drizzle the mixture with lime juice, then mix until well combined. You may also add finely sliced fresh artichokes to make it even heartier and more filling, or enjoy the salad.

Kale and Brussels Sprouts Salad

Kale is an excellent food for sprucing up Brussel sprouts - something we all wish for. You'll also need toasted almonds (slivered if possible), toasted sesame seeds, red pepper flakes, maple syrup, tahini, a flavored vinegar of your choice, and some water. Wash, dry, chop, and place the kale into a bowl. Slice the stem of the Brussel sprouts, then cut them into bite-sized chunks. Add them to the kale, and then make the dressing in a smaller bowl. Pour the vinegar, maple syrup, red pepper flakes, and tahini into the bowl, and mix until well combined. Add some water to get a smoother consistency. Coat the salad with the dressing and mix everything once again. Top it off with the toasted sesame seeds and almond slices.

Disclaimer

Lastly, it's important to note that a professional nutritionist hasn't created this chapter; therefore, it must be treated only as a general guide on what foods can contribute to your Anahata health. For the best results, it's always a good idea to check in with a nutritionist with experience in chakra healing before making any drastic changes in your diet. A professional can assess your needs and determine which foods your body and mind require for optimal health. By assisting you with creating a personalized meal plan, they can also help you incorporate these items into your regular diet. If you have any underlying conditions, you'll also need to consult your health care specialist to avoid making the issues worse. They can determine how a particular new diet could affect your body and mind.

Once your doctor and your nutritionist have given you the green light, you can start to make the changes to unblock, heal or balance your heart chakra. When doing so, remember to eat food you enjoy and not just because they are recommended. Even though a varied diet full of greens will improve your physical and mental health, your Anahata will still suffer if you don't find joy in your meals. You must nourish your soul to have your heart center fully open and its function as a bridge for the natural energy in your body employed at all times.

Keep in mind that many raw green veggies contain organic compounds that can be toxic if consumed in high quantities. This is particularly true for leafy greens like spinach and kale, containing oxalate, a compound linked to kidney stones. While baby green contains lesser amounts of oxalate, you still want to be careful how often you consume them. Make sure to rotate your leafy greens daily to avoid ingesting too many toxic compounds. It will also help to incorporate as many of them as possible into your diet to avoid getting bored. Although greens can go a long way to balance Anahata, having a well-balanced diet will ensure you stay happy and healthy, and your heart chakra stays open for positive energy.

Chapter 10: Anahata Chakra Seven-Day Routine

Now that you've read almost the entire book, you probably realize that opening your heart chakra can't be done overnight. You need to try various activities and experiment with different methods to understand what works best for you. The thing with the chakra system is that it requires ongoing care and maintenance. If you finally release the blockages in the heart chakra but never follow up, the Anahata will likely fall out of balance as soon as you're met with a series of negative events and emotions. We can't always prevent bad things from happening, but we can learn how to respond in healthy, mindful, and accepting ways. Everything we've mentioned in the previous chapters, from mantras, mudras, and meditation to crystals and diets, will help you work toward this goal.

When you embark on the journey that is opening your chakras and balancing them, you have to realize that the changes you make to your lifestyle should be sustainable. Following a seven-day routine whenever you feel like you're starting to fall behind can help you stay on track. Even if it's just for one week, this routine will help remind you of your goal and what matters the most. It can be hard to get yourself out of bed to start a meditation session. However, if you feel obliged to do it as a part of your weekly routine, you'll be reminded of how much fun it is and how great it makes you feel. It takes the average person around 21 days to build a habit and 90 days to set a lifestyle in stone. You can follow this routine every week until you make these positive activities a habit. Hopefully, when you get the hang of it, you can make some changes to mix it up a little.

The first seven days will be fun and will feel like a breeze. However, the longer you continue, the more danger there is of becoming demotivated and worn out. When this happens, don't be afraid to hit pause for a day or two before carrying on with the routine. You can also decrease the intensity or take some tasks out of each day. Remember that consistency is key, and you can't stay consistent if you're too tired and lack motivation. Don't stress yourself out! This is supposed to be a fun and experiential way to balance your Anahata.

This chapter includes a seven-day routine that will allow you to open your heart chakra and enhance different aspects of your life. The routine comes with a mix of mantras, mudras, affirmations, and diet recommendations to help you work toward your goal. As we mentioned above, you can repeat this routine whenever you want. After you've completed this routine as many times as needed, you can retake the quiz in chapter two to re-assess the status of your heart chakra.

Seven-Day Routine for Balancing the Heart Chakra

Each day of the week focuses on a certain theme, so you focus on a different aspect of the heart chakra each day.

Day 1: Go Green

Green is the color of nature on a universal level. It symbolizes trees, plants, meadows, and pastures. When hearing the word "green," most people envision vast forests, think of the scent of freshly mown grass or the refreshing fragrance of rain and earth, recall the feel of dewy leaves, or hear the sounds of the chirping birds in their heads. The color green also happens to be that of the heart chakra.

We feel inspired, safe, reinvigorated, and at peace when we see the color green. This color also promotes positive emotions like optimism, hope, compassion, and harmony. Green has been scientifically proven to make the mind and heart feel at peace. These are all elements e essentially associated with the Anahata chakra. Besides the trees and plants, the color green also corresponds to the nature of the human body. It is a symbol of good health and great well-being. When the heart chakra is at its optimal state, it lives up to the correspondences of the color green. It grants you peace of mind and allows you to feel calm and relaxed. An open heart chakra allows you to connect easily with everyone and everything around you, including nature. So, it only makes sense that you dedicate a day in your routine to going green.

The Routine

Affirmation: *"I live harmoniously with all other beings."*

This is your main affirmation for day 1 of the routine. If you wish, you can combine it with other affirmations to set your intention for the day.

Take a long walk in nature.

Go for a half an hour walk in nature. Listen to relaxing music, observe the various hues of green, and notice the animals and their behaviors. You can take your shoes off and feel the grass or earth beneath your feet. Fully immerse yourself in the experience, and don't forget to take deep breaths, filling your lungs with the crisp air.

Have a green, hearty bowl of salad.

Gather all the green ingredients you can get your hands on, like peas, romaine lettuce, cucumbers, green onions, kale, and avocados, and make the greenest salad you can eat.

Practice the Lotus Mudra.

This mudra is great for the heart chakra and allows you to stay grounded. Besides being representative of nature, this mudra is known to offer mental purity.

Carry an Aventurine.

This green crystal can help you release negative feelings and emotions. It also allows you to welcome new opportunities and challenges, making it the perfect crystal for day 1 of the routine.

Day 2: Build Boundaries

Boundaries are limits you need to set within all your relationships (yes, even your relationship with yourself. They are necessary to preserve your mental, emotional, physical, and spiritual health. When you don't have strong and healthy boundaries, your heart chakra is prone to falling out of balance. If you find it difficult to set much-needed limits for your social, romantic, and professional interactions, then this is the time to do something about it.

Day 2 of the routine is all about pinpointing the areas in your life in which you allow people to overstep your set limits. Do you often say yes to other people's requests and favors even when they compromise your own needs and well-being? Do you or others set very high standards and expectations for you? Today, you'll put yourself first and practice being assertive.

The Routine

Affirmation: *"I prioritize nourishing my spirit, soul, and body."*

The main affirmation for day 2 of the routine will help you set the intention for your day: practicing assertiveness and self-care.

Practice the Anahata Balancing Meditation.

Refer to chapter five for instructions on how to carry out this meditation. When you lack personal boundaries, you risk burning yourself out and promoting a hindrance in energy flow through your heart center. This meditation will help restore balance and release negativity.

Say "No."

Think of this day as an opportunity to just say "no" to anything you don't feel like doing. It may feel uncomfortable, but it will spare you your mental and spiritual health. Repeating the day's affirmation to yourself will help you stand your ground.

Use essential oils.

You can either put essential oils in a diffuser or add a few drops to your bath as a form of self-care. This will help you relax and relieve some of your tension, and essential oils like Ylang, Frankincense, and Sandalwood can help balance your heart chakra.

Day 3: Love Yourself

An imbalance in the heart chakra comes with a disrupted state of self-love and compassion. When the Anahata is overactive or imbalanced, we tend to seek validation, compassion, and acceptance from those around us. Individuals with an unhealthy heart chakra find it hard to achieve self-sustenance and resort to tactics like people-pleasing and desperation.

To restore balance to your heart chakra, you have to practice self-love. Day 3 of the routine focuses on treating oneself with compassion and tolerance.

The Routine

Affirmation: *"I deeply accept and love myself."*

This is the primary affirmation for day 3. You can combine it with similar self-love-related affirmations to help reinforce the goal for the day.

Chant the YAM mantra.

Find a comfortable space to chant the YAM matra for at least 10 minutes. This will help you find peace and compassion toward yourself and others.

Do the Camel pose.

Refer to chapter six for instructions on doing the Camel or Ustrasana pose. The Camel opens your heart and helps you build self-trust and faith. Nothing promotes self-love like a yoga pose that allows you to embrace your body and its strength.

Don't suppress your thoughts and emotions.

On day 3 of the routine, avoid suppressing any thoughts or emotions you may receive. Allow yourself to feel all your emotions, even negative ones. Take the time to reflect on them and accept them. Similarly, don't be afraid to speak your truth even when someone challenges your beliefs.

Carry an Amazonite.

This crystal will help you settle emotional disturbances. It will also help you stand for what you believe in and embrace your passion and compassion.

Day 4: Spread Love

The heart chakra is all about being loving, compassionate, and tolerant toward yourself and others. We were all created to interact and communicate with others. A blocked heart chakra can make you closed off and lonely. To break this cycle, you need to get comfortable with giving and receiving love. This is the main focus of day 4 of the routine.

The Routine

Affirmation: *"I am open to receiving and giving love."*

Day 4's affirmation declares your openness to giving love to others and receiving it back. On this day, you'll not resist compassionate exchanges.

Chant the YAM mantra.

Chant the YAM mantra for as long as you need to be able to cultivate feelings of love and compassion in your interactions.

Reconnecting with Your Heart Chakra Meditation

Refer to chapter five for instructions. This meditation will help you reconnect with your Anahata chakra and open it for love. It will teach you to repair relationships and let go of negative emotions.

Do a random act of Kindness.

Day 5: Cleanse Your Heart

When you have a blocked heart chakra, you'll hold onto negative emotions and grudges. You repress feelings and find it hard to let go of past traumas and unpleasant experiences. The more you feed into this, the more challenging it becomes to unblock your heart chakra. It's a vicious cycle.

The Routine

Affirmation: *"I let go of past hurt."*

Day 5's affirmation allows you to let go of previous hurtful experiences, which is the main scope of the day.

Practice forgiveness.

Feel all the negative emotions, such as regret, guilt, sadness, and grief, that are currently weighing you down. Write as many letters as you need to, to anyone who has hurt you (even if it's yourself). Express your emotions and how their (or your) actions have affected you. Once you let it all out, burn these letters and visualize all the negative emotions dissipating with the smoke.

Open Your Heart with Visualization Meditation.

Refer to chapter five for instructions. This meditation will help you replace negative emotions with more fulfilling sensations.

Do the Cow Pose.

The cow pose will help you invite love and positive emotions throughout your day. Refer to chapter six for instructions.

Day 6: Breathe

Breathing deeply is one of the ultimate solutions for healing the chakras. It allows you to revitalize the life force flowing through your body. Breathing exercises can help you release the pent-up pain and negativity in your body, allowing you to make the space for pure love and peace.

The Routine

Affirmation: *"My heart space emits vigorous green light."*

Day 6 is all about revitalizing your heart space and learning to control your emotions through breathing exercises.

Go for a long walk.

Take a long walk and allow yourself to clear your mind. Draw deep breaths in and out of your lungs, and focus on breathing at an adequate, collected pace.

Practice Bhramari pranayama.

Refer to chapter six for instructions. This breathing exercise will help you let go of frustration and anxiety. It's a simple technique that helps you calm your mind.

Day 7: Reflect

Many of us carry traumas and negative life experiences throughout our life journeys. The longer we hold onto them, the more challenging they are to release. This undoubtedly makes it impossible to keep the heart chakra balanced.

The Routine

Affirmation: *"I free myself of feelings of resentment."*

This affirmation sets the tone for the final day of the routine: reflection.

Take up journaling for the day.

Reflect on all the traumas or undesirable feelings you've dragged along throughout your life. Think about how they hinder the quality of your life. What can you do about them? Can any of the activities you did during the seven-day routine (including journaling) potentially help you deal with those negative emotions?

Write about the different ways (even if they're subtle) this routine has changed the quality of your day.

Do the Hridaya mudra.

Refer to chapter four for instructions. This mudra can help you let go of stress and other unwanted emotions that weigh you down.

Do the Mindfulness Exercise for Healing and Self-Compassion.

Refer to chapter five for instructions. This exercise promotes spiritual growth, making it the perfect way to end your routine.

Following this routine can be a very good opportunity to test your patience, resilience, and determination. It will also expose you to new and healthy activities while elevating various aspects of your life. While this routine is fun, you have to keep in mind that you may lose your excitement if you plan on doing it every week. Know when to cut back so you don't wear yourself out.

Bonus: Rising into the Upper Chakras

As we have explored the enchanting world of the heart chakra, we've seen that it holds a vital place in ensuring the longevity of our overall well-being. Have you always struggled with trusting or loving others around you, or perhaps it has always been hard to connect with others? People who struggle with balancing their heart chakra often have issues relating to their relationships or connections. You'll also see them having trouble forgiving others and tend to hold deep-rooted grudges against others. They may also struggle with the problem of social anxiety. This bonus chapter will talk about the benefits of balancing your heart Chakra and how to move up to the higher chakras.

A Glance at the Heart Chakra

As we've learned, the heart chakra in Sanskrit means "Anahata" or "unhurt" and is located at the center of the chest. The element of air is linked with this Chakra, and its color is "green." In general, the Anahata or heart chakra brings stability to relationships with others and self by improving the ability to forgive or love oneself or others. However, an imbalance in this Chakra may bring the big guns out - the feelings of jealousy, hatred, or selfishness and their empathy, forgiveness, and compassion for self and others. In other words, the energy centers in our bodies have an important role in developing psychological, emotional, spiritual, and physical well-being. With the main chakras balanced well, you can swiftly embark upon a healthy style of living.

To encompass all the benefits and prosperity that opening up Anahata can bring is beyond the scope of this book. This is because of the expansiveness of the heart chakra and all the numerous benefits associated with it. It is a mystical link between the upper and lower chakras and connects the spiritual and physical realms.

Opening the Anahata

There are various reasons to open or unblock the heart chakra, and one of the most obvious is to ascend to other upper chakras. For instance, if you want to move up to the throat, third eye, or crown chakra, you must ensure that the Anahata is already balanced. To open the heart chakra, you can start implementing four simple things in your day-to-day routine.

The first thing to help balance the Anahata is burning incense and using essential oils because aromatherapy has strong healing attributes. It is also helpful in uncovering the feelings of forgiveness and love. You can use essential oil and scented incense (lavender, orange, rose, jasmine, or sandalwood scent). This ritual has a generally calming impact on the nerves.

The next significant activity that you must make an integral part of your daily routine is to rehearse positive affirmations about embracing the energy of love. You can formulate any sentence that solidifies this emotion. The primary aim is to set powerful intentions that help you break away from the old habits and move towards the healthier (newer) ones. So, any affirmation that speaks about compassion and love would be helpful to open the Anahata and keep it in balance. You can also try the postures that are helpful with opening the heart chakra, including the camel, bridge, and upward-facing dog posture.

One of the most essential things to keep in mind is to ensure that you welcome the emotion of love. To do this, you have to be in a position of exchange, meaning you have to "give love" before receiving it. So, think daily about all the things that you can do in your day to make others around you happy by expressing your love. It could be as simple as smiling at someone looking at you, letting go of old arguments, or parting ways with criticism or gossip. Showing appreciation and acknowledging the efforts of those around you'll also help open the heart chakra.

You don't have to confine yourself to these few ideas to balance your heart Chakra and move up to other higher chakras. You'll have to give more than you're expecting. You have to think outside the box and simply *outdo your best self*. Now that we have discussed ways to balance the heart chakra, we will be exploring more about opening the crown chakra, throat chakra, and the third eye chakra.

An Overview of Throat Chakra

The throat chakra belongs to the group of upper chakras and is also known as the "Vishuddha chakra." It is associated with the element of "space" or "sound" and is represented by the color blue. The linked crystals include turquoise, blue stones, and aquamarine. The Vishuddha chakra is primarily responsible for self-expression and better communication. Having a well-balanced throat chakra means that you can speak your truth openly, without any hindrance or hesitation. Before you can think about working to balance this upper Chakra, you have to recognize the possible blocks that are often linked with this Chakra and how to remove those blocks.

Since the throat chakra plays a role in creative expression, communication, and self-expressivity, any block or imbalance in the Vishuddha chakra will lead to difficult ineffective communication. A blockage in the throat chakra may manifest as:

- fear of sharing your truth with the world
- having difficulty practicing self-expression
- feeling extremely anxious about communicating or speaking your truth

As long as the Vishuddha chakra remains unbalanced and unattended, there may be sudden shifts in behavioral expressions. For instance, the person may exhibit emotional outbursts or opposite (than normal) emotions. A fifth chakra (heart chakra) imbalance results in extreme criticism towards self and others. The person may also suffer from "raspy throat," "mouth ulcers," laryngitis, sore throat, thyroid challenges, or TMJ disorders. Below are some quick tips to help you resolve these obstacles to balancing your throat Chakra without any further delay.

The first thing you can do is add more of the color blue to your day-to-day life. You can go for blue-colored crystals because the throat chakra is related to sound energy and resonance. This means that the crystals will be quite effective in working to open the blockage in this Chakra. You can either wear a ring or another piece of jewelry using these blue stones. *(Wearing a necklace is recommended since it's hanging close to your throat.)*

Stretching your neck is another helpful strategy to deal with the blocked throat Chakra. These neck exercises don't have to be complex, and neither would you need to perform any type of headstand. You can start working towards opening your throat Chakra with a simple neck or throat area exercise that prevents buildup or stress from your neck.

The next quick and simple tip is to pay attention to your breathing pattern. You'll have to use the breathing strategy known as the lion's breath. It is quite helpful in getting rid of the toxins and stimulates your chest and throat areas by releasing the stress or tension buildup.

You can also perform yoga poses that relieve your body of the tensions around this area. Also, yoga would generally help you keep the stored energy flowing. You can practice the yoga pose of "stand, plow, and fish."

Another intuitive option is to try a reiki healing session. Reiki is beneficial to all the chakras in our body, so it is worthwhile investing in this.

In addition to the tips, you can add journaling to your daily routine and ensure that your neck is in natural alignment with the spine while sitting. Working with Bija Mantra also helps with the throat upper chakra.

People are often confused about the signs pointing toward an unbalanced throat Chakra, but they are quite hard to miss if you observe closely. The person with a blocked throat Chakra may experience low self-esteem, depression, or anxiety. They may also show difficulty in expressing themselves and an inability to speak. It is necessary to unblock this Chakra if you want to be an effective communicator. With a balanced and healthy throat chakra, anyone can speak their mind and at the same time be compassionate with how they speak and what they say.

An Overview of Third Eye Chakra

Some people label the third eye chakra as a sixth sense and often point its location to the middle of both eyes. Ajna, or third eye chakra, is the sixth one in the wheel of energy chakras and is thought to be linked with spiritual ascension, awareness, and perceptual clarity. According to popular belief, having an open third eye chakra helps with insight and wisdom and enhances the spiritual links. This Chakra is considered to be a doorway to the spiritual realm.

A blocked Ajna would cause various issues, including cynicism, pessimism, confusion, lack of purpose, and uncertainty. While working towards opening this Chakra, you can enjoy a serene mental clarity, clarity of self-expressiveness, a sense of bliss, and improvement in concentration span. The person with an open Ajna will also have very strong qualities of intuition and decisiveness. To activate your third eye chakra, you can try one of the following and explore what works best for you.

You can start at the activation phase by sending a message of gratitude to the third eye.

You may also need to detoxify and eat pure food to strike a balance in your third eye chakra.

When opening the third eye, using essential oils is also an integral part of the healing ritual.

Another method is to try to sun gaze, and although you may not be able to maintain eye contact for long, this exercise can be very helpful in opening up the third eye chakra for you. Meditation and chanting different affirmations are also quite helpful with unblocking eye chakra.

An Overview of Crown Chakra

This Chakra is particularly linked with thoughts, and, as an element, it controls spiritual connections. It also helps you connect with the universal consciousness and touch the realm of wisdom and self-knowledge. The color linked with this Chakra is violet, reflecting its connection with enlightenment or spirituality.

The Crown chakra happens to be the uppermost Chakra and has a big part in the enlightenment and self-actualization process of an individual. A blocked crown chakra will manifest as a general imbalance in different areas of your life, poor coordination, and substantially decreased physical functionality.

If you are planning to work with this Chakra, you'll have to spend a decent amount of time reflecting on the world as it exists around you. Give some thought to yourself and practice introspection. You may want to ask yourself some bigger questions, like, "How to be better than today?" or "How do the world and I connect with one another?" or "How to remove the confusion about my role in the Universal plan?"

Understandably, if you are struggling with a blocked chakra, you'll feel confused in general, and there will be a diminished connection to the world around you. It is also possible to experience hyper-spiritualization or a decline in mental functioning. To avoid all the negative effects of an imbalance in the crown chakra, you must align it. Since crown chakra is recognized as a gateway to super-consciousness, it would not be wise to leave it unattended. You can achieve this by practicing the pranayama for this Chakra. Another way to unblock crown chakra is by investing time in reading books and gaining knowledge. You can also activate your crown chakra by practicing "silence." When you are quiet, you listen actively, enabling information acquisition.

While working with your upper chakras is necessary *(and aligning them will manifest various physical, psychological, emotional, and spiritual benefits)*, you must remember that it is not mandatory. However, given the benefits and potential of growth, it is certainly a worthwhile endeavor to indulge in.

Conclusion

Often linked to love, innocence, and compassion, Anatha is the fourth Chakra in your energy system. Located at your heart, it acts as a bridge between your lower and upper chakras, making it one of the most influential chakras. When obstructed, the heart chakra can affect the function of all the other energy centers, particularly the lower ones. This effect can manifest as solely within an inactive or overactive Anatha, although this is rarely the case. Physical, emotional, and cognitive symptoms in organs governed by the other chakras are just as common.

At the same time, the blocked or unbalanced lower chakras will not allow energy to flow freely toward Anatha, hindering its health functions. For this reason, when dealing with heart chakra blockage, you mustn't focus only on opening this center. You must explore the lower centers as well. You'll find that, often, the solution to your problem lies in clearing up the negative energy in your other chakras.

This negativity is often caused by traumas from your past affecting your emotional health in the present - something you weren't aware of until you decided to look deeper into the issue. This book contains user-friendly tools that will help you assess your symptoms and determine the current status of your Anatha.

With Anatha being linked to so many powerful emotions - including the sense of trust, peace, fearlessness, security, generosity, ability to change, grow, establish boundaries, develop emotional control, and love for yourself - there are plenty of reasons for keeping your heart Chakra in balance. Fortunately, there are many ways to achieve this, whether by nourishing this center or the lower ones.

After establishing a strong chakra foundation, you can move on to exploring the mantras and the mudras. Remember that these are slightly different from typical affirmations as their effect on your body and mind is infinitely greater. You may also find solace in the range of meditation and visualization techniques designed for opening Anahata. Some techniques appeal to a wide audience, whatever your lifestyle or knowledge of yoga, meditation, or any other mindful philosophies. The deep breathing and similar mindfulness techniques you learn can also come in handy if you decide to try yoga poses for your heart. After all, yoga isn't just about maintaining your posture - it grounds you and intertwines with many other layers of chakra healing. Apart from physical activity, you'll also need to pay attention to your diet and nutrition and consume food that promotes your heart chakra's opening. The use of aromatherapy may also bring you some benefits on this front, along with healing crystals and stones.

Due to being an essential part of the flow of energy towards higher chakras, balancing the heart chakra opens up the possibility of raising your energy in the upper centers. If you are experiencing problems with a blocked throat, third eye, or Crown Chakra, the solution may be found in your Heart Chakra. Not only that but balancing them could bring the harmony you need in your life. It's not a necessary step, but it may just be what you need to improve your life and grow spiritually.

Part 5: Throat Chakra

The Ultimate Guide to Unblocking, Balancing, and Opening Vishuddha

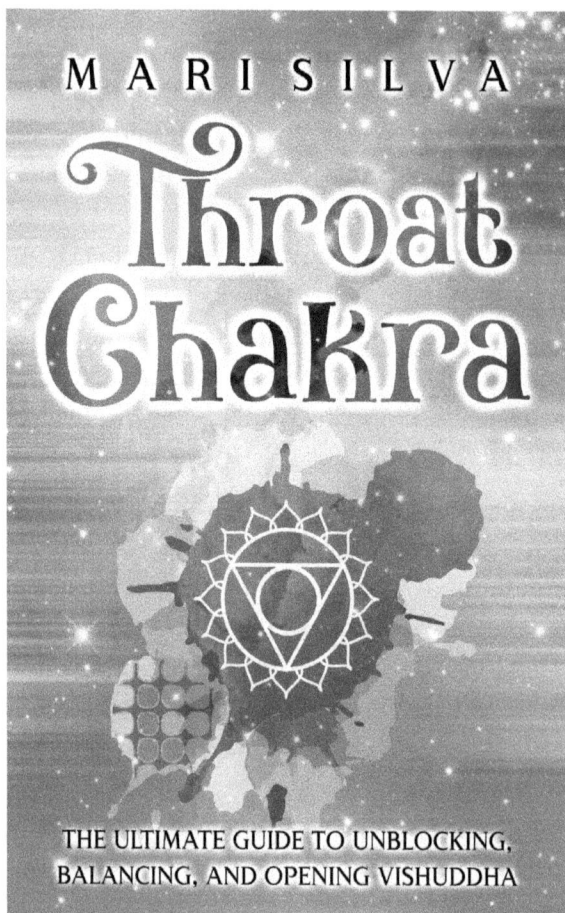

Introduction

You could not have chosen a better book to learn about the subject of the throat chakra and how it affects your life in so many ways. Unfortunately, few people understand just how vital this chakra is and why they should take the time to make sure they heal it and keep it in balance. However, you are a different breed. How do I know this? Because you are reading this right now. Whether through study or an intuitive nudge, you realize the importance of your throat chakra, and you know that when you get to work on it, you'll experience radical shifts in your life. What you may not know is how to go about sorting out the energy flow in this chakra, and that is what this book seeks to help you accomplish.

Certain habits are vital to human existence. For instance, if you want to make sure that your physical body is in tiptop condition, it is a good idea to take a bath, eat good food, get enough sleep, work out your muscles, and do regular checkups so that you can be certain that you are doing just fine. In the same way, you have to take care of your spirit. You must care for the energy body and learn to be discerning about the sort of energies that you are receiving and putting out there, for they will ultimately dictate the sort of life you live, over and above everything else you could do physically. You are already doing the smart thing by looking into how to take care of your Vishuddha, and this is something commendable. Not everyone takes the time and effort to look into this, and because you have, you'll definitely be rewarded.

Unlike other books on the market that make the concept of chakras unnecessarily complicated, you'll find this one is a very simple and easy-to-understand read. Subs and ideas presented here are given to you in plain English so that there is no confusion about what you are doing at any given point in time. You'll have hands-on, practical instructions that you can begin to implement to create the change you desire with your throat chakra. Even if you are already familiar with the idea of energy centers, there is sure to be something new that you discovered from reading this book. By the time you have finished reading this book, you'll not just be an expert on the throat chakra but will know exactly what steps you need to take to ensure that this energy center remains healthy and open. From yoga and mudras to crystals and mantras (and so much more), this book has everything you'll need to begin working with your Vishuddha in an empowering way. If you are ready to discover the power of your throat chakra, let's dive in and explore. You are going to have a good time. Fasten your seatbelt.

Chapter 1: What Is Vishuddha?

What On Earth Is a Chakra?

No, it's not short for Chaka Khan. Okay, all kidding aside, you have definitely heard of chakras, and I know this because not only are you reading about it right now, but you have also chosen a book about the throat chakra, which hopefully means that you have taken the time to look into the other chakras that come before the throat chakra and to do the work to get them working optimally.

So, what is a chakra? It's a ball of energy that spins, and you have seven of those. Actually, you have more than seven, but those are the major ones in your body. The interpretation of this Sanskrit word is literally "wheel" or "disk." The chakra is an energy center responsible for how you process chi, also called *prana* or *life force*. This life force is, well, literally *the force of life*. It is why you move, breathe, think, and have a beating heart and organs that know what to do at every point. It's also why your health, love life, friendship, finances, and everything in life are the way they are for you. The more life force you allow to flow through you, the more love, abundance, prosperity, health, and peace of mind you get to experience in life. That is just the way it works.

Now, back to the chakras. All seven happen to be stacked on top of each other in a straight line along your spine. They also extend in front of and behind you, so don't assume they're only contained in your middle. They are:-

- The root chakra or Muladhara
- The sacral chakra or Svadhisthana
- The solar plexus chakra or Manipura
- The heart chakra or Anahata
- The throat chakra or Vishuddha
- The third eye chakra or Ajna
- The crown chakra or Sahasrara

What Is the Energy Body?

The truth about who you really are is that you are more than just your mind and your physical body. In fact, you have several bodies, but for the purpose of this book, let's just focus on the energy body, which is an invisible framework for your physical body. If you are clairvoyant, you'll be able to see the energy body as a field of light that extends out of the physical body as far as five inches or even more. This body is connected with the physical one, so whatever you do to one will affect the other. Some people refer to this energy body as your etheric body or your etheric double because it is composed of pure ether. Your chakras are part of this energy body. They allow you to channel energy as needed to various aspects of your body and your life as well. Without the energy body, you would not be able to exist, nor would you be able to interact with the knowledge that lies outside this 3D world. You would not have such a thing as your intuition, nor would you feel any connection to spiritual matters and know that there is so much more to life than what appears to be physical. Also, even if you do not care for matters of the spirit, the fact is that this energy body is responsible for keeping the physical one alive and thriving.

Why are we talking about the energy body when the core topic is the throat chakra? Well, because your chakras act as portals to feed your energy body, which in turn can assist your physical one with its own needs and functions. It also affects your mind and emotions, too. So, you can see why it matters. If you do not have open energy centers or the flow of prana through them is impeded in any way, this could have an adverse effect on your energy body, which in turn will have horrible repercussions for you physically, mentally, emotionally, and spiritually if you allow these blockages to continue unchecked.

About the Vishuddha

This chakra or energy center is the fifth one in the entire energy system. Vishuddha is a Sanskrit word etymologically rooted in two other words, *Vi,* a word used to intensify the meaning of whatever word comes after it (like the English equivalent "very") *Suddhi,* meaning pure. It is called the throat chakra because it is located in the same area as the throat. Its color is blue.

The thing about this energy center is that it is where your divinity begins. Where the other chakras before it are more material in nature, working with the energy from here is less about the physical things of life and more about spiritual matters. From this point, you begin to think outside the realm of the mundane. You go beyond just seeing the physical world the way it appears – and you begin to actually *touch the truth.* There is no other way to describe this. When you come from this energy in all you do, you are no longer selfish in your motivations. You are more selfless, more in tune with your noble qualities. When your consciousness rises to the Vishuddha level, you begin to awaken your supernatural nature.

This chakra is a gateway to your upper chakras – and the gifts that they have in store for you. In other words, before you can truly harness the power of the third eye and crown chakras, you have to make sure that you have done the work to balance out the energy of the Vishuddha.

Physically, this chakra connects with your parathyroid and thyroid glands, both of which are extremely vital. When you have too much hormonal secretion from them, this results in a condition known as hyperthyroidism. When you experience this, you'll notice heart palpitations, issues with eating, weight loss, trouble with your breathing, and more. When you have too little secretion going on, the reverse is the case as you have to deal with feelings of persistent heaviness, constipation, and unusual weight gain. These glands are also important for your brain health and mind, which are connected to the Vishuddha. When you awaken this chakra, you'll notice that you think clearer. Your energy is sharp in a smooth and non-disruptive way.

The throat energy center has a lot to do with the sense of hearing and sound in general. When you have a clear and strong Vishuddha, you'll have no issues expressing your thoughts, and those who have done the work on this chakra tend to speak clearly with a strong voice. In fact, you could almost say that there is a sort of musicality to the way they say everything, to the point where even their silent pauses are pregnant with meaning and beautiful to listen to. You get the sense that there is true compassion in all they say, and it is just a joy to hear someone with a balanced Vishuddha speak. They tend to be very charismatic people who can galvanize people into action or bring concepts to life as no one else can.

This chakra is about the finer senses, far above the basic nature of animals and humans, and for this reason, it allows you to have access to the worlds beyond this one, cutting through the illusions of space and time. It is where you are blessed with omniscience or claircognizance, the ability to know the truth of a matter without any evidence needing to be presented to the physical senses. Thanks to this chakra, you can begin to access mystical and occult knowledge and understand the concepts presented on matters of spirit with ease. As you develop this chakra, your psychic self awakens powerfully.

Symbol and Origin

Throat Chakra Symbol
https://pixabay.com/images/id-2533108/

The symbol for this energy center is a circle with sixteen petals around it. Hindu tradition holds that you can express your thoughts clearly because of this energy center. This symbol is the representation of communication in its truest form. Communication is not necessarily just about speaking with others to get your message across but also about receiving messages from the divine and your higher self.

The origin of the system of chakras is in India from the period 1500 to 500 BC. These energy centers were first mentioned in the Hindu Vedas, which are ancient, sacred religious texts and some of the oldest we have. They are also mentioned in the Upanishads.

The symbology of the chakras goes back to the yajna's five symbols. The yajna itself is an old ritual that must be performed before a fire is considered holy. The original symbols are the circle, square, half-moon, triangle, and dumpling.

Let us circle back to the symbol of the Vishuddha chakra. It represents consciousness, wisdom, and sound. Often the symbol is depicted with a bright blue color. The color blue represents the concepts of purity, wisdom, faith, and implicit trust. The symbol's crescent shape is drawn from the moon itself. This symbol is the representation of divine sound, which is absolute purity. You'll notice that purity is an important concept with this particular chakra. When I mention purity, I am not just speaking about spiritual matters, but purity in your mind and body. The chakra symbol also represents ether, which is one of the classical elements. All sixteen petals are connected to the seven musical tones that we have. The seed sound of this mantra is HAM, and you can see it inscribed in the symbol, written in white.

Themes of Your Throat Chakra

Authenticity and Voice: This energy center is all about being able to express your aspirations and confidently state your dreams. Because of this center, we can speak with clarity and confidence about what we are here on this earth to accomplish. This is what allows us to express ourselves to others, regardless of what they may think or whether or not they support us. For this chakra to work the way it is supposed to, confidence is key. You have to understand that it is your divine right to express who you really are and not try to camouflage or filter yourself.

Purity and Honesty: According to the Eightfold Path of Buddhism, one of the best ways to end suffering in life is to choose the right speech all the time. This means that you'll not indulge in lying or using your mouth to slander or hurt others. You do not engage in any conversation that serves to make someone else look bad or cause strife and anger. You are only supposed to say things that will lift other people up at every point in time. If it does not illuminate yourself or another person, then it should not pass through your lips. When you have a thorough grasp of how detrimental gossip, prejudice, and assumption can be as you speak, you'll choose to be very mindful about the words you utter.

Using the power of your tongue for all the wrong purposes is a great way to make sure that your throat chakra remains blocked and inactive. So, before you ever open your mouth to say anything, you should ask yourself, *is this true?* The next thing you should ask yourself is if what you're about to say will *serve the other person for good.* When you figure out that what you have to say is a good thing for them to hear, the next thing you should ask is, "*Why am I about to say this? What is my motive here?*" You should ask yourself if the words you are about to say are truly your own or if you are only regurgitating what other people or society has conditioned you to say.

To communicate from a place of truth and purity, you must make sure that you know how you really feel and that you are speaking exactly that out loud. This does not mean that you should become an utterly terrible person and bluntly hurt people's feelings, but that you must make sure that you are only ever being honest at all times. Finding out your personal truth will require some time and observation on your part. If you ever wonder whether something you are saying is true, all you have to do is notice the way you feel in your body when you utter the words. When there is any bit of dishonesty or lies in your words, you'll sense a little shift in energy in your body – almost like you are becoming weaker than usual. Every time you notice that sensation, pause for a moment and reflect on the actual truth of the matter and verbally express it right away.

It may appear that this chakra is all about words, words, and more words - but that is not the case. It is about being intentional when you speak and honoring the need for silence. You see, words may communicate many ideas, but silence is heavy with meaning, if not heavier than words.

Functions of the Vishuddha

The third chakra is an energy center that makes it possible for you to do such things as study, plan, and so on. It is also said to be strongly correlated to the Svadhisthana, which is the sex chakra or sacral chakra. Both of these chakras have to do with creativity. Where the lower chakra is more about physical creation, the higher chakra is about spiritual and mental creation. The connection between the two is why you'll notice that really creative people tend to have exceptionally powerful sex drives. However, that does not mean that you'll need to take it as an absolute; don't believe that you'll have power just because your sacral chakra is powerful.

Physiologically speaking, this chakra is connected to your mouth and everything you require to create sound. It also shares a connection to your lymphatic system. Your throat, esophagus, vocal box, and saliva glands also fall under the purview of the throat energy center. The Vishuddha can also help you process prana from the food you eat. Spiritually speaking, this chakra is absolutely essential for you to ascend in consciousness. The road to spiritual ascension means watching what comes out of your mouth because, as the Bible says, that has an even more detrimental effect on you than what goes into it. Just because you should not say things that will hurt people does not mean that you have free reign to at least think those negative thoughts. The idea behind the concept "out of the abundance of the heart, the mouth speaks" is that you can only say what you are saying if it is what you are thinking and feeling. So, you should focus on keeping your words pure and making sure that your mind is just as pure. This may seem like a difficult thing to do at first, but really, it is not that hard. All you have to do is decide that you are the kind of person who only wants to think and see the best in everything and everyone around them, and it will be difficult for negative thoughts to make a home in your mind.

Chapter 2: When Your Throat Chakra Is Blocked

When it comes to blockages in the chakra, it is not the same thing as having a blockage in some vital organ of your body. This is because the chakras are not physical. However, that does not mean that blockages cannot cause very real and terrible effects. When the chakras are blocked, what happens is that prana cannot flow as freely as it should to allow you to truly thrive in health, wealth, and all other areas of life. This is why you must make sure you keep the energy centers free and clear so that you can continue to draw on prana as needed.

What Causes Chakra Blocks?

Meet the Twins — Anxiety and Stress: Stress and anxiety are two of the chief causes of blocked chakras. The world that we live in is very fast-paced. The struggle to keep up is more than enough to cause even the most relaxed person a bit of stress at least once a week. Information continues to fly at us at the speed of light, making it difficult to keep up with what is going on in the world. The way society is structured would imply that you have to know what is going on at every point in time, which is an impossibility. Social media, magazines, books, and news all want you to consume as much as possible.

To consume as much as possible, you have got to go to work. Sometimes that means you have to overwork because the more you work, the more money you make, and then the more you can consume. So, you wind up working a little too hard, too long, and too late, increasing your stress and anxiety levels. These two factors have a very real and noticeable effect on your energy body. Continue living this way, and you'll inevitably develop blocks in your chakras.

Now, more than ever, you must learn how to protect your energy because if you allow stress and anxiety, they can give way to other problems like addiction and depression – all of which will have a terrible effect on your energy centers. Negative emotions are just like toxins, you see, and they can create a horribly ill energy body.

Illness: Remember how we mentioned that the physical body could have a real effect on the energy body as well? Whenever you have issues with your body, it could easily translate to a blocked chakra. It is so important to treat your body like a temple. It is not a great idea to indulge in illicit drugs. It is horrible for you if you insist on living life like a couch potato or not getting enough sleep, water, or sunlight. Stress is also a great way to invite illness into your life, so you have to find ways to play more and relax a little bit. Having said that, please do not take this as an invitation to only treat your illnesses on an energetic level. We have professional medical doctors for a reason, and it is smart to seek their counsel about what you should do to feel better about your body. Keep that in mind with every recommendation concerning your health and well-being as we go through this book.

Karmic Issues: Karma is a Sanskrit word that means "action," it is the accumulation of all our deeds, whether good, bad, or neutral. For instance, you get good karma if you do something good for someone without expecting anything in return. When you cheat or lie, you accrue bad karma points. When you do something neutral like brush your teeth, that is neutral (at least you won't chase people away with your garlic breath or something, so there is that).

You can build up Karma in a lifetime and carry it on to other lifetimes. In other words, you live several lives. This is not your first rodeo. So, you could be carrying some good and bad karma from a previous life that needs to be balanced out. Bad karma can show up as a block in your chakras, so whenever you realize that nothing you do or try is working, it may be a good idea to work towards balancing out possible bad karma by doing good things. Even so, there's a catch-22 here. If you're trying to do good to accrue good karma, that would be a self-serving reason, and it would not count. So, it is better to decide that you'll be a good person whether or not there is something in it for you, and allow yourself to be inspired by this decision to naturally do the right thing at the right time.

Another spiritual issue that can cause blockages to your chakras is the refusal to come to terms with who you really are and explore your true purpose here on earth. This could be very detrimental, especially for the higher chakras.

Symptoms of a Blocked, Weak, and Overactive Vishuddha

A healthy throat chakra is cooperative, fruitful, and nurturing. This usually means that the throat chakra helps you to feel safe when you speak up and has room for your creativity. But if your throat chakra is out of balance, it can cause your voice to change and make you feel afraid to speak. It may also be easy for you to choke or cough on foods or liquids, leading to more health problems.

When the throat chakra is weak or blocked, it can cause various throat symptoms such as sore throat, hoarseness, and difficulty swallowing. Some people also experience itching in the throat area, pus from an abscessed tooth in their mouth, a lump in their throat when they swallow saliva, a runny or stuffy nose, and/or swelling of the tonsils. Weak or blocked chakras can be caused by chronic stress on the body's immune system and nervous system, poor diet, and poor sleeping habits. When you have a weakened throat chakra, you'll tend to have difficulty catching your breath. You may also find that you are more likely to become sick and have colds or flu symptoms.

A blocked or weak throat chakra can be a source of chronic stress as it leads to pain in the body's lower back and neck area. The throat chakra is linked to the thyroid gland, which may help you to understand why some of the symptoms of an unbalanced or blocked throat chakra are related to thyroid difficulties. These symptoms may include:

- deformation of the neck area and/or facial features
- problems swallowing, including pain and choking
- cold hands or feet with bluish coloring under nails
- puffiness around the eyes
- bloating in the face, hands, and feet
- sensitivity to temperature changes, such as when coming into a warm room from outdoors on a summer day

People with blocked or weakened throat chakra may also have difficulty swallowing and find it difficult to have enough saliva flow to protect their throats. A blockage can also cause the voice to change, making it difficult to talk clearly. People with an unbalanced or overly active throat chakra may have physical signs such as coughs, colds, runny nose, and sore throats that keep coming back. They may also experience changes in their moods.

An overactive throat chakra can result in a person talking excessively and often dominating conversations because they feel entitled to have everyone listen to their opinion or story. They may also be overly concerned with food and eating habits. They may tend to bloat and gain weight easily. Other symptoms of an overactive throat chakra may include poor storytelling abilities, poor listening skills and interrupting others' stories, self-centeredness, or feeling entitled to everyone's attention.

An underactive throat chakra can lead to a quiet person, withdrawn, contemplative, suddenly shy or paranoid, and overly critical of others' behavior. People with an underactive throat chakra may find it difficult to speak up for themselves for fear that what they have to say will not be heard. They may also refrain from speaking up because they feel threatened by being heard. Other symptoms of an underactive throat chakra may include:

- A change in voice or speech, such as stopping mid-sentence with no explanation
- Repeating a sentence you have just heard in your head
- Difficulty speaking clearly and articulately, such as stumbling over your words or not finding the right word to use
- Not being able to fit a full sentence into a conversation without pausing for thought
- Saying too little or not speaking at all

Signs of Balance in the Vishuddha

When you have a balanced Vishuddha, you are very clear with others and yourself. You have no trouble standing up for what you believe in, and if you need to set a boundary with someone who is trying to manipulate you or goad you into doing something, you do it clearly and confidently. You feel no shame whatsoever because that has no place when it comes to knowing how to assert yourself in the world around you. You can also listen closely without getting swayed by emotions or other outside factors.

You can avoid any unnecessary patterns of behavior. You are anchored in the present moment and grounded. You can distinguish between what is true in the present moment and what is not. Your mind focuses on what is real from the outside, not on your inner desires. When this energy center is blocked, you'll notice that your thoughts are plagued with delusions and confusion, making it hard for you to express emotions clearly because your words have no meaning anymore. You'll also have difficulty trusting others because they do not seem real to you. They aren't always who they claim to be either.

A balanced Vishuddha means that you'll notice that you feel fulfilled and satisfied. You have a sense of purpose in life, and you are enthusiastic about that purpose. You can feel compassion without getting lost in it. It is truly integrated compassion, meaning you can walk away from a miserable situation and know that you made a difference and that people's lives might be slightly better off because of your actions.

With this chakra open, you'll be correct when it comes to how law works, truth works, and reality works. You'll be able to easily follow the path of true healing and find joy in being able to help others. As a result, you'll have no problems with confidence, intuition, and the ability to make the right decisions. You'll also have no difficulties with anger management or the ability to keep yourself on track when dealing with anger issues.

When your Vishuddha is in balance, you feel strong, especially when it comes to your inner self. You do not let others get in the way of you feeling good about yourself, and you do not let fear or any similar feelings flood your body because when they try to surface, you just breathe and move on. Life is too short to let things like that hold you back. You have no problems with your daily personal practice. You'll know that you are never out of tune with your true self. Learning comes easy to you and is automatically applied in the right context.

Quiz: How Balanced Is Your Vishuddha?

The following quiz will show you how in balance or out of balance your Vishuddha chakra is:

- Do you often feel like you are struggling with something or someone?
- Do you find it difficult to communicate with others easily?
- Do you struggle to really understand what is happening in the world around you?
- Do you have trouble keeping your composure in awkward situations?
- Are most of your friendships superficial and without depth?
- Have others ever tried to manipulate or use your true nature against you?
- Do you struggle with telling the truth?

- Do you have trouble sustaining any emotions or relationships because you feel you cannot speak your mind?

- Does your heart often feel heavy and burdened with worry?

- Do you have trouble with hearing the truth, no matter how ugly it is?

- Is there discord within your family life?

- Are you constantly suppressing your true thoughts even when you should speak up?

- Do you always feel like you're "not good enough?"

- Do you tend to talk way too much or way too little?

- Are you always being betrayed?

If You Have 8 Yes Answers or More: You have a **blocked** throat chakra, or it is really weak from a lack of use or excessive use. You have to do what you can to bring balance to this chakra so you can express your truth in love.

If You Have 6 to 7 Yes Answers: Your Vishuddha is on the verge of becoming blocked.

If You Have 4 to 5 Yes Answers: It means your Vishuddha is **fairly active**, but you could gain a lot from doing some work on this chakra.

If You Have 2 to 3 Yes Answers: Your Vishuddha is doing quite well. Just make sure that you are proactive about keeping it this way.

If You Have 0 to 1, Yes: You have a **balanced** Vishuddha. You are also open to the energies flowing from the lower chakras and ready to work with the higher chakras, which is excellent for you.

Benefits of Healing Your Vishuddha

Once you clear your Vishuddha, you'll find that the world around you becomes brighter and more beautiful. You'll be able to see what is real without any doubts about anything anymore. You'll feel a sense of satisfaction in knowing that you are on the right path in life and that you can be happy with others around you no matter what problems come up. Even when others are angry with one another or going through a rough time, you'll be the rock they turn to because they know that they can count on your unconditional love, which is never conditional upon how they act or how they treat you.

Chapter 3: Building Upon the Other Chakras

To make the most of the process of opening up your throat chakra, it is best to work with the lower chakras first so that their energies can flow freely upwards into the Vishuddha. You need to make sure that the lower chakras are also open and balanced. It is quite risky to work on the higher chakras (throat, third eye, and crown) without first beginning from the very bottom, working your way up from the Muladhara to the Anahata before taking on the Vishuddha, Ajna, and Sahasrara. In this chapter, we will take a look at the chakras that come before the Vishuddha so that you can ascertain that yours are nice and open and that everything is prepared to give you the right energy. Think of it this way... you would never build a house without a foundation unless you want that house to collapse into nothing, would you? In the same way, when it comes to your energy body and centers, you must start from the very bottom. As Fraulein Maria once trilled, *"Let's start from the very beginning; a very good place to start."*

The Root Chakra or Muladhara

The root chakra is located at the base of the spine, one-third to two-thirds of the way up from the coccyx. It is your connection to all that is solid and stable in life. Your root chakra is about survival, about you being able to go over any obstacle and keep going. It is about being able to survive hard times and move forward in life with strength and perseverance. Your root chakra keeps you grounded in the present moment when there are challenges around you. It helps you make good decisions without getting swayed by anger or depression, and it also helps set boundaries when necessary. The color of this chakra is red.

When your root chakra is balanced, you are grounded and connected to your surroundings. Your life has meaning and purpose, and you know that you are exactly where you need to be at any one moment in time. You know when it is time to leave the past behind and move forward, which is the only way that you can free yourself from negativity. This center helps you let go of pain because it connects to the negative energy that is stored within your body. When this chakra is functioning properly, you'll feel very connected with other people because they no longer feel like strangers. They are family; they are people just like yourself trying to make their way through life just like everyone else.

Symptoms of a Blocked Root Chakra

When your root chakra is blocked, the stress and anxiety in your life start to come out. You'll find it hard to stay grounded when there are challenges around you and the world begins to feel more painful than it has before. You'll find it hard to set boundaries because you start taking everything personally, leaving you feeling very used and taken advantage of.

You may miss out on opportunities because of fear. For example, if someone asks you to do something with them and you are scared that time will get away from you, then say no even though deep down inside, that is what you really want to do. It stinks when this happens all the time in your life because the opportunities are just passing by.

For example, if someone asks you to do something and you say no for whatever reason, then that person gets angry with you. When this happens, it is as if all the stress in your life rises up and surrounds you, making it even harder for you to handle day-to-day life because there are now so many more problems on your plate.

Healing Your Root Chakra

If you want to bring this energy center back into balance, there are so many ways to do so. You just need to find what works best for you, and you can only do that by trying all the methods you learn.

You Can Meditate and Visualize: There's really no better way to start working on your chakras than by meditating. This is the process of simply focusing all of your attention on the here and now by either paying attention to your breath, a sound, a sensation, something you can see, or anything else. When you focus all of your attention on one thing, it forces your attention to be here and now, which grounds you. You can then use that grounded energy to work on your chakras, and your root chakra is no exception. A simple way to meditate is to focus on your breath, and when your mind begins to wander away from your breath, simply notice and then bring your attention with love and care back to your breath. Do not let it get to you, no matter how often you get distracted. It happens to the best of us, and if you beat yourself up, you'll only slow yourself down.

You Can Work on Your Food and Nutrition: You can also help bring balance back into your root chakra by eating the right foods and drinking plenty of water. Your body needs vitamins, minerals, and phytochemicals that all help bring balance and protein, and healthy fats. Focus on getting plenty of nutrients, whether you are eating a healthy meal or just grabbing something on the go. Your body will naturally know how much it needs without having to guess. Also, it helps to incorporate a lot of red foods into your diet.

You Can Work with Essential Oils: Essential oils are a very good way to help heal your root chakra. Use any of the following oils to help bring balance back into your life: black pepper, cardamom, cinnamon, clove, eucalyptus, frankincense, geranium, ginger, helichrysum, myrrh, and patchouli. If you do not feel like picking out a single oil, use a blend of two or more oils, as they can help each other and also add another layer of energy to your healing process.

You Can Do Yoga: Yoga is one of the best ways to bring balance back into your root chakra. There are plenty of yoga poses that you can get in touch with this energy center, which will allow you to relax and focus on the present moment. Yoga is a great way to spend some time meditating as well. You should definitely check it out if you want to work on opening up your root chakra.

The Sacral Chakra or Svadhisthana

What is the sacral chakra? This is the second energy center, also known as the Svadhisthana. It is responsible for our emotions, creativity, and sexuality, as well as our ability to express ourselves and communicate. The sacral chakra is about emotional sensitivity and its expression in positive or negative ways. It is about maintaining a healthy emotional state with the ability to express yourself. Think of it as the bridge between your spiritual self and your physical body.

The sacral chakra is associated with the color orange, the element water, and the planet Venus. Its emotional association is happiness. This second energy center has to do with emotions and creativity, so you can heal it by focusing on your own emotional well-being. Orange objects are said to stimulate this chakra and help you reconnect your interpretation of the world with your emotions.

What aspects of emotions can be healed by healing the sacral chakra? Let's talk about anxiety. Emotions are a major player in anxiety. Being too emotional can be a way of avoiding your fear. Instead of dealing with what makes you anxious, you get lost in your drama and forget the reason why you are anxious in the first place. But if emotions are not expressed or released appropriately, they can turn into something destructive. Emotions are energy, and to live fully and happily, we have to learn how to honor that energy and express it properly.

To open and balance the sacral chakra, we must first recognize its role in serving us in our daily lives. Once this is understood, we can more clearly see how to gain control of this vital energy center, which will ultimately bring us closer to our spiritual nature.

Symptoms of a Blocked Sacral Chakra

One of the symptoms of a blocked Svadhisthana is an inability to feel love, joy, and pleasure. When someone has a blockage in this energy center, they may be in denial of the emotional needs that they have. They may not express gratitude or appreciation for the people in their life or their surroundings. They may experience difficulty opening up to others about their personal lives and find it hard to form deep emotional connections with others or feel comfortable making decisions about their lives.

Another thing that is often noticed with sacral chakra trouble is that breathing patterns can get rather dramatic and fast or labored and constricted. If this is you, you may have noticed that you find it hard to breathe if you are too upset. You might also have a shallow breathing pattern or irregular breathing pattern.

You may experience physical symptoms like low back pain or urinary disorders with a blocked sacral chakra. Other physical problems may include tension in the pelvic area and a constant feeling of pressure in that area. You may have a hard time relaxing because of the stress in your life. Sometimes that stress can get so bad that you may also experience problems with your digestive system, such as diarrhea or constipation. You might experience problems with weight gain or loss.

Emotional symptoms include agitation, fear, insecurity, and depression. Sufferers of sacral chakra blocks may feel like they lack emotion or do not have any feelings of joy or happiness. They might also experience anxiety which may lead to panic attacks. There may be feelings of confusion and frustration in their lives and feeling like a victim to others. They may truly believe that they cannot get ahead in their life, do not know what they want out of their existence, or that there is no point in wanting anything. These emotions could possibly lead them to thoughts of suicide or self-harm.

Healing Your Sacral Chakra

Your Sacral Chakra needs to be healed to recognize your full potential and connect with your spiritual self. You can apply the same ideas from the section on healing your root chakra, except that you'll place your focus on the sacral chakra. Following are more things you can do to specifically bring balance to your chakra by working with your emotions and mind:

Start by clearing any limiting beliefs that you have about yourself. Tell yourself that you are a special and unique person who deserves unconditional love and acceptance. If any doubts or insecurities are floating around in your mind, tell yourself that they do not define you as a person but merely as someone who is grieving their own loss. Remind yourself of the qualities and traits about you that make you valuable, beautiful, smart, and talented. Write down things you love about yourself and keep them somewhere you can read them every day.

Learn to appreciate the things in life that make you happy, even if they seem small. Find happiness in your life, no matter what it is. Tell yourself daily that you deserve to be happy and to feel loved. If you have any negative beliefs about yourself or your ability to be happy, take a moment and repeat those statements to yourself until they are replaced with gratefulness for who you are and what your life brings.

Start living in the present moment by practicing full awareness of your thoughts, emotions, and actions daily. When you are with others, give them your full attention and show them an appreciation for who they are. Your awareness will allow you to respond appropriately in all situations.

Practice loving yourself unconditionally, no matter what you have done or how you feel. Have compassion for yourself and understand that it is perfectly normal to sometimes feel sad, angry, betrayed, or lonely. This does not mean that you do not deserve love and acceptance. Ask for forgiveness when necessary. Learn from your mistakes so that you can become a stronger person. Look at the good things in your life and try to focus on the positive aspects of it. Visualize yourself as beautiful and happy while performing loving acts toward yourself daily.

Practice patience and show tolerance for your loved ones. Understand that everyone is human and makes mistakes from time to time. Let go of grudges and learn to forgive others for their wrongdoings. Fighting will only bring negativity into your life. Try to maintain a loving, peaceful environment in which you can live comfortably.

Learn to set goals for yourself, but do not become attached to the outcome of these goals. Do not make decisions based on your emotions but rather through logic, reason, and consideration of the overall picture of what is best both for yourself and those around you. Remember that your goals do not have to be perfectly set in stone. You can change them as needed, but try to avoid creating impractical or unrealistic goals.

Focus on your strengths and abilities. Try to find a balance between what you can do and what will benefit your life and relationships in the long term. Ask for help when you need it and let others help you when they offer to. Share your talents with others, whether it be through simple acts such as volunteer work or large gestures, including going back to school to further education which will make you more employable in the future (depending on your present circumstances).

Focus on your physical health as well as your mental and spiritual health. Eat nutritious meals five times a day and take vitamins to promote overall well-being. Exercise regularly to keep the blood flowing, strengthen your muscles, improve your immunity, and stay in the best shape possible. Spend at least 10 minutes a day meditating or doing yoga exercises so that you can relax and focus inward for just a moment. Spend time in nature or find activities that can rejuvenate you spiritually, such as learning about different cultures or volunteering for charitable causes.

Surround yourself with positive people who will support you in all aspects of your life. Be positive yourself, but do not be afraid to speak your mind if you disagree with others on matters of importance. Stand up for what you believe in but try to choose your battles wisely. Nurture those important relationships and allow yourself to get close to those who will love and support you unconditionally.

Try new things to keep your life interesting and exciting. Explore the world around you with an open mind, even if it means traveling out of your comfort zone (but also be careful not to travel too much or spend money frivolously). Consider moving somewhere new (if finances permit) or trying a different career path that will take you down a new path in life.

The Solar Plexus Chakra or Manipura

The solar plexus chakra is associated with the element of fire and the color yellow, while its related body parts are the stomach and large intestine. This center is located in the abdomen, stretching from below the navel up to the breastbone. It governs personal power, willpower, self-confidence, and ambition.

The Solar plexus chakra is connected to the center of being and our willpower. Our life force is usually centered here, but we may have neglected this area for a long time. You can tell if you have neglected your solar plexus chakra when you are in a situation where you are emotionally charged but feel "out of control." This may be during a difficult or challenging moment, when someone is rude or unsupportive, or when you are under tremendous stress in some way. You may have also been feeling this way for some time. Before you let yourself stay in one emotional place too long, take a moment to see if you are still connected to your solar plexus chakra.

Symptoms of a Blocked Manipura

When our emotions overwhelm us and make us feel powerless, we lose connection with our solar plexus chakra. When I get caught up in my emotions, and I can't keep them from overwhelming me (especially a negative emotion), I feel like I am losing control over my life, as if my "higher self" is not there guiding me anymore. I have been known to feel like a small kid whose feelings are in control of me.

I know this may sound funny, but I have often compared it to the feeling I get when one of my children throws a tantrum. You know, the feeling when you see your child being out of control when they do not get their own way, and they are crying and screaming at the top of their lungs, or even becoming physically violent. When they are in this state, and we do not know what else to do, we sometimes just hold them tight with our arms around them in an attempt to keep them safe. We can only get them to calm down by having our arms around them and physically restraining them from running away or doing something else out of control. I am sure that most of you have had this experience.

For me, it is an overwhelming feeling of being "out of control." With the solar plexus chakra being where our life force is located, it feels like it is not there to guide me anymore and that I have lost my connection to my higher self. It may be difficult for some of you to get a sense of what this really feels like when experiencing an emotion that takes over your being.

You may feel angry and hateful towards someone or certain situations for no reason. You may be critical and judgmental of others or things in general, including judging yourself. You may envy someone who has a nicer life or more resources than you do. You may feel like you have to have something that someone else has or that you are not getting your fair share.

You may also experience these symptoms when you find yourself in a situation where you feel powerless and out of control. You may be in a situation where someone is in authority over you but does not agree with your views or values. You may not have enough resources to support yourself, such as food and money. You might find yourself in a situation where you can't get what you want or need, whether it is through no fault of your own or because something has gone wrong over which you had little control.

Healing Your Manipura

Use the Mantra RAM: Chanting this for a few minutes a day can really help you to bring this chakra back into balance. You can do this while practicing your meditation or while doing breathwork like the bumblebee breath.

Use Breath-work: A great form of this is the ujjayi breath, the bumblebee breath I just mentioned. We will get into this in detail in a later chapter, so make sure you keep an eye out for that.

Eat Yellow Foods: Make sure that these foods are natural. Go for oats, bananas, papayas, lemons, almonds, nuts, etc. As long as it is wholesome and not processed, you'll enjoy the effects these foods will have on your chakra. Bonus points if you eat them mindfully, too.

Do Some Yoga: The best poses for this chakra are the chair pose, bow pose, and revolving triangle pose.

Use Affirmations: These are just short sentences that affirm that you are in touch with yourself and help you heal this chakra. For instance, you could try the following:

- My solar plexus chakra is whole and balanced
- I am at peace with myself and the world
- I am in touch with my creative side
- I am comfortable expressing myself through play
- My life is my playground, and every day is a fun day
- I see the beauty in one and all

If you need more information on how to work with these three chakras, I strongly advise that you do some more research and read more books on them to truly do the work required before healing your throat chakra.

Chapter 4: Mantras and Mudras

What Is a Mantra?

A mantra is a word, sound, or phrase that is repeated to gain a particular benefit. They are spiritual words that are used to stimulate energy. You can use these to center yourself and focus your energy on the important things in your life. In our efforts to heal, we must first find out what it is that is keeping us from moving forward and then figure out how we can change or remove these obstacles in our path so that we can move forward with our healing. This process is not easy to do, so we turn to mantras because they have the power to create the changes that we seek and make them really stick for good.

The most powerful mantras happen to be in Sanskrit and form the basis for much of the Tantric philosophy. They are said to have been delivered by Lord Shiva to his consort Parvati. Mantras are not only used to heal ourselves but also to connect us with our higher selves. It is a tool that helps us in connecting with our spirituality.

What Is the Difference between Mantras and Affirmations?

Affirmations are positive statements that we repeat regularly, such as "I am healthy" or "I am happy." These can help us to make good changes in our life by building a positive mindset. However, they cannot be used to heal ourselves but only to facilitate the process of healing through positive thinking. They are not life-changing in themselves. On the other hand, Mantras do not make a direct statement about what you want but essentially work through the psychic system to contribute to your healing. This is why mantras are powerful. The way they stimulate energy is much more dynamic than affirmations.

Mantras are not only the words, but they also contain the energy that is embedded in those words, so they are much more potent. The power of a mantra lies in the fact that it is a vibration that corresponds to a particular vibration that has very specific effects on the brain. This allows us to be able to "talk" to our higher self and soul. This is very powerful for healing, as it allows us to tap into the energies and knowledge of our higher self and soul, knowledge that goes beyond who we are physically.

One Mantra to Rule Them All

Mantras can help you get more out of life, but they also can be used to heal our chakras. They are capable of stimulating energy in a very positive way that has the power to improve your health and well-being. When we repeat a mantra regularly, we are energizing the chakra in question while also imprinting it with the energy created by the mantra's vibrations.

Each of our chakras corresponds to a particular part of ourselves, so we need to familiarize ourselves with these parts and their corresponding mantras before starting to work with them. While you may already know some of the mantras that correspond to each chakra, it is important to ensure that your knowledge is correct.

You may have heard someone say "OM" and wonder what it means. While many of you may hear this and think that it is merely a common sound, it is actually a very powerful mantra. The most important thing about this mantra is that we are not only saying the name of God, but we are also exaggerating its sound so that when the sound is released through our lips, which happens when we pronounce OM, there will be a vibration or wave-like energy traveling through our being and into the universe.

OM is believed to have been created by Lord Shiva as a universal sound that can be used for healing. It is an incredibly powerful mantra and one of the most effective. This is because it helps us tap into the power of the divine and use it in our lives, and it also allows us to become more aware of the blessings that we have. In this way, we can see our spiritual connection and begin to feel more connected with others around us. The divine energy that OM generates induces a feeling of love in the body, which allows our chakras to open up more easily.

The bija mantra or seed sound specifically connected to the throat chakra is HAM, pronounced H-Ah-M, and not "ham" as in "hamburger." You can chant this sound repeatedly for explosive results with this chakra.

Affirmations for the Throat Chakra

Affirmations can help your throat chakra by way of the law of attraction. Ask yourself, "*What do I want to manifest in my life?*" and reaffirm it several times throughout the day. You'll start to attract more positive and happy things into your life, leading you to a richer and more fulfilling existence. With that being said, affirmations can also help with opening up opposition or disbelief around what you are trying to manifest.

The following are excellent affirmations you can use for your throat chakra:

- I speak my truth with confidence and clarity
- I am a powerful, positive, confident person
- I feel powerful and clear when expressing myself
- I speak my truth clearly with joy
- My voice is strong, clear, authoritative, and inspiring

- I speak with clarity and truth as if there was no doubt in the world
- My words are spoken with clarity of purpose and sincerity
- I speak from my heart, only with love
- I am happy and fulfilled
- I have the gift of the gab
- My thoughts are positive and supportive
- I find joy in helping others
- My words are golden
- I speak up for myself

This list could go on forever, as there are thousands of affirmations you can use to help improve your throat chakra. You have the option of creating your very own affirmations if you would like. All you have to do is think about the particular ways in which your throat chakra blockage manifests for you and affirm the opposite is true. For instance, if you notice that you have trouble speaking up and with confidence, you can affirm, "I speak the truth with boldness, always."

Why do affirmations work? Affirmations are a great way to get your subconscious mind to work for you. They bypass the conscious mind, which is where most blocks and fears reside, and straight to the subconscious mind, which controls your creative abilities. Your conscious mind is the critical judge of what you are thinking, but affirmations loosen up a bit and let the subconscious handle its job while focusing on other things like meditation.

Your Mind and Mantras

How come mantras have such a powerful effect on the brain despite them being in Sanskrit? Sure, these words may seem completely foreign to those who do not know the language, but even if you only speak your native tongue, you'll still be better able to recognize the effect these meaningful phrases have on your psyche.

The Sanskrit words are acoustically more complex than letters in other languages, and they provide the opportunity for chanting, making use of the energy from the sounds themselves. For instance, Om is a sound that transcends duality. It is theorized that these sounds affect the brain's neural activity, providing a release from stress associated with routine practice and engagement.

Using mantras as therapy has been around for centuries, and we have only just begun to explore its potential applications. Mantras are translated to be "sacred words" and usually have a meaning in the original language. A mantra can be repeated repeatedly as part of a mediation practice or a spiritual discipline. These words are chosen because they are easy to remember and strike a chord with the person who is chanting them.

The power can come from the frequency they create as they are chanted or because practitioners view mantras as special. They offer insight into what spiritual seekers aspire to be, devoid of everyday distractions such as perceptions and judgment that usually come with using regular affirmations or meditating with no mantra in mind.

Mudras for Your Vishuddha

Mudras are hand gestures.
https://www.pexels.com/photo/woman-in-white-dress-holding-mans-hand-8710846/

Mudras are hand gestures. For centuries, they have been used in Indian culture and other Eastern cultures, such as Tibet and Japan. People use various kinds of hand gestures to communicate specific meanings, and they can also be used to heal others or as part of spiritual practices. There are over 500 known types of Auspicious Mudras from Hinduism and Buddhism. Some variations involve the whole body rather than just the hands or fingers. Mudras can act as a conduit through which crystals can pass energy to the body and mind. Each hand gesture worked with a specific crystal to increase its effectiveness.

Why are they so powerful? There are three main reasons. Firstly, each mudra has a specific vibration that encourages the body's energy field to resonate at that same frequency, ultimately strengthening and balancing it. Secondly, each mudra activates certain glands and organs within the body that correspond with its vibration. Thirdly, each mudra sends positive energy into the chakras. Mudras are an effective way to direct the mind, body, and spirit in the direction of healing and consciousness.

Although mudras can be done with the fingers individually, they are often done with both hands to make them more powerful. They are usually combined with either pranayama (breathing exercises) or meditation. In addition to being used as a direct healing tool, mudras can be used to help diagnose problems or encourage awareness of how we use our bodies. When combined with pranayama, mudras help balance the chakras and enhance meditative states of mind by improving the energy flow through each one.

Granthita Mudra: This is also known as the *knot mudra,* and it is absolutely perfect for your throat chakra. It will help you to activate it – and not only that – it will cause your voice to sound much clearer and even more music to the ears. You'll also find that this mudra will work on your thyroid gland to help it function better, and it is said to have a healing effect on those who have cancer. However, you should not use this as a substitute for whatever your doctor prescribes, but only as a supplement. You should always consult with your professional medical doctor on whatever problems you may have with your health. Here's how to do the Granthita mudra:

- Clasp your fingers together.
- Connect your right index finger and thumb at the tips to form a circle.
- Take the index finger and thumb of your left hand and create a circle with it as you did with the right fingers, but you're going to interlock the fingers around the circle formed by the right fingers. In other words, you should have two interlocking circles with these fingers while the other fingers are interlocked with one another as if in prayer.
- Make sure you're sitting when doing this mudra and that you've got your spine straight and neutral.
- Hold this mudra right in front of the Vishuddha.
- Breathe deeply as you relax into your body, and meditate on the Vishuddha.
- Envision blue light filling your throat chakra.
- Remain in this position for the next 5 to 10 minutes as you breathe regularly.
- You can focus on an affirmation as you hold this mudra. Try the following: *"My Vishuddha is opening up. All impurities are now gone."*

Vishuddha Mudra: This mudra is for your Vishuddha and will help you restore balance to the energy flow there. Here's how to do it:

- Sit comfortably with your spine erect.
- With your palms facing the sky, interlock your fingers.
- Press your thumb tips against each other.
- Place this mudra close to your belly button, letting your hands relax on your thighs.
- You can do this while chanting HAM and imagine that the breath you are inhaling is a brilliant, cool blue light that clears out your throat chakra.
- Do this for 5 to 10 minutes.

Shankh Mudra: this is also known as the shell mudra because it really does look like a shell. Here's how to do it:

- Wrap all the fingers of your right hand around your left thumb.

- Place your right thumb tip against the tip of your left middle finger. If you're doing this right, your hand should resemble a conch's shell.

- Hold this mudra in front of your breast bone.

- Chant the OM mantra or HAM mantra seven times, then remain in silence as you sit there for the next 15 minutes.

- You can imagine that your hands are literally a seashell and that your thumb is the pearl within.

The left thumb represents the higher self, and your right hand is love, so you are enveloping yourself in the energy of love, which does wonders for your throat chakra.

Udana Mudra: This one works with the energy of air, and it happens to be the very framework of sound itself. Here's how to do it:

- Put the tips of your index, middle, and ring fingers together, and let them connect to your thumb tip.

- As for your pinky, let it stick out.

This particular mudra is lovely because you can use it to help you with the Vishuddha and bring you optimism and joy, helping you feel even more creative and willing to express yourself as it increases your self-worth.

Shunya Mudra: If you notice that you have trouble really listening to people, or you sense that lately, you have been feeling disconnected, uncentered, and ungrounded, then this is the mudra for you. You can use it to help you feel more connected to one and all, more rooted in life, clear in your thoughts, and able to communicate those thoughts with no trouble at all. You'll also be able to truly listen to people instead of just waiting for them to finish so you can get your own words in. Here is how to do it:

- Fold the middle finger on each hand to connect with the bottom of your thumb.

- Place your thumb over the middle finger to hold it down in place.

- Extend the rest of the fingers to be nice and long.

Keep in mind that you are doing this same mudra on both hands.

You must continue to practice these mudras regularly if you want to get powerful results. You cannot just do it once and assume that that is the end of that! Making it a daily practice will cause your throat chakra to finally free itself of all blocks and come back into balance if it happens to be underactive or overactive. You can use them whenever you like, but it is a lot better for you to make sure that you have a set time to do them to be really disciplined and not miss a day because you forgot. Also, it is helpful to set a timer before you begin so you can focus on the mudra instead of worrying that you are taking too much time.

Chapter 5: Meditation and Visualization

Meditation reduces stress.
https://pixabay.com/images/id-1851165/

What Is Meditation?

It is the process of focusing one's mind on a particular thing, such as breathing, to calm oneself. Meditation is a practice that is supposed to help reduce stress and tension, increase your ability to concentrate, and bring more relaxation into your life. It has been said that the best time to meditate is in the morning. However, any time can be the best time for meditation if you want to do it. It just takes a few minutes of uninterrupted focus.

Many studies have been done on meditation and its effects on patients suffering from depression, anxiety, or chronic pain disorders such as fibromyalgia and arthritis in recent years. These studies show us that meditation really does have a calming effect on people who are suffering from one or more of these conditions.

There is some medical proof that meditation does, in fact, help people reduce stress. Several scientific studies show that people who regularly meditate have lower heart rates, breathe slower and deeper, and also have lower blood pressure than those who do not meditate. These physical factors help people to cope with stress better without getting into a physical frenzy. A person's emotional state will also be more positive after they meditate because the body is at rest and calmer, thus helping the mind to be clearer and more positive as well.

There is also the alternative theory that meditation helps people to find a deeper meaning in their lives. People who meditate can accept themselves and their problems and gain a new perspective on life's difficulties. Meditation helps people see the bigger picture and change their thinking patterns to create a side benefit of increased quality of life.

In short, there is scientific proof that meditation works. Some people have been known to have great success after only one meditation session, while others will take weeks or even months to really experience the full benefits of this practice. Meditation can do wonders for you. You may be fed up with your mind running at top speed, catastrophizing about what might happen in the future, or worrying about things that happened yesterday. You just want a break from your thoughts. It can feel like you are trying to fill a leaky bucket that never gets full, and you are always trying to catch up to it instead of moving forward. Meditation can help tame those anxieties and free your mind of all those convoluted worries that have been keeping you stuck in place.

You may be feeling physically out of sorts and looking for something that can help you restore balance in your body. Meditation has been proven to have a calming effect on the body, releasing muscle tension, supporting better sleep, lowering blood pressure, and improving cardiovascular health.

You have probably heard the term "mindfulness" bandied about by now. It is the good-for-your-brain habit of exercising your control over your thoughts and feelings instead of surrendering to them. Meditation helps you train your mind and focus on what is important. It is like taking a mini-vacation from all the constant chatter in your head, which can be refreshing and energizing.

Who Can Meditate?

Meditation is accessible to one and all. All you need is yourself, your ability to breathe, and a few minutes each day. It is recommended that you have an open mind to the different ways of meditation and try a few until you find one that works for you. When people are stressed or anxious, they will usually think the best way to relax is by getting drunk or using illegal substances to chase a high that never lasts. However, if they continue to use these harmful tools to relax, they will become addicted and suffer physical and emotional harm later in life. By frequently engaging in meditation, people can find a new way to relax that works wonders for the body, mind, and spirit to boot. Meditation is one of the few activities you can enjoy for free and has little to no negative effects. However, meditating regularly for a certain time for a certain period of time can potentially have incredible impacts on your health and well-being.

The best time for meditation is when your mind is open, your heart is happy, and your body feels good with all three aspects of yourself being at peace at the same time. Although there are many different types of meditation, generally, it helps to focus on one thing at a time and do it for at least 15 minutes every day. Meditation is supposed to be an easy process that simply involves focusing on the present and being in the moment.

There are numerous ways to meditate, but most of them will involve sitting comfortably, either upright or laying down, with eyes closed or open at half-mast. You may choose a technique that works for you, such as counting your breath, simply observing it, focusing on a flower or plant in the garden outside your window, or anything really.

Meditation allows people to relieve their stress by focusing on one thing, their breathing, which then allows them to become more relaxed and able to cope with stress much better in the future. This does wonder not just for your physical body but for the energy body, too.

The following are reasons why you should meditate:

- Reduces stress
- Improves health
- Increases happiness
- Increases life span
- Increases focus
- Boosts concentration
- Enhances creativity and productivity
- Helps fight depression and anxiety
- Boosts immune system strength
- Provides relief from chronic pain
- Reduces blood sugar and promotes weight loss
- Increases positive energy while decreasing negative energy
- Improves physical performance and athletic skills
- Helps sleep better, deeper, and easier

What Is Visualization?

Meditation is a practice that helps you cultivate inner peace and awareness. It is the art of being still, learning to go with the flow, and noticing everything that arises in your mind without judgment or analysis. Meditation has been shown to have many health benefits, such as stress reduction and anxiety relief. Together, meditation and visualization are potent for straightening out relationship issues and healing past wounds related to heartache or other painful life experiences.

It can be compared to a tuning fork in that the vibration it emits will soothe any imbalances within the body. Keeping your energy balanced can help you achieve optimum health and well-being, so mastering meditation is so important. Your energy flows through your physical body, emotions, and thoughts, creating a chain reaction responsible for many of the physical ailments that come our way. Your goal with meditation is to get in tune with these flows of energy and heal yourself from within. The stronger your energy flow, the more you'll be able to handle any obstacles that come your way.

What is visualization? Visualization is the process that lets you create images in your mind's eye. It is a great way to tune out your surroundings and focus on one thing at a time. You can learn to do it at home or listen to someone guide you through visualization exercises.

Imagination and visualization are often used interchangeably, but this can prove to be inaccurate in some instances. Recent research shows that imagination is not as much a mental imagery process as it is a mental activity that involves cooperation between your perception and action systems. Imagination can involve diverse components such as emotion, motivation, and visualization. This is further supported by the fact that the same mental processes leave a different trace in the brain depending on whether they are linked to action or perception. This can support the use of imagination and visualization interchangeably, but I prefer to use imagery as it is more commonly used.

Visualization is a great way to support the throat chakra during your meditation sessions. When combined with meditation, visualization for the Throat Chakra is an excellent way to relax and open up this energy center, allowing new possibilities into your life. It is important to set that intention before you begin to get the most out of your visualization for the throat chakra.

Guided Meditation for the Opening of the Vishuddha

Close your eyes and take a moment to ground and center yourself. Breathe deeply and slowly, becoming more aware of your breath as you inhale and exhale. Imagine that you are breathing through the center of your chest, right below your throat, where the Vishuddha Chakra is located. As you breathe in, breathe all the way down into that region of your body. As you exhale, imagine all of the tension leaving this area of your body.

When you feel ready, pick up a white candle and set it in front of you. Light the candle with a lighter or matches. Take a moment to enjoy its glow as it flickers before you, then close your eyes again.

As you breathe in and out of your relaxed belly, imagine that you are breathing into the white candle. Feel the warm glow of the candle as it emanates light through your chest and throat. As light and energy move into this area of your body, you may feel heat or tingling sensations or even see colorful lights in front of your eyes.

When you are ready, focus on the throat chakra as it opens up to receive more energy and light. Take a few minutes to absorb this energy before continuing on with your visualization of the throat chakra. After a few minutes, open your eyes again. Take a moment to focus on the candle's flame, then shut your eyes and resume seeing it in your mind's eye.

As you focus on the candle, picture it growing taller and taller, almost like a tree with branches. Picture a seed growing deep inside the candle. Feel it starting to grow as light and energy move into your throat chakra from it. You may see white flowers or seeds rising from the candle. Keep up your visualization until the candle burns out or until 15 minutes have elapsed, whichever happens first. You have finished this visualization for the throat chakra.

Guided Meditation for Healing the Vishuddha

Sit somewhere comfortable and quiet where you'll neither be disturbed nor distracted for the next 15 minutes. Shut your eyes and take a few moments to focus on the way you are breathing. Breathe in through your nose and slightly part your lips to exhale. When you notice that you feel relaxed and comfortable, it is time to visualize.

See a blue ball of energy spinning in your throat slowly in your mind's eye. Pay close attention to this ball of energy and notice how brilliant the color is. How fast or slow is it moving? Do you see any dark colorations in it? If it is moving too slowly and you notice that there is some darkness in it, that means that there are blockages that you must get rid of.

Take a deep breath in, and as you do so, imagine that you were inhaling brilliant blue light through your throat chakra. Feel the sensation of this energy as it goes into your chakra, healing it and causing it to move faster. As you exhale, notice that the darkness leaves through the chakra as well, leaving your energy center slightly brighter and more brilliant than before. Continue visualizing the darkness leaving your throat chakra until there is nothing left in it than brilliant blue power.

Now imagine that a small ball of blue light is right in front of you. As you continue to breathe in through your chakra, imagine that this ball grows brighter and brighter before you. Pay attention to the sound that comes from this energy ball and notice how it grows louder and louder the bigger it gets. Allow this energy ball to become so big that it fills the entire room in your mind's eye. Now imagine that you are dissolving into this ball of blue light so that you no longer exist as yourself, but you are the light itself. Feel how powerful you are. This is the true essence of you. Embrace it. You allow this light to be absorbed by your throat chakra until it is glowing within this energy center instead of the room. When you are ready, you can come out of this visualization and open your eyes.

Guided Meditation with Touch to Unblock the Vishuddha

Place your thumbs on the Vishuddha, just above your collarbones. Inhale deeply and exhale completely three times. Feel the air moving out of your lungs and through your throat. Let go of any tension in this area by breathing deeply for a few more moments.

Next, place one hand on the back of your head and one hand on the base of your throat.

Inhale deeply through your nose and exhale completely. Imagine that the air moving through your throat and down your spine clears any remaining blockages in your throat chakra. With each exhalation, continue to let go of any tension around the Vishuddha until you feel the area relax completely.

Finally, when you are ready, place both hands together over your heart. Inhale deeply through both nostrils and exhale completely three times, feeling thankful that your throat chakra is now functioning as it should. Feel yourself filling with lightness in the throat chakra as your breath unblocks all parts of it. This completes the guided meditation.

Guided Meditation to Receive Details on How to Heal Your Throat Chakra

Find a comfortable place to sit or lie down. Focus on your breathing. When you breathe in, fill your lungs and stomach as much as possible. Focusing on the breath is a way to enter a meditative state of mind, which will help you relax.

Roll your shoulders back and release any tension from them. Tense muscles can make it hard for you to focus for long periods of time, so be sure to take care of that first.

Close your eyes and imagine opening the door before you (or behind you if that feels more comfortable). This door leads into the place where all intuition manifests. In this place, everything is possible.

Through the door, you see a small blue light in the distance. It is a small glowing ball that moves toward you, getting bigger as it gets closer. It stops at arm's length and then slowly moves down your body and comes to rest in your throat chakra. See the light radiate so brightly that it touches the sky above, connecting you with spirit. In this light, notice the many beautiful shades of blue and the different geometric patterns that change and move as your chakra vibrates more strongly.

Looking at this ball of light in your throat chakra, notice what it makes you feel. Focus on the symbols or shapes inside the ball. If you are unsure what the symbols mean, ask your angels or spirit guides or the universe for assistance.

Ask your angels and spirit guides if there is anything they want you to know about the throat chakra. What seems important right now? Trust your intuition when it comes to receiving information from *spirit* - even if it seems strange at first.

If you are receiving a message, ask your angels to help you accept it and bring it into your consciousness.

Say "yes" to what you are being asked to know or to do at this time by trusting that the required information is being downloaded into your Vishuddha. Now that your throat chakra knows what it needs and wants, these answers will come through into your conscious mind in the future.

Ask yourself, "*What am I supposed to do now?*" See if any of the ideas you receive would benefit your throat chakra. If you do not like any of them, go with the one that feels best for now.

End the meditation by thanking your spiritual helpers for their help and sending them light and love. Relish in the feeling of the energy in your throat chakra, knowing that you can always come back to this sacred place at any time.

Tips for Doing Guided Meditations

My first tip is to always remember this is your time. It is nobody's business what you are doing during your meditation, so do not worry about letting other people down by "wasting time." I also recommend that when getting started with guided meditations, you should record them and play them back so you can follow along without having to refer to this book and lose your concentration. Another great benefit to recording them is that you can listen to them as you fall asleep so that you'll be able to get the added benefits of having your subconscious mind programmed for success with your goal of unblocking your Vishuddha.

You may notice that you cannot seem to stop your mind from wandering while listening to your meditations. You may have tried several times, but you find yourself drifting off into your thoughts no matter how hard you try. How do you fix this? Do not worry about it! You are not alone in this struggle. Many people can attest to the challenge of keeping their minds from wandering when listening to a guided meditation. When you are ready, a great idea would be to follow the recording with a journal entry where you write down some of your thoughts as they come up so that you do not forget about them later on. These journal entries do not have to be lengthy, but it is important to get the words down before they fade from your memory.

Another great tip for doing guided meditations is setting up a comfortable environment and making sure that you'll not be disturbed. Turn your cell phone off and tell your family not to bother you except in case of an emergency. The idea is for you to keep distractions to a minimum so that your mind can focus on the meditation without being tugged away from it by something as simple as a phone call or someone's knock at the door.

One more tip for doing guided meditations is to prepare yourself mentally before starting. I have talked about the power of expectation and how the conscious mind often does not know the difference between something that is real and something that is not, although you know it is not real. The belief in your subconscious mind can help you make a self-fulfilling prophecy come true! Suppose you are prepared for this guided meditation as though you have already experienced a positive result from it Since you believe it. In that case, your subconscious mind will believe in its reality and help to create the end result.

I myself have found that the best time to do guided meditations is first thing in the morning. I find that it is easier to keep my mind on what I am doing and less likely to wander off into trying to figure out all the things that I need to do for the day. It is also a good idea to set up your meditation area the night before, rather than making do with whatever messes might be there waiting for you in the morning if you do not prepare everything on time. Having everything laid out beforehand will give you a sense of accomplishment as your mind and body wake up, and you are less likely to skip your meditation session.

Going into a guided meditation, you should use the same kind of mentality when entering your meditative state. This means that you should have no expectations of what will happen and that you should be completely open to any form of manifestation. I like to put myself in a quiet place with as little noise around me as possible. I put on some calming background music and bring myself into a relaxed meditative state. Like most forms of meditation, it is important for you to just do what feels right for you and stick with it. If guided meditation is still new to you, there is no need to feel pressured or uncomfortable by following someone else's advice on where to set up or how they do it.

Chapter 6: Pranayama and Yoga

What Is Pranayama?

The word pranayama is Sanskrit for "control of breath." Breathing techniques practiced in yoga are called pranayama. Breath-control techniques and exercises, such as deep breathing, are practiced before or during meditation as a way to energize the body and focus the mind.

Yoga experts say that you can learn to control your autonomic nervous system through breath-control exercises with practice. The ability to calm yourself without medication can be hugely beneficial for people who suffer from anxiety disorders or depression. Yoga breathing practices also help built-up release tension in muscles and joints.

Pranayama is thought to be one of the oldest yoga practices, and it involves a series of breathing techniques that are combined with other yoga exercises. A variety of pranayama techniques are used to focus and calm the mind, release tension in the body, or provide energy during meditation. A person who practices yoga may improve their overall health by practicing pranayama regularly.

Prana is the Sanskrit word for "life force" or "breath." In yogic practice, it refers to the vital energy that fills the entire body. As you breathe with these very special techniques, you practice contemplation, which happens when one's breath and mind become still. This can happen through various practices, such as dhyana or meditation.

When practiced properly, pranayama can induce various effects, including slowing and balancing brain waves, detoxifying the body, reducing anxiety and stress levels, increasing energy levels, improving focus and concentration, and improving moods and creativity. It also has some anti-anxiety properties in general.

All methods of pranayama share certain common features, including the use of sound and silence, breaths focused on a specific part of the body, an even tempo, and the harmonious use of breath and concentration.

Why Is Pranayama Good for You?

Pranayama is a powerful and revitalizing technique and has many beneficial effects. It is especially good for people with anxiety disorders or depression and those who suffer from physical pain or exhaustion.

This practice is popular among people who want to become more relaxed and those seeking to reduce their anxiety levels. It also helps people who want to be more grounded, focused, and aware of the body's rhythms.

When you practice a pranayama technique regularly, you'll find that it improves the function of essential systems in the body, including:

- breathing regulation
- muscle tone
- circulation
- digestion
- endocrine function
- cell metabolism (energy production)
- immunity enhancement
- detoxification
- relaxation
- meditation benefits

Long-term benefits of pranayama include enhanced relaxation and focus, better sleep, better health, and a more positive outlook.

Sanskrit for the union. Yogic breathing exercises are one of the six classical divisions of yoga. The word yoga comes from the Sanskrit word for "union." There are four goals in classical yoga, spiritual enlightenment, self-realization, intellectual perfection, and liberation from bondage to material objects.

The main purpose of pranayama is to help you control your mind, body, and breath so that your physical and psychological actions complement each other, or, put differently; they work in unison with each other. It is a tool that assists with achieving the highest goal of yogic practice, samadhi, a state of meditative consciousness.

The second purpose of pranayama is to awaken the inner sound and guide you in communicating with your internal being. The goal is to achieve complete self-knowledge through opening your heart channels and developing a harmonious connection between your mind and body. Also, since you are waking up your inner sound, it is going to do wonders for helping your Vishuddha work far better than it already does, and you'll see this translate into very real, positive results in your life.

Pranayama exercises are designed to help you develop control over your breath to use it as an instrument for deeper meditation, tranquility, and a sense of peace within yourself. The goal is to balance actions with concentration, which helps you gain greater emotional clarity, improve focus, and increase sensitivity in dealing with reactions towards both doing a particular action or not doing it at all. All of these things will inevitably assist your energy body in general.

Why Pranayama Matters in Yoga and Meditation

Pranayama is essential to yoga and meditation. They are interconnected groups of practices with some of their roots in the same spiritual principles, but they are not the same. Yoga is a group of techniques designed to help the body gain flexibility, develop strength and endurance, and improve posture and breathing techniques through various poses and postures known as Asanas. Asanas can be combined with the pranayama breathing exercises or "breath-work," According to Patanjali's Yoga Sutras (dated 200 BCE), Asanas should be practiced with an empty stomach. Yoga aims to help you achieve enlightenment by achieving Samadhi, a state of meditative consciousness and enlightenment, by practicing Kriya, a series of actions combined with meditation. Yoga teaches you to open your heart and connect to a higher consciousness or make friends with your inner being to achieve samadhi. This involves learning how to control your mind, body, breath, emotions, and speech to gain self-knowledge.

On the other hand, meditation is a form of consciousness that includes closing your eyes and focusing on the present moment mindfully and without judgment. The goal is to achieve peace and tranquility and bring awareness to your inner being. This action will help you break the cycle of negative thought patterns, allowing you to think clearly, form positive thoughts, and have a greater ability to communicate on all levels. The ability to communicate effectively is the sign of a healthy Vishuddha, and therefore it is worth your time to make pranayama, yoga, and meditation a part of your daily routine. According to The Yoga Sutras of Patanjali (dated 200 BCE), to achieve enlightenment, a practitioner must first develop the ability to focus attention, which comes from meditation and pranayama techniques.

Pranayama for Your Throat Chakra

The thing about communication is that we cannot escape it. It is an essential part of our day-to-day lives. If you do not think so, I challenge you to go a few days without communicating. And no, I am not just talking about a vow of silence. Try not writing, not making any signs, or using anything to signal your intent and meaning to the people around you, not even making faces. You'll start to see how we cannot escape communication. If you accept my challenge and somehow do well, try not receiving messages or communicating with your own mind or not getting any messages from your body about being hungry or needing to use the bathroom. You see, you cannot escape it! You should definitely practice pranayama so that you cannot just communicate, but do so effectively, which means that you never miss a beat when it comes to sending and receiving the true meaning and intent of the messages from without, within, and from the divine. With that in mind, let us talk about some of the best pranayama techniques for you to use and how to do them right.

The Victorious Breath Is Also Called Ujjayi Pranayama: Sometimes, you'll hear this one being referred to as "oceanic breath" because it mimics the ocean's sounds as it rises and falls. This breath will bring you to a state of pure calmness. It will also increase the flow of oxygen in your body and generate internal heat if you feel cold. The idea behind this technique is that you are breathing with your lips sealed, working with your nostrils only. However, as your lips are sealed, you'll pay attention to your throat. Think of it as if you are trying to breathe through a very thin straw.

I would like to take this time to caution you about creating tension in your jaw. Just because your lips are sealed does not mean you should close them firmly. Be gentle about it. Also, beware of tension in your neck, and try not to clamp your teeth together.

Note that the inhales and exhales should be a smooth continuous motion with no breaks in between so that you cannot tell the difference between one and the other. Also, both should be even, so you could practice this with a metronome or a metronome app, working with 75 beats per minute. You should breathe in for four counts and out for another four counts. You must also make sure that each breath fills your lungs and belly completely, so that is another thing for you to consider as you work to get better at this. If you are just starting out, in the beginning, it is a good idea to breathe with your mouth open so that you can become familiar with what the back of your throat and the sound of your breath are like before you move to seal your lips. Here is what to do:

- Sit comfortably in a way that feels natural and grounded, making sure your weight is evenly distributed on your sit bones. You should ideally have your knees lower than your hips. If you are using a chair, make sure that your head is sitting over your neck, your shoulders are square, and your spine is nice, long, and neutral. Your ribs should also be right in line with your hips, and keep your chin parallel to the ground.

- Open your mouth and breathe out through it. Pretend that you are trying to fog up your glasses or a mirror. You should hear the "ocean sound" if you do it right. You can hold up a palm to your mouth to notice your warm breath if you wish.

- When you breathe in again, make the same sound. Repeat this ten times, with each repetition having one inhale, one exhale, and each breath in and out being four counts. Pay attention to which part you struggle with, whether that is the inhale or the exhale.

- When you sense that you have gotten the hang of it, you can close your mouth when you breathe in but open it when you breathe out. Notice if you can keep the sound the same even when your lips are together.

- Next, try breathing in with your mouth open and exhaling with it shut, making sure the sensation of fogging up a glass remains in your throat and that the sound does not change. Do this for the next 5 to 10 repetitions.

- When you are ready to proceed, put your hand down in your lap to join the other one, and then fully settle into your meditation with ujjayi pranayama. You might find that it is good to set a timer so that you do not get carried away. A metronome will help you make sure that you keep each inhale and exhale at exactly four counts.

As you practice, notice what you are struggling with so that you can pay more attention to that in subsequent sessions.

The Bumblebee Breath or Bhramari Pranayama: This is a soothing, calming practice. It is named after the bumblebee because your breathing should sound like that to you. It is lovely not only for awakening your throat chakra but also for getting rid of stress, which allows you to heal even more on an energetic and, subsequently, physical level. You can also use this to help you drop your blood pressure and experience some relief from hypertension. It is excellent for sleep, too. However, if you have these health issues, please do not rely on this pranayama alone, but reach out to a medical professional for expert advice and supervision. Here is how to do this breathwork:

- Begin by sitting down in a comfortable position. Please make sure you'll not be distracted and wear loose and comfy clothing.

- Use your index fingers to block both of your ears, then shut your eyes.

- With both ears now blocked, breathe in deeply with your nose.

- Exhale until your lungs are empty, making a buzzing sound as you do so. Think of it almost like humming.

- Repeat this repeatedly until 5 to 15 minutes have elapsed. You can take breaks in between if it gets uncomfortable for you.

Yoga for Your Vishuddha

Yoga is a set of movements that will help the energy flow better in your etheric and physical bodies, so it is worth practicing. You can do specific poses that will help your throat chakra, in particular, to improve the energy flow there. Let us get into them right away.

The Camel Pose or Ustrasana

Camel Pose

- Begin by kneeling on your yoga mat or carpeted floor. If you have neither, you can work with a blanket or something soft so that you do not hurt your knees.

- Bring both hands up your sides to the rib cage. Place your thumbs on your back and let the other fingers hold your sides and front with your elbows extended. From here, work with your hands to raise your chest and rib cage to the sky.

- With your chest still lifted, reach each hand behind you, one after the other, to hold on to your heels. If you notice that you need some more height, you can tuck your toes beneath you. If not, you can just let the top of each foot remain connected to the ground.

- Draw your hips towards the front of the room. You want them to remain over both knees.

- Drop your head back to open your throat chakra to the sky if you feel you can. If you cannot handle that extension, it is okay to leave your chin tucked.

- Come out of this position by bringing the chin to the chest and returning your hands one at a time to your hips, engaging your core muscles to support you as you come back to kneeling upright.

The Baby Cobra Pose or Bhujangasana

- Start off by lying down on your belly.

- Put both hands on the floor, palms down. They should be lined up with your shoulders.

- Bring your elbows to your sides as you bend them to point towards the back of the room.

- Root your hips into the ground while staring at the floor, making sure your neck is in a neutral position.

- Take a deep breath in as you raise your chest off the ground, rolling back both shoulders while making sure that your lower ribs are still on the floor. Pay attention to your elbows and make sure they are still connected to your sides, not sticking out away from you.

- When you are ready to come out of this pose, breathe out as you return to lying prone.

The Fish Pose or Matsyasana

The fish pose.

- Start off by lying on your mat on your back.

- Lift yourself onto your elbows, keeping both forearms on the mat, palms down. Your upper arms will be at a 90-degree angle to the ground.

- With your forearms and palms placed firmly on the floor, push out your chest to the sky. To do this, just roll both shoulders back while you tuck in your shoulder blades to create firm support. You will feel your back bending.

- Push into the ground with your palms. If this is not comfy for you, you could put them just beneath your sit bones to feel more stable in this pose.

- Bring down the top of your head to reach for the floor, and your throat chakra is open to the sky.

- Check both legs and feet and make sure that the muscles there are strong and engaged as you hold this pose and breathe.

- When you are ready to release the pose, push down into your palms and forearms once more and lift the crown of your head off the ground. Then, allow your upper body to come back down to earth.

Final Notes

Keep in mind that it is not just about the poses when you are practicing yoga. You are working to heal your throat chakra, so that means you should focus on it by working with all of the information in this book and layering it all for a truly immersive and life-transforming experience. In other words, why not do the victorious breath as you work through these poses? Could you do a mudra as well? Also, could you add some visualization exercises on top of that? What about crystals, stones, and essential oils? Do not worry; we'll talk about all the other stuff in later chapters, and it will absolutely rock your world when you put all of this together. If you want a stellar plan for making all of this work together, I recommend taking a peek at the final chapter, where you'll find routines to heal your Vishuddha.

Chapter 7: Using Crystals and Stones

Crystals
https://www.pexels.com/photo/close-up-photo-of-assorted-crystals-4040644/

Crystals and gemstones are yet another layer that you can add to your yoga, meditation, pranayama, and visualization practices to help your throat chakra get the most out of your energy healing work.

What Are Crystals?

Crystals are naturally occurring, inorganic solids that offer healing power and energy to the body. They can be found in natural rock deposits or soil, but they also occur as unique formations within volcanic rocks, when sedimentary layers of earth or sandstone are subjected to heat, pressure, and/or water. Humans have used crystals for thousands of years. In Central and South America, they were used in ritualistic practices from 1500 BC. The Aztecs held quartz crystals in high regard since they believed the crystals had energy-healing properties. Ancient Egyptians used lapis lazuli and carnelian for eye ailments, while the Mayans and Aztecs used malachite to aid sleep and calm children.

Today, people use crystals in jewelry, tiled floors, countertops, and home decorating. Some people even have them implanted underneath their skin. Yet modern technology has not fully explored or defined the true nature of crystals until recently. It has been discovered that crystals can support the health of a particular organ or system in the body and regulate important physiological processes. Crystals are unique to each individual. While they may have similar internal structures, they do not behave in exactly the same way. In fact, every crystal has its own unique energy flow pattern.

What is a crystal made of? All crystals are made from the same basic elements, such as calcium and oxygen. These active elements interact with each other in various ways to create their structure and form. Crystals are formed when one material is buried under another material for an extended period of time, causing it to react and form new compounds or minerals based on its own chemical properties. Once crystals have formed, they can be transformed into many different forms of minerals depending on the surrounding material. The process of crystal formation is similar to a root system.

The process of crystal formation is similar to a root system. Crystals are also thought to carry out "work" such as balancing energy levels and purifying the body. They can absorb negative energy and transform it into positive energy in the form of healing energy or electricity. They can be used to balance and unblock the energy flow of organs within the body, facilitating the flow of necessary nutrients and elimination of toxins.

Crystals can also be used to amplify certain energies, like sound or vibration, and therefore can help heal in many ways. Some crystal healing methods involve placing crystals in the temple, on the various chakras, and on other important areas of the body to amplify their energy healing properties. Some even use crystals as a form of alternative medicine.

How does a crystal work? When you put a crystal under your pillow or hold them in your hand, you are indirectly connected to that particular crystal. An energetic link between yourself and the crystal allows it to absorb your thoughts, feelings, and intentions. Crystals have been used throughout history for many different purposes. For example, they are used to help with vision problems such as glaucoma or cataracts and also to help with respiratory disorders such as asthma and bronchitis.

Are Crystals and Gemstones the Same?

Many people assume they are, but that is not necessarily the case, although it can be easier to just call them all stones. The key difference between crystals and gems is that gems can only be found in certain parts of the world, and they are often rather limited and rare, while crystals are quite defined in structure. Some crystals are considered gems, but a gem is not a crystal. Another key difference between the two is that when it comes to the classification of crystals, it is dependent on their structure and shape. Gems or gemstones are classified based on their chemical makeup.

Gemstones are formed underground, while crystals form as a part of the earth's natural forces. Gemstones are made up of organic materials that contain different minerals and metals. For example, diamonds, rubies, and emeralds are all made up of carbon. Crystals are usually made up of inorganic minerals such as quartz, feldspar, and calcite, which are mostly void of any metal or organic ingredients.

Also, crystals consist of smaller particles than gemstones, making them denser for the same volume. They also have fewer impurities than gemstones since they do not grow larger during creation due to pressure from air or water molecules. For the context of this chapter, we shall be referring to them interchangeably.

How Stones Heal Your Chakras

How can crystals and gems work to heal the chakras? Crystals work to regulate the flow of energy in the body. This is done by absorbing and releasing energy in everything they come into contact with, which means they can balance each of the chakras in our body and a part of our physical health.

Crystals can be used to stimulate or promote specific functions within the body, whether it is balancing energy levels, strengthening health, or regulating hormonal processes. We constantly need a balance of energy. These crystals can regulate this process for us to maintain equilibrium without experiencing any imbalance or imbalance due to outside influences, like excessive amounts of stress.

For example, too much attention given to one area will cause an imbalance within your chakra system. Certain stones will help promote balance, while others can help stimulate a particular chakra.

Crystals can regulate the overall energy flow in the chakras, which is crucial for the body's well-being. Since every aspect of your health and well-being is intertwined, you cannot maintain optimum health if any of your chakras are blocked or not functioning correctly. Each of your chakras works together to keep harmony in your body, mind, and emotions.

How can you tell which stone might do well for your throat chakra? One obvious giveaway would be the color of the stone. If it happens to match the blue of the Vishuddha or is really any shade of blue, you'll experience its healing effects if you use it on that energy center. This is the way it is because the color is a clear expression of which energies are or are not a match with each other. So, opting for the blue stones will likely be a good idea.

Another thing you must consider is your intuition. Sometimes a stone calls to you, and you can sense this in your gut. It could even be a stone that is not typically considered to be a Vishuddha stone, but you should always trust what Spirit is telling you and go for it.

Stones for the Vishuddha

Aquamarine: Aquamarine is a powerful clouded blue crystal known as the "stone of courage." It has been known to naturally attract abundance, love, and happiness into its user's life. Aquamarine also helps calm the mind, promoting increased levels of creativity, wisdom, and self-possession. Aquamarine can help you with your throat chakra by helping you to speak your truth and express yourself fully without holding in your thoughts and feelings.

Lapis Lazuli: Lapis lazuli is one of the oldest stones known to man. The Egyptians believed that this stone contained the soul of their ancestors. Because of its ability to help you speak your mind without reservation or judgment and give you total courage for your decisions is also known as the stone of truth. Lapis lazuli can help to activate the throat chakra by allowing you to be authentic in your words and share your feelings more openly with others. It can also be used in meditation to help relieve physical and emotional tension and enhance inner strength, balance, and wisdom.

Blue Howlite: This is an excellent stone for those going through a difficult time in their lives. Howlite can help you find inner peace and strength to keep moving forward, no matter your circumstances. It also helps to share your emotions with others without fear of judgment or being ridiculed. Howlite can help you balance your throat chakra by allowing you to express yourself fully and freely without fear of looking bad or being judged. You'll become more comfortable speaking to others and using your voice as a powerful tool for good.

Blue Lace Agate: This stone is believed to have a healing effect on the throat chakra and can help to relieve the pain that occurs when this chakra is blocked. Blue lace agate works in harmony with the throat chakra by helping you speak your truth, promoting self-expression and honesty in all aspects of your life. It brings clarity and peace of mind. If you are feeling uncertain or lacking confidence, this stone will bring balance back into your life so that everything can be experienced as it is. It has many energies that help to activate the throat chakra allowing you to speak without reservation or judgment and giving you total courage for your decisions. Blue lace agate can also be used in meditation to help relieve physical and emotional tension and enhance inner strength, balance, and wisdom.

Chrysocolla: This stone is used in meditation to help relieve physical and emotional tension and enhance inner strength, balance, and wisdom. It can give energy directly to the body, giving it strength and vitality. If you feel exhausted all of the time, this stone will bring vigor back into your life to get more out of life instead of just sitting on top of it all day. The vibrations of this stone help to stimulate the throat chakra, helping you learn when to speak and when to be silent. It gives you the courage to be who you are *fully* - without holding back anything from others. It has a soothing, healing energy that helps you balance yourself and put your physical body at ease, allowing for an easier expression of your voice and creativity in all areas of life.

Blue Chalcedony: This is one of the most calming stones for the throat chakra and is known to bring love and happiness into one's life. It helps you to speak your truth and express yourself fully without holding in your thoughts or feelings. It will assist you in developing patience and wisdom to let others grow at their own pace and let them experience their own lessons in their own time. Blue chalcedony allows you to balance your throat chakra by giving you the ability to speak honestly, openly, and clearly about how you feel about something, allowing others to learn how to communicate back with the same honesty, openness, and clarity. It will show you the best way to phrase things so that you do not hurt people, but at the same time, you do not skew the truth into a lie because you are trying to spare their feelings.

Blue Kyanite: This stone has deep, calming energy and is used in meditation to help you get in touch with the divine and learn the truth about who you really are and how you could achieve your goals. Sometimes, we are not honest with ourselves about what we really need to do to become the person we would like to be. This stone can help us cut through the fog of ego and allow our higher selves to communicate the truth to us. Blue kyanite is known to calm the mind, promoting increased levels of creativity, wisdom, and self-possession. This stone will bring balance back into your life to get more out of life instead of just sitting on top of it all day. It strengthens self-confidence, assisting you in authentically speaking your truth, ensuring that those who prefer lies and deceit will not find a home or excellent company with you and have to look elsewhere.

Azurite: A very soothing stone for the throat chakra. You'll have a hard time allowing lies to escape your lips when you work with this beautiful azure stone. It is the stone of purity and light, and all true thoughts or feelings will be exposed. It will assist you in developing patience and wisdom to let others grow at their own pace and let them experience their own lessons in their own time. Azurite can help you balance your throat chakra by giving you the ability to speak honestly, openly, and with clarity about how you feel about something. This will allow others to learn how to communicate back with the same honesty, openness, and clarity. It gives you the courage to be who you are fully without holding back anything from others. Also, it will help you cut through the fluff in other peoples' words and actions and see through to the heart of the matter, so you can hear not just what is said but what is being withheld—a truly powerful stone.

Celestite: This stone has a very high vibration that also has a calming effect on the mind and spirit. It helps to clear up confusion and gives you the courage to face your challenges with wisdom, strength, and honesty. Celestite has several spiritual effects, like helping you see the bigger picture and allowing you to see that things are not always as they seem. It helps us to be more honest and truthful in our everyday lives. It can bring balance into your life by bringing inner peace and harmony into the throat chakra, allowing you to communicate clearly so that everyone involved understands your words. This stone will also improve your ability to listen to others as well. This is good for the Vishuddha because sometimes we get so carried away thinking about our own responses to others that we *miss what is being said.* As a result, we could miss out on opportunities for bonding, healing, and growth with those we love as a result. If you notice that you are always arguing and fighting with others (and you can be honest with yourself that it's not that toxic people surround you), then you should become best friends with this stone. It will help you speak the truth with honey and hear what others have to say without feeling like you are being attacked. Celestite is truly a celestial stone, and it provides support during times of change or stress, bringing clarity of thought and a sense of being grounded when you are feeling stressed, scattered, or overwhelmed.

How to Cleanse Your Crystals

Crystals and gemstones act as a physical healers and can also guide you to a higher state of consciousness. But when they are used too often, they lose their potency. This happens because their energy becomes too heavy, and it takes more effort for them to vibrate the numbers on your scale. They need cleansing so that the energy can return to its optimum level. Also, all kinds of people may have handled and touched the stones you are working with before they get to you, meaning that other energies may or may not be good for your throat chakra and your energy system. Better safe than sorry, so cleanse your crystals once you buy or find them, and make sure that you cleanse them periodically when your intuition tells you that it is time.

To cleanse your crystal, you can do any of the following:

- Bury them in the sand for a day
- Cleanse them in saltwater (if they're the sort that is water-friendly)
- Breathe on your crystals thrice through your mouth and say, "I cleanse you."
- Bury them in the soil of a potted plant
- Place them on the windowsill to absorb sunlight for an entire day
- Let them absorb the moonlight, which will cleanse them
- Use other crystals like quartz to cleanse and charge your crystal by simply placing them together

- Sitting with your hands over them, visualize white light coming through your palms to clear out their energy. You can do this for 5 to 15 minutes or as long as you feel is necessary. Stop when you sense that they are fine.

Chapter 8: Throat Chakra Aromatherapy

Before anything else, you should know that if you are experiencing any health issues, it is best to consult a licensed medical practitioner and not just rely on the contents of this book. Everything here should be considered supplementary, at best, to whatever professional recommendations and medications you have been instructed by you r healthcare provider to take for any medical conditions with which you are dealing. Also, please do not ingest essential oils to heal yourself, as this could be potentially risky for your health. With that out of the way, let's talk about aromatherapy.

What Is Aromatherapy?

Aromatherapy is the therapeutic use of essential oils for healing and promoting wellness. Essential oils contain chemicals (such as terpenes) that are capable of interacting with the human body to produce beneficial and often therapeutic effects. An aromatherapist can affect health by emitting these volatile compounds into the air by diffusing the fragrance, applying it topically in massage therapy, or inhaling it through steam inhalation.

Essential oils are extracted from plants by distillation. Distillation is a process that involves heating a liquid to vaporize it without burning it. The vaporized material comes out as a fine mist called the distillate. Because essential oils are volatile, they evaporate quickly and are prone to spoilage if kept on their own. They also tend to oxidize quickly at room temperature. It takes between 1–3 years for pure essential oils to mature after being distilled from the plant matter.

How Does Aromatherapy Work?

When your chakra is out of balance and wreaking havoc on your life, it is good to work with essential oils. You would be right to wonder why, though. How can some random plant oil extract work on your energy body? Is this just more "woo-woo" stuff? Let me bring you back to the source and origin of all things, energy.

You see, at the heart of everything and everyone is energy. That is the stuff that we are made of. All things vibrate at various frequencies, but they vibrate nonetheless. When you interact with substances like drugs, alcohol, and other harmful chemicals, naturally, their energy will affect your energy by causing you to vibrate at their rate. In the same way, certain things will raise your vibration when you interact with them so that you can experience health, wellness, abundance, and so on. Essential oils do the same thing in much the same way that crystals and stones can help you with your energy body. They carry the vibration and intelligence of plants, living beings that have the ability to heal, or, at least, certain plants. You can use essential oils to help you heal your chakras. All you need are the right ones that match the chakra in question.

Being Safe with Essential Oils

It is important to note that before you work with any essential oil by applying it to your skin, you must do a patch test to ensure it will not irritate you. Even when you find out that the oil is safe for you, it is still a good idea to mix it into a carrier oil like coconut or jojoba oil before using it in your baths or on your skin. This is just to be extra sure that you'll be okay.

You must pay attention to the instructions on the bottle regarding the dosage and how much it needs to be diluted. Note that this will be different from one brand to another, and even then, you have to use some practical sense because some parts of the body are more sensitive than others. Also, if you are working with oils on kids, you have to use much less than you would use on yourself as an adult. The same thing goes for pets.

Another thing that you need to think about is who will be in the same vicinity as you are, breathing this scent in. Not everyone reacts positively to the smell of these oils, you see. For instance, if you have a loved one who struggles with asthma, it might become a problem if you use too much of your oils. They may not be able to remain in a room with a working diffuser. On top of that, you have to think about your pets because certain oils will be toxic to them. So, it is important to do your own research before you get oils and begin working with them.

One final thing to note is that as helpful as these oils are, the Food and Drug Administration does not closely look at how pure the oils being sold really are, and it doesn't thoroughly scrutinize whether they are truly safe or not. So, you should always reach out to your medical doctor or another professional healthcare official before you start working with these and look for a brand with a good reputation.

Essential Oils for the Vishuddha

Before we talk about which oils work well for healing the Vishuddha, I would like to clarify that these are not the only ones you can work with. You might find that you are intuitively drawn to work with an oil that is not on this list or is not even conventionally known to work for the throat chakra. This is fine. Above all else, you should follow your gut and do what feels right. Everyone is different when it comes right down to it, and as the old saying goes, "one man's meat is another man's poison." Now let us look at the oils.

Lavender: This happens to be one of the oils you could use for so many purposes. It works well for cleansing energies and for helping you relax when you feel anxious or stressed out. It can be combined with any oil you like to make the effects of the other oil more powerful.

The thing about being human is that we are at our best when we are the most relaxed. This is when we are our truest selves and have no trouble expressing that. This is when our thoughts are clear, and our minds are free from the shackles of fear, which means that we can make decisions that serve our evolution, and more importantly, we will be able to manifest our desires faster and with ease. For thousands of years, lavender has induced this state of ease and flow.

Records show that this oil was used as far back as 2,500 years ago by the ancient Egyptians to preserve their mummies and as a natural fragrance. It is still used in skin care products – and small wonder, too, since it cleanses on an energetic and spiritual level. It is also good for working through anxiety and will balance you out emotionally, spiritually, and physically.

Peppermint: This is a great oil to use if you want to open up your throat chakra. You can add peppermint to any oil you like and make it stronger and more potent. If you need to feel more creative or inspired, try using peppermint with other oils that help you become more expressive, such as mandarin, lavender, and bergamot. If you are one of those people who are worried about having enough courage in your life, peppermint will work wonders for your growth in this area. If this is something that has been holding you back from living life fully and achieving the success that is possible for you, peppermint will help you start feeling more confident too. It is also a great way to help you become more productive and avoid taking on too much to make time for what is truly important.

Eucalyptus: This oil will help you clear out the energy in your home and office, and if you use it with other oils, the results can be amazing. Use eucalyptus with peppermint and lavender if you want to rid yourself of anxiety or tension. You should be able to feel a change within minutes of applying this blend. It will make you feel as if your body has been completely cleansed. If you have been working too hard recently and do not have time to relax, try using eucalyptus with a few drops of patchouli, jasmine, or sandalwood oil to help get you through the day without feeling overworked or burned out. This can make you feel as if you are taking a nice, long nap, and from this state, you'll be more in tune with your truth. Remember, relaxation is our natural state of being.

Frankincense: It inspires heightened mental functions and makes you more aware of subtle energy levels. If you apply frankincense and a few drops of myrrh oil to your skin, the impact will be powerful and immediate. You'll feel clearer about what it is you want to say, and best of all, you'll understand that what is coming from you is authentic because it is coming from your heart. This is especially good for people who have been using words to cover up their real feelings or present an image that is not really them.

Geranium: This is a very potent oil that you should use with caution. You can combine it with other oils to make it less intense, but even then, you should be careful. When geranium is used on its own, the results are often very profound and noticeable immediately. It will purify your mind of past and future concerns, bringing into sharp focus the present moment and your true desires. If you are too overwhelmed to know what to do next, this is the oil to reach for.

Ylang Ylang: This is another oil that is best used in combination with others rather than on its own. It is very powerful, and if you use it on its own, you could easily get a headache from the intense change occurring in your energy system. Adding Ylang Ylang to other oils such as frankincense, cinnamon, and neroli oil helps release your fears and clear out anything holding you back. When you use Ylang Ylang oil for your throat chakra, it will help you to understand your true purpose and make your energy lighter and more positive. This is a great oil to use if you are a teacher or a coach, especially when working with others on their spiritual journeys.

Rose: This is one of the oils people are most concerned about using, simply because it is so strong. To avoid problems, you'll want to use it in combination with other oils rather than on its own. Rose essential oil will enhance your intuitive nature and make you feel that higher forces are guiding you. It is not uncommon for people new to this oil to become emotional when they first use it simply because they have recently been disconnected from their intuition. Working with rose essential oil on your throat chakra will cause you to feel more in touch with your feelings and your desires.

Sage: Sage is another of those oils which are best used in combination with others. When it is used on its own, it is almost too powerful for some people and, in many cases, will leave you feeling physically drained. I have had both positive and negative experiences with this oil, so it is really something that you have to be careful about using. One of the most common uses for sage essential oil is to get rid of unwanted energy and break bad habits that no longer serve us. In my experience, sage works best when combined with other oils such as lemon, peppermint, or eucalyptus. When you work with it to balance your Vishuddha, you can feel a sense of calm and connectedness with everything around you, including your own soul. Sage will help you get rid of anger and resentment, and it can dispel fear or worry instantly. This is why it has been used as a cleansing agent or magical tool throughout the ages.

Jasmine: This is another great oil if you use other oils to balance your Vishuddha. Jasmine will increase energy flow in this chakra, no matter what type of essential oils you use with it. If you have trouble with self-expression or lack confidence in this area, jasmine is just what you need. It will make you feel like you can express every aspect of yourself with ease, and that can be a major step forward if you are just starting out on your spiritual journey.

Rosemary: Rosemary will help to protect you against fear, even if you are afraid of change and loss. Fear of this kind is one of the biggest blocks to growth, so anything you can do to remove it from your life is important somehow. Rosemary essential oil can also be used on the throat chakra to release anxiety and nervousness. The ancients believed that this was one of the most important oils to have on hand to make your life more fulfilling. For this reason, you should use it regularly, even if you do not know what sort of bad habits or blocks you are dealing with at the moment. They could be buried deep within your subconscious mind and getting ready to pop up at any moment. Until you can take care of these issues, it is best not to say or do anything that might make them surface.

Meditating with Essential Oils

You do not need too much when you want to meditate with essential oils. You only need a drop or two applied to your collarbone or jawline behind the ear so that you can smell it. Then you can work with the energy of the oil. Here is how to meditate with oils to heal your Vishuddha:

- First, make sure that you are wearing loose and comfortable clothing.

- Sit somewhere you won't be bothered for the next 5 to 15 minutes. Make sure that you are in a position that is comfortable for you.

- Apply your essential oil to your jawline or collar bone.

- Shut your eyes and focus on your breathing to be in the moment.

- Breathe as deeply as you can, allowing the air to fill with the scent of the oil.

- As you breathe in your mind, imagine that the essential oil scent is actually energy and that you are breathing it right into your throat chakra. See this energy as a brilliant blue light.

- As you inhale, imagine that the essential oil's scent supercharges your throat chakra, clearing it of all blockages.

- As you exhale, imagine the darkness in a blockage in this energy center is being released as a puff of gray or black smoke.

- After a few minutes of inhaling, exhaling, and visualizing, in order to channel energy from your hands into the chakra, put your fingers on the area between your collarbone and neck.

- When you are finished, sit for another minute or so and just focus on your breathing.

- When you are ready, open your eyes and slowly stand up.

Chapter 9: Vishuddha Diet and Nutrition

Let me state right off the bat that I am no nutritionist, and I do not have any license that makes it legal for me to tell you what to do with your diet. So, before you decide to make any changes based on what you learn from this chapter, please check with a licensed nutritionist or another medical expert first, especially if you are dealing with some preexisting condition that could worsen.

Blue Foods for Vishuddha

The throat chakra is associated with blue, indigo, and turquoise colors. These colors are soothing, calming, and persuasive. A diet rich in these colors will improve communication at the throat chakra, which means you'll be able to share your ideas more clearly and effectively.

You need to eat foods high in antioxidants, such as blueberries, purple grape juice, and turmeric, to promote clear speech. Blueberries are high in antioxidants and anthocyanins, which help block free radicals that damage your vocal cords. Blueberries are also rich in flavonoids that reduce inflammation of the vocal cords, thus reducing damage caused by free radicals.

Blue foods contain anthocyanins, which are antioxidants and anti-inflammatory. Anthocyanins present in blue foods provide healthy skin, prevent inflammation, and fight free radicals. Anthocyanins can also support the throat chakra by maintaining the integrity of the vocal cords, increasing breath control, supporting smooth and strong vocal cords, and controlling cholesterol levels.

The best types of food to incorporate into your diet are fruits and vegetables, green tea, and organic meats. These foods provide the ingredients necessary for your body to combat stress efficiently. MSG-free soy sauce, tamari, and miso can also benefit your throat chakra health by providing a vital source of glutamic acid, which benefits throat chakra function. Because the brain cannot synthesize its own glutamic acid in good amounts due to an enzyme shortage caused by stress, a diet rich in foods naturally rich in glutamic acid can be vital for improved brain function.

Spices such as cinnamon, cardamom, ginger, and turmeric are great for nourishing the throat chakra. These herbs and spices can be added to your diet via cooking with them or by drinking their essential oils. Many essential oils are extremely concentrated and must be used sparingly to avoid ingestion that exceeds safe levels. Do your own research before ingesting any essential oil, particularly if you have a condition that is aggravated by spicy foods, such as heartburn or ulcers. A word of caution, any time that you ingest an herb or spice, always make sure it is properly prepared through techniques like steeping (in warm water) or roasting. When consuming essential oils of any kind, make sure they are used safely by using an essential oil safe for ingestion, diffusion, or topical application and in the correct dosage.

Another nourishing herb that is great for the throat chakra is echinacea, which helps to boost the immune system. Keep a cup of echinacea tea handy when you feel like you are coming down with something. At the first sign of illness, immediately increase your intake of vitamin C-rich foods such as berries (especially strawberries), citrus fruits (oranges, lemons, limes), and kiwis.

Mindful Eating

Eating mindfully is a good way to balance your energy body. This should not just be about whipping your Vishuddha into shape but also about doing what is best for yourself. The decision only to eat foods that are good for you is more than enough to help your throat chakra. However, mindful eating is more than just choosing to eat wholesome, natural foods. It is also about being aware of the eating process itself.

Decide that you'll be fully aware of everything about how you feed yourself, from how you prepare the meal to the way it looks on the plate and how the textures and tastes are in your mouth. You cannot be eating mindfully while watching your favorite TV show. You have got to make sure that your attention is only on your food. You need to understand that you are not just eating food but actual energy and light. You can channel this energy towards whatever it is you want the food to help you accomplish, and you'll get results.

Recipes for Your Vishuddha

Chia Blueberry Pudding

This is such a lovely meal that you'll find absolutely delightful to have first thing in the morning.

You'll Need:

- 2 tablespoons coconut flakes
- 2 cups blueberry
- ¼ cup maple syrup
- 1 cup oat milk
- ½ cup chia seeds

Instructions:

- Take a bowl and mix your maple syrup with the milk and chia seeds. Allow this to sit in your refrigerator for just 8 hours.
- Take a small saucepan and put your blueberries in it. Cook them for the next 20 minutes using low heat to ensure the liquid

reduces halfway.

- When your chia is ready, you can serve it in separate bowls and top it off with the blueberry jelly and garnish with your coconut flakes.

Blue Quinoa Kale

This is a good one to have for lunch, and it tastes as good as it looks. You can keep the leftovers for a day or two in your fridge.

You'll Need:

- ½ cup sprouts
- 2 cups kale leaves
- 1 cup lentils (properly rinsed)
- 1 cup blueberries
- 1 cup quinoa (uncooked)

For the vinaigrette:

- 1 tablespoon maple syrup
- 1 teaspoon lemon zest
- 2 teaspoons lemon juice
- ¼ cup olive oil
- Salt (to taste)
- Pepper (to taste)

Instructions:

- Prep your quinoa the way the package says you should, and then set it aside to cool.
- Take a bowl and mix your sprouts, lentils, kale, blueberries, and cool quinoa.
- Now it's time to make the vinaigrette. All you have to do is mix the pepper, salt, map syrup, lemon juice, and olive oil together.
- Mix in your lemon zest.
- Add your blueberries to the mixture and combine thoroughly.

Blue Chicken Salad Wrap

This is a lovely light wrap you can have when you are feeling peckish but do not want to eat anything particularly heavy.

You'll Need:

- ½ cup blueberries
- 4 Boston lettuce leaves
- ½ teaspoon garlic powder
- 2 tablespoons plain yogurt
- 2 cups chicken (cooked and chopped fine)
- ¼ cup onion (chopped fine)
- 1 celery stalk (chopped fine)
- Fresh basil (to taste)
- Salt (to taste)
- Pepper (to taste)

Instructions:

- Put your garlic powder, yogurt, onion, celery, and chicken into a big enough bowl for you to mix and season as needed.
- Place the mix on your Boston lettuce leaves.
- Top it with blueberries and fresh basil.

Vishuddha Smoothie

This is a very simple recipe for a refreshing smoothie that your throat chakra will thank you for.

You'll Need:

- 2 cups plant milk
- ½ cup blackberries (frozen)
- 1 ½ teaspoon spirulina
- 1 cup blueberries

- 2 frozen bananas
- Chia seeds (optional)
- Bee pollen (optional)
- Ice

Instructions:

- Blend everything until nice and smooth.
- Serve and enjoy.

Blue Cauliflower Cream

This one does wonders for the Vishuddha. You are sure to feel it when you eat this.

You'll Need:

- 1 teaspoon blue spirulina
- ¼ cup cashews (raw and unsalted) or ½ cup coconut milk (full fat)
- 1 cauliflower head (large, chopped)
- 1 tablespoon sesame oil (you can use grapeseed or coconut oil instead)
- ½ fennel bulb (or yellow onion)
- 2 garlic cloves (minced. You can use less or skip it for the pitta)
- 1-quart veggie broth
- ½ teaspoon sea salt (add a little extra to taste)
- 2 tablespoons hemp seeds (for garnishing)

Instructions:

- Heat some oil over medium heat.
- Add in your garlic and onion and sauté them for three minutes. You want a touch of brown to them.
- Throw in the cauliflower and let it sauté for a minute more.
- Add your veggie broth, then turn the heat up so the mixture can

boil.

- When it comes to a boil, turn the heat down to a simmer, leaving the pot uncovered. Cook until cauliflower is tender. This should take 20 minutes to half an hour.

- Take your soup off the heat and allow it to cool down a bit so that it is at room temperature.

- Pour your soup into a blender and some cashews and blend at a high setting until everything is creamy and smooth. This should not take longer than a minute.

- Add in your blue spirulina and blend for a short moment. Keep in mind that the heat from the blending will take away from the nutrients, so keep it brief.

- Mix in some salt to taste.

- Top it with your hemp seeds.

Vishuddha Parfait

This one is full of ingredients that will nourish your throat chakra and the other ones, promoting excellent energy flow all through the etheric body.

You'll Need:

- ½ cup water

- 2 tablespoons chia seeds

- ¼ cup yogurt (plant-based. You might love vanilla-flavored coconut for this one)

- 4 to 8 raspberries (halved)

- 1 kiwi (peeled, diced)

- ½ orange (cut into supremes, with no pith)

- ½ banana (cut into circles)

- 8 blueberries (more or less halved)

- 8 blackberries (more or less halved)

- ⅛ teaspoon cloves

- ⅛ teaspoon cardamom

- ¼ teaspoon nutmeg

- ½ teaspoon ginger (ground)

- 2 teaspoons cinnamon

- 2 teaspoons coconut oil

- 1 tablespoon maple syrup

- 2 tablespoons white almond butter (brown can work too)

- 1 cup (5 ounces) purple sweet potato (cooked, peeled)

- 1 tablespoon chia seeds

- 1 teaspoon vanilla extract

- ¼ teaspoon lemon juice

- 1/16 teaspoon sea salt

- 1 to 1 ¼ cups water (more or less according to preference)

Instructions:

- In a glass container, whisk your yogurt and water.

- Add in the chia seeds bit by bit as you whisk. You want it to be thoroughly mixed in.

- Allow the chia to sit for 5 minutes. Start whisking again, then allow it to sit for 10 minutes. Whisk once more. (Don't skip this, or the seeds will lump together).

- Cover the mixture and let it rest in your fridge overnight or for a couple of hours if you are in a hurry.

For the parfait:

- Take a glass and arrange the fruits the way you want to, working with chopsticks to help you put them in the glass in circular layers, working from the outside of the circle to the inside.

- As you put one layer of each fruit, add a layer of your chia pudding before adding another layer of fruits. The purple sweet potato should be your final layer.

For the purple sweet potato pudding:

- Set a pan on low heat and melt some coconut oil.

- Add in your spices and combine them with your wooden spoon, stirring until you begin to smell them. Take them off the heat.

- Mix your almond butter, maple syrup, water, sea salt, and sweet potato in a blender, using the high setting, until smooth.

- Drop to a slower setting, and then add in your vanilla extract and lemon juice. Stop blending when everything is nicely incorporated.

- Pour half a cup of your smoothie into a cup. You can drink the rest too, or you can save it for another time.

- Whisk your chia seeds into the mix, and then let it sit for two hours or overnight.

If you want this parfait to taste even sweeter, using a natural sweetener like honey or maple syrup is best. You can drizzle them on the chia layers. It is also good to opt for the kind of coconut yogurt that does not have whitening agents, gums, carrageenan, and added sugars. Also, if you do not want to use coconut, any other plant-based yogurt is fine.

Blueberry Loaf

This is a yummy meal that you are sure to enjoy, physically and energetically.

You'll Need:

- 1 teaspoon cinnamon

- 1 teaspoon vanilla extract

- 1 teaspoon baking soda

- 1 egg (can use 1 teaspoon of flaxseed meal and 2 tablespoons of sunflower oil instead)

- ⅔ cup brown sugar (can use coconut or date sugar instead)

- 3 to 4 tablespoons sunflower oil or butter

- 1 ½ cups baking flour (can opt for gluten-free flour)
- 1 cup blueberries
- ¾ cup walnuts
- 2 cups dates (dried, chopped)
- 1 cup strong coffee (or boiling water)

Instructions:

- Preheat your oven to 350 degrees Fahrenheit.
- In a bowl, add your vanilla, cinnamon, baking soda, sugar, oil (or butter), and chopped dates.
- Pour your hot coffee or water over the mix. Allow to cool for 15 minutes.
- Chop your walnuts.
- Mix your wet ingredients with your flour.
- Grease your pan, and then pour this mixture into it.
- Bake this for the next 35 to 40 minutes. When you can pierce it with a butter knife or toothpick, and it comes out clean, it is ready.

Note that you can use the batter to make yourself some muffins instead of a loaf.

Blueberry Thumbprint Cookies

This is a sweet treat that you can have anytime, anywhere.

You'll Need:

- 1 teaspoon cinnamon or vanilla
- ¼ cup oil
- ¼ cup protein powder
- ⅓ cup natural blueberry jam
- ½ cup peanut butter
- ½ teaspoon baking powder

- ½ teaspoon salt

- 1 cup coconut flour (or any other gluten-free flour)

- 1/s cup sugar (you can use date or coconut sugar instead)

- 1 egg (can be skipped if you're vegan and replaced with 3 extra tablespoons of peanut butter)

- A spoon or your thumb

Instructions:

- Preheat your oven to 350 degrees Fahrenheit.

- Mix your dry ingredients.

- Mix your wet ingredients.

- Mix both the wet and dry ingredients together slowly.

- When your dough is not as thick or sticky as it was at first, you can use parchment paper or a coffee measuring spoon to scoop it and place it on a baking sheet.

- With your thumb or a spoon, push down in the middle to create a depression in the middle.

- Fill this depression with your jam.

- Stick it in the oven for 15 minutes. You want the dough to turn a nice, golden brown.

- Allow to cool – then serve and enjoy!

How to Eat

When you are eating, sit and pay attention to the colors of the food. Take your time to express your gratitude for the energy with which they are about to imbue your Vishuddha. Place both hands over them, and imagine white light flowing from your hands to the food. As you chew and eat, imagine that you are actually eating blue energy. See and feel this energy move right into your throat chakra, recharging and clearing it. Feel gratitude with each bite and swallow. Think about how you would like your life to be better, whether that means you want to speak up for yourself more or you want to be able to relate with others better. Eat with thanks, knowing that the food will help you and your chakra to accomplish your desire.

Please treat your mealtime just as you would your meditation. In other words, you should not be watching the television, looking at your phone, or having a conversation with someone. Your focus should be entirely on your eating and visualization to get the most out of this practice.

Chapter 10: Vishuddha Chakra 7-Day Routine

You have learned an awful lot from the start of this book to this point. The question becomes, how do you put it all together? In this chapter, I will offer you a routine that you can follow for the next seven days. But before we get into the routine, we need to lay some ground rules.

Consistency Is Key

First things first, you must understand that you'll not get the results you seek if you are not consistent with this routine. Some people erroneously assume that all they have to do is sit down for several hours at a go, and they will have mastered a practice. That is not how this works. You'll get far better results by consistently doing this 5 minutes a day than by trying to cram several days' worth of work in a single session.

There will be times when, for some reason, you are not able to do your session. When this is the case, you need to be mindful of two things. First, you should never skip up to two days in a row if you can possibly avoid it. Second, if you do miss a day, you should never begin again from the first day. Instead, pick up where you left off so that you do not wind up in an endless cycle of starting and never finishing. If you keep starting from day one each time you skip a day, you'll eventually find that you are no longer motivated to start, let alone finish.

Your Body, Your Pace

Another thing I must emphasize is that you'll unblock your throat chakra at your own pace. It is a very bad idea to try to put a time limit on this. With the routine, you were given for seven days, and if you are intuitively led to do it again, then follow your gut. However, do not assume that you should have unlocked your throat chakra's full potential just because you have done the routine once. Some people will begin to notice effects from the first day, and others will need a week or even longer. You are not doing yourself any favors by comparing your experiences with someone else's.

On that note, you should know that sometimes you may feel a definite shift in your energy, and other times you may feel nothing. This is quite natural. It is also why I strongly suggest that you go into this seven-day routine with no expectations whatsoever. When you have expectations that do not play out as you thought they would, you might feel discouraged and choose not to bother with this altogether. It is far better for you to simply run through the exercises without worrying about the outcome. The results will come when they come.

Think of it like working out after being a couch potato for a very long time. If you assume that you can perform like an elite athlete after the first few days, you'll find yourself very disappointed. If you try to go at the same pace as someone who has been working out for decades, you'll wind up either hurting yourself or not being pleased with your results. In the same way, you should know that you need to take your time with this routine. Do not put yourself under unnecessary pressure to perform or impress. Patience is key. You'll be tempted to try to accomplish far more than you should, and when that happens, remind yourself that this is a marathon, not a sprint.

Trust Your Intuition

The routine outlined in this book has been specifically crafted to give you phenomenal results. However, it is possible that you may find yourself being drawn to an entirely different exercise on some days. Your intuition may be leading you down a different path than the one outlined in this book because that is what your throat chakra needs at that time. If this happens, go with your gut. Do not be confused or upset at having to disregard the exercises for the day.

On Visualization

Some people have serious trouble seeing images in their minds. If you are one of them, then pay attention. You don't have to work only with your imaginal sense of sight. You see, some of us are more dominant in a certain sense than others. For instance, I find that I do particularly well with hearing and touch. I can also visualize things in my mind's eye, but those senses are stronger than my sight sense. So, if you have trouble visualizing a blue ball of light, you may feel its energy. It is also possible to hear what that sounds like.

However, it is worth learning how to see with your imaginal sense of sight in the long run. To do this, pick a small, simple object around you and study it intricately. It could be an apple, a computer mouse, or your cell phone. Notice the little details about it, then shut your eyes. Now, in your mind's eye, recreate the objects you studied as accurately as possible. Open your eyes once more and see if there are any details that you may have missed. Shut your eyes once more and picture the image again until you finally get it right. With time, you can begin visualizing entire rooms, checking to see how accurately you recreate them in your mind.

You can also train the other imaginal senses of touch, hearing, smell, and taste if you like. Why should you bother? Because in addition to working with the sense of sight, you can really deepen the experience of your visualizations by incorporating the other senses, which means you'll get much more powerful results. To improve your sense of smell, you can spray a napkin with perfume or dab some essential oil on it, take a whiff, and then leave the room. Try to recreate the scent in your mind. When you get good at this, you'll find you can actually work with the energy of essential oils without actually having them!

For the sense of hearing, you have to listen to people around you and then recreate what they said in your mind's ear. It is a simple matter of trying to feel different objects with your mind's hands for touch. Don't just notice the texture, but also the weight of things. As for taste, recollecting different foods will help here.

Day 1

- As soon as you are up in the morning, chant HAM out loud for five minutes.

- For the next five minutes, do the victorious breath.

- Later, contemplate these affirmations for ten minutes: *"I speak my truth with confidence and clarity."* You should say the affirmation aloud and give yourself at least 30 seconds in between each one to soak up the meaning.

- Do the granthita mudra as you meditate with essential oil for the Vishuddha. The essential oil should be on your collar bone or beneath both ears on your jaw. Hold the mudra for five minutes, and picture blue energy moving from the oil and the mudra into your throat chakra.

- Do the camel pose for five minutes as you practice the victorious breath. Please take breaks as you need.

Reflection: What does truth mean to me?

Day 2

- This morning, chant the EE vowel sound aloud for five minutes (EE as in "sleep"). This is the vowel sound for the Vishuddha.

- When you get out of bed, spend five minutes doing the baby cobra pose while doing the victorious breath. Please take breaks during this time as needed.

- Later in the day, sit with your hands in the Vishuddha mudra as you repeat this affirmation: *"I speak my truth clearly with joy."* Remember to take 30 seconds in between each repetition to contemplate what this means.

- For ten minutes, do the bumblebee breath while visualizing your chakra being cleared. You can place your preferred crystals around you and use any essential oil combination you want.

- Perform the guided meditation for healing the Vishuddha (from chapter five).

Reflection: What is my truth, and how can I live it more?

Day 3

- Begin the day contemplating this affirmation: *"My words are golden."* Do this for ten minutes, and feel the truth in what you are saying.

- When you get out of bed, get right into the fish pose. You are going to do this pose for five minutes. Take breaks in between as needed. You can incorporate an essential oil if you wish while doing the victorious breath.

- Sit with your preferred crystal or stone and place your hands in the shankh mudra. Chant the HAM mantra for the next ten minutes.

- Prepare yourself a throat chakra meal (if it is easier, just eat one blue, natural food). Eat mindfully, imagining its blue light imbuing the Vishuddha with power.

- As you go to bed tonight, chant HAM until you're fast asleep.

Reflection: How do I recognize truth every day?

Day 4

- Start off your day chanting HAM for five minutes. Then switch over to the EE vowel sound for five more minutes.

- For the next ten minutes, flow from camel pose to baby cobra pose to fish pose while doing the victorious breath. Take breaks from both breathing and posing as needed.

- Prep a meal for your throat chakra and eat it mindfully. Offer it thanks when you start and when you're done.

- Do the guided meditation for healing the Vishuddha (from chapter five).

- Chant this affirmation for ten minutes while doing the udana mudra: *"I speak from my heart, only with love."*

Reflection: How can I listen to the truth more?

Day 5

- Start off your day chanting EE for ten minutes with your hands in the shunya mudra.

- Contemplate and repeat the following affirmation for ten minutes: *"I am a powerful, positive, confident person."* You can do this with your preferred essential oil.

- Meditate on a crystal. In your mind, see and feel it filling you with loving blue energy for ten minutes.

- Think about something you have been meaning to say to someone. For five minutes, repeat to yourself, *"I speak the truth with love."* Call them or sit them down and say what you must.

- Wrap up the day by chanting HAM for fifteen minutes before bed.

Day 6

- Start your day by chanting HAM for fifteen minutes with your hands in the Vishuddha mudra.

- Prep a meal for your Vishuddha. Before you eat it, let your hands hover above it and chant HAM five times. Imagine vibrant blue light emanating from your hands and mouth to bless the food. Then eat mindfully.

- For ten minutes, do the baby cobra, camel, and fish poses while doing the victorious breath. Take breaks as needed, please.

- For ten minutes, sing a song. Do not try to sound pleasant, and don't worry about how you sound. Sing at the top of your lungs, and have fun with it. Notice any temptation to feel self-conscious, and then gently let it drop as you return your mind to having fun.

- End the day by chanting EE as you drift off to sleep.

Reflection: How can I be bolder each day?

Day 7

- Chant HAM, but do so in your mind for just 7 minutes. Then switch over to chanting EE in your mind for the next 7 minutes. Keep your attention on the Vishuddha and your hands in the granthita mudra.

- Practice the bumblebee breath while imagining that you are nothing but a powerful, big, bright blue ball of energy. Do this for ten minutes.

- For ten minutes, you are going to sing again. If you notice that you want to keep singing for longer, continue. If anyone judges you, do not take it to heart. It is about them, not you. If you feel uncomfortable, sing louder, and decide to have fun with it.

- Prep a throat chakra meal and infuse it with energy from your hands and mouth as you chant EE. Eat mindfully, and thank the meal for helping your Vishuddha.

- End your day by envisioning yourself as a ball of blue light for fifteen minutes while you do the victorious breath and the shankh mudra. You can supercharge this with your preferred oils and crystals.

Reflection: How can I be more of myself regardless of the world around me?

Want more powerful results? When you are done with the first seven days, you can repeat this for the next 21 to 30 days. You can switch up the mudras, mantras, and affirmations as you wish. You should also definitely do your own research to see what other yoga poses will help you with this chakra and learn more about what you can visualize to help you along your journey. Keep in mind that some days you may really not feel like doing this, but consistency will pay off in the end. So, stick with it. You do not have to feel like doing something before you do it.

Bonus: The Chakras Ahead

Now you know all that you must to clear your throat chakra. You have also learned that you have to work on the chakras before them before you do that, so you have a solid foundation. However, your journey does not end here. You are developing your entire energy body, which means every energy center must be addressed. This is why I have included this bonus section in this book for you to continue your work on the chakras above your Vishuddha. So, let us take a quick look at each one.

The Third Eye Chakra

Sanskrit Name: Ajna (command center)

Location: Between and above the brows

Element: Light

Function: Intuition, imagination

Blocked By: Illusions

Color: Indigo

Seed Sound: Om

Vowel Sound: Mmm

Foods: Blue foods and all entheogens that cause a shift in consciousness are often used in religious and spiritual contexts to tap into the world beyond this one.

Stones: Quartz, lapis lazuli, amethyst

The third eye chakra centers our intuitive mind and higher consciousness. This chakra regulates our thoughts, dreams, visions, and imagination. It tells us what will help us manifest our goals and dreams in a way that is aligned with who we are as individuals. Our intuition comes from this center of the body.

As we move into our higher consciousness, the third eye chakra grows larger to accommodate a greater sense of understanding of things as they truly are. Our third eye chakras are closed at birth, but every human being has a small opening in this energy center which allows for clairvoyance or second sight on occasion. The key to opening the third eye chakra is listening to our intuition and acting on it for the greater good. Your intuition can come to you in many ways, a feeling, a vision, a dream, or from hearing your inner voice. An intuitive message could mean that something needs to change in your life, or you may be given insights into someone else's life.

The third eye chakra is associated with psychic abilities, clairvoyance, and clairaudience.

Symptoms of a Blocked Third Eye Chakra

- Feeling cut off from your intuition or your spiritual side
- Not being able to trust your own inner voice Feeling that you are not good enough or do not deserve to succeed in life
- Difficulty making decisions or trusting your instincts when faced with a difficult situation
- Having a difficult time dreaming and fulfilling those dreams. Having trouble manifesting the things you want in life.
- Difficulty being creative or inspired in life
- Feeling like you do not quite fit in or are not doing anything meaningful with your life
- Feeling disconnected from other people

- Not accepting yourself as a person and not being able to identify with yourself.

- Headaches

- Migraines

- Issues with eyesight

- Nightmares

How to Balance Your Third Eye Chakra

- Visualize the color indigo emanating from your third eye chakra

- Meditate, listening to your inner voice or intuition. If you do not hear anything, expect to hear something soon. You'll start to hear guidance from your higher self as you meditate and practice listening.

- Keep a dream journal. Write down what you dream about when you wake up in the morning. This can give you insights into your future.

- Find a way to take action on your dreams and follow through with that action. Use your imagination to make those dreams come true.

- Get out of your head a little more and make decisions based on what feels right for you at the moment. Take action from your heart. Make decisions from love.

- Practice acceptance of yourself and others. Be compassionate with yourself and others.

- Use the power of positive thinking in life.

- Do things that you find meaningful and fulfilling in life.

- Be honest with yourself about what is holding you back from being more successful in life.

- Find a meaningful purpose in life and engage your passion.

Affirmations for the Third Eye Chakra

- I am intuitive and in tune with my spiritual side

- I trust myself and have faith in my inner voice

- I listen to my intuition and follow it daily

- I am good enough

- I am here to fulfill my soul's purposes and desires

- I am a positive, loving, and wise person

- I trust myself, and I trust my intuition

- I know that I can make good choices that are aligned with who I am

The Crown Chakra (Sahasrara)

Sanskrit Name: Sahasrara (Thousand-fold)

Location: On top of the head

Element: Thought

Function: Bliss and understanding

Blocked By: Attachment

Color: White, violet

Seed Sound: None

Vowel Sound: Ng (as in long)

Foods: Broccoli, beet tops, blackberry, garlic, plums, purple grapes

The crown chakra is the center of our higher spiritual selves, connection with the divine, spirituality, and enlightenment. The crown chakra regulates our mental, spiritual, emotional, and physical well-being. When the crown chakra is balanced and open, you feel on top of the world. When this center is blocked or inactive, it can also lead to an imbalance in other energy centers.

The Sahasrara brings us our higher consciousness and our ability to connect with higher levels of understanding. It is part of the body of light that we are all made up of as human beings, called "the Christ consciousness." The crown chakra will open naturally as we move through our journey of enlightenment, but it also needs to be consciously worked on to open the chakra.

When you are in a state of higher consciousness, your soul shines through, and you feel truly awake and alive in every way. You can manifest all that you desire in this reality, including healing any illness or disease that you have within your physical body. You'll have a greater understanding of life and all of its purpose for being here. This is when we truly come alive and feel connected with all living things on this planet.

Symptoms of a Blocked Crown Chakra

- Feeling like you have nothing left to live for. Feeling depressed and suicidal
- Feeling disconnected from your spiritual side
- Not feeling that the things you do in life are meaningful and fulfilling
- Having difficulty believing in yourself and putting your faith in yourself to achieve what you want in life
- Having no sense of value or purpose in life or feeling like a failure as a person
- Feeling overwhelmed with life in general
- Having difficulties finding balance in your life
- Feeling like you never have enough time to do everything
- Feeling disconnected from other people and feeling exhausted after social interaction.
- Having no connection with your Higher Self

How to Balance Your Crown Chakra

- Visualize the color violet emanating from your crown chakra.
- Reach for the feeling of being connected to a higher purpose

and direction.

- Make meditation a regular practice
- Listen to your gut and learn to trust it
- Ask questions about your true purpose for being on this planet
- Use positive affirmations to manifest the things that you want in life
- Get out of your head a little more and use the power of positive thinking in life
- Remember that you are a powerful divine being, worthy and deserving of love, attention, and health
- Notice how you feel about certain things. Notice how those feelings influence your energy body
- Contemplate what it means to be fully alive in this life and why this reality exists for us
- Practice progressive relaxation techniques and positive affirmations (to give yourself faith)
- Learn and practice astral projection
- Let go of negativity and learn to see the good in everyone

Affirmations

- I am a divine being.
- I am fearlessly and beautifully alive.
- I celebrate the abundance in my life, and I thrive in it.
- Life flows through me as easily as water over rocks.
- I see my divine purpose.
- I enjoy being me.
- I love feeling balanced and centered.
- My mind is open to creativity and new ideas.

- I fully accept myself as a whole person, with all my flaws and strengths.

- I express love in every single action I take.

- The world is transformed into the beauty around me from this place of harmony, peace, and joy inside me.

Conclusion

We have finally come to the end of his book, and it has been quite a journey! You have a lot of information available to you that will help bring your throat chakra to its optimal condition. *But it is not enough to know what you know.* You have to put in the work. Practice is where the magic happens. I must warn you that you are about to experience the sort of transformation that you never envisioned possible. The techniques that you have been given in this book are very powerful and have worked in the past for countless people, so it is sure to work for you as long as you remain consistent.

Your decision to work on your Vishuddha means that you'll affect your energy system for the better, which means all other chakras will indirectly benefit from your work. You'll experience some interesting effects as a result. What will you experience? That differs from person to person, and there is only one way to find out. Practice.

Here is a note of warning that I must share with you. Sometimes, it will feel as if you are not making any progress with any of this. Do not be deceived by the seeming nothingness. You see, it is especially in times like that when you must persevere and continue with your practice because there is something brewing on an energetic level. By the time it begins to manifest in your physical world, you'll be absolutely shocked and positively delighted by all the quantum leaps you'll make. You'll be glad that you did not give up on yourself when that happens. Just be easy on yourself and never try to put a deadline or any other form of pressure. Relax and trust the process. Results are sure to come.

There is no doubt in my mind that you are definitely going to practice all that you have learned. I know this because you have actually made it to the end of the book, which says a lot about your intentions for your life. Please note that your throat chakra is the beginning of higher consciousness, and so as you develop it, you'll begin to experience certain interesting phenomena. In other words, you may notice that you are more in touch with your psychic side. Now is as good a time as any to ask you to please be responsible for the gift you are given and not allow your ego to take over you. The temptation to allow all that power to get to your head is very real and always present. If you give in to it, you'll effectively stunt your spiritual growth, and you'll not be able to access the higher levels of consciousness that are waiting for you to tap into them.

Please do not limit yourself to the information you have gotten from this book. Do your own research to find out better ways that you can help your chakra to function as it should. When it comes to matters of spirit and energy, always remember that there is no such thing as limits. Now go out there and see how high you can fly.

Part 6: Third Eye Chakra

The Ultimate Guide to Awakening, Balancing, and Healing Ajna

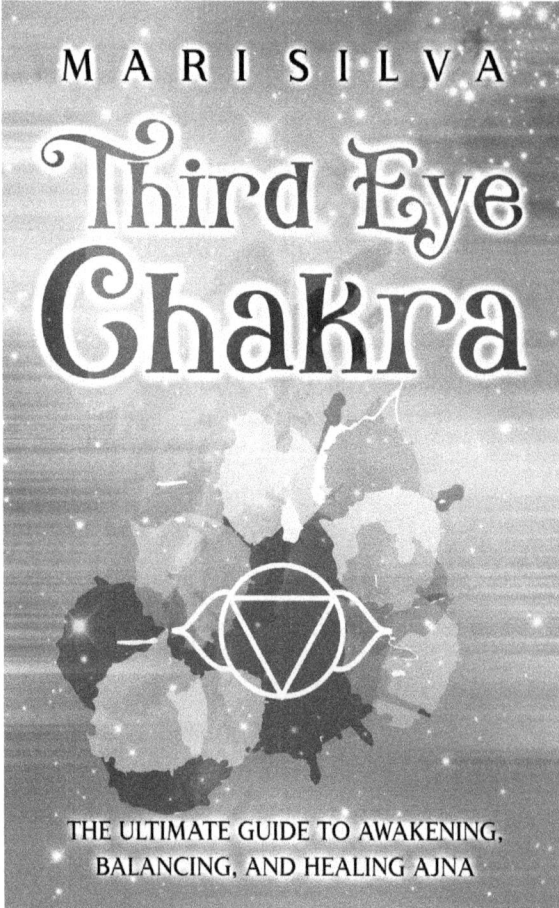

MARI SILVA

Third Eye Chakra

THE ULTIMATE GUIDE TO AWAKENING, BALANCING, AND HEALING AJNA

Introduction

"There is deep wisdom within our very flesh; if we can only come to our senses and feel it." - Elizabeth A. Behnke

Are you curious about the third eye chakra? Do you want to know how to open it and what benefits you can experience from this awakening?

The third eye chakra, also called the Ajna chakra, is located between the eyebrows in the center of the forehead. It is the sixth chakra of our body and is associated with intuition, imagination, wisdom, and psychic abilities. While the crown chakra is our connection to the Divine, the third eye chakra is our connection to our inner guidance, also known as our "gut feeling."

The third eye chakra is about more than just intuition. It is also associated with our ability to focus, concentrate, and see the big picture. This guide will introduce you to the third eye chakra and provide tips on opening it. By the end of this guide, you'll better understand it and how to balance it.

The first chapter provides an overview of the third eye chakra, including its location, color, element, and associated body parts. Chapter two will explore the blockages that can prevent it from functioning properly. Chapter three will discuss the importance of balancing the other chakras before working with the third eye chakra.

Chapter four introduces mantras and mudras, powerful tools for opening the third eye chakra. In chapter five, we'll explore meditation and visualization techniques. Chapter six introduces yoga and breathing techniques that can also be used to balance the third eye chakra.

In chapter seven, we'll discuss using crystals and stones to balance the third eye chakra. Chapter eight introduces the concept of Ajna aromatherapy and provides recipes for blends that can be used to balance the third eye chakra. Chapter nine will discuss diet and nutrition for the third eye chakra. Finally, chapter ten provides a seven-day routine for balancing the third eye chakra.

We've also included a bonus chapter that provides a cheat sheet on the third eye chakra and the crown chakra connection for those who want a quick reference. Known as the seventh chakra, the crown chakra is found at the top or crown of the head and is associated with our connection to the Divine. The third eye chakra is often called the "eye of the soul."

The benefits of balancing the third eye chakra are diverse and plentiful. With this book to guide you, you'll soon be on your way to experiencing the many benefits of a balanced third eye chakra. The tips, techniques, and information provided in this guide are meant to be used as a starting point on your journey of self-discovery. Remember that you are the only one who can determine what is best for you. Trust your intuition and allow your third eye to guide you on your path to balance and harmony.

We hope you enjoy this guide on the third eye chakra. May it provide you with the guidance and knowledge you need to open your third eye and experience the many benefits that come with it.

Chapter 1: What Is Ajna?

Chakras are energy centers found along the spine that control different areas of our physical, mental, and emotional bodies. The dormant chakras can be awakened through meditation, yoga, and other spiritual practices. While there are other chakras, we will focus on Ajna, also known as the third eye chakra.

This chapter will lay out a general overview of what chakras are, explain the origins of Ajna, and provide information on its location, color, and traits. We will also discuss the function of the third eye chakra and how it is connected to intuition and psychic powers.

What Are Chakras?

Chakras are energy centers in the human body responsible for processing and distributing vital energy throughout the body. There are seven located along the spine, from the base to the crown of the head. Each has a different physical, emotional, and mental function.

Chakras are energy centers.

1. The Muladhara (or root chakra) is the first one and is responsible for survival and grounding.

2. The Svadhisthana (or sacral chakra) is the second one and is responsible for sexuality and creativity.

3. The Manipura (or solar plexus chakra) is third and is for self-esteem and personal power.

4. The Anahata (or heart chakra) is fourth – and is for compassion and love.

5. The Vishuddha (or throat chakra) is fifth and is for expression and communication.

6. The Ajna (or third eye chakra) is sixth and is responsible for psychic powers and intuition.

7. Finally, the Sahasrara (or crown chakra) is responsible for spiritual enlightenment and connection to the divine.

Chakras are believed to be spinning wheels of energy that receive, process, and transmit it throughout the body. They are also believed to be connected to the endocrine system and its production of hormones in the body. As they are said to be interconnected, each one impacts the others. When one or more of the chakras are blocked, a person experiences physical, mental, and emotional imbalances.

When these energy centers are balanced and flowing freely, we experience good health and well-being. Chakras can be balanced through various methods such as meditation, yoga, and Reiki.

The Energy Body

The human energy body is a complex system made up of chakras, the nadis, and the auric field. The chakras spin at different rates and vibrate at different frequencies, and are responsible for nourishing the physical body with life-force energy. The nadis are subtle energy channels that connect the chakras throughout the body.

The auric field is an electromagnetic field that surrounds the body and extends out from it. It comprises three layers: the innermost layer is closest to the physical body, the middle layer is connected to the emotional body, and the outermost layer is connected to the mental body. Together, these three components make up the human energy body.

The Role of the Chakras

The Kundalini is a potent energy that resides at the base of the spine. This energy is responsible for our spiritual awakening and growth. As we raise our Kundalini energy through the chakras, we experience different states of consciousness.

The first is Muladhara, or root chakra, found at the spine's base. This chakra is responsible for our survival instincts and is associated with the element of earth. The Svadhisthana, or sacral chakra, is the second chakra, and it is located just below the navel. This chakra is responsible for our creativity and sexuality, and it is associated with the element of water.

The Manipura, or solar plexus chakra, is the third chakra, and it is located just above the navel. This chakra is responsible for our power and self-esteem, and it is associated with the element of fire. The fourth is the Anahata, or heart chakra, which is found in the center of the chest. This chakra is responsible for love and compassion and is associated with the element of air.

The Vishuddha, or throat chakra, is the fifth chakra, and it is located in the throat. This chakra is responsible for communication and expression and is associated with the element of ether. The Ajna, or third eye chakra, is the sixth chakra, and it is located between the eyebrows. This chakra is responsible for intuition and psychic powers and is associated with the element of mind.

The Sahasrara, or crown chakra, is the seventh chakra, and it is located at the top of the head. This chakra is responsible for our connection to the divine and spiritual enlightenment and is associated with the element of spirit. When all of the chakras are open and balanced, we experience good health and well-being. However, when one or more of the chakras are blocked, it can lead to physical, mental, and emotional imbalances.

Ajna: The Third Eye Chakra

The Ajna chakra is the seat of our inner vision, so being located between our eyes makes perfect sense. When this chakra is balanced, we can see things clearly both visually and emotionally, externally and internally. When everything is working properly, we have a strong connection to our intuition and can trust our gut instincts without any worry. We may also find that we become more introspective and aware of our thoughts and feelings. We may even start to experience psychic phenomena, such as clairvoyance or precognition.

When the Ajna chakra is out of balance, migraines, insomnia, or headaches are commonplace, and we're generally feeling bad-tempered and out of sorts. We may also find it difficult to focus and are indecisive. If you feel you need to bring more balance to your Ajna chakra, there are several things you can do. Meditation and visualization are two very popular methods for accessing the third eye chakra: crystals or essential oils. By bringing balance to your Ajna chakra, you can access your inner vision and intuition back and live your life with greater clarity and purpose.

Origins

The Ajna chakra is one of the most important ones in the human energy body, and its origin can be traced back to the Vedas, a collection of ancient Indian texts. The Ajna chakra is often called the third eye chakra because it is connected to inner vision."

The Vedas reveal a connection between the Ajna chakra and the pineal gland, which is found in the brain. The pineal gland produces melatonin, a hormone responsible for regulating sleep cycles. It is also said that the Ajna is connected to the pituitary gland, which is responsible for the production of hormones that regulate growth and development.

Together with these associations, the Vedas inform us that the "third eye" is also connected with the elements of space and light. When we meditate on the Ajna chakra, we can access the depths of our consciousness and connect with the infinite space that surrounds us as well as our ability to see clearly both externally and internally.

The Vedic texts also reveal that the Ajna chakra is connected to the sun. The sun is said to be the source of all life, and it is through the sun that we can see clearly. The sun is also the source of our inner vision. When we meditate on the Ajna chakra, we can connect with the sun and access our inner vision.

Symbolic Representation

A symbolic eye often represents the third eye chakra because the term "Ajna" means both "command" and "perception," lending credence to the connection it has with both intuition and intellectual insight. The eye symbolism also echoes the belief that Ajna is the "eye of the soul." In other words, it is through Ajna that we access our innermost wisdom. And just as a physical eye needs light to see, Ajna also needs to be open and receptive to perceive clearly.

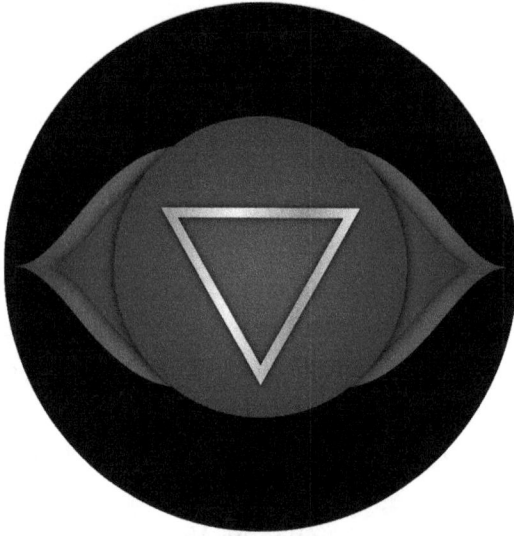

The symbol of Ajna also contains two lotus petals, which represent the duality of our nature. The lotus is a sacred flower in many cultures, and it is often seen as a symbol of purity and enlightenment. The two lotus petals in the Ajna symbol represent the two sides of our nature – the light and the dark, the positive and the negative. We all have these two sides to us, and it is crucial to learn to balance them. The lotus petals remind us that we can achieve this balance by rising above our lower nature and expanding our consciousness.

When Ajna is balanced, we see ourselves and the world around us with greater clarity. We are also more likely to experience moments of intuition and inspiration. If Ajna is out of balance, we'll find it difficult to focus or make decisions. We are both physical and spiritual beings, and Ajna helps us to remember this. By bringing balance to this chakra, we access our rich inner world vision and intuition and live our lives with clarity and purpose.

Color

The Ajna chakra is traditionally associated with the color indigo. The blue indigo color has many hues and is most often seen as a deep blue, but it can also have purple or even red tones. Indigo is said to represent wisdom and intuition. In many cultures, it is associated with royalty and wealth because pure indigo is a very rare color to find, and only those with royal blood or great wealth could afford to wear cloth dyed with it.

The indigo color is also said to be linked to the night sky. This is because when we look up at the night sky, we are reminded of the vastness of the universe and our place in it. When we meditate on the Ajna chakra, we can connect with this vastness and access our inner wisdom. Our psychic powers are also said to be associated with indigo, and logically, inner visions would emanate from the Ajna chakra. When our Ajna chakra is balanced, we can tap into our psychic abilities and use them for good.

Traits

All these traits - wisdom, intuition, insight, imagination, creativity, clarity, and focus - come from this mystical chakra. The third eye chakra governs our ability to see clearly both physically and intuitively. We can see ourselves and the world around us with greater clarity with a balanced third eye chakra. We are also more likely to experience moments of intuition and inspiration. If our third eye chakra is out of balance, we may find it difficult to focus or make decisions. We may also experience headaches, blurry vision, or eye strain. We may also find it difficult to trust our intuition or have doubts about our psychic abilities.

Function

The third eye chakra is responsible for our ability to see clearly in every way, both externally and internally. Through Ajna, we can perceive the world around us and understand our place in it. Ajna is also responsible for our ability to see into the future and access our intuition. We can tap into our higher wisdom and intuition with our third eye open. This chakra helps us to see beyond the physical world and connect with the spiritual world.

When Ajna is in balance, we can see things as they truly are. We are not misled by our own biases or the illusions of the world. We can also tap into our psychic abilities and extrasensory perception. When Ajna is out of balance, we may find it difficult to focus or make decisions. We may also experience nightmares, headaches, or eye problems.

Benefits of Aligning the Third Eye Chakra

1. Intuition

When Ajna is in balance, we are likely to experience more moments of intuition and inspiration. We see things from a higher perspective and connect with our inner wisdom. We may also find that we are more attuned to the subtle world around us and that we pick up on energy patterns and intentions that we would not have been aware of before. In short, when Ajna is balanced, we see the big picture and find guidance from within. We trust our gut instincts more and follow our hearts.

2. Clarity

When our Ajna is in balance, we see ourselves and the world around us more clearly. We can make decisions more easily and feel more confident in our choices. We may also experience enhanced mental powers, such as telepathy or precognition. To keep our Ajna in balance, we can meditate on the color indigo and visualize a bright blue light shining from our third eye. We can also eat blue or purple foods, such as blueberries or grapes.

3. Wisdom

When this chakra is in balance, we access our inner wisdom and knowledge. We see the bigger picture and find meaning in our lives. We also make choices that are in alignment with our highest good. When Ajna is out of balance, we may feel lost and confused. We may have trouble focusing or making decisions. We may also experience headaches, eyestrain, or sinus problems. Keeping our Ajna balanced can help us maintain our inner peace and wisdom.

4. Creativity

When this chakra is in balance, we see things from a different perspective and find new solutions to problems. We are also more open to new ideas and ways of doing things. We may feel more inspired, motivated, and excited to pursue our goals. Our communication with others is also improved as we express ourselves more clearly. We are better able to connect with our spiritual side. So, if you're looking to boost your creativity and innovation, keep your Ajna chakra in balance.

5. Focus

When our Ajna chakra is in balance, we find it easier to focus and stay on task. We are less easily distracted and have better concentration overall. This can be beneficial in work, school, or any other area of life where we need to maintain our focus. When our Ajna is out of balance, we may find ourselves constantly being pulled away from what we are trying to do. We may feel scattered and have a hard time completing even simple tasks.

6. Psychic Powers

When Ajna is in balance, psychic abilities or extrasensory perception becomes more common, and these abilities can help us to see things that we'd not be able to see otherwise. We may be able to communicate with other people through thoughts or energy. We may also see into the future or receive guidance from our higher selves. If you are interested in developing your psychic abilities, keep your Ajna chakra balanced and open.

7. Connection to the Spiritual World

When Ajna is in balance, we feel more connected to the spiritual world. We may have a strong sense of intuition and receive guidance from our higher selves or our spiritual guides. We may also use astral travel or have out-of-body experiences. The veil between the physical and spiritual world is also thinner, so we may see or communicate with spirits more easily. Keep your Ajna chakra open and balanced if you want to strengthen your bond with the spiritual realm.

8. Insight

We have greater insight into ourselves and our world with a balanced Ajna. We see things from a different perspective and find hidden meanings. We're also better able to tackle issues and make decisions. We find clarity and direction in life when the Ajna chakra is in balance. To achieve this balance, we can meditate on the color indigo and visualize a bright blue light shining from our third eye. We can also eat blue or purple foods, such as blueberries or grapes.

9. Balance

When Ajna is in balance, we bring balance to our lives. We see both the light and the dark sides of ourselves and learn to accept both. We find balance in our relationships and see the positive and negative aspects of the people in our lives. We're able to stay grounded and centered even amid chaos. The key to achieving this balance is to keep our Ajna chakra open and clear.

10. Unity

A well-functioning third eye gives us a sense of unity with the universe. We feel connected to all of life and see the interconnectedness of all things. We also feel a sense of oneness with the Divine. This can be a very powerful and transformative experience. If you're seeking to deepen your spiritual connection, keep your Ajna chakra in balance. With a balanced Ajna chakra, we can approach life with a sense of peace and harmony.

11. Imagination

Our imagination frees itself, and we can start dreaming of wonderful things again when Ajna is in balance. We see things that are not yet physical. We can also create our reality and manifest our desires. When the Ajna chakra is in balance, we are limitless in what we can create. We can use our imagination to solve problems, come up with new ideas, or simply have fun. The sky's the limit when our third eye is open.

12. Power

There is a sense of personal power that comes with a healthy Ajna. We are confident and self-assured. We know our worth, and we stand up for ourselves. We also have a strong sense of personal boundaries. We know what we will and will not tolerate. When the Ajna chakra is in balance, we are empowered to create the life we want. If you want to feel more powerful and confident, keep your Ajna chakra in balance.

13. Manifestation

When Ajna is in balance, we manifest our desires, create our reality, and bring our dreams into physical form. We can also better understand the laws of the universe and how to work with them. All of our manifesting power comes through the Third Eye. If you want to improve your manifestation skills, keep your Ajna chakra in balance. By focusing on the indigo color and visualizing a bright blue light shining from our Third Eye, we can bring balance to this chakra.

This vital chakra is associated with intuition, psychic powers, and manifestation, and we feel empowered and confident when it is balanced. We can manifest our desires and create our reality. We also have a strong sense of intuition and can see things from a different perspective.

The key to unlocking these abilities is to keep the Ajna chakra in balance. This can be done by meditating on the color indigo and visualizing a bright blue light shining from the Third Eye. You can also eat blue or purple foods, such as blueberries or grapes. Keeping the Ajna chakra in balance brings balance to our lives, provides access to our imagination, and gives a sense of personal power. We can also better understand the laws of the universe and how to work with them.

If you want to feel more connected to the divine, manifest your desires, or simply live a more balanced life, continue to read on!

Chapter 2: When Your Third Eye Is Blocked

To recap what we learned in the first chapter – The third eye or Ajna chakra is a sixth of seven in the systems found between our eyes. It's associated with clarity of thought, intuition, imagination, and insight. When this chakra is blocked or imbalanced, it can lead to poor concentration and a lack of focus on daily tasks.

But what does it actually mean when it is said your third eye is blocked? This chapter will explore the symptoms of a blocked third eye chakra (and the causes), as well as some real-life stories. At the end of this chapter, you'll find a quiz to test how in-balance your Ajna chakra is.

Blocked Third Eye Chakra

Being connected to the pineal gland, which regulates sleep patterns and produces melatonin, when this chakra is blocked, it can lead to sleep problems, such as insomnia or nightmares. You may also find it difficult to focus on tasks or find that you are very indecisive. You may feel stuck in a rut and unable to see the bigger picture. While a blocked third eye chakra can be caused by physical problems, such as a tumor on the pineal gland, it is more often due to mental or emotional issues.

Symptoms of a Blocked Third Eye Chakra

The most common symptom of a blocked third eye chakra is eyestrain or headaches. You may also experience pressure in the head, neck, and shoulders. If you have a blocked third eye chakra, you may find it difficult to concentrate or focus on tasks. You may also feel like you are in a fog, and your thoughts are jumbled. You may have trouble remembering things or making decisions. Other symptoms include:

- Anxiety
- Depression
- ADD/ADHD
- OCD
- PTSD
- Schizophrenia

Causes of a Blocked Third Eye Chakra

There are many possible causes of a blocked third eye chakra. A common one is an excess of negative emotions – anger, fear, or sadness. These emotions can prevent us from seeing the world clearly and lead to bad decision-making based on our intuition. Other potential causes include physical ailments, such as headaches or eyestrain, and being more susceptible to blockages caused by electromagnetic radiation from electronic devices. By understanding the causes of a blocked third eye chakra, we can take steps to unblock it and restore balance to our lives.

- Negative emotions: anger, fear, sadness, etc.
- Physical ailments: headaches, eyestrain, etc.
- Energetic blockages: electromagnetic radiation, etc.

Real-Life Stories

Andy had been dealing with anxiety and depression for years. He had tried medication and therapy, but nothing seemed to help. He was feeling stuck in his life and unable to see the bigger picture. Then, he heard about the third eye chakra and decided to give it a try. He started by meditating and visualizing a bright light in between his eyebrows. He also started making time for things he enjoyed, such as painting and hiking. After a few months, he noticed a difference. He was able to focus better on work, and his anxiety was manageable. He felt like he had a new lease on life.

Out of Balance Third Eye Chakra

When the third eye chakra is in balance, we tend to have a strong intuitive sense and can see beyond the physical world. We become more creatively imaginative and have a better understanding of our dreams. However, when the third eye chakra is out of sync, we may have trouble seeing clearly both physically and metaphysically. If you find yourself struggling in these areas, there are a few things you can do to help bring your third eye chakra back into balance. By taking some time to focus on your third eye chakra, you can bring more harmony and balance into your life.

Real-Life Stories

Ronald started having migraines shortly after he started working at a new job. He was under a lot of stress and felt like he had no control over his life. His migraines were so severe that he sometimes had to miss work. He tried medication, but it didn't seem to help. His doctor suggested he try meditation and focus on his third eye chakra. After a few weeks of regular practice, Ronald started to feel better. His migraines became less frequent, and he felt more in control of his life. He was even able to reduce his medication.

Another story is that of Harry. He was diagnosed with cancer and given only a few months to live. He was scared and didn't know what to do. A friend suggested he try meditation and focus on his third eye chakra. He was skeptical, but he decided to give it a try. After a few weeks of regular practice, Harry started to feel better. He had more energy, and his pain was manageable. He even started to feel hopeful about the future. While he knows he can't completely cure his cancer, he feels that the meditation has helped him to make the most of the time he has left.

Emma was in a car accident that left her with severe injuries. She was in a lot of pain and had trouble sleeping. Her doctor prescribed medication, but it made her feel fuzzy-headed and out of balance. Her mom suggested she try meditation and focus on her third eye chakra. After a few weeks of regular practice, Emma started to feel better. Her pain was manageable, and she was able to sleep through the night. She even started to feel more hopeful about her recovery.

These real-life stories demonstrate the power of the third eye chakra. Our physical eyes only see a small percentage of the world, but we can see beyond this world by opening our third eye – it just takes practice and intent.

Weak Third Eye Chakra

When the third eye chakra is weak, we may have trouble trusting our intuition, and others may easily sway us. We can become gullible and easily manipulated. We may also find it difficult to focus on tasks or make decisions. If you find yourself struggling in these areas, there are a few things you can do to help strengthen your third eye chakra. Spend time in nature, meditate, or practice yoga. You can also try using crystals, like amethyst or lapis lazuli, which are known for their ability to open and balance the third eye chakra.

Symptoms of a Weak Third Eye Chakra

We may doubt our intuition and second-guess our decisions. We may also feel disconnected from the world around us and find it difficult to understand complex concepts. Other symptoms of a weak third eye chakra include:

- Indecisiveness
- Disorganization
- Confusion
- Lack of focus
- Easily distracted
- Memory problems

Causes of a Weak Third Eye Chakra

Many factors can contribute to a weak third eye chakra, including diet, lifestyle choices, and unresolved traumas. Eating foods that are high in toxins can cause the third eye chakra to become sluggish, as can spending too much time in front of screens or living a generally chaotic lifestyle. Unresolved emotional trauma can also block this chakra, preventing us from accessing our inner wisdom. By taking steps to clean up our diet and lifestyle choices and heal our past wounds, we can help to bring balance back to the third eye chakra.

Real-Life Story

After years of working in a high-stress job, Karen began to feel disconnected from her intuition. She found it difficult to make decisions, and when she did make them, she often second-guessed herself. She was also easily distracted and had trouble focusing on tasks. Her therapist suggested she try meditation and yoga to help balance her third eye chakra. After a few weeks of regular practice, Karen began to feel more in tune with her intuition. She was able to make decisions more easily, and her focus improved. She also felt more connected to the world around her.

Overactive Third Eye Chakra

An overactive chakra means your chakra energy is too high. It can cause you to be paranoid, anxious, and think too much. You might also see or hear things that other people don't. If your third eye chakra is overactive, you may become obsessed with spiritual ideas and lose touch with reality. You may also have trouble sleeping and become easily agitated. You may see or hear things that others don't, which can lead to feelings of paranoia.

If you find yourself struggling with these symptoms, there are a few things you can do to help bring balance back to your third eye chakra. Spend time in nature, meditate, or practice yoga. You can also try using crystals, like amethyst or lapis lazuli, which are known for their ability to open and balance the third eye chakra.

Symptoms of an Overactive Third Eye Chakra

An overactive third eye chakra can cause you to be paranoid, anxious, and think too much. You may also have trouble sleeping and become easily agitated. You may also see flashes of light or colorful geometric patterns. Feeling as though you are being watched or followed, even when there is no one there, is also a common symptom of an overactive third eye chakra. Other symptoms of an overactive third eye chakra include:

- Paranoia

- Anxiety

- Insomnia

- Agitation

- Visual hallucinations

Causes of an Overactive Third Eye Chakra

There are several possible causes of an overactive third eye chakra. One is simply having too much yin energy in the body. This can be caused by spending too much time indoors, working too hard, or being overly emotional. Another possible cause is an imbalance in the other chakras. When one or more of the other chakras are out of alignment, it can throw the whole system off balance and lead to an overactive third eye chakra. Finally, an overactive third eye chakra can also be a sign that you are psychic or have some other type of extrasensory ability. If you find yourself experiencing any of these symptoms, it may be worth exploring whether you have an overactive third eye chakra.

Real-Life Story

Gina had always been a highly sensitive person, but after a traumatic experience, she began to feel as though she was going crazy. She was jumpy and paranoid all the time, and she started seeing things that no one else could see. Her friends and family began to worry about her, and she was eventually diagnosed with an overactive third eye chakra. Her therapist suggested she try meditation and yoga to help balance her chakra. After a few weeks of regular practice, Gina began to feel better. She could focus more clearly, and she no longer felt as though she was being followed or watched. She also slept better, and her overall anxiety level decreased.

Common Symptoms of a Blocked and Overactive Ajna Chakra

When the third eye chakra is blocked, we have trouble seeing things clearly, both literally and figuratively. We have trouble focusing our eyesight, and we also find it difficult to be empathetic and see things from other people's perspectives. Alternatively, when the Ajna chakra is overactive, we experience visual hallucinations or become overly fixated on one particular point of view. We also find it difficult to sleep, as the constant flow of images can be overwhelming. Ultimately, whether the Ajna chakra is blocked or overactive, it is crucial to seek balance to maintain our mental and physical health. Here are some common symptoms of a blocked or overactive third eye chakra:

1. Inability to Focus

There are a few common symptoms of a blocked and overactive Ajna chakra, and one of the most noticeable ones is an inability to focus. When your Ajna chakra is unbalanced, it can be difficult to concentrate on anything for more than a few minutes. You may find yourself constantly getting distracted, or your mind may feel foggy and overwhelming. This can make it hard to get work done, study for exams, or even carry on a conversation. If you're struggling with an inability to focus, it may be a sign that your Ajna chakra needs some attention.

2. A Feeling of Being Stuck

Another common symptom of an unbalanced Ajna chakra is feeling stuck. This can manifest in several ways, such as feeling like you're in a rut, feeling uninspired, or feeling like you're just treading water and not moving forward. If you're stuck, it may be because you do not see the bigger picture. When our third eye is unbalanced, we can get caught up in the details and miss the forest for the trees. If you're feeling stuck, it may be time to step back and get some clarity on your situation.

3. Depression

Depression is another common symptom of an unbalanced Ajna chakra. When our third eye is out of balance, we may feel hopeless, helpless, and unworthy. We may also lose interest in things that we used to enjoy and may withdraw from social activities. If you're struggling with depression, it's important to seek professional help. Depression is a serious condition that can be difficult to overcome on your own.

4. Anxiety

Anxiety is another common symptom of an unbalanced Ajna chakra. When we're anxious, we may feel like we're constantly on edge. We may be worried about things that haven't even happened yet, and we may find it hard to relax. If you're struggling with anxiety, it's important to seek professional help. Anxiety can be a debilitating condition that interferes with your daily life.

5. Headaches and Migraines

When your Ajna chakra is blocked or overactive, you may experience headaches or migraines. This is because of the positioning of the Ajna chakra. If this energy center is imbalanced, it can cause tension in the muscles and nerves around your head, leading to pain. Other common symptoms of a blocked Ajna chakra include eye strain, neck pain, and dizziness.

If you're experiencing any of these symptoms, it's vital to see a doctor or holistic health practitioner to rule out other possible causes. However, balancing your Ajna chakra may be worth exploring if you're seeking relief from chronic headaches or migraines. There are many simple and effective ways to do this, such as meditation, yoga, and aromatherapy.

Test Your Knowledge! (Quiz)

Now that you know some of the symptoms of a blocked, weak, out of balance, or overactive Ajna chakra, it's time for you to take a quiz to see where your chakra stands. Choose any one answer for each of the 10 questions from the list below and answer them as honestly as possible. Remember, there are no right or wrong answers, so just go with your gut.

1. **Do you find it difficult to focus on anything for more than a few minutes?**
   a) My mind is always racing, and I can't focus on anything for long. (Blocked)
   b) I can usually focus when I need to, but my mind does wander sometimes. (Weak)
   c) I can usually focus on what I need to, but I do get distracted easily. (Out of Balance)
   d) I can focus on what I want for as long as I need to. (Overactive)

2. **Do you have a hard time remembering your dreams?**
   a) I don't usually remember my dreams. (Blocked)
   b) I sometimes remember my dreams, but not always. (Weak)
   c) I usually remember my dreams, but they don't always make sense. (Out Balance)
   d) I always remember my dreams, and they usually make a lot of sense. (Overactive)

3. **Do you worry about things that haven't happened yet?**
   a) I'm always worrying about something. (Blocked)
   b) I sometimes worry about things, but not all the time. (Weak)
   c) I don't usually worry about things, but I sometimes have a hard time letting go of my stress. (Out of Balance)
   d) I don't usually worry about things, and I can easily let go of my stress. (Overactive)

4. **Do you have a hard time falling asleep at night?**
   a) I have a hard time falling asleep and staying asleep. (Blocked)
   b) I usually fall asleep all right, but I sometimes wake up in the middle of the night. (Weak)
   c) I usually fall asleep fine, but I sometimes have trouble staying asleep. (Out of Balance)
   d) I usually have no problem falling and staying asleep. (Overactive)

5. **Do you see things that other people can't see?**
   a) I sometimes see things that other people can't see. (Blocked)
   b) I sometimes see things that other people can't see, but I'm not sure if they're real. (Weak)
   c) I sometimes see things that other people can't see, but I know they're not there. (Out of Balance)
   d) I never see things that other people can't see. (Overactive)

6. **Do you feel like you have a hard time understanding yourself?**
   a) I don't understand myself. (Blocked)
   b) I sometimes understand myself, but other times I feel lost. (Weak)
   c) I usually have a pretty good understanding of myself, but there are still some things I'm exploring. (Out of Balance)
   d) I have a very clear understanding of myself. (Overactive)

7. **Do you have a hard time communicating your thoughts and feelings?**
   a) I have a hard time communicating my thoughts and feelings. (Blocked)
   b) I sometimes have a hard time communicating my thoughts and feelings. (Weak)
   c) I usually have no problem communicating my thoughts and feelings, but there are still some things I'm exploring. (Out of Balance)
   d) I always have no problem communicating my thoughts and feelings. (Overactive)

8. **Do you find yourself getting lost in your thoughts?**
   a) I often get lost in my thoughts, and it's hard for me to focus on anything else. (Blocked)
   b) I sometimes get lost in my thoughts, but I can usually snap out of it. (Weak)
   c) I don't usually get lost in my thoughts, but there are times when my mind does wander. (Out of Balance)

d) I never get lost in my thoughts. (Overactive)

9. **Do you have a hard time being in the present moment?**

a) I'm always in my head, and it's hard for me to be present. (Blocked)

b) I sometimes have a hard time being present, but I'm working on it. (Weak)

c) I usually have no problem being present, but there are times when my mind does wander. (Out of Balance)

d) I'm always present, and I never have a problem with being in the moment. (Overactive)

A blocked third eye chakra can result in several physical and mental problems. If your third eye is blocked, you may have trouble sleeping, seeing things that other people can't see, or understanding yourself, and you might struggle to get your feelings and thoughts across to others. It's important to work on unblocking your third eye chakra so that you can live a more balanced and fulfilling life.

If you think your third eye chakra may be blocked, you can do a few things to help unblock it. The following chapters will provide more information on how to do this.

Chapter 3: Balancing Your Other Chakras First

One of the essential things to know about chakras is that they are interconnected. While it is possible to open the third eye chakra without opening the other chakras, it is not advisable. This is because the third eye is located at the very top of the chakra system, and energy needs to be able to flow freely through all of the chakras for it to be properly balanced.

Energy needs to flow freely for your chakras to be balanced.
https://pixabay.com/es/photos/meditar-mujer-yoga-zen-meditando-1851165/

When the other chakras are open and in balance, energy can flow freely through them and up to the third eye chakra. This chapter will provide an overview of the six chakras, from the root chakra up to the throat chakra. First, we will provide an overview of the chakra's symbol and role – and symptoms when it is blocked.

The Connection between the Chakras

The seven chakras are energy centers located along the spine. Each chakra is associated with a different area of the body and a different aspect of our lives. When all of the chakras are open and in balance, we feel healthy and whole. However, when one or more chakras become blocked, we may experience physical, emotional, or spiritual problems. The best way to awaken Ajna, or the third eye chakra, is first to make sure that the other chakras are open and balanced.

How Awakening Ajna Works Best When the Other Chakras Are Open

When it comes to openings chakras, it's often said that it's best to start from the bottom and work your way up. However, things are different when it comes to the Ajna chakra, also known as the third eye chakra. The Ajna chakra is located at the very top of the chakra system, and while it can be opened on its own, it typically works best when all of the other chakras are open as well. Here's a look at why that is and how you can go about opening your Ajna chakra for optimum results.

If there is a blockage in any of the lower chakras, energy will not be able to flow freely upwards. As a result, it will be difficult to access Ajna's higher abilities. To ensure that the energy can flow freely, it is vital to eat a healthy diet, exercise regularly, and engage in activities that promote relaxation and self-awareness. Awakening Ajna will be much easier once the lower chakras are open and balanced. By opening Ajna, we can access our inner wisdom and connect with our higher selves.

The Best Way to Start Preparing Is by Working on the Self

One of the best ways to prepare for opening the third eye is by working on the self. This means looking at the other chakras and ensuring that they are open and balanced. If there is a blockage in any of the other chakras, it will be difficult to open the Third Eye. The best way to clear blockages is by eating a healthy diet, exercising regularly, and engaging in activities that promote relaxation and self-awareness. Once the other chakras are open and balanced, awakening the third eye will be much easier.

The third eye chakra is associated with intense spiritual experiences and psychic abilities, which can be overwhelming for someone unprepared for it. It is, therefore, crucial to do some work on balancing the other chakras first. This will help prepare you for opening the Third Eye chakra and ensure that you can handle its intense energies.

These include things like psychic abilities and spiritual experiences. To help you get started, we have provided an overview of each of the other six chakras, from the root chakra up to the throat chakra

The Root Chakra

At the base of the spine is the root chakra, connected with survival, security, and safety. It is the foundation of the chakra system and is responsible for our physical health and well-being, and we feel grounded, safe, and secure when it is in balance. We meet our basic needs and feel confident in our ability to do so. Therefore, the root chakra governs the physical body and is the most important chakra to focus on when it comes to physical health and well-being.

Root Chakra's Symbol and Roles

The root chakra, known as the Muladhara in Sanskrit, is associated with the element of earth. It's also connected to the sense of smell. The root chakra's symbol is a four-petaled lotus flower. It is red and is associated with the element of earth. The role of the root chakra is to provide a foundation for the other chakras. It governs the physical body and is responsible for our physical health and well-being.

Blockage Symptoms

When your root chakra is blocked, you may feel disconnected from your body and the Earth. You may also experience feelings of anxiety or insecurity, and you may find it difficult to trust others. Physical symptoms of a blocked root chakra include problems with the feet, legs, hips, and lower back pain. You may also suffer from constipation or digestive issues.

Simple Ways to Balance It

To open your root chakra, try spending time in nature, eating grounding foods like root vegetables, and practicing yoga or other forms of exercise. Red is the color associated with the root chakra, so you can also try wearing red clothing or carrying red stones like garnet or ruby. By opening your root chakra, you'll feel more connected to yourself and the world around you.

The Sacral Chakra

The sacral chakra, located just below the navel, is linked to pleasure, creativity, and sexuality. It is in charge of emotions and our ability to feel pleasure and pain. We feel confident in our physical selves and creative abilities when the sacral chakra is balanced. We can enjoy pleasure without any attachments or attachments. The sacral chakra also controls our physical energy and desires.

The Sacral Chakra's Symbol and Roles

Known as the Svadhisthana in Sanskrit, it is associated with the element of water. It is also connected to the sense of taste. The sacral chakra's symbol is a six-petaled lotus flower associated with the orange color. The role of the sacral chakra is to provide us with pleasure, creativity, and energy. It governs our emotions and is responsible for our ability to feel pleasure and pain.

Blocked Symptoms of Sacral Chakra

When your sacral chakra is blocked, you'll feel disconnected from your creative side and physical energy. You may feel apathetic and unable to enjoy the things you used to love. You may find yourself craving things that are bad for you or engaging in self-destructive behaviors. You may feel numb and unable to experience pleasure. You may also experience physical symptoms, such as infertility, impotence, urinary problems, or lower back pain.

How to Balance the Sacral Chakra

To open the sacral chakra, we can try activities that promote creativity, such as painting or dancing. We can also try to connect with our sexuality more consciously, whether that means exploring our fantasies or enjoying more intimate moments with a partner. The color associated with the sacral chakra is orange, so we can also try wearing orange clothing or carrying oranges with us. By opening the sacral chakra, we can bring more vitality and pleasure into our lives.

The Solar Plexus Chakra

The solar plexus chakra is found above the navel and is connected to self-esteem, self-confidence, and power. It is responsible for our ability to assert ourselves and take control of our lives, and when it is in balance, we are confident and feel more in control of ourselves and our lives. We can set boundaries and stand up for ourselves.

The Solar Plexus Chakra's Symbol and Roles

The solar plexus chakra is also called by the Sanskrit name Manipura and is connected to the fire element. It is also connected to the sense of sight. The solar plexus chakra's symbol is a ten-petaled lotus flower associated with the yellow color. The solar plexus chakra helps us with self-esteem, self-confidence, and personal power. It is responsible for our ability to assert ourselves and take control of our lives.

Blocked Symptoms of Solar Plexus Chakra

When your solar plexus chakra is blocked, you may feel powerless and out of control. You may feel like you are not good enough and do not deserve success. You may find yourself second-guessing everything you do – and avoiding risk. You may also experience physical symptoms, such as digestive problems, ulcers, or diabetes.

How to Balance the Solar Plexus Chakra

To open the solar plexus chakra, we can try activities that promote personal power, such as assertiveness training or public speaking. We can also try to connect with our power more consciously by setting boundaries and standing up for ourselves. The color associated with the solar plexus chakra is yellow, so we can also try wearing yellow clothing or carrying yellow objects with us. By opening the solar plexus chakra, we can bring more confidence and power into our lives.

The Heart Chakra

Located in the center of the chest, the heart chakra is connected to forgiveness, love, and compassion. It is responsible for our ability to give and receive love. When the heart chakra is balanced, we feel loved, and we can give love. We feel compassion for others, and we can forgive.

The Heart Chakra's Symbol and Roles

The heart chakra is also known by its Sanskrit name, the Anahata, and is connected with the air element and our sense of touch. Its symbol is a lotus flower with twelve petals, and it also has a connection to the color green. The heart chakra's role is to help us with forgiveness, love, and compassion. It is responsible for our ability to give and receive love.

Blocked Symptoms of Heart Chakra

You may feel unloved and unworthy of love when your heart chakra is blocked. You may find it difficult to give or receive love. You may also feel disconnected from others, and you may have difficulty feeling compassion. You may experience physical symptoms, such as heart problems, respiratory problems, or immune system problems.

How to Balance the Heart Chakra

To open the heart chakra, we can try activities that promote love, such as giving or receiving a hug, writing love letters, or spending time with friends and family. We can also try to connect with our heart chakra more consciously by meditating on love or practicing yoga. The color associated with the heart chakra is green, so we can also try wearing green clothing or carrying green objects with us. When we open the heart chakra, we invite compassion and love into our lives.

The Throat Chakra

Found at the dead center of the throat, this chakra is associated with self-expression, communication, and truth, helping us speak our truth and learn how to express ourselves. When the throat chakra is balanced, we can communicate clearly and truthfully. We feel confident in our ability to express ourselves, and we can listen to others.

The Throat Chakra's Symbol and Roles

The throat chakra, known as the Vishuddha in Sanskrit, is associated with the element of sound. It is also connected to the sense of hearing. The throat chakra's symbol is a sixteen-petaled lotus flower associated with the blue color. Its role is to help us learn to express ourselves and speak our truth.

Blocked Symptoms of the Throat Chakra

If you struggle to express yourself, it's likely your throat chakra is blocked. You may find it difficult to communicate, and you may have difficulty speaking your truth. You may also feel that you are not being heard, and you may have a hard time listening to others. You may experience physical symptoms, such as throat problems, mouth problems, or teeth problems.

How to Balance the Throat Chakra

Try activities that promote communication and self-expression, such as singing, writing, or painting, to open the throat chakra. Also, try to connect with your throat chakra more consciously by meditating on communication or practicing yoga. The color associated with the throat chakra is blue, so we can also try wearing blue clothing or carrying blue objects with us. We can bring more communication and self-expression into our lives by opening the throat chakra.

The Crown Chakra

Found at the top of the head, the crown chakra is connected with spirituality, enlightenment, and our connection to the divine. It is responsible for our ability to connect with our higher selves and the world around us. When the crown chakra is balanced, we feel spiritually connected and aligned with our highest purpose. We feel a sense of peace and connection to all.

The Crown Chakra's Symbol and Roles

The crown chakra, known as the Sahasrara in Sanskrit, is connected with the element of consciousness and your sense of intuition. The crown chakra's symbol is a thousand-petaled lotus flower associated with the violet color. The role of the crown chakra is associated with enlightenment, spirituality, and connection to the divine. It is responsible for our ability to connect with our higher selves and the world around us.

Blocked Symptoms of the Crown Chakra

When your crown chakra is blocked, you may feel disconnected from your spirituality. You may find it difficult to connect with your higher self or with the world around you. You may also feel like you are not living your highest purpose. You may experience physical symptoms, such as headaches, migraines, or problems with your nervous system.

How to Balance the Crown Chakra

To open the crown chakra, activities that promote spirituality and connection to the divine, such as meditation, yoga, or prayer, are the exercises to do. We can also try to connect with our crown chakra more consciously by meditating on our connection to the universe. The color associated with the crown chakra is violet, so we can also try wearing violet clothing or carrying violet objects with us. By opening the crown chakra, we can bring more spirituality and connection to the divine into our lives.

Simple Ways for Balancing Your Chakras

There are many ways to balance your chakras. Some people may find that they need to work on one chakra more than others. Here are some simple ways to get started:

1. Wear the corresponding color for each chakra. For example, if you want to focus on your crown chakra, wear violet.
2. Carry objects of the corresponding color with you. For example, carry a green stone with you if you want to focus on your heart chakra.

3. Meditate on the associated element for each chakra. For example, if you want to focus on your root chakra, meditate on the element of earth.

4. Visualize the corresponding color for each chakra. For example, visualize the color yellow if you want to focus on your solar plexus chakra.

5. Do yoga poses that correspond to each chakra. For example, if you want to focus on your throat chakra, do a yoga pose that opens the throat, such as the camel pose.

6. Read books dedicated to each chakra. For example, if you want to focus on your crown chakra, read a book about enlightenment or spirituality.

The chakras are seen as the seven energy centers, corresponding to three states: physical, emotional, and spiritual. When the chakras are balanced, our minds and bodies are aligned. There are many ways to balance our chakras. We could wear the corresponding color, carry objects of the corresponding color, meditate on the associated element, or visualize the corresponding color. We could also do yoga poses corresponding to each chakra and read books dedicated to each chakra. Choose the method that resonates with you, and start balancing your chakras today!

Chapter 4: Mantras and Mudras

Mantras and mudras are great tools for opening and balancing the third eye chakra. They are sacred words or sounds repeated during meditation in any language but are often in Sanskrit. Mudras are hand gestures also used during meditation. The power of mantras and mudras lies in their ability to focus the mind.

The third eye chakra can be opened and balanced using these exercises. This chapter will cover mantras and mudras and their benefits for opening the third eye chakra. It will also provide a few example affirmations and tips for creating your own original mantras.

Mantras

One way to clear away blockages and open up the third eye chakra is through the use of mantras. These are the sacred sounds that can help focus the mind and connect us with our spiritual nature. Many different mantras can be used for the third eye chakra, but some of the most popular include *"Om Namah Shivaya"* and *"Aham Brahma Asmi."* Simply repeating these mantras aloud or in your mind can help open up the third eye chakra and bring you closer to your true nature.

Definition

A mantra is a word or phrase repeated often, usually as part of religious or spiritual practice. The word "mantra" comes from the Sanskrit "mam," meaning "to think," and "trai," meaning "to protect." In Hinduism and Buddhism, mantras are often repeated during meditation as a way to focus the mind and connect with the divine. Mantras can also be recited for other purposes, such as promoting healing or bringing good luck.

While mantras are typically associated with Eastern religions, they can be found in other spiritual traditions as well. For example, some Christians recite the Lord's Prayer as a mantra, and Native Americans may use mantras in their ceremonial chants. Ultimately, a mantra is simply a tool that can be used to promote peace of mind and connection with the higher self.

Difference between Mantras and Affirmations

A mantra is a sacred utterance, a numinous sound, a syllable, a word or phonemes, or a group of words in Sanskrit believed by practitioners to have psychological and spiritual powers. Mantras are used as tools for contemplation, reflection, and meditation. Affirmations are positive statements that can help you challenge and overcome self-sabotaging and negative thoughts.

You can bring about positive changes to your life by repeating affirmations as often as possible and truly believing in them. For example, if you want to believe you can run a marathon, an affirmation could be, *"I am a strong and powerful runner."* Repeating this to yourself multiple times, especially if you doubt your ability to run the marathon, can help increase your belief that you can do it.

Mantras are often more general than affirmations and less specific to an individual goal. They are also usually repeated numerous times (108 is considered a sacred number in many Eastern religions), while affirmations are typically only said once or twice. Mantras are also usually chanted or spoken aloud, while affirmations can be either spoken aloud or just repeated silently in your mind.

Affirmations are about changing your beliefs to empower you to take action and achieve your goals, while mantras are more about connecting with the divine or your higher self.

Examples of Affirmations

Affirmations are simply positive statements that you repeat to help you challenge negative thoughts and overcome self-sabotage. When you believe in what you are saying and repeat them often, affirmations can help you change the negative in your life into positive. Here are some examples of affirmations that could be used to open up the third eye chakra:

If you want to increase your self-awareness:

"I am attuned to my intuition."

"I am open to guidance from my higher self."

"I trust my inner knowing."

"I am connected to my higher power."

If you want to overcome negative thinking:

"I am releasing all negativity."

"I am filled with positive energy."

"I am worthy of love and happiness."

"I am grateful for all the good in my life."

Tips for Creating Your Affirmations

Creating your affirmations is a great way to boost your self-confidence and bring positive changes into your life. Here are a few tips to get you started:

First, choose affirmations that are realistic and achievable. If you're telling yourself that you're going to be a millionaire by the end of the year, it's not likely to happen, and you'll just end up feeling disappointed. However, if you focus on attainable affirmations, such as *"I am worthy of love and respect,"* you'll be more likely to believe them.

Second, make sure your affirmations are in the present tense. For example, rather than saying *"I will be successful,"* say *"I am successful."* This helps to program your mind to believe that success is happening right now, not in the future.

Finally, repeat your affirmations regularly. The more often you say them, the more likely you are to believe them. So, make a point of repeating them several times each day, either out loud or in your head. Put them up where you'll see them often, such as on your bathroom mirror or your fridge.

By following these tips, you can create powerful affirmations that will help improve your life in many ways.

Effects of Mantras on the Body and Brain

The act of repeating a mantra can help to focus the mind, still your thoughts, and bring about a sense of inner calm. But what many people don't realize is that mantras can also have a powerful impact on the body and brain. Studies have shown that mantra repetition can help to lower blood pressure, improve breathing, and reduce stress levels.

In addition, Mantras can also help to increase focus and concentration, improve memory, and boost cognitive performance. So, the next time you are feeling stressed or overwhelmed, try repeating a mantra to yourself. You may be surprised at how quickly it helps to center your thoughts and ease your tension.

The "AUM" Mantra

The "AUM" mantra is also a powerful tool for activating and balancing the third eye chakra. AUM is the sound of the universe, and it is considered the most sacred sound in Hinduism. The word AUM comprises three parts: A, U, and M. These three parts represent the waking, dreaming, and sleeping states of consciousness. These are three Sanskrit letters: A, U, and M. Each letter has a specific meaning and purpose. "A" stands for the waking state, "U" stands for the dreaming state, and "M" stands for the sleeping state. When these three states are united, they form the unified field of consciousness that is necessary for activating the third eye chakra.

By chanting the "AUM" mantra, we create a bridge between the conscious and subconscious mind, which allows us to access our higher wisdom. The mantra's vibration also helps cleanse and purify the third eye chakra, promoting clarity and vision. In short, the "AUM" mantra is an invaluable tool for anyone seeking to awaken their third eye chakra.

Other Mantras for the Third Eye Chakra

As well as the "AUM" mantra, there are many other mantras that can be used to activate and balance the third eye chakra. Some of the most popular third eye chakra mantras include:

"Om Mani Padme Hum" (Pronunciation: Aum Ma-nee Padme Hum)

From the Tibetan Buddhist tradition, this mantra means "Hail to the jewel in the lotus." It is often used for purification and protection purposes. It is also said to be incredibly powerful for opening the third eye chakra and developing psychic abilities.

"Om Namah Shivaya" (Pronunciation: Aum Na-ma-ha Shi-va-ya)

This mantra is from the Hindu tradition, and it means "I honor the divine within myself." This mantra is often used for cleansing and purification. It is also said to be very helpful for opening the third eye chakra and accessing higher states of consciousness.

"So, Hum" (Pronunciation: Soo Hum)

This mantra is from the Vedic tradition, and it means "I am that." This mantra is often used for self-realization and awakening and is also thought to help you open your third eye chakra and gain access to higher states of consciousness.

Mudras

Mudras are hand gestures and formations often used in yoga and meditation practices. They can be used to help focus the mind, direct energy flow, and promote relaxation. There are many different mudras, and each one has a different purpose. For example, the Gyan Mudra is often used for promoting concentration and aiding in meditation. Many different mudras can be used for various purposes. Experiment with different mudras to see which ones work best for you.

When and How to Use Mudras

Mudras can be used anytime and anywhere. They are a great way to focus the mind and direct energy flow when you are feeling scattered or unfocused. Mudras can also be used to promote relaxation and calm the mind. If you are new to mudras, start by practicing them for a few minutes each day. You can use mudras throughout the day as needed or practice them for a specific purpose, such as meditation or relaxation.

Mudras for Third Eye Chakra

Mudras are a great way to unblock and balance your third eye chakra. If you are having trouble meditating or accessing your psychic abilities, try using one of the mudras listed below. Another way of doing it is by combining mudras with other third eye chakra exercises, such as visualization or affirmations. Experiment and find what works best for you.

Many different mudras can be used to activate and balance the third eye chakra. Some of the most popular third eye chakra mudras include:

Shambhavi Mudra (Pronunciation: Shaam-baa-vee Moo-dra)

Shambhavi means "conqueror of the mind." This mudra is said to be very helpful for concentration and meditation. It is also said to help open the third eye chakra and access higher states of consciousness.

Sit in a comfortable position with your spine straight to do this mudra. Focus your attention on the space between your eyebrows. Next, slowly and gently bring your eyebrows together. You can hold this mudra for as long as you like.

Bhumisparsha Mudra (Pronunciation: Boo-mee-spar-she Moo-dra)

Bhumisparsha means "touching the earth." This mudra is said to be specifically designed to help you get grounded and stable and can help open your third eye chakra, accessing higher states of consciousness.

Sit in a comfortable position with your eyes closed to do this mudra. Focus your attention on the space between your eyebrows. Next, slowly and gently bring your right hand to your right knee with your palm facing down. Then, place your left-hand palm-up on your lap. You can hold this mudra for as long as you like.

Anjali Mudra (Pronunciation: Aan-jaa-lee Moo-dra)

Anjali means "offering." This mudra is said to be very helpful for promoting peace and calm, helps with unblocking the third eye chakra, and helps with accessing higher states of consciousness. This mudra is often used as a gesture of respect or prayer. You can also add a slight bow if you like.

Anjali Mudra.
https://pixabay.com/es/photos/budismo-theravada-budista-monja-1769528/

Sit in a comfortable position with your eyes closed to do this mudra. Focus your attention on the space between your eyebrows. Simply bring your palms together in front of your chest with your fingers pointed up. This mudra can be used anytime you feel the need to connect with your higher self or the divine.

Gyan Mudra (Pronunciation: Jee-yan Moo-dra)

Gyan means "knowledge." This mudra is very useful for promoting concentration and aiding in meditation. It also helps you unlock the third eye chakra, thus gaining access to higher states of consciousness. Sit in a comfortable position with your spine straight to do this mudra.

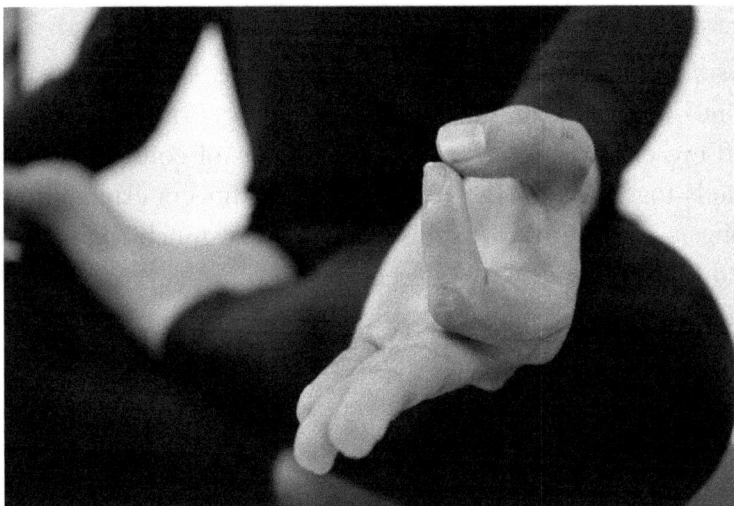

Gyan Mudra.

Focus your attention on the space between your eyebrows. Next, bring your index finger and thumb together to form a circle. The other three fingers should be extended. You can hold this mudra for as long as you like.

Shakti Mudra (Pronunciation: Shaak-tee Moo-dra)

Shakti means "power." This mudra is said to help increase energy and motivation, unblock the third eye chakra, and access higher states of consciousness. Bring your hands together in front of your heart with your palms facing each other to do this mudra. Next, fold your index and middle fingers into your palms. The ring and pinky fingers should be extended. You can hold this mudra for as long as you like.

Apana Mudra (Pronunciation: Aa-paa-na Moo-dra)

Apana means "downward moving." This mudra helps promote detoxification and aids in digestion. It is also helpful for opening the third eye chakra and accessing higher states of consciousness. Sit in a comfortable position with your spine straight to do this mudra. Focus your attention on the space between your eyebrows. Next, bring your thumb, middle finger, and ring finger together. The other two fingers should be extended. You can hold this mudra for as long as you like.

Kalesvara Mudra (Pronunciation: Kaal-ay-shvaara Moo-dra)

Kalesvara translates to "lord of time," and is said to help give you insight into your past, present, and future. It is also helpful for healing the third eye chakra and accessing higher states of consciousness. Bring your hands together with the middle and ring fingers extended and the other fingers tucked in to do this mudra. Next, touch the tips of your extended fingers to the space between your eyebrows. You can hold this mudra for as long as you like.

Mudras and mantras are powerful tools that can open the third eye chakra and access higher states of consciousness. While mudras are physical gestures that activate specific energies in the body, mantras are sacred sounds that create specific vibrations in the mind. Both mudras and mantras can be used together or separately to achieve the desired results. Many mantras and mudras can be used to help unblock and balance the third eye chakra. Experiment with different mudras and see which ones work best for you.

Chapter 5: Meditation and Visualization

Meditation and visualization are powerful tools for opening and balancing the third eye chakra. The practice of meditation can help still the mind and quiet mental chatter, providing a space for inner stillness and peace. Visualization can be used to help focus and direct attention inward towards the third eye chakra.

With regular practice, meditation and visualization can help to open and balance the third eye chakra, promoting greater clarity of thought, intuition, and psychic ability. This chapter will explore some basic techniques for third eye chakra meditation and visualization. There is no one "right" way to meditate or visualize. Experiment with different techniques and find which works best for you.

The Power of Meditation

Meditation has been practiced for centuries, and it has many benefits. It can help to improve mental and physical health, and it can also promote creativity and well-being. One of the key benefits of meditation is that it helps to reduce stress levels. When we meditate, we focus on our breath and let go of all other thoughts. This allows us to find a sense of inner peace and calm. As a result, we are less likely to feel overwhelmed by stressors in our life.

Meditation can also help to improve focus and concentration. By regularly practicing meditation, we train our minds to be more present and tune out distractions. This can be extremely beneficial in both our personal and professional life. Added benefits are that meditation can help to boost our mood and increase our sense of well-being.

Studies have shown that regular meditation can decrease anxiety and depression and increase self-esteem and happiness. If you're looking for a way to improve your overall health and well-being, then look no further than meditation. It is a simple and effective way to promote relaxation and stress relief.

Benefits of Meditation for Third Eye Chakra

Meditation is described in a lot of guides as the primary way to calm the mind. While this is certainly one of its benefits, meditation can also be used to develop greater clarity and insight. One of the critical areas of focus in meditation is the third eye chakra. By bringing our attention to the third eye chakra, we can begin to develop a deeper understanding of our experiences. We can learn to see beyond the surface level and gain a more intuitive sense of what is happening around us.

In addition, by opening up the third eye chakra, we can also increase our ability to connect with our higher selves and receive guidance from our intuition. As we develop a stronger connection to the third eye chakra, we can experience greater clarity and insight in our lives. With regular practice, we can learn to trust our intuition more and use it to make better decisions in all areas of our lives.

How to Meditate for the Third Eye Chakra

For those who are new to meditation, the idea of opening the third eye chakra can seem daunting. However, with a little practice, anyone can learn to meditate and not only for the third eye chakra. The first step is to find a comfortable place to sit or lie down. Once you are comfortable, close your eyes and take a few deep breaths. Imagine a white light entering your body through your forehead as you inhale. Visualize the light moving down to your third eye chakra, located in the center of your forehead.

Imagine the white light expanding outward from your third eye chakra as you exhale. Continue to breathe deeply and focus on the light until you feel your third eye chakra begin to open. You may also feel a tingling sensation or see colors or images behind your eyelids. When you are ready, slowly open your eyes and take a few moments to ground yourself before getting up. With practice, you'll be able to open your third eye chakra with ease and enjoy all its positivity.

Meditation Techniques for the Third Eye Chakra

One of the most important things you can do for your mind, body, and soul is to meditate. Meditation has improved mental and physical health and relationships, and work life. However, many people find it difficult to meditate, as they cannot clear their minds or focus on their breath. If this sounds like you, then you may benefit from unblocking your third eye chakra.

As you meditate, breathe deeply, and let go of any thoughts or worries that are taking up space in your mind. With practice, you'll be able to clear your mind and connect with your higher self. If you feel like your third eye chakra is blocked, it may be helpful to meditate on the color purple. Here are some meditation techniques to help you unblock, heal, and balance your third eye chakra:

1. Visualization

Visualization is a powerful meditation technique that can be used to focus and balance the third eye chakra. To begin, find a comfortable place to sit or lie down. Close your eyes and take a few deep breaths. Once you are relaxed, begin to visualize a glowing purple ball of light in the center of your forehead. See the ball getting brighter and brighter until it fills your entire field of vision.

Feel your third eye chakra opening and expanding as you gaze at the ball of light. Then, imagine beams of light radiating out from the center of the ball, filling your whole body with energy and light. Take some time to simply enjoy the experience of being filled with this peaceful and healing energy. Slowly open your eyes and take a few deep breaths before getting up when you are finished.

2. Candle Gazing

One popular meditation technique is *candle gazing*, which involves fixing your gaze on a lit candle flame. The key is to keep your gaze soft, allowing your vision to blur slightly. You may find it helpful to practice this meditation with your eyes closed at first until you get the hang of it. As you focus on the candle flame, allow your mind to become still and simply observe any thoughts or feelings that arise.

Candle gazing.
https://pixabay.com/es/photos/las-manos-abierto-vela-1926414/

If your attention wanders, gently bring it back to the present moment. You can also visualize the candle flame as a purple ball of light and imagine it opening and expanding your third eye chakra. With regular practice, you'll develop greater clarity and focus, and you may start to notice subtle shifts in your perceptions and awareness.

3. Mindful Meditation

Mindful meditation is a simple yet powerful technique that can be used to focus and calm the mind. Find a comfortable place to sit or lie down, close your eyes, and take a few deep breaths. Then, simply focus your attention on your breath and the sensations in your body.

Notice the rise and fall of your chest, the feel of the air moving in and out of your lungs, and the sensation of your feet on the ground. Consciously draw your attention back to your breath if your mind starts wandering. If your mind begins to wander, simply bring your attention back to your breath. With practice, you'll develop greater focus and concentration, and you may find that your mind becomes calmer and more at ease.

4. Sound Meditation

Sound meditation is another effective way to unblock and balance the third eye chakra. Find a comfortable place to sit or lie down, close your eyes, and breathe in deeply a few times. Then, simply focus your attention on the sound of your breath.

You may also want to focus on a mantra or affirmation that you repeat to yourself. The key is to simply observe the sound of your breath and the mantra without getting caught up in thinking about them. If your mind begins to wander, gently bring it back to the present moment. With regular practice, you'll develop greater focus and concentration, and you may find that your mind becomes calmer and more at ease.

Tips and Tricks for the Third Eye Chakra

If you are having trouble meditating or opening your third eye chakra, here are a few tips and tricks that may help:

1. Record Yourself

If you find it difficult to meditate on your own, try recording yourself reading a guided meditation or visualization. Record yourself for posterity so you can look back on your progress and see where you've been and how far you've come. Writing down your thoughts is a great way to get clarity and raise your vibration. When you record yourself, be sure to use a soothing voice.

Now find somewhere comfortable to sit or lie down and press play. As you listen, let go of any expectations or goals. Simply relax and allow the words to flow through you. If your mind wanders, simply bring your attention back to the sound of your voice. This can be a great way to relax and focus your mind, and it can also help you to connect with your higher self.

2. Incorporating Breathing Techniques

Incorporating breathing techniques into your daily routine is another way to balance the third eye chakra. For example, you can try inhaling inhale through your nose deeply and slowly exhale through the mouth. You can also try holding your breath for a few seconds after exhaling. When you focus on your breath, it can help to still the mind and allow you to connect with your higher self.

There are also several more breathing exercises that you can do to help open up your chakra. One of the more popular exercises is known as the "breath of fire." Sit with your spine straight and take a deep breath through your nose. Then, exhale forcefully through the mouth, making a "ha" sound. Continue this rapid breathing for up to one minute. You may feel lightheaded or dizzy at first – this is normal. Just be sure to listen to your body and take breaks as needed.

These techniques will help to clear your mind and allow you to focus on your inner vision. With regular practice, you'll start to see the world around you in a new light. The third eye chakra is associated with the element of light, so it's important to incorporate some form of light into your practice. This could be anything from candles to sunlight.

3. Wear Purple

The color purple is associated with the third eye chakra, and wearing it can help to encourage balance in this energy center. In addition to promoting psychic awareness, purple is also said to help relieve tension headaches and improve communication. If you seek to open your third eye chakra, try wearing purple next time you meditate or do some other form of energy work. You may just find that it helps you tap into your innate wisdom.

The purple color is also associated with the crown chakra, located at the top of the head. Wearing purple can help to encourage balance in both of these energy centers. Another way to incorporate the color purple into your life is to eat purple foods. Some great options include grapes, eggplant, and blueberries.

4. Use Essential Oils

Essential oils can be used to promote balance in the third eye chakra. Some of the best options include lavender, frankincense, and peppermint. These oils can be used in a diffuser or added to a bath. You can also add a few drops to a cotton ball and inhale the aroma. When using essential oils, be sure to start with a small amount and increase as needed.

Most oils can be applied directly to the skin, but some may need to be diluted first. Read the label carefully and follow the instructions. If you have any concerns, speak to a qualified aromatherapist. These oils can help open your third eye chakra and promote psychic awareness with regular use.

5. Connect with Nature

Spending time in nature is a great way to connect with the third eye chakra. This energy center is associated with the element of light, so spending time in the sun is a very easy way to get your fill of light. This will help to energize and balance the third eye chakra. In addition to spending time outdoors, you can also bring nature into your home. This could be anything from plants to crystals.

One of the best ways to connect with nature is to spend time in the forest. This is because forests are full of negative ions, which can help to improve your mood and mental well-being. If you don't have access to a forest, try spending time near a body of water. The sound of the waves can help to still the mind and encourage reflection.

6. Try Crystal Healing

Crystal healing is a popular method for balancing the third eye chakra. Some of the best crystals for this purpose include amethyst, lapis lazuli, and sodalite. You can wear these stones in the form of jewelry or place them somewhere on your body when you meditate. They can also be kept in your office or home to encourage peace and calm wherever you are.

If you're new to crystal healing, starting with a stone that resonates with you is important. Once you've found the right crystal, hold it in your hand and take a few deep breaths. As you exhale, visualize the negative energy being released from your body. You can also place the stone on your third eye chakra during meditation; *just be sure to cleanse it regularly to remove any negative energy.*

7. Get a Massage

A massage is a great way to promote balance in the third eye chakra. This energy center is located in the center of the forehead, so massaging this area can help to encourage psychic awareness. In addition to traditional massage, there are also some specific third eye chakra massage techniques that you can try. These include acupressure and reflexology.

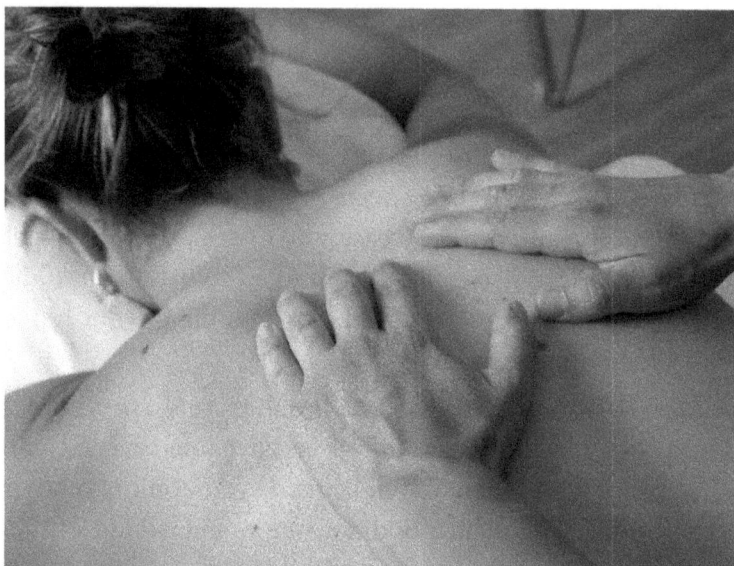

Get a massage.
https://pixabay.com/es/photos/mujer-las-manos-masaje-masajeando-567021/

When massaging the third eye chakra, it's important to use light pressure. This area is delicate, so you don't want to apply too much pressure. If you're unsure how to massage this area, consider seeking a qualified therapist. With regular massage, you can help to open your third eye chakra and promote psychic awareness.

8. Practice Meditation Regularly

Meditation is one of the most convenient and best ways to balance the third eye chakra. This practice helps to still the mind and encourages introspection. When meditating, you can focus on your breath or a mantra. You can also visualize a particular color or symbol.

There are many different ways to meditate, so it's important to find a method that works for you. If you're new to meditation, there are some great online resources. With regular practice, you can help to open your third eye chakra and promote psychic awareness.

9. Eat a Balanced Diet

What you eat has a direct impact on your third eye chakra. This energy center is associated with the element of light, so include plenty of fruits and vegetables in your diet. These foods are high in antioxidants, which can help to protect the body from free radicals. In addition to eating a healthy diet, it's also important to stay hydrated. This will help to flush toxins from the body and promote balance in the third eye chakra.

10. Get Plenty of Sleep

The third eye chakra is associated with the pineal gland, responsible for regulating sleep. This means that getting enough sleep is essential for balancing this energy center. If you're having trouble sleeping, you can do a few things to promote restful sleep. These include establishing a regular sleep schedule, avoiding caffeine before bed, and creating a calm and relaxing environment in your bedroom.

Meditation and visualization are two great ways to balance your chakra. With regular practice, you can help to open your third eye chakra and become more proficient at psychic awareness. In addition to these practices, it's also important to eat a balanced diet and get plenty of sleep. By taking care of your body and mind, you can help to encourage balance in the third eye chakra.

If you wish to learn more about yoga and breathing techniques, continue reading the next chapter.

Chapter 6: Yoga and Breathing Techniques

Pranayama, or controlled breathing, is crucial for the exercise of meditation and yoga. Pranayama routines can help to balance and heal the third eye chakra. If you have ever tried meditating or doing yoga, breathing is a key element of both practices. The word "pranayama" comes from the Sanskrit words "prana," meaning life force or breath, and "Ayama," meaning control or extension.

It is often said that pranayama helps to still the mind, making it easier to focus on meditation. However, even if you are not interested in meditation, pranayama can still be beneficial for your overall health. So next time you roll out your yoga mat or sit down to meditate, take a moment to focus on your breath and see how it affects your practice. This chapter will focus on pranayama exercises and yoga poses particularly helpful for balancing the third eye chakra.

Pranayama

Pranayama is the practice of controlling your breath to improve your overall health and well-being. There are a lot of different pranayama techniques, but all of them involve regulating the breath in some way. Pranayama can be practiced on its own or as part of a larger regimen of yoga practice.

Pranayama.
https://commons.wikimedia.org/wiki/File:The_Sundhya_Plate_6_Fig_3.jpg

Pranayama is a great way to balance the third eye chakra. It's a type of yoga that focuses on breath control. By controlling our breath, we can better control our thoughts and emotions – think of what happened with your breathing the last time you were startled, and that will give you an idea of the role breathing plays in controlling emotions. Traditionally associated with the element of space, it's important to create a sense of spaciousness in the mind when practicing pranayama.

To do this, focus on deep, slow breathing. Allow your inhales and exhales to be equal in length, and allow your belly to expand fully on each inhale. As you exhale, envision your thoughts and worries floating away on the breath. You'll find it easier to quiet your mind and access your intuition with regular practice.

The Importance of Controlled Breathing

Breathing is obviously an essential function of life, but it's also one that we often take for granted. When we're feeling calm and relaxed, our breathing is slow and steady. However, our breathing can become shallow and rapid when we're under stress. This change in breathing can profoundly impact our body, physically and mentally.

Slow, deep breathing triggers the body's relaxation response, lowering stress levels, heart rate, and blood pressure. Controlled breathing can also help to ease anxiety and promote feelings of calmness. In other words, it's not just important to breathe – it's important to breathe correctly. By taking a few minutes each day to focus on our breath, we can help to improve our overall health and well-being.

Pranayama Exercises for the Third Eye Chakra

Pranayama exercises are a great way to help bring the third eye chakra back into balance. Many different pranayama exercises can help balance the third eye chakra. Below are a few of our favorites.

1. Nadi Shodhana (Alternate Nostril Breathing)

Nadi Shodhana, also known as Alternate Nostril Breathing, is a simple but powerful breathing technique that can be used to refresh and rejuvenate the body and mind. It requires you to block and open your nostrils alternately, thus creating an energy balance between the right and left sides of your body. The left side of the body is associated with the moon; the right side of the body is associated with the sun. Nadi Shodhana helps to balance these two energies and bring them into harmony.

In addition to promoting relaxation, Nadi Shodhana has been shown to improve concentration, reduce stress levels, and boost immunity. The best part is that it can be done anywhere, at any time. So, if you're looking for a quick and easy way to center yourself and bring some peace into your day, give Nadi Shodhana a try.

First, sit comfortably with your spine straight. Rest your left hand on your left knee and use your right index finger and thumb to block off your right nostril by pressing it closed. Take a deep breath through your left nostril and then block off your left nostril with your right ring finger. Exhale through your right nostril deeply and slowly, and inhale again. Swap sides; use your right ring finger to block the right nostril and unblock your left one. Continue for between five and ten minutes, alternating sides.

2. Bhastrika (Bellows Breath)

Bhastrika is a type of pranayama involving forceful exhales and deep inhalations. The practice is said to resemble the sound and movement of a blacksmith's bellows, hence the name. Bhastrika is an invigorating breath that can help to increase energy levels and vitality.

The practice is best suited for mornings – or anytime you need an energy boost. However, it is not recommended for people with high blood pressure or heart conditions. If you have any concerns, please consult with your doctor before trying Bhastrika.

To start, sit comfortably, keep your spine straight, and breathe in deeply. Forcefully exhale your breath through your nose. Repeat this for 10-15 breaths, making sure that each exhalation is stronger than the last. Then take a few deep breaths and return to your normal breathing pattern.

3. Kapalabhati (Skull Shining Breath)

Kapalabhati is a type of pranayama that involves rapid and forceful exhales. The practice is said to resemble the sound of a drum, hence the name. Kapalabhati is an invigorating breath that can help to increase energy levels and vitality. The practice is said to be beneficial for the respiratory system and can help to clear the sinuses.

The practice involves exhaling forcefully through the nose while drawing the belly in and then inhaling deeply through the nose while expanding the belly. Kapalabhati can be performed for a variety of specific reasons, including improving respiratory function, increasing energy levels, and reducing stress. The practice is said to cleanse the lungs and sinuses and help to clear the mind.

Kapalabhati is not recommended for pregnant women or those with high blood pressure, heart disease, or epilepsy. However, this breathing exercise can offer a host of benefits for healthy adults. Try incorporating Kapalabhati into your daily routine and see how it affects your overall well-being.

Yoga

Yoga has been around for centuries and is a great way to exercise your body and mind. There are many different types of yoga, but they all have one thing in common: the use of poses, or asanas, to stretch and strengthen the body. Yoga can be practiced by people of all ages and levels of fitness. It's a great way to relieve stress, increase flexibility, and improve your overall health. Whether you're looking for a gentle workout or a more vigorous practice, there's a yoga class for you. You might just find that yoga is exactly what you need.

The Benefits of Yoga in Balancing Ajna

A key benefit of this ancient art is its ability to balance Ajna. When Ajna is in balance, we can better access our higher selves and connect with our true purpose. Yoga helps to bring Ajna into balance by promoting stillness and introspection. As we quiet the mind and focus on our breath, we create space for insights and guidance to arise. Oga also helps strengthen and cleanse the Third Eye, improving our ability to see clearly both externally and internally. We can keep Ajna in balance by practicing yoga regularly, enhancing our wisdom, intuition, and clarity.

Asanas for the Third Eye Chakra

Asanas are physical yoga poses that help to stretch, strengthen, and promote flexibility in the body. There are many different asanas, and each one has its benefits. Here are a few asanas that are particularly beneficial for the third eye chakra:

1. Ustrasana (Camel Pose)

Ustrasana, or Camel Pose, is a great way to open up the front of the body and improve flexibility in the spine. This pose also helps to stimulate the third eye chakra. It's a gentle pose that people of all levels can practice. When performing Ustrasana, be sure to keep the spine long and engage the core muscles.

Ustrasana.

lululemon athletica, CC BY 2.0 <https://creativecommons.org/licenses/by/2.0>, via Wikimedia Commons https://commons.wikimedia.org/wiki/File:Ustrasana_-_Camel_Pose.jpg

To get into the pose, start on your hands and knees in a tabletop position. Then, place your hands on your lower back with your fingers pointing down. As you inhale, press into your feet, and send your hips forward, arching your back. Allow your head to fall back as you continue to lengthen through the spine.

Once you reach your maximum range of motion, hold for a few breaths before releasing back to tabletop position. This pose can be challenging for beginners, so it's important to go slowly and listen to your body. Remember to breathe deeply throughout the entire pose.

2. Matsyasana (Fish Pose)

Matsyasana, or Fish Pose, is a yoga posture that helps to activate the third eye chakra. This pose is also said to improve posture, relieve back pain, and increase flexibility in the spine. When performed regularly, Matsyasana can help to keep the spine healthy and reduce the risk of injury.

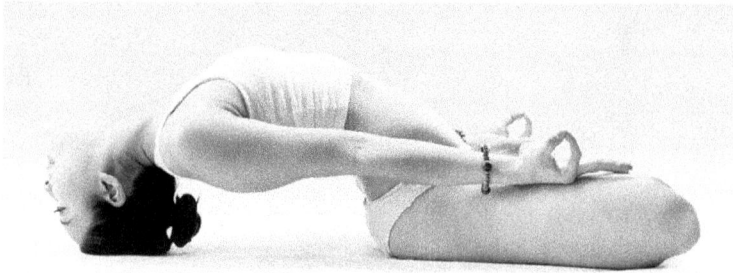

Fish Pose.

To practice Matsyasana, begin by lying on your back with your knees bent and your feet flat on the floor. Then, place your hands under your buttocks with the palms facing up. Next, slowly arch your back and lift your chest off the floor. Finally, press your head back and place the top of your head on the floor. Hold this pose for at least 30 seconds. As you inhale and exhale deeply, focus on opening up the third eye chakra.

You may feel a sense of pressure in the center of your forehead as you do this pose. Matsyasana is a gentle way to open up this chakra and improve your mental clarity and focus. With regular practice, you'll notice an increase in your ability to think clearly and make decisions with ease.

3. Halasana (Plow Pose)

Halasana is otherwise known as the Plow Pose and is used to open your third eye chakra and balance it. Start by lying on your back, extending your legs out. Inhale deeply, lift your feet using your abdominal muscles, and raise your legs above your head. Try to put your hands flat on the floor next to you and maintain a straight, flat back as you bring your feet to the floor behind your head.

If you cannot touch the floor, keep your legs elevated and rest your weight on your shoulders. Hold the pose for at least five deep breaths before slowly returning to starting position. Third eye chakra imbalances can manifest as headaches, insomnia, or difficulty concentrating. If you are experiencing any of these symptoms, give Halasana a try!

4. Sarvangasana (Shoulder Stand)

Sarvangasana, or shoulder stand, is a yoga pose that comes with a wide variety of benefits. It helps to improve circulation, increase energy levels, and calms the mind. It can also help relieve stress and tension headaches. For the third eye chakra, Sarvangasana helps to open up the space around the eyes and forehead, improving circulation and allowing for greater mental clarity.

To perform Sarvangasana, begin by lying on your back with your legs straight. Next, slowly bring your legs up towards the ceiling, keeping your back and buttocks flat against the floor. Once your legs are vertical, support your lower back with your hands and press your shoulders and head into the floor. You can walk your hands up your back and interlace your fingers behind your head for a deeper stretch.

Hold the pose for as long as is comfortable before slowly lowering your legs back to the floor. With regular practice, you'll soon be enjoying all the benefits of Sarvangasana!

5. Prasarita Padottanasana (Wide-Legged Forward Fold)

Prasarita Padottanasana, or Wide-Legged Forward Fold, is a fantastic pose for beginners. It helps to stretch the hamstrings and open up the hips while also providing a gentle forward bend. The pose can be done with the hands on the hips or interlaced behind the back. If you interlace the hands behind the back, make sure to keep the shoulders down and away from the ears.

To come into the pose, start from Standing Mountain Pose. Step your feet wide apart, with your toes pointing out to either side. Bend forward from the hip joints, keeping the spine long. If you can, place your palms flat on the floor in front of you. Otherwise, place your fingertips on a block or a yoga strap. Hold for five to eight breaths before coming back to Standing Mountain Pose.

These are just a few yoga poses and breathing techniques that can help open and balance the third eye chakra. With regular practice, you'll soon be enjoying all the benefits of a balanced third eye chakra.

6. Utthan Pristhasana (Lizard Pose)

One of the most underrated yoga poses is *Utthan Pristhasana,* or lizard pose. This simple yet effective asana offers a host of benefits, from increased flexibility to improved circulation. Lizard pose can be performed by anyone, regardless of their fitness level or experience with yoga.

Start in a low lunge position, stretching your right leg out in front of you and your left leg behind. Lower your forearms to the ground, and open your hips so that your left leg is parallel to the mat. Gently sink into the pose, keeping your core engaged. You should feel the stretch in your hips and hamstrings. Hold it for between 30 seconds and a minute, and then swap sides.

Utthan Pristhasana is an excellent pose for beginners because it helps to build strength and improve flexibility in the legs and hips. It is also a great way to release tension in the lower back and improve circulation throughout the body. For more experienced yogis, Utthan Pristhasana can be used as a preparatory pose for deeper hip openers such as Kapotasana (pigeon pose) or Eka Pada Rajakapotasana (one-legged king pigeon pose).

Putting It All Together – A Comprehensive Practice

When people think of yoga, they often envision someone contorting their body into an impossible-looking pose. However, yoga is much more than just physical postures. The asanas (yoga poses) are just one layer of the practice. If you are interested in working with the third eye chakra, it is also necessary to focus on meditation and pranayama (breathwork).

The poses described above can help open up the energy centers in the body, but the breathwork and meditation will help calm and focus the mind. And don't forget to include mudras (hand gestures) in your practice. Mudras are a powerful way to direct energy throughout the body and can be very helpful in balancing the third eye chakra. By including all of these layers into your practice, you'll create a well-rounded routine that will help heal and balance all your chakras, particularly your third eye chakra.

The third eye chakra is a powerful energy center that can be used to enhance your psychic abilities and connect with your intuition. However, the third eye chakra is just one part of a larger system. To maintain balance in your life, keeping all of the chakras in alignment is crucial.

If you find that your third eye chakra is out of balance, several yoga poses and breathing techniques can help open and heal this energy center. In addition to physical postures, it is also important to focus on meditation and pranayama. By including all of these elements into your practice, you'll create a well-rounded routine that will help to bring balance back into your life.

Chapter 7: Using Crystals and Stones

If you find yourself highly critical, over-thinkers, or worried about what others think of you, your third eye chakra is probably out of balance. Crystals can be powerful tools in balancing the Ajna chakra. This is the chakra of intuition and clarity, so you'll likely find yourself more decisive, clear-minded, and confident when it is in balance.

Crystals and stones.
https://pixabay.com/es/photos/cristales-piedras-roca-cristal-1896077/

Just as practicing meditation or yoga can help to balance your chakras, using crystals is a form of healing with energy that can promote balance within the body. Each crystal has its unique vibrational frequency that can help to restore balance and harmony. This chapter will teach you everything you need to know about using crystals and stones for the third eye chakra.

To help you get started, let's take a look at what crystals are and how they help balance the Ajna chakra.

What Are Crystals?

Crystals are solid minerals that have a repeating atomic structure. This gives them their characteristic shape and hardness. They are found in many different colors, depending on the minerals present. For example, quartz is made up of silicon and oxygen atoms, which gives it a clear or white color.

Crystals are often used as jewelry, but they can also be used for their metaphysical properties. Each crystal has its unique vibrational frequency that can help to promote balance and harmony within the body. The science behind this is still being studied, but anecdotal evidence suggests crystals can help balance the chakras.

Crystals and Ajna Chakra

Crystals can be used to help balance and heal the Ajna chakra. For example, amethyst is a purple crystal that is associated with calmness and peace, used to reduce anxiety and stress, and promotes relaxation and restful sleep. Other crystals that can be used to balance the Ajna chakra include lapis lazuli, sodalite, and turquoise. When placed on or around the third eye chakra, these crystals can help to promote clarity of thought and intuition.

But it's not just the stones themselves that are important; it's also the energy that you put into them. Before we get into how to use crystals for the third eye chakra, it's crucial first to understand the concept of intent. Your intent is a powerful force that can be used to manifest your desires. When you set an intention for your crystals, you are essentially programming them to vibrate at a certain frequency. This helps to align their energy with your own, making it easier for you to receive their healing benefits.

How Do Crystals Help Balance the Third Eye Chakra?

Crystals work by absorbing, storing, releasing, and regulating energy. They can balance the energies in the body and promote a sense of well-being. When you hold a crystal or place it on your body, you are exposed to its vibrational frequency. This can shift your energy into a balanced state.

In addition to their vibrational frequency, crystals also have a physical structure that can help to promote balance in the body. For example, tourmaline is a black crystal that is often used to ground and protect the body. It has a pyramid-like structure that helps to dissipate negative energy and promote a sense of calm and peace.

Incorporating Crystals in Daily Life

Now that you know a little more about crystals, let's take a look at how you can incorporate them into your daily life to help balance the third eye chakra. There are a few different ways that you can use crystals. One is to simply carry them around with you throughout the day. You can also place them on your body, either on the third eye chakra itself or around it.

Another way to use crystals is to meditate with them. This can help to quiet the mind and allow you to focus on your breath. When you focus on your breath, you can better connect with your intuition. If you're not sure how to meditate with crystals, plenty of resources are available online.

One final way to use crystals is to make them into an elixir. This can be done by adding crystals to water and allowing them to infuse for 24 hours. Once the elixir is ready, you can drink it or use it as a topical application. However, not all crystals are safe to ingest. If you're unsure whether or not a crystal is safe to ingest, it's best to consult with a qualified professional.

Stones vs. Crystals

Stones and crystals have been used for centuries for their purported healing properties. But what's the difference between these two substances? Stones are typically made of minerals, while crystals are composed of atoms that have been arranged in a highly-ordered structure. As a result, crystals tend to be more vibrant and sparkly than stones. They're also believed to vibrate at a higher frequency, making them ideal for use in energy healing.

Stones, on the other hand, are said to be more grounding. Their slower vibration can help to calm and balance the mind and body. Whether you prefer stones or crystals is a matter of personal preference. However, both can be effective tools for promoting wellness and relaxation. Crystals are often used to promote clarity of thought and intuition in the third eye chakra, while stones are more commonly used to ground and protect the body.

What Makes a Stone or Crystal Good for Ajna

Not all stones and crystals are equally beneficial for Ajna chakra balancing. The ideal stone for this purpose resonates with the energy of the sixth chakra, which is associated with intuition, clairvoyance, and inner wisdom. Some of the most popular stones for Ajna balancing include amethyst, lapis lazuli, and sodalite. These crystals can help open up the third eye chakra, promoting psychic awareness and protection.

When choosing a stone or crystal for Ajna chakra work, it is important to select one that resonates with your energy. Other stones that are helpful for Ajna chakra balancing include quartz crystal, moonstone, and tourmaline. Doing a little research on the different stones and crystals can help you to identify the ones that will be most beneficial for you. Expecting results overnight is not realistic, but you should begin to see improvements in your intuitive abilities with regular use.

Here are some factors that you should consider when choosing a stone or crystal for the third eye chakra:

Color

The color of the stone or crystal can help determine its energy. Blue or purple stones and crystals are typically associated with the sixth chakra. This is because these colors are associated with the element of water, which is connected to emotions and intuition. Some other colors that are said to be helpful for the third eye chakra include white, silver, and gold.

Properties

When selecting a stone or crystal for the third eye chakra, you'll want to choose one that resonates with the energy of this chakra. Amethyst, tourmaline, lapis lazuli, quartz crystal, sodalite, and moonstone are said to be the best ones for the third eye chakra. These stones are associated with intuition, clairvoyance, and inner wisdom.

Formation

The formation of the stone or crystal can also help determine its energy. Stones and crystals are formed naturally to have a higher vibration than man-made ones. For this reason, it is often recommended to choose stones and crystals that are naturally formed. When selecting a stone or crystal for the third eye chakra, you'll want to choose one that is smooth and rounded. This is because sharp edges can be too stimulating for the third eye chakra.

Different Types of Stones and Crystals for Ajna Chakra

There are a variety of stones and crystals that can be used to activate and balance the Ajna chakra. Some of the most popular stones for this purpose include amethyst, sodalite, and lapis lazuli. Each of these stones has its unique energies and properties that can support the development of greater intuition and psychic ability.

Labradorite

Labradorite is a stone of transformation which can assist you in clearing and balancing your Ajna chakra. This stone helps bring about change in your life by providing clarity and insight into your journey. It also helps to dissipate negative energies and promote a sense of inner peace.

Labradorite.
https://pixabay.com/es/photos/labradorita-cristal-roca-1430906/

Labradorite can be used in meditation or placed on your third eye chakra during yoga. You can also wear this stone as jewelry or carry it in your pocket or purse. Whichever way you choose to work with this stone, it can help open and balance your Ajna chakra, promoting psychic abilities and spiritual insights.

Clear Quartz

Clear quartz is an excellent stone for balancing and clearing Ajna chakra. It helps to open up psychic abilities and enhances spiritual understanding. Meditating with clear quartz can help bring about a deep sense of peace and clarity. Quartz can also be used to connect with your higher self and the realm of the divine. If you seek guidance or clarity on your spiritual path, quartz can be a helpful ally. While meditating, position a clear quartz stone on your Ajna chakra. Alternatively, wear jewelry that includes the stone to ensure its energies remain close to you all day.

Selenite

Selenite is a powerful crystal for clearing and opening the Ajna chakra. It helps to clear away any congestion or blockages in this chakra so that energy can flow freely. It also helps to increase our clarity of thought and intuition. For this reason, selenite is an excellent crystal to use during meditation or when you are trying to connect with your higher self. If you are looking for stones and crystals to help balance your Ajna chakra, selenite is a great choice.

Lapis Lazuli

The blue stone of wisdom, Lapis Lazuli, is said to be highly effective when used to adjust the Ajna chakra. By meditating with Lapis Lazuli, we can begin to open ourselves up to new levels of understanding. The stone also helps to release negative emotions such as anger and grief, making it easier to move on from the past. In addition, Lapis Lazuli is known for boosting psychic abilities and expanding consciousness. If you seek greater clarity and insight, this may be the stone for you.

Amethyst

Amethyst is a violet stone that has long been associated with the Ajna chakra. This stone is said to enhance psychic abilities and spiritual understanding. Amethyst can also help to open up the third eye chakra, promoting greater clarity and insight. The stone is also known for its ability to calm and soothe the mind, making it a great choice for meditation. If you are looking for a stone to help balance your Ajna chakra, amethyst may be the right choice. It's also very pretty and can be incorporated into your jewelry.

Sodalite

Sodalite is a blue stone that is said to help balance and open the Ajna chakra. This stone helps to enhance psychic ability and intuition. It also helps clear away any blockages or congestion in this chakra, promoting greater clarity and understanding. During yoga practice, sodalite can be used in meditation or placed on the third eye chakra. You can also wear this stone as jewelry or carry it in your pocket or purse. Whichever way you choose to work with sodalite, it can help to open and balance your Ajna chakra.

These are just a few stones and crystals that can be used to balance and clear Ajna chakra. If you seek greater clarity, insight, and understanding, consider working with one or more of these stones. You may also want to consult with a qualified crystal therapist or energy worker to find the right stones.

Caring for Your Stones and Crystals

Stones and crystals are more than just pretty objects - they can also have powerful healing energies. If you're drawn to the metaphysical properties of stones and crystals, it's vital to protect and cleanse them regularly. Doing so will help to preserve their energies and keep them working effectively.

Cleansing

There are a few different ways to cleanse your stones and crystals. One is to simply rinse them with water - either from a natural source like a river or stream or from your tap at home. You can also use salt water, which is thought to be especially cleansing. If you choose this method, make sure to rinse your stones well afterward with fresh water. Stone cleansing can also be done using sage smoke or incense. Simply hold your stone in the smoke for a few minutes, then allow it to air out before using it again.

Crystal Grid

In addition to cleansing, it's also important to regularly care for your stones and crystals in addition to cleansing. One way to do this is by setting up a crystal grid. This involves creating patterns with your stones that can help to amplify and focus their energies. You can also place your stones in specific areas of your home or office that correspond with the type of energy you want to attract. For example, you might place a prosperity stone in your home's entryway to attract abundance or a love stone in your bedroom to promote relationships.

Storage

There are a few things to keep in mind when it comes to storing your stones and crystals. First, it's important to store them in a safe place where they won't be damaged. Second, it's best to keep them away from other objects that might drain their energies. Finally, it's best to cleanse your stones regularly, especially if they've been in storage for a while. The best way to store your stones will depend on the type of stone and the size of your collection. Smaller stones can be stored in a pouch or box, while larger stones may need their own dedicated space.

With proper care, your stones and crystals can be a valuable asset on your journey to self-discovery and growth. By taking the time to cleanse, charge, and store them correctly, you can ensure that they will provide you with the maximum benefit.

Tips for Working with Stones and Crystals

1. **Choose The Right Stone:** When selecting a stone or crystal, choose one that resonates with you. If you're unsure which stone to choose, consult with a qualified crystal therapist or energy worker.

2. **Cleanse Regularly:** Be sure to cleanse your stones and crystals regularly. This will help to preserve their energies and keep them working effectively.

3. **Store Properly:** When storing your stones and crystals, be sure to keep them in a safe place where they won't be damaged. It's also good to keep them away from other objects that might drain their energies.

4. **Use for Intention:** When using your stones and crystals, be sure to set your intention. This will help to focus their energies and amplify their effects.

5. **Trust Your Intuition:** Always trust your intuition when working with stones and crystals. If you're not sure how to use a particular stone, ask your guides for guidance.

Using crystals and stones for the third eye chakra can be a powerful way to connect with your intuition and higher self. When selecting stones, be sure to choose ones that resonate with you. Remember to cleanse and charge your stones regularly, and store them in a safe place.

Most importantly, always trust your intuition when working with these powerful tools. You can ensure that you get the most out of your experience by following these tips.

Chapter 8: Ajna Aromatherapy

Essential oils can be very helpful in balancing Ajna, the third eye chakra. Oils help purify and cleanse the body and mind and eliminate negative thought patterns and emotions while enhancing clarity, concentration, and intuition.

This chapter will focus on the essential oils that encourage balancing the third eye chakra. We will first talk about how essential oils help balance Ajna and what makes an essential oil appropriate for this task. We'll explain each oil's properties, why it helps open Ajna, and how to use it. You'll also find a list of recommended oils to help open Ajna.

Essential Oils

Essential oils are concentrated liquids that contain the essence of a plant. They are extracted through a steam distillation process or cold pressing, and they have several uses. Some people use essential oils for their healing properties, while others simply enjoy their pleasant aroma.

There are many different kinds of oils available, each with its unique scent and benefits. Some of the most popular are lavender, lemon, and peppermint. When used properly, essential oils can be a safe and effective way to improve your health and well-being.

Some of the best oils for third eye chakra work include lavender, frankincense, and sandalwood. These oils can be used in a diffuser or applied topically to the area between the eyebrows. You can also try placing a drop of oil on each wrist and inhaling deeply whenever you need to attune to your inner guidance.

By working with all of these supportive oils, you can bring balance to your Ajna chakra and reclaim your power of perception. Once this chakra is open and balanced, you'll be able to see, make wise decisions, and connect with your intuition.

Benefits of Aromatherapy

Aromatherapy is an alternative medicine that uses essential oils to promote relaxation and well-being. The oils are diluted in a carrier oil and then applied to the skin or inhaled. Aromatherapy offers several health benefits, including reducing stress, improving sleep, and relieving pain.

Some research has shown that aromatherapy can indeed help manage certain conditions. For example, one study found that lavender oil may help reduce anxiety, while another showed that peppermint oil could improve cognitive performance. However, more research is needed to confirm these effects.

Aromatherapy is generally considered safe when used properly. However, some people may experience skin irritation or an allergic reaction to certain essential oils. If you're interested in trying aromatherapy, be sure to consult with a qualified practitioner.

Here are some benefits of aromatherapy that may help you balance your third eye chakra:

- Reduces stress
- Improves sleep
- Relieves pain
- Boosts cognitive performance
- Fights depression and anxiety
- Aids indigestion

- Regulates hormones
- Lowers blood pressure

How Essential Oils Help Balance Ajna

Some more oils for this chakra are basil, frankincense, and sandalwood. Basil helps to sharpen focus and increase clarity, Frankincense opens the third eye and balances the mind, and Sandalwood calms the nerves and promotes introspection. We can begin to bring Ajna back into alignment by using these oils regularly. As our third eye chakra becomes balanced, we will find it easier to trust our intuition and make choices that are in line with our highest good.

What Makes an Essential Oil Appropriate for This Task?

There are a few things to keep in mind to make sure you're choosing the right one for you when it comes to essential oils. First, ask yourself what you want to use the oil for. Is it for relaxation? For energy? For focus? Once you've determined that, you can start to narrow down your choices.

Next, take a look at the ingredients list and make sure you're not allergic to any of them. Once you've found an oil that meets both of these criteria, you can start to experiment with different scents to see which one you like the best. And finally, when you're ready to purchase, make sure you're getting the oil from a reputable source.

When choosing an essential oil to support Ajna, look for one that is grounding and has a calming effect on the mind. Some of the best oils for this chakra are basil, frankincense, and sandalwood. These oils will help open the third eye and promote clarity of thought. With a little bit of research, you can find the perfect essential oil to help balance your Ajna chakra.

Suggested Essential Oils

Essential oils can be used to help balance Ajna. Some other suggested oils include rosemary, sage, frankincense, and lavender. Rosemary is a stimulating oil that can help increase mental clarity and focus, while sage is a cleansing oil that can help purify the mind and release negativity. Frankincense is a grounding oil that encourages stillness and promotes inner wisdom, and lavender is a soothing oil that can offer comfort and peace. Using these essential oils can help bring Ajna into balance and encourage harmony within ourselves.

Apart from the above-suggested essential oils, some other options that might help balance Ajna include pure cypress, myrrh, and juniper. Here's a look at the properties of each of these oils and how they can help to support Ajna.

1. Pure Cypress

Cypress essential oil is said to be a powerful tool for balancing the Ajna chakra. It has a fresh, woody scent that helps to ground and center the mind. It can be used to ease anxiety and stress, promote clarity of thought, and boost concentration. Cypress oil is also said to help open the third eye chakra, promoting psychic awareness and intuition. Pure cypress essential oil is an excellent tool for those seeking to balance their Ajna chakra.

2. Myrrh

Myrrh oil has a wide range of benefits, but it is particularly well-suited for use on the Ajna chakra. It can help rebalance the Ajna chakra by promoting clarity of thought and inner peace. It is also said to enhance spiritual connection and intuitive guidance. To use Myrrh oil for Ajna chakra balance, simply add a few drops to your diffuser or apply it directly to your skin. You can also add it to a bath or massage it into your temples and forehead. For best results, repeat this process daily or as needed.

3. Juniper

Juniper oil has long been used in traditional medicine for its many health benefits. Today, it is still prized for its ability to soothe and relax the mind and body. One of the most popular uses for juniper oil is in massage therapy. When used in massage, juniper oil can help to ease muscle tension and relieve pain. It is also thought to promote circulation and improve lymphatic drainage. Juniper oil can also be used in aromatherapy.

When diffused, it can help to purify the air and reduce stress levels. Juniper oil can also be used topically on the skin. When diluted with a carrier oil, it can help to improve complexion and reduce inflammation. Juniper oil is a versatile oil with many potential health benefits. Whether you use it in massage, aromatherapy, or skincare, it is sure to leave you feeling refreshed and rejuvenated.

4. Basil

Basil oil is a refreshing and uplifting oil. It has a sweet, herbaceous scent that promotes mental clarity and focus. Basil oil is also said to help reduce stress and anxiety. Adding a few drops of basil oil to your diffuser or on your skin can help you balance your Ajna chakra. You can also add it to a bath or massage it into your temples and forehead. For best results, repeat this process daily or as needed.

When diffused, basil oil can help to purify the air and reduce stress levels. In addition, basil oil can be used topically on the skin. When diluted with a carrier oil, it can help to improve complexion and reduce inflammation.

5. Rosemary

Rosemary oil is a stimulating oil. It has a sharp, refreshing aroma which helps to clear the mind and promote concentration. It can also help to ease headaches and encourage mental clarity. Add a few drops of rosemary oil to a diffuser or massage it into your temples and forehead. You can also add it to a bath or use it in a compress. Repeat this process daily or as needed.

6. Peppermint

If you're looking for a way to improve your focus and concentration, consider using peppermint oil. Peppermint oil has long been used to remedy mental fatigue and concentration problems. The refreshing scent of peppermint oil can help to clear your mind and improve your focus.

In addition, peppermint oil is said to stimulate the Ajna chakra, which is the energy center associated with intuition and insight. To use peppermint oil for the Ajna chakra, add a few drops to a diffuser or apply it directly to your forehead. You can also try massaging it into your temples or the back of your neck.

7. Lavender

Lavender oil is a versatile oil that can be used to support the Ajna chakra. This oil has a calming, floral scent that promotes relaxation and inner peace. Lavender oil is also thought to help reduce stress and anxiety. In addition, lavender oil helps promote relaxation and sleep. This can be beneficial for those who tend to have a lot of anxiety or stress, as it can help ease tension and allow the mind to relax.

As with basil oil, applying lavender oil directly to your skin or using it in a diffuser can help balance your Ajna chakra. You can also add it to a bath or massage it into your temples and forehead. For best results, repeat this process daily or as needed.

How to Use Essential Oils for Ajna Chakra Balance

There are many ways to use essential oils to support the Ajna chakra. While some people may prefer to use one method, others may find that a combination of methods works best for them. The most important thing is to find what works best for you and to be consistent with your practice.

1. Diffuse

One of the most popular methods is diffusing, which involves dispersing the oil into the air to be inhaled. This allows the oil to enter the bloodstream and travel to the brain, which can have a balancing effect. To diffuse essential oils, you'll need an essential oil diffuser. These come in various styles, but all work by heating the oil and releasing it into the air. Diffusing essential oils allows you to enjoy their aroma while also benefiting from their therapeutic properties.

2. Topical Application

Essential oils can also be applied directly to the skin. Simply add a few drops of oil to the area between your eyebrows or massage the oil into your temples. You can also create a more powerful impact by blending the oil with a carrier agent such as coconut oil and then applying it to your forehead in a circular motion.

The key is to use just enough oil to absorb it into the skin easily. If you find that the oil is not being absorbed, you can add a little more carrier agent. The goal is to create a balanced blend that will not be too oily or too dry. Applying essential oils topically is a great and effective way of helping to balance the Ajna chakra, but only when done correctly.

3. Baths

Adding essential oils to your bath is a great way to enjoy their relaxing and balancing effects. To do this, simply add a few drops of oil to your bathtub before getting in. You can also add the oil to a cup of Epsom salt and then add the mixture to your bath. This will help the oil disperse evenly and provide you with a more concentrated dose. Soaking in an essential oil bath is a great way to relax and unwind after a long day.

4. Inhale

Inhaling essential oils is a quick and easy way to enjoy their balancing effects. You can simply add a few drops of oil to a tissue or handkerchief and inhale deeply. You can also add a few drops of oil to your diffuser and inhale the aroma as it is released into the air. If you don't have a diffuser, you can add a few drops of oil to a pot of boiling water and then inhale the steam.

5. Massage

Massaging essential oils into the skin is a great way to enjoy their relaxing and balancing effects. You can add a few drops of oil to a carrier agent such as coconut oil and then massage the mixture into your temples and forehead. You can also add a few drops of oil to your favorite lotion and massage it into your skin. The goal is to create a balanced blend that will not be too oily or too dry. When done correctly, massage can be a very effective way to promote balance in the Ajna chakra.

6. Compress

Compresses provide another effective method of benefitting from essential oils without directly applying them to your skin. To create a compress, simply add a few drops of oil to a bowl of hot water and then soak a cloth in the mixture. Wring it out once the cloth is saturated, and then lay it on your forehead.

You can also add a few drops of oil to a bowl of cold water and then soak a cloth in the mixture. Once the cloth is saturated, wring it out and then apply it to the forehead. The goal is to find a comfortable temperature for you, which will help promote balance in the Ajna chakra.

7. Supplements

Several supplements can also be of great help to balance the Ajna chakra. One such supplement is omega-3 fatty acids. These are found in fish oil and can help to support the health of the brain and nervous system. Another supplement that can be helpful is magnesium. This is a mineral involved in a variety of biochemical reactions in the body and can help support the health of the nervous system. You can find magnesium in supplements or foods such as dark leafy greens, nuts, and seeds.

Essential oils offer a natural and effective way to promote balance in the Ajna chakra. When used correctly, they can be a safe and powerful tool for supporting your mental and emotional health. Essential oils are an effective way of helping you boost your concentration and focus, improve memory, and relieve stress by balancing your Ajna chakra.

Disclaimer: The content is not intended to be a substitute for professional medical advice, diagnosis, or treatment. Always seek the advice of your physician or another qualified health provider with any questions you may have regarding a medical condition. Always read the label of their essential oil and be careful when using them around pets, people with allergies, pregnant women, or children.

Chapter 9: Ajna Diet and Nutrition

You are what you eat, as the saying goes. And that's never been truer than when it comes to the Ajna diet. Keeping your mind, body, and spirit in balance is key to good health. And the best way to do that is to fuel your body with nutritious foods full of the energy you need to live a healthy, happy life.

The Ajna diet is based on the principle of eating for balance. It emphasizes wholesome, nutrient-rich foods that are easy to digest and provide the body with the energy it needs to function at its best. This chapter will discuss the best foods and nutrition for the third eye chakra.

The Role of Diet in Ajna Chakra Healing

The role of diet in Ajna chakra healing is firstly to nourish. When the body is not getting the proper nutrition, physical and mental imbalances become more prevalent. One of the most important things we can do is eat a healthy diet. Foods high in antioxidants, such as blueberries and dark leafy greens, can help cleanse and purify the Ajna chakra.

Other balancing foods include Himalayan salt, which helps to ground excess energy, and ghee, which lubricates and calms the mind. Eating a diet rich in these nutrient-dense foods can help keep the Ajna chakra in balance and support our overall health and well-being.

Fasting Techniques for Opening and Healing Ajna

If you're seeking to open and heal your Ajna chakra, fasting techniques can also help. The idea of fasting is to help cleanse the body and mind, providing a blank slate on which to focus your intentions. It can also help to reduce stress and promote clarity of thought. When fasting for the Ajna chakra, focus on eating light, purifying foods that will help to detoxify and cleanse the body. Good choices include fruits and vegetables, lean protein, and plenty of water. Avoid processed foods, caffeine, and alcohol.

There are many different ways to fast, so find the best method for you. Here are different types of fasting techniques you can try:

Water Fasting

When we hear the word "fasting," we usually think of going without food for some time. However, water fasting is a different kind of fast altogether. Instead of abstaining from all food, water fasters consume nothing but water for a set period, generally 24 hours or more. While water fasting can have many benefits, it is important to consult with a health care provider before embarking on such a fast.

When done correctly, water fasting can help to cleanse and purify the body, and it can also be an effective way to open and heal the Ajna chakra. Water fasting helps to open and clear the Ajna chakra, facilitating greater clarity and understanding. In addition, water fasting can help to improve concentration and mental focus.

If you are considering a water fast, be sure to do your research and consult with a health care provider beforehand. Done correctly, water fasting can be a powerful tool for opening and healing the Ajna chakra.

Juice Fasting

One way to help open and heal the Ajna is through juice fasting. This cleansing practice helps to purge the body of toxins and negative energy, creating space for new growth. When combined with meditation and visualization, juice fasting can be a powerful tool for opening and healing the third eye.

When juice fasting, it's important to use fresh, organic fruits and vegetables. Juices should be made in a juicer or blender, and they should be consumed immediately. If you're new to juice fasting, start with a one-day fast and work your way up to longer durations. If you seek to improve your intuition and connect with your higher self, consider giving juice fasting a try.

Intermittent Fasting

Intermittent fasting is a type of fasting that involves periods of abstinence from food, followed by periods of eating. The most common form of intermittent fasting is the 16/8 method, which involves fasting for 16 hours and eating for 8 hours. Other popular methods include the 5:2 diet and the warrior diet.

Intermittent fasting can have many benefits, including weight loss, improved mental clarity, and increased energy levels. When done correctly, intermittent fasting can also help to open and heal the Ajna chakra. Intermittent fasting helps to clear the mind and facilitate greater clarity of thought. In addition, intermittent fasting can help to improve concentration and focus.

Dry Fasting

Dry fasting is a type of fasting that involves abstaining from both food and water. While dry fasting can have many benefits, it is important to consult with a health care provider before embarking on such a fast. Dry fasting helps cleanse and purify the body, and it can also be an effective way to open and heal the Ajna chakra. Dry fasting also helps clear the mind and facilitate greater clarity of thought. In addition, it can help to improve concentration and focus.

Foods That Help Unblock or Balance Ajna

Certain foods can be eaten to help unblock or balance the Ajna chakra. For example, foods that are high in magnesium and potassium are believed to be helpful. These include dark leafy greens, bananas, avocados, and nuts. Additionally, eating blue or purple foods is thought to be beneficial for the Ajna chakra. This is because these colors are associated with spiritual awareness and intuition. So, next time you're looking to unblock or balance your Ajna chakra, try incorporating some of these foods into your diet.

Many different types of foods can help unblock or balance Ajna. Here are some examples:

Purple Foods

Several purple foods can help to unblock or balance Ajna. Purple grapes, for example, are rich in antioxidants and flavonoids, which have been shown to improve cognitive function. Blueberries are another excellent choice, as they support healthy brain function and memory. Finally, lavender is a popular herb that has long been used to promote relaxation and sleep.

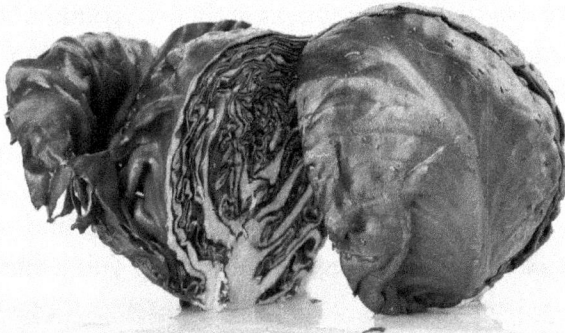

Purple Cabbage
https://pixabay.com/es/photos/vegetal-alimentos-col-4357039/

You can also benefit from other purple foods, such as purple carrots, eggplant, blackberries, blueberries, and purple cabbage. These foods can help to unblock or balance Ajna, promoting feelings of peace and well-being. When choosing purple foods, it's important to select those that are organic and free of pesticides.

Magnesium-Rich Foods

Magnesium is a mineral that plays an important role in brain function. It's also been shown to promote relaxation and reduce stress levels. Foods that are high in magnesium include dark leafy greens, nuts, seeds, and legumes. Pumpkin seeds, spirulina, and dark chocolate are also excellent choices. If you're looking to unblock or balance your Ajna chakra, try incorporating some of these foods into your diet.

Potassium-Rich Foods

Potassium is a mineral essential for proper brain and nerve function. It is also one of the key nutrients that help to keep Ajna in balance, so incorporating potassium-rich foods into your diet is a great way to support this important chakra. Some excellent sources of potassium include bananas, avocados, potatoes, Swiss chard, and lentils. So, if you're looking to unblock or balance your Ajna, be sure to load up on these delicious potassium-rich foods.

Whole Grains

Many whole grains can help unblock or balance Ajna, the third eye chakra. Brown rice is a great grain, as it helps ground the chakra's energy. Quinoa is another grain that can be helpful because it is high in magnesium which is known to help relieve stress.

Oats are also beneficial, as they contain avenanthramides which have been shown to improve blood flow to the brain. Lastly, barley is a wonderful grain for Ajna balance as it helps to calm and soothe the mind. Eating any of these grains regularly can help you achieve a more balanced third eye chakra.

Fruits and Vegetables

A few key fruits and vegetables are particularly beneficial for unblocking or balancing the Ajna chakra. Some of the best options include:

- **Pineapple:** This tropical fruit is not only delicious, but it also contains bromelain, an enzyme that helps break down proteins and reduce inflammation.

- **Cucumber:** Cucumbers are refreshing and hydrating, making them ideal for Ajna chakra. They also contain silica, a mineral that helps to strengthen connective tissue.

- **Green Beans:** Green beans are a nutrient-rich vegetable that can help to improve circulation and detoxify the body.

- **Spinach:** Spinach is another vegetable that is high in nutrients and antioxidants. It can help to boost energy levels and promote overall health.

These are just a few of the many fruits and vegetables that can help to unblock or balance the Ajna chakra. Incorporating them into your diet is a simple and delicious way to support your health and well-being.

Fun, Healthy, and Simple Recipes

With the above ingredients, you can make some delicious and healthy recipes that will help to unblock or balance the Ajna chakra. Here are a few ideas to get you started:

1. Pineapple Cucumber Smoothie

This refreshing smoothie is perfect for a summertime snack or breakfast. It is packed with nutrients and only takes a few minutes to make. Simply combine fresh pineapple, cucumber, yogurt, and honey in a blender and blend until smooth. For an extra boost of flavor, add a squeeze of lime juice. If you find the smoothie too thick, add a little water or ice until it reaches your desired consistency. Enjoy your pineapple cucumber smoothie immediately, or store it in the fridge for later. Either way, you're sure to love this delicious and healthy treat.

2. Green Bean Salad

This simple, healthy salad is perfect for a light lunch or side dish. It is packed with nutrients and flavor and takes just minutes to make. Simply combine cooked green beans, diced tomatoes, chopped red onion, and crumbled feta cheese in a bowl. Whisk together olive oil, lemon juice, and garlic for the dressing. Season the salad with salt and pepper to taste. Toss everything together and enjoy. This salad can be served immediately or stored in the fridge for later. Enjoy!

3. Spinach Quinoa Bowl

This hearty and filling bowl is perfect for a quick and easy lunch or dinner. It is packed with protein and fiber and can be made in just a few minutes. Simply cook quinoa according to package instructions. Then, add cooked quinoa, spinach, diced tomatoes, and shredded chicken to a bowl. Whisk together olive oil, balsamic vinegar, and garlic for the dressing. Season the salad with salt and pepper to taste. Toss everything together and enjoy. This salad can be served immediately or stored in the fridge for later.

4. Purple Superfood Smoothie

This nutrient-rich smoothie is perfect for a quick and easy breakfast or snack. It is packed with antioxidants and flavors and takes just minutes to make. Simply combine fresh or frozen berries (such as blueberries, blackberries, and raspberries), yogurt, and honey in a blender and blend until smooth. For an extra boost of flavor, add a squeeze of lemon juice. If you find the smoothie too thick, add a little water or ice until it reaches your desired consistency. Enjoy your purple superfood smoothie immediately, or store it in the fridge for later. Either way, you're sure to love this delicious and healthy treat.

5. Easy Purple Chakra Bowl

This simple and healthy bowl is perfect for a quick and easy lunch or dinner. It is packed with antioxidants and flavors and can be made in just a few minutes. Simply cook quinoa according to package instructions. Then, add cooked quinoa, diced tomatoes, blackberries, and shredded chicken to a bowl. For the dressing, whisk together balsamic vinegar and garlic. Season the salad with salt and pepper to taste. Toss everything together and enjoy.

6. Beet, Berry, and Chia Seed Bowl

This nutrient-rich bowl is perfect for a quick and easy breakfast or snack. It is packed with antioxidants, protein, and fiber and takes just minutes to make. Simply combine cooked beets, fresh or frozen berries, chia seeds, and yogurt in a bowl. For the dressing, whisk together honey and lemon juice. Season the salad with salt and pepper to taste. Toss everything together and enjoy. This bowl can be served immediately or stored in the fridge for later.

7. Rainbow Chakra Bowl

This colorful and healthy bowl is perfect for a quick and easy lunch or dinner. It is packed with antioxidants and flavors and can be made in just a few minutes. Simply cook quinoa or rice according to package instructions. Then, add cooked quinoa or rice, diced tomatoes, blackberries, raspberries, and shredded chicken or tofu to a bowl. For the dressing, whisk together balsamic vinegar, honey, and garlic. Season the salad with salt and pepper to taste. Toss everything together and enjoy.

8. Lavender Lemonade

This refreshing and calming drink is perfect for a hot summer day. It is packed with flavor and takes just minutes to make. Simply combine fresh lemon juice, water, honey, and lavender in a pitcher. Stir until the honey is dissolved. Then, add ice and enjoy. If you find the lemonade too tart, add a little more honey. If you find it too sweet, add a little more lemon juice. Either way, you're sure to love this delicious and healthy drink.

9. Eggplant Parmesan

This classic Italian dish is perfect for a quick and easy dinner. It is packed with flavor and can be made in just a few minutes. Simply cook eggplant slices in a pan. Then, add tomato sauce, mozzarella cheese, and Parmesan cheese to the pan. Cook until the cheese is melted. Serve with a side of bread or pasta. Enjoy your eggplant Parmesan immediately, or store it in the fridge for later.

These are just a few of the many recipes that you can make with the above ingredients. With a little creativity, you can easily find ways to incorporate these foods into your diet and support your health and well-being.

Diet and Nutrition Tips

Certain diet and nutrition tips can help maintain the Ajna chakra's balance. Firstly, it is important to eat plenty of fresh fruits and vegetables, because they are packed with vitamins and minerals essential for good health. Secondly, whole grains are also beneficial for the Ajna chakra, as they help to promote mental clarity and focus. Third, it is also important to eat plenty of protein-rich foods, such as lean meats, tofu, beans, and nuts.

Protein provides the building blocks for all biochemical processes in the body, including those that take place in the brain. Finally, it is also important to stay hydrated by drinking plenty of water throughout the day. Water helps flush toxins from the body and allows all cells to function properly.

In conclusion, the diet and nutrition tips for Ajna chakra balance are:

- Eat plenty of fresh fruits and vegetables.
- Eat whole grains.
- Eat plenty of protein-rich foods.
- Stay hydrated by drinking plenty of water.
- Avoid processed foods.
- Avoid caffeine and alcohol.
- Eat slowly and mindfully.

While many foods are beneficial for the Ajna chakra, a few should be avoided. Processed foods, caffeine, and alcohol can all lead to imbalances in this chakra.

Processed foods are often high in sugar, which can cause anxiety and irritability. Caffeine can also cause these symptoms, as well as restlessness and insomnia. Alcohol can lead to dehydration, which can then cause problems with concentration and focus.

It is vital to eat a balanced and healthy diet to keep the Ajna chakra in balance. By following the diet above and the nutrition tips, you can easily incorporate these foods into your diet and support your health and well-being.

Disclaimer: The information provided in this article is for informational purposes only and is not intended to replace the advice of a medical professional. If you have any concerns or questions about your health, you should always consult with a doctor or other health care professional.

Chapter 10: Third Eye Chakra 7-Day Routine

Are you now ready to open your third eye chakra and develop your intuition? You've read in the previous chapters a wealth of information about the third eye chakra, and the time has come to put that knowledge into practice. Keeping the Ajna chakra in balance will allow you to live more fully in the present moment and trust your intuition. With regular practice, you'll develop a stronger connection to your intuition and begin to see the world through the lens of your Third Eye.

This chapter provides a seven-day routine for opening and balancing the third eye chakra. Every day, you'll be given specific yoga poses and meditation to practice and other exercises that will help open your third eye chakra. You'll also have the opportunity to try out additional things that can help you balance this chakra, such as reading spiritual books, spending time in nature, and practicing gratitude.

Here is a seven-day routine to help you open and balance your third eye chakra:

Day 1

Yoga Poses

Half Camel Pose, Cat-Cow Pose, Child's Pose, Three-Legged Downward Dog Pose

To start, practice some basic yoga poses that will help to open up the third eye chakra. Half Camel Pose is a good one to start with, as it releases tension in the neck and shoulders. Cat-Cow Pose is also beneficial, as it increases flexibility in the spine. Child's Pose is a restorative pose that can help to calm the mind and nervous system. Finally, Three-Legged Downward Dog Pose is a great pose for stretching the entire body.

Meditation

When you're ready, sit in a comfortable position and close your eyes. Begin by taking some deep breaths and allowing your body to relax. Once you're feeling calm, begin to focus your attention on your third eye chakra. Visualize a glowing ball of light in the center of your forehead. Spend a few minutes focusing on this light, and then allow your mind to wander.

Additional Exercise

Spend time in nature today, and take some time to soak up the sun. Also, be sure to read a spiritual book or article for at least 10 minutes. The more you can immerse yourself in spiritual teachings, the easier it will be to open your third eye chakra. At the end of the day, reflect on the following questions:

- How did I feel today?

- What did I notice about my thoughts and emotions?

- Did I have any intuitive insights?

Day 2

Yoga Poses

Cobra Pose, Downward Dog Pose, Fish Pose, Seated Forward Fold Pose

Today, start with some basic backbends to release tension in the spine. Cobra Pose is a good pose to start with, as it helps to open up the chest and shoulders. Downward Dog Pose is also always beneficial, as it stretches the entire back side of the body. Fish Pose is a restorative pose that can help to open up the chest and lungs. Finally, Seated Forward Fold Pose is a great pose for stretching the hamstrings.

Mantras

Ajna Chakra Mantra – "Om Namah Shivaya"

This mantra is used to connect with the energy of Lord Shiva, which is associated with the third eye chakra. When you repeat this mantra, visualize the energy of Lord Shiva opening and balancing your third eye chakra. You can find more information about this mantra in the chapter "Mantras and Mudras."

Second Mantra – "Om Shreem Maha Lakshmiyei Namaha"

This mantra is used to connect with the energy of Maha Lakshmi, which is associated with the third eye chakra. This mantra focuses on abundance, so when you repeat it, visualize your third eye chakra opening and receiving the energy of abundance. If you'd like to learn more about this mantra, you can find more information online.

Additional Exercise

Take some time for yourself today to reflect on your goals and dreams. What do you want to achieve in the next month, year, or even in your lifetime? Visualize achieving these goals and seeing yourself succeeding. Also, be sure to Journal for at least 10 minutes. At the end of the day, reflect on the following questions:

- What are my goals and dreams?

- What steps can I take to achieve these goals?

- What are some things that are holding me back?

Day 3

Pranayama:

Nadi Shodhana (Alternate Nostril Breathing)

This pranayama helps calm the mind and nervous system, and it helps balance the right and left hemispheres of your brain.

Sit in a comfortable position with your eyes closed. Place your right hand in Vishnu Mudra (see chapter "Yoga and Breathing Techniques" for more information). Block your right nostril with your index finger and thumb and breathe in deeply through the left one. Then use your pinky and ring fingers to block your left nostril and exhale through the right one. Continue alternating sides for several minutes.

Mudra

1. **Gyan Mudra (Mudra of Knowledge)** – This mudra helps to stimulate the third eye chakra and promote clarity of thought.

   To practice this mudra, sit in a comfortable position and close your eyes. Place your hands in your lap with your palms facing upwards. Bend your index finger and touch the tip of your thumb. The other fingers should remain extended. Rest your hands in your lap and breathe deeply for several minutes.

2. **Shuni Mudra (Mudra of Patience)** – This mudra helps calm the mind and promote feelings of peace.

To do the Shuni Mudra, simply touch the tip of your index finger to the pad of your thumb. The remaining three fingers should be extended outward. This mudra represents a state of complete single-mindedness, and it is often used during meditation and prayer. The Shuni Mudra can help to still the mind, promoting a sense of peace and tranquility. It is believed to foster qualities such as patience, wisdom, and compassion.

The mudra can also be used to connect with your higher self. By assuming the Shuni Mudra, you align yourself with your highest purpose and open yourself up to divine guidance. Whether you use it for meditation or self-reflection, the Shuni Mudra is a powerful tool for personal growth.

3. **Akasha Mudra (Mudra of Space)** – This mudra helps to promote a sense of spaciousness and openness.

The Akasha Mudra, or Mudra of space, is one of the most basic and versatile mudras. It is often used as a starting point for other mudras, as it helps to center and focus the mind. The Akasha Mudra is traditionally performed by touching the tips of the thumbs and index fingers together, but it can also be done with the middle and ring fingers.

This mudra helps to promote ideas of expansiveness, openness, and vulnerability. It can be used to connect with others on a deep level or to simply open oneself up to new possibilities. The Akasha Mudra is a powerful tool for promoting personal and spiritual growth. Try incorporating it into your daily practice, and see what unfolds.

Additional Exercise

Today, take some time to reflect on your spiritual practice. What are you doing to grow spiritually? Are you reading spiritual books? Listening to audio teachings? Practicing meditation regularly? Doing yoga? Find something that you can do to deepen your spiritual practice. At the end of the day, reflect on the following question:

- What is my spiritual practice?
- Am I happy with it?
- If not, what can I do to change it?

Day 4

Affirmations

Take some time to read through the following affirmations and choose one or two that resonate with you. Repeat these affirmations to yourself throughout the day, either out loud or silently in your mind.

- I am open to new ideas and perspectives.
- My third eye is open, and I see clearly.
- I trust my intuition and listen to my inner voice.
- I am connected to my higher self.
- I am wise, and I make good decisions.

- I am attuned to the energies around me.

Gratitude Practice

Take some time to reflect on what you are grateful for in your life. Write them down in a journal, or just spend some time thinking about them. Be sure to focus on the positive things in your life, no matter how small they may seem. Write down a few things that you are thankful for, or even better, share your gratitude with someone in your life.

Additional Exercise

Find a quiet place to sit or lie down and practice meditation for at least 10 minutes. If you need some guidance, you can find meditation audio or video online or in the chapter "Meditation and Visualization." After your meditation, reflect on the following question:

- How do I feel after my meditation?

- What am I grateful for today?

- What are some things that I take for granted?

Day 5

Yoga Sequence

1. **Sarvangasana (Shoulder Stand)** – This yoga pose helps to improve circulation, stimulates the thyroid gland, and calms the mind.

To practice this pose, lie down on your back with your feet together and your arms by your sides. Slowly lift your legs up and over your head, keeping your back and shoulders flat on the ground. Use your hands to support your lower back once your legs are perpendicular to your torso. Breathe deeply and hold the pose for several minutes.

2. **Halasana (Plow Pose)** – This yoga pose helps to improve circulation, stimulates the thyroid gland, and calms the mind.

To practice this pose, lie down on your back with your feet together and your arms by your sides. Slowly lift both your legs up together and over your head, keeping your back and shoulders flat on the ground. Use your hands to support your lower back once your legs are perpendicular to your torso. Breathe deeply and hold the pose for several minutes.

3. **Karnapidasana (Ear Pressure Pose)** - This yoga pose helps to improve circulation, stimulates the thyroid gland, and calms the mind.

To begin the position, begin by sitting in a comfortable cross-legged position. Then, place your hands on the floor beside you and slowly lean back, allowing your head to fall backward. You should feel a mild stretch in the front of your neck. If you feel any pain, stop and rest in Child's Pose.

To exit the pose, simply roll back up to seated and slowly come up to standing. Karnapidasana is a great way to release built-up tension in the neck and shoulders and can be done anytime, anywhere.

Visualization Exercises

1. **The Color Orange** - Imagine a bright orange ball of light in front of you. See the color fill your entire field of vision. Feel the warmth and energy of orange permeate your entire being. Now, see the ball of light slowly move into your third eye chakra between your eyes. See the orange light fill up your chakra and wash away any negativity or blockages. Breathe deeply and relax into the visualization.

2. **The Lotus Flower** - Imagine a beautiful lotus flower in front of you. See the petals slowly open up, and the center of the flower begins to glow. This is your third eye chakra opening up and activating. See the light emanating from the center of the flower enter into your third eye chakra and fill it up with light. Breathe deeply and relax into the visualization.

4. **The Sun** - Imagine a bright, shining sun in front of you. See the rays of light reaching out and touching your third eye chakra. Feel the warmth of the sun fill up your chakra and activate it. Now, see the sun slowly start to rise, taking your third eye chakra with it. The sun represents your higher self, and as it rises, you feel yourself becoming more enlightened and wiser. Breathe deeply and relax into the visualization.

Creative Expression

Today, spend some time doing something creative. This can be anything from painting and drawing to writing and gardening. Let your imagination run wild and have fun with it. At the end of your creative session, reflect on the following questions:

- How did I feel while doing something creative?
- Did I enjoy it?
- What did I create?
- What could I have done differently?

Day 6

Yoga Sequence:

1. **Paschimottanasana (Seated Forward Bend Pose)** – Paschimottanasana is a seated forward bend pose that is often practiced in yoga. The name of the position comes from the Sanskrit words "Pascha," meaning "west" or "back," "Uttana," meaning "intense stretch," and "asana," meaning "pose." This pose stretches the entire backside of the body, including the hamstrings, back, and shoulders. It also helps to calm the mind and improve overall flexibility.

   To practice Paschimottanasana, begin by sitting on the floor with your legs extended straight out in front of you. Then, slowly lean forward from your hips, reaching your hands toward your feet. If you can't reach your feet, you can place your hands on your shins or thighs. Hold this pose for at least 30 seconds before releasing and repeating it as needed. Remember to breathe deeply throughout the exercise to help relax your body.

2. **Ardha Matsyendrasana (Half Spinal Twist Pose)** - This posture gets its name from Matsyendra, a legendary yoga teacher who was said to be able to twist his body into all sorts of shapes. While you may not achieve quite the same level of flexibility, this pose will still help stretch and lengthen your spine, simultaneously releasing tension from your neck and shoulders.

Sit on the floor, stretching your legs out in front of you. Bring your right knee up and over your left one, and place your foot flat on the ground beside your left hip. Twist your body to the right, so your left elbow is on the outer of your right thigh. Twist further, breathing in and out deeply, and support yourself with your right hand on the floor behind you. Hold, breathing in and out deeply five times, and then release. Repeat on the other side.

3. **Anjaneyasana (Low Lunge Pose)** - Anjaneyasana, also known as the low lunge pose, is a great way to stretch the hip flexors and psoas muscle. To enter the pose, start standing upright with your feet hip-width apart. Step forward on your right foot, bending your knee at an angle of 90 degrees. Put your hands flat on the ground on either side of your foot. Then, straighten your left leg and rest your left knee on the ground. You can either keep your hands on the ground or place them on your right thigh.

To deepen the stretch, you can lean forward and press your pelvis down into your right thigh. Hold the pose for 30 seconds to 1 minute, then repeat on the other side. Anjaneyasana is a great way to prepare for more challenging poses like Warrior III and Camel Pose. It's also a great way to release tension in the hips and lower back.

Compassion

Today, show compassion to someone in your life. This could be a family member, friend, or even a stranger. You can do something as simple as holding the door open for someone or complimenting them. Take a moment to reflect on how you felt after showing compassion. Did it make you feel good? Why or why not?

Day 7

Reflection and Integration

Take some time today to reflect on your third eye chakra journey. What did you learn about yourself? What challenges did you face? How did you grow? What are some things you still want to work on? Write down your thoughts in a journal or share them with a friend. This will help you integrate the lessons you've learned and solidify your understanding of the third eye chakra.

Here are some things you can do to further integrate the third eye chakra into your life:

- Read spiritual books or listen to podcasts.
- Create a vision board.
- Start a daily gratitude practice.
- Meditate for at least 10 minutes each day.
- Spend time in nature.
- Practice yoga or another form of exercise.
- Do something creative each day.
- Avoid processed foods, caffeine, and alcohol.
- Make sure you're getting enough sleep.
- Limit your time spent on electronics.
- Spend time with supportive people.
- Be patient with yourself. Remember that growth takes time. Rome wasn't built in a day!
- Most importantly, trust your intuition and be open to change.

The seven-day routine to open and heal your third eye chakra is now complete. Remember, it's important to be patient with yourself and trust the process. The most important thing is that you're taking the time to nurture your mind, body, and soul.

Opening and balancing the third eye chakra can be a challenge, but it's so worth it! By following the tips and exercises in this book, you'll be well on your way to a more balanced and healthier third eye chakra. Keep up the good work, and enjoy the journey!

Bonus: Third Eye and Crown Connection Cheat Sheet

Do you ever feel as if you have a higher power or intuition guiding you? Do you wonder how you can connect with the divine and receive clear messages? By working with both the third eye and Crown chakras, you can develop a deeper connection with the spiritual realm to improve your life in every way.

While the third eye chakra is associated with intuition and our connection to the divine, the crown chakra is known as the "thousand-petaled lotus flower" and is our connection to the universe. Through this chakra, we receive guidance and insight from a higher power.

So how can we work with both of these chakras to develop a stronger connection with the spiritual realm? This chapter will give you all the information and exercises you need to get started on this journey. It will cover the role of the Crown chakra, its symbol, how to open and balance it, and some tips on visualization exercises you can do to work with both the third eye and crown chakras.

The Crown Chakra

The crown chakra is the seventh and highest chakra. It is found at the top of the head and is associated with spirituality, enlightenment, and cosmic consciousness. The crown chakra is often illustrated as a thousand-petaled lotus, and it is considered to be the doorway to higher states of consciousness.

When the crown chakra is in balance, we feel connected to our higher selves and the divine. We feel inspired, creative, and in tune with our purpose in life. We may also experience feelings of bliss, ecstasy, and oneness with all that is. However, when the crown chakra is out of balance, we may feel disconnected from our surroundings, confused about our life path, or like we are searching for something that is just out of reach.

If you are seeking to balance your crown chakra, there are many ways to do so. Visualization and energy healing are all excellent methods for clearing blockages and restoring balance to the crown chakra.

The Role of Crown Chakra

Being the gateway to higher consciousness, this chakra is responsible for our connection with the spiritual realm. A balanced crown chakra will give us a sense of bliss, peace, and unity with the universe. We are open to new ideas and perspectives, and we feel connected to something larger than ourselves. However, when the crown chakra is out of balance, we may feel disconnected from our spirituality, lost in confusion or mental chaos. We may also experience headaches, insomnia, or spaced-out feelings.

Meditation, yoga, and breathwork are all excellent practices for opening up this energy center. You can also try wearing purple or white clothing or placing crystals on your forehead while you sleep. By taking some time to nurture your crown chakra, you can expand your consciousness and connect with your highest self.

The Relation between Third Eye and Crown Chakra

The crown chakra, or Sahasrara, is associated with the color violet and the element of thought. The third eye chakra, or Ajna, is just below it in the center of the forehead. It is associated with the color indigo and the element of light. Both chakras are considered very powerful, and they are often seen as interconnected.

The crown chakra is the gateway to higher realms of consciousness. It is associated with wisdom, understanding, and enlightenment. The third eye chakra is the seat of intuition and insight, associated with psychic abilities, clairvoyance, and intuition. When both chakras are open and balanced, we can access our highest potential and live our lives with passion, purpose, and clarity.

The relation between the third eye and crown chakras is very close. Before we can open our crown chakra and connect with our higher selves, we must first open our third eye and expand our consciousness. The third eye is the key that unlocks the door to the crown chakra.

The Blockage Symptoms of Crown Chakra

The blockage symptoms of crown chakra can be manifest in both physical and mental ways. On the physical level, a blocked crown chakra can lead to headaches, scalp problems, and difficulties with hearing or vision. One may also feel spacey or disconnected from their body. Mentally, a blockage in the crown chakra can manifest as feelings of depression, apathy, or disconnection from others.

One may also struggle with spiritual beliefs or feel isolated from a higher power. When the crown chakra is balanced, however, one feels confident in their beliefs and connected to a higher power. They may also feel more creative and open-minded. If you are struggling with any of these symptoms, there are many ways to balance your crown chakra and improve your overall well-being.

Tips to Open Up Your Crown Chakra

There are many ways to open up your crown chakra and improve your connection to the spiritual realm. This section will provide some tips on how to get started.

1. Meditation

One of the best ways to open up your crown chakra is through meditation. It quietens your mind and connects to loftier places within yourself. Find a comfortable place to sit or lie down, close your eyes, and focus on your breath. As you inhale and exhale, imagine a white light emanating from the top of your head and filling your entire body. The light may represent divine energy or pure consciousness. Allow yourself to absorb this energy and feel it fill you with peace, love, and joy.

Spend 5-10 minutes focusing on your breath and visualizing the white light. You can do this meditation daily or whenever you need to feel spiritually connected. There are many different ways to meditate, so find a method that works best for you. If you're new to meditation, plenty of resources are available to help you get started. The key is to be patient and consistent with your practice.

2. Visualization Exercises

Visualization exercises are another great way to open up your crown chakra. These exercises can be done with or without meditation. The aim is to focus your attention on the crown chakra and imagine it opening up and expanding.

There are many ways to balance and unblock the crown chakra. One approach is through visualization exercises. Below are three crown chakra visualization exercises that you can try:

1. Visualize a white light emanating from the top of your head. See this light expanding and enveloping your entire body. Feel the light penetrating every cell, filling you with a sense of peace and connection.

2. Visualize yourself in a beautiful natural setting – a field of wildflowers on top of a mountain peak beside a pristine lake. Fill your senses with the beauty around you and breathe in the purity

of the air. Feel your connection to all of nature and know that you are one with all that is.

3. Imagine yourself surrounded by loving energy. See this energy as a soft white light emanating from the hearts of those around you. Feel this love enter your body and fill you with a sense of warmth and connection. Know that you are loved and supported.

Choose one of these visualization exercises or create your own. Spend 5-10 minutes visualizing yourself in a peaceful and beautiful setting. Focus on your breath and imagine the crown chakra opening up and expanding.

3. Connect with Nature

One way to open up your crown chakra is to spend time in nature. Surrounded by the beauty of the natural world, we can let go of our concerns and connect with something larger than ourselves. Breathe in the fresh air, feel the sun on your skin, and listen to the sounds of birdsong and waves crashing against the shore. We can recharge our batteries and open up our crown chakras by spending time in nature. As a result, we feel more connected to the world around us and at peace with ourselves.

4. Spend Time with Like-Minded People

Another way to open up your chakra is to spend time with like-minded people. When we are around others who are on a similar spiritual path, we feel more supported and less alone on our journey. We can also learn from each other and gain new insights into our spiritual practice. In addition, spending time with like-minded people can help us to feel more connected to the larger community of which we are a part.

5. Be Open to New Experiences

When we are open to new experiences, we feed our crown chakras. We expand our horizons and open ourselves up to new possibilities by trying new things. We may also discover new interests and talents that we never knew we had. So, step out of your comfort zone and be open to new experiences. You never know what you might discover.

6. Practice Mindfulness

Mindfulness is a state of being present in the moment. When we are mindful, we are not living in the past or worrying about the future. We are simply present in the here and now. Mindfulness can help us connect with our innermost selves and open up our crown chakras.

Mindfulness helps us become more present and aware of our thoughts and feelings, providing a sense of calm and clarity. In addition, mindfulness can help us connect with our higher selves and access our inner wisdom. As such, it is an ideal practice for those seeking to open up their crown chakras.

7. Connect with Your Higher Power

Another way to open up your crown chakra is to connect with your higher power. This can be done through prayer, meditation, or simply spending time in nature. When we connect with our higher power, we open ourselves up to guidance and wisdom. We also feel a sense of connection with something greater than ourselves. This can help us let go of our fears and concerns and feel more at peace.

8. Let Go of Attachment

One of the biggest obstacles to opening up our crown chakra is attachment. When we are attached to material possessions, our egos, or our opinion of ourselves, we block the flow of energy to our crown chakras. As a result, we feel disconnected from our higher selves and the rest of the world.

We need to let go of attachment to open up our crown chakras. This doesn't mean that we have to get rid of all our possessions; it simply means that we need to let go of our attachment to them. We can also let go of our attachment to our ego, our opinion of ourselves, and our need for approval from others. When we let go of attachment, we make space for the energy of the Universe to flow through us.

9. Be Grateful

Another way to open up your crown chakra is to be grateful. When we are grateful, we open ourselves up to receive the good that the Universe has to offer. We also send out a vibration of love and appreciation, which attracts more good into our lives. So, if you want to open up your crown chakra, start by being grateful for all the good in your life and write your own gratitude list.

10. Listen to Your Intuition

One of the best ways to open up your chakra is to listen to your intuition. When we listen to our intuition, we are connecting with our higher selves and the wisdom of the Universe. We are also opening ourselves up to guidance and guidance from our guides and angels. So, if you want to open up your chakra, listen to your intuition.

These are just a few of the many ways you can open up your crown chakra. Experiment and see which ones work best for you. Remember, there is no one right way to do this. Just follow your heart and trust that your higher self is guiding you.

Understanding the Symbol

The crown chakra is often symbolized by a lotus flower with 1000 petals. This symbolizes the infinite nature of the universe and the human potential for spiritual awakening. A thousand petals also represent the many different aspects of our being that are integrated and united through the crown chakra. It also symbolizes our connection to the divine and our ability to blossom into our highest potential.

Other symbols associated with the crown chakra include a jeweled crescent moon, a shining sun, and a radiant diamond. Each of these symbols represents a different aspect of the crown chakra. The crescent moon symbolizes the waxing and waning of life, the sun represents the light of knowledge, and the diamond represents the purity of consciousness.

Together, these symbols remind us that we are constantly growing and evolving and that we have the potential to reach our highest levels of consciousness. Remember that the crown chakra is not just about spirituality; it's also about our connection to the natural world and all of life. To achieve balance in this chakra, we must be open to new experiences and perspectives.

The Colors Associated with the Crown Chakra

The colors associated with the crown chakra are violet, white, and gold. Violet is the color of transformation and spiritual awareness, while white is the color of purity and truth, and gold is the color of enlightenment and wisdom. These colors represent the highest levels of consciousness that we can reach.

The crown chakra is also sometimes depicted as being clear, like a crystal. This represents the clarity of mind and the pure consciousness that we can achieve when this chakra is in balance. The crown chakra is also sometimes symbolized by a rainbow, representing the many different aspects of our being united through this chakra.

How Can the Third Eye and Crown Chakras Improve Your Life

When the third eye and Crown chakras are open and balanced, you can experience a number of benefits. These include:

1. A deeper connection to your intuition and inner wisdom.
2. A greater sense of peace, calm, and clarity.
3. Improved concentration and focus.
4. Greater creativity and imagination.
5. Increased psychic abilities and intuition.
6. A deeper connection to your higher self, guides, and angels.
7. Improved mental and emotional health.

Key Takeaways

- The crown chakra is located at the top of the head. It is associated with the color purple or white.

- The crown chakra is our connection to the divine. Through this chakra, we receive guidance and wisdom from our higher selves.

- The crown chakra is responsible for our sense of connection with the Universe. When it is blocked, we may feel disconnected from our higher selves and the rest of the world.

- There are many ways to open up your crown chakra. Some of these include meditation, mindfulness, connecting with your higher power, letting go of attachment, and being grateful.

- Listen to your intuition and trust that your higher self is guiding you. There is no one right way to open up your crown chakra. Just follow your heart and trust that your higher self is guiding you.

The crown chakra is associated with spirituality, enlightenment, and connection to a higher power. When this chakra is open, we feel connected to something greater than ourselves and experience a sense of peace and bliss. We may find ourselves drawn to meditation or other spiritual practices.

If you're looking to open up your crown chakra, there are a few things you can do. First, try to spend time in nature and connect with the beauty around you. This can be as simple as taking a walk in the park or spending time in your garden. You can also meditate on the color purple or white, which are associated with the crown chakra.

Take some deep breaths and focus on your breath entering and leaving your body. Visualize a purple or white light shining down from above and filling your entire being with divine energy. As you do this, feel your connection to the infinite source of love and wisdom that is available to you.

Allow yourself to relax into this energy and feel it flow through you, cleansing and purifying your body, mind, and soul. You may also want to try chanting "om" or another sacred sound while focusing on your breath. This can help to open up your crown chakra and connect you with the divine.

Remember, there is no right or wrong way to do this. Just allow yourself to be open to the experience and see what comes up for you.

Conclusion

"We have two eyes to see two sides of things, but there must be a third eye which will see everything at the same time and yet not see anything. That is to understand Zen." - D.T. Suzuki

The third eye chakra is known as the Ajna chakra in Sanskrit. It is located between the eyebrows and is associated with the color violet or white. The third eye chakra is connected to our ability to see clearly physically and intuitively. When this chakra is balanced, we have a strong sense of intuition and can see beyond the physical world.

When the third eye chakra is out of balance, we may experience problems with our vision, both physically and metaphorically. We may have trouble seeing the bigger picture or be unable to see beyond our perspective. We may also suffer from headaches, migraines, or sleep problems.

This guide covered everything you need to know about the third eye chakra, from its location and color to its associated qualities. The first chapter explored the Third Eye chakra and how it affects our lives. We also learned about the chakra's connection to our intuition and ability to see beyond the physical world.

In the second chapter, we explored how the third eye chakra can become blocked in the second chapter. We also learned about some of the signs that indicate a third eye chakra imbalance. Chapter three taught us how to balance our other chakras before working on the third eye chakra.

In chapter four, we learned about mantras and mudras that can help us activate and balance the third eye chakra. Chapter five explored meditation and visualization techniques for the third eye chakra. Chapter six covered yoga and breathing exercises to help balance the third eye chakra. In chapter seven, we learned about using crystals and stones to balance the third eye chakra.

Aromatherapy and diet were covered in chapters eight and nine, respectively. Finally, in chapter ten, we created a 7-day routine to help balance the third eye chakra. The bonus chapter looked at the connection between the third eye chakra and the Crown chakra. We also explored ways you can tell if your third eye chakra is out of balance.

The third eye chakra is associated with our ability to see clearly, both physically and intuitively. To open and balance the third eye chakra, we can use mantras and mudras, meditate, visualize, do yoga and breathing exercises, and use crystals and stones. We can also balance our third eye chakra by eating a nutritious diet and using aromatherapy. Finally, we can follow a daily routine that includes these activities.

By following the tips in this guide, you'll be on your way to a balanced third eye chakra. Be patient and consistent with your practice, and trust that the answers will come in time. Remember, it is crucial to work on balancing all of your chakras before focusing on one chakra in particular. The most important thing is to be patient and consistent with your practice. With time and dedication, you'll begin to see results.

Part 7: Crown Chakra

The Ultimate Guide to Clearing, Opening, and Balancing Sahasrara

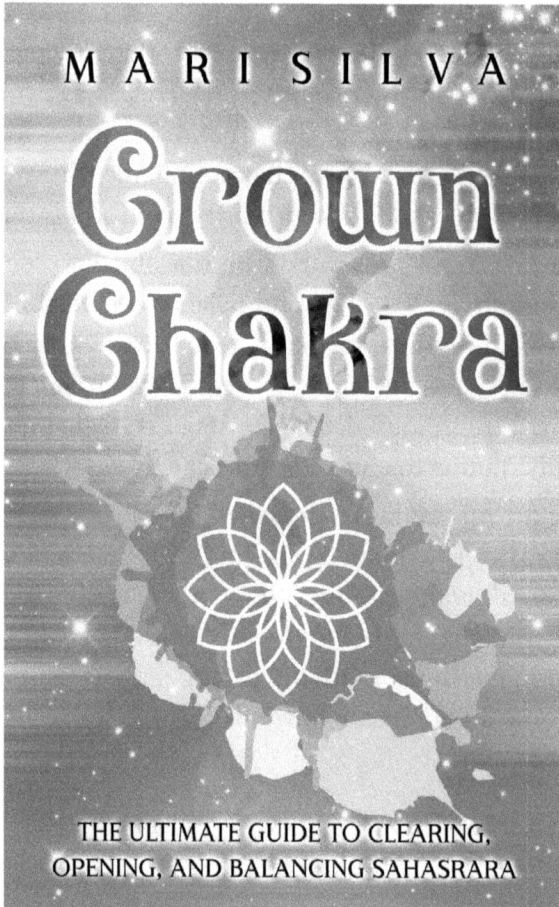

Introduction

Unlocking the mysteries of the seventh and highest chakra can be life-changing. The Sahasrara, or crown chakra, is located at the top of the head and is associated with higher consciousness, enlightenment, and self-awareness. When this chakra is blocked or out of balance, you may feel disconnected from your spiritual self or experience difficulties in critical thinking and problem-solving.

In this guide, we will explore the basics of the crown chakra and provide tips on opening and energizing it. We will also discuss how the Sahasrara can be blocked and offer guidance on how to remedy these issues.

The first chapter will provide a general overview of what chakras are, what the energy body is, and discuss the roles chakras have in the energy flow through the body. The second chapter will explain the symptoms of a blocked, out of balance, weak, or even overactive crown chakra.

The third chapter will offer a variety of techniques to raise your energy through the chakras. These include yoga poses, meditation, mantra and mudra use, and aromatherapy.

Chapter four will focus specifically on the mantras and mudras that can be used to energize and open the Sahasrara. Chapter five will discuss different types of meditation and visualization techniques that stimulate the crown chakra. Chapter six will provide information on pranayama and yoga asanas that can be used to balance and open the Sahasrara.

In chapter seven, we will explore the use of crystals and stones for crown chakra healing. We will discuss the properties of some of the most popular crystals and stones for this purpose and provide a guide on how to use them. In chapter eight, we will look at aromatherapy for crown chakra healing. We will discuss the properties of some of the most popular essential oils for this purpose and provide a guide on how to use them.

Chapter nine will focus on nutrition and the appropriate diet for the crown chakra. We will provide a guide on eating in alignment with the crown chakra's energy and discuss some of the most beneficial foods. The tenth chapter of this guide offers a 7-day routine for opening and energizing the crown chakra.

Finally, you'll find a bonus chapter on the Chakras Cheat Sheet – a comprehensive guide to all of the main chakras and the entire chakra system. It will include information on the location of each chakra, its colors, and its roles.

Unlike other chakra guides, this one will also include information on how to heal and balance each chakra. So, this guide has something for you, whether you're just starting your journey to enlightenment or you are a seasoned pro. You'll discover everything you need to know about the crown chakra and how to open it. May it help you open the door to higher consciousness and enlightenment and allow you to experience the bliss of self-awareness.

So, let's begin our journey!

Chapter 1: What Is the Sahasrara?

When you hear about yoga, a few things may come to mind, such as meditation, breath-work, and the practice of being mindful. But did you know that yoga is a system used for self-improvement and is a means of connecting with the Universe?

The chakras are energy centers or portals within our bodies that connect us to life force energy or "prana." Through this connection, we can receive nourishment and healing and find our sense of purpose in life. Understanding the chakras can optimize our physical, mental, and emotional health.

The Sahasrara is the seventh primary chakra, according to Hindu tradition. The word means "thousand" in Sanskrit, and the Sahasrara is also known as the crown chakra. It's located at the top of the head, just above where the soft spot is on a baby.

This chapter will help you to understand the chakras, the energy body, and the role of the Sahasrara chakra in overall well-being. We'll explore its origins, what the early scriptures of the Vedas reveal about it, and why some texts omit to mention this chakra.

We'll also analyze its symbol, discuss where this chakra is located, its color, and talk about its traits and function. Finally, we'll touch on the benefits of aligning this chakra.

The Chakras

Human beings are complex bodies of energy. Our physical body comprises billions of cells, each with consciousness and intelligence. Our mind is also made of energy, as are our emotions and feelings. In addition, we have an energy body that exists in three dimensions and mirrors our physical body in every way. This energy body is known as the subtle body or the aura.

There are seven major energy centers within the subtle body referred to as chakras. These chakras are responsible for sending and receiving various energies within the different dimensions.

There are seven main chakras:

1. **Manipura** (or Solar Plexus Chakra)
2. **Muladhara** (or Root Chakra)
3. **Vishuddha** (or Throat Chakra)
4. **Ajna** (or Third Eye Chakra)
5. **Swadhisthana** (or Sacral Chakra)
6. **Sahasrara (or** Crown Chakra)
7. **Anahata** (or Heart Chakra)

They are essential for our health and wellness, and they offer us balance and harmony when it comes to all levels of our consciousness: physically, emotionally, mentally, and spiritually. They act like antennas that absorb and transmit energy from higher realms. If they become blocked by negative emotions or thoughts, they cause interference in our lives and even lead to disease.

The Energy Body

In addition to the physical body, each of us has an energy body composed of multiple layers of subtle energy fields called auric bodies. Through these subtle layers, we connect with the world around us. The chakras are located at specific points aligned with this energetic anatomy, and these act as gateways to transmit information between the physical and subtle bodies.

The energy body is in constant motion, sending and receiving information through the chakras. Through this exchange, a person interacts with their environment and receives the nourishment and healing they need to maintain balance in their lives.

The energy body is a subtle energy system that surrounds and pervades the physical body. It consists of the chakras, the nadis, and the aura. The chakras are the main energy centers of the body. The seven main chakras spin at different speeds and vibrate at different frequencies. They absorb, process, and distribute energy throughout the body.

The nadis are the energy channels through which the life force (prana) flows. There are thousands of nadis in the body, but there are three main nadis; Ida, Pingala, and Sushumna. Ida and Pingala intersect at each chakra, while Sushumna runs through the center of the chakras.

The aura is the energy field that surrounds and permeates the physical body. It consists of the chakras, the nadis, and the subtle bodies. With training, one can learn to see and feel the aura.

The Role of the Chakras

The chakras are important parts of our energy system. They are powerful wheels of energy that sit at different points along the spine. There are seven chakras, each connected to a different part of your physical and spiritual being. Each chakra has its role within your body and unique characteristics to help you understand and work with it.

Each of the seven main chakras is responsible for certain functions, from creativity to intuition to sexuality. They can each work alone or together to fulfill each of our functions. Each of these chakras has a color, symbol, and corresponding crystals and oils. Let's take a closer look at the roles of chakras when it comes to the energy flow throughout the body.

The Root Chakra

You'll find this chakra on your lower back at your spine's root (base). It is generally associated with the color red, and the power that comes from it is often displayed through our in-built survival instinct. The root chakra is the foundation of our energy body and provides a sense of stability and grounding. It helps us feel safe and secure in our environment.

The Sacral Chakra

Located on the front of your body under the naval. It is responsible for our sexuality and is associated with the color orange. The sacral chakra helps us create and maintain healthy relationships. It also gives us the ability to feel pleasure and enjoy our bodies.

The Solar Plexus Chakra

The solar plexus chakra is located just above the navel. Yellow is the color of the solar plexus chakra, and it helps us channel our strength and power. The solar plexus chakra helps us assert our power and to be in control of our lives. It also gives us the ability to take action and make things happen.

The Heart Chakra

As you might expect, the heart chakra is located where your heart is. Green is the color of the heart chakra, and though green represents the heart chakra, it is still associated with love, both for ourselves and toward others. It also gives us the ability to forgive and let go of the past.

The Throat Chakra

Just like the heart chakra, the throat chakra's name gives away the location. Blue is the color of the throat chakra. The throat chakra helps us communicate our needs and desires. It also gives us the ability to express ourselves creatively.

The Third Eye Chakra

You might have seen pictures of a third eye - always located on the forehead. As the name suggests, this chakra is about seeing the unseen - powering our subconscious and intuition. The color for this chakra is purple, and it also gives us the ability to connect with our higher self.

The Crown Chakra

Just as a crown would sit on top of your head, your crown chakra is located at the very top of your person. It is responsible for our spiritual connection and is associated with the color violet. The crown chakra helps us connect with our higher purpose. It also gives us the ability to see the world from a higher perspective.

Sahasrara: Origins

The Sahasrara is often depicted as a lotus flower with a thousand petals, representing the many ways we can connect to the Divine. The chakra is believed to be the point of connection between the physical and spiritual worlds. When activated, it can help us transcend the physical body's limitations and connect with our highest selves.

The origins of the Sahasrara are unclear, but it is believed that the Vedas, the oldest texts in Hinduism, may have mentioned it. Some scholars believe that the chakra was first mentioned in the Vedas as the "seventh lotus."

Sahasrara: The Vedas

The Vedas were the first record of Indian thought. They were written between 1500 and 1000 BCE and contain more than 100 hymns to praise different deities who represented different aspects of nature. One of those deities was Indra, who was associated with thunderstorms and lightning bolts.

Indra has 1,000 eyes representing the Sahasrara chakra that he uses to see all aspects of reality. Indra is described as "the thousand-eyed one in the Rig Veda." This may be a reference to the Sahasrara chakra.

In the Vedas, Sahasrara is associated with pure consciousness and spiritual transcendence. The sacred text helps us understand Sahasrara, detailing it as a lotus flower. The lotus has one thousand petals, each relating to a facet of reality. When all of the petals are open, one is said to achieve enlightenment.

While the path to enlightenment may be long and difficult, the rewards are more than worth the effort. Those who reach Sahasrara are said to experience a deep sense of peace and bliss and a profound understanding of the nature of reality.

Whether you're just beginning your journey or nearing the end, the Sahasrara is a powerful symbol of the potential for spiritual growth and transformation.

Sahasrara: Omissions

While the Sahasrara is often mentioned in scriptures and texts, some omit it. The Svetasvatara Upanishad, for example, only mentions six chakras. It's conceivable that the omission of Sahasrara was deliberate, as the Upanishad was written for beginners who were not yet ready to deal with the complexities of the seventh chakra.

It's also possible that the omission was simply a mistake. The Svetasvatara Upanishad was written in the 6th century BCE, and maybe the author was not aware of the Sahasrara chakra then. Since this chakra is associated with spiritual transcendence, it may not have been understood yet in the 6th century BCE.

Regardless of the reason, the Sahasrara is an important part of the chakra system. It is the culmination of our spiritual journey and the point at which we can connect with our highest selves. The Sahasrara is a symbol of our potential for growth and transformation.

Sahasrara: Symbolism

In Sanskrit, Sahasrara means "thousand-petaled." It is described as the lotus of a thousand petals that lies either on or slightly above the crown of the head. In Tibetan Buddhism, it is known as "The Diamond Realm."

The Sahasrara is often depicted as being oval, and each of the thousand petals is a different color. The center has a golden ring around it, and within that ring is a full white moon. The unfolded petals represent the Vrittis of all mental modifications (Chitta Vritti). At its center is a flame, representing consciousness and said to be white or very light pink. By attaining the knowledge of this center, one can know everything about the past, present, and future.

The thousand-petalled lotus symbolizes the highest state of consciousness, and each petal represents a different aspect of reality. The lotus is often seen as a symbol of spiritual growth and transformation, as it grows from the soil of the Earth toward the light of the sun.

The Thousand Petal Lotus.

Sahasrara: Color

The Sahasrara, or crown chakra, is traditionally associated with the color violet. Violet is the highest frequency of visible light and represents our connection to the Divine. When the Sahasrara is in balance, we feel a sense of oneness with all of creation. We see the beauty in everything and feel compassion for all beings. We experience a deep sense of peace and joy.

When the Sahasrara is out of balance, we may feel disconnected from our spirituality. We may feel anxious or depressed, and we may also suffer from headaches, insomnia, or memory problems. Balancing the Sahasrara can be as simple as spending time in nature or meditating in violet light. You can also wear violet clothes or jewelry or surround yourself with violet flowers.

The Sahasrara is traditionally associated with the color violet, but it can also be represented by white or gold. These colors are often used to symbolize wisdom and spiritual understanding. Regardless of the specific colors used, the Sahasrara is typically seen as a place of enlightenment and peace. Those who can open their Sahasraras are said to be able to see beyond the physical world and connect with the Divine.

Sahasrara: Traits

Some say the Sahasrara represents universal compassion, while others believe it represents a union of heaven and earth. It is also said to represent a reflection on knowing and understanding the self-realization of one's mind concerning humanity as a whole.

It is where we experience pure consciousness and start to understand our place in the Universe beyond our physical bodies (Atman). In this state, we can begin to tap into our inner wisdom from past experiences, which can lead us toward enlightenment.

When this chakra is balanced and open, you'll have a sense of connection with all living things and have feelings of peace and compassion toward yourself and others. You can quickly take in new information while processing what you already know to make intelligent decisions about life situations.

Sahasrara: Function

The Sahasrara is associated with pure awareness, integration of opposites, and transcendence of the physical world. The connection to our identity is loosened here to favor a more expansive sense of our place in the Universe.

When the Sahasrara Chakra is balanced and open, a person will feel enlightened, spiritually aware, and in sync with the Universe. This includes feelings of self-realization and spiritual fulfillment. A person will also be able to tap into their intuition, wisdom, and understanding of how they fit in the world. They will have no problem finding answers to questions that are important to them in life.

The Sahasrara can become blocked when a person feels uninspired or does not feel like they have a purpose. When this happens, a person may feel depressed or lack the energy needed for day-to-day activities. A blockage can also manifest as a feeling of isolation from others or a lack of connection with one's spirituality. This can cause someone to feel confused and unable to find answers about the meaning of life in general.

Benefits of Aligning Your Sahasrara

Aligning your Sahasrara can bring about a sense of clarity and peace. You may feel more connected to your spirituality and have a greater understanding of your place in the Universe. You may also notice an improvement in your memory and ability to focus. But that's not all! Many other benefits come with aligning your Sahasrara. Some of these benefits include:

1. Increased Creativity

When your Sahasrara is open and aligned, you may find that your creativity levels increase. This is because you are no longer limited by the simplicity of your thoughts and beliefs. You can tap into a higher level of consciousness full of creative ideas. This chakra is also associated with the element of aether, which is the substance from which all things are made. This means that when your Sahasrara is open, you can connect with the creative force within all things.

2. Improved Intuition

One of the benefits of aligning your Sahasrara is that you can start to trust your intuition more. This is because your rationality no longer limits you. When your Sahasrara is open, you can connect with your higher self, which knows all things. You can receive guidance and answers to questions you may have about your life.

3. Enhanced Psychic Abilities

Another benefit of aligning your Sahasrara is that you may start to develop psychic abilities. This is because you are not limited anymore by your physical body. When your Sahasrara is open, you can connect with the spiritual realm. You can receive messages from your spirit guides and angels. You might also see things that are not of this world.

4. Greater Connection with the Divine

When your Sahasrara is open, you can connect with the Divine Source of all things. This connection can bring about a sense of peace and bliss. You may also start to feel a sense of oneness with all that is. Many people report feeling a deep connection with nature when their Sahasrara is open.

5. Increased Wisdom

One of the benefits of aligning your Sahasrara is accessing the Akashic Records. This is a library of all knowledge that is stored in the aether. When you align your Sahasrara, you can tap into this store of knowledge and wisdom. You may also find that you can remember all your past lives. It's also said that you can access the Akashic Records in your dreams.

6. Improved Health

When your Sahasrara is open and aligned, your health improves since the energy flow in your body is balanced. When your chakras are in alignment, your body can heal itself. Many people report feeling more vibrant and alive when their Sahasrara is open. A balanced Sahasrara can also prevent disease.

7. Increased Happiness

A feeling of ecstasy or bliss is one of the most common benefits of aligning your Sahasrara. The connection with the Divine can bring about a sense of joy and happiness. Immense love is also said to be felt when the Sahasrara is open. You may find yourself feeling more loving and compassionate toward others. When your Sahasrara is open, the entire world may start to look different to you.

8. A Sense Of Oneness

If you're looking for a sense of oneness with the Universe, aligning your Sahasrara is a good place to start. When your Sahasrara is open, you can tap into the collective consciousness. This is the part of the Universe that contains all knowledge. All of humanity is connected to the collective consciousness. When you align your Sahasrara, you can feel this connection.

The Sahasrara (crown chakra) sits on the top of your head like a crown. The traditional depiction is a lotus with a thousand petals, each a different color. The crown chakra represents your consciousness (being close to your mind), and the other chakras gain their energy from the crown chakra. This chakra is responsible for your nervous system and brain function.

If you're looking to improve your life, aligning your Sahasrara is a good place to start. The benefits of aligning your Sahasrara are many. When your Sahasrara is open, you can tap into a higher level of consciousness. You may also start to develop psychic abilities and a greater connection with the Divine.

Aligning your Sahasrara can also bring about increased wisdom, improved health, increased happiness, and a sense of oneness with the Universe. If your crown chakra is blocked, you may experience disconnection, loneliness, and depression. You may also suffer from headaches, memory problems, and fatigue.

To learn more about the Sahasrara and how to align it, turn the page to the next chapter. We'll discuss the steps you need to take to open your Sahasrara and reap the benefits.

Chapter 2: When Your Crown Is Blocked

Have you ever felt like your brain is running at a million miles an hour, and there's no way to slow it down? Or perhaps you feel an invisible wall between yourself and the world? Do you feel like you're always missing something, but you can't figure out what it is?

If either of these situations sounds familiar to you, you may have a blocked crown chakra.

A blocked crown chakra can lead to all kinds of problems in your life. It could be why you're feeling disconnected from everything around you. It could be why your brain is constantly working overtime, even when your body wants to relax. It could be why you're feeling stuck or hopeless about getting past the things holding you back.

A blocked crown chakra can cause stress.
https://unsplash.com/photos/wuo8KnyCm4I

Your crown chakra is your connection with your inner self and the Universe. It helps you feel centered, secure, and at peace with who you are. Unfortunately, like all chakras, it can become blocked by stress, negative emotions, and physical ailments.

When you connect with your crown chakra, you can begin to understand yourself as part of a larger whole. And when this chakra is blocked, you may feel as if your life has no meaning or purpose.

Let's look at how imbalances in this energy center can manifest in your life, how to recognize these signs, and how to correct them.

Causes of a Blocked Crown Chakra

When the crown chakra is balanced, we feel spiritually connected and aligned with our highest purpose. However, when it is blocked, we may feel disconnected from our spirituality and grounded in material concerns. Several things can cause a blockage in the crown chakra, including:

1. Lack of Self-Awareness

One of the most common causes of a blocked crown chakra is a lack of self-awareness. When we're not aware of our thoughts and emotions, they can take control of us and prevent us from connecting with our higher selves. If you're not sure what's going on inside you, it can be difficult to connect with your spirituality.

2. Fear of The Unknown

Another common cause of a blocked crown chakra is fear of the unknown. When we're afraid of change or new experiences, we can hold ourselves back from growth. This fear can prevent us from exploring our spirituality and connecting with a higher power. We can become stuck in a rut when we're afraid to let go of our old ways.

3. Attachment to Material Possessions

Another cause of a blocked crown chakra is attachment to material possessions. When we're more focused on acquiring things than on our spiritual growth, we can lose sight of what's truly important in life. This attachment can prevent us from connecting with our higher selves and the Universe. People who are overly attached to their possessions may be more likely to experience greed, envy, and other negative emotions.

4. Negative Emotions

Negative emotions like anger, fear, and jealousy can also block the crown chakra. When we're caught up in these emotions, we cannot see the beauty in life or connect with our higher purpose. These negative emotions can also prevent us from connecting with others and experiencing true love and compassion.

5. Physical Ailments

Physical ailments can also block the crown chakra. It can be difficult to focus on anything else when dealing with pain or illness. This can prevent us from connecting with our spirituality and finding inner peace. With a blocked crown chakra, we may also be more susceptible to anxiety and depression.

6. Trauma

Trauma can also block the crown chakra. When we've experienced a traumatic event, it can be difficult to let go of the past and move on. This can prevent us from connecting with our higher selves and living in the present moment. Trauma can also cause us to experience flashbacks, nightmares, and intrusive thoughts.

7. Lack of Creativity

A lack of creativity can also block the crown chakra. When we're not expressing our creative side, we may feel like we're not living up to our potential. This can prevent us from connecting with our spirituality and finding our true purpose in life. A lack of creativity can also lead to boredom, depression, and a feeling of hopelessness.

8. Shutting Down Emotions

When we shut down our emotions, we cannot properly process them, and this can lead to a build-up of negative energy in the crown chakra. When we don't allow ourselves to feel our emotions, we may struggle to connect with our higher selves and miss out on important life lessons.

Why Most People Have a Blocked Crown Chakra

The crown chakra is the highest, and it is associated with spirituality. Because of this, many people have a hard time opening it up. They may feel like they're not worthy or may be afraid of what they might find if they open up spiritually.

If you're having difficulty opening your crown chakra, know that you're not alone. Many people struggle with this issue. But you are worthy of opening up spiritually. The more you tap into your crown chakra, the more you'll see and sense the world you are in. When our crown chakra is blocked, we may experience various symptoms. These can include physical, mental, and emotional issues. We may find ourselves feeling disconnected from our spirituality in our day-to-day lives. We may also feel like we're not living up to our potential.

As we live our lives, it's natural for our crown chakras to become blocked. Many things can cause this to happen, such as negative thinking, a lack of spirituality in your life, trauma, and stress. If you're dealing with any of these issues, seek help so that you can open your crown chakra and live a more balanced life.

Symptoms of a Blocked Crown Chakra

A blocked crown chakra can feel like you have a weight on your shoulders. It can manifest physically as headaches or migraines, making you feel like you're constantly tired. You may also suffer from depression, anxiety, or feelings of disconnection. If your crown chakra is blocked, you may find it difficult to focus during meditation.

Here are some common symptoms of a blocked crown chakra:

1. Headaches or migraines
2. Fatigue
3. Depression
4. Anxiety
5. Feelings of Disconnection

6. Difficulty focusing during meditation

7. Insomnia

8. Sensitivity to light or sound

9. A feeling of being lost or confused

10. Memory problems

If you're experiencing any of these symptoms, it's a sign that your crown chakra is blocked. While these symptoms can be alarming, there are ways to unblock your crown chakra and get back on the path to spiritual growth.

Symptoms of an Out of Balance Crown Chakra

An unbalanced crown chakra often presents itself in the form of mental stress. Over time, this can cause physical health problems as well. Aches and pains (especially in the back of the neck and head) are common. You may experience migraine headaches, confusion, mood swings, or a loss of motivation. Over time, serious issues like Alzheimer's disease or dementia may develop if your crown chakra remains unbalanced.

Here are some common symptoms of an out of balance crown chakra:

1. Headaches or migraines

2. Aches and pains

3. Confusion

4. Mood swings

5. Loss of motivation

6. Alzheimer's disease

7. Dementia

8. Impaired ability to think clearly or make decisions

9. Feeling disconnected from your body

10. Feeling disconnected from reality

These are just some of the symptoms when your crown chakra is out of balance. An out-of-balance crown chakra can be a serious issue, so it's important to take steps to restore balance.

Symptoms of a Weak Crown Chakra

An underactive crown chakra can lead to a sense of loss or despair. It can feel as though you've lost something important but don't know what it is, making it even more frustrating. You may experience feelings of loneliness despite being surrounded by people who support you. You may feel disconnected from the world around you and find it difficult to connect with your spirituality. Here are some common symptoms of a weak crown chakra:

1. A sense of loss or despair
2. Feelings of loneliness
3. Disconnection from the world around you
4. Difficulty connecting with your spirituality
5. A feeling that something is missing from your life
6. A sense of being lost or confused
7. A lack of purpose in life
8. Depression
9. Anxiety
10. Addictions

If you're struggling with any of these symptoms, it's a sign that your crown chakra is weak. It's imperative to take steps to strengthen your crown chakra so that you can live a more balanced, fulfilled life.

Symptoms of an Overactive Crown Chakra

An overactive crown chakra can feel like you have too much going on in your head. You might have difficulty focusing on one task or feel like your thoughts are racing. You might also experience anxiety, mania, or hallucinations. An overactive crown chakra can be a sign of mental illness, so it's important to seek help from a professional if you're struggling.

Here are some common symptoms of an overactive crown chakra:

1. Difficulty focusing
2. Thoughts that race or are hard to control
3. Anxiety
4. Mania
5. Hallucinations
6. Mental illness

If you're struggling with any of these symptoms, it's important to seek professional help. An overactive crown chakra can signify a serious mental illness, so it's important to get the help you need.

Real-Life Stories

There are many instances in which the crown chakra becomes blocked, out of balance, weak, or even overactive. Here are some real-life stories of people who have experienced these issues:

Maria was born into a family of devout Catholics. From a young age, she was taught that God was all-powerful and that her purpose in life was to serve Him. As she got older, Maria began to question her faith. She started to read about other religions and philosophies and realized that there was more to life than what she had been taught. However, Maria didn't want to upset her family, so she kept her questions to herself.

Eventually, Maria's questioning led her to doubt her faith entirely. She lost her connection to God and felt lost and confused. Maria began to experience symptoms of a weak crown chakra, including depression and anxiety. She felt like something was missing from her life but didn't know what it was.

Maria's story is a common one. Many people experience a loss of faith at some point in their lives. This can be difficult, but it's important to find your truth and connect with your spirituality.

Another tale is that of Sarah, who was always a bright and outgoing person. She had many friends and was always the life of the party. However, when Sarah turned 30, she began to feel like something was missing from her life. She started to withdraw from her friends and stopped going out altogether. Sarah began to experience symptoms of a weak crown chakra, including loneliness and disconnection from the world around her.

Many people feel like they're missing something when they reach a certain age. This can be a difficult time, but it's crucial to find your truth and connect with your spirituality. A blocked crown chakra can prevent you from living your best life, but there are many ways to unblock it and live a more balanced life.

John is an example of someone who has an overly active crown chakra. John was always a bright and outgoing person. However, when he turned 30, he began to experience symptoms of mania. He would have racing thoughts and found it hard to focus on one task. He was also extremely agitated and had a hard time sleeping. John's doctor diagnosed him with bipolar disorder, and he began to receive treatment.

John's story is a reminder that an overactive crown chakra can be a sign of a serious mental illness. If you're struggling with overactive crown chakra symptoms, it's important to seek professional help.

The Crown Chakra Quiz

Take the following quiz to get an idea of how balanced your crown chakra is. Simply select the answer that best describes your current state.

1. How connected do you feel to your spirituality?
   a) I don't believe in anything spiritual.
   b) I believe in a higher power but don't feel particularly connected to it.
   c) I feel a strong connection to my spirituality, and it's an important part of my life.
   d) I'm not sure; I'm still exploring my spirituality.

2. How often do you experience symptoms of anxiety or depression?
   a) Rarely
   b) Occasionally
   c) Frequently

d) Almost always

3. Do you feel like you're missing something in your life?

    a) No, I'm happy with my life.

    b) Sometimes, I feel like something is missing, but I'm not sure what it is.

    c) Yes, I feel like something is missing, but I don't know what it is.

    d) Yes, I feel like something is missing, and I know what it is.

4. Do you have a hard time sleeping?

    a) No, I generally sleep well.

    b) Sometimes, I have trouble sleeping, but it's not a regular occurrence.

    c) Yes, I have trouble sleeping regularly.

    d) No, I don't need to sleep; I only need 3-4 hours of sleep.

5. Do you find it hard to focus on one task?

    a) No, I can focus when I need to.

    b) Sometimes, I have trouble focusing, but it's not a regular occurrence.

    c) Yes, I have trouble focusing regularly.

    d) No, I don't need to focus. I can multi-task easily.

6. Do you feel disconnected from the world around you?

    a) No, I feel connected to the world around me.

    b) Sometimes, I feel disconnected, but it's not a regular occurrence.

    c) Yes, I often feel disconnected from the world around me.

    d) No, I don't feel the need to be connected to the world; I prefer to be alone.

7. Do you have a hard time meditating?

    a) No, I can easily clear my mind and focus on my breath.

    b) Sometimes, it's hard for me to clear my mind, but I can eventually focus on my breath.

c) Yes, it's very hard for me to clear my mind, and I can never seem to focus on my breath.

d) No, I don't need to meditate. I can easily clear my mind without focusing on my breath.

8. Do you see colors and shapes when you close your eyes?

a) No, I don't see anything.

b) Sometimes, I see colors or shapes, but it's not a regular occurrence.

c) Yes, I often see colors or shapes when I close my eyes.

d) No, I don't need to close my eyes to see colors and shapes. I can see them with my eyes open.

9. Do you feel like you have a lot of unresolved anger?

a) No, I generally don't get angry.

b) Sometimes, I get angry, but I usually deal with it in a healthy way.

c) Yes, I have a lot of unresolved anger that I don't know how to deal with.

d) No, I don't get angry. I only feel love and compassion.

10. Do you have a hard time remembering your dreams?

a) No, I generally remember my dreams.

b) Sometimes, I have trouble remembering my dreams, but it's not a regular occurrence.

c) Yes, I have trouble remembering my dreams regularly.

d) No, I don't need to remember my dreams; I can have lucid dreams.

The Results of the Quiz

Once you've answered all of the questions, tally up your results to see how balanced your crown chakra is.

If you mostly selected:

a) Your crown chakra is blocked. This means that you're disconnected from your spirituality, and you may be experiencing symptoms of anxiety or depression. You may feel like you're missing something in your life, but you're not sure what it is. You may have trouble sleeping, focusing, or meditating. You may also feel disconnected from the world around you and have unresolved anger.

If you mostly selected:

b) Your crown chakra is weak. This means that you're partially disconnected from your spirituality. You're likely experiencing some symptoms of anxiety or depression. Very occasionally, you may feel like you're missing something in your life or have trouble sleeping, focusing, or meditating. You may also feel disconnected from the world around you occasionally, but it's not a regular occurrence. You may have some unresolved anger, but it's not a major issue.

If you mostly selected:

c) Your crown chakra is in balance. This means that you have a good connection to your spirituality. You likely don't experience any symptoms of anxiety or depression. However, you may feel like you're missing something in your life or have trouble sleeping, focusing, or meditating every now and then. You may also feel disconnected from the world around you on occasion, but it's not a regular occurrence. You may have some unresolved anger, but it's not a major issue.

If you mostly selected:

d) Your crown chakra is overactive. This means that you have a strong connection to your spirituality. You likely don't experience any symptoms of anxiety or depression. You may feel like you're missing something in your life, but you likely know what it is. You may have trouble sleeping, focusing, or meditating. You may also feel disconnected from the world around you and have unresolved anger. But you're likely able to deal with these issues healthily.

When talking about the seventh chakra, you're talking about your connection to the higher divine. You're talking about being able to communicate with the Universe and being completely aware of your connection to the rest of existence.

In the same way that a clogged drain prevents water from flowing freely, a blocked crown chakra can prevent your energy from flowing freely through your body. When this happens, you may experience physical symptoms such as headaches, chronic fatigue, and emotional symptoms such as confusion, frustration, and depression.

If your crown chakra is blocked, weak, or out of balance, there are several things you can do to heal and unblock it. Raising energy up to the crown chakra can help unblock and balance it. This can be done through meditation, visualization, affirmations, or energy work. The following chapter will go into more detail about how to do this.

Chapter 3: Raising Energy through Your Chakras

The chakras are energy centers in your body, and they work together to help you do all sorts of magical things. They start at your root chakra and move outward like a flower blooming until they reach your crown chakra. Sahasrara is the highest chakra, and it is associated with your spiritual connection to the Universe. To awaken your Sahasrara, it is best to have all of your other chakras open and in balance so that energy can flow freely through them up until it reaches it.

The first chapter of this guide covered the basics of the chakras and how they work. If you need a refresher, please refer back to that chapter. We will go through each chakra, from the Root up to the Third Eye. For each chakra, we will first provide an overview of symptoms that the chakra is blocked. Then, we will list a few simple ways to balance it.

Sahasrara and the Other Chakras

Sahasrara is the seventh and final chakra, located on the crown of the head. It is associated with enlightenment, pure consciousness, and bliss. Although it is the highest chakra, Sahasrara is not separate from the other chakras. It is intimately connected to them.

Each chakra provides energy and information to Sahasrara, which, in turn, affects our state of consciousness. For example, balancing our Muladhara chakra helps us feel more grounded and stable. If the Ajna chakra is balanced, we can access our intuition and inner wisdom. By keeping all of our chakras in balance, we can maintain our connection to higher states of consciousness.

The energy of the chakras also flows upward from the root chakra to the crown. This flow of energy is known as kundalini, which allows us to connect with our higher selves. We can think of Kundalini energy as a coil, often a snake, that wraps around our spine from the bottom to the top (and only positively).

When the kundalini energy is blocked, we may feel stuck in our lives, or like we are not reaching our full potential. By clearing blockages and opening our chakras, we can allow kundalini energy to flow freely, which will help us reach our highest potential.

Muladhara: The Root Chakra

The root chakra is located at the bottom of our spine. It is associated with the element of earth, and it is responsible for feeling safe and secure. When Muladhara is balanced, we feel grounded, stable, and safe. We can handle difficult situations with grace and feel like we belong in the world.

Red is the color of the root chakra. Red is the color of passion, vitality, and security. It is the color of our physical body and our connection to the earth. The root chakra is the foundation of our energy system, and it is critical to keep it balanced so that we can feel grounded and stable in our lives.

Overview of Blocked Symptoms

If Muladhara is out of balance, we may experience many different symptoms. Here are some of the most common ones:

- Feeling unsafe or insecure.
- Feeling like you don't belong in the world.
- Feeling anxious or stressed.

- Difficulty concentrating or focusing.

- Feeling spaced out or disconnected from your body.

- Aches and pains in the body.

If you feel like these things describe you, try starting with some simple yoga poses and breathing exercises to help clear out the stagnant energy in your root chakra. Once that's done, try to stay positive and focused on your goals. We have covered some simple ways to do this in the next section.

Ways to Balance Muladhara

There are many ways to balance Muladhara. Here are a few of the most effective:

- Practice Tadasana (Yoga Pose).

- Spend time in nature.

- Wear red clothing or surround yourself with red objects.

- Eat root vegetables.

- Do grounding exercises such as yoga or Tai Chi.

- Get a massage.

- Spend time with animals.

Swadhisthana: The Sacral Chakra

The second chakra is Swadhisthana, located just below the navel. It is associated with the element of water, and it is responsible for pleasure and creativity. When Swadhisthana is balanced, we feel confident and desirable. We have the freedom to appreciate our physical selves. We feel creative and connected to our emotions.

Swadhisthana is also associated with the sacral chakra color orange. Orange is the color of joy, enthusiasm, and pleasure. It is the color of our sexuality and creativity. The sacral chakra is the foundation of our emotional body, and it is critical to keep it balanced so that we can feel confident and creative.

Overview of Blocked Symptoms

If Swadhisthana is out of balance, we may experience many different symptoms. Here are some of the most common ones:

- Difficulty experiencing pleasure.
- Low self-esteem or confidence.
- Sexual dysfunction.
- Creative blocks.
- Emotional instability.
- Mood swings.

Ways to Balance Swadhisthana

There are many ways to balance Swadhisthana. Here are a few of the most effective ones:

- Practice Matsyasana (Yoga Pose).
- Wear orange clothing or surround yourself with orange objects.
- Eat citrus fruit.
- Do creative activities such as painting or writing.
- Dance or playfully move your body.
- Spend time in the water.
- Connect with your sensual side.

Manipura: The Solar Plexus Chakra

Chakra number three, the solar plexus chakra, is located around your naval area. It is associated with the element of fire, and it is responsible for power and vitality. When Manipura is balanced, we feel confident and in control of our lives. We can set boundaries and achieve our goals.

Yellow is the color of your Manipura. Yellow is the color of clarity, wisdom, and intellect. It is the color of our mental body and our ability to think clearly. The solar plexus chakra is the foundation of our power, and it is critical to keep it balanced so that we can feel confident and in control of our lives.

Overview of Blocked Symptoms

If Manipura is out of balance, we may experience many different symptoms. Here are some of the most common ones:

- Low self-esteem or confidence.
- Difficulty setting boundaries.
- People pleasing.
- Codependency.
- Control issues.
- Anger or resentment.
- Feeling powerless or victimized.

Ways to Balance Manipura

There are many ways to balance Manipura. Here are a few of the most effective ones:

- Practice Paschimottanasana (Yoga Pose).
- Wear yellow clothing or surround yourself with yellow objects.
- Eat yellow fruit and vegetables.
- Do mental activities such as puzzles or Sudoku.
- Spend time in the sun.
- Visualize yourself as powerful and in control.
- Affirm your power.

Anahata: The Heart Chakra

Your heart chakra is located where your heart is. Being close to your lungs, the heart chakra has an air symbol, and like your heart, it deals in the emotions of love and compassion. When Anahata is balanced, we feel loving and compassionate toward ourselves and others. We can unconditionally give and receive love.

Green is the color of your heart chakra. Green is the color of healing, growth, and abundance. It is the color of our physical and emotional bodies, and it is critical to keep the heart chakra balanced so that we can feel love and compassion in our lives.

Overview of Blocked Symptoms

If Anahata is out of balance, we may experience many different symptoms. Here are some of the most common ones:

- Difficulty giving or receiving love.

- Lack of compassion.

- Emotional numbness.

- Bitterness or resentment.

- Jealousy or envy.

- Difficulty forgiving others or yourself.

Ways to Balance Anahata

There are many ways to balance Anahata. Here are a few of the most effective ones:

- Practice Anahatasana (Yoga Pose).

- Wear green clothing or surround yourself with green objects.

- Eat green fruit and vegetables.

- Spend time in nature.

- Visualize yourself surrounded by love.

- Affirm your capacity to give and receive love.

- Be kind and compassionate to yourself and others.

Vishuddha: The Throat Chakra

You might have already guessed (or know) where the throat chakra is located – in your three areas. It is associated with the element of ether, and it is responsible for our ability to communicate our truth. When Vishuddha is balanced, we can express ourselves clearly and honestly. We are also able to listen to others with openness and respect.

Blue is the color of the throat chakra. Blue is the color of communication, expression, and truth. It is the color of our mental body, and it is critical to keep the throat chakra balanced so that we can communicate our truth with integrity.

Overview of Blocked Symptoms

If Vishuddha is out of balance, we may experience many different symptoms. Here are some of the most common ones:

- Difficulty communicating.
- Fear of speaking your truth.
- Dishonesty.
- Gossiping or talking behind others' backs.
- Manipulative or passive-aggressive communication.
- Lying.

Ways to Balance Vishuddha

There are many ways to balance Vishuddha. Here are a few of the most effective ones:

- Practice Halasana (Yoga Pose).
- Wear blue clothing or surround yourself with blue objects.
- Eat blue fruit and vegetables.
- Do vocal activities such as singing or chanting.
- Visualize yourself communicating with ease and confidence.
- Affirm your right to express yourself freely and truthfully.

Ajna: The Third Eye Chakra

Your third eye chakra is located on your forehead, and you might have seen depictions of a third eye chakra in various media. It is associated with the element of light, and it is responsible for our ability to see clearly. When Ajna is balanced, we can clearly see the world around us and make wise decisions. We learn to trust our intuition and follow our inner compass.

Ajna is also associated with the third eye chakra color indigo. Indigo is the color of intuition, insight, and psychic ability. It is the color of our spiritual body, and it is critical to keep the third eye chakra balanced so that we can see clearly and make wise decisions.

Overview of Blocked Symptoms

If Ajna is out of balance, we may experience many different symptoms. Here are some of the most common ones:

- Difficulty making decisions.
- Confusion.
- Lack of focus.
- Brain fog.
- Anxiety.
- Depression.

Ways to Balance Ajna

There are many ways to balance Ajna. Here are a few of the most effective ones:

- Practice Ajna Mudra (Yoga Pose).
- Wear indigo clothing or surround yourself with indigo objects.
- Eat indigo fruit and vegetables.
- Visualize yourself, making wise decisions with ease.
- Affirm your ability to trust your intuition and follow your inner guidance.

Sahasrara: The Crown Chakra

A crown sits on top of your head, and so does the crown chakra. It is associated with the element of thought, and it is responsible for our ability to connect with our higher selves. When Sahasrara is balanced, we feel connected to something greater than ourselves. We feel enlightened and at peace.

Sahasrara is also associated with the crown chakra color violet. Violet is the color of spirituality, enlightenment, and connection. It is the color of our divine body, and it is critical to keep the crown chakra balanced so that we can feel a sense of connection to the Divine.

Overview of Blocked Symptoms

If Sahasrara is out of balance, we may experience many different symptoms. Here are some of the most common ones:

- A sense of disconnection from something greater than yourself.
- Feelings of emptiness or loneliness.
- A lack of purpose or meaning in life.
- Depression.
- Anxiety.

Ways to Balance Sahasrara

There are many ways to balance Sahasrara. Here are a few of the most effective:

- Practice Sahasrara Mudra (Yoga Pose).
- Wear violet clothing or surround yourself with violet objects.
- Eat violet fruit and vegetables.
- Visualize yourself connected to the Divine.
- Affirm your connection to something greater than yourself.

Opening All Your Chakras

Now that you know more about the chakras, you may wonder how to open them up. To experience utter bliss, you'll need to have all seven chakras open and balanced. If a single chakra is out of balance, it can throw your entire system off balance.

Your energy body is the network of energy that runs through and around you. When this energy flows freely and easily, you feel happy and healthy. But when it gets blocked or sluggish, you can sometimes feel depressed or run down.

While there is no one-size-fits-all approach to opening your chakras, there are a few things you can do to get started. Here are a few suggestions:

A Healthy Diet

What we put into our bodies is so important for our energy. Eating lots of processed foods and junk food can make you feel sluggish and slow, whereas a healthy diet that includes lots of whole grains, leafy greens, and clean proteins will help your energy body run smoothly.

Healthy eating is crucial to keep your chakra balanced.
https://unsplash.com/photos/jUPOXXRNdcA

One of the best ways to open your chakras is to eat healthily. Eating foods associated with the chakras can help balance and open them up. So, if you're looking to open your root chakra, eat plenty of red fruit and vegetables. For example, to open your sacral chakra, eat orange fruit and vegetables.

Ensure that you have lots of whole grains, fruits and vegetables, and lean protein in your diet. Foods that are high in sugar and fat can sap your energy. If you're hungry or tired, try eating an apple or a handful of nuts for a quick pick-me-up.

In addition to eating the right foods, it's also important to drink plenty of water. Water is essential for proper chakra function. It flushes out toxins and keeps the body hydrated.

Yoga

Yoga is an excellent way to open your chakras and get your energy flowing. There are several different yoga poses you can do to target each of the chakras. For example, if you're looking to open your heart chakra, you can do a heart opener like Camel Pose. Or, if you're looking to open your root chakra, you can do a grounding pose like Mountain Pose.

Doing yoga regularly can keep your chakras open and balanced. If you're new to yoga, plenty of resources are available to help you get started. You can find yoga classes at your local gym or community center or even find instructional videos online.

Each chakra has a different color associated with it. When you're doing yoga, try to wear clothing that is the color of the chakra you're trying to open. Your heart chakra is represented by green, so wear green clothing if you want to fully open that specific chakra. It doesn't have to be a lot, just enough to help you feel more connected to the chakra.

Start with just a few minutes of yoga each day and gradually increase the amount of time you spend as you get more comfortable with the practice. Focus on the root chakra at first since it's the foundation of the chakra system. Once that's open and balanced, you can move on to the other chakras.

Meditation

Meditation is another excellent way to open your chakras and promote healthy energy flow. Meditation calms the mind and allows you to focus on the present moment. When you focus on the present moment, you can tune into your body and energy.

There are many different ways to meditate, so find one that works best for you. You can try a guided meditation, where someone talks you through the process, or you can meditate on your own. You can also try a walking meditation, where you focus on your breath and your footsteps as you walk.

It is best to start small and grow. A few minutes each day is all that you should try in the beginning so you can hold focus the entire time as you build up your meditation endurance. Chakra balancing doesn't have to be difficult or time-consuming – A little time put aside will work wonders for balancing and opening your chakras.

Grounding

Grounding is a great way to center yourself and connect with the Earth. You release excess energy when you ground yourself and connect with the Earth's grounding energy. This can calm and center you, and it can also open and balance your chakras.

There are many different ways to ground yourself. You can try walking barefoot, gardening, or doing grounding meditation. You can also try eating grounding foods, such as root vegetables, or using essential oils like vetiver or sandalwood.

Take a minute or two each day to work on grounding, and increase your dedicated grounding time as you become more comfortable with it. Grounding will help you feel more connected to the Earth and your own body, and it can also open and balance your chakras.

Affirmations

Affirmations are positive statements you can say to yourself to help shift your mindset. You effectively train your brain to focus on the positive when you repeat affirmations. This can open and balance your chakras by promoting healthy energy flow.

You can use many different affirmations, so find those that resonate with you the most. Some examples of affirmations you can use to open and balance your chakras include:

- "I am safe."
- "I am loved."
- "I am worthy."
- "I am enough."
- "I am strong."
- "I am healthy."
- "I am happy."
- "I am abundant."

Start by repeating affirmations to yourself for just a few minutes each day. As your skill in affirmation progresses, you can spend more time each day. You can also try writing your affirmations down and repeating them to yourself throughout the day.

Visualizations

Visualizations are another great way to open and balance your chakras. You create mental images that can shift your energy and promote a healthy flow when you visualize. Some examples of visualizations you can use to open and balance your chakras include:

- Visualize a white light shining down from the sky and filling your body with light.
- Visualize each of your chakras as a spinning wheel of energy.
- Visualize your chakras opening and balancing as you breathe in and out.

You do not need a lot of time to visualize, and it is best to start small and grow the process. Visualizations are a great way to shift your energy and promote healthy chakra flow.

Chakra balancing is a great way to promote healthy energy flow in the body. By incorporating a few simple practices into your daily routine, you can keep your chakras open and balanced. Many great books and resources are available if you're interested in learning more about chakra balancing.

Just remember to start slowly and increase the time you spend on each practice as you get more comfortable with it. With a little time and effort, you'll be on your way to a more balanced and healthy life.

Chapter 4: Mantras and Mudras

A balanced crown chakra allows you to feel connected to others and the Universe as a whole, be open-minded and open to learning, and live in the present moment. However, it can be more difficult to balance because the crown chakra is so far from our other chakras.

Luckily, two very powerful tools can help you open your crown chakra: mantras and mudras. Let's look at what these are and how you can use them.

What Mantras Are

The way we use mantras varies according to the school and philosophy related to the mantra. However, mantras, which are considered sounds, syllables, and a group of words, can create the ultimate transformation. They're mainly used as spiritual conduits or vibrations that provide sharp focus and concentration. They're also included in religion and ceremonies to attract wealth, protect you from danger, and push away enemies.

Mantras are an ancient practice of singing, chanting, or repeating a word or phrase to yourself to achieve a goal. They are highly effective tools for clearing out old thought patterns and replacing them with new ones. They can help you achieve peace and serenity, and they can also help you set and achieve goals.

Mantra combines two Sanskrit words: "manas" (the mind) and "tra" (to deliver). The mind is a very powerful tool, so the idea behind mantras is that by repeating something repeatedly to your subconscious mind, you'll be able to manifest what you want in life.

Mantras have been used for thousands of years by people who have wanted to achieve specific goals. Studies show that our brains are very receptive to positive thoughts. The science behind mantras has been proven by studies showing that our brains are very receptive to positive thoughts. Our brains release chemicals called neurotransmitters when we think positive thoughts. These neurotransmitters help us feel happier and more relaxed. And when we feel happier and more relaxed, we're more likely to be successful in achieving our goals.

Mantras are easy to learn and use because they require nothing but your voice. You don't need any special equipment or training. And they can be used anywhere, at any time.

The Difference between Mantras and Affirmations

In modern psychology and cognitive therapy, affirmations are any form of positive self-talk statement designed to affect the conscious mind. These statements can be anything from "I love myself unconditionally" to "I am good at my job" to "I am healthy." As such, mantras fall under this category.

In yoga and Ayurveda, mantras are believed to have a much deeper impact on the conscious mind and more far-reaching effects throughout our entire being – past the conscious mind and into the subconscious mind and body.

Mantras and affirmations are similar in that they are both positive statements we repeat to ourselves. The difference is that mantras are usually based on ancient wisdom, while affirmations are more modern and secular. Mantras are also usually based on sacred texts, while affirmations are not.

Affirmations are more focused on the conscious mind, while mantras are designed to penetrate the deeper layers of the subconscious mind.

Our beliefs, thoughts, and feelings about ourselves reside in the subconscious mind. It's also the part of the mind that controls our automatic behaviors and habits.

Because mantras are designed to penetrate the deeper layers of the subconscious mind, they are more powerful and effective than affirmations.

Affirmations to Open the Crown Chakra

There are many affirmations you can use to open your crown chakra. Here are a few examples:

- I am connected to the infinite wisdom of the Universe.
- I look for guidance and direction from my Higher Self.
- I am worthy of love, respect, and abundance.
- My thoughts are clear and focused.
- I am surrounded by love and light.
- I am at peace with myself and the world around me.

If you're having trouble with the above affirmations, you can also write your own. The important thing is that the affirmations are positive and in line with what you want to achieve. Here's a quick guide on how to make your affirmations.

1. List of Qualities

Make a list of the qualities you want to cultivate in yourself. For example, if you want to open your crown chakra, you may want to list qualities such as peace, love, joy, and wisdom. Look at your list and choose one quality you want to focus on.

2. Make a Statement

Once you've chosen a quality, turn each quality into an "I am..." statement. For example, if you've chosen peace, your statement would be, "I am at peace with myself and the world around me."

3. Repeat Your Statement

Repeat your statement out loud multiple times a day. The more you repeat it, the more likely you'll believe it. It's also helpful to write it down and put it somewhere you'll often see it on your mirror or desk. If you struggle to remember your affirmation, set a reminder on your phone or create a mantra ringtone.

4. Visualize

In addition to repeating your statement, visualize yourself as already having the qualities you want to cultivate. For example, if you're working on the quality of peace, visualize yourself as a peaceful person. See yourself surrounded by peace and calm. Feel the peace within you. Create a visual board or picture to help you with this visualization.

5. Believe in Yourself

The most important step to crafting affirmations is to believe in yourself. As you visualize yourself with the qualities you want to cultivate, believe that you can achieve them. Trust that you are worthy of having these qualities. The more you believe in yourself, the more likely you'll achieve your goals.

How Mantras Affect the Body and Brain

Mantras are sounds you say to yourself that have a lot of power. They can affect your body and brain, even if they are just words. Studies related to Sanskrit mantras have shown that they can help to reduce stress, anxiety, and depression. They can also improve sleep and increase focus and concentration.

Mantras work by affecting the brainwaves. When you say a mantra, it creates vibrations in your vocal cords. These vibrations then travel to your brain and change your brainwaves. Depending on the mantra you say, you can change your brainwave patterns to those associated with relaxation, sleep, or concentration.

Mantras can also affect the body. When you say a mantra, it creates vibrations in your body. These vibrations o release tension, improve circulation and boost the immune system. When it comes to stress relief and energy healing, there's some evidence that mantras work by affecting the body's vibrational frequency – the speed at which molecules move.

Mantras have a profound effect on the mind and body. They can help you heal, become more mindful, or open up the energy channels in your body. One of the greatest benefits of this practice is that it can be done anywhere. You don't need to live in an ashram to practice mantras!

Try a few rounds of mantra meditation if you're looking for a quick way to feel calmer, more focused, or just need a break from everything going on around you.

The "OM" Mantra

In Hinduism, Om (or Aum) is the sound of the Universe. It's considered the most sacred sound and is often used in meditation. This sound represents the vibration of the Universe and all its energy. If you're feeling disconnected from your sense of purpose, this mantra can help ground you back into yourself and restore balance.

The pronunciation of Om is aum, with a long "o" sound. The "u" sounds like the "oo" in "moon." The "m" sounds like the "ng" in "sing." The mantra should be said with the mouth slightly open as if you're about to take a sip of water.

When you say Om, it's important to connect with the vibration. Feel the sound move through your body and notice how it makes you feel. Don't worry about getting the pronunciation perfect – just let the sound flow through you.

You can chant "Om" three times at the start and end of your meditation or yoga. Chant the first with your eyes wide open, the second after closing your eyes, and the third after you open your eyes again.

How to Chant "Om"

1. Sit in a comfortable position with your back straight.
2. Take a deep breath and close your eyes.
3. When you're ready, begin chanting "Om."
4. Repeat the mantra as many times as you want.
5. Take two more deep breaths and open your eyes again.

If you're new to mantra meditation, start with three rounds of Om. Once you get the hang of it, you can increase the number of rounds to nine, eighteen, or even thirty-six.

Mantras That Correspond with the Chakras

Each chakra comes with its own chant. Each has its unique sound that vibrates at a different frequency and stimulates a particular area in the body. Here are the 7 chakras and their corresponding mantras:

1. Root Chakra: "Lam."
2. Solar Plexus Chakra: "Ram."
3. Sacral Chakra: "Vam."
4. Throat Chakra: "Ham."
5. Heart Chakra: "Yam."
6. Crown Chakra: "Ah."
7. Third Eye Chakra: "Om."

When selecting a mantra, choose one that resonates with you. If you're not sure which mantra to use, try out a few and see which one has the most positive effect on your mood and energy levels.

Other Mantras

1. The Gayatri Mantra

The Gayatri Mantra is a powerful Hindu prayer traditionally used for healing. This mantra helps to enhance peace and harmony within and balances body and mind. When chanted with intention, it can help you connect with your higher power and find guidance in your life.

Mantra:

Om Bhur Bhuvah Svah (Aum Boor Buh-vah Ss-vah)

Tat Savitur Varenyam (Tut Sah-vee-toor Vah-ren-yum)

Bhargo Devasya Dhimahi (Bar-goh Day-vah-syah Dee-muh-hee)

Dhiyo Yo Nah Prachodayat (Dee-yoh Yoh Nuh Pray-cho-duh-yut)

Translation:

To get the most out of your mantra meditation, focus on the meaning of the words, not just the sound. To help you remember the mantra, here's a rough translation:

We meditate on the transcendental glory of that divine sun (Savitur),

Who imparts knowledge through the science of light (Gayatri),

May He inspire and enlighten our intellects (Dhiyo Yo Nah).

2. The Maha Mrityunjaya Mantra

The Maha Mrityunjaya Mantra is a Hindu prayer that promotes healing and protects against disease. This mantra is also known as the "Death Conquering" or "Great Death-Defying" mantra.

Mantra:

Om Tryambakam Yajamahe (Aum Tree-yahm-bah-kahm Yah-jah-mah-heh)

Sugandhim Pusti-vardhanam (Soo-gund-heem Pus-tee-var-dha-nahm)

Urvae Rukamiva Bandhanan (Oor-vay Roo-kah-mee-vah Buhn-dha-nahn)

Mrityor Muksheeya Maamritat (Muh-ree-tohr Mook-shee-yah Mah-muh-ree-tut)

Translation:

We worship the three-eyed (Tryambakam) Lord Shiva

Who is fragrant (Sugandhim) and nourishes all beings (Pusti-vardhanam),

And liberates from bondage (Bandhanan) like the cucumber (Rukamiva) from its vine (Urvae),

May He liberate us from death (Mrityor) for the sake of immortality (Muksheeya), just as (Maamritat) the ripe cucumber (Rukamiva) is freed from its bondage (Urvae).

3. The Om Namah Shivaya Mantra

This mantra is used to honor Lord Shiva, who is one of the main deities in Hinduism. The mantra translates to "I bow to Shiva," which promotes peace, patience, and self-control.

Mantra:

Om Namah Shivaya (Aum Nah-mah Shee-vah-yah)

Translation:

I bow to Shiva.

Mudras are a way to get into deeper meditation.
https://www.pexels.com/photo/woman-in-white-dress-holding-mans-hand-8710846/

4. Mudras

Mudras are hand and body gestures that form a symbolic seal. In Sanskrit, mudra means "seal" or "closure." Mudras are used in yoga and meditation to channel energy throughout the body, and they can be used alongside mantras. These gestures activate the flow of energy throughout your body and mind. They can help you concentrate, balance, and heal yourself and others. Mudras are a meaningful way to help you get into deeper meditation, and they can also help open your chakras. Each chakra has a specific mudra that opens and activates it. For example, the Gyan Mudra is said to help open the Third Eye Chakra.

Mudras are perfect to use when you meditate because they help you focus on the area of the body that's being manipulated by the mudra and the associated chakra. This will help you open up that specific chakra, helping it become balanced and harmonious.

Mudras are thought to help guide your energy flow so that you can direct it toward an intention or a focus. This can mean anything from opening specific chakras to bringing yourself into a more mindful state. While they're often associated with ancient Indian religions like Hinduism and Buddhism, mudras are becoming more popular in modern yoga practices.

Mudras are simple to perform and don't require special training or skills. You can use them while sitting down or standing up, and you don't need any fancy equipment (although using a meditation pillow or blanket can help).

How and When to Use Mudras

Mudras can be used at any time, but they're especially useful during meditation. To get the most out of your mudra practice, here are a few tips:

1. Choose a Comfortable Position

You can sit in a chair with your feet on the floor or sit cross-legged on the ground. You can also stand up or lie down. You just need to be comfortable to focus on your breath and the mudra. Make sure your spine is straight so that energy can flow freely up and down your body. It's also important to relax your shoulders and release any tension in your body.

2. Focus on Your Breath

Mudras are meant to help you focus your energy, so it's crucial to be aware of your breath. Inhale and exhale deeply and evenly. Your mind might wander, and if it does, focus on your breathing and slowly bring your mind back to the meditation. The goal is to clear your mind and focus on the present moment. When you're ready, you can begin your mudra practice.

3. Use a Mudra for a Specific Intent

Mudras can be used for specific purposes, such as opening a chakra or promoting healing. If you have a specific intention in mind, choose a mudra that aligns with that intention. For example, if you want to heal your heart, you may try the Anjali Mudra. If you're having trouble sleeping, you may try the Shunya Mudra. There are also mudras for more general purposes, such as increasing concentration or relaxation.

4. Hold the Mudra for 3-5 Minutes

Once you've chosen a mudra, take a few deep breaths and then begin. Hold the mudra for 3-5 minutes while focusing on your breath. You can increase the time as you get more comfortable with the mudra. Take a few deep breaths and release the mudra when you've finished.

You can then go about your day or continue with your meditation practice.

Mudras to Open the Crown Chakra

The following three mudras can be used to open the crown chakra:

1. Gyan Mudra (Mudra of Knowledge)

The Gyan Mudra is said to help open the Third Eye Chakra. It's often used during meditation and can also be used during yoga practice. First, find a comfortable place to sit and sit with your back straight to perform this meditation. Place the backs of your hands on your knees with palms open and facing upward. Bring your index finger and thumb together. Breathe in and out, focusing on your breath for the entire 3-5-minute duration.

Mudra of knowledge.
https://pixabay.com/images/id-6170664/

According to ancient texts, the Gyan Mudra increases concentration and memory. It can help with stress and tension. When your index finger and thumb touch, it activates the pressure point known as the Hoku spot. This spot is said to relieve stress. This mudra also releases serotonin, which is a neurotransmitter that's associated with happiness and well-being.

2. Shunya Mudra (Mudra of Emptiness)

The Shunya Mudra is said to open the crown chakra. It's often used to promote peace and relaxation. To perform this meditation, find a comfortable seat, and sit with a straight back. Place the backs of your hands on your knees with fingers pointing upward. Touch your middle finger to your thumb and keep the other fingers straight. Focus on your breath and hold the mudra for 3-5 minutes.

The Shunya Mudra is said to reduce stress, anxiety, and insomnia. It's also said to help with migraines and headaches. This mudra activates the pressure point known as the Neiguan point. This point is located on the inner wrist and is said to help relieve stress and anxiety.

3. Sahasrara Mudra (Mudra of a Thousand Petals)

The Sahasrara Mudra is said to help open the crown chakra. It's often used during meditation and can also be used during yoga practice. Sit in a comfortable position with your back straight and relaxed to perform this meditation. Place the backs of your hands on your knees, bring your thumbs and index fingers together to point upward in triangular shapes, and point your other fingers upward too. Focus on your breath and hold the mudra for 3-5 minutes.

The Sahasrara Mudra is said to promote concentration and memory. A useful meditation for managing stress and anxiety. When your index fingers and thumbs touch, it activates the pressure point known as the Ajna point. This point is located between the eyebrows and is said to help relieve stress and anxiety.

Many other mudras can be used to open the crown chakra. Experiment with different mudras and see which ones work for you. If you're new to mudras, it's best to start with the simpler mudras and work your way up to the more complex ones. Learn as much as you can about each mudra before you try it. This will help you get the most out of your practice.

Mantras and mudras are two powerful tools that can be used to open the crown chakra. You can balance and heal this energy center by repeating a mantra and performing a mudra. Start with the mantras and mudras mentioned in this chapter and see how they affect you. Remember to be patient and to be kind to yourself. The crown chakra is a delicate energy center, and it can take time to open up. With regular practice, you'll eventually be able to open your crown chakra and experience the blissful state of enlightenment.

Chapter 5: Meditation and Visualization

"The mind is everything. What you think, you become." - Buddha

While mantras and mudras cleanse and balance the chakras, meditation and visualization will ultimately still the mind and provide a sense of inner peace. These are two powerful tools you can use to improve your mental, emotional, and physical health. Science has shown that training your mind to focus on specific images, thoughts, emotions, or feelings can reduce stress, increase energy levels, help you get better sleep, boost your immune system, and more.

Meditating.
https://pixabay.com/images/id-1851165/

This chapter will talk about how to meditate and practice visualization to strengthen your crown chakra. First, we'll cover these practices and why they're so effective. Then we'll go over some tips on meditating and visualizing like a pro. Finally, we'll give you some guided exercises you can use to get started with meditation and visualization for the crown chakra!

Defining Meditation and Visualization

Meditation and visualization are different ways of reaching an altered state of consciousness, and they can work together to help you achieve your goals. They both share a common goal: to help you focus your thoughts or energy on a specific aspect of your life. The differences? Visualization is typically used as a tool for mental exercise, whereas meditation is more about focusing *inward.*

Meditation is easy to learn and hard to master, but there are numerous benefits when you start to master it. The practice will help you live more in the moment and let go of your worries. During meditation, you can use visualization to focus your thoughts on a specific image, goal, or intention. When you visualize, you create a mental picture of what you want to achieve. This can be anything from feeling calmer and relaxed to increasing your wealth or improving your health.

At its core, meditation is the practice of being still, both physically and mentally. We're so used to constant motion and thinking that meditation can feel strange at first. But that feeling of discomfort comes from a place of resistance – our minds will resist the quiet, and our bodies will resist the stillness. The more we practice, the more comfortable we become.

Visualization is a technique that involves using our imagination to create mental images of things we wish to experience or have in our lives. When we visualize something, it becomes much more tangible than an abstract idea. It's easier to believe it's possible because we can "see" it happening in our minds. So, when we want to achieve something like growing our hair or improving our posture, visualization can make it much easier for us to stay motivated and focused on reaching that goal.

The Benefits of Meditation and Visualization

In today's society, people are constantly moving from one day to the next, from one sense-based experience to the next. They're often so mentally exhausted from just trying to make it through each day that they can't stop talking about how they want to take a break from constantly moving through life.

While there are many things we can do to reduce our stress and anxiety, meditation is a proven method that has been used for centuries to help us slow down and enter a deeper level of awareness. When we meditate, we focus on our breath and the present moment, which calms the mind and allows us to feel more relaxed.

Meditation and visualization have countless benefits. Here are just a few of the ways these practices can improve your life:

1. Improve Self-Awareness

Meditation and visualization help us focus on the present moment, which can improve our self-awareness. We can better manage our thoughts and emotions when we're more aware of them. We can also become more aware of our triggers and how to avoid them. The more we meditate, the more in control we feel of our lives.

2. Reduce Stress and Anxiety

Stress and anxiety are two of the most common mental health issues people face today. Meditation has been shown to effectively reduce stress and anxiety by slowing down the heart rate and promoting a state of relaxation. When we're less stressed, we're better focused on our goals and more likely to achieve them. Visualization also reduces stress by allowing us to focus on a positive image or outcome.

3. Improve Sleep

Meditation and visualization can also improve sleep. When we're stressed, our bodies are in a constant state of "fight or flight." This means that our bodies prepare for danger, even when there isn't any. This can make it difficult to fall and stay asleep. Meditation calms both the mind and body, which allows us to fall asleep and stay in a deep sleep state.

4. Boost Immunity

Meditation and visualization have also been shown to boost immunity. When we're stressed, our bodies produce more of the stress hormone cortisol. This can weaken our immune system and make us more susceptible to illness. The relaxation response, which is the opposite of the stress response, boosts immunity by reducing cortisol levels.

5. Accessible Anywhere

You can meditate and visualize anywhere, at any time. You can meditate in your clothing (as long as it is comfortable), and there is no additional equipment needed. It's great for people who have busy schedules or who travel often. All you need is a couple of minutes a day. When implementing these practices into your life, the sky's the limit. You can do it on your own or with the help of a guided meditation or visualization app.

6. Improve Concentration and Focus

Meditation and visualization also improve concentration and focus. When we're constantly multitasking, our brains become overloaded, and we have trouble focusing on one thing. Meditation helps us focus on one thing at a time and clear our minds of distractions. This allows us to be more productive and efficient in our work.

7. Increase Creativity

Meditation and visualization can also increase creativity. When we're constantly thinking about the past or worrying about the future, we're not present in the moment. This prevents us from thinking creatively. When we meditate, we allow our minds to wander and explore new ideas. This can lead to more creative solutions to problems.

8. Improve Emotional Health

Meditation and visualization can also improve emotional health. When we're constantly thinking about negative experiences, it can lead to depression and anxiety. Meditation helps us focus on the present moment and appreciate the good in our lives. This can improve our mood and help us cope with difficult emotions.

9. Connects Us with Our Spiritual Side

For many people, meditation and visualization are also ways to connect with their spiritual side. When we quieten our minds, we can access a deeper level of consciousness. This can help us connect with our higher selves and experience a sense of peace and calm. The spiritual connection we experience can improve our physical and mental health.

10. It's Free

Meditation and visualization are free. You don't need to spend any money to get started. Comfort is key, and as long as you are seated or lying comfortably, there is no cost involved. Regardless of how you choose to meditate or visualize, the important thing is that you do it.

The benefits of meditation and visualization are vast and far-reaching. If you're looking for a way to improve your health and well-being, these practices are a great place to start. Remember, the key to success is consistency. The more you meditate and visualize, the better the results will be. So, find a quiet place to sit or lie down, close your eyes, and let the healing begin.

How to Get Started with Meditation and Visualization

If you're new to meditation and visualization, it can all feel a little overwhelming at first. It's hard, for example, to know where to start. Should you focus on your breathing? On repeating a mantra? Or on applying the techniques you've learned from past meditative experiences? And once you have that figured out, how should you mentally prepare yourself for the experience? What expectations should you set? How can you stay focused and present while traveling through your mind?

Meditation and visualization are essential practices to help you gain control of your mind and emotions. To get started, create a meditation area in your home. It should be clean, quiet, and uncluttered. Find a comfortable chair or cushion where you can settle in for ten to twenty minutes.

If you're using a chair, sit upright with a slight curve in the spine. If using a cushion, make sure your hips are higher than your knees, which allows for better circulation in the legs. Sit with your hands resting on your lap or the arms of the chair. If you prefer, you may close your eyes, but it's also okay to keep them open and focus on an object or candle flame.

Now that you've settled in, begin by taking several slow and deep breaths through the nose. Take a deep breath in through your nose, and exhale out your mouth. Repeat this until you feel relaxed and ready to begin meditating.

If thoughts arise during meditation, don't try to push them away; instead, acknowledge them with acceptance and then let them go by refocusing on your breathing or whatever object you have in front of you. Practice this several times per week and watch how your life transforms.

Here are a few tips to help you get started:

1. Start with the Basics

When you're first starting, it's crucial to keep things simple. Focus on your breath and on repeating a mantra. Once you have the hang of it, you can start to experiment with other techniques. Find a quiet space where you won't be disturbed. Grab a blanket or mat you can sit on if that makes it more comfortable for you.

2. Set an Intention

Before you begin, it's a good idea to set an intention for your practice. This can be something as simple as wanting to relax or wanting to connect with your higher self. When you have an intention, it gives you something to focus on while meditating. It also keeps you motivated when things get tough.

3. Don't Force It

Meditation is the practice of letting go. If you try to force it, you'll only feel frustrated. So let go of any expectations you have and simply be present at the moment. Accept whatever comes up without judgment. Your mind might wander, but be conscious of it and slowly bring it back to the meditation. Being gentle and patient with yourself is key here.

4. Practice Every Day

The more you meditate, the better the results will be. Set aside time each day to sit down and meditate. The more consistent you are, the easier it will be to quiet your mind and enter a state of deeper consciousness.

5. Join a Meditation Group

If you're having trouble getting started, consider joining a meditation group. There's nothing like the support of others to help you stay motivated and on track. You can find groups in your local community or online. The important thing is to find a group that feels right for you.

The process is simple, but it does need practice. The more you practice, the better the results will be. So, find a quiet place to sit or lie down, close your eyes, and let the healing begin.

Guided Meditation and Visualization Exercises for the Crown Chakra

1. The Inner Light

Close your eyes and imagine a tiny point of light floating in front of you. Slowly move your gaze toward the light until it fills your entire field of vision. Then, focus on a spot behind the light, as far away from you as possible, and watch it slowly drift backward until you can no longer see it. This exercise will help open your crown chakra.

2. The White Light

Imagine a column of white light descending from the sky and entering through the top of your head. Feel the light moving down your spine and into your root chakra. Then, visualize the light moving up through your chakras, one by one, until it reaches your crown chakra. Allow the light to fill your entire being, cleansing and purifying as it goes.

3. The Lotus Flower

Visualize a lotus flower blooming at the top of your head. Feel the petals opening and the light of the sun shining down on you. Breathe in the fresh, clean air and feel the tension leaving your body. As you exhale, let go of all your worries and concerns. Allow yourself to drift off into a state of blissful relaxation.

4. The Crystal Palace

Imagine yourself inside a beautiful crystal palace. You are surrounded by sparkling walls of amethyst, rose quartz, and selenite. Feel the peaceful energy of the crystals soothing and calming your mind and body. In the center of the room is a throne made of pure diamond. Sit on the throne and feel the power of the crystals flow through you.

5. The Stargate

Visualize a giant stargate opening up above you. Through the gate, you see a brilliant white light. Step into the light and feel yourself being drawn upward toward the stars. As you travel higher and higher, you leave your body behind and enter a state of pure consciousness. You are one with the universe, connected to all that is.

These are just a few of the many meditation and visualization exercises you can do to balance your crown chakra. You'll know the one that works best for you when you find it, so be sure to try many for the best results.

Meditation Practices When Commuting

If you have a long commute, you can use that time to meditate. Here are a few ideas to get you started:

1. Listen to Guided Meditations

Many guided meditations are available online and on apps like iTunes and Spotify. Find one you like and press play. Close your eyes and follow along. Depending on the length of your commute, you may not be able to finish the entire thing, but that's okay. The important thing is to take a few minutes to relax and de-stress.

2. Repeat a Mantra

Choose a short, simple mantra you can easily remember. Close your eyes and repeat it over and over. Focus on the sound of your voice and the feeling of the words vibrating in your body.

3. Visualize Your Ideal Commute

If your commute is usually stressful, use visualization to create your ideal commute. Close your eyes and imagine yourself driving or taking public transportation without any traffic or delays. Visualize yourself arriving at your destination feeling calm and relaxed.

4. Practice Deep Breathing

One of the quickest and easiest ways to reduce stress is taking deep breaths. Close your eyes and inhale slowly through your nose, letting your stomach expand. Then, exhale slowly through your mouth. Repeat this several times. You can also count to four as you inhale and exhale.

5. Listen to Relaxing Music

If you don't want to meditate, you can still use your commute to relax by listening to some calming music. Choose slow, relaxing, and instrumental songs. This will help quiet your mind and ease you into a more relaxed state. The key is to find the music you enjoy that doesn't distract you from your drive; if you're driving, that is.

By taking just a few minutes out of your day to meditate, you can reduce your stress and improve your overall well-being. So, the next time you're stuck in traffic, use that time to your advantage and try one of these meditation techniques.

Tips for Successful Meditation and Visualization

1. Get Comfortable

The first step to successful meditation and visualization is to get comfortable. Sit comfortably or lie down in a relaxing position. Try to eliminate or at least decrease any distractions from your environment, such as noise or bright lights. Be sure that there are no interruptions around you.

2. Breathe Deeply

Once you're comfortable, take a few deep breaths and allow your body to relax. Allow your eyes to close, and focus on breathing in and out. Feel the air fill your lungs and then slowly release it. Repeat this process for a few minutes until you feel your body loosening up.

3. Set a Purpose

Before you begin your visualization, take a moment to set an intention. What do you hope to achieve from this session? Are you looking to reduce stress, increase creativity, or heal a specific wound? Keep your intention in mind as you progress through your visualization.

4. Be Patient

It takes time and practice to master the art of meditation and visualization. Don't get discouraged if you don't see results immediately. Don't get discouraged if it does not work straight away – it takes time. The benefits will come, so try to enjoy the process and see it as its own reward.

5. Keep a Journal

One of the best ways to track your progress is to keep a journal. Every time you meditate or visualize, make a note of what you did and how you felt afterward. Over time, you'll be able to look back and see how far you've come. It's also a great way to keep track of your goals and intentions.

Meditation and visualization are powerful tools that can be used to improve your overall well-being. The benefits of balancing and opening your crown chakra include spiritual growth. You'll find you have a deeper connection with life and nature, a feeling of calm, clarity of thought, greater intuition, and a sense of purpose. With regular practice, you can achieve a greater sense of balance and harmony in your life.

By taking a few minutes out of your day to practice meditation and visualization, you can reduce stress, improve your mental and emotional state, and achieve a greater sense of balance in your life. Give it a try and see how it can help you on your journey to wellness.

Chapter 6: Pranayama and Yoga

Pranayama is a practice that uses breathing to control the life force energy or prana. The breath is the link between the body and the mind. It is an aspect of our physiology that we can control, and it also has a strong connection with our emotions. Breathwork can bring calmness and quiet to busy minds, but it can also stimulate us when we need more energy. On a physical level, it oxygenates the tissues, increasing vitality.

Like meditation, breathing is a powerful tool to focus the mind and connect with our higher selves. This chapter will focus on pranayama and yoga for the crown chakra. It will include controlled breathing exercises (pranayama) and yoga poses (asanas). We'll also discuss the benefits of yoga and how it can balance the crown chakra.

Defining Pranayama

Pranayama is the yoga practice of controlled breathing. It is one of the eight limbs of yoga, a system developed by an ancient sage named Patanjali that is meant to guide practitioners toward enlightenment. The word is derived from two Sanskrit words; "prana," meaning life force or vital energy, and "Yama," meaning control. In yoga, pranayama is used as a way to harness your energetic flow and ultimately help you connect with your higher self.

The practice of Pranayama encompasses many different methods of breathing, with each one having its particular focus. For example, some types of Pranayama are meant to cleanse the body and mind, while others are used in meditation to help you achieve a state of deep relaxation.

Pranayama is the practice of controlling and managing your breath through various techniques and exercises. The goal is to help you become more aware of how you breathe, how it affects your state of mind, and the overall quality of your life. Pranayama isn't limited to one specific religion or spiritual path; it's open to anyone who wants to learn how to manage their breathing and improve their sense of well-being.

There are many types of pranayama exercises, each with its benefits. Some focus on balancing the energy in your body by opening up your energy channels (known as nadis), while others focus on getting rid of toxins in your system by helping you eliminate carbon dioxide from your lungs.

Controlled Breathing

To practice pranayama, you need to first understand how to control your breath. You can count your breaths as you breathe in and out, counting the whole breath or each half of it – this gives your mind a focus and a distraction. You can also count the time – breathe in and count to five as you do, taking the breath for the entire duration. Then, breathe out and count to five, allowing the exhale to last as long as the inhale. You can repeat this cycle as many times as you like, for as long as you like.

As you become more comfortable with the practice, you can experiment with different ratios of inhales to exhales. For example, you can inhale for a count of four and exhale for a count of eight. Or you can inhale for a count of six and exhale for a count of twelve. There are no right or wrong ratios. Feel free to play around and see what feels best for you.

In addition to counting your breaths, you can also focus on the quality of your breath. Take your time. Fill your lungs with as much air as possible, and then exhale until your stomach is completely flat. The goal is to eventually be able to control your breath without having to count. This can take some time, so be patient and don't expect to master it overnight. The more you practice, the better you'll become at it.

Importance of Pranayama

Pranayama is important because it helps us control our breath, which helps us control our mind. When we're stressed, our breathing becomes shallow and fast, exacerbating the stress response. By learning how to control our breath, we can learn how to control our minds.

Pranayama has many benefits, both physical and mental. Physically, it can improve our respiratory function, increase our lung capacity, and strengthen our immune system. Mentally, it can reduce stress and anxiety, improve our focus and concentration, and promote feelings of calmness and relaxation.

Pranayama is also said to be beneficial for the chakras. Each chakra is associated with a certain element, and by working with the breath, we can balance the energy in each chakra. The crown chakra, for example, is associated with the element of aether. Aether is the most subtle of all the elements, and it's said to be the link between our physical bodies and the cosmos. Balancing the energy in our crown chakras promotes a sense of connection with the universe.

Pranayama for the Crown Chakra

Understanding the seven chakras can help you understand where you should focus your pranayama practices for different results – the crown chakra deals with our understanding of spirituality and connectedness. Like a crown, the crown chakra is located at the top of the head. The crown chakra is associated with thought, enlightenment, wisdom, and more.

When this chakra is open and balanced, we feel complete both within ourselves and in our connection with everything around us. If this chakra is blocked or unbalanced, we may feel disconnected from our spirituality or like we're not living up to our potential.

There are three pranayama techniques we can use to balance and open our crown chakra:

Nadi Shodhan (Alternate Nostril Breathing)

Nadi Shodhan focuses on our breathing and the flow of breath. It's said to help balance the energy in the body and promote a sense of calm. The Word "Nadi" means "channel" in Sanskrit, and "Shodhan" means "purification." This technique is said to purify the energy channels in the body, thus promoting balance and harmony.

To utilize this technique, ensure that you are seated comfortably with a straight back. Take your right thumb and press and hold the side of your right nostril, closing the air passage. Inhale and exhale through the open left nostril. Count fifteen breaths in and out before you alternate to the other nostril.

Brahmari (Humming Bee Breath)

Brahmari is a pranayama technique that involves making a "buzzing" sound with your throat as you breathe. The word "Brahmari" comes from the Sanskrit word "Brahma," which means "creator." This technique is said to help us connect with our creative energy and promote feelings of calm and peace. Great for relieving stress and tension.

To practice Brahmari, first sit in a comfortable position with your back straight. Place your hands on your knees, close your eyes, and take a few deep breaths. As you exhale, make a "buzz" sound with your throat. You can also place your fingers over your ears to amplify the sound. Continue for 10-15 breaths.

Ujjayi (Victorious Breath)

Ujjayi is a pranayama technique that involves partially constricting your throat to control the flow of breath. It's said to promote relaxation and reduce stress. The word "Ujjayi" comes from the Sanskrit word "Uj," which means "to conquer." This technique is said to help us conquer our fears and doubts and promote feelings of courage and strength.

For best results, find a comfortable seated position and sit with a straight spine. Place your hands on your knees, close your eyes, and take a few deep breaths. As you exhale, partially constrict your throat to make a "ha" sound. The air will naturally flow through your constricted throat when you inhale, making a soft "hissing" sound. Continue for 10-15 breaths.

Defining Yoga

Yoga is a practice of physical and mental exercises that originated in India. Although it began as a spiritual practice, today, it's typically associated with yoga poses or asanas. Yoga has been shown to have many health benefits, including increased flexibility and strength, better breathing, relaxation, and even improved sleep.

Yoga is an ancient meditation practice, breathing exercises, and physical stretching. The word "yoga" comes from the Sanskrit root word "Yuj," which means "to yoke" or "to unite." The goal of yoga is to connect your body and mind so that you can experience the union between them.

Yoga was originally developed as a science and philosophy to help us better understand our place in the world and how to live in harmony with ourselves and others and the world around us. It is an ancient practice that can help us achieve a balance between the body and mind, leading to better health, peace of mind, and overall happiness.

Benefits of Yoga for the Crown Chakra

Opening the crown chakra is a sure way to rise above the challenges and stresses of everyday life. For yogis, the physical poses of yoga are just the beginning. To truly maximize your benefits from practicing yoga, you also need to consider the chakra system. When combined with yoga poses and proper breathing techniques, the crown chakra, or Sahasrara, can offer some amazing benefits.

Here are some benefits of practicing yoga for the crown chakra:

1. Improves Focus and Concentration

Yoga improves focus and concentration by teaching you how to control your breath. When you can control your breath, you can better control your thoughts. This is because your thoughts and emotions are directly linked to your breath. If you're feeling anxious or stressed, your breath will be shallow and fast. But if you're feeling calm and relaxed, your breath will be slow and deep.

2. Reduces Stress and Anxiety

The feeling of calm and peace that comes with yoga can reduce stress and anxiety. Yoga clears your mind of negative thoughts and allows you to focus on the present moment. This can reduce stress and anxiety because you're not worrying about the future or dwelling on the past. Staying in the moment can eliminate most of the stress and anxiety from your life.

3. Increases Energy Levels

Practicing yoga can increase your energy levels by increasing circulation and improving the function of your respiratory system. When your body breathes more efficiently, it can get more oxygen to your cells. This can improve your overall energy levels and make you feel more alert and awake. Breathing consciously and deeply through yoga can also calm your nervous system, leading to increased energy levels.

4. Improves Sleep Quality

If you're struggling with insomnia or poor sleep quality, yoga can help. The deep breathing exercises that are a part of yoga can help relax your body and mind, leading to better sleep. Yoga can also increase your energy levels during the day, leading to improved sleep at night.

According to Sadhguru, an Indian spiritual teacher, "If you are tired during the day, sleep will come more easily at night."

5. Boosts Immunity

Yoga can boost your immunity by increasing circulation and improving the function of your respiratory system. When your body breathes more efficiently, it can get more oxygen to your cells. This can improve your overall health and immunity. Most importantly, yoga can reduce stress, a major contributor to mental and physical illnesses.

6. Increases Flexibility

Yoga increases flexibility by stretching and lengthening your muscles. This can improve your range of motion and make your joints and muscles more flexible. Flexibility is important for overall health because it reduces the risk of injuries. The more flexible your body is, the less likely you are to injure yourself.

7. Improves Balance

Yoga improves your balance by strengthening your core muscles. Stronger core muscles stabilize your body and keep you upright. This is especially important as you age when your risk of falling increases. Improving your balance can help you stay active and independent as you grow older. Many yoga poses require you to stabilize your body, which can help to improve your overall sense of balance.

Asanas (Yoga Poses) for the Crown Chakra

Several yoga poses can help you re-align the crown chakra and lead you to a place of peace. This section will explore some of the most effective poses for this chakra and step-by-step instructions on doing them correctly.

1. Sirsasana (Headstand)

Known as the "King of all Asanas," Sirsasana is an inversion pose that improves circulation and increases blood flow to the brain. It also calms the mind and relieves stress and anxiety. This pose is so effective for the crown chakra because your head is below your heart when you're upside down. This improves circulation and gets more oxygen to your brain.

Headstand pose.
https://www.pexels.com/photo/flexible-barefoot-woman-performing-yoga-exercise-on-green-field-4127305/

Step-by-Step Instructions:

1. Start in a tabletop position with your hands and knees on the ground.

2. Place your forearms on the ground and interlace your fingers.

3. Place the top of your head on the ground in front of your hands.

4. Slowly walk your feet toward your head.

5. Once your feet are close enough, slowly straighten your legs and lift your hips toward the sky.

6. Hold the pose for as long as possible once you're in an inverted "V" position.

7. Slowly bend your knees and lower your hips toward the ground to exit the pose.

8. With your feet planted on the ground, come back into a tabletop position.

2. Padmasana (Lotus Pose)

Lotus pose.

Bryan Helfrich, Alias52, CC BY-SA 3.0 https://creativecommons.org/licenses/by-sa/3.0, *via Wikimedia Commons:* https://commons.wikimedia.org/wiki/File:Lotus_position.svg

Padmasana is a sitting pose that improves circulation and digestion. It also promotes relaxation and peace of mind. This pose is so effective for the crown chakra because it opens up the hips and lower back, which can release any blockages in those areas. The release of these blockages can improve circulation and increase blood flow to the brain.

Step-by-Step Instructions:

1. Start in a sitting position with your legs extended in front of you.

2. Bring your right foot up until the bottom of your foot is rested against your left thigh.

3. Repeat the same action with your left foot, resting it against your right thigh.

4. Place the backs of your hands on your lap, palms facing upward

5. Allow your eyes to close and take three deep breaths, in and out.

6. To exit the pose, slowly release your legs and come back into a sitting position with your legs extended in front of you.

3. Vriksasana (Tree Pose)

Tree pose.
https://www.pexels.com/photo/serious-woman-doing-yoga-in-white-studio-6311499/

Vriksasana is a standing pose that improves balance and coordination. It also strengthens the legs and feet. This pose is so effective for the crown chakra because it opens up the hips and lower back, which can release any blockages in the lower chakras. When these blockages are released, they can help increase blood flow to the brain and improve overall circulation.

Step-by-Step Instructions:

1. Start in a standing position with your feet together.

2. Shift your weight onto your left foot and place your right foot on your left ankle, calf, or thigh.

3. Place your hands in a prayer position in front of your chest.

4. Focus your gaze on a point before you and take several deep breaths.

5. To exit the pose, slowly release your right foot and come back into a standing position with your feet together.

4. Sarvangasana (Shoulder Stand)

Shoulder stand.

Mr. Yoga, CC BY-SA 4.0 https://creativecommons.org/licenses/by-sa/4.0, via Wikimedia Commons: https://commons.wikimedia.org/wiki/File:Mr-yoga-unsupported-shoulderstand.jpg

Sarvangasana is an inversion pose that improves circulation and increases blood flow to the brain. It also calms the mind and relieves stress and anxiety. This pose is so effective for the crown chakra because when you're upside down, your head is below your heart. This improves circulation and gets more oxygen to your brain.

Step-by-Step Instructions:

1. Start by lying on your back with your legs extended in front of you.
2. Place your hands on your lower back with your palms facing down.
3. Use your hands to help lift your legs and hips off the ground.
4. Once your hips and legs are in the air, continue to lift your torso and head off the ground.
5. Place your hands on your lower back with your palms facing up.
6. Hold the pose for as long as you can.
7. To exit the pose, slowly lower your hips and legs to the ground.
8. Use your hands to help lower your torso and head to the ground.

Yoga Isn't Just Asanas

While asanas are an integral part of yoga, they are not the only component. To fully reap the benefits of yoga, you must also practice pranayama (controlled breathing) and meditation. The information provided throughout this guide will help you understand and incorporate these practices into your own life. These practices and recommended routines can be intertwined with your asana practice or done independently.

For example, meditation and pranayama can be done while you're in a seated position, lying down, or even walking. You can chant your mantra when you're in the Padmasana (Lotus Pose) or choose to meditate. Asanas can be done in a group setting or individually. You can attend a yoga class, or you can practice at home.

Chanting the Om sound is a form of meditation that helps focus the mind and connect with the Divine. It can be combined with asanas, pranayama, or done on its own. There is no right or wrong way to meditate – the best way to meditate is to find what works for you. The important thing is that you find a practice that works for you and that you stick with it.

Pranayama, yoga, and meditation are excellent practices for the crown chakra. They improve circulation, increase blood flow to the brain, and calm the mind. When combined, these practices can open up the crown chakra and allow for a greater connection with the Divine. The breathing techniques and yoga pose for the crown chakra can be done on their own or combined with other practices. The important thing is that you find a routine that works for you and that you stick with it.

Chapter 7: Using Crystals and Stones

Crystals.
https://unsplash.com/photos/5IvyH1qk-JQ

Sahasrara is our gateway to all universal energy, spirit, and consciousness. This chakra can be difficult to heal because it's hard to know when it's out of balance. After all, the symptoms are subtle. But by using crystals or stones that correspond to Sahasrara, you can bring your Crown chakra back into balance.

Over the years, crystals and stones have become increasingly popular for all kinds of uses, from jewelry to decor, and you've probably seen them around a lot. However, there's also a growing interest in using these healing stones for their metaphysical properties, like balancing your seven chakras.

People often use the words "crystals" and "stones" interchangeably, but they refer to two different things. This chapter will introduce you to the world of crystals and stones, explaining how they can be used to balance your chakras and some of the best stones for Sahasrara.

Crystals and Stones

Crystals are minerals that have been formed over millions of years by geological processes. They have a regular, repeating atomic structure that gives them their unique shape. Crystals are often used to balance the Crown chakra. Different stones are known to vibrate at different frequencies, and these vibrations can balance your energy centers. Some stones are also aligned with certain elements, which can help you work with them on an elemental level as well.

According to metaphysical beliefs, each type of crystal has its unique properties that can be used for healing. Whether you're looking to balance your chakras or manifest your dreams, a crystal out there can help. The best way to figure out which crystals are right for you is to follow your intuition. There are no "right" or "wrong" crystals, so go with your gut and see what resonates the most with you.

When it comes to working with chakras, each chakra is associated with a different color. Violet is associated with the crown chakra, so if you are looking for accessories and want to focus on your crown chakra, look for violet accessories. Or you might look for a crystal with properties that correspond to the Crown chakra, like intuition or spiritual connection.

How Crystals Can Help Balance the Crown Chakra

The crown chakra is our connection to the Divine, and it is often seen as the most spiritual of all the chakras. Crystals can be used to balance the Crown chakra by opening and expanding our awareness. Amethyst, clear quartz, and selenite work well. These crystals can be used in meditation or worn as jewelry to keep the crown chakra in balance.

While the crown chakra is often seen as the most spiritual of the chakras, it is also the most fragile. This chakra can easily become imbalanced, leading to feelings of disconnection and disorientation. Wearing a crown chakra crystal can protect this energy center and keep it balanced. However, there's a difference between stones and crystals, and not all stones are appropriate for the crown chakra.

The Difference between Stones and Crystals

Stones are rocks that have been broken down over time by weathering and erosion. They don't have the same regular atomic structure as crystals, so they don't have the same geometrical shape. Stones are often more opaque than crystals, and they tend to be less shiny.

While stones and crystals are beautiful and have their unique properties, they are not the same. Stones are more commonly used in jewelry, while crystals are more commonly used for their metaphysical properties. The type of stone or crystal you use is up to you, but it's important to be clear on the difference between the two.

For the crown chakra, you want to use stones and crystals that have properties that correspond to the chakra. Amethyst, clear quartz, and selenite can open and expand your awareness, and they can also protect this energy center. Many other stones and crystals can be used for the crown chakra, so follow your intuition and see what resonates with you.

Choosing a Stone or Crystal

When it comes to choosing a stone or crystal for the Crown chakra, here are a few things to keep in mind:

1. The Color

The Crown chakra is associated with the color violet, so you might want to look for a violet stone or crystal. For example, amethyst is a violet stone often used to balance the crown chakra. However, you can also choose a stone or crystal with properties corresponding to the crown chakra, like intuition or spiritual connection. These include crystals like Celestite, Lapis Lazuli, and Turquoise.

2. The Shape

The shape of the stone or crystal can also be important. Some people believe that certain shapes have different energies and can be used to balance the chakras. For example, crystals like amethyst and quartz come in various shapes, including points, clusters, and geodes. You can also find stones and crystals in the shape of a pyramid or obelisk. These shapes are often used to focus energy on meditation.

3. The Size

The size of the stone or crystal also plays a role in its energy. Smaller stones and crystals are often used for meditation, while larger stones and crystals can be used in the home or office. If you're not sure what size to get, it's always best to err on the side of caution and go with a smaller stone or crystal. Choose a size that feels right for you. When in doubt, go with your intuition.

4. The Quality

The cut and polish of the stone or crystal are also significant factors. You want to make sure you're getting a high-quality stone or crystal when it comes to crystals. This means that the stone or crystal should be free of any nicks, scratches, or damage. A well-cut and polished stone or crystal will have a high vibration, which can be beneficial for the crown chakra. However, spending a lot of money on a stone or crystal is unnecessary. You can find high-quality stones and crystals at your local gem show, crystal shop, or online.

5. The Energy

Each stone and crystal have its unique energy, which can help balance the chakras. For example, amethyst is a stone that has a high vibration and can be used to open the third eye chakra. It's also a stone that is associated with the element of water, which can help balance emotions. If you're not sure what type of energy you need, it's always best to consult with a professional.

Crystals and Stones for the Crown Chakra

Now that you know what to look for, here are some suggested stones and crystals for the crown chakra:

1. Amethyst

Properties: Intuition, Protection, Spiritual Connection

Amethyst is a violet stone often used to balance the crown chakra. It's a stone with a high vibration and can be used to open the third eye chakra. Amethyst helps with headaches and migraines. It also promotes peace, tranquility, and protection from negative energy.

Why It Works: Amethyst is a stone that can open and expand your awareness. It's also a stone associated with the element of water, which can balance emotions.

How to Use It: Amethyst can be placed on the forehead during meditation. Some people also like to wear amethyst jewelry, like a necklace or earrings. It can be worn as jewelry, placed in your home or office, or used in meditation.

2. Celestite

Properties: Clarity, Communication, Divine Connection

Celestite is a blue stone that is often used to balance the crown chakra. It's a stone that may assist you in opening and broadening your cognition. Celestite is a stone associated with the element of air, which can help to promote communication. It eases the pain of migraines and headaches. The Celestite crystal can also be used to cleanse and purify your energy field.

Why It Works: According to crystal experts, Celestite exhibits a very high vibration – making it perfect for prayer and meditation. This stone can help you connect with the Divine. The presence of Celestite can create a sense of peace and calm.

How to Use It: If you're looking for a stone to help with meditation, Celestite is an excellent choice. This stone can also be worn as jewelry, placed in your home or office, or used in meditation. Some people also like to keep a piece of Celestite in their pocket or purse. It can also be placed on the forehead during meditation.

3. Clear Quartz

Properties: Clarity, Manifestation, Amplification

Clear quartz is a white or colorless stone often used to balance the crown chakra. Clear quartz is a stone that can be used for a variety of purposes, including healing, manifestation, and protection. Clear quartz is also a stone associated with the element of fire, which can promote motivation.

Why It Works: Clear quartz has a very high vibration. It's also a stone that is known for its ability to amplify the energy of other stones and crystals. This makes it an excellent choice for meditation and prayer.

How to Use It: Clear quartz can be used in various ways, including meditation, jewelry, and home decor. Since it balances all chakras, it's a good stone to use during a chakra balancing meditation. You can also wear clear quartz jewelry, like a necklace or earrings.

4. Fluorite

Properties: Clarity, Intuition, Protection

Fluorite is a green or purple stone that is often used to balance the Crown chakra. Fluorite is associated with the element of air, which can promote communication. When used in crystal healing, it's said to calm the mind and help with focus. With its high vibration, Fluorite is also said to be a stone of protection.

Why It Works: Fluorite is known for calming the mind and promoting focus. It's also a stone that is said to be helpful for those who are easily distracted. The high vibration of Fluorite can also protect you from negative energy.

How to Use It: Fluorite is a great stone to use during meditation. Many people like to wear Fluorite jewelry, like a necklace or earrings. It can also be placed in your home or office.

5. Selenite

Properties: Clarity, Protection, Divine Connection

Selenite is a white or colorless stone that is often used to balance the Crown chakra. Selenite is associated with the element of water, which can promote emotional balance. It's a stone said to be helpful for those seeking clarity. Selenite is known for its ability to cleanse and purify your energy field.

Why It Works: Selenite has a very high vibration. It's also helpful for those seeking clarity. The presence of Selenite can also create a sense of peace and calm.

How to Use It: To get the most out of Selenite, it's best to use it during meditation. While Selenite can be placed in your home or office, keeping it away from moisture is important. Selenite is a delicate stone, and it can easily sustain damage. When meditating with Selenite, you can hold it in your hand or place it on your forehead.

6. Moonstone

Properties: Emotional Balance, Feminine Energy, Intuition

Moonstone is a white or colorless stone that is often used to balance the Crown chakra. Moonstone is associated with feminine energy and the element of water. It's helpful for those seeking emotional balance. Moonstone is known for its ability to promote intuition and psychic abilities.

Why It Works: Moonstone is known for its emotional balance and intuition properties. It's also helpful for those seeking to connect with their feminine energy. Moonstone is said to be helpful for psychic abilities because it's associated with the moon.

How to Use It: Moonstone can be used in a variety of ways, including meditation, jewelry, and home decor. Moonstone is a great stone to use during meditation or prayer. You can also wear Moonstone jewelry, like a necklace or earrings.

7. Lapis Lazuli

Properties: Inner Wisdom, Truth, Royalty

Lapis lazuli is a blue stone that is often used to balance the Crown chakra. Lapis lazuli is associated with the element of water and the planet Venus. It's helpful for those seeking inner wisdom. Lapis lazuli is known for its ability to promote self-awareness and help you access your higher self.

Why It Works: Lapis lazuli is known for its properties of inner wisdom and truth. It's helpful for those seeking to connect with their higher self. The blue color of Lapis lazuli promotes peace and calm.

How to Use It: Lapis lazuli is a great stone to use for meditation, jewelry, and interior design. If you're using Lapis lazuli for meditation, you can hold it in your hand or place it on your forehead. You can also wear Lapis lazuli jewelry, like a necklace or earrings. You can also use Lapis lazuli in your home or office decor.

Many stones and crystals can be used to balance the Crown chakra. The ones listed here are just a few of the more popular ones. If you're drawn to a particular stone or crystal, trust your intuition and go with what feels right for you.

Cleansing and Charging

When using stones and crystals for the Crown chakra, it's important to regularly cleanse and charge them. This will ensure that they are working effectively and that their energy is fresh and vibrant. There are various ways to cleanse and charge your stones and crystals:

1. Use Running Water

Use running water as a cleanser. This can be done using a faucet or natural running water, like a river or stream. Gently rub the stone or crystal under the water, and envision the water washing away any negativity or impurities. When you've finished, allow the stone or crystal to air dry. The running water will cleanse the stone or crystal of any negative energy.

2. Use Salt Water

Another popular cleaning method is to use saltwater. This can be done by adding salt to a bowl of water and stirring until the salt is dissolved. Then, add your stones and crystals to the bowl and allow them to soak for at least 24 hours. The saltwater helps remove any negative energy from the stones and crystals. It's important to rinse the stones and crystals off with fresh water after being in the saltwater.

3. Use Incense

Incense is another popular way to cleanse your stones and crystals. The smoke from the incense removes any negative energy from the stones and crystals. To use this method, simply hold your stone or crystal in the incense smoke for a few minutes. If you're using multiple stones and crystals, you can place them on a plate or in a bowl and hold the incense over them. With this method, it's important to make sure that the burning stick does not come into direct contact with the stones or crystals, as this can damage them.

4. Use Sunlight or Moonlight

Sunlight and moonlight are also great ways to cleanse your stones and crystals. Find a place where your stone can be under direct sunlight and moonlight for twenty-four hours. Both types of light remove negative energy from your crystals and stones.

5. Use a Crystal or Stone Cleaning Kit

You can purchase a crystal or stone cleaning kit that contains everything you need to cleanse your stones and crystals. These kits usually come with a cleansing spray, a charging crystal, and a storage pouch. This is a great option if you have a lot of stones and crystals or want to be sure that you're using the proper cleaning method.

Charging your stones and crystals is just as important as cleansing them. This replenishes their energy and keeps them working effectively. Place them in sunlight and moonlight for twenty-four hours to charge them. You can also place them on a selenite charging plate or use a crystal quartz crystal to charge them.

Storing your stones and crystals is also important. This keeps their energy fresh and prevents them from getting damaged. It's best to store your stones and crystals in a cool, dark place. A jewelry box, drawer, or closet are all great options. You can also purchase a stone or crystal storage pouch to keep them in.

When using stones and crystals for the crown chakra, it's important to choose ones that correspond with the chakra's energy. Some great options for the crown chakra include amethyst, selenite, and clear quartz. Amethyst is a purple stone associated with the crown chakra. It's said to have calming and relaxing properties. Selenite is a white or transparent stone that has cleansing and purifying properties. Clear quartz is a clear stone that has amplifying and energizing properties.

When using stones and crystals for the crown chakra, regularly cleanse and charge them. This keeps their energy fresh and prevents them from getting damaged. Store them in a cool, dark place when you're not using them. Choose stones and crystals that correspond with the chakra's energy for the best possible results!

Chapter 8: Using Aromatherapy

Aromatherapy is a holistic medicine that uses essential oils extracted from plants to improve mental health. Aromatherapy is a great way to keep your crown chakra open and balanced. Essential oils interact with your emotions, which can heal your mind and activate different energy centers in your body.

Aromatherapy.
https://unsplash.com/photos/r40EYKVyutI

When a chakra is under-active or overactive, it can cause physical or mental problems. Essential oils can help heal the chakras and bring them back into balance. This chapter will focus on the essential oils that balance the crown chakra. It will cover how essential oils help balance Sahasrara and what makes an essential oil appropriate for this task. You'll also find a list of recommended essential oils for the crown chakra, explaining their properties and how to use them.

Essential Oils and the Crown Chakra

Essential oils are botanical extracts that can be used for various purposes. One of the best ways to cleanse and balance your crown chakra is to use essential oils. These oils can be used to promote feelings of euphoria, bliss, and enlightenment. They're all-natural, accessible, and easy to use, making them great for those just starting on their spiritual journey or looking for an easy addition to their current spiritual practices.

To help release the blockage and open your crown chakra, you can use essential oils to assist your efforts. They are a powerful tool that can help you to improve your physical, emotional, and mental health.

There are a wide variety of essential oils that can help balance the crown chakra. As you choose an oil, consider its properties and how they match up with what you are hoping to achieve. Many essential oils have multiple purposes, so don't be afraid to experiment until you find the perfect oil or combination of oils for you.

How Essential Oils Work

Essential oils are composed of tiny molecules that our bodies can easily absorb. These molecules enter our bloodstream when we inhale them. They can also be absorbed through our pores when the oils are applied to the skin. Once in the bloodstream, the molecules interact with our emotions and can trigger different responses.

The limbic system is the part of the brain that controls our emotions. It's also responsible for our sense of smell. When we inhale essential oils, the molecules interact with the limbic system and can trigger different emotions. This is why essential oils are so powerful and can be used to promote different emotional states.

The active ingredients in essential oils are known as volatile organic compounds (VOCs). These molecules are easily vaporized at room temperature, which is why you can often smell them before you even see the plant. Once inhaled, VOCs interact with the body in a variety of ways.

Some VOCs stimulate the olfactory system, which is responsible for our sense of smell. This can help to improve our mood and energy levels. Other VOCs interact with the limbic system, which controls our emotions and memory. This is why certain essential oils can be used to help with anxiety, depression, and stress. VOCs can also interact with the hypothalamus, regulating our body temperature, hunger, and thirst. This is why some essential oils can be used to help with weight loss and cravings.

How to Use Essential Oils for the Crown Chakra

In aromatherapy, essential oils can bring balance to the crown chakra. Remember that a little goes a long way when using essential oils for the crown chakra. Start with one or two drops and increase as needed. Here are some easy ways to open your crown chakra using aromatherapy:

1. Use a Diffuser

If you have a diffuser that disperses essential oils into the air, you can use it to open your crown chakra. You need to add a few drops of essential oil to the diffuser and allow it to disperse while meditating or doing yoga. You'll soon find yourself feeling more relaxed than ever before.

The diffuser will open up your crown chakra by releasing the oil into the air. The oil will be absorbed through your nose and into your bloodstream. This will allow the oil to trigger certain emotions and bring about a sense of balance.

2. Drop into Hot Water

If you don't have access to a diffuser, you can still use essential oils by putting some drops in hot water and sprinkling them onto surfaces in your home or office space. This will help release any negative energy and allow you to focus on the task at hand with ease. If possible, try meditating while doing so because it will make all the difference.

Many people choose to add essential oils to their baths as well. If you decide to do this, make sure you use a carrier oil such as jojoba oil or sweet almond oil to help disperse the oil evenly. You don't want to add too much essential oil because it can be overwhelming and potentially irritating to your skin.

3. Apply Directly to Your Skin

If you want to experience the full benefits of essential oil, you can apply it directly to your skin. This method is best for those looking for an immediate response. The oil will be absorbed quickly into your bloodstream, which will allow it to interact with your emotions and bring about a sense of balance.

Don't forget to use carrier oil to dilute the essential oil. You don't want to use too much essential oil because it can irritate your skin. Start with one or two drops and increase as needed.

4. Inhale Directly from the Bottle

If you're looking for a quick way to open your crown chakra, you can simply inhale the essential oil directly from the bottle. This method is best for those looking for an immediate response. If possible, try to find a quiet place to sit or stand while you do this. Allow your eyes to close and breathe in and out slowly.

You can also place a few drops of oil on a cotton ball and inhale that. This method is best if you're sensitive to smells or don't want the oil to be too potent. Also, if you're using this method, keep the cotton ball away from your face to avoid getting the oil in your eyes.

Recommended Essential Oils for the Crown Chakra

Using essential oils that have properties that help to open the crown chakra is a great way to help you feel in tune with yourself spiritually. Here are some of the best essential oils for the crown chakra:

1. Pure Frankincense

Frankincense has a sweet, woody, and slightly spicy scent known for its ability to promote relaxation and peace. It's also believed to reduce stress and anxiety. Frankincense is a great essential oil to use for the crown chakra because it encourages feelings of connection and oneness.

Frankincense is a very popular oil that's used in many different applications. It's often used in meditation because it helps one feel centered and focused. It's also said that frankincense aids emotional healing, especially when feeling more connected with others.

- **Properties**

Frankincense has many healing properties. It has been used for thousands of years in religious ceremonies, cosmetics, and perfumes. It has antibacterial properties that make it a great oil for treating acne-prone skin. It also boosts immunity by reducing inflammation and strengthening the immune system.

In addition to balancing hormones and reducing inflammation, frankincense can help you feel more grounded, which can help open your crown chakra. Its woody scent with a hint of spice promotes feelings of grounding, balance, and calmness. It also helps one feel more connected to their mind, body, spirit, and surroundings.

- **Why It Helps Open the Crown Chakra**

Frankincense helps us connect more deeply with ourselves because its aroma resonates very subtly. Frankincense is a strong oil due to its high levels of sesquiterpene ketones, which have been shown to have anti-cancer properties in animal studies. Frankincense can open and balance the crown chakra when used for spiritual purposes.

One reason why frankincense is so effective at opening the crown chakra is its ability to combat fear and anxiety. When our crown chakra is closed, we feel disconnected from others and afraid of our inner wisdom. By using frankincense, not only do we feel more connected with ourselves, but we also become more connected to those around us as well.

- **How to Use**

If you're looking for a more spiritual experience, you can add a few drops of frankincense to your bathtub and enjoy a relaxing soak. You can also add it to massage oil and give yourself a massage. You can use frankincense oil by adding 2–3 drops to a diffuser or by diluting it with a carrier oil (like jojoba oil) and applying it to your chest or the back of your neck.

There are many ways to use frankincense. You can add a few drops to your diffuser and inhale the aroma throughout the day. You can also add it to your lotions and creams to reduce the appearance of scars and stretch marks.

2. Myrrh

Myrrh has a warm, earthy, and slightly sweet scent that promotes relaxation and eases stress. Myrrh is also known for its ability to boost immunity and fight infection. It's a great essential oil to use for the crown chakra because it encourages feelings of connection and oneness.

Myrrh is a resin that's derived from the Commiphora myrrha tree. It's been used for centuries in religious ceremonies and as a natural remedy for various ailments. Myrrh is a warm oil with spicy and peppery notes. In addition to its aromatic properties, myrrh is also known for its anti-inflammatory, antifungal, antibacterial, and antiviral qualities. It's been used medicinally throughout history to treat wounds, respiratory infections, and other conditions like athlete's foot and acne.

- **Properties**

Myrrh has many healing properties. It's been shown to treat colds, coughs, and sore throats. It's also a natural expectorant, which means it can loosen phlegm and ease congestion. Myrrh is also a powerful anti-inflammatory agent. It can reduce swelling, redness, and pain associated with various conditions like arthritis and carpal tunnel syndrome. It can also reduce inflammation throughout the body, promoting overall health and wellness.

In addition to its physical benefits, myrrh also promotes emotional well-being. It's often used to ease stress, anxiety, and depression. Myrrh has been linked to emotional healing in terms of spirituality and emotional wellness. It can help you connect with your spiritual side by making you feel more connected to the universe at large and yourself as part of that universe. The emotional properties of myrrh make it an excellent choice for opening up the crown chakra.

- **Why It Helps Open the Crown Chakra**

The crown chakra is associated with our connection to the Divine. When this chakra is out of balance, we may feel disconnected from our spirituality or a higher power. Myrrh encourages feelings of connection and oneness. It also assists in spiritual growth and enlightenment.

Myrrh grounds you while connecting you to the Divine, helping you open your crown chakra with the confidence that comes from knowing what you're doing and how it could help others. The oil can also be used to anoint the crown of your head during meditation or prayer.

- **How to Use**

Myrrh is available in several forms, including incense and essential oil. You can use the oil to create a diffuser blend that connects you to your spirituality. Mix the myrrh oil with frankincense oil in a diffuser and allow it to fill the room while you meditate or perform yoga. It's also possible to ingest myrrh as a supplement or an herbal tea.

Myrrh can be used in a diffuser, or you can add a few drops to a warm bath. You can also dilute it with a carrier oil (like jojoba oil) and apply it to your skin. Mix 10 drops of myrrh essential oil into ½ cup of olive oil (or any carrier oil). Apply to the base of your neck, head, temples, and ears. For the best results, apply twice a day - once before bed and once after you wake up.

3. Sandalwood

Sandalwood is a sweet, woody essential oil often used in aromatherapy. It has a rich, creamy texture with a warm, earthy scent. Sandalwood is known for its ability to promote relaxation and ease stress. It also facilitates focus and concentration.

- **Properties**

Sandalwood is a natural moisturizer. It is an excellent choice for dry skin, eczema, and psoriasis. It can reduce inflammation and redness.

Sandalwood has many helpful properties for your mental health. It can increase mental clarity and boost your mood. It's also considered an aphrodisiac.

Sandalwood is also known for its calming properties. This makes it an excellent choice for easing stress, anxiety, and depression. It's also been linked to helping you fall asleep faster. The oil can also be used to ease headaches and migraines.

In addition to its physical benefits, sandalwood also aids spiritual well-being. It's often used in meditation and prayer for its ability to encourage a sense of calm and inner peace. It's also helpful to promote self-awareness and clarity of thought.

- **Why It Helps Open the Crown Chakra**

Sandalwood encourages feelings of connection and oneness. It has a deep, earthy scent with a slightly sweet undertone. It is known to have strong anti-inflammatory properties and has been used in alternative medicine as a treatment for anxiety, depression, and insomnia. These properties could explain why sandalwood is an excellent oil to use if you have trouble connecting with the spiritual side of your crown chakra – as it helps relieve stressors in the mind and body.

- **How to Use**

Sandalwood is available in several forms, including incense and essential oil. You can use the oil to create a diffuser blend that helps you connect with your spirituality. Mix the sandalwood oil with frankincense oil in a diffuser and allow it to fill the room while you meditate or perform yoga. It's also possible to ingest sandalwood as a supplement or an herbal tea.

Sandalwood can be used in a diffuser, or you can add a few drops to a warm bath. You can also dilute it with a carrier oil (like jojoba oil) and apply it to your skin. Mix 10 drops of sandalwood essential oil into ½ cup of olive oil (or any carrier oil). Apply to the base of your neck, head, temples, and ears. For the best results, apply twice a day - once before bed and once after you wake up.

Other Essential Oils for the Crown Chakra

1. Rose

Rose is a delicate, floral essential oil with a sweet, romantic scent. Rose oil is known for its ability to boost your mood and ease stress. It promotes self-confidence and self-esteem. The oil can also be used to ease headaches and migraines. It also promotes wound healing.

Rose oil encourages feelings of self-love and self-acceptance. It boosts feelings of peace and calm. The oil can be used to ease stress, anxiety, and depression. These properties could explain why rose oil is an excellent choice for opening your crown chakra.

Rose oil is available in several forms, including essential oil and an absolute. You can use the oil to create a diffuser blend that helps you connect with your spirituality. Mix rose oil with lavender oil in a diffuser and allow it to fill the room while you meditate or perform yoga. It's also possible to ingest rose oil as a supplement or an herbal tea.

2. Jasmine

Jasmine is a sweet, floral essential oil with a romantic scent. The oil can be used to boost your mood and ease stress. It promotes self-confidence and self-esteem. Jasmine can help your spiritual well-being. It's often used in meditation and prayer for its ability to encourage a sense of calm and inner peace.

Jasmine oil can be used to create a diffuser blend that helps you connect with your spirituality. Mix jasmine oil with rose oil in a diffuser and allow it to fill the room while you meditate or perform yoga. Jasmine oil is associated with the body's natural healing process, so if you have any long-term health issues, it might help you through them.

3. Lavender Oil

Lavender oil is associated with introspection and peace, so you can use it in meditation or to help you relax at night. The oil is thought to have a calming effect on the nervous system, easing stress and promoting relaxation. It's also helpful in promoting feelings of self-love and self-acceptance.

Lavender oil can be diffused or added to a bath. You can also dilute it with a carrier oil (like jojoba oil) and apply it to your skin. Mix 10 drops of lavender essential oil into ½ cup of olive oil (or any carrier oil). Apply to the base of your neck, head, temples, and ears. For the best results, apply twice a day - once before bed and once after you wake up.

Disclaimer: Do not substitute the information in this chapter for medical advice. You should always consult a doctor first before starting any treatment, and this guide is intended to highlight the options available to you. Always read the essential oil label and be careful when using them around pets, people with allergies, pregnant women, or children.

Essential oils can be used to encourage the balancing of your crown chakra. The best essential oils for the crown chakra are pure frankincense, myrrh, and sandalwood. These oils are associated with feelings of peace and calm. They can be used to ease stress, anxiety, and depression. Use two or three drops in a diffuser, or combine with a carrier oil if you are applying to the skin. For the best results, apply twice a day - once before bed and once after you wake up.

Chapter 9: Nutrition and Diet

Food is an incredible healer, and it's one way we can get our energy to flow again freely. The relationship between nutrition and the crown chakra has been studied for many years now, with scientists looking at everything from fasting to eating specific foods. When it comes to the crown chakra, a balanced diet is key to keeping this chakra open and functioning properly.

Though some people consider that the Crown chakra, being the most spiritual, requires only spiritual practices or meditation to open and maintain, some consider that each chakra is associated with a certain type of food. This chapter looks at the relationship between the crown chakra and nutrition, including fasting and the foods that help unblock or balance it. You'll also find several recipes that use the ingredients known to help the crown chakra.

The Relationship between the Crown Chakra and Nutrition

We often think of food as just the fuel for our bodies, but our relationship with it is complex. It's about pleasure, it's about connection, and it's about how we honor ourselves.

Psychologists have found that healthy eating habits are connected to a well-functioning crown chakra. When your options for food are limited, or your access to food is restricted in any way, you may struggle to take care of yourself and feel secure and grounded in the world.

This can affect your access to the wisdom of the crown chakra - the wisdom that can help you make sense of the world around you. That's why nutrition and diet are so important! The foods we choose and how we acquire them can affect our mental well-being and spiritual health.

Because the crown chakra has such an active connection with the mind, body, and spirit, it also involves aspects of how you eat and how you move. Even if you don't consider yourself spiritual or you're not into things like yoga, it's still important to understand that the food you consume can greatly impact your mental wellness.

The crown chakra helps you connect with yourself and others. A healthy diet and nutrition plan are essential for keeping it balanced. Eating foods rich in carbohydrates can help balance this chakra, as can eating foods high in sodium or potassium. However, it is important not to overdo it.

When you eat foods that are not good for you or not in line with your body's needs, you can cause an imbalance in your chakras. This makes it difficult to connect with your spirit and maintain healthy relationships with others. The foods that tend to cause an imbalance in the crown chakra include:

- Refined sugar
- Processed meat
- Alcohol
- Caffeine
- White flour

How Fasting Impacts the Crown Chakra

Fasting is a practice that has been used for centuries to cleanse the body and mind, and it can be a great way to reset your system. Fasting gives your body, especially your digestive system, a break - this will give your mind more focus as the body is working on fewer tasks.

Fasting can also open up the crown chakra. When you're not focused on food, you can focus on your connection to the Divine. This can help you feel more connected to your higher self and the universe. There are many different ways to fast, and you can choose the right method for you. Some people fast for a day or two, while others fast for a week or more.

Fasting detoxifies the body and clears the mind. It's a great way to reset your system and focus on your spirituality. If you're interested in fasting, it's important to talk to your doctor first.

Foods that Help Unblock or Balance the Crown Chakra

One of the best ways to rebalance your Sahasrara is through what you eat and drink. Eating white or purple foods is a great place to start, as these colors offer a direct connection to the crown chakra. Foods like coconut, onions, ginger, watermelon, and garlic might not be your favorite, but they're all terrific choices if you want to rebalance your Sahasrara.

Try adding chromium-rich foods to your diet. Chromium is a metal that's been used to treat diabetes mellitus by lowering blood sugar in the body. This is a perfect example of an element of the physical world directly impacting the spiritual world. You can also try foods high in antioxidants, like blueberries, dark chocolate, and acai berries. Antioxidants protect the body from damage caused by free radicals.

When you're incorporating more of these foods into your diet, make sure they're free from pesticides, other harmful chemicals, or that haven't been sitting around for weeks (like frozen vegetables). Many different types of food can unblock or balance the crown chakra, and it's important to find the ones that work best for you.

Ginger

In addition to being one of the most powerful healing foods on the planet, ginger is easy to add to your diet and can calm inflammation and lower blood pressure – which is exactly what your crown chakra needs. If you're used to drinking coffee throughout the day, try replacing it with ginger tea to manage stress and get more restful sleep.

Onion

A great place to start with onions is white onion. It has antibacterial properties that can reduce inflammation. Additionally, onions are high in chromium, an element that helps balance blood sugar and manage hunger pangs. It also helps lower cholesterol and triglycerides, so you feel less weighed down by meals.

Coconut

Many people believe that coconuts are a fruit of the gods – and why not? Coconut is great for detoxing, and the nutrients and minerals have been shown to reduce inflammation, reduce blood sugar levels, and boost your metabolism and energy. It's the perfect food to balance your crown chakra. You can easily make coconut milk at home; simply blend a can of coconut milk with fresh water until smooth, and add it to smoothies or use it in place of cow's milk.

Chamomile

Chamomile is a type of flower that's often used to make herbal tea. This tea is a great way to relax before bed and get some restful sleep. Chamomile tea also helps with anxiety and stress. If you're feeling particularly tense, try adding a chamomile sachet to your bathwater for a relaxing soak. Chamomile is the perfect way to soothe an overactive crown chakra with its calming properties.

Sage

Sage is an herb that's often used in cooking, but it can also be burned as incense. Burning sage is said to help cleanse the mind and body of negative energy. It's a great way to start your day or prepare for meditation. There are many different ways to use sage, so find the one that works best for you. You can also try adding sage to your diet in small amounts. Try using it to flavor chicken, fish, or vegetables.

Fennel

Fennel is a type of herb that's often used in cooking. It has a slightly sweet taste and can be added to several dishes. Fennel is also said to have some health benefits, including improving digestion, reducing inflammation, and promoting weight loss. Adding fennel to your diet is a great way to help balance the crown chakra.

Honey

Honey is often used in baking and as a natural sweetener for tea. It has many health benefits, including boosting energy levels, improving digestion, and fighting off infections. It is also said to be a natural anti-inflammatory. Adding honey to your diet is a great way to balance the crown chakra since it's packed with nutrients beneficial for the body.

Acai Berry

Acai berry is a type of fruit native to Brazil. It's often used in smoothies and juices. Acai berry is said to have many health benefits, including the ability to improve digestion, reduce inflammation, and promote weight loss.

Maca

Maca is a type of root vegetable native to Peru. It's often used in powder form. Maca is said to have many health benefits, including improving energy levels, boosting mood, and promoting fertility. If you're looking for a natural way to support the crown chakra, adding maca to your diet is a great option.

Pineapple

Pineapple is often used in smoothies, juices, and salads. Pineapple works wonders for the digestive system to be part of a weight loss program and reduce inflammation. To get the most benefit from pineapple, it's best to eat it fresh. You can also try adding it to your diet in small amounts. The sweetness of pineapple can help counteract the bitterness of some of the other foods on this list.

Cucumber

Cucumber is often used in salads, sandwiches, and juices. Cucumber can aid in digestive issues, promote weight loss, and deal with inflammation. A great way to get the most benefit from cucumber is to eat it raw. You can also try adding it to your diet in small amounts. The cool, refreshing taste of cucumber can help soothe an overactive crown chakra.

These are just some foods that can help unblock or balance the crown chakra. Remember, the goal is to eat clean, whole foods packed with nutrients. Processed foods, sugary snacks, and alcoholic beverages can contribute to an imbalance in the crown chakra. So, make sure to avoid them as much as possible. Instead, focus on eating foods that are nourishing and good for your crown chakra.

Recipes

If you're looking for specific recipes to help unblock or balance the crown chakra, you can try a few fun, healthy, and simple recipes.

Acai Berry Smoothie

This delicious smoothie is made with acai berry, banana, and almond milk. It's a great way to start your day or enjoy a healthy snack. The acai berry is packed with antioxidants and vitamins that are great for the crown chakra. If you don't have acai berries, you can also use frozen blueberries or raspberries.

Ingredients:

- 1 cup frozen acai berries
- 1 banana
- 1 cup almond milk
- ½ cup pineapple
- 1 tablespoon of honey

Directions:

1. Add all ingredients to a blender and blend until smooth.
2. Pour into a glass and enjoy.
3. You can also add some ice cubes if you want a thicker smoothie.

Pineapple and Curry Chicken Stir Fry

This quick and easy stir fry is a great way to get a dose of crown chakra-supporting foods. The pineapple provides sweetness and vitamins, while the curry boosts flavor. If you don't have chicken, you can use shrimp or tofu.

Ingredients:

- 1 lb skinless, boneless chicken breast – cubed
- 1 diced onion
- 1 tbsp olive oil
- 1 cup diced pineapple
- 1 diced red bell pepper
- 2 cloves minced garlic
- ½ cup green beans
- ½ cup chicken broth
- 1 tbsp curry powder
- Salt and pepper

Directions:

1. Heat the olive oil over medium-high heat in a large pan.
2. Add diced chicken and brown.
3. Add the onion, curry powder, garlic, and pineapple – cook for 5 minutes.
4. Add the green beans, bell pepper, chicken broth, salt, and pepper – cook for 10 minutes.
5. Serve with rice, pasta, or quinoa.

Cucumber and Mint Salad

This refreshing salad is perfect for a summer day. The cucumber and mint are cooling and help soothe the crown chakra. If you don't have mint, you can use basil or cilantro.

Ingredients:

- 2 cucumbers, diced
- 1 red onion, diced
- ½ cup chopped mint

- 3 tablespoons olive oil
- 2 tablespoons of white vinegar
- Salt and pepper to taste

Directions:

1. In a large bowl, combine the cucumbers, red onion, mint, olive oil, white vinegar, salt, and pepper.
2. Stir until all the ingredients are coated with the dressing.
3. Let the salad sit for about 30 minutes so the flavors can meld together.
4. Serve and enjoy.

Cucumber and Honeydew Melon Soup

This delicious soup is ideal for a summer afternoon. Since it's made with cucumber and honeydew, it's refreshing, and it soothes the crown chakra. The soup can also be made with cantaloupe if you don't have honeydew.

Ingredients:

- 2 cucumbers, peeled and diced
- 1 honeydew melon, peeled and diced
- ½ cup plain yogurt
- 2 tablespoons of honey
- 1 tablespoon of lime juice
- Salt and pepper to taste

Directions:

1. In a blender or food processor, combine the cucumbers, honeydew, yogurt, honey, lime juice, salt, and pepper.
2. Blend until smooth.
3. Chill in the fridge for about an hour.
4. Serve and enjoy.

Maca Chocolate Bark

This recipe is a fun and easy way to get your daily dose of maca. It's also a great way to satisfy your sweet tooth. The maca powder balances the crown chakra, and the chocolate provides a dose of antioxidants. If you don't have dark chocolate, you can also use milk or white chocolate.

Ingredients:

- 1 cup dark chocolate chips
- 2 tablespoons of maca powder
- 1 teaspoon of vanilla extract
- ½ cup chopped nuts (optional)

Directions:

1. Line a baking sheet with parchment paper.
2. Melt the chocolate chips in the microwave in 30-second increments, stirring in between.
3. Stir in the maca powder and vanilla extract.
4. Pour the chocolate onto the prepared baking sheet and spread it into a thin layer.
5. Sprinkle with the chopped nuts.
6. Place the bark in the fridge for about an hour or until the chocolate is firm.
7. Break into pieces and enjoy.

These are just a few ideas to get you started on your crown chakra diet. Remember, the key is to eat foods that are cooling and soothing to the chakra. So, get creative and experiment with different foods and recipes. And most importantly, enjoy!

Many different foods can help unblock or balance the crown chakra. And by incorporating these foods into your diet, you can keep your chakra in alignment. So, get creative in the kitchen and enjoy exploring different recipes. And most importantly, remember to listen to your body. It will tell you what it needs. Trust your intuition and let it guide you on your journey to a healthy and balanced crown chakra.

Note: The information in this chapter is not intended to replace the advice of a medical professional. If you have any concerns or questions about your health, please speak with your doctor.

Chapter 10: Crown Chakra 7-Day Routine

An unbalanced crown chakra can lead to feelings of loneliness, isolation, depression, meaninglessness, cynicism, or self-righteousness. When it's blocked or overactive, you may feel disconnected from others and the world around you. And if you don't find a way to balance it soon enough, it could even lead to mental illnesses such as schizophrenia or bipolar disorder.

To avoid these issues, it's important to establish a routine that balances the crown chakra and keeps it in tune with the rest of the other chakras. This will help you feel connected to others and even give you a sense of purpose in life.

This chapter provides a 7-day crown chakra routine you can follow to balance and open your crown chakra. Each day, you'll find a mix of yoga poses, mantras, affirmations, mudras, pranayama, and meditation exercises that you can try. Add in other activities and exercises you enjoy – the key is fun and relaxation.

The Importance of Having a Routine for Balancing the Crown Chakra

From a spiritual perspective, the crown chakra is the gatekeeper to your connection with the Universe. When it's unbalanced, you'll feel disconnected from your higher power and your soul's purpose. As a result, you might feel unmotivated, anxious, depressed, or hopeless.

Having a daily routine that includes activities that benefit your crown chakra will help you feel more connected to yourself and your environment. This way, you can trust yourself and others more easily. You'll also find it easier to make decisions because you'll see things from a more intuitive perspective. Your ability to focus will also improve because you'll be easily able to tune out distractions.

When you regularly balance your crown chakra, you'll feel more at peace with yourself and your world. You'll also find it easier to connect with others because you won't be holding onto any feelings of isolation or loneliness.

7-Day Crown Chakra Routine

Day 1: Yoga Poses, Mantras, Affirmations, Mudras, and Pranayama

Start your day by doing some gentle yoga stretches. Include a mix of standing, seated, and supine poses. After your yoga session, sit down in a comfortable position and recite some of the following mantras:

- *Om Namah Shivaya (Aum and salutations to Shiva)*
- *So, Hum (I am that)*
- *Sahasrara Hum (I am the crown chakra)*
- *Aham Brahmasmi (I am the Universe)*
- *Lokah Samastah Sukhino Bhavantu (May all beings everywhere be happy and free)*

After you've recited the mantras, spend a few minutes practicing some of the following affirmations:

- I am connected to all that is.

- I am surrounded by love and light.

- I am worthy of love and respect.

- I am open to receiving guidance from the Universe.

- I am safe, protected, and guided.

After you've said the affirmations, spend a few minutes practicing some mudras. You can go back to chapter 4 for instructions on how to do them. The main mudras for the crown chakra are the Shuni Mudra (finger mudra), which balances the mind, and the Gyan Mudra (thumb and index finger mudra), which increases concentration and memory.

Finally, spend a few minutes practicing some pranayama. Try the following exercises:

- **Alternate Nostril Breathing:** Sit up straight. Relax your left hand and arm. Use your right thumb (or a finger) to close your right nostril, sealing the airway. Inhale deeply through your left nostril. Bring up your left hand and close off your left nostril, sealing the airway – release the right nostril. Exhale slowly through your right nostril. Repeat this, alternating between inhaling and exhaling, and switch your nostrils halfway through.

- **Breath of Fire:** Sit up straight. Lay your palms on your knees. Inhale and exhale rapidly through your nose, keeping your abdominal muscles contracted. Try to breathe from your diaphragm and not your chest. Do this for a minute or two, and then take a few deep breaths.

Day 2: Meditation Exercises and Reading Spiritual Books

Today, start by doing a few minutes of mindfulness meditation. Try to focus on your breath and the sensations in your body. Your mind might wander, and that is okay – slowly bring it back when it does. After your mindfulness meditation, spend some time doing a visualization exercise. Picture yourself surrounded by a soft white light. This light is full of love and compassion. It surrounds you and fills you with a sense of peace and calm. Take a few deep breaths and let the light fill your entire being.

After your visualization, spend some time reading a spiritual book. You can choose any book that resonates with you. Some good choices include The Power of Now by Eckhart Tolle, A New Earth by Eckhart Tolle, The Untethered Soul by Michael A. Singer, and The Alchemist by Paulo Coelho.

Day 3: Creating a Gratitude Practice

Start your day by spending a few minutes writing down things you're grateful for. Include things like your health, family and friends, home, job, pets, etc. Try to think of at least 10 things you're grateful for.

After you've written down what you're grateful for, spend a few minutes reflecting on why you're grateful for those things. For example, if you're grateful for your health, think about how much worse your life would be if you were sick. If you're grateful for your family and friends, think about how much they add to your life and how you would feel if you didn't have them.

Day 4: Connecting With Nature

Spend some time today connecting with nature. Go for a walk in a park, sit in your backyard, or just enjoy looking out the window and appreciating the beauty of the natural world around you. Take a few deep breaths and try to clear your mind of all thoughts. Just focus on the present moment and the sensations around you.

After you've spent some time connecting with nature, spend a few minutes reflecting on how you feel. Do you feel more connected to the world around you? Do you feel more at peace? Make a note of how you feel so you can refer back to it in the future.

Day 5: Opening Up To Love and Compassion

Today, spend some time focusing on love and compassion. Start by thinking about someone you love and care about. Picture them in your mind and send them all of your love and positive energy. Try to feel the love in your heart as you picture them.

After you've done that, spend a few minutes thinking about someone you don't know very well. Again, picture them in your mind and send them all of your love and positive energy. Try to feel compassion in your heart as you picture that person receiving positive energy.

Day 6: Forgiveness Meditation

Spend some time today doing forgiveness meditation. First, think of someone you need to forgive. It could be someone who has hurt you in the past or someone who you're currently having problems with. Picture them in your mind and send them all your love and positive energy.

Then, focus on the forgiveness itself. Picture the act of forgiveness as a light that surrounds and engulfs both you and the other person. This light is full of love, understanding, and compassion. It forgives all wrongs and sets you both free. Take a few deep breaths and let the light fill your entire being.

Day 7: Connecting With Your Higher Self

Spend some time today connecting with your higher self. Start by picturing yourself in a beautiful place. It could be somewhere you've been before or somewhere you always wanted to go. Remember to breathe evenly through this all.

Once you are picturing yourself in a location, see a bright, white light everywhere. Feel that the light is full of love and wisdom. It knows who you are, and it loves you – it is here to guide you on your journey. Continue to breathe in and out as the light fills your being.

When you're finished, spend a few minutes reflecting on your feelings. Are you more connected to the person you are? Do you feel more at peace? Make a note of how you feel to refer back to it in the future.

Reflecting on Your Progress

Spend a few minutes reflecting on your progress at the end of each day. How did you feel during the chakra balancing exercise? How did you feel after connecting with nature, love and compassion, your higher self, or forgiveness? Make a note of your progress to look back on it in the future.

When you're finished with your reflection, spend a few minutes writing down any goals or intentions you have for the future. What do you want to work on next? What do you want to achieve? Write down your goals and refer back to them often to keep yourself on track.

By following the crown chakra routine, you'll be able to balance your chakras and live a more fulfilling life. Remember to mix and match the different exercises to find what works best for you. Also, don't forget to include additional things you enjoy doing every day, such as reading spiritual books or spending time in a quiet space. Finally, make sure to reflect on your progress to see how far you've come.

Bonus: Chakras Cheat Sheet

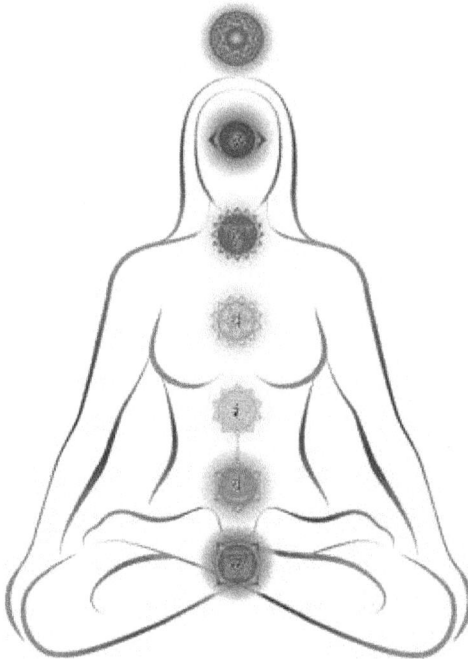

Woman in the lotus pose with 7 chakras placed in their locations.

RootOfAllLight, CC BY-SA 4.0 https://creativecommons.org/licenses/by-sa/4.0, via Wikimedia Commons: https://commons.wikimedia.org/wiki/File:7ChakrasFemale.png

The chakra system is an important part of many Eastern philosophies and religions, including Hinduism and Buddhism. There are said to be seven main chakras. They are believed to be energy centers located along the spine. Each chakra is associated with a different color, affirmation, sound, and role in the body.

This bonus chapter will provide you with a cheat sheet on all of the main chakras to learn more about them and how they work.

Chakra 1: Root or Muladhara Chakra

Muladhara chakra.
Atarax42, CC0, via Wikimedia Commons: https://commons.wikimedia.org/wiki/File:Chakra1.svg

The root chakra, or Muladhara chakra, is located at the base of the spine. It is associated with the color red, the affirmation "I am safe," the sound "Lam," and the element of earth. The root chakra is responsible for feelings of safety and security. The root chakra is said to be the most important chakra, as it is the foundation of the entire chakra system.

The kundalini, or life force energy, is said to be located at the base of the spine in the root chakra. This energy is what is responsible for the movement of energy up the spine and through the other chakras.

Chakra 2: Sacral or Svadhisthana Chakra

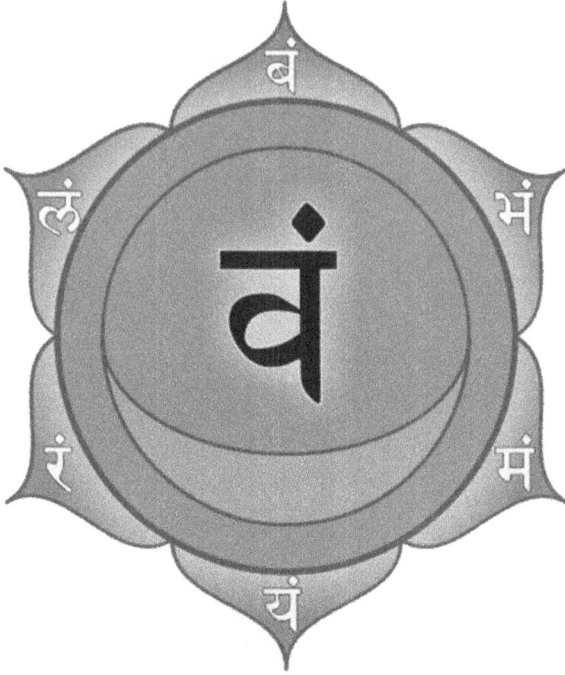

Svadhisthana chakra symbol.
Atarax42, CC0, via Wikimedia Commons: https://commons.wikimedia.org/wiki/File:Chakra2.svg

The sacral chakra, or Svadhisthana chakra, is located just below the navel. It is associated with the color orange, the affirmation "I am creative," the sound "Vam," and the element of water. The sacral chakra is responsible for feelings of creativity, pleasure, and sexuality.

The sacral chakra is the center of our emotions and desires. It is associated with the water element, which is said to be ever-changing and flowing. The Sacral chakra is very important, as it is responsible for our ability to feel pleasure and enjoy life.

Chakra 3: Solar Plexus or Manipura Chakra

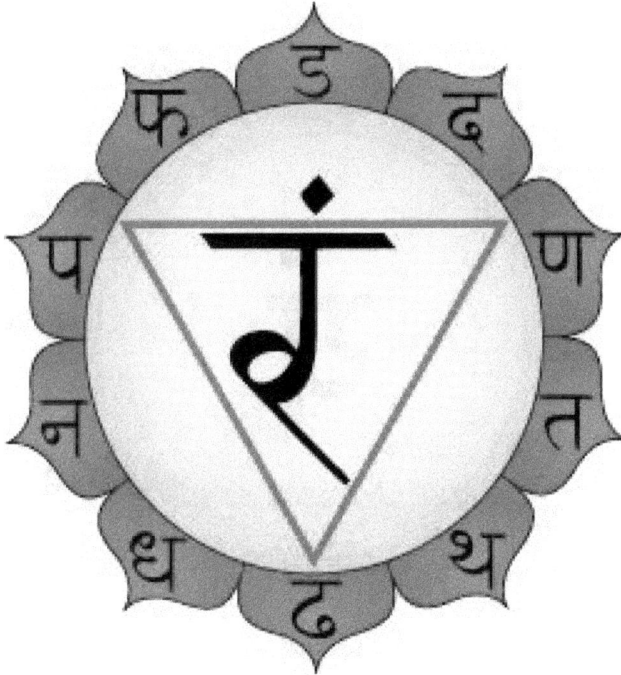

Manipura chakra symbol.
Wikipedia:User:AndyKali, modified by User:Iṣṭa Devatā, CC BY-SA 3.0
https://creativecommons.org/licenses/by-sa/3.0, via Wikimedia Commons:
https://commons.wikimedia.org/wiki/File:Manipura_cakra_with_correct_bijas.png

The solar plexus chakra is located just above the navel. Yellow is the color of the solar plexus chakra. Use the chant "Ram," focus on the fire element, and find confidence in this chakra. This is where your confidence and power originate.

The solar plexus chakra is the center of our power. It is associated with the fire element, which is said to be transformational and purifying.

Chakra 4: Heart or Anahata Chakra

Anahata chakra symbol.
Mirzolot2, CC BY-SA 3.0 https://creativecommons.org/licenses/by-sa/3.0, via Wikimedia Commons: https://commons.wikimedia.org/wiki/File:Anahata_green.svg

The heart chakra, or Anahata chakra, is located in the center of the chest. Green is the color of the heart chakra, "Yam," is the chant of the heart, and you can use the affirmation: "I am filled with love." The heart chakra is responsible for love and compassion.

The heart chakra is the center of our ability to love and be loved. It is associated with the air element, which is said to be expansive and supportive. The heart chakra is very important, as it is responsible for our ability to feel love and compassion.

Chakra 5: Throat or Vishuddha Chakra

Vishuddha chakra symbol.
Atarax42, CC0, via Wikimedia Commons: https://commons.wikimedia.org/wiki/File:Chakra5.svg

The throat chakra, or Vishuddha chakra, is located in the center of the throat. It is associated with the color blue, the affirmation "I am heard," the sound "Ham," and the element of aether. The throat chakra is responsible for communication and self-expression.

The throat chakra is the center of our ability to communicate and express ourselves. It is associated with the aether element, which is said to be expansive and limitless. The throat chakra is very important, as it is responsible for our ability to communicate effectively.

Chakra 6: Third Eye or Ajna Chakra

Ajna chakra symbol.
Atarax42, CC0, via Wikimedia Commons: https://commons.wikimedia.org/wiki/File:Chakra6.svg

The third eye chakra, or Ajna chakra, is located between the eyebrows. It is associated with the color indigo, the affirmation "I see clearly," the sound "OM," and the element of mind.

The third eye chakra is the center of our ability to see clearly, both literally and figuratively. It is associated with the mental element, which is said to be sharp and focused. When we have strong intuition, it is because of our third eye chakra – we can sense the intent in other people and see clearly both in the present and what is yet to come.

Chakra 7: Crown or Sahasrara Chakra

Sahasrara symbol.
https://pixabay.com/images/id-1340083/

Just like a crown, the crown chakra sits atop our head. It is associated with the color violet, the affirmation "I am connected," the sound "Silence," and the element of spirit. The crown chakra is responsible for spirituality and connection to the Divine.

The crown chakra is the center of our ability to connect with the Divine. It is associated with the spiritual element, which is said to be expansive and all-encompassing. The crown chakra is very important, as it is responsible for our ability to connect with our spirituality. The health of your crown chakra influences how connected you feel to a higher power, your spiritual beliefs, and your ability to access wisdom.

The chakras are an important part of our overall health and well-being. By understanding each chakra's role in our lives, we can better balance our energy and maintain a healthy mind, body, and spirit. Starting with the root chakra and moving up to the crown chakra, we can see how each chakra is interconnected with the others to create a well-rounded system. By taking care of our chakras, we take care of ourselves as a whole.

Conclusion

In this guide, we've covered a lot of information on the Sahasrara. We've discussed what it is, its associated color and location, and how to keep it healthy. We've also gone over some of the ways you can tell if your crown chakra is blocked. With this knowledge, you can start on the path to opening and balancing your crown chakra.

The first chapter of this guide introduced the concept of the crown chakra and what it represents. In chapter two, we explored some of the signs that your crown chakra is blocked. In chapter three, we discussed how you could raise energy through your chakras. Chapter four introduced the concept of mantras and mudras and how they can be used to improve the health of your chakras.

In chapter five, we explored different ways you can meditate to improve the health of your crown chakra. Chapter six introduced the concept of pranayama and yoga and how they can be used to improve the health of your chakras. In chapter seven, we discussed how you could use crystals and stones to improve the health of your crown chakra.

In chapter eight, we discussed how you could use aromatherapy to improve the health of your crown chakra. Essential oils are a great way to improve the health of your chakras. In chapter nine, we discussed how nutrition and diet could be used to improve the health of your crown chakra. Finally, in chapter ten, we went over a seven-day crown chakra routine you can follow to improve the health of your Sahasrara.

The different techniques we covered in this guide can be interlinked and used to improve the health of your crown chakra. Do not rely only on this book, but use it as inspiration – find what works for you, and continue to practice that. Remember, the most important thing is to be consistent with your practice. A routine will help keep your crown chakra healthy and balanced.

We hope you enjoyed this guide and find the information helpful. If you suspect that your crown chakra is blocked, the tips provided throughout this guide can help you unblock it. Try some of the exercises we've discussed, such as meditation, visualization, and pranayama. You can also use crystals and stones, aromatherapy, and diet to support your crown chakra.

Remember, the journey to a healthy crown chakra is an ongoing one. It's important to be patient with yourself and to trust the process. The information in this guide can help you get started on the path to a healthy and balanced crown chakra.

Disclaimer: Always consult with a doctor if you are starting a treatment plan or have any ailments or illnesses. This guide is intended as a guide and should be used alone as a cure or treatment.

Here's another book by Mari Silva that you might like

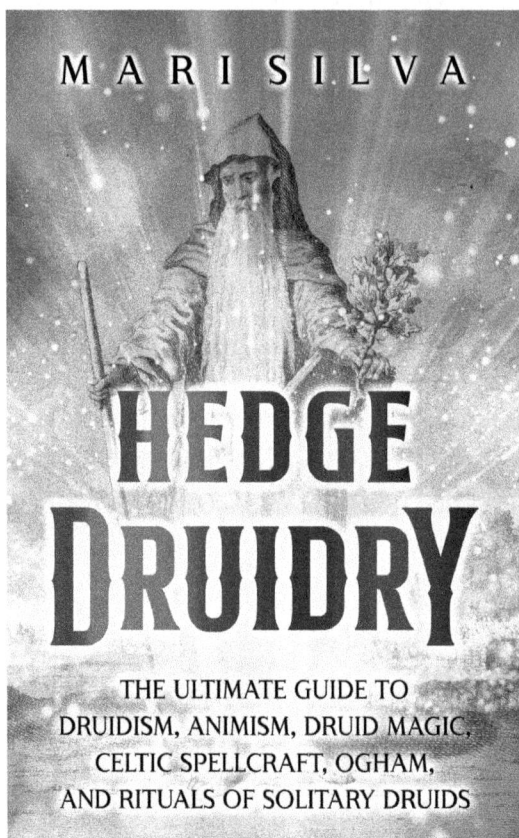

MARI SILVA

HEDGE DRUIDRY

THE ULTIMATE GUIDE TO
DRUIDISM, ANIMISM, DRUID MAGIC,
CELTIC SPELLCRAFT, OGHAM,
AND RITUALS OF SOLITARY DRUIDS

Your Free Gift
(only available for a limited time)

Thanks for getting this book! If you want to learn more about various spirituality topics, then join Mari Silva's community and get a free guided meditation MP3 for awakening your third eye. This guided meditation mp3 is designed to open and strengthen ones third eye so you can experience a higher state of consciousness. Simply visit the link below the image to get started.

https://spiritualityspot.com/meditation

References

Davis, F. (2021, February 24). Chakra frequencies: What they are & how to achieve resonance. Cosmic Cuts. https://cosmiccuts.com/blogs/healing-stones-blog/chakra-frequencies

Drollinger, J. (2021). Root chakra: Activating, balancing, and healing: Mind-body and soul connection. Independently Published.

Fishman, D. (2021, June 24). Sex and the root chakra. Center for Holistic Mental Health and Sexual Therapy. https://chmhst.com/sexual-behavior/sex-and-the-root-chakra/

Fondin, M. (2020, October 7). The root chakra: Muladhara. Chopra. https://chopra.com/articles/the-root-chakra-muladhara

Kelly Neff, M. A. (2019, August 23). 7 chakra-clearing affirmations to enhance your sex life. Mindbodygreen. https://www.mindbodygreen.com/0-12926/7-chakraclearing-affirmations-to-enhance-your-sex-life.html

Lindberg, S. (2020, August 24). What are chakras? Meaning, location, and how to unblock them. Healthline. https://www.healthline.com/health/what-are-chakras

MacKinnon, H. (2019, September 30). The first chakra: Root Chakra —. Small Seed Bar. https://www.smallseedbar.com/blog/root-chakra

Novak, S. (2022, January 26). The crazy link between an awesome sex life and your chakra system. Organic Authority. https://www.organicauthority.com/energetic-health/the-crazy-link-between-the-chakra-system-and-having-an-awesome-sex-life

Pfannkuch, K. (2016, January 11). The 7 core chakras and how they influence creative expression. Creative Katrina. https://creativekatrina.com/the-7-core-chakras-and-how-they-influence-creative-expression/

Shirley, P., & Joy. (2018, February 6). Bad yogi blog. Bad Yogi Blog. https://www.badyogi.com/blog/demystifying-muladhara-the-root-chakra/

Snyder, S., Editors, Y. J., Indries, M., Marglin, A. T. to, & LaRue, M. B. (2021, August 11). Everything you need to know about the root chakra. Yoga Journal. https://www.yogajournal.com/yoga-101/chakras-yoga-for-beginners/intro-root-chakra-muladhara/

Stokes, V. (2021, October 25). Root chakra healing: The science, traditions, and techniques. Healthline. https://www.healthline.com/health/mind-body/root-chakra-healing

The energy body in yoga. (2015, December 8). Ekhart Yoga. https://www.ekhartyoga.com/articles/practice/the-energy-body-in-yoga

The Root Chakra: Your personal guide to balance the first chakra. (n.d.). Art Of Living (United States).

Dadabhay, Y. (2021, December 30). 11 blocked or underactive root chakra warning signs to be aware of. Subconscious Servant. https://subconsciousservant.com/blocked-or-underactive-root-chakra/

Lindberg, S. (2020, August 24). What are chakras? Meaning, location, and how to unblock them. Healthline. https://www.healthline.com/health/what-are-chakras

Brown, K. J. (2020, March 9). How to open your root chakra, according to reiki masters. Well+Good. https://www.wellandgood.com/how-to-open-root-chakra/

A daily mindful walking practice. (2017, July 17). Mindful. https://www.mindful.org/daily-mindful-walking-practice/

Ashish. (2021, October 5). Root Chakra meditation: How to do, benefits & practice tips. Fitsri. https://www.fitsri.com/articles/root-chakra-meditation

Balter, J. (2015, June 16). 7 ways to easily incorporate meditation into your life. Wanderlust. https://wanderlust.com/journal/7-ways-to-easily-incorporate-meditation-into-your-life/

Brown, K. J. (2020, March 31). How a successful root chakra meditation makes you feel more grounded. Well+Good. https://www.wellandgood.com/root-chakra-meditation/

Cherry, K. (n.d.). What Is Meditation? Verywell Mind. https://www.verywellmind.com/what-is-meditation-2795927

Daga, R. B. (2017). Walking Meditation. Journal of Sleep Disorders & Therapy, 06(05). https://doi.org/10.4172/2167-0277.1000279

Editors, Y. J., Husler, A., Land, R., Herrington, S., & Rosen, R. (2017, March 8). Meditation seal. Yoga Journal. https://www.yogajournal.com/poses/dhyana-mudra/

Fernandez, C. (2019, September 18). These profound thich Nhat Hanh quotes will bring you peace today. Oprah Daily. https://www.oprahdaily.com/life/g29092056/thich-nhat-hanh-quotes/?slide=7

Heger, E. (2020, May 18). 7 benefits of meditation and how it can affect your brain. Insider. https://www.insider.com/benefits-of-meditation

Holmes Place. (2018, April 6). 3 ways to include meditation in your daily schedule. Holmes Place. https://www.holmesplace.com/en/en/blog/wellness/3-ways-include-meditation-daily-schedule

Ishak, R. (2015, November 3). How to start meditating & 6 ways to include it in your daily life. Bustle. https://www.bustle.com/articles/121407-how-to-start-meditating-6-ways-to-include-it-in-your-daily-life

Kable, R. (2019, February 3). 20 powerful tips to help you meditate better —. Rachael Kable. https://www.rachaelkable.com/blog/tips-to-help-you-meditate-better

Kurt. (2017, July 4). Finding your center: Grounding meditation techniques. Earthing Canada. https://earthingcanada.ca/blog/grounding-meditation-techniques/

Long commute: How to reduce rising stress. (2019, July 17). Insight Timer Blog. https://insighttimer.com/blog/long-commute-meditation-stress/

Matson, M. (2019, March 17). Muladhara: Root chakra meditation for healing and balancing [VIDEO]. Brett Larkin Yoga. https://www.brettlarkin.com/muladhara-root-chakra-meditation-healing-balancing/

Meditation. (n.d.). Art of Living (India). https://www.artofliving.org/in-en/meditation

Rebecca Cairns, Z. I. (2021, July 1). What is meditation? The history and health benefits of meditation — and how you can get started. Insider. https://www.insider.com/meditation-definition

Root chakra meditation. (n.d.). KiraGrace. https://www.kiragrace.com/blog/root-chakra-meditation/

Scott, S. J. (2019, April 22). Mindful commuting: Making Time for mindfulness during free moments. Develop Good Habits. https://www.developgoodhabits.com/mindful-commuting-making-time-mindfulness/

Stibich, M. (n.d.). How to fit meditation into your day. Verywell Mind https://www.verywellmind.com/how-to-fit-meditation-into-your-day-every-day-2224118

Stokes, V. (2021, October 25). Root chakra healing: The science, traditions, and techniques. Healthline. https://www.healthline.com/health/mind-body/root-chakra-healing

Yoga, K. (2015, June 10). What exactly are Mudras, and why use them in yoga practice? —. Korsi Yoga. http://www.korsiyoga.com/korsi-blog/2015/6/10/what-exactly-are-mudras-and-why-use-them-in-yoga-practice

Ashish. (2019, November 27). Gyan Mudra: Meaning, How to Do, Benefits & Precautions. Fitsri. https://www.fitsri.com/yoga-mudras/gyan-mudra

Muladhara Mudra Yoga. (n.d.). Tummee.Com. https://www.tummee.com/yoga-poses/muladhara-mudra

Yele, K. (2021, March 30). (Earth Mudra) Prithvi Mudra Meaning and its Benefits for Hair Growth & Weight Gain. Vedic Yoga Ayurveda. https://vedicyogayurveda.com/prithvi-mudra/

Saradananda, S. (2015). Mudras for Modern Life. Watkins Publishing.

Nunez, K. (2020, May 15). Pranayama Benefits for Physical and Emotional Health. Healthline. https://www.healthline.com/health/pranayama-benefits

Learn Pranayama Breath Control and Its Positive Effects on Your Health. (n.d.). Art Of Living (United States). https://www.artofliving.org/us-en/blog/learn-pranayama-breath-control-and-its-positive-effects-on-your-health

Pranayama for Root Chakra. (n.d.). Yogateket. https://www.yogateket.com/blog/pranayama-for-root-chakra

Hughes, A. (2020, May 4). Balancing Muladhara: How to Realign Your Root Chakra. Yogapedia.Com; Yogapedia. https://www.yogapedia.com/balancing-muladhara-how-to-realign-your-root-chakra/2/12056

Nadi Shodhana. (n.d.). Yogapedia.Com. http://www.yogapedia.com/definition/5322/nadi-shodhana

Sitali Pranayama. (n.d.). Yogapedia.Com. http://www.yogapedia.com/definition/6518/sitali-pranayama

Mackenzie A. 8 root chakra poses for balance and stability of muladhara. YOGA PRACTICE. Published October 25, 2020. https://yogapractice.com/yoga/root-chakra-yoga-poses/

Snyder S, Indries M, Varshney P, Schettler RM, Land R, Hunter F. Root chakra tune-up practice. Yoga Journal. Published January 1, 2015. https://www.yogajournal.com/practice/yoga-sequences/root-chakra-muladhara-tune-up-practice/

Hughes A. Balancing muladhara: How to realign your root chakra. Yogapedia.com. Published May 4, 2020. https://www.yogapedia.com/balancing-muladhara-how-to-realign-your-root-chakra/2/12056

Root Chakra Stones: Balancing Crystals for the Base Chakra. (n.d.). Shawacademy.Com. https://www.shawacademy.com/blog/root-chakra-stones/

Beads, T. (2020, December 14). What Is The Difference Between Crystals & Gemstones? Tejas Beads. https://www.tejasbeads.com/blogs/the-geologist/the-difference-between-crystals-and-gemstones

Oakes, J. (2021, April 7). Root Chakra Stones: These 11 Crystals Are Crucial For Healing. Tiny Rituals. https://tinyrituals.co/blogs/tiny-rituals/root-chakra-stones

Oakes, J. (2021, March 27). How To Cleanse Crystals: 9 Crucial Practices You Need To Know. Tiny Rituals. https://tinyrituals.co/blogs/tiny-rituals/how-to-cleanse-crystals

Harutyunyan, M. (2021, November 9). Root Chakra Stones: What Are The 7 Best Root Chakra Crystals? Conscious Items. https://consciousitems.com/blogs/practice/root-chakra-stones

Find The Best Healing Crystals For You. (n.d.). HealingCrystalsForYou.Com. https://www.healing-crystals-for-you.com/

TNN. (2019, August 1). The science behind healing crystals explained! The Times of India; Times Of India. https://timesofindia.indiatimes.com/life-style/health-fitness/home-remedies/the-science-behind-healing-crystals-explained/articleshow/70482968.cms

12 professionals share their favorite essential oils & blends for the root chakra. (n.d.). Sacred Soul Holistics. https://www.sacredsoulholistics.co.uk/blogs/news/root-chakra-essential-oils-blends

How to use essential oils to balance your chakras. (n.d.). Releaseyoga.Com. http://releaseyoga.com/blog/2015/12/01/how-to-use-essential-oils-to-deepen-your-yoga-practice

Knight, A. (2016, April 11). Root Chakra. Aromacare. https://aromacare.com.au/blogs/aromatherapy-services/root-chakra

Pure Essential Oils to balance your Root Chakra. (n.d.). Meraki Essentials. https://merakiessentials.com/blogs/meraki-essential/pure-essential-oils-to-balance-root-chakra

Simone, D. (2019, September 22). The key to balancing your energy might be aromatherapy. XoNecole: Women's Interest, Love, Wellness, Beauty. https://www.xonecole.com/chakra-attunement-using-aromatherapy-to-balance-your-energy/

Stokes, V. (2021, February 17). Essential oils for chakras: Balance and heal with scents. Healthline. https://www.healthline.com/health/essential-oils-for-chakras

3 recipes for your root chakra. (n.d.). Daily Life https://dailylife.com/article/recipes-for-your-root-chakra?ref=tfrecipes

Caron, M. (2018, November 5). Healing the root chakra with food. Sivana East. https://blog.sivanaspirit.com/hl-sp-root-chakra-food/

Chakra foods for healing & health. (2018, March 27). Deborah King. https://deborahking.com/7-foods-to-heal-7-chakras/?doing_wp_cron=1649895609.0356950759887695312500

Easterly, E. (2020, June 16). Eating to balance your chakras. Chopra. https://www.chopra.com/articles/eating-to-balance-your-chakras

Fondin, M. (2020, October 7). The root chakra: Muladhara. Chopra. https://chopra.com/articles/the-root-chakra-muladhara

Give energy with root (Muladhara) chakra recipes. (2019, March 21). Chakrashealth.Com.

Kaiser, S. (2020, February 21). Get grounded with these 3 root chakra soups.... Spirituality & Health. https://www.spiritualityhealth.com/articles/2020/02/21/get-grounded-with-these-3-root-chakra-soups-bonus-recipe

Moone, A. (2018, December 30). 6 foods to balance your root chakra. Plentiful Earth. https://plentifulearth.com/6-foods-to-balance-your-root-chakra/

The. (n.d.). Chakra foods: 7 chakras food chart. 7 Chakra Store https://7chakrastore.com/blogs/news/chakra-foods

The best foods for each chakra. (2016, June 18). Parsnips and Pastries. https://www.parsnipsandpastries.com/chakra-food-pairing-balancing-healing-energy-centers-food/

The root chakra: Foods to ground and strengthen. (n.d.).

Food for your chakras. Times Of India. https://timesofindia.indiatimes.com/life-style/health-fitness/diet/food-for-your-chakras/articleshow/19661214.cms

Drollinger, J. (2021). Root chakra: Activating, balancing, and healing: Mind-body and soul connection. Independently Published.

Mackenzie, A. (2020, October 25). 8 root chakra poses for balance and stability of muladhara. YOGA PRACTICE. https://yogapractice.com/yoga/root-chakra-yoga-poses/

Stokes, V. (2021, October 25). Root chakra healing: The science, traditions, and techniques. Healthline. https://www.healthline.com/health/mind-body/root-chakra-healing

The Tribune India. (2018, December 5). Muladhara chakra How to keep one grounded? The Tribune India

Stelter, G. (2016, October 4). Chakras: A Beginner's Guide to the 7 Chakras. Healthline. https://www.healthline.com/health/fitness-exercise/7-chakras

Burton, N., Derisz, R., Fay, Z., & Dowling, A. (2021, December 5). How to Unblock Chakras: A Complete Guide to Getting Clear from Root to Crown. Goalcast. https://www.goalcast.com/how-to-unblock-chakras/

Muladhara Chakra – The Most Important Chakra. (n.d.). Ishafoundation.Org https://www.ishafoundation.org/ta/blog/muladhara-chakra.isa

Freshwater, S. (2017, November 21). 1st Chakra Root Muladhara. Shawna Freshwater, Ph.D. https://spacioustherapy.com/1st-chakra-root-muladhara

Editors, Y. J., Indries, M., Marglin, A. T. to, & LaRue, M. B. (2021, April 27). What you need to know about the sacral chakra. Yoga Journal. https://www.yogajournal.com/yoga-101/intro-sacral-chakra-svadhisthana/

Estrada, J. (2022, April 1). How to heal your sacral chakra and get your creative—and sexual—energy free-flowing again. Well+Good. https://www.wellandgood.com/sacral-chakra-healing/

Jain, R. (2020, August 26). Svadhishthana - Sacral Chakra: All you need to know. Arhanta Yoga Ashrams. https://www.arhantayoga.org/blog/svadhishthana-chakra-all-you-need-to-know-about-the-sacral-chakra/

Regan, S. (2020, July 16). 6 ways to balance your sacral chakra, A hotspot for creativity & sexuality. Mindbodygreen. https://www.mindbodygreen.com/0-5332/6-Ways-to-Balance-Your-Sacral-Chakra.html

The Refinery Team. (2018, January 31). The Sacral Chakra. The Refinery. https://therefinerye9.com/the-sacral-chakra/

The Sacral Chakra: Discover and align the second chakra. (n.d.). Art Of Living (United States).

Using the Sacral Chakra to Engage with your Sexuality. (2017, June 6). Viva Center. https://www.vivapartnership.com/optimal-living/using-sacral-chakra-to-engage-with-your-sexuality/

Want to deepen your sensuality? Look to the sacral chakra. (2021, December 6). Healthline. https://www.healthline.com/health/mind-body/sacral-chakra

Arora, I. (2010, December). Chakra Meditation with Mudra and Mantra. In International Symposium on Yogism.

Atwell, H., McManus, D. J., & Carr, H. H. (2013). The OSI Model and the Seven Chakras of Hinduism: A Comparative Analysis. International Journal of Applied.

Battaglia, S. (2009). Practical guide to chakras and aromatherapy. Australia: Perfect.

Bhetiwal, A. The Role of Musical Notes and Color Frequencies for Balancing Chakras in the Human Body.

Greenwood, M. (2006). Acupuncture and the chakras. Medical Acupuncture.

Herring, B. K. (2009). Asanas for the chakra system. Yoga Journal.

Krishna, A. B. (2016). Spirituality and science of yogic chakra: A correlation. Asian Journal of Complementary and Alternative Medicine.

Kumaar, S. S. (2022). A critical analysis of chromotherapy (color therapy) and its impact on married life.

Nazari, N. A. A., Fauzi, N. M., Rosli, N. F., Zakaria, S. N., Jalil, S. Z. A., & Noor, N. M. (2017, September). Physiological studies of human fatigue using human electromagnetic radiation. In 2017 IEEE International Conference on Signal and Image Processing Applications (ICSIPA).

PS, J., Gopal, U. B., & Simon, R. K. (2021). NEUROLOGICAL UNDERSTANDING OF SHAD CHAKRA WITH SPECIAL REFERENCE TO VATA DOSHA. International Journal of Ayurveda and Pharma Research.

Sanyal, K. Chakra Meditation and Five Elements Engagement of the Chakras with Five Elements in Nature. Role of Arts, Culture, Humanities, Religion, Education, Ethics, Philosophy, Spirituality and Science for Holistic Societal Development.

Simpson, L. (1999). The book of chakra healing. Sterling Publishing Company, Inc.

Stux, G., & Pomeranz, B. (1995). Additional methods of treatment. In Basics of Acupuncture. Springer, Berlin, Heidelberg.

Stux, G. (2003). 8.1 Chakra Acupuncture. Basics of acupuncture.

Wills, P. (2002). Chakra Workbook: Rebalance your body's vital energies. Springer Science & Business.

Zeltzer, C. (2002). The role of the third chakra in the psychology of terrorism. Psychological Perspectives

Lindberg, S. (2020, August 24). What are chakras? Meaning, location, and how to unblock them. Healthline. https://www.healthline.com/health/what-are-chakras

4 powerful benefits of healing your heart chakra & affirmations + sound bath music to open your heart chakra. (2022, January 19). Meditative Mind. https://meditativemind.org/4-powerful-benefits-of-healing-your-heart-chakra-affirmations-soundbath-music-to-open-your-heart-chakra

An overview of the Heart Chakra. (2019, October 11). Popular Vedic Science. https://popularvedicscience.com/heart-chakra

Anahata Nada. (n.d.). Yogapedia.Com. https://www.yogapedia.com/definition/9104/anahata-nada

Borohhov, D. (2011, May 15). Chakra meaning. Ananda. https://www.ananda.org/yogapedia/chakra

Brown, M. (2022, January 31). Your guide to the 7 chakras — and how to know if yours are depleted, according to experts. InStyle. https://www.instyle.com/lifestyle/astrology/what-are-chakras

Cameron, Y. (2021, October 29). Everything you've ever wanted to know about the 7 chakras in the body. Mindbodygreen. https://www.mindbodygreen.com/0-91/The-7-Chakras-for-Beginners.html

Chakra. (n.d.). Etymonline.Com. https://www.etymonline.com/word/chakra

Das, S. (n.d.). What you need to know about the Vedas—India's most sacred texts. Learn Religions. https://www.learnreligions.com/what-are-vedas-1769572

Heart chakra essentials – connecting with Anahata. (2021, November 12).
UniGuide.

https://www.uniguide.com/heart-chakra-anahata

Jain, R. (2019, June 13). Complete guide to 7 chakras. Www.Arhantayoga.Org.
https://www.arhantayoga.org/blog/7-chakras-introduction-energy-centers-effect

justbewell. (2020, August 25). What is the energy body? Justbewell.Info.
https://justbewell.info/what-is-the-energy-body

Kandanarachchi, P. (2013a). Heart Chakra. Lulu.com.
https://www.yogapedia.com/definition/5524/heart-chakra

Kandanarachchi, P. (2013b). Heart Chakra. Lulu.com.
https://www.anahana.com/en/yoga/heart-chakra

Kristin. (2021, February 10). Heart chakra: Everything you need to know. Be
My Travel Muse. https://www.bemytravelmuse.com/heart-chakra

Lindberg, S. (2020, August 24). What are chakras? Meaning, location, and how
to unblock them. Healthline. https://www.healthline.com/health/what-are-
chakras

Negus, S. (2021, January 13). 5 simple ways to unblock your chakras that will
change your life. Glamour UK.
https://www.glamourmagazine.co.uk/article/what-are-chakras

Oils, R. M. (n.d.). Exploring your heart chakra. Rockymountainoils.Com.

https://www.rockymountainoils.com/learn/exploring-your-heart-chakra

Pathshala, V. (2020, September 21). Anahata - the Heart Chakra. School of
Wisdom and Knowledge. https://vedapathshala.com/2020/09/21/anahata-the-
heart-chakra

Pugle, M., Burton, N., & Derisz, R. (2021, August 26). Heart chakra:
Everything you need to know about the fourth Chakra. Goalcast.
https://www.goalcast.com/heart-chakra

Arora, I. (2010, December). Chakra Meditation with Mudra and Mantra. In
International Symposium on Yogism.

Atwell, H., McManus, D. J., & Carr, H. H. (2013). The OSI Model and the
Seven Chakras of Hinduism: A Comparative Analysis. International Journal of
Applied.

Battaglia, S. (2009). Practical guide to chakras and aromatherapy. Australia:
Perfect.

Bhetiwal, A. The Role of Musical Notes and Color Frequencies for Balancing Chakras in Human Body.

Greenwood, M. (2006). Acupuncture and the chakras. Medical Acupuncture.

Herring, B. K. (2009). Asanas for the chakra system. Yoga Journal.

Hoshawk, C. M. (2018). Stilling the Mind: The Journey of Consciousness in the Mental-Egoic Era. Journal of Conscious Evolution.

Krishna, A. B. (2016). Spirituality and science of yogic chakra: A correlation. Asian Journal of Complementary and Alternative Medicine.

Kumaar, S. S. (2022). A critical analysis of chromotherapy (color therapy) and its impact on married life.

Kumar, S. Fostering Mental Wellbeing by Healing Chakras through Music Therapy.

Nazari, N. A. A., Fauzi, N. M., Rosli, N. F., Zakaria, S. N., Jalil, S. Z. A., & Noor, N. M. (2017, September). Physiological studies of human fatigue using human electromagnetic radiation. In 2017 IEEE International Conference on Signal and Image Processing Applications (ICSIPA).

PS, J., Gopal, U. B., & Simon, R. K. (2021). NEUROLOGICAL UNDERSTANDING OF SHAD CHAKRA WITH SPECIAL REFERENCE TO VATA DOSHA. International Journal of Ayurveda and Pharma Research.

Redmond, L. (2012). Chakra meditation: Transformation through the seven energy centers of the body. Sounds True.

Sanyal, K. Chakra Meditation and Five Elements Engagement of the Chakras with Five Elements in Nature. Role of Arts, Culture, Humanities, Religion, Education, Ethics, Philosophy, Spirituality and Science for Holistic Societal Development.

Shumsky, S. G. (2005). Exploring Chakras: Awaken Your Untapped Energy. Motilal Banarsidass.

Simpson, L. (1999). The book of chakra healing. Sterling Publishing Company, Inc.

Slayton, K., & Grigorievskiy, A. CHAKRAS EXPLAINED-BEGINNER'S GUIDE The Ultimate Guide to CHAKRAS| How to Unblock For Full 7 CHAKRA Energy! (POWERFUL!) Everything You Need to Know About Chakras De 7 chakra's en wat voor mega impact het op jou heeft. How to Awaken the Chakras: Open the Sahasrara Crown Chakra (Ep. 8).

Stux, G., & Pomeranz, B. (1995). Additional methods of treatment. In Basics of Acupuncture. Springer, Berlin, Heidelberg.

Stux, G. (2003). 8.1 Chakra Acupuncture. Basics of acupuncture.

Wills, P., & Gimbel, T. (1992). 16 Steps to Health and Energy: A Program of Color & Visual Meditation, Movement & Chakra Balance. Llewellyn Worldwide Limited.

Wills, P. (2002). Chakra Workbook: Rebalance your body's vital energies. Springer Science & Business

All you need to know about third eye meditation. (2019, December 10). The Times of India; Times Of India. https://timesofindia.indiatimes.com/life-style/health-fitness/home-remedies/all-you-need-to-know-about-third-eye-meditation/articleshow/72458177.cms

Cameron, Y. (2022, February 7). An introduction to the third-eye chakra + how to heal it. Mindbodygreen. https://www.mindbodygreen.com/0-97/Third-Eye-Chakra-Healing-for-Beginners.html

Jain, R. (2020, October 7). Ajna Chakra, your Third-Eye Chakra awakening. Arhanta Yoga Ashrams. https://www.arhantayoga.org/blog/ajna-chakra-your-third-eye-chakra-awakening/

Kristin. (2021, February 13). Third eye chakra: Everything you need to know. Be My Travel Muse. https://www.bemytravelmuse.com/third-eye-chakra/

Secrets of Third Eye Activation. (n.d.). Art Of Living (India). https://www.artofliving.org/in-en/meditation/secret-of-third-eye-activation

Stokes, V. (2021, May 6). How to open your third eye chakra for spiritual awakening. Healthline. https://www.healthline.com/health/mind-body/how-to-open-your-third-eye

Weingus, L. (2019, May 27). How to open your third eye with 15 tips from experts. Well+Good. https://www.wellandgood.com/how-to-open-your-third-eye

Chakra healing: How to open your crown chakra. (n.d.). Goodnet., https://www.goodnet.org/articles/chakra-healing-how-to-open-your-crown

Crown chakra. (n.d.). Anahana.Com. https://www.anahana.com/en/yoga/crown-chakra

Jain, R. (2020, October 8). Crown chakra: The divine energy of Sahasrara chakra. Arhanta Yoga Ashrams. https://www.arhantayoga.org/blog/crown-chakra-divine-energy-of-sahasrara-chakra/

Kristin. (2021, February 14). Crown chakra: Everything you need to know. Be My Travel Muse. https://www.bemytravelmuse.com/crown-chakra/

Lindberg, S. (2020, August 24). What are chakras? Meaning, location, and how to unblock them. Healthline. https://www.healthline.com/health/what-are-chakras

Snyder, S., Editors, Y. J., Indries, M., Marglin, A. T. to, & LaRue, M. B. (2021, August 18). Everything you need to know about the crown chakra. Yoga Journal. https://www.yogajournal.com/yoga-101/chakras-yoga-for-beginners/intro-sahasrara-crown-chakra/

Team SEEMA. (2021, November 14). Everything to know about the purple-crown chakra. Seema. https://www.seema.com/everything-to-know-about-the-purple-crown-chakra